THE POLITICS OF SEXUALIT

PITT LATIN AMERICAN SERIES

John Charles Chasteen and Catherine M. Conaghan, Editors

THE POLITICS OF SEXUALITY IN LATIN AMERICA

A READER ON LESBIAN, GAY, BISEXUAL, AND TRANSGENDER RIGHTS

Edited by Javier Corrales and Mario Pecheny

UNIVERSITY OF PITTSBURGH PRESS

Published by the University of Pittsburgh Press, Pittsburgh, Pa., 15260

Copyright © 2010, University of Pittsburgh Press

Manufactured in the United States of America

Printed on acid-free paper

10 9 8 7 6 5 4 3 2 1

Library of Congress Cataloging-in-Publication Data

The politics of sexuality in Latin America : a reader on lesbian, gay, bisexual, and transgender rights / edited by Javier Corrales and Mario Pecheny.

     p. cm. —(Pitt Latin american series)

  Includes bibliographical references and index.

  ISBN 978-0-8229-6062-1 (pbk. : alk. paper)

    1. Sex—Political aspects—Latin America. 2. Gay rights—Latin America. 3. Sex and law. I. Corrales, Javier, 1966– II. Pecheny, Mario.

  HQ23.P663 2010

  323.3′264098—dc22

                          2010002369

CONTENTS

FOREWORD

Lisa Baldez

GENDER EQUALITY was barely conceivable thirty years ago in Latin America, but the region has since made remarkable improvements in women's rights. Every country in the region has ratified CEDAW, the United Nations' Convention to End All Forms of Discrimination Against Women. Every country has passed domestic violence legislation. Twelve Latin American countries have adopted gender quota laws that require that women make up 30 percent of all the candidates nominated for legislative office. These changes and others came about largely in response to women who mobilized to demand more rights amid transitions to democracy. Latin American women still have a long way to go to achieve full equality, but they have established a permanent place on the political scene.

Achieving equal rights for gays, lesbians, bisexuals, and transgendered people is the next human-rights challenge for Latin America in the twenty-first century. The region has already made significant strides. In June 2008, for example, the Organization of American States adopted a resolution condemning violence based on sexual orientation and gender identity.[1] Many, but not all, Latin American countries have one or more GLBT organizations.[2] Nonetheless, the GLBT movement in Latin America is small, young, and incipient in comparison to the more established women's movement. The magnitude of organizing within the GLBT community, in Latin America and elsewhere, is small in comparison to women's organizing, in part because of their respective numbers—GLBT people are a small percentage of the population, while women are half of it. Although some GLBT organizations formed alongside feminist groups in the late 1970s, most are newer: *Comunidad Homosexual Argentina* formed in 1984, Chile's *Movimiento de Integración y Liberación Homosexual* (MOVILH) and Nicaragua's *Puntos de Encuentro* emerged in 1991, and *Colombia Diversa* was created in 2003.

What other comparisons between these two movements might we draw? This volume, as a collection of writings about GLBT politics in Latin America, provides us with an opportunity to reflect on the role that writing and academic research have played in fostering social movements. To what extent has scholarly writing served the strategic goals of these two movements? In this foreword, I examine the extent to which writing and research have contributed to the feminist movement and to the achievement of gender equality in Latin America, and I highlight some points of comparison with the GLBT movement. I demonstrate some of the ways in which writing has strengthened feminism in Latin America, including creating a community of adherents, expanding awareness of key issues, and amplifying political influence. I also discuss some of the limitations associated with writing and academic research. I draw my examples primarily from Chile, the case with which I am most familiar.

Writing is one of the spaces in which a movement exists. Activists do not simply write about the feminist movement; in writing, they constitute it. While writing is (usually) done in isolation, it represents an effort to create a community. The audience for what one writes can be infinite. A published work will be distributed to bookstores, libraries, and universities around the world, accessible to future generations. Writing allows activists to explain their actions to the public and establishes the movement's foothold in the historical record.

Accounts of the history of Chilean feminism typically highlight demonstrations, *encuentros*, and conferences, but the texts that accompanied these events were at least as important as the events themselves. The first time Chilean feminists staged a protest, in May 1983, they distributed leaflets printed with what would become the leading slogan of feminism throughout the region: "Democracy in the country and in the home." This slogan conveyed the central idea of feminism in Latin America: an end to authoritarian government at the national level was linked to an end to violence and gender inequality in relationships between men and women. In their second demonstration, held in August 1983, feminist protesters carried a banner that said "Democracy Now—The Feminist Movement of Chile." This statement explicitly linked the political struggle of the opposition with women's struggle for equality. Writing thus defined each of these actions.

The publication of newsletters and *samizdat* literature in the early stages of a movement creates the underground infrastructure for mobilization—particularly in a context of fear and repression. These early communiqués foster recognition among readers that they are not alone and preserve key moments for future generations. Pamphlets and newsletters allow activists to communicate with one another, to articulate their ideas and goals and foster discussion about strategies and tactics. One of the most important feminist organizations in Chile was Isis International, a group that served as an information clearinghouse. Isis gathered all the materials it could find and created a publicly accessible database and network of activists in Chile and around the world. Its slogan expressed the essential role of movement publications: "Information is for action."[3]

Social science research played a particularly important role in the feminist movement in Chile, for two reasons. First, many of the women who became active in feminist politics were among those academics, men and women alike, whom the military had cast out of university life after the coup. When the military junta seized power in 1973, it replaced university administrators with military officials, fired professors, and made it impossible for many students to return. Second, scores of left-leaning intellectuals who remained in Chile after the coup went to work for think tanks and nongovernmental organizations, where they produced mountains of research documenting the country's socioeconomic situation. Several of these focused specifically on women, including the *Centro de Estudios de la Mujer* (CEM), an interdisciplinary study group dedicated to social science research on the status of women in employment, education, and citizenship, and *Fundación Instituto de la Mujer*, an NGO that focuses on women's rights. Doing research allowed many scholars to survive financially, thanks to international funding. It also provided a way for men and women on the Left to reflect on the past and to rebuild politically.[4]

Research on women fueled feminist mobilization by legitimizing women as political actors and documenting the extent of gender inequality. Two books that stand out in the Chilean case are Julieta Kirkwood's *Ser política en Chile*, published by *Facultad Latinoamericana de Ciencias Sociales* (FLACSO) in 1986, and *Mundo de mujer: continuidad y cambio*, produced by CEM in 1988. In *Ser política en Chile*, Kirkwood makes visible the participation of women in partisan politics in the early part of the twentieth century, highlighting the relationship between "*feministas*" and "*políticas*" (between activists and partisans), a dichotomy still characterizes Chilean politics today. Kirkwood and others showed that feminism was not a bourgeois Trojan horse, as its critics on the Left claimed, but an enduring part of Chile's history.

For Chilean feminists, academic work could not be isolated from opposition politics. The two were closely fused. In the prologue to *Ser política en Chile*, Kirkwood explicitly acknowledges the relationship between writing the book and her intense political involvement:

> During the months of October and November 1984 . . . I attended 30 meetings of the Feminist Movement, one of the Movement of Women for Socialism, two for the Socialist Bloque, one in CEPAL [*Comisión Económica para América Latina y el Caribe*], weekly assemblies; we had a dialogue with MEMCH [*Movimiento para la Emancipación de la Mujer Chilena*] that was for us like a small earthquake that re-equilibrated and settled our relationship with women in the parties; personally, [I attended] a presentation about Feminism and Politics and some other talk; I went to Lima, to Buenos Aires; I read and comprehended various things, conducted sixteen interviews with political women and feminists for my next book; I attended conversations of the socialist women in Buenos Aires; I thought yes or no about this and that; the women's issue became huge, diffuse and important; various sociologists, lawyers, historians began to concern ourselves with presentations and commentaries; we staged seven demonstrations under the slogan "democracy in the country and in the street."[5]

The second book, *Mundo de mujer*, documents discrimination against women in the arenas of health, education, law, work, culture, and politics. Read today, twenty years later, the book comes across as a straightforward and rather arid account of women's status. When first published, its content and its purpose were revolutionary. When I interviewed Eugenia Hola, one of the authors, in 1990, she said, "We wrote *Mundo de mujer* as a diagnostic overview of the Chilean woman, so that when democracy returned, we would be ready to go" in terms of implementing policies that would promote women's rights. The work that feminist scholars did during the dictatorship served as the basis of the women's rights agenda when the new democratic government came to power in 1990.

Chilean feminist writing became a way to raise consciousness and to extend feminism to new generations of activists. In the 1990s, the feminist group *La Morada* offered workshops that explored feminist theory and praxis. Margarita Pisano, one of the leaders of feminism in Latin America and a prolific writer, taught many of the workshops. The twenty-something women (both in age and in number) in one of these classes went on to form their own organization, *las feminarias*. They became active in the Autonomous Feminist Movement, even contributing their own writings to an eponymously titled book.[6] *La Morada*'s workshops illustrate how print sources can reach those as yet unwilling to attend a meeting or a march, thus expanding the reach of an activist community.

Research produced by the international community further fueled feminist activism at the domestic level. When the United Nations convened a conference to kick off the Decade of the Woman in 1975, the mostly male leaders of many UN member countries insisted that women already enjoyed full equality with men. The data gathered on the status of women, which was required of all countries that desired to participate in the conference, suggested otherwise. The information collected in anticipation of this and future UN World Conferences on Women revealed the glaring inequalities between men and women in every corner of the world. Research on the status of women shocked many into acknowledging problems that had not previously been defined as such. Each of the UN World Conferences on Women (held in Mexico City in 1975, Copenhagen in 1980, Nairobi in 1985, and Beijing in 1995) produced "platforms for action" that provided snapshot assessments of the priorities of UN member countries with regard to women's rights. For the UN and other international organizations, these documents identified specific goals and illustrated the achievement of consensus around certain issues.

Writing and research propelled feminism forward in some ways but limited progress in others. The process of documenting the activities of organizations necessarily distorts how events will be interpreted. While writing can legitimize mobilization, it can also crystallize certain facts, thus reifying the movement. A single account of a particular event can unwittingly become a synecdoche for the entire movement; that is, a part of the movement, as it exists at a specific point in time, can come to represent the whole. Women's movements have long been plagued by the problem of a small group of women claiming to represent all women, and a written history can easily be interpreted in a way that exaggerates the importance of a particular event. We read texts of speeches that were given at demonstrations, but we don't know how many people attended, whether anyone was listening, or how the audience reacted—factors that are at least as important as what was said.

Another disadvantage of relying upon writing and research is that the version of an action that gets written down sometimes bears little resemblance to what actually happened in a particular event. The "official version" (even if written by someone within a marginalized group) may fail to convey the substance of conflicts and compromises that lay behind specific decisions. Writing privileges the perspectives of those with a facility for writing and communicating clearly. Many activist-scholars are part of an international academic elite whose proficiency connects them to funding from NGOs in the developed world and crowds out what is written by those less lettered. Writing can thus exacerbate already deep class divides among activists.

Another limitation associated with academic writing pertains to the relationship between Latin American scholars and their counterparts abroad, particularly in North America and Europe. The by-now enormous literature on Latin American feminism includes excellent work by scholars from many regions, each of whom brings distinct perspectives to the production of knowledge about feminism. In Latin America, most scholars wrote to inform their activism. Explosive levels of mobilization among Latin America women captured the imaginations of North American and European scholars, women in particular, who were interested in democratization and were struck by the absence of attention to women's issues. Within political science, writing about feminist movements and the participation of women for (and against) democratization provided a way for American and Canadian scholars to find their (our) own voices and to claim spaces within the academy.[7] Northerners, in seeing things from an outsider's perspective, may write things that locals would never see or might not be able to say because of fear of reprisals, unspoken loyalties, partisan connections, or unwillingness to violate the trust of friends. Nonetheless, too few Northern scholars, myself among them, sought to promote collaboration with Southern scholars to the extent we might have and too few of us translated our work into Spanish and Portuguese to make it more widely accessible.

The Internet intensifies both the benefits and limitations of writing and research as a movement strategy. As Elisabeth Friedman's essay demonstrates, the Internet has multiplied exponentially the opportunities for GLBT movements to "get the word out," thus reducing the isolation of individuals in geographically remote locations, expanding the scope of interaction among activists, and providing a safe place to be "out" and yet protected from discrimination. The Internet diminishes the authority and centrality of certain individuals and organizations as voices of the movement. It disperses authority and authenticity, but may disperse them so widely as to render the Internet ineffectual as a vehicle for social and policy change: it provides no mechanisms for the aggregation of individual voices into a collective "we," other than by means of hyperlinks on a Web site.

The publication of this volume on GLBT politics represents an inaugural effort to disseminate research on this important topic within political science. Several of the chapters within it highlight the important role that writing and research play within the GLBT movement in Latin America. James Green's contribution underscores the importance of mimeographed newsletters, passed hand to hand among trusted individuals, in building awareness, debating pragmatic political strategies, raising theoretical issues about identity, and providing news about friends. As Green writes of the journal *Lampião da Esquina*, "This tabloid-sized newspaper, produced by a collective of writers and intellectuals from Rio de Janeiro and São Paulo, declared itself to be a vehicle for the discussion of sexuality, racial discrimination, the arts, ecology, and machismo." Eduardo Gómez addresses this also. Tim Frasca's chapter describes how activists came to conduct research that suited their goals better than "the academic disciplines [which] seemed to offer only ambition and mediocrity, rather than useful tools . . . Years later the Ford Foundation would support us to conduct this research directly through our non-professional health promoters." Finally, because this volume includes work by North American, Latino, and Latin American scholars alike, it establishes a model of transnational collaboration for future scholars.

When people think of the kinds of activities in which social movement activists engage, they envision protest marches, sit-ins, and demonstrations. Writing and research are at least equally as powerful in terms of their ability to facilitate networking, generate public awareness, and increase political clout. Writing and research can reveal the complexities that surround previously unproblematic issues and provide empirical evidence around which debate can form, thus setting the political agenda.

Notes

1. Human Rights Watch. 2008. "OAS Adopts Resolution to Protect Sexual Rights," June 5, http://hrw.org/english/docs/2008/06/06/colomb19049.htm (accessed August 3, 2008).

2. Human Rights Watch, "LGBT Web Resources," http://hrw.org/english/docs/2007/07/11/global16375.htm (accessed August 3, 2008).

3. Isis International. 1988. *Women's Database: Bibliographical Information*, vol. 1, no. 1–2: v. Santiago, Chile: Isis International.

4. Jeffrey Puryear. 1994. *Thinking Politics: Intellectuals and Democracy in Chile, 1973–1988*. Baltimore: The Johns Hopkins University Press.

5. Julieta Kirkwood. 1986. *Ser política en Chile: los nudos de la sabiduría feminista*, 10. Translation by author. Santiago, Chile: FLACSO.

6. See Sandra Lidid and Kira Maldonado, eds. 1997. "Capítulo 6: Taller de Escritura Feminista 1996." In *Movimiento Feminista Autónomo*, 137–60. Santiago, Chile: Ediciones Número Crítico.

7. I wish I could say that work on women and gender broadened the scope of discussion about democratization within political science, but I'm afraid it has not, as I argue in "The Gender Lacuna in Comparative Politics," *Perspectives on Politics* 8, no. 2 (2010).

ACKNOWLEDGMENTS

WE ARE grateful to Amherst College and the University of Buenos Aires for their financial support. Ronald (Alex) Clark provided invaluable help in the early stages of the project. Seguin Strohmeier, Lucy Zhou, Sarah Harper, and Brittany Berckes provided long hours of research, as well as administrative and copyediting assistance. We want to thank the various translators, whose contributions, we are embarrassed to admit, were underpaid. Last but not least, we are deeply grateful to Malú Moreno, who was involved in every stage of this process. She kept us focused, organized, and more important, sane. She is a friend and colleague like few others.

We are also grateful to all the publishing houses that granted permission to include reprints. Many of the authors provided excerpts of their texts, often within a tight schedule. In some cases, the authors shaped their excerpts, which was crucial for preserving the integrity of those texts. In other cases, we the editors did the excerpting. In addition to excerpting, some of the reprinted texts have undergone minor editorial alterations to create stylistic consistency within this volume.

THE POLITICS OF SEXUALITY IN LATIN AMERICA

Introduction

The Comparative Politics of Sexuality in Latin America

Javier Corrales and Mario Pecheny

POLITICAL SCIENTISTS who study Latin America have not been sufficiently attentive to the genesis of gay, lesbian, bisexual, and transgender (LGBT) politics and tribulations in the region. Few studies on LGBT issues in Latin America have been published in political science journals in the United States. This is not the case in sociology, anthropology, history, and cultural studies, in which LGBT issues have become highly theorized and almost obligatory subjects of study. The inattention to LGBT politics by political scientists seems inexplicable given the field's preeminent role in studying issues of state formation, citizenship, democratization, civil rights, inclusionary politics, bargaining, social movements, identity, public policy, and more recently, issues surrounding the quality of democracy. Political scientists who study Latin America have produced novel theories and empirical studies on each of these subfields. Few of them have focused on LGBT issues.

The paucity of studies on LGBT politics in Latin America could give the impression that LGBT groups and issues are insignificant in the region's politics. The purpose of this reader is to show otherwise. Collectively these readings demonstrate that LGBT topics have been salient affairs in Latin American politics during the current "third wave of democratization," as well as in previous waves.

This reader assembles complete or excerpted works by scholars, analysts, activists, and politicians on the politics of advancing LGBT rights. We tried to select works that were written in the 2000s and to ensure as much regional and thematic coverage as possible. The authors exhibit variations in disciplinary training, theoretical bent, methodological approach, country of origin, and units of analysis, yet, despite these differences, they share two beliefs. First, the authors agree that LGBT politics cannot be omitted from the study of democratization. If democracy is inconceivable in the absence of respect for "cultural diversity" and "the right to difference" (Hagopian 2007), the authors in this reader would insist that LGBT rights are fundamental components of diversity and difference. In essence, the authors are united behind the idea that there is a fundamental "democratic right to sexuality" (Raupp Rios 2005; Raupp Rios this volume). Second, they agree that studying LGBT politics offers different and sometimes new insights about the democratization process—how it advances, stagnates, or reverses. These are insights that are not easy to visualize when studying other social groups claiming rights. In short, LGBT affairs are essential and distinct topics of democratization.

What do these works reveal collectively? At the risk of downplaying the diversity of ideas contained in this reader, we identify two major themes. First, the struggle for LGBT rights in Latin America has made unprecedented inroads in the first decade of the twenty-first century, but not in every domain, nor everywhere in the region. In several countries and cities, it is now common to find laws and policies against discrimination based on sexual orientation, legal recognition of same-sex couples and gender changes, policies against homophobia, and the inclusion of LGBT activists within government. In many other domains, regions, or countries, there has been little progress, if any. Several pieces in this reader document and seek to explain this uneven progress.

Second, these inroads, where they have occurred, were long in coming, far longer than one would have expected given the progress achieved by LGBT groups in many democracies elsewhere, and the progress achieved by other social movements in Latin America (see Baldez, Thayer in this volume). Furthermore, it is unclear whether inroads will continue to be made or even endure. Many of the readings here discuss the factors that have hindered and may continue to hinder the progress of LGBT movements in the region.

This reader is therefore about the uneven and late achievement of LGBT rights in Latin America, and the potential for that achievement to stagnate. In this introduction, we would like to offer some insights, drawn mostly from our authors, about these topics. We begin with a brief conceptualization of LGBT politics in democratization studies, and then proceed to a discussion of the political factors that have blocked or propelled LGBT rights in the region.

Fighting Heteronormativity

At its core, LGBT politics is about challenging heteronormativity. This term refers to the tendency of societies to organize social relations and citizen rights based on the notion that reproductive heterosexuality is ideal. In most contemporary societies, leaders and opinion makers often apply the standard of reproductive heterosexuality in judging a person's worth and eligibility for rewards such as acceptance, inheritance, pensions, social status, welfare benefits, and job promotions. Heteronormativity imposes on individuals the expectation of having sexual and affective partnerships with members of the opposite sex, raising children in heterosexual environments, and performing gender-based roles that align with traditional (binary) or majoritarian definitions of *male* and *female*.

LGBT politics focuses on creating a safe space for individuals who do not conform to these heteronormative expectations. These include people who feel attraction to members of the same sex (gays, lesbians, and bisexuals); those whose gender identity and/or expression depart from binary canons (female vs. male, heterosexual vs. homosexual) and those who feel that their "nature-given anatomy," their identity attributed at birth, or both are in conflict with their true gender identity (Pecheny 2008, 14).

A heteronormative environment is typically uncomfortable with diversity. This discomfort affects nonconforming individuals not just at the psychological level, but also politically. Heteronormativity places all nonconforming citizens within any polity at high risk of feeling or actually experiencing exclusion, denigration, discrimination, ostracism, victimization by hate crime, forced migration, and neglect by state security and welfare policies. LGBT politics is therefore the struggle against the conditions that give rise to these experiences and the feeling of living with the threat of these experiences.

Distinguishing among Desires, Identities, Public Expressions, and Practices

Although LGBT social movements and citizens may be united in their opposition to heteronormativity, not all share the same political concerns. Scholars face a number of complications in trying to classify the array of concerns for all LGBT citizens (see Moreno in this volume for a discussion of the complexity of identity and politics in the Buenos Aires GLTTB movement). These complications arise from the occasionally overlapping nature of some of these concerns. One way to understand these complications is to think in terms of the differences between desires, sexual practices, identities, and behaviors (see table 1.1).

Table 1.1. Heteronormativity and nonheteronormativity: desire, identity, and expression

	Desire (sexual orientation)	(Self-)identity	Gender and identity expression vis-à-vis others
Heterosexual	Predominant or exclusive attraction to the opposite sex (includes asexual individuals by default)	May not be an issue	May or may not deviate from heteronormativity (e.g., macho/effeminate men; tomboy/feminine women)
Homosexual (men are referred to as gays; women, as lesbians)	Predominant or exclusive attraction to the same sex	May or may not consider him- or herself a LGBT individual	May or may not deviate from heteronormativity (e.g., macho/effeminate men; tomboy/feminine women), with one caveat: may display different degrees of "outness" in the family, work and community
Bisexual (women and men)	Attraction to the opposite and the same sex	May or may not consider him- or herself a LGBT individual	May or may not deviate from heteronormativity (e.g., macho/effeminate men; tomboy/feminine women), with one caveat: may display different degrees of "outness" in the family, work and community
Transgender (women and men)	May or may not be an issue	Rejects the gender identity that was assigned at birth	May or may not deviate from heteronormativity (e.g., macho/effeminate men; tomboy/feminine women), with one caveat: may display different degrees of "outness" in the family, work and community
Transsexual (women and men)	May or may not be an issue	Rejects the gender identity that was assigned at birth	Changes appearance, and maybe anatomy
Effeminate men and masculine women	Attraction to the opposite and/or the same sex	May or may not be an issue	Mannerisms deviate from heteronormative standards
Intersex	May or may not be an issue	May or may not be an issue	May or may not change anatomy, but experiences social pressure to possess physical anatomy, particularly genitalia, that match male or female heteronormative standards

For gay men and lesbians, the main political concerns tend to be the ability to express their sexual orientations or desires without discrimination or any other social penalty, and to have their sexual and loving relationships be socially recognized. Sexual orientation refers to a person's capacity for profound emotional, affectionate, and sexual relations with others (The Yogyakarta Principles 2007). Men who experience same-sex desire predominantly are often referred to as *gays*, and same-sex attracted women are referred to as *lesbians*. If they experience this desire for both women and men, they are referred to as *bisexual*. Notice that the translation of desires into sexual practices is not crucial: homosexuals, like heterosexuals, may practice celibacy, monogamy, nonmonogamy, or frequent changes in sexual partners. What is crucial for defining gay/lesbian sexual orientation is a preponderance of desire for emotional, affectionate, and sexual relations with members of the same sex, although denominations and terms for these orientations may differ across cultures, generations, and settings. Multiple local denominations exist across societies and within sexual subcultures.

For transgendered individuals, on the other hand, the main issue is the recognition of their gender identity, and the end of their exclusion from almost every social domain of life (education, employment, social networks). Gender identity refers to a person's deeply felt internal and individual sense of gender, which may or may not correspond with the sex/gender assigned at birth, including the personal sense of the body. To them, the key issue is self-identification (what is between their ears), more than their sex (what is between their legs) (Girshick 2008). Transgender individuals may or may not choose to modify bodily appearance or function (by medical, surgical, or other means) or alter expressions of gender, including dress, speech, and mannerisms (The Yogyakarta Principles 2007). They depart from heteronormativity on the basis of identity, but not necessarily in any other category in table 1.1.

Some people wish to adapt their appearances (partially or fully, permanently or occasionally, anatomically and/or through clothing and makeup) and social identities (beginning with their names) away from the gender identities attributed to them at birth, to reflect their true gender identities. Citizens with this desire are called *transgender*, *transvestite*, or *transsexual*. Those who undergo deeper forms of change in their gender expression, for instance, those who engage in anatomical change or hormone therapy, dislike the term *change of sex* to describe their transition, preferring instead to state that they have "adapted" their genitalia and/or physical appearance to their true gender and sexual identities. Many transgenders stop referring to themselves as *transsexuals* after they complete their "transition," preferring instead to be called *men* or *women*. However, this process of adaptation may or may not proceed according to binary terms (i.e., *male* or *female*, as exclusive alternatives); it may include elements that could be called *feminine* and elements that could be called *masculine*. A school of thought typically denominated as the "queer approach" specifically challenges the idea that gender and sexuality are binary: male and female, masculine and feminine, straight and gay, and so on.

Some scholars talk about gender as a cultural and social construction of (biological) sexual difference, while others affirm that gender language precedes even the understanding of material bodies: one "sees" bodies only through received gender lenses, and gender differences and practices are continually performed. According to this perspective, the discussion about whether gender attributes correspond or not to each "sex" is pointless, since there is no "sex" outside or before gender constructions. In a heteronormative construction of sex and gender, there are two sexes and two genders, and individuals are expected to conform more or less to this binary construction. Looking through a nonheteronormative lens, however, one perceives that gender varies along a continuum.

Recently, in Latin America, transvestites have become politically visible in relation to sex work and their encounters with the police. Cultural and psychosocial factors, as well as factors related to the impossibility of entering the job market, have made sex work almost the exclusive source of income for female transgender individuals. In everyday life, transgendered people suffer multiple forms of hardship: transphobia (irrational aversion to transgenderism), intolerance toward sex work, police abuse in the form of "rape, assault, and extortion," poverty, underemployment, exposure to HIV/AIDS, and crime. These forms of oppression act in synergy (Human Rights Watch 2009; Parker and Aggleton 2003; Modarelli in this volume).

While identity is an unavoidable issue for transgendered citizens, it is not necessarily salient for all LGB individuals. Having same-sex desires and behaviors does not necessarily produce LGB identities. Some citizens exhibiting LGB desires and behaviors actually expend great efforts disguising their desires from others to avoid being assigned a label. LGB citizens might not necessarily develop an LGB identity or even a public expression of their desires. Though same-sex desires have been recorded for millennia, LGB identities are more recent and vary across historical periods, cultures, and even circles of friends, indicating that expression is not a necessary outgrowth of LGB desires (Balderston and Guy 1997; Sigal 2003; Gutiérrez 2007). In some other cases, gender expression is also at stake: for effeminate men, for instance, as well as for masculine women (regardless of sexual orientation and/or actual sexual practices), especially during childhood and adolescence, harassment and discrimination may occur because of this apparent incoherence between their gender identities as men or as women and their respective effeminate or masculine manners.

Intersex people comprise yet another group negatively affected by heteronormativity. *Intersex* is a general term to describe a person who is born with a reproductive or sexual anatomy that

> doesn't seem to fit the typical definitions of female or male. For example, a person might
> be born appearing to be female on the outside, but having mostly male-typical anatomy

on the inside. Or a person may be born with genitals that seem to be in-between the usual male and female types—for example, a girl may be born with a noticeably large clitoris, or lacking a vaginal opening, or a boy may be born with a notably small penis, or with a scrotum that is divided so that it has formed more like labia. (Intersex Society of North America 2009)

Scientists estimate conservatively that at least 1.7 percent of people are born with a possible intersexual condition (*The Economist,* 2009). In most countries, surgery to "normalize" sexual appearance as either male or female is often performed. In adulthood, intersex people may come to regret this decision for a number of reasons (not least because one possible consequence of surgery is diminished sexual sensitiveness and sterility). Others who did not undergo surgery may choose surgery in adulthood.

Finally, women fighting heteronormativity often contend that they are simultaneously fighting other more primordial issues, such as patriarchalism and gender hierarchy, which can be considered part of heteronormativity. Because homophobia directed at women combines both heteronormative standards and patriarchalism, women often feel that homophobia directed at them is more hostile than that directed at males; lesbians also find fewer public gathering spaces in which to meet than do gay and bisexual men (see Friedman; Babb; Guinea, Desh, and Peroni in this volume).

It is crucial to reiterate that desire and identity are different from actual behavior. Not all gay, lesbian, and bisexual desires translate into gay, lesbian, and bisexual practices or public behaviors. Likewise, not all transgender identities produce actual efforts to change and adapt, cosmetically or bodily, one's gender appearance. In short, many individuals with same-sex desires and many transgender individuals opt not to engage in LGBT practices or public behaviors.

The Politics of Advancing LGBT Rights: Small Minorities and Large Closets

The starting point of LGBT politics (and of LGBT individuals acting in ordinary politics) is the realization that, in a heteronormative society, converting LGBT desires and identities into actual behaviors and expressions entails costs, obstacles, and risks. These costs, obstacles, and risks may be expected to cause enough trauma to preclude actual LGBT behaviors and expressions. Heteronormativity thus conspires against the fundamental freedoms of expression and association.

Politics, together with social hostility, thus influence LGBT behavior and identity, though generally not desires. This means that a nonheteronormative environment may lead to freer LGBT expressions, but it will not make heterosexual individuals suddenly experience homosexual desires. Degrees of recognition and tolerance, socialization, and legal practices shape a person's self-acceptance (the degree to which one acknowledges homosexual attractions or a challenging gender identity), activities (the degree to which one engages in homosexual sex and loving relationships), and expression (the degree to which one decides to hide fully, hide partially, reveal partially, or reveal openly one's nonconformance to heteronormativity) (see Espinosa Miñoso in this volume for a discussion of the link between lesbianism and feminist activism). Politics will not fix or change a person's sexual orientation, but politics can influence identity and expression, as shown in table 1.1.

This brings us to a dilemma in LGBT politics. For LGBT rights to advance in any society, it is necessary for a group of LGBT rights-demanders to coalesce. However, such a group is likelier to coalesce when nonheterosexual individuals publicly develop LGBT (or other nonheterosexual) public identities (see Brown in this volume). This raises a double paradox: first, LGBT citizens must challenge the notion that sexualities and gender identities are fixed (i.e., sexual and gender boundaries are more "inessential" and "fluid" than is conventionally believed), but at the same time, they must develop strong identities themselves to gain political power (Gamson 1995). Second, a comfort zone seems to be a prior necessity for these identities to form. Thus, advancing LGBT rights presupposes an expansion of LGBT identity, and yet, this expansion of LGBT identity is likelier if there are minimal political opportunities for it to surface. A crucial element of LGBT politics consists of figuring out how to escape from this conundrum.

Yet another dilemma in the politics of LGBT rights has to do with the problem of numbers. According to most social movement theories, there is a strong connection between numbers and power. The greater the number of adherents, real or perceived, to any given cause, the greater the chance of influencing politics. This poses a dilemma for LGBT politics in three ways.

First, the proportion of the population comprised by LGBT citizens is typically a minority, even if we suspect that people who do not conform to heteronormative standards could in theory constitute a large group. The smallness of this population represents a structural impediment to the bargaining leverage of LGBT groups in any political struggle. As an interest group participating in democratic politics, LGBT groups will never constitute a large group, and thus, will never achieve sufficient influence unless they acquire allies within other societal groups (see Brown, Green in this volume). Moreover, minority status means not only (or mainly) a small size, but also relegation to "minoritization" or subordinate status through some type of political process.

Second, the possibility of hiding one's desires, identity, and behavior (an available option for most gays, lesbians, and bisexuals, but not for transgenders) and of managing one's public identity make the structural impediment of small numbers even more restricting. The closet (the informal practice endemic to LGB citizens of disguising their LGB behaviors and identities) hurts the strength of LGBT forces in ways that are not relevant among many other nondominant groups. Most people who are discriminated against based on physical appearance (e.g., targets of racism, ageism, nativism, sexism) cannot easily hide their physical appearance, and thus do not have the closet option, but LGB people can avoid the stigma by staying—totally or partially—in the closet. Almost all LGB people, at some point or another, especially in their younger years, engage in some form of effort to remain undetected, to "pass" as heterosexual (i.e., conforming to heteronormativity). Hiding is the first thing LGB individuals and groups learn to do when they begin to experience heteronormativity and think about gender and sexual public expression. Some LGB people pursue the closet option for a very long time, even an entire lifetime. The closet is a seeming safe haven for many LGB citizens, but it is a serious impediment to overcoming the small-constituency problem inherent in LGB politics. To use the language of public choice theories, the closet option is tantamount to the "free rider problem" as an obstacle to collective action: the closet means that a large number of people are unwilling to shoulder the costs of action, thus thwarting the capacity of associations to mobilize constituents and affect policy.

Third, sexual categories are not a priori social groups with identifiable bonds and settings. Often, members of social groups are visible to each other: workers may form unions, or members of religious minorities may worship at the same place. In contrast, because sexuality is a feature mainly expressed in intimate settings, members of sexual social groups are not necessarily visible. Establishing social (and political) bonds requires an active effort of visibility, internal and external (see Pecheny, "Sociability, Secrets, and Identities: Key Issues in Sexual Politics in Latin America," in this volume for further discussion of the closet and how the "secret" of homosexuality influences realms of sociability).

A central issue of LGBT politics is therefore fighting not just homophobic institutions and attitudes, but also what Eskridge has called the "apartheid of the closet," that is, the tendency of LGBT people themselves to seek the closet in order to find security and freedom (Eskridge 1999). The paradox of LGBT politics is that the closet might be a necessary place for citizens to enter, at least occasionally, in order to find protection and even freedom, but staying in the closet undermines the prospects for LGBT activism, since it reduces the number of adherents to the cause, impeding the achievement of greater protection and freedom.

However serious, it is important not to overstate the problems posed by smallness of group size and closet issues. There are plenty of examples of small interest groups in democracies that become influential in politics. We know from public choice theories since Mancur Olson (1965; see also Becker 1983) that small associations enjoy advantages that allow them to capture policy. A lot depends on each group's internal organization, the nature of its demands, its tactics, its allies and foes across society, and larger structural issues such as overall economic conditions. We will turn our attention to these endogenous and exogenous factors and how they have influenced the bargaining leverage of Latin America's LGBT movements. But first, we offer a review of progress thus far.

Latin America's Coming Out in the 2000s

During the first decade and a half after the return to democracy (early 1980s through mid 1990s), LGBT issues in Latin America remained in the closet or were discussed only in very small circles. Unquestionably, autocratic rule was not generally gay friendly. In Brazil and Argentina, some tiny but visible "homosexual liberation groups" emerged in the 1970s and took a beating from authoritarian regimes. In Cuba, LGBT citizens were placed in labor camps in the 1960s. Yet, the transition to democracy was not that progay either, at least initially. Shortly after the transition to democracy, LGBT movements were in early stages or heavily wounded. They thus had less visibility and impact than other social movements. A combination of a false sense of triumph (the new democratization), other priorities (framing new political institutions, dealing with past human-rights violations, economic travails), and the overall weakness of LGBT movements in the region meant that LGBT rights in the early 1980s and 1990s did not advance greatly.

However, since the late 1990s, Latin America has experienced a significant "coming-out" experience, albeit not evenly. LGBT issues have become more openly debated topics in most countries (at least in some circles), and more importantly, the political and legal environment in favor of LGBT rights has begun to expand in some countries (see Raupp Rios in this volume for a legal analysis of LGBT rights in Latin America).

In 1998, for instance, Ecuador adopted a new constitution that included protections against discrimination based on sexual orientation. In 1999, Chile decriminalized same-sex intercourse. In 2000, Rio de Janeiro's state legislature banned sexual-orientation-based discrimination in public and private establishments. In 2002, the city of Buenos Aires guaranteed all couples, regardless of gender, the right to register their civil unions. In 2003, Mexico passed a federal antidiscrimination law that includes sexual orientation. In 2004, the government of Brazil initiated *Brasil sem Homofobia* (Brazil without Homophobia), a comprehensive program combining the resources of NGOs and government agencies to change social attitudes toward LGB people. In 2006, Mexico City approved the Cohabitation Law, granting same-sex couples marital rights identical to those established for common-law relationships between men and women. In 2007, Uruguay passed a new law granting access to health benefits, inheritance, parenting rights, and pension rights to all couples who have cohabited for at least five years, and Bogotá and other Colombian cities established public policies specifically addressed to LGB populations. In 2008, Nicaragua reformed its penal code to decriminalize same-sex relations, and Cuba's new president, Raúl Castro, authorized free sex-change operations for qualifying citizens. The 2008 LGBT parade in São Paulo,

Brazil, was attended by more than three million people, making it the biggest public gathering in Brazilian history, bigger even than those at the time of *Diretas Já!* (the massive civil movement demanding direct presidential elections in 1984), and the largest LGBT demonstration in the world. And at the end of 2009, Mexico and Argentina moved forward with same-sex marriage (see appendix timeline in this volume).

Policy areas have also seen progress. By 2007, for instance, approximately three-quarters of persons needing antiretroviral treatment for HIV/AIDS in the Americas were receiving that treatment—the highest coverage in the developing world (Pan American Health Organization 2007). As some pieces in this reader indicate, this is a triumph for LGBT movements and patients, many of whom have concentrated on this policy issue. Furthermore, Latin American cities are becoming increasingly "gay friendly," defined as having a high density of LGBT establishments per capita. In some cases, Latin American cities score higher than richer cities in other democracies (see Corrales in this volume). Large cities like Rio de Janeiro, Buenos Aires, and Mexico City, as well as smaller cities like Puerto Vallarta and San Miguel de Allende in Mexico, often rank high as LGBT destinations in international travel guides. Academically, LGBT studies have become part of higher education in Brazil, Argentina, Mexico, Peru, Colombia, and Chile.

LGBT issues have thus become increasingly salient in Latin America and are part of public debate and political contestation. This is astounding because levels of homophobia in the region, we now know for sure, are profound. A survey by Americas-Barometer, the only survey of public opinion and democratic behavior that covers all of the Americas, hosted by Vanderbilt University in Nashville, Tennessee, revealed shocking degrees of homophobia across the region. People in 2006–07 were asked whether they approve or disapprove of the right of homosexuals to run for public office. In Canada and the United States, a large majority expressed approval (76.2 and 69.7 percent, respectively). In Latin American countries, except Mexico, Brazil, and Uruguay, the vast majority, sometimes more than 60 percent of respondents, disapproved of extending this basic democratic right to homosexuals (Orces 2008). The survey was not asking whether to extend homosexuals the right to marriage, adoption, inheritance, and pensions, which are typically controversial, but simply, the right to run for office. Homophobia in the region is so profound that it gives rise to public support for suppressing basic democratic rights. Given this attitudinal context, the region's achievements in advancing LGBT rights seem remarkable.

Two key questions are worth highlighting. First, why did this coming-out experience occur at this particular historical moment? Second, will the progress continue? Answering these questions requires looking more closely at the factors that tend to promote or retard the expansion of LGBT issues worldwide and in Latin America in particular, and that shape the specific patterns of these processes.

In the following sections, we focus on the extent to which Latin America, as a whole, may differ from other democratic regions in terms of the following: (1) prolonged homestay, which, given that homophobia begins at home, tends to distort and delay the rise of a gay identity; (2) the dilemmas faced by independent youths; (3) the availability of the closet(s); (4) the role of income and competing economic issues; (5) the role of shocks and horrors in drawing attention to LGBT rights; (6) the role of religion; and (7) the difficult interaction between political parties and LGBT social movements.

Homophobia Begins at Home

A key problem facing LGBT movements in Latin America is the extent to which young people, typically the biggest engines of social movements, live with their parents or extended families. The problem with this living arrangement is that it exposes too many young people to a type of discrimination that is not that common among members of other nondominant groups in any society: household discrimination (see Pecheny, "Sociability, Secrets, and Identities," in this volume). Usually, the most feared and cruelest forms of homophobia begin at home or in small towns. A major trauma for many LGBT youths is that the very people who are closest (affectively and biologically)—immediate relatives—are the ones who have the hardest time accepting LGBT identities and practices.

Evidence of household-based discrimination for LGBT citizens in Latin America is growing. A survey of participants in the Buenos Aires 2005 gay pride march revealed that 26.5 percent of respondents felt "excluded and marginalized by their families" (Jones, Libson, and Hiller 2006) (see figure 1). This was the third most frequent form of discrimination, preceded by discrimination by "teachers and classmates" and discrimination by "neighbors." A similar survey of participants in the 2007 gay pride march in Santiago, Chile, placed the number even higher: 29.8 percent of participants report having "felt excluded or marginalized within their family" (Barrientos et al. 2008). The Santiago survey goes further by providing data for different subgroups: for lesbians, the percentage increases to 33.8 percent; for transgendered people, the percentage is 47.4 percent. The survey also reveals that 70.8 percent have been subjected to "verbal aggressions" and 22.8 to "physical aggression." A 2005 survey in Mexico revealed that 21 percent of surveyed LGBT individuals felt they were denied jobs, 11 percent felt they were denied access to a school, and 30 percent felt they were discriminated against by the police (Figueroa 2006). In Colombia, a survey asked people to state whom they would prefer not to have as neighbors; the answers included "thieves, paramilitaries, ex guerrillas, prostitutes, homosexuals, and people with AIDS" (Salazar 2006).

For most people suffering discrimination and exclusion, such as members of religious or racial minorities, the household normally serves as a safe haven in an otherwise inhospitable world. Black parents, for instance, do not reject black children for being black—on the contrary, they often teach them how to cope with outside dis-

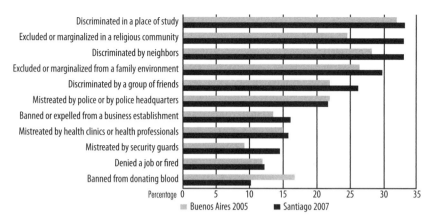

Figure 1. Survey of participants in gay pride marches

crimination. In contrast, straight parents may have intense reactions to their children's deviations from heteronormativity, sometimes more intense than their reactions to strangers' deviations. For transgender youths, rejection is much stronger, and thus, the incidence of migration to other cities or countries and severing of ties with families of origin are more frequent.

Of course, there are exceptions. The 1985 Mexican movie, *Doña Herlinda y su hijo* (*Doña Herlinda and Her Son*), depicts the story of a mother in Guadalajara who tolerates her gay son and his male lover. But the fact that the film draws humor from a mother's acceptance is a testament to how unusual this practice is. Furthermore, the acceptance in the movie comes with certain conditions: the son must still marry a woman and keep his gay relationship secret, suggesting household tolerance more for what we could call an "open closet" than for open LGBT behavior per se (further discussed below).

In general, therefore, LGBT citizens, in contrast to many others within nondominant social categories, are likelier to find the household to be an uncomfortable and even unsafe environment—a place where it is dangerous to exhibit LGBT desires, identities, and behaviors, and where discrimination can bring about the direst consequences, such as ostracism, harassment, mistreatments, even economic destitution. However, household and parental homophobia is not always cruel or long-lasting. Frequently, household environments do change for the better, becoming quite supportive. But it is hard for most young LGBT citizens to discount household homophobia, at least initially. Coming out to parents and close relatives is typically a nerve-racking experience that individuals from other nondominant groups seldom experience, and LGBT youths must confront this hardship early in their lives.

Latin American Youths Stay Home Longer

In high-income, advanced democracies, a typical solution to the problem of "homophobia begins at home" is household exodus: LGBT youths leave their homes, sometimes their hometowns, in search of greater freedom, new experiences, and supportive groups. But for LGBT individuals in Latin America, this exit option is considerably less prevalent. The 2007 Santiago gay pride poll revealed that 51.3 percent of participants lived with "a mother, a father, or both"; 81 percent of those in that category were in the 18–25-year-old age group (Barrientos et al. 2008). In Buenos Aires, 62.3 percent of 20–24-year-olds and 34.3 percent of 25–29-year-olds lived with "parents and relatives" (Jones, Libson, and Hiller 2006). In Latin America, it seems, the household exit option is not as prevalent for LGB people, even in higher-income countries like Argentina and Chile. This may not be the case for transgendered youths, many of whom report household exodus. But for the vast majority of LGB people in their early twenties, and a large majority of LGB people in their late twenties, household exodus is atypical.

There are several reasons for this stay-with-family phenomenon. First, incomes are lower and job opportunities are scarcer for young citizens in Latin America. Young people cannot, therefore, afford an independent lifestyle. Second, families still expect unmarried children to stay within the household, either as a cultural preference or out of economic necessity. Third, many cities and towns have a housing shortage, forcing different generations to share dwellings (see Larson in this volume).

Table 1.2 shows differences in household structure, comparing Latin America and the Caribbean to the United States. The table shows that the exodus option is relatively rare in the general population in Latin America. The share of people living alone is less than one-third of those in the United States. Most of these live-alone youths are concentrated in the urban areas of Argentina and Uruguay (Arriagada 2004). Latin Americans in the bottom three deciles of income rarely live alone—less than 2 percent, in contrast to the 6–7 percent figure of the United States (Inter-American Development Bank 1998, 65). Evidence from Colombia, Chile, and Mexico shows that 80 percent of young adults still live with their "family of origin" rather than within their "own family," resulting in "delayed autonomy" (Economic Commission for Latin America and the Caribbean 2004, 27). Most Latin American youths (between 70 and 90 percent) live in nuclear (two parents) or extended households (another relative in addition to parents) (Inter-American Development Bank 1998). In the United States in 2003, in contrast, 55 percent of adults aged 18–24 years old lived with at least one parent, most likely in a nuclear family (rarely an extended family). The percentage drops to 10 percent among adults 25–34 years old (Fields 2004). In Latin America, where extended families are still more prevalent, typically a grandparent constitutes this third person in extended families, suggesting that more youths in Latin America live with older-generation relatives. Insofar as homophobia is stronger

Table 1.2. Structure of households, United States (2003), Latin America (2002), and the Caribbean (2002)

	Latin America and the Caribbean (%)	United States (%)
Single-headed households	8.4	26.4
Nonnuclear households	4.8	6.1
Nuclear families (two parents with children)	42.8	23.5
Nuclear without children (married childless couple or two parents)	7.7	28.2
Extended families (parents and at least one more relative) and composite families (at least one nonrelative, not including domestic workers, resides in the household)	22*	No data
Youth old enough to live independently, but living with original family	70–90†	45‡

Sources: For Latin America and the Caribbean, Arriagada (2004); for United States, Census Bureau (Fields 2004).

* estimate; † age of youth group unspecified; ‡ 18–24 years old.

among older-generation adults (Kornblit et al. 1997), the prevalence of extended families in Latin America suggests that heteronormative pressures on Latin American youths are greater.

Whatever the reasons, household exodus is limited in Latin America, and the average Latin American household is more intergenerational. This situation has implications for LGBT politics. It means that many young people are exposed to household discrimination, possibly delaying or inhibiting LGBT behaviors, identities, and expression, potentially causing more trauma among LGBT youths in Latin America than in other democracies. As a generalization, one could say that LGBT youths in the United States leave their households, whereas in Latin America, they stay home, complicating their coming-out experience. The number of young LGBT people who feel ready to join a political struggle on behalf of LGBT rights is relatively small—youths in Latin America may still be hiding their nonheterosexuality from their parents and even themselves.

Household Exodus Brings Problems

While youth household exodus is limited in Latin America, when it does occur, it may bring its own set of problems that can hinder the rise of LGBT groups. Given the lack of job and housing opportunities for young people in Latin America, poor young people living outside their families in Latin America face onerous economic problems. Furthermore, there is evidence that household exodus among low-income young people may lead to street living. In Honduras and Nicaragua, for instance, the World

Bank calculates that 8–12 percent of all children below the age of 18 are working or living in the streets—or both. These household leavers come from poverty and stay in poverty.

Latin America's street youths might be free from household homophobia—and relatively free to engage in sex (and sex work)—but they are nonetheless burdened by new hardships such as poverty, crime, abandonment, teenage pregnancy, and overall insecurity, as famously depicted in the 1981 Brazilian movie *Pixote*. These street youths become *disconnected*, a term used in the United States to refer to citizens who are disengaged from productive activities, such as employment and schooling, and thus are not preparing for a self-sufficient life.

Disconnected street youths in Latin America may display LGBT behavior, but do not necessarily harbor a positive LGBT identity or the will and chance to be part of any LGBT civic group. They are too preoccupied with other difficulties of life, detached not only from productive activity, but from civil society in general. They are not necessarily available for political mobilization.

Class difference reveals itself here. For some reason, there are more transgender expressions in the lower strata of society, and these transgenders have less to lose from household exodus. Middle-class people, in contrast, are less likely to choose household exodus, and there are fewer known transgenders in this income group (Kulick 1998; Berkins and Fernández 2005; Berkins 2008; Fernández in this volume).

A more drastic form of exodus is emigration. The need to leave a country to escape homophobia is a topic that, not surprisingly, appears frequently in novels (see Foster 2002) and movies with LGBT themes in Latin America (e.g., *No se lo digas a nadie* [*Don't Tell Anyone*], *Conducta impropia* [*Improper Conduct*], *Fresa y chocolate* [*Strawberries and Chocolate*], *Antes que anochezca* [*Before Night Falls*], *XXY*). Immigration affords LGBT Latin Americans a chance at relief from an array of hardships, such as poor economic opportunities, political persecution, and societal and household homophobia, but pursuing this chance comes with very high costs and risks: the costs of leaving one's own community and the risks of crossing tough immigration barriers and adapting to an alien environment (see Ocasio in this volume). Emigration also brings the risk of turning LGBT people into "double minorities" (immigrants and non-heterosexuals) and thus plunging them into double hardships. In both *No se lo digas a nadie* and *XXY*, the main LGBT characters, from Peru and Argentina, respectively, are in the end unable to find safety through emigration (for Mexicans in the United States, see Carrillo et al. 2008).

Latin America's Multiple Closets

An ancient route through which young people "exit" household-based heteronormativity and discrimination is heterosexual marriage. This exit strategy—again, historically pervasive among LGBT people worldwide—raises the issue of closet living. The more "comfortable" the closet in any given society, or alternatively, the more closet options there are, and the higher the perceived costs of coming out, the fewer the number of citizens available for mobilization for LGBT rights. It is precisely because of this inverse relationship between closet options and power that LGBT movements worldwide devote efforts to encouraging people to come out, and that pride marches often focus on the issue of visibility.

In some Latin American societies, not only are the pressures to remain hidden stronger, but the closet options are arguably more "comfortable" and abundant than in Europe or in the United States. Societies vary according to the number of ways in which people can hide their LGBT sexuality in order to be accepted by heteronormative standards. In Latin America, heterosexual married life can become compatible with closet homosexual practices in a number of ways. Many anthropologists and sociologists argue that there are multiple "closet options" available. In addition to the standard closet of simply disguising one's own desire, identity, and behavior, the following closets exist:

1. The marital-life closet, linked to a gendered double standard (what is expected for a man versus for a woman): the degree to which a spouse tolerates extramarital affairs, heterosexual or otherwise

2. The good-parent closet: the idea that as long as a parent is a reliable provider in the household, any behavior outside the family is tolerated

3. The top-versus-bottom closet: the idea that as long as one performs certain sexual roles and not others, one need not be considered LGBT. For instance, in some circles, a sexual penetrator, a nonkisser, or simply the man who sets the rules of sexual activity can still be considered compliant with heteronormativity

Michael Musto has argued that in the United States this tolerance for semihidden LGBT behavior, what he calls the "glass closet," is mostly associated with Hollywood celebrities (2007). But it seems that in Latin America the "glass closet" is available to many more citizens, especially in upper income brackets.

The 1998 Peruvian film *No se lo digas a nadie*, based on the novel by journalist Jaime Bayly, offers examples of all three glass closets. In the movie, a young gay man from Lima's upper middle class faces discrimination by family and society as an "out" homosexual; however, he gains reacceptance by the end of the movie by tacitly promising to live according to heteronormative standards, even though his peers, family, and potential girlfriend know perfectly well that he will lead a double life. The young man is afforded this "luxury" of a double life because he will be discreet and, it seems, is willing to fulfill the other functions of heterosexual matrimony. In addition, there are scenes in which some of his sexual partners reject a gay self-identity, despite their sexual orientation, in part because of the role they play while having sex.

For women, these multiple closets might be less available than for men, which may create fewer freedoms for lesbians (see Friedman in this volume). On the other hand, friendship between two women has served as a form of camouflage for loving homosexual relations, practiced by lesbians who have children or are divorced from men. In Latin America, this camouflage has historically been more easily accepted for women than for men.

Although one could argue these closets and camouflages are becoming less available in general, they have not disappeared, and in some circles, they remain quite prevalent (Pecheny, "Sociability, Secrets, and Identities" in this volume). Insofar as visibility is a necessary condition for effective collective action, these multiple closets and forms of camouflage unquestionably hamper the potential progress of LGBT movements. Many potential allies, especially in the middle and upper class, are unavailable as political members of these groups because they enjoy many comfortable closets in which to hide while still finding societal toleration—which is not the same as social acceptance or recognition.

Income Levels and Competing Priorities

Income levels affect LGBT politics in a number of ways. In general, albeit with exceptions, LGBT rights have expanded the most in the world's richest countries. This makes sense. Social movements, especially those advocating for postmaterialist concerns (i.e., concerns one considers once basic material needs for food, shelter, etc. are met), are likelier to move forward as incomes at the national and individual levels rise. By the same token, poor economic conditions may be associated with fewer opportunities for expansion of LGBT rights. For many citizens, economic problems such as unemployment, poverty, precarious income, lack of job security, and insufficient savings tend to trump issues of sexuality as a political priority. Thus, when economic conditions are precarious within the nation, the community, the household, or the individual's pocketbook, citizens may be less inclined to treat LGBT issues as a priority. In other words, the struggle for LGBT rights is often a postmaterialist concern: it is likelier to rise to the top of the agenda when material concerns become less urgent (see Thayer in this volume for a discussion of new social movement theory).

This income argument and the existence of larger urban middle-class groups explain why Latin America as a whole has stronger LGBT movements than do Africa and South Asia, but has weaker movements than do most Organisation for Economic Co-operation and Development (OECD) countries, where income levels and urban populations are higher (Cáceres et al. 2008).

However, although income conditions in Latin America are producing a more favorable environment for LGBT progress, macroeconomic conditions in general might still be causing delays. Since the late 1980s, Latin America as a whole has been plagued by profound macroeconomic problems such as debt (in the 1970s), inflation and recession (in the 1980s), economic adjustment and financial volatility (in the 1990s), and persistent inequality and poverty (Corrales 2003; Corrales 2008). Voters thus may remain focused on economic issues, rather than LGBT issues. This might explain why LGBT movements and issues took so long to become salient even in the high-income countries of the region: economic issues took precedence. One could argue that as long as the region continues to suffer from serious economic problems, LGBT rights will face strong competition and may remain a secondary concern even among sympathetic people and LGBT people themselves (see Merentes in this volume; Saavedra 2004).

Finally, in the United States, there is evidence suggesting that as a person's socio-economic status increases, the chances of harboring homophobic attitudes diminishes, in part because improved socioeconomic status yields higher education levels, and homophobia in the United States declines with education (Pew Research Center 2003; Pew Research Center 2006; Pew Research Center 2008). In Latin America, at least traditionally, anthropologists and filmmakers often provide examples of the exact opposite: homophobia is particularly virulent among high-income groups (see *No se lo digas a nadie* and the 2003 Bolivian film *Dependencia sexual* [*Sexual Dependency*]), and tolerance of open LGBT behavior may be more common—though far from widespread—among poor and working-class neighborhoods (see the 2002 Brazilian movie *Madame Satã*, the 2000 Colombian film *La Virgen de los sicarios* [*Our Lady of the Assassins*], and the anthropological study *Mema's House, Mexico City: On Transvestites, Queens, and Machos* [Prieur 1998]). This is consistent with the idea that in Latin America, the upper classes are far more tolerant of "open closets" (acceptance of gay behavior as long as heterosexual stereotypes are observed) than open homosexuality. Whether this income-related difference in attitudes toward homophobia and the closet is pervasive or still in existence, and, if so, why, are topics that require further research.

The Depletion of Shock

The LGBT rights movement, not just in Latin America but throughout the world, suffers from one major impediment: it depends too heavily on the shock effect. The influence of most human-rights social movements on policy increases following moments of national shock. In the area of human rights in Latin America, for instance, the work done by truth and reconciliation commissions in documenting the extent of human-rights abuses during the dictatorships of the 1970s produced in many countries a sense of shock that made possible significant progress in legislation and enforcement of human-rights norms in the 1980s and 1990s.

Likewise, the AIDS epidemic in Latin America had a similar shock effect that drew attention to LGBT movements (Pecheny 2003). The epidemic demonstrated how ill prepared the state was to address the health concerns of and rights of the LGBT community, one of the first to be affected by the epidemic. It was not surprising that some of the advances in terms of health care, counseling and rights protection for LGBT citizens emerged following the initial onslaught of the AIDS epidemic in Latin America, as elsewhere (Klein 1998; see also Núñez González, Gómez in this volume).

One problem with horror as a propellant of rights is that it is not a sustainable resource. After an initial shock, societies and individuals can learn to live with otherwise horrific conditions. Shock can easily transition into complacency and indifference. This is what has happened with the AIDS epidemic. Now that the epidemic has become more contained—and thus, less shocking—interest in addressing the plight of the LGBT community may have waned in many countries, and may remain low until another shock shakes public opinion. For example, Tim Frasca's essay in this volume discusses how, with the containment of the AIDS epidemic, society has settled back into traditional patterns.

A similar pattern occurs with hate crimes. There is evidence that LGBT citizens are systematically subjected to not just verbal and physical abuse, but also murder (UNAIDS 2009). The International Lesbian and Gay Association (ILGA) reported that a gay man was killed every two days in Latin America in 2005 solely because of his sexuality (*The Economist* 2007). Brazil is often described as leading the world in the murder of homosexuals, with one study documenting 122 homophobic murders in Brazil in 2007, compared with 35 in Mexico and 25 in the United States (Phillips 2008). A previous study claimed that between 1980 and 2006 at least 2,680 gay people were killed in Brazil, mostly as a result of homophobic violence. The problem is that in a region where homicide may be so prevalent, these hate-crime statistics, however horrific, become commonplace and therefore insufficiently disturbing to generate public outcries.

Organized Religion

Social movement strength depends not just on numbers (people available to mobilize) and material resources (income levels), but also on the degree of political obstacles faced. Scholars agree that organized religion poses one of the most powerful political obstacles to sexual rights (Vaggione 2007). Most Christian churches, both in the United States and in Latin America, officially consider homosexual behavior to be immoral and sinful. This doctrinal position translates into an open rejection of LGBT rights. In the Santiago and Buenos Aires surveys of gay pride parade participants, 33.1 percent and 24.6 percent of respondents, respectively, report having been discriminated against by a "religious community" (see figure 1).

The influence of religious institutions, particularly the Catholic Church and Evangelical communities, as forces in opposition to LGBT rights is one major difference between today's struggle for LGBT rights and many previous democratic struggles in the Americas, such as ending slavery in the nineteenth century, establishing women's suffrage in the early twentieth century, and advancing labor, human, and indigenous rights since the 1940s. These earlier democratic struggles did not face the same overt, and often virulent, opposition from churches. Many times, in fact, church groups became major advocates on behalf of these democratic struggles. Only feminist and reproductive rights, particularly abortion, face the same type of religious opposition as LGBT rights (Petracci and Pecheny 2007).

Nevertheless, it is incorrect to assume that religion is a homogenously insuperable barrier to LGBT rights. Both Catholic and Protestant church communities are diverse within and across countries, producing different degrees of opposition. The Catholic Church, for instance, tends to be more influential in the policy arena (lobbying against legislation, restricting discourse, blocking agendas) than in launching witch hunts against LGBT church members. That is, it tends to be more tolerant of lifestyles than of legislation (for a discussion of this distinction as it plays out in Brazil, see Delpotte 2007). In contrast, Protestant churches in the predominantly Catholic countries of Latin America tend to have less influence in the public policy arena (than in the United States), but can be more active than the Catholic Church in efforts to regulate behavior within communities (as in the United States).

These are, of course, generalizations. Even within each denomination, there are variations. Evangelicals and especially Pentecostals in Latin America are becoming influential in policy circles (e.g., successfully opposing legislation in Brazil—see Marsiaj in this volume), not just in household affairs (Miller Llana 2007). Some Catholics are becoming more outspoken against homosexual behaviors, part of the worldwide trend toward a conservative approach to sexuality and reproductive rights—the so-called pelvic issues (Allen 2008).

On the other hand, in some countries, Catholic parishes are moving in the opposite direction: becoming less interventionist in public policy, less concerned with topics of sexuality relative to other issues, and/or less institutionally strong in terms of influencing politics. Officially, the Catholic Church condemns homosexual behavior, but even the conservative Catholic Church in Chile, for instance, offers assistance for gay AIDS patients. Often the Catholic Church, worried as it is about defections among parishioners, is not eager to condemn Catholic individuals, even if they strongly ignore Catholic doctrines.

This ambiguity on the part of the Church's opposition may partly explain why Latin America's predominantly Catholic countries do not officially criminalize, or in some cases recently decriminalized, homosexual acts in their civil codes (Panama was the last country to decriminalize homosexuality), whereas a majority of predominantly Protestant countries—mostly in the English-speaking Caribbean basin—ban homosexuality, following their Anglo-Saxon Common Law tradition, which includes an antisodomy norm: Antigua and Barbuda, Barbados, Belize, Dominica, Grenada,

Guyana, Jamaica, St. Kitts and Nevis, St. Lucia, St. Vincent and the Grenadines, Trinidad and Tobago (Ottosson 2008; see Wilets in this volume).

This legal difference between Hispanic America and Anglo-America might have to do with different historical legal traditions (see Wilets in this volume). A stereotype describes Latin America as having a powerful tradition of machismo and homophobia in comparison to more tolerant societies in Europe and Anglo-America. Some historiographies of the nineteenth and early twentieth centuries also portray Latin America as intolerant. However, the sexual legislation of Latin America tended to be more liberal than in the United States and Northern Europe, because antisodomy codes were entrenched in Anglo-Saxon legal traditions. In contrast, following the Napoleon Code, most Latin American countries decriminalized homosexuality during the nineteenth century. The antisodomy laws of Northern Europe and the United States had no parallel in Hispanic America. The police still persecuted LGBT expressions (see Ben in this volume), but perhaps did so to a lesser extent.

Latin Americans' choices related to contraception and/or premarital sex have shown that many people tend not to follow their church's prescriptions, so it is incorrect to assume that religion in Latin America is an insuperable damper on LGBT rights. For example, while the Catholic Church opposed same-sex civil unions in Buenos Aires, the bill passed nonetheless (see Saavedra 2004). In some cases, pastors and priests provide comfort, and even empowerment, for many nonheterosexual worshipers. Churches in large Latin American countries appear to be part of the double standard that characterizes Latin America in terms of sexuality and reproduction (Shepard 2000).

Nevertheless, most scholars agree that churches often serve as veto players, objecting to nonheteronormative behaviors, if not in a person's life, at least in the policy realm. In sum, the rise of sexual issues into the political arena is shaped by the degree of separation between the Church and the state, and this is still too abstract in many Latin American and Caribbean nations.

The Party-Movement Divide

LGBT movements—because of their small constituencies, the multiplicity of closets, the prevalence of rival (economic) struggles, and the strength of opponents—are in dire need of strong political allies. On their own, they lack sufficient bargaining leverage to change policies and practices. On the face of it, political parties seem to be the obvious candidates for political alliances. Because parties on the right, across most democracies, are typically unwilling to serve as allies of LGBT causes, most LGBT movements gravitate toward leftist parties (Escobar and Alvarez 1992). However, in Latin America, cooperation between LGBT movements and leftist parties has not been easy to accomplish, as many articles in this reader discuss (especially Marsiaj). In the 1980s, for instance, some Sandinista supporters were lesbians and gays, but they were not allowed to form a group or march openly (see Thayer, Babb in this volume). In 1999, Venezuela's constituent assembly rejected a proposal to insert a constitutional ban on LGBT discrimination while the assembly was dominated almost entirely by leftist, pro-Chávez delegates (see Merentes in this volume). In Ecuador in 2008, there were divisions within the very same movement that was advocating progressive changes (see Xie and Corrales in this volume). Feminists also have problems forging alliances with leftist parties. In 2008, for example, the Uruguayan president from the leftist *Frente Amplio* (Broad Front), Tabaré Vásquez, vetoed an abortion law approved by the congress.

Scholars recognize that in Latin America, social movements and parties historically have had a difficult time finding mutually acceptable forms of collaboration (Eckstein and Wickham-Crowley 2003). However, the tensions between organized parties of the Left and LGBT (and feminist) movements seem to be stronger than those between the Left and other social movements. This party-movement divide contrasts sharply with Spain, where the leading leftist party, the *Partido Socialista Obrero Español* (PSOE, Spanish Socialist Workers' Party), established a close alliance with the LGBT movement in the late 1990s, a key reason that Spain became one of the few European countries to enact LGBT marriage legislation in 2005 (Calvo 2007). For Latin America, in contrast, scholars document real hostility from leftist parties toward LGBT movements. In many instances, leftist parties have actually condemned, not just excluded, LGBT demands.

The 1985 Brazilian-American film *Kiss of the Spider Woman*, based on the novel by Argentine author Manuel Puig, depicts the relationship between inmate Molina, a gay, transgendered man, and his cellmate, Valentín, a conventional, macho revolutionary leader, and could be seen as a statement on the divide between LGBT movements and the traditional Latin American Left. In the movie, Molina shows no interest in revolutionary affairs, one could even say in politics; Valentín shows utter disdain for Molina's concerns, and even perpetrates an act of homophobic aggression. Although the movie concludes with a dramatic rapprochement between the two characters, in real life, rapprochements between LGBT movements and leftist forces have been less predictable.

One reason why leftist and populist parties have been less sympathetic to LGBT groups is that many of these parties aspire to become catch-all parties, and thus prefer to avoid polarizing issues that seem to matter only to a generally "tiny minority." Another reason is that LGBT movements have resented being lumped together with other forms of social vindication, because they feel that becoming one more group in a larger coalition of progressive forces dilutes their visibility and thus threatens one of their central demands: social recognition for their difference.

A third reason is that activists on the Left have historically focused on social class issues, which they deem to be the central issues within any capitalist system, and thus treat LGBT rights as secondary (or even petit bourgeois) concerns. The Cuban government itself, the flag bearer of the radical Left in Latin America, has a well-documented history of repression (in the 1960s), prosecution and expulsion (in the 1970s), and seclusion (in the 1990s) of LGBT citizens, often justified with a rhetoric of valuing the protection of the proletariat nation above any other nonclass interest (see Ocasio, Larson in this volume). Furthermore, in terms of political rhetoric, male leaders on the Left have historically used a macho style of imagery and vocabulary to discuss issues like nation building, consciousness raising, and guerrilla warfare, which reifies heteronormativity and homophobia (see Bejel, Ben in this volume). In relation to sexuality, therefore, members of the Left have sometimes been as reactionary as their right-wing counterparts. The difficulty that LGBT movements experience in forming strong alliances with large leftist parties is one reason that these movements rely heavily on forming alliances with other social movements (e.g., human-rights movements) or small and new parties.

Perhaps one of the most positive developments of the 2000s is that this historical animosity between leftist parties and LGBT movements has somewhat abated in some countries. Some of the most important legal accomplishments of LGBT movements in Latin America have come following close political collaboration with leftist or populist parties (see Vianna and Carrara in this volume). In June 2008, the president of Brazil, leader of the Workers' Party, launched a conference to promote LGBT rights, a first for any head of state in the world (see President Luiz Inácio Lula da Silva's opening speech in this volume). Even in Cuba, crucial members of the ruling party, such as Raúl Castro's own daughter, are making inroads on behalf of LGBT rights (see Haydulina in this volume). In short, although leftist parties are inconsistent or hesitant in their support for LGBT demands and still harbor lingering homophobia, the situation is changing.

The Future: Democratization, Globalization, and the Paradox of Coming Out

We can now summarize some of the conditions that lie behind the late and uneven bloom of LGBT issues in Latin America relative to the United States, Canada, and many European countries. First, at the individual level, LGBT youths stay in their original households for much longer, confronting a homophobia that can be so intense that it hinders coming out and self-acceptance; LGBT youths also find more numerous and more comfortable closets after they leave their original families, and this too hinders coming out. Second, at the structural level, other political and economic priorities, such as the needs to fight authoritarianism and settle human-rights abuses, to institutionalize democracy, and to solve macroeconomic problems, dominated the agenda in the 1980s and 1990s. Third, at the institutional level, both organized religion and organized party life pose problems. The Catholic Church acts as a strong policy veto player, while Protestant churches attempt to regulate private behavior. The party-based problem consists of a historical aversion on the part of Latin America's leftist and populist parties to embracing postmaterialist social movements in general, and LGBT demands in public.

The future of LGBT politics in Latin America will depend, therefore, on the future of the struggle against each of these obstacles. LGBT movements, like all minority movements, benefit from allies and safe spaces. A crucial start is the household: parents (and neighbors) could become less homophobic. Simultaneously, closets could become less comfortable and available. Material conditions—of countries, communities and individuals—could continue to improve to make room for postmaterialist demands in the nation's national agenda, although it is not automatic that gay rights rise with rising incomes. Organized religion could become more pluralistic and tolerant (just as it has become in its response to divorce, premarital sex, and interracial marriage), and the separation of churches and state could become more concrete. Courts and security forces could become less homophobic and better enforce anti-discriminatory protections. And finally, political parties and other social movements could become stronger allies of LGBT movements, since, alone, LGBT movements lack sufficient leverage to influence politics. Furthermore, we should not forget that LGBT causes encompass diverse (and dissimilar) realities related to sexual orientation and gender identity, intersecting with class, race, ethnicity, language, and other potential sources of social oppression.

In short, the future of LGBT movements depends on the very same factors that determine the quality of democracy elsewhere: individual empowerment, structural conditions, and institutional quality. Furthermore, progress in one dimension will not guarantee progress in other dimensions, although deficiencies in a cluster of these dimensions normally lead to deficiencies in all others (Diamond and Morlino 2004).

The evolution of LGBT politics depends not just on the extent to which obstacles diminish, but also on the extent to which the forces that propel LGBT rights gain strength in the region. Perhaps the most powerful of such forces is globalization. LGBT movements in Latin America are not strongly opposed to globalization, the way so many progressive social movements in developing countries tend to be. Some LGBT movements express profound reservations about the commodification of LGBT culture, but many others welcome globalization, learning to use the resources provided by globalization and local-global markets to sharpen their own strategies and enhance their bargaining leverage at home (see Moreno, de la Dehesa, and Green in this volume).

LGBT movements, for instance, use traditional and new media such as the Internet to actively monitor—and adapt to local circumstances—the strategies adopted by LGBT movements elsewhere on the planet (see Brown, Friedman in this volume). As far back as Cuba prior to the 1959 revolution, LGBT people welcomed tourism as an economic force that can turn both the state and the business sector more LGBT friendly. LGBT groups have learned that demonstrating (even exaggerating) the spending power of LGBT people allows them to earn allies in business and government.

Migration, another component of globalization, continues to serve as an exit opportunity, albeit a costly and traumatic one. Likewise, the return of emigrants to their home countries, and the close contacts kept with emigrants who are abroad, serve as an information bridge, a mechanism through which international ideas and trends get transmitted to Latin America (see Babb in this volume). Latin American universities have also become more globalized, accepting more exchange students, hiring more international faculty, participating in regional and international research collaborations, and forging ties with academic institutions in Europe and the United States, all of which helps inject more acceptance in places of study. Likewise, courts and lawyers in Latin America embrace "transnational jurisprudence" to a greater degree than do those in the United States. Judges and legal experts (not just economists and technopols) are fairly accustomed to the notion of "importing and exporting" knowledge, expertise, precedent, and evidence, first from Europe and now from the United States and their own neighbors (Domínguez 1997; Dezalay and Garth 2002). All of this helps spread nonheteronormative values in Latin America.

LGBT movements are thus beneficiaries and exploiters of globalization forces, and this is encouraging news for Latin American LGBT citizens. After Asia, Latin America —especially its largest cities and most educated population centers—often scores highest on most indices of globalization. The more globalized portions of Latin America have a higher chance of becoming more hospitable to LGBT politics.

Despite this long list of region-specific factors that favor or hinder LGBT rights, we must conclude on a more sobering note. The LGBT movement worldwide will always be haunted by one special problem endemic to all movements dedicated to fighting on behalf of minorities. Let's call this the paradox of success: when these movements achieve any type of success in lessening levels of discrimination, they may paradoxically also lessen the extent to which people outside the movement feel that the issue remains problematic and thus worthy of more attention. With any new victory, citizens can feel that the war, rather than the battle, has been won. This can end up creating obstacles or complacency, neither of which is conducive for future progress.

The paradox of success for LGBT rights is therefore that as more progress is achieved, the struggle for LGBT rights becomes both easier and harder. It becomes easier because, as we argued in the beginning, the creation of more comfort zones helps LGBT citizens to engage in collective action on behalf of their rights, creating a snowball effect that makes non-LGBT people more accustomed to this type of citizenship diversity. But it also makes progress harder in that the expansion of comfort zones may make the cause appear less urgent to non-LGBT people. More alarmingly, growing comfort zones might actually make homophobes sharpen their attacks by making homophobes more aware of their targets. Just as comfort zones encourage LGBT citizens to come out and act collectively, they can draw out homophobic sentiments as well. For many members of society, therefore, an isolated victory for LGBT groups might appear sufficient, or even excessive. For LGBT people, who are keenly aware of the scale of heteronormativity in all societies, no victory is ever final or irreversible. For LGBT movements worldwide, not just in Latin America, convincing all citizens of this latter point may very well be the highest hurdle of all.

Note

We are most grateful to Lee Badgett, Lisa Baldez, Pablo Ben, Stephen Brown, Dorine Jennette, Juan Marsiaj, and Malú Moreno for their comments.

References

Allen, J. L., Jr. 2008. The Catholic Church: Think Again. *Foreign Policy* (November–December): 32–38.

Arriagada, I. 2004. *Estructuras familiares, trabajo y bienestar en América Latina.* In *Cambio de las familias en el marco de las transformacione globales: Necesidad de políticas públicas eficaces,* 42. Santiago, Chile: CEPAL/Naciones Unnidas.

Balderston, D., and D. Guy, eds. 1997. *Sex and Sexuality in Latin America: An Interdisciplinary Reader.* New York: New York University Press.

Barrientos, J., P. Meza, F. Gómez, S. Catalán, J. Longueira, and J. Silva. 2008. *Política, derechos, violencia, y diversidad sexual: Primera encuesta, marcha del orgullo y diversidad sexual, Santiago de Chile 2007.* Rio de Janeiro: Centro Latinoamericano de Sexualidad de Derechos Humanos (CLAM).

Becker, G. S. 1983. A Theory of Competition among Pressure Groups for Political Influence. *Quarterly Journal of Economics* 98:371–99.

Berkins, L., ed. 2008. *Cumbia, copeteo y lágrimas: Informe nacional sobre la situación nacional de las travestis, transsexuales, y transgéneros.* Buenos Aires: Editorial Lilith.

Berkins, L., and J. Fernández. 2005. *La gesta del nombre propio: Informe sobre la situación de la comunidad travesti en la Argentina.* Buenos Aires: Ediciones de las Madres de Plaza de Mayo.

Cáceres, C. F., M. Pecheny, T. Frasca, and R. Raupp Rios. 2008. Review of Legal Frameworks and the Situation of Human Rights related to Sexual Diversity in Low and Middle Income Countries. Study commissioned by UNAIDS. June.

Calvo, K. 2007. Sacrifices that Pay: Polity Membership, Political Opportunities, and the Recognition of Same-Sex Marriage in Spain. *South European Society and Politics* 12 (3): 295–314.

Carrara, S., and A. Vianna. 2007. Sexual Politics and Sexual Rights in Brazil: A Case Study. In *Sex Politics: Reports from the Front Lines,* ed. R. Parker, R. Petchesky, and R. Sember, 27–52. New York and Rio de Janeiro: Sexuality Policy Watch. http://www.sxpolitics.org/frontlines/book/pdf/sexpolitics.pdf (accessed December 3, 2009).

Carrillo, H., J. Fontdevila, J. Brown, and W. Gómez. 2008. *Risk across Borders: Sexual Contexts and HIV Prevention Challenges among Mexican Gay and Bisexual Immigrant Men.* San Francisco: Center for AIDS Prevention Studies, University of California, San Francisco.

Corrales, J. 2003. Market Reforms. In *Constructing Democratic Governance in Latin America,* 2nd ed., ed. J. I. Domínguez and M. Shifter, 74–99. Baltimore: Johns Hopkins University Press.

———. 2008. The Backlash against Market Reforms. In *Constructing Democratic Governance in Latin America,* 3rd ed., ed. J. I. Domínguez and M. Shifter, 39–71. Baltimore: Johns Hopkins University Press.

Delpotte, L. 2007. *Brazilië, in de schaduw van het kruis* (Brazil in the Shadow of the Cross). *De Morgen,* August 7, 10–11.

Dezalay, Y., and G. B. Garth. 2002. *The Internationalization of Palace Wars: Lawyers, Economists, and the Contest to Transform Latin American States.* Chicago: University of Chicago Press.

Diamond, L., and L. Morlino. 2004. An Overview: The Quality of Democracy. *The Journal of Democracy* 15 (4): 20–31.

Domínguez, J. I., ed. 1997. *Technopols.* University Park: Penn State University Press.

Eckstein, S., and T. P. Wickham-Crowley, eds. 2003. *Struggles for Social Rights in Latin America.* New York: Routledge.

Economic Commission for Latin America and the Caribbean. 2004. *Social Panorama of Latin America.* Santiago, Chile: ECLAC/United Nations.

The Economist. 2007. Gay Rights in Latin America: Out of the Closet, and into Politics. March 8.

———. 2009. Intersexuality: A Question of Sex. October 15.

Escobar, A., and S. Alvarez, eds. 1992. *The Making of Social Movements in Latin America: Identity, Strategy, and Democracy.* Boulder, Colo.: Westview Press.

Eskridge, W. N., Jr. 1999. *Gaylaw: Challenging the Apartheid of the Closet.* Cambridge, Mass.: Harvard University Press.

Fields, J. 2004. America's Families and Living Arrangements: 2003. *Current Population Reports,* no. P20-553. Washington, D.C.: U.S. Census Bureau.

Figueroa, A. 2006. *México frente al espejo. BBC Mundo,* September 5. www.bbcmundo.com.

Foster, D. W. 2002. The Homoerotic Diaspora in Latin America. *Latin American Perspectives* 29 (123): 163–89.

Gamson, J. 1995. Must Identity Movements Self-Destruct? A Queer Dilemma. *Social Problems* 42 (3): 390–407.

Girshick, L. B. 2008. *Transgender Voices.* Hanover: University Press of New England.

Gutiérrez, R. 2007. Introduction to the Special Issue on Latin American Sexualities. *Journal of the History of Sexuality* 16 (3): 349–54.

Hagopian, F. 2007. Latin American Citizenship and Democratic Theory. In *Citizenship in Latin America,* ed. J. S. Tulchin and M. Ruthenburg, 11–57. Boulder, Colo.: Lynn Rienners.

Human Rights Watch. 2009. "Not Worth a Penny": Human Rights Abuses against Transgender People in Honduras. Human Rights Watch, May 28. http://www.hrw.org/en/reports/2009/05/28/not-worth-penny (accessed December 3, 2009).

Inter-American Development Bank. 1998. *Facing Up to Inequality in Latin America: Economic and Social Progress Report, 1998–1999.* Washington, D.C.: Inter-American Development Bank.

Intersex Society of North America. 2009. What Is Intersex? www.isna.org/faq/what_is_intersex (accessed November 5, 2009).

Jones, D., M. Libson, and R. Hiller. 2006. *Sexualidades, política y violencia: La marcha de orgullo* GLTTBI *Buenos Aires 2005*, 2nd ed. Buenos Aires: Antropofagia.

Klein, C. H. 1998. From One "Battle" to Another: The Making of a *Travesti* Political Movement in a Brazilian City. *Sexualities* 1 (3): 327–42.

Kornblit, A. L., M. Pecheny, and J. Vujosevich. 1997. *La homofobia en la ciudad de Buenos Aires.* *Acta Psiquiátrica y Psicológica de América Latina* 43 (3): 221–40.

Kulick, D. 1998. *Travesti: Sex, Gender, and Culture among Brazilian Transgendered Prostitutes.* Chicago: University of Chicago Press.

Miller Llana, S. 2007. How Pentecostals Brought "The Fiesta Spirit" to Church in Latin America. *The Christian Science Monitor*, December 17.

Musto, M. 2007. The Glass Closet. *Out*, May 17.

Olson, M. 1965. *The Logic of Collective Action.* Cambridge, Mass.: Harvard University Press.

Orces, D. 2008. Problems of Political Tolerance. AmericasBarometer Research Notes, Vanderbilt University. http://sitemason.vanderbilt.edu/lapop/AmericasBarometerResearchNotes (accessed September 18, 2009).

Ottosson, D. 2008. *State-Sponsored Homophobia: An* ILGA *Report.* International Lesbian and Gay Association. http://www.ilga.org/statehomophobia/ILGA_State_Sponsored_Homophobia _2008.pdf (accessed December 4, 2009).

Pan American Health Organization. 2007. *Health in the Americas 2007.* Washington, D.C.: Pan American Health Organization.

Parker, R., and P. Aggleton. 2003. HIV and AIDS-related Stigma and Discrimination: A Conceptual Framework and Implications for Action. *Social Science and Medicine* 57 (1): 13–24.

Pecheny, M. 2003. Sexual Orientation, AIDS, and Human Rights in Argentina. In *Struggles for Social Rights in Latin America*, ed. S. Eckstein and T. P. Wickham-Crowley, 253–70. New York: Routledge.

———. 2008. *Investigar sobre sujetos sexuales.* In *Todo sexo es político*, ed. M. Pecheny, C. Figari, and D. Jones, 9–17. Buenos Aires: Del Zorzal.

Petracci, M., and M. Pecheny. 2007. *Argentina: Derechos humanos y sexualidad.* Buenos Aires: CEDES-CLAM.

Pew Research Center. 2003. Religious Beliefs Underpin Opposition to Homosexuality: Republicans Unified, Democrats Split on Gay Marriage. The Pew Research Center for the People and the Press and the Pew Forum on Religion and Public Life, November 18. http://people-press.org/report/197/religious-beliefs-underpin-opposition-to-homosexuality (accessed September 18, 2009).

———. 2006. Less Opposition to Gay Marriage, Adoption and Military Service: Only 34% Favor South Dakota Abortion Ban. The Pew Research Center for the People and the Press, March 22. http://people-press.org/report/273/less-opposition-to-gay-marriage-adoption-and-military-service (accessed September 18, 2009).

———. 2008. Gay Marriage Is Back on the Radar for Republicans, Evangelicals but Overall Opposition to Gay Marriage Is Less than in 2004. The Pew Research Center for the People and the Press, June 12. http://pewresearch.org/pubs/868/gay-marriage (accessed January 3, 2009).

Phillips, T. 2008. The "Rainbow Killer" Stalks Brazilian Gays. *The Observer*, December 14, 44.

Prieur, A. 1998. *Mema's House, Mexico City: On Transvestites, Queens, and Machos.* Chicago: University of Chicago Press.

Raupp Rios, R. 2005. *Towards a Democratic Right to Sexuality.* São Paulo: CLAM. http://www
.clam.org.br/pdf/roger_demrigsex_eng.pdf (accessed December 4, 2009).

Saavedra, R. M. 2004. Same-Sex Marriage under Capricorn's Tropic. *Feminism and Psychology*
14 (1): 47–51.

Salazar, H. 2006. Violencia homofóbica en Colombia. *BBC Mundo*, September 4. www
.bbcmundo.com.

Shepard, B. 2000. The "Double Discourse" on Sexual Reproductive Rights in Latin America:
The Chasm between Public and Private Action. *Health and Human Rights* 4 (2): 121–43.

Sigal, P., ed. 2003. *Infamous Desire: Male Homosexuality in Colonial Latin America.* Chicago:
University of Chicago Press.

UNAIDS. 2009. HIV Prevention Hampered by Homophobia, January 13. http://www.unaids.org/
en/KnowledgeCentre/Resources/FeatureStories/archive/2009/20090113_MSMLATAM.asp
(accessed December 4, 2009).

Vaggione, J. M. 2007. The Politics of Dissent: The Role of Catholics for a Free Choice in Latin
America. In *Women, Feminism, and Fundamentalism*, ed. I. Dubel and K. Vintges. Amsterdam: Humanistic University Press.

The Yogyakarta Principles. 2007. Principles on the Application of International Human Rights
Law in Relation to Sexual Orientation and Gender Identity. http://yogyakartaprinciples
.org/principles_en.htm (accessed September 18, 2009).

PART I

Nation-Building and Heteronormativity

Male Same-Sex Sexuality and the Argentine State, 1880–1930

Pablo Ben

PREVIOUS STUDIES of sex between men in the late nineteenth and early twentieth centuries claim that repression is the key to understanding the relationship between the state and sexuality during this period in Argentina. [...] In fact, repression is frequently the central focus of scholarly work on all forms of sexual expression south of the Rio Grande. Intolerance and machismo, or male chauvinism, are frequently perceived as innate characteristics of the region, and indications to the contrary are taken as exceptions to the rule. Within this framework, the existence of a liberal sexual legislation since the mid- to late-nineteenth century throughout the region has been overlooked. [...]

The Legislation of Male Same-Sex Sexuality

Historians of sexuality have usually overlooked the existence of liberal sexual legislation in Latin America. The decriminalization of all sexual practices between consenting adults in the private sphere that is characteristic of most Latin American penal codes stands in sharp contrast to the scholarly focus on the persecution of sexual outcasts. In addition, the influence of liberalism in Latin America has been obscured by a historiography that tends to assume a high degree of arbitrary state intervention on civil society throughout the region. Although liberal sex laws failed to stop the policing of sexuality throughout Latin America, the lack of a legal ground for the persecution of men who had sex with other men granted them a higher degree of freedom than that experienced by men in those countries where such sexual practices were outlawed. [...]

The French Revolution profoundly affected the law of sexuality in Europe and the Americas. The new liberal approach, premised on limiting the intervention of the state in civil society, led to the decriminalization of all forms of private and consensual sexuality between adults. With the military expansion of France across continental Europe, the decriminalization of sodomy under the Napoleonic Code was enforced in the occupied regions.[1] Despite the defeat of Napoleon in 1815, the French legislation continued to influence other countries. In 1822, the Spanish penal code omitted sodomy, and the influence of this change was felt throughout Latin America after independence in the early nineteenth century. [...] Argentina, then, along with Brazil, Mexico, and Colombia, followed the liberal French tradition of decriminalizing previously punishable acts of private and consensual sex between adults.

Although in Argentina the legal decriminalization of sodomy only took place formally in the 1880s, it seems that in practice sodomy was not considered a crime from the mid-nineteenth century onward, as the nation-state was emerging. [...] Colonial laws concerning sodomy continued to exist formally until 1886, when a new penal code was issued by the national congress. However, as early as the 1860s, the old laws concerning sexuality were not enforced. Whereas in 1813, a group of foreigners were expelled from Buenos Aires for committing sodomy,[2] by the 1860s the punishment of sodomy did not seem to be effective. Effeminate men had become the object of derision rather than legal persecution. In an article published in a major newspaper in 1862, the author satirically assumed the guise of a woman, asking the police to persecute effeminate men who could be seen cruising in search of other men throughout Buenos Aires. This article suggests that such men were enjoying some degree of freedom if they circulated visibly throughout the city.[3] In addition, the sentences of sodomy trials that took place in the decade prior to the introduction of the penal code were not based on colonial legislation. On the contrary, sodomy was treated as if decriminalization had already taken place.[4] In 1886, the new penal code completely eliminated legal punishment for all forms of private adult consensual sexuality, thus finally formally decriminalizing sodomy.[5]

The history of sexual legislation in countries that followed the French legal tradition, such as Spain, Brazil, Mexico, Colombia, and Argentina, was the result of a liberal approach to the relationship between state and civil society. State intervention was limited to guaranteeing basic rights, such as the defense of life, private property, and freedom of speech. According to this view, morality was a realm of civil life that should be independent from any state interference. Even if male same-sex sexuality was morally condemned in civil life, the state had no right to persecute men who engaged in such sexual practices. Other countries of the Atlantic basin, however, followed a very different path. [...]

Liberal Penal Codes vs. Repressive Police Edicts

Despite the striking difference between the laws outlawing male same-sex sexuality in some countries and the decriminalization of sodomy in the French-influenced penal codes, countries that did liberalize sexual legislation did not put an end to the policing of men who had sex with other men. Liberal legislation only made the policing milder. The countries decriminalizing consenting sexual acts between adults in private frequently gave the police power to punish public displays of all forms of non-normative behavior, including same-sex sexualities. Although in Brazil, same-sex sexuality was not outlawed in the penal code, the police could still deprive an individual of his or her freedom for committing a "public scandal" or involvement in "disorderly conduct."[6] As James Green argued, the legal situation of same-sex sexuality could not be properly understood through an analysis of the crimes explicitly listed in the penal code. Although sodomy "had been decriminalized in the early nineteenth century ... criminal codes with vaguely defined notions of proper morality and public decency, as well as provisions that limited cross-dressing and strictly controlled vagrancy, provided a legal net that could readily entangle those who transgressed socially sanctioned sexual norms." So even though "homosexuality" was not outlawed, the Brazilian police and the courts used those vague notions of morality inherent in the penal code to control same-sex sexuality.[7] William Peniston describes a similar panorama operating in Paris after sodomy decriminalization: legal discrimination against same-sex sexuality was erased from the penal code, but it continued to exist in practice. The 1810 penal code [...] outlawed rape and sexual assaults, public offenses against decency, the incitement of youths to debauchery, and adultery and bigamy. These laws did not distinguish between same-sex and different-sex sexual activities. However, they "were used extensively against men who had sex with other men, especially if their activities took place in public."[8]

Brazil and France have very different histories, but similar relationships between the state and civil society in terms of how these two spheres address non-normative sexuality, as well as other forms of urban disorder and unrest to which elites objected. The model of French legislation limits the power of the state over civil society. Ideally, under this legal system the police should only be concerned with the violations of the penal code. However, Brazil and France provide numerous examples of persecution taking place despite the spirit of the law. The contradiction between state social control and legislation happened in different ways. Sometimes the police resorted to vaguely defined notions of morality in the penal code; in other cases, the forms of social control were explicitly specified in police codes or dispositions. [. . .]

In strict legal terms, police codes in these countries not only contradict penal codes, but also imply an intrusion of the executive power over the legislative one, as they are issued by the police—a branch of the executive—rather than by the parliament.[9] According to William Peniston, while the French penal code implied a limitation of the arbitrary power of the state over the elites, the police code of Paris facilitated the enforcement of public order among the urban poor.[10] Since male same-sex sexuality was considered a threat to public order, the police—with the approval of police codes—continued persecuting this form of sexuality in those countries where this sexual practice had technically been decriminalized.

Although the Argentine state followed a path similar to Brazil and France regarding the control of sexuality, in Buenos Aires, the police did not issue any specific regulation against sex between men until the 1930s.[11] As in France, the Buenos Aires police issued their own regulations aimed at controlling forms of urban unrest that were not outlawed in the penal code, but their focus was not sexuality. These regulations, known as "police edicts," existed from 1880 and remained in place until 1996.[12] Police edicts violated the tripartite division of political power written into the constitution of 1853, since the police were technically a branch of the executive power and therefore should not have issued legal regulations. However, as in France and Brazil, this legal contradiction did not prevent the Buenos Aires police from enforcing such edicts. In a book published by the city police in 1910, issuing edicts to defend morality and maintain the social order is listed as one of the proper attributes of the police since its creation.[13] The absence of any police edict against sex between men would suggest that such sexual practice was not an immediate concern for an institution whose explicit aim was to combat threats to morality and the social order.

The impetus for issuing police edicts in the early 1880s was the federalization of the city and its separation from the surrounding province. With the exception of female prostitution, these edicts rarely referred to any aspect of sexuality. There was one reference to "bestiality," but only as an argument that the "penal codes of civilized nations, such as ours, do not mention this rare and degrading crime of the human species, which is actually a fault that should be buried in silence."[14] In 1885, the sheriff of Buenos Aires circulated a note to all police stations establishing the first systematic set of police edicts.[15] These edicts regulated issues such as the possession and carrying of arms, drunkenness in the public sphere, "disorders" and "scandals," balls, vagrancy, playing cards, the behavior and circulation of minors in the city and the celebration of carnival.[16] As I will discuss in the following section, while the police sometimes used the edicts in the name of "disorder" and "scandal" to persecute effeminate men and male same-sex sexuality, the persecution of male same-sex sexuality was not systematic. In fact, male same-sex sexuality was not officially considered an actual form of disorder or scandal, according to the police edicts.

Although the primary terms in the two police edicts, *disorder* and *scandal*, were vague and potentially broad, the definitions of violations included in these categories were quite precise and did not include any reference to same-sex sexuality. In these two edicts, there were only two references to sexuality. One alluded to female prostitutes standing in front of brothel windows in order to attract men in the streets; the other involved men saying "obscene" words to women who passed by. All other forms of interaction described in the edicts regarding "disorder" and "scandal"—such as public demonstrations, fights among unarmed men, false fire alarms, corruption of minors, urinating or bathing in public places, public nudity, and loud music at night —were not aimed at same-sex sexuality. In fact, the eventual use of these edicts against men who had sex with other men entailed an ad hoc extension of police power rather than—as Jorge Salessi suggests in his book on male same-sex sexuality and the nation-state[17]—a coherent and well-conceived plan carried out in response to a "homosexual panic."

In his analysis of the Argentine penal code, Cristian Berco has interpreted the end of the penalizing tradition as an official attempt to erase same-sex sexual practices from the public scene.[18] Although the previously discussed 1881 police order referring to "bestiality" declared a hope that this fault would be "buried in silence," there isn't sufficient evidence to prove that this was the aim of legislators who passed the penal code or the sheriffs who issued police edicts.[19] Indeed, in parliamentary discussions on the penal code, deputies did not mention anything about the social control of sexuality. Although some laws (such as laws concerning adultery and abortion) clearly implied state control over sexuality (especially female sexuality), the penal code was passed as a whole, without parliamentary debate on issues related to sexuality. The main concern expressed explicitly in the discussion among deputies in the congress was the danger posed by the lack of a unified penal law that could legitimize the rule of the state. Deputies claimed that no modern society could function without a standardized legal system where individuals could know what to expect from the law. To these deputies, the code symbolized a proper and "modern" set of rules, and its enactment reflected a desire for the homogenization of the whole legal system into a hegemonic liberal tradition, rather than official concern about the spreading of non-normative sexuality.[20]

The shifting meaning of the legal concept of *sodomy* in Argentina provides an insight into the understanding of how the state handled sexual acts between men. As discussed earlier, before the passage of the penal code, the term *sodomy* was legally defined as an "act" in which a man would anally penetrate another man, a woman, or an animal. This was the definition used in all of the sixteenth-century European codes mentioned previously. The distinctions between private and public sexual acts or between consensual and forced acts had no meaning in this old legislation. The law exempted legal minors from punishment, but the punishment applied to adults was the same if they performed a sexual act with another adult or with a minor. In the new Argentine penal code of 1886, the word *sodomy* continued to exist, but since this code did not punish consensual acts between adults in the private sphere, sodomy acquired a new meaning. The word was now used to refer to what U.S. law classifies as "statutory rape." Sodomy no longer designated all forms of anal penetration. Only men performing sexual acts with boys were condemned under the late-nineteenth-century sodomy law, and anybody accused of performing sodomy was subjected to the same legal conditions that applied to those men who performed sexual acts with female legal minors. When an adult man had sex with a boy, the code used the sodomy category, whereas in the case of sex between adult men and girls, the code referred to rape. Despite these different categories, the number of years in prison did not vary according to the sex of the victim, but according to extenuating or aggravating circumstances.

According to Cristian Berco, shifting the meaning of *sodomy* to indicate statutory rape expressed official panic towards adult pederasts who might corrupt Argentine children, thus threatening the future of the nation. However, the symbolic association of children with the future of the nation only began to emerge in the 1920s; it was consolidated several decades later with the rise to power of Juan Domingo Perón (1946–55), who made the statement that children should be the only people with privileges.[21] Indeed, the state was not particularly concerned with the situation of children in turn-of-the-century Argentina. In Buenos Aires, most children worked in the streets, factories and workshops from the age of nine. There was no law against child labor until 1907;[22] furthermore, after the law was passed, it took the state many years to actually enforce it effectively.[23] In terms of sexuality, the state did not protect children from systematic abuse.[24] In many sodomy trials during this period, the victims were poor boys engaged in urban prostitution. The state had no policies to prevent the widespread sexual abuse of minors by adults, which was fueled by the vulnerable economic situation of the youngest portion of the urban population.[25] In fact, the new concept of *sodomy* was in itself inadequate to deal with the prostitution of minors—both girls and boys. Minors on the streets who turned to prostitution were unlikely to press charges against those adults who had sex with them.[26] The penal code requirements to punish somebody for committing sodomy demonstrate that the state followed a liberal path, considering such a crime a private concern rather than a practice that deserved the attention of the state.

In the 1886 penal code, sodomy was considered a crime against an individual, not against the state. This meant that legal prosecution could only take place if the victim pressed charges, and in the case of minors, only their parents were allowed to do so.

[. . .] By allowing (plebeian) parents to decide, [legislators] handed the authority to punish to a group of people portrayed by most turn-of-the-century bibliographies as violent, irresponsible, and irrational. This was certainly not the best option if legislators wanted to protect children from sexual abuse. It could be argued that the embarrassment associated with sodomy led legislators to pass a law that allowed the victims to avoid going through the experience of a trial. Under this law, if parents failed to press charges, there would be no trial, which could save the victim and his family from opprobrium, but at the same time left the accused unpunished. If this was the case, embarrassment seemed to have more weight than the "future of the nation." It is impossible to grasp the intentions of legislators, especially when they are not expressed in the records of parliamentary debate. The available evidence, however, suggests that the sodomy law was not the product of fear for the nation and its children. It was the result of the emergence of a new body of liberal laws that legislators did not care to debate closely.

Sodomy law followed the general liberal trend of sexual legislation established by the 1886 penal code. Although criminologists and psychiatrists advocated the persecution of all kinds of "sexual deviants," this persecution was not legal. Neither the penal code nor police edicts mentioned any sanction for same-sex sexuality expressed by consenting adults, nor was the law biased in cases of statutory rape. An analysis of the real situation of men who had sex with other men, however, should address the information provided by the actual proceedings of repressive institutions rather than simply focusing on legal, psychiatric, and criminological discourses. [. . .]

Not Especially Targeted for Persecution

The history of sexuality has frequently focused on elite representations of sexual deviance. From such descriptions, historians have usually emphasized the persecution of sexual outcasts. My analysis of the relationship between the state and same-sex sexuality, however, suggests a more complex situation in turn-of-the-century Buenos Aires. Professionals and state officials turned to the category of "sexual inversion" when depicting same-sex sexuality as an obstacle to nation-building that would influence the order required for progress. However, it is important to explore the social control of sexuality independently from the elite representation of the threat posed by deviance. In fact, elite textual representations are not the best vehicle for assessing the actual procedures of the police and other repressive state institutions. On the contrary, the role of the police in relation to same-sex sexuality is better understood in reference to the history of sexual legislation. Because historians have developed an analysis shaped by the "repressive hypothesis," however, they have diminished the importance of legal history for understanding the experiences of men who had sex with other men. A historiographical approach that goes beyond the analysis of sexual repression should attend to the worldwide influence of the liberalization of sex laws.

[...] [I]n the case of French-influenced liberal laws regarding sexuality, lifting the ban on same-sex activities did not necessarily imply a final end to the persecution of men who had sex with other men. In the context of the social control of the lower urban strata of Buenos Aires, police officials could manipulate the laws or even create their own edicts, harassing or arresting female prostitutes and other sexual outcasts, drunkards, workers on strike, and any other "threats" to the social order. Although the Buenos Aires police enacted edicts to control urban unrest beginning in the 1880s, male same-sex sexuality was not especially targeted for persecution.

Notes

1. "With the rise of the nation-state, homosexuality was regarded as particularly dangerous, although, as James D. Steakley points out in his important study on the origins of the homosexual emancipation movement, 'In France, the revolutionary Constituent Assembly had enacted a penal code in 1791 that removed homosexuality from the list of punishable offences. This action was reaffirmed in the Napoleonic Code.' French thinking on this matter was to have a liberalizing influence on several of the German states, especially Bavaria." Richard Plant, *The Pink Triangle: The Nazi War Against Homosexuals* (New York: Henry Holt and Company, 1986), 31.

2. D. Juan Madera, "*Nota del Dr. D. Juan Madera al Intendente de Policía sobre la introducción del vicio de sodomía resultante de un número de hombres de diferentes países,*" in *Índice del Archivo del Departamento General de Policía desde el año de 1812* (Buenos Aires: Imprenta de La Tribuna, 1859), 44:5. The original document referred to in this index of the nineteenth-century police archive can be found at the *Archivo General de la Nación*.

3. "*Los Maricones,*" La Nación, Buenos Aires, November 21, 1862, 2; the article continued the next day, November 22, 1862, 2.

4. The following are records, located in the *Tribunales Criminales* of Argentina's *Archivo General de la Nación*, of sodomy trials previous to the penal code that actually applied the legislation that such code made legal a few years later: *1869, Legajo G, "L.G."; 1876, Legajo E, "E., I. Prófugo por delito de sodomía cometido en la persona del menor M. V."; 1877, Legajo B, "B., P. Por sodomía en la persona del Menor C."; 1879, Legajo B, "B., A., Acusado de conato de sodomía y heridas al menor F. L."*

5. *Código Penal de la República Argentina* (Buenos Aires: *Imprenta de Sud América*, 1887).

6. See Robert McKee Irwin, "The Famous 41: The Scandalous Birth of Modern Mexican Homosexuality," GLQ: *A Journal of Lesbian and Gay Studies* 6. 3 (2000): 353–77; see also James Green, *Beyond Carnival: Male Homosexuality in Twentieth-Century Brazil* (Chicago: University of Chicago Press, 1999).

7. Ibid., 23.

8. There were a number of articles on sexual crimes in the penal code, but "None of these laws specifically mentioned sodomy, pederasty, acts against nature, or any other term used at that time for same-sex sexual behavior." In fact, they "all applied to sexual crimes between men and women, as well as between men and men and women and women." William Peniston, *Ped-*

erasts and Others: Urban Culture and Sexual Identity in Nineteenth-Century Paris (New York: Harrington Park Press, 2004), 17.

9. The human-rights movement in Argentina has questioned the very existence of the police edicts on these grounds since the coming of democracy in 1984.

10. "The distinction made between a police code and a criminal code reflected the legislator's concern to redefine the relationship between state and society. The police code was designed to limit the arbitrary power of the state without depriving it of the means to enforce public order. It dealt, therefore, with infractions that could be modified to fit the needs of the state. The criminal code, on the other hand, was created to protect the citizens' natural rights in terms of their properties and persons. It defined crimes (i.e., felonies) which were, theoretically, universal. Whereas the police code was enforced by officers, the criminal code fell within the domain of lawyers and judges, and it became the primary concern of legal experts both within and outside the Ministry of Justice." William Peniston, *Pederasts and Others*, 17.

11. *República Argentina, Policía de la Capital, Disposiciones de la policía. Leyes—Decretos del P. E.—ordenanzas municipales, edictos y disposiciones de la jefatura. Resoluciones varias, en vigor, 1880–1923* (Buenos Aires: Imprenta y Encuadernación de la Policía, 1924). For an analysis of the dispositions on disorder and scandal between 1880 and 1923, see pp. 234–39. Other publications compiling police edicts did not include any reference to male same-sex sexuality either. See Eugenio Soria, *Digesto municipal de la ciudad de Buenos Aires. Leyes, ordenanzas, acuerdos y decretos vigentes. Publicación oficial* (Buenos Aires: Imprenta de Biedma e Hijo, 1907); *República Argentina, Repertorio de Policía. Compilación de las disposiciones vigentes comunicadas por la "orden del día" de la Policía de la Capital, 1880–98. Hechas bajo la dirección del Dr. M. Mujica Farías, Secretario General de Policía* (Buenos Aires: Imprenta y Encuadernación de la Policía de la Capital, 1899).

12. In 1996, the legislature of the city of Buenos Aires eliminated the police edicts and passed what is now known as the *Código de Convivencia Urbana* (Code for Urban Public Behavior). Although this code has been legally voted on by the legislative power, its very existence is legally problematic because it overlaps with the penal code and in some cases there are contradictions between them. This is why GLBTT and human-rights groups in Argentina have questioned the existence of the code, which is still used to persecute transgender people, political demonstrations, and the young and urban poor. See Guillermo Rafael Navarro, *Código Contravencional de la Ciudad de Buenos Aires: Código de Convivencia Urbana y otras leyes locales actualizadas* (Buenos Aires: *Pagina 12*, 1998). For an analysis of the recent history of police edicts and the new Code for Urban Public Behavior, see Mercedes S. Hinton, *The State on the Streets: Police and Politics in Argentina and Brazil* (London: Lynne Rienner Publishers, 2006) 34–35 and 55–57.

13. *Policía de la Capital. La Policía de la Capital Federal* (Buenos Aires: Imprenta y Encuadernación de la Policía, 1910), 3–5.

14. "*Los códigos penales de las naciones civilizadas, así como el nuestro, no hacen mención de este delito, raro y degradante de la especie humana, que más bien es una falta cuya existencia debía quedar sepultada en el silencio.*" *República Argentina. Policía de la Capital. Memoria del Departamento de Policía de la Capital* (Buenos Aires: Tipográfica La Pampa, 1881), 272.

15. See *República Argentina. Policía de la Capital. Libro de Ordenes del Día. Buenos Aires, 20 de abril de 1885.*

16. *República Argentina. Policía de la Capital. Disposiciones de la policía. Leyes—Decretos del P. E.—ordenanzas municipales, edictos y disposiciones de la jefatura. Resoluciones varias, en vigor, 1880–1923* (Buenos Aires: Imprenta y Encuadernación de la Policía, 1924), 230–61.

17. Jorge Salessi, *Médicos maleantes y maricas: Higiene, criminología, y homosexualidad en la construcción de la nación Argentina, Buenos Aires 1874–1914* (Rosario: Beatriz Viterbo, 1995).

18. Cristian Berco, "Silencing the Unmentionable: Non-reproductive Sex and the Creation of Civilized Argentina, 1860–1900," *The Americas*, 58.3 (2002), 419–41. See also *Código Penal de la República Argentina* (Buenos Aires: Imprenta de Sud América, 1887).

19. Osvaldo Bazán argues that the decriminalization of same-sex sexuality was an attempt to silence its existence. Outlawing sex between people of the same gender could have rendered such sexual activity visible as trials caused sexual scandals. Decriminalizing instead allowed the Argentine state to avoid those scandals. And Bazán thinks that Argentine legislators were seriously concerned with the image of the country abroad. To prove this point, Bazán argues that the professionals who analyzed the project for a legal code quoted a text by Adolphe Chaveau in which he argued in favor of silencing same-sex sexuality to avoid scandals. The fact that such a reason was not debated in the congress, however, points out a lack of interest in the topic. A single quote among a few of the people who debated the project should be placed in the context of the whole debate over the code. The interest in adopting a coherent liberal body of laws was the prevailing interest of legislators. See Osvaldo Bazán, *Historia de la homosexualidad en la Argentina de la conquista de América al siglo XXI* (Buenos Aires: Marea, 2006), 77 and 426.

20. Lila Caimari, *Apenas un delincuente: Crimen, castigo, y cultura en la Argentina, 1880–1955* (Buenos Aires: Siglo Veintiuno, 2004), 37.

21. See Donna J. Guy, "The State, the Family, and Marginal Children in Latin America," in *Minor Omissions: Children in Latin American History and Society*, ed. Tobias Hecht (Madison: University of Wisconsin Press, 2002), 139–64.

22. Congreso Nacional. *Diario de Sesiones de la Cámara de Diputados. Año 1906*. Tomo I. Sesiones Ordinarias, Abril 22–Septiembre 28 (Buenos Aires. Talleres Gráficos de la Penitenciaría Nacional, 1907).

23. In 1906, when the law against child labor was issued, a popular magazine published an article about a chocolate mill. A few shots of the collective of workers at the company show a majority of children among the workers; see *Caras y Caretas*, 1906, Year IV, No. 378. Three years after the banning of child labor, *Caras y Caretas* was still publishing pictures of children at work; see *Caras y Caretas*, 1910, Year XIII, no pages. An article about a publishing house considered a "model" by the same magazine also showed numerous pictures of minors among the workers, which confirms Juán Suriano's hypothesis that the law was not enforced until later in the century; see "Las artes gráficas en la República. Un establecimiento modelo," *Caras y Caretas*, May 7, 1910, Year XIII, No. 605. See also Juan Suriano, "Niños trabajadores: Una aproximación al trabajo infantil en la industria porteña de principios de siglo," in *Mundo urbano y cultura popular. Estudios de historia social Argentina*, ed. Diego Armus (Buenos Aires: Sudamericana, 1990), 253; Eduardo Ciafardo, *Los niños en la ciudad de Buenos Aires, 1890–1910* (Buenos Aires: Centro Editor de América Latina, 1992).

24. See the analysis of sodomy cases in chapter 3 of my dissertation, "Male Sexuality, the Popular Classes and the State: Buenos Aires, 1880–1955" (PhD diss., University of Chicago, 2009). Although a study conducted by José Ingenieros showed that newspaper boys in the streets in many cases turned to prostitution, the state did not pass any legislation or take any measure to prevent children from selling sex for money. See José Ingenieros, "Los niños vendedores de diarios y la delincuencia precoz," *Archivos de Psiquiatría, Criminología, y Ciencias Afines*, 1908, 7:329–48.

25. For an analysis of the vulnerable economic situation of minors in turn-of-the-century Buenos Aires, see Ricardo Salvatore, "Criminology, Prison Reform, and the Buenos Aires Working Class," *Journal of Interdisciplinary History* 23, no. 2 (1992), 279–99.

26. Donna J. Guy, "Parents Before the Tribunals: The Legal Construction of Patriarchy in Argentina," in *Hidden Histories of Gender and the State in Latin America*, ed. Elizabeth Dore and Maxine Molyneux (Durham, N.C.: Duke University Press, 2000), 172–93; Eduardo Ciafardo, *Los niños*; Carlos de Arenaza, *Menores delincuentes, su psicopatología sexual* (Buenos Aires: Jesús Menéndez, 1919), chapter 8 on child prostitution.

Cuban CondemNation of Queer Bodies

Emilio Bejel

In spite of the universality of the modern concept of nationhood and the obsession of nationalist discourses with claiming a natural essence, the construct of any nation is a historical artifact, discontinuous and adaptable, whose ideology is neither reactionary nor progressive in and of itself. This is why diverse forms of nationality have, in modern history, adapted themselves to liberalism, fascism, and socialism, to peace and war, and to images of the past and hopes for the future, according to the circumstances and formative discourses of each nation. This adaptability and diversity are related to the discursive precariousness of nationalism—that is to say, to its extreme dependence on practices and definitions (always variable, multiple, and changing) that attempt to contain its discursive limits. Indeed, the very intelligibility of each nation depends on such practices and definitions, since nationhood rather than an identity (something identical to itself) is a relational category whose meaning is derived from a system of differences. Thus, so-called national identity is determined to a large extent by what it is not, or rather what it presumes not to be at any given moment. Nevertheless, this does not imply that the production of what we could call the ideological field of nationality is exclusively a process of negative or excluding oppositions. National discourse also consolidates itself based on mechanisms of identification and of "shared memory" among its citizens. But it must be emphasized that, for the discourse of nationality to have referential validity, there would have to exist a homogeneous horizontal community that could express itself through time in spite of time—that is to say, in spite of changes and temporal differences, in spite of accidents and the plurality of contingency. This would imply a nonarbitrary linguistic sign, a lack of separation between discourse and reality. As Homi Bhabha says, "the political unity of the nation consists in a continual displacement of its irredeemably plural modern spaces."[1]

In the modern world, everyone is expected to have nationality, just as everybody is expected to have a gender.[2] Discourse on nationality, as well as on gender, seeks to naturalize itself in order to anchor its limits and privileges in essentialist bases, since its foundations are, in fact, quite precarious. Moreover, the discourses of nationality and heterosexism support each other, and this alliance has deeply affected the relationship between the categories of homosexuality and nationalism. Nevertheless, studies on Cuban nationalism have dealt almost exclusively with race, class, colonization, the role of women, and U.S. and foreign relations; there are few current studies dealing with the role of homosexuality in Cuban nationalism.[3]

This essay will examine how homosexuality has shaped Cuban nationalism. I will deal with this question particularly (although not exclusively) as it manifests itself in the last half of the nineteenth century—that is to say, during the emergence of a modern Cuban society. During this period, Cuba was undergoing a marked transition in several areas: deeper economic and political divisions between the colony and Madrid, and complex tensions between whites and blacks, as well as between *criollos* (whites born on the island) and *peninsulares* (Spaniards). Class structure was in transition, cultural forms were in flux, and relations with Spain were progressively worsening. Moreover, during these years of transition, economic and cultural relations between Cuba and the United States increased dramatically. As Cubans became more and more discontented and disaffected with colonial structures, they developed new attitudes toward several aspects of American society. Slave labor was under severe attack, although wage labor was slow in developing (slavery lingered in Cuba until 1886). By the 1880s, Cuba had fallen almost completely under the economic sway of the United States. By midcentury, the Cuban economy had already made substantial connections to world markets and was using modern production technologies and transportation facilities, in spite of the fact that its colonial status forced it to function within Spain's old-fashioned colonial structures. But despite these drawbacks, by the second half of the nineteenth century, Cuba had crossed a threshold into dynamic capitalism, and the middle class had expanded. Moreover, in the midst of this commotion, many thousands of Cubans traveled to the United States, and some returned to the island with a new perspective on their own society. American influence was deepening on all fronts.[4]

It was precisely at this time that a modern Cuban homophobic discourse emerged, based on ideological precepts that saw the "homosexual" as a body that endangered the body of the nation. And since bodies, far from being given, unproblematizable entities, are always endowed with connotations that go beyond themselves, nationalist discourse tends to perceive some bodies as healthy and desirable and others as queer and dangerous.[5] This is the fundamental reason why Cuban national discourse (along with the majority of national discourses) has invested so much time and effort in placing a series of controls and normalization mechanisms on certain bodies and their sexualities—mechanisms that give rise to practices of containment, negation, and repression. While forms of capitalism developed in Cuba and cultural changes followed, some leaders of modernization, ironically, attacked some of the very changes their leadership produced. One of the main casualties of this contradiction was the homosexual, who was perceived as a threat to modern nationalist aspirations and coherence.

Therefore, in Cuba, the modern definition of *homosexual identity* is closely related to that of modern *national identity*, which was developed in the last thirty years of the nineteenth century. As Doris Sommer has shown, in relation to Latin America in general, the modernist project of bringing coherence to the "imagined community" used the image of the heterosexual bourgeois family, symbolically employing the erotic attraction between the lovers (with its corresponding elements of jealousy and loyalty) to allegorize the building of the modern Latin American nation. In this symbolic system, the citizen-father marries the earth-mother, impregnates her, and protects her from "internal" and "external" queer bodies. The earth-mother (the nation) is the object of desire that the citizen must possess and impregnate in order to achieve harmony and legitimacy. Not only the project but also the process of bourgeois consolidation had to be based on marriage, both literal and figurative. Production implied reproduction.[6]

However, in this sense, Cuba has perhaps been more complex and contradictory than the majority of Latin American countries, since at the end of the nineteenth century it was still in the hands of Spain and frequently at war. The image of the military hero, far from having been supplanted by that of the productive, home-dwelling citizen, was still at its peak during the wars of independence against Spain, which started in 1868 and did not reach their conclusion until 1898. Cuba experienced its struggle for independence from Spanish colonization as certain modern capitalist structures were emerging, and as an expansionist threat from the United States was beginning. The image of the homosexual as one of the main rejects of the modern Cuban nation emerged in the midst of this complex crisis. By the 1880s, the Cuban was not just defined in contrast to Spanish colonization (a contrast that had been developing for a long time, but which after the end of the last war of independence in 1898 began to lose its importance), but also in contrast to blacks and mulattos, who since the war years had been moving toward a complex and contradictory national integration. The Cuban was also defined in contrast to American neocolonialism (which by that time had begun to affect Cuba economically and culturally), and in contrast to the importation of European ideals (which some nationalist leaders, especially Martí, considered pernicious). He was defined in contrast, as well, with the representation of women (who had barely begun the process of effectively questioning masculine hegemony), and in relation to class struggle (a problematic that was very late in being widely recognized). It is my contention that the Cuban of that time was also defined in opposition to the "homosexual body" (and other "queer bodies"), which at that moment in history had been constituted as one of the main abjections of Cuban society, that which national discourse repudiated most.

But the formation of an abject homosexual in Cuba toward the end of the nineteenth century is not just the product of discursive necessities. Social and economic circumstances allowed for the symbolic possibilities of that historical construct. In the period between the end of the Ten Years' War (1868–78) and the start of the final war of independence (1895–98), Cuban society experienced a great socioeconomic transformation. As the Cuban historian Manuel Moreno Fraginals has explained in great detail, in the years between the wars the most profound change in Cuba was the transition from a slave-based mode of production to wage labor.[7] This is important to our study, since in countries affected by capitalism, the modern concept of homosexuality was formed in the second half of the nineteenth century as a result of the dramatic increase in wage labor and other social changes that emerged with capitalism, which was spreading over much of the world. Of course, capitalism did not create homosexuality, but with capitalism a new discourse on homosexuality came to dominate society.

According to the American historian John D'Emilio, as a consequence of the new social and economic capitalist system, family unity ceased to operate according to its traditional structure of interdependence, and became instead a social institution that depended for its survival on the salary of one or more of its members. This profoundly changed the interdependence of family members and the very definition of heterosexual relationships, since procreation no longer had the same economic function as in a feudal structure. Moreover, the freedom of family members was considerably increased in this new situation, because they now depended on wages and not collective work to produce the goods they consumed.[8] Thus, toward the end of the nineteenth century, the new role of women in Cuban society was an important factor in the redefinition of the family and of gender roles. Moreover, by the first two decades of the twentieth century, women's political activity was beginning to emerge in Cuba, as women demanded their social and labor rights.[9] In addition to wage labor and the emergence of women's-rights movements, other factors contributed to the drastic change in traditional Cuban family roles at that time: the wars of independence and the immigration of foreigners to Cuba in search of work, as well as the emigration of Cubans to other countries. Perhaps because of the freedom from family pressure, it was possible for persons attracted to others of the same sex to group together (usually in large cities), which facilitated the formation of subcultures based on this identification, and on a sense of "identity" as a subjectivity based on sexual orientation. Michel Foucault insists that the social conditions of the last three decades of the nineteenth century are what allowed the change from homosexuality as an "act" to homosexuality as a "species" ("identity") to take place.[10]

The most important factor in the emergence of urban homosexual subculture and the new definition of this "homosexual identity" was the change in the structure and meaning of the traditional family due to growing bourgeois values. It seems that modern bourgeois Cuban nationalism, without being aware of it, created the material conditions necessary for the formation of homosexual subcultures and "identities," but at the same time defined those social formations as the abjections responsible for its social instability and fragmentation. This also reflected capitalism's contradictory position in regard to the nuclear family.[11] Aided by modernism and nationalism, the phenomenon of homosexuality acquired a new social meaning that it had previously lacked. Before the emergence of modern nationalism in Cuba, homosexuality mainly had been considered a sin; by the end of the nineteenth century, its practitioners were viewed as sick and deviant. Physiological and mental causes for homosexuality were sought; its cause was also looked for in race and in the degeneration of customs. Thus it was that homosexuality, which in religious discourse was considered a sin against nature, was now subject not only to that prejudice (old forms and prejudices did not disappear completely, but rather aided the new ones), but also to those articulated by positivist science, which had as its fundamental objective to leave nothing uninvestigated or unclassified. The consequence of all these changes was that now homosexuality was not simply a sin (for those with religious beliefs), but rather the homosexual, the individual, was carefully studied in order to discover the causes of his illness, of his disease. By that time, homosexuality was already an "identity": if it was found out that someone had had a homosexual encounter, that person (his "identity" or "being" in its totality) was defined as "a homosexual" or by one of several other equivalent terms.

These social and economic changes are part of the transformation of Cuba into a modern nation. Moreover, this modernization was mediated by the United States. If Cuba, which was still under Spanish rule, wanted to modernize itself and to progress, it had to follow the example of its northern neighbor.[12] In fact, approaching the turn of the twentieth century, the Cuban economy depended to a large extent on the United States.[13] And, I believe, with even greater relevance to our study, that the modern Cuban abjection of the homosexual was intertwined and mixed up not only with the internal social and economic changes in Cuba, but also with the expansionism and homosexual panic that was taking place in the United States at that time, as will be shown later in this study.

By the end of the 1880s and the beginning of the 1890s, the United States was well on its way to becoming a world power with expansionist aspirations, and with them came an obsessive preoccupation with masculinity and what some Americans perceived as the danger of male homosexuality. Theodore Roosevelt himself warned of the dangerous effects of "effemination" during times of peace: "The greatest danger that a long period of profound peace offers to a nation is that of [creating] *effeminate* tendencies in young men" (emphasis added).[14] This preoccupation with what was perceived by some as the danger of effemination of young American men was extended (with contradictory implications and goals) to the bodies of entire nations. In regard to Cuba, the accusation was both direct and generalized. On March 6, 1889, the *Philadelphia Manufacturer* published an article titled "Do We Want Cuba?" written by several influential Republican congressmen. In this article, the advantages and disadvantages of annexing Cuba to the United States were discussed. The advantages cited were generally economic and strategic. Insofar as the disadvantages were concerned, the Cuban character was seen as the most problematic:

> What would be the result of an attempt to incorporate into our political community a population such as Cuba's? The Cubans are not much more desirable [than the Spaniards]. Added to the defects of the paternal race are *effeminacy* and an aversion to all effort, truly to the extent of illness. They are helpless, lazy, deficient in morals, and incapable by nature and experience of fulfilling the obligations of citizenship in a great and free republic . . . Our only hope of qualifying Cuba for the dignity of statehood would be to Americanize her completely, populating her with people of our own race; and there would still remain unresolved at least the question of whether our race would not degenerate under a tropical sun and under the conditions necessary to life in Cuba (emphasis added).[15]

The U.S. congressmen, with an obviously positivist rhetoric, make the whole of Cuba out to be a nation of "effeminates," which implies not only a gender-based condemnation, but also one based on race and imperialism. On one hand, since the Cubans are "effeminate," they might contaminate the Americans; on the other hand, their "effeminacy" shows the Cubans to be an inferior race and, therefore, a people who need to be "virilized" through annexation. This annexation must be accompanied by a "masculinization" of the "effeminate" bodies. In this context, the Cuban, the "effeminate man," is a sort of barbarian who needs the modernizing power of the civilized man. All this must have influenced the attitude of Cuban nationalist rhetoric toward homosexuality. From that point on, this rhetoric was complicated by ideas and prejudices about the effeminate male body that came from the United States, the modern country par excellence, which Cuba was supposed to emulate and which now was showing imperialist intentions. Since Cuban society was made up of opposing discourses, the abject position of the homosexual was heightened by the struggle for political power both within and without Cuba. The direct and public characterization of all Cubans as effeminate was part of an attitude both generalized and implicit in many U.S. actions toward Cuba. This attitude probably affected the reactivist posture of Cuban nationalism and its compulsive machismo.

The accusations of the U.S. congressmen in the *Philadelphia Manufacturer* were answered by José Martí in the *New York Post* on March 25, 1889. In his response, Martí shifts the emphasis of the accusations toward the Spanish government.

> We have suffered impatiently under tyranny; we have fought like men, sometimes like giants, to be freemen . . . But because our government [the Spanish government] has systematically allowed after the war [the Ten Years' War of independence] the triumph of criminals; . . . because our half-breeds and city-bred young men are generally of delicate physique, or suave courtesy, and ready words, hiding under the glove that polishes the poem the hand that fells the foe—are we to be considered as the *Manufacturer* does consider us, an "effeminate" people? These city-bred young men and poorly built half-breeds knew in one day how to rise against a cruel government . . . These "effeminate" Cubans had once courage enough, in the face of a hostile government, to carry on their left arms for a week the mourning-band for Lincoln.[16]

Noteworthy in Martí's answer, first of all, is the absence of the positivist rhetoric used by the Americans. Furthermore, as we shall later confirm, Martí's rhetoric with respect to this article is very different from the positivist positions of Enrique José Varona and Dr. Benjamín de Céspedes. Despite Martí's enormous importance in the construction of Cuban nationalism, the most dominant Cuban rhetoric and attitudes toward homosexuality during the nineteenth century and later closely follow a mixture of Catholic and positivist positions. Although Martí defends Cuban men in his answer to the *Philadelphia Manufacturer,* affirming that they constitute a valiant people (and, as this logic implies, those of a sort that cannot be "effeminate,") at no time in his article does he refer to the "effeminate man" in injurious terms, and certainly not when the issue at stake was nationalistic: the Cubans had been accused of being effeminate by U.S. congressmen. In this sense Martí, using rhetorical questions at one point, seeks to cast doubt on the accusation of the congressmen. Nevertheless, it is only fair to point out that in other works Martí adopts a quite different position with respect to homosexuality. For example, Martí reacts negatively to the homosexual (or rather queer) manner of dress adopted by Oscar Wilde at a conference talk he gave in New York that was attended by Martí.

Martí's reaction to Wilde, like that of other Latin American *modernistas*, shows a contradictory position in terms of so-called fin de siècle decadence, for on one hand there is an admiration for the world of the "decadent" Europeans (Martí and the *modernistas* greatly admired their love of art and beauty), but on the other hand, the insistence on building a coherent nationalism leads to a rejection of any sign of homoeroticism. In those times, homoeroticism was thought by nationalists to be an assault on the coherence of the nation.[17] Insofar as homoeroticism (or queerness) among women is concerned, Martí, in his novel, *Amistad funesta* (*Fatal Friendship*, 1885), obliquely refers to the "fatal" homoerotic relationship between the characters Sol and Lucía as an element that impedes the nationalist project of the male character Juan Jerez. As is common in the Latin American novel, Martí's is a form of national allegory in which love and jealousy symbolize the positive and negative paths that the nation will encounter, and Martí's story clearly implies that Lucia's queerness (which is supposedly due to her jealousy for the love of Juan, although she is actually more passionate for Sol's beauty than for Juan's qualities) interrupts Juan's wonderful national ideals and objectives.[18]

The growing Cuban homophobia at the end of the nineteenth century becomes much more evident and clearly defined in the sociological and medical treatises of the period. In 1888 Dr. Benjamin de Céspedes published a study in Havana called *La prostitución en la Ciudad de La Habana* (*Prostitution in the City of Havana*) with a section on "male prostitution," in which the Cuban physician gave the results of his research on homosexuality in certain neighborhoods of Havana, and above all in the centers of clerks ("*centros de dependientes*"). Young, recently arrived Spanish immigrants, for the most part unemployed and in difficult financial circumstances, lived temporarily at these centers. Dr. Céspedes's study concludes that these young Spaniards (and other male prostitutes) were corrupting the Cuban nation because they supported themselves by selling their bodies to other men (presumably wealthy Cubans). In his representation of homosexuality, Dr. Céspedes mixes a pseudoscientific positivist rhetoric with a strident homophobic morality while, ironically, including elements of religious rhetoric:[19]

> *Y aquí en La Habana, desgraciadamente, subsisten con más extensión de lo creíble y con mayor impunidad que en lugar alguno, tamañas degradaciones de la naturaleza humana, abortos de la infamia que pululan libremente, asqueando a una sociedad que se pregunta indignada, ante la invasión creciente de la plaga asquerosa; si abundando tanto pederasta, habrán aumentado los clientes de tan horrendos vicios; si habremos retrogradado hasta los bochornosos días de la Roma decadente, revolcados en el lodo de esas ciudades alcanzadas por la cólera y el fuego celestes.*[20]

[Unfortunately, here in Havana, there exist in greater number than can possibly be believed, and with greater impunity than in any other place, enormous degradations of human nature, abortions of infamy that freely swarm, sickening a society that indignantly asks itself, before the ever-growing invasion of this disgusting plague; if there abounds such pederasty, then the numbers of clients of such horrendous vices must have increased; if we have regressed to the shameful days of Roman decadence, wallowed in the slime of those cities touched by heavenly fire and wrath.]

Dr. Céspedes's work does provide us, however, with relevant information on various aspects of homosexuality in the Cuba of the 1880s: it offers irrefutable proof that there was a homosexual subculture in the Cuban capital at that time and that such activity was seen by some (at least by some of the nationalists in a position to publish their studies in the national press) as something abominable, both for the individuals who engaged in such practices and for the nation as a whole. Dr. Céspedes's "discovery" of this homosexual activity in Havana, as is usually the case, set the stage for political incrimination. Céspedes accused the Spaniards of corrupting national morality, and the next year, in 1889, the Spaniard Pedro Giralt, in reply to Dr. Céspedes, turned this logic around to accuse the Cubans (the supposedly rich *criollos* who picked up young Spaniards for sex) of being the true corrupters of society. According to Giralt, the entire matter had to do with economic class: the Spaniards engaged in this behavior out of economic necessity, whereas the *criollos* did it out of perversion.[21]

In his study, Dr. Céspedes does not limit himself to reporting behavior, but classifies this behavior and endows those individuals who engage in it with an "identity" based on their sexual activities. Perhaps without being aware of it, Dr. Céspedes is acting as the agent of discursive power that most typifies the moment of emergence for modern Cuban nationalism: the pseudoscientist with positivist ideas who researches, classifies, names, and morally judges individuals who have sexual relations with other individuals of the same sex, and thereby contributes to the formation of a Cuban modernity that identifies the homosexual body as one of the main abjects of the nation. Céspedes calls those men who engage in sex with other men "pederasts" and says that they are "the kinds of men who have inverted their sex to deal in these bestial tastes" ("*tipos de hombres que han invertido su sexo para traficar con estos gustos bestiales*").[22] Dr. Céspedes also makes a distinction between "active" and "passive" "pederasts," lending support to a defining binary that continues in Cuban society up to the present day, in which the "passive" participant is the most scorned and at times the only one classified as a homosexual. It is also important to point out that Céspedes's book contains a preface by Enrique José Varona, one of the most distinguished Cuban intellectuals and positivists of that period, and a supporter of Cuban independence. Varona's preface rails against what he considers to be vices brought from Europe:

[E]l que lea estas páginas se convencerá pronto de que, si Cuba participa imperfectamente de la cultura europea, en cambio ha recibido sin tasa el virus de su corrupción pestilente. A los ojos del lector atónito se descubre una nueva faz de la colonización europea; y penetra en el fondo sombrío de estas setinas donde la codicia y la concupiscencia humanas han amontonado los detritus de las viejas civilizaciones, revueltos y mezclados con los elementos *étnicos más disímiles. Allí verá lo que han dejado las piaras de ganado negro, transportadas del África salvaje, los cargamentos de chinos decrépitos en el vicio, arrancados a su hormiguero asiático, y los cardúmenes de inmigrantes europeos sin familia, desmoralizados por la pobreza y la ignorancia, dispuestos a vivir como en aduar o campamento, regido todo por el burócrata soberbio y licencioso, hinchado de desdén por la tierra cuyos despojos se reparte, dispuesto a ser pregonero de su atraso y de su inmoralidad, que él mismo en primer término fomenta, y de que él exclusivamente es responsable.*[23]

[He who reads these pages will soon become convinced that, if Cuba participates only partially in European culture, it has in exchange received the virus of its pestilent corruption without measure. A new facet of European colonization is revealed to the astonished eyes of the reader; and he penetrates into the darkest reaches of these degradations where human greed and concupiscence have piled high the detritus of the old civilizations, stirred up and mixed with the most dissimilar ethnic elements. There he will see what the herds of black cattle, transported from darkest Africa, have left, and the burdens of the Chinese, corrupt in their vices, torn from their Asian anthill, and the human shoals of family-less European immigrants, demoralized by poverty and ignorance, willing to live as in douars or camps, governed by the arrogant and licentious bureaucrat, full of disdain for the land whose spoils he distributes, ready to be spokesman for its backwardness and immorality, which he himself has fomented first and foremost, and for which he is exclusively responsible.]

Varona, referring to all the "vices" studied by Dr. Céspedes, states that Cuba has received from Europe "the virus of its pestilent corruption" ("*el virus de su corrupción pestilente*"), and he expresses his conviction that all this is also related to "decrepit" races (*razas "decrépitas"*) and "demoralized" economic situations (*situaciones económicas "desmoralizadas"*). Some of these charges show that Varona is using the typical positivist discourse of the time, in which sexuality was intimately related to physical, racial, and moral issues, and in which the blame for the "corruption" of society falls on the "Old World" and the black and yellow races. But Varona's declarations mixing sexual orientation with anti-European attitudes constitute a very different stance from his other works (Varona wrote several pieces on this issue, and his opinion changed over time), where he insists that Cuba should follow the modern European model—excepting, of course, that of Spain, which was considered by Varona and most nationalists as premodern and backward.[24] As is evident, Varona's strident position and rhetoric are quite different from Martí's: Varona's was a positivist-racist position, while Martí's was more typical of the contradictory position of the Spanish American *modernistas*.

Despite their obvious differences, the writings of Varona, Giralt, and Dr. Céspedes, as well as the article by the U.S. congressmen, and Martí's response and his novel, show that by the 1880s, the conflict between homosexuality and Cuban nationalism had found one of its primary targets in the abject body of the homosexual, in whose symbolism a series of tensions and struggles, not only of gender but also of nationality, race, and class, is inscribed. The Cuban homosexual has now been turned into a new barbarian who must be fenced in, dominated by the civilized (or civilizing) rationalist discourse of modern nationalism. It is precisely due to this complex, fluctuating, and precarious oppositionality that Cuban nationalism has dealt so obsessively with naturalizing itself—that is, with trying to halt the constant dissemination of its limits. To do so, an essentialist discourse of "national identity" has been employed. In this discourse, the naturalization of heterosexuality is used to mark, in a radical and frequently abusive manner, those bodies which it is believed ought to be expelled from the interior of the nation.[25] The homosexual is represented in nationalist Cuban rhetoric as an inversion of gender roles, which are represented as natural and essential. The health of the body of the nation is perceived as depending to a large extent on the effectiveness with which one can "cure" (expel, repress, contain, or hide) the queer homosexual body, which contradicts the heterosexual image of the ideal or idealized citizen. Moreover, the body of the nation, with its need to acquire a sense of coherence, constantly appeals to a complex series of symbols, feelings, assimilations, and rejections, which are grouped around the naturalization of heterosexuality and its relation to the body of the nation. This is the discursive matrix of the Cuban heteronational symbol system. It is precisely this matrix which must be called into question, since heterosexism is not only a sexual orientation but also a complex value system which carries with it a series of socially and economically exploitative relationships.[26]

The Unsettling Return of the Excluded

As the twentieth century drew to a close and the twenty-first began, there were clear indications of a crisis in the Cuban public imaginary regarding the supposedly natural relationship between heterosexuality and citizenship. The Cuban revolution of 1959 destabilized the previous system and then tried to institutionalize structures and practices of power and ethical concepts that it was unable to fix (just as the previous bourgeoisie was unable to fix its practices and concepts, creating a sense of void and instability that the revolution used in its favor). This is why the position of authority of the revolutionary Cuban subject is part of an ambivalent process of identification. It is precisely in the midst of that ambivalence, of that unavoidable fracture of the system, that the category of homosexuality installs itself, frequently in order to bring about a criticism of nationalist discourse in general and *machista* discourse in particular. The metaphor that often is adopted from cultural expressions of Cuban gay marginality is that of a transformation that displaces the center of power. To transform and translate the nation from the margins is a reading of the category of homosexuality in relation to that of nationality that points toward a metaphorical process that could be interpreted from our position as a metaphor of crisis.

The questioning of the relationship between heterosexuality and citizenship in Cuban society is manifest in cultural phenomena such as, among others, the critical and popular success of the film *Fresa y chocolate* (*Strawberry and Chocolate*); some documentaries depicting Cuban gay and transvestite life, such as *Conducta impropia* (*Improper Conduct*), *En busca de un espacio* (*Looking for a Space*), *Mariposas en el andamio* (*Butterflies on the Scaffold*), and *Gay Cuba*;[27] popular songs like Pablo Milanés's "*Pecado original*" ("Original Sin") and Pedro Luis Ferrer's "*El tiene delirio de amar varones*" ("He's Crazy about Boys"), which defend the right to romantic relationships between people of the same sex; the work and persona of Reinaldo Arenas;[28] and numerous poems and short stories, mainly by young writers, dealing with gay/lesbian issues in a new light. Among such authors, the following merit special note: Abilio Estévez, Miguel Mejides (whose story has been recreated by Francisco López Sacha), Pedro de Jesús López, Marilyn Boves, Leonardo Padura, Roberto Urias, Norge Espinosa, Ena Lucía Portela Arzola, Jacqueline Herrans Brooks, Alberto Acosta Pérez, Mirta Yanez, Fatima Paterson, Manelic R. Ferret, Alejandro Aragón L'Oria, Senel Paz, Alexis Pimienta, Juan Carlos Valls, Francisco Morán Lull, and Damaris Calderón.[29] Many of these writers' texts, most published since 1988, portray a terrible world of *machista* discrimination that tries to repress and suppress all that is "homosexual." But I believe that simply talking about this matter from a gay or queer perspective, especially given the abundant number of texts published in the span of just a little over one decade, is already a clear indication of a radical departure from *machista* Cuban culture. If we compare this situation with that of the extreme repression during the UMAP (*Unidades Militares de Ayuda a la Production* [Military Units to Aid Production]) era of 1965–68, to the First Congress of Education and Culture in 1971, or even to the Mariel boat lift in 1980, we must conclude that there has been a substantial change in Cuba on matters regarding homosexuality.

Although lacking institutional bases that would permit the consolidation of its territory, the category of homosexuality in Cuban culture at the end of the twentieth century started to position itself as a marginality from which the abject homosexual criticizes—directly or indirectly—dominant national culture. This new attitude casts doubt on a tortuous, discontinuous, and paradoxical historical relationship whose genealogy, as we have seen, extends back for more than a century. In spite of the enormous efforts to expel that queer body, or precisely because of them, the specter of homosexuality has constantly haunted Cuban national discourse since at least the nineteenth century. The category of homosexuality, as a part of the construction—due to rejection and negation—of modern Cuban national discourse becomes, ironically, a constitutive element of that discourse. And so, as with every ideological field, that of Cuban nationality contains a structural contingency that assures a permanent state of instability. In that sense, since homosexuality is a constitutive part of the interpellation of Cuban national subjectivity, the category of homosexuality can offer the possibility of a new way of looking at Cuban nationalism.

In some ways, the most radical and explicit articulation of the destabilizing return of the homosexual in Cuban culture has to be the work and persona of Reinaldo Arenas. In almost all of his works, but especially in *Viaje a la Habana* (*Trip to Havana*), *Otra vez el mar* (*The Sea Again*), *El color del verano* (*The Color of Summer*), and *Antes que anochezca* (*Before Night Falls*), Arenas attacks the most fundamental principles upon which nationalist and patriarchal discourses are based.[30] These texts do not seek admittance into a more tolerant society, nor do they propose a "new" vision of the nation with broader bases in a liberal style. Rather they are based on a radically queer position in the sense of constituting themselves through a desire for constant destabilization which resists approaching any kind of normalization.[31] Arenas antagonizes the implicit power of generalization that the dominant discourse assigns itself. This process of significant "singularity" resists totalization and serves to interrupt power and knowledge, producing in this fashion other spaces of subaltern meaning. I conclude, reflecting with Homi Bhabha on the famous idea of Frantz Fanon, that the people inhabit the zones of instability; that is to say, that it is in such zones that the living people is found, not in those described in the official national narrative. Perhaps forgetting this narrative is the basis for remembering the nation, for populating it anew, for imagining the possibility of other contestatory forms of cultural identification. Only from a position of radical alterity can the traces of the genealogy of the Cuban national narrative and the patches and voids of the monumentality of its historicism be illuminated, and only by living in the margins of gender, race, class, and group will we be able to position ourselves to translate the differences among these categories into a form of solidarity.[32]

Notes

1. Homi K. Bhabha, "DissemiNation: Time, Narrative, and the Margins of the Modern Nation," in *Nation and Narration*, ed. Homi K. Bhabha (London: Routledge, 1990), 300.

2. See Benedict Anderson, *Imagined Communities: Reflections on the Origin and Spread of Nationalism*, rev. ed. (London: Verso, 1991).

3. The most recent collection of articles and discussions on the topic of Cuban national identity of which I am aware is *Cuba, cultura e identidad nacional* (Havana: Cuban Writers and Artists Union and the University of Havana, 1995). After I had finished writing this article, I obtained a copy of Víctor Fowler Calzada's *La maldición: Una historia del placer como conquista*. Here he discusses several Cuban texts that deal with homosexuality.

4. See Manuel Moreno Fraginals, *El ingenio: Complejo económico social cubano del azúcar*, vol. 2 (Havana: Editorial de Ciencias Sociales, 1978), esp. chap. 2, 174–221. Also see Louis A.

Pérez, Jr., *Cuba: Between Reform and Revolution*, 2nd. ed. (Oxford: Oxford University Press, 1995), esp. chaps. 4–7, 70–188. For an informative and interesting article on the influence of American culture in the last thirty years of the nineteenth century in Cuba, see Louis A. Pérez, Jr., "Between Baseball and Bullfighting: The Quest for Nationality in Cuba, 1868–1898," *Journal of American History* 81, no. 2 (September 1994): 493–517. I thank my friend Lou Pérez for his comments and suggestions regarding the present article.

5. As far as these ideas on the body and its abjections are concerned, see Judith Butler, *Bodies That Matter: On the Discursive Limits of "Sex"* (New York: Routledge, 1993). In this work I have concentrated on the image of the "effeminate man" due to the space available, and also due to the specific research that a study of lesbianism in Cuba would require.

6. Doris Sommer, "Irresistible Romance: The Foundational Fictions of Latin America," *Nation and Narration*, ed. Homi Bhabha (London: Routledge, 1990), 71–98. Sommer develops all the ideas from this article in her book *Foundational Fictions: The National Romance of Latin America* (Berkeley: University of California Press, 1991). I thank my friend Doris for having read an early draft of this study and for her opinion on it.

7. Moreno Fraginals, *El ingenio*, esp. chap. 2, 174–221.

8. See John D'Emilio, "Capitalism and Gay Identity," *The Lesbian and Gay Studies Reader*, ed. Henry Abelove, Michèle Aina Barale, and David M. Halperin (New York: Routledge, 1993), 467–76.

9. For a fairly recent study on the feminist movement in Cuba from the turn of the century, see K. Lynn Stoner, *From the House to the Streets: The Cuban Woman's Movement for Legal Reform, 1898–1940* (Durham, N.C.: Duke University Press, 1991).

10. Michel Foucault, *The History of Sexuality: An Introduction*; originally published in French as *Histoire de la sexualité, 1: la volonte de savoir* (Paris: Gallimard, 1976).

11. For a discussion of the contradiction of capitalism in relation to the nuclear family, and specifically with reference to a queer leftist critique of this contradiction, see, among others, Rosemary Hennessy in her "Queer Theory, Left Politics," *Marxism beyond Marxism*, ed. Saree Makdisi, Cesare Casarino, and Rebecca E. Karl (New York: Routledge, 1996), 214–42.

12. For a development of this idea, see Louis A. Pérez, Jr., "Identity and Nationality: The Sources of Cuban Separatism, 1868–1898." This unpublished manuscript was provided to me through the generosity of Louis Pérez.

13. For a detailed analysis of Cuba's economic dependence on the United States during this period, see Moreno Fraginals, *El ingenio*, vol. 2.

14. Cited in Joe L. Dubbert, *Man's Place: Masculinity in Transition* (Englewood Cliffs, N.J.: Prentice Hall, 1979), and in David E Greenberg, *The Construction of Homosexuality* (Chicago: University of Chicago Press, 1988), 393.

15. See "Do We Want Cuba?" in José Martí, *Our America: Writings on Latin America and the Struggle for Cuban Independence* (New York: Monthly Review Press, 1977), 229–30.

16. On March 25, 1889, Martí responded to the article in the *Philadelphia Manufacturer* with his own article, "A Vindication of Cuba," in the *New York Evening Post*. We have taken this article from Martí, *Our America*, 234–41.

17. For an insightful study on the attitudes of Martí and the *modernistas* in relation to the idea of "decadence" and homosexuality, see Sylvia Molloy, "Too Wilde for Comfort: Desire and

Ideology in Fin-de-Siècle Spanish America," *Social Theory* 31/32 (1992): 187–201. Oscar Montero also has dealt intelligently with this issue regarding Martí in "Before the Parade Passes By: Latino Queers and National Identity," *Radical America* 24 (1990): 15–26, esp. 18–24.

18. See José Martí, *Amistad funesta* (Charleston, S.C.: Biblio Bazaar, 2007).

19. See Oscar Montero, "Julián del Casal and the Queers of Havana," ¿Entiendes? Queer Readings, Hispanic Writings, ed. Emilie L. Bergmann and Paul Julian Smith (Durham, N.C.: Duke University Press, 1995): 92–112. Dr. Céspedes's book is *La prostitución en la ciudad de La Habana* (Havana: Establecimiento Tipográfico O'Reilly, 1888; reproduction microfilm New Haven, Conn.: Research Publications, 1977).

20. Céspedes, *La prostitución*, 190.

21. Pedro Giralt, *El amor y la prostitución: Réplica a un libro del Dr. Céspedes* (Havana: Ruíz y Hermano, 1889; reproduction microfilm New Haven, Conn.: Research Publications, 1976).

22. It is apparent from the type of research, the ideas, and the rhetoric of Dr. Céspedes that he is an adherent to scientific positivism. This is emphasized by the fact that the preface to his book, *La prostitución en la Ciudad de La Habana*, is by Enrique José Varona, the most distinguished Cuban positivist at the time.

23. Enrique José Varona, Introduction to Céspedes, *La prostitución*, viii–xi.

24. There are various studies on positivism in Cuba in general, and on the positivism of Varona in particular. Of special interest is chapter 11 of Medardo Vitier, *Las ideas en Cuba: Proceso del pensamiento político, filosófico y crítico en Cuba, principalmente durante el siglo XIX* (Havana: Editorial Trópico, 1938); Jorge Mañach, "*La filosofía de Varona*"; and Elio Alba-Buffill, *Enrique José Varona: Crítica y creación literaria* (Madrid: Hispanova de Ediciones, 1976).

25. About the naturalization of heterosexuality, see Butler, *Bodies That Matter*, esp. chaps. 1, 7, and 8.

26. The political philosophy of Butler's *Bodies That Matter* is oriented toward Ernesto Laclau and Chantal Mouffe's concept of "radical democracy" in *Hegemony and Socialist Strategy: Towards a Radical Democratic Politics* (London and New York: Verso, 2001), and Laclau, *Reflections on the Revolution of Our Time* (London and New York: Verso, 1990). Rosemary Hennessy's critique of the ideas and implications of "radical democracy" is found in her article "Queer Theory, Left Politics."

27. Besides *Conducta impropia* (*Improper Conduct*), the famous documentary by Néstor Almendros from the early 1980s, there are several recently produced documentaries that deal with gay/lesbian issues in present-day Cuba. Among them are *Gay Cuba* (1995), directed by Sonja de Vries; *En busca de un espacio* (*Looking for a Space: Lesbians and Gay Men in Cuba*) (1993), directed by Kelly Anderson; and *Mariposas en el andamio* (*Butterflies on the Scaffold*) (1996), directed by Luis Felipe Bernaza and Margaret Gilpin.

28. The work and even the persona of Reinaldo Arenas are in many ways the greatest return of the repressed homosexual in Cuban culture. See my "*Antes que anochezca: autobiografía de un disidente cubano homosexual*," *Hispanoamérica* 25, no. 74 (1996): 29–45.

29. Most of these authors live in Cuba at present, but others have left the island and reside permanently outside their country of origin. I owe some of the information about these recent authors and texts to Sonia Rivera-Valdés, Víctor Fowler Calzada, and Ambrosio Fornet.

30. For a discussion of these ideas in some of Arenas's texts, see, among others, Carmelo Esterrich, "*Locas, maros y demás mariconadas: El ciudadano sexual y el estado en* Otra Vez el Mar *y* El Color del Verano *de Reinaldo Arenas*," *Confluencia* 13, no. 1 (Fall 1997): 178–93.

31. The queer reading is one of the interpretative possibilities of Arenas's texts, in the sense of a desire to constantly destabilize the dominant power. Nevertheless, this reading must be accompanied by other readings of other aspects of his work: for example, that which sees an antigay position in various areas of his texts. Arenas was against what activists would call the principles of the gay liberation movement. The idea of a political organization with objectives other than destabilization seemed to Arenas limiting and oppressive. For Arenas, homosexual desire was always and exclusively promiscuous and dissident.

32. See Frantz Fanon, "On National Culture," in his *The Wretched of the Earth* (Harmondsworth: Penguin, 1969), 174–90. Homi Bhabha discusses and elaborates on Fanon's ideas on national culture in his "DissemiNation," 302–3. On page 320, Bhabha expresses this idea but mentions just gender and race.

Mexico

Stephen O. Murray

THE POPULATION of Mexico, the country of 1,923,040 square kilometers immediately south of the United States, recently exceeded 100 million (with an estimated annual rate of increase of 1.5 percent). Thirty percent of the population is entirely or predominantly *indígeno* (Amerindian), sixty percent *mestizo* (mixed Amerindian and Spanish descent), nine percent of entirely European descent (*blanco*), and one percent other.

Preconquest Mexico

Maize (corn) was first domesticated in what is now Mexico and was the staple of diets in civilizations that rose and fell before the sixteenth-century Spanish invasion—most notably, the Olmec, Maya, Teotihuacán, and Toltec. The Nahuatl-speaking Mexicas (Aztecs) built an empire from a base in the valley of Mexico where the current capital, Mexico City, is located. The city of Tenochtitlán at the time the Spaniards arrived was larger than any European city except Paris.

The Mexicas held public rituals that were at times very erotic, but they were very prudish in everyday life. The Mexicas' pantheon offers a sense of their understanding of gender and sexual power. In their pantheon, the Mexicas worshipped a deity, Xochiquetzal (feathered flower of the maguey), who was the goddess of nonprocreative sexuality and love. Originally the consort of Tonacatecutli, a creator god, Xochiquetzal dwelled in the heaven of Tamoanchan, where she gave birth to all humankind. However, subsequently she was abducted by Tezcatlipoca, a war god, and raped. This event transformed her character from the goddess of procreative love to the goddess of nonreproductive activities.

Xochiquetzal was both male and female at the same time, and in her male aspect (called Xochipilli), s/he was worshipped as the deity of male homosexuality and male prostitution. Xochiquetzal had a positive and a negative aspect. In Xochiquetzal's positive aspect, s/he was the deity of loving relationships and the god/dess of artistic creativity; it was said that nonreproductive love was like art—beautiful and rare. In his/her negative aspect, s/he was the deity of sexual destruction; s/he incited lust and rape, and inflicted people with venereal disease and piles.

The Mexicas' mythical history, like those of other Mesoamerican peoples, asserted that there had been four previous worlds. During the immediately preceding one, the "Age of the Flowers, of Xochiquetzal," the people supposedly gave up the "manly virtues of warfare, administration, and wisdom," and pursued the "easy, soft life of *sodomy*, perversion, the Dance of the Flowers, and the worship of Xochiquetzal."

There is also a classic Nahuatl word, *patlacheh*, for a woman "playing the role of a man" penetrating women. The *patlacheh* is described at some length (as a scandal) in the Florenine codes (one of the two major extant collections of writings about the Aztecs).

Although the Aztecs were publicly sexually exuberant and privately prudish, their subjects varied greatly in their sexual customs. For example, the area which is now the state of Veracruz was very well known for practicing same-sex sodomy. When Bernal Díaz del Castillo reached Veracruz with Cortés, he wrote of the native priests: "the sons of chiefs, they did not take women, but followed the bad practices of sodomy." Their practices included boy prostitutes and cross-dressed adults.

Although this claim's veracity is somewhat suspect, since such revelations were used to rationalize the European conquest, Cortés wrote his king, the Emperor Charles V, "We know and have been informed without room for doubt that all [*Veracruzanos*] practice the abominable sin of sodomy."

Colonial Mexico

The Mexicas had not conquered all the peoples, particularly those living on both the Pacific and the Gulf coasts, who were most notorious for their sexual availability. Thus, the Spanish were able to make alliances against the Mexicas. Malinche, the coastal woman who became the sexual partner of conquistador Hernán Cortés and aided the Spanish conquest, became the prototype of the "fucked/fucked over" Mexican. In Octavio Paz's analysis of Mexico's fatalistic national character, *El laberinto de la soledad*, the mixed-blood (mestizo) children are "*hijos de la chingada*," the children of the fucked one, *la Malinche*.

The Spaniards condemned homosexuality more vociferously than the Aztecs had. After the conquest, all pagan rituals were banished and their rationale discredited. Mestizo culture came to exhibit a melding of Aztec attitudes towards private homosexuality and those of the Spaniards. The former ritual tradition that celebrated homosexuality as communion with the gods was lost.

In early colonial times, when Bishop Zumarraga was the apostolic inquisitor of Mexico, homosexuality, and particularly sodomy, was a prime concern for the Inquisition. The usual penalties for homosexuality were stiff fines, spiritual penances, public humiliation, and floggings. However, homosexuality was tried by the civil courts as well, from whence people were sentenced to the galleys or put to death.

The only records providing a glimpse of homosexual social life during the colonial period are the records of court proceedings when homosexual scandals occurred. Of such events, a purge that took place in Mexico City between 1656 and 1663 is the best known. It resulted in a mass execution.

Whereas heretics and Jews were burned in the Alameda, now a park near the center of Mexico City, homosexuals were burned in a special burning ground in another part of the city, San Lázaro, because homosexuality was not a form of heresy and thus fell into an ambiguous category of offenses. Thus, the group to be executed was marched to San Lázaro, where the officials first garroted them. They were "done with strangling all of them at eight o'clock that night . . . then they set them afire." Novo states that several hundred people came from the city to watch the event. It should be noted that strangling the victims before burning them was considered an act of mercy; for burning was such terrible agony that it was feared that the prisoners would forsake their faith in God and thus lose their immortal souls.

The purge seems to have ended when the superiors in Spain wrote back to Mexico that they did not have papal authority to grant the jurisdiction the Mexican Holy Office requested, and that the inquisitors were "not to become involved in these matters or to enter into any litigation concerning them."

Postcolonial Mexico

Mexican independence from Spain in 1821 brought an end to the Inquisition. The intellectual influence of the French Revolution and the brief French occupation of Mexico (1862–67) resulted in the adoption of the French legal code, in which sodomy was not a crime.

This decriminalization of sodomy did not grant people the right to be overtly homosexual, for included in the "minimum ethics indispensable to maintaining society" were laws against solicitation and any public behavior considered socially deviant or contrary to the folkways and customs of the time. Such vagueness in the law accorded wide latitude to interpretation by police. Shaking down (demanding money and jewelry from) those who a policeman decides are an "affront to public morality" has provided a source of supplementary income for policemen, some of whom have also demanded (and received) sexual favors.

On the night of November 20, 1901, Mexico City police raided an affluent drag ball, arresting forty-two cross-dressed men and dragging them off to Belén Prison. One was released. The official account was that she was a "real woman," but persistent rumors circulated that she was a very close relative of President General Porfirio Díaz, so in Mexican slang *cuarenta y dos* (number forty-two, the one who got away) refers to someone who is covertly *pasivo* (a male who is sexually receptive to other males).

Those arrested were subjected to many humiliations in jail. Some were forced to sweep the streets in their dresses. Eventually, all forty-one were inducted into the Twenty-fourth Battalion of the Mexican Army and sent to the Yucatán to dig ditches and clean latrines. The ball and its aftermath were much publicized, including illustrated broadsides by caricaturist Guadalupe Posada (who provided the cross-dressed men with mustaches and notably upper-class dress). The raid on the dance of the forty-one *maricones* was followed by a less-publicized raid of a lesbian party on December 4, 1901, in Santa María.

The spectacular growth of Mexico City in the 1930s was accompanied by the opening of homosexual bars and baths, which supplemented the traditional cruising locales of the Alameda, the Zócalo, Paseo de la Reforma, and Calle Madero (formerly Plateros). Those involved in homosexual activity continued to live with their families. There were no homophile publications or organizations, so homosexual activity was practiced clandestinely or privately.

In the absence of a separate residential concentration, the lower classes tended to accept the stereotypes of unions between masculine insertors (*activos*) and feminized insertees (*pasivos*). While some in the cosmopolitan upper classes rejected the stereotypical effeminacy expected of *maricones* ("faggots"), they tended to emulate European dandies of the late nineteenth century.

During World War II, ten to fifteen gay bars operated in Mexico City, with dancing permitted in at least two, *El África* and *El Triunfo*. Relative freedom from official harassment continued until 1959 when, following a grisly triple murder, Mayor Uruchurtu closed every gay bar under the guise of "cleaning up vice" (or at least reducing its visibility).

The perceived failures of masculinity of *maricones* made (and makes) them "fair game" to be robbed, beaten, and used as sexual receptacles by males upholding conventional "macho" notions of masculinity, particularly policemen. However, in both

Mexico City and Guadalajara, there have been short-lived gay liberation groups since the early 1970s. For example, *El Frente Liberación Homosexual* formed in 1971 to protest the firing of gay employees by Sears stores in Mexico City. *El Frente Homosexual de Acción Revolucionaria* organized protests of 1983 roundups in Guadalajara, and small gay-rights organizations have continued to pop up and fade away in large Mexican cities.

There are now annual gay pride marches, gay publications, and gay and lesbian organizations in touch with organizations in other countries.

Constructions of Homosexuality

Although there have been challenges to the dominant conception of homosexuality as necessarily related to gender crossing, simplistic *activo-pasivo* logic ("I'm a man [*hombre*]; if I fuck you, you're not a man") continues to direct thought and behavior in Mexico, as elsewhere in Latin America.

The *norteño* (North American) conception that males who have sex with males, regardless of the sexual role taken, are "homosexual" is not unknown and may account for some of the unease and outright denial sociologists Murray and Prieur elicited from *activos*. There is also a recognition that some seemingly ultramasculine men could be penetrated.

This phenomenon of "flipping" is frequently discussed among male transvestite prostitutes, and the pleasure of "surrender" to penetration is not inconceivable to masculine-appearing males. Indeed the prospect frightens more than a few males who have penetrated males and directly observed the reactions of the penetrated. "If I let him fuck me I'd probably like it and then I'd do it again, and then I'd be queer," is consciously articulated. "You don't know how your body might react, or your mind. Morally, you don't know what might follow. And if I am a man, I want to stay like that forever," an interviewee named Roberto told Prieur. There is even a term, *hechizos* (made ones), for former *mayates* (insertors) who have become passive partners in anal intercourse over time. Still, the feared anal penetration does not turn everyone who has experienced it into a *maricón*. Nor does it inevitably compromise masculine deportment or end masculine self-conception, especially if the stigmatized behavior occurs with those who live outside one's *barrio* (neighborhood).

The homosexual involvement of some persons is an open secret, that of others is not discussed, and some homosexual involvement is genuinely secret. Reticence usually prohibits discussing one's own homosexuality and/or that of one's friends and family members. Moreover, there is the tendency to bundle sex(uality) and gender into the *activo/pasivo* role dichotomy: those who are perceived as not being able to take care of themselves will "naturally" get both fucked and fucked over.

Although this understanding remains dominant in the lower classes, it is regarded as backward by middle- and upper-class male and female Mexican homosexuals who pride themselves on their modernity and cosmopolitanness. Those who reject being categorized as either *pasivo* or *activo* are labeled *internacional*, a term with positive connotations of sophistication and modernity.

Héctor Carrillo's 2002 study of changing sexual patterns and conceptions in Guadalajara explores middle-class sexual modernity. Surveys of self-reported sexual behavior find roles less dichotomized now than they were when the ethnography of Joseph Carrier began in the late 1960s, especially in Mexico City.

References

Carrier, J. M. *De los Otros: Intimacy and Homosexuality among Mexican Men.* New York: Columbia University Press, 1995.

Carrillo, H.. *The Night Is Young: Sexuality in Mexico in the Time of AIDS.* Chicago: University of Chicago Press, 2002.

Idell, A. *The Bernal Diaz Chronicles.* New York: Doubleday, 1956.

Irwin, R. M., et al., eds. *The Famous 41: Sexuality and Social Control in Mexico 1901.* New York: Palgrave, 2003.

Izazloa-Licea, J. A., et al. HIV-1 Seropositivity and Behavioral and Sociological Risks among Homosexual and Bisexual Men in Six Mexican Cities. *Journal of AIDS* 1 (1991): 614–22.

Kimball, G. Aztec Homosexuality: The Textual Evidence. *Journal of Homosexuality* 26.1 (1993): 7–24.

Lumsden, I. *Homosexuality, Society and the State in Mexico.* Toronto: Canadian Gay Archives, 1991.

Morris, J. B., ed. *Five Letters [of Hernán Cortés], 1519–1526.* London: G. Routledge, 1928.

Murray, S. O. *Latin American Male Homosexualities.* Albuquerque: University of New Mexico Press, 1995.

Novo, S. *Las locas, el sexo, los burdeles.* Mexico: Novaro, 1972.

Paz, O. *El laberinto de la soledad.* Mexico: Fondo de Cultura Económica, 1993.

Prieur, A. *Mema's House, Mexico City: On Transvestites, Queens, and Machos.* Chicago: University of Chicago Press, 1998.

PART 2

Sexuality-Based Political Struggles

More Love and More Desire

The Building of a Brazilian Movement

James N. Green

THE YEAR 1978 was a magical time in Brazil. After more than a decade of harsh military rule, the generals' demise seemed imminent.[1] Hundreds of thousands of metalworkers, silent for a decade, laid down their tools and struck against the government's regressive wage policies. Students filled the main streets of the states' capitals, chanting, "Down with the dictatorship!" Radio stations played previously censored songs, and they hit the top of the charts. Blacks, women, and even homosexuals began organizing, demanding to be heard.

During the long, tropical summer that bridged 1978 and 1979, a dozen or so students, office workers, bank clerks, and intellectuals met weekly in the city of São Paulo, Brazil's largest metropolis. Rotating from apartment to apartment, sitting on the floor for lack of adequate furniture, they plotted the future of the first homosexual rights organization in Brazil. The meetings randomly alternated between consciousness-raising and discussion. The participants, mostly gay men with a few lesbians moving in and out of the group, debated the most recent antigay statements in *Noticias Populares*, a large-circulation, scandal-driven newspaper, and the appropriate responses to come from their newly founded organization, *Nucleo de Ação pelos Direitos dos Homossexuais* (Action Nucleus for Homosexuals' Rights). They closely followed every new issue of the recently launched gay monthly publication *O Lampião da Esquina*. This tabloid-sized newspaper, produced by a collective of writers and intellectuals from Rio de Janeiro and São Paulo, declared itself to be a vehicle for the discussion of sexuality, racial discrimination, the arts, ecology, and machismo.

As the summer progressed, the group's name became a topic of heated debate. Did the name Action Nucleus for Homosexuals' Rights discourage new members from joining the group because it too boldly declared a political agenda? Perhaps the tone of activism in the group's name was the reason that only a dozen people at any given time came to the semisecret meetings. Some wanted to change the name of the group to *Somos* (We Are) to pay homage to the publication put out by the Argentine Homosexual Liberation Front, South America's first gay-rights group, which had come to life in Buenos Aires in 1971 and disappeared in the long night of the military dictatorship in March 1976. Others proposed a name that would clearly express the purpose of the organization: *Grupo de Afirmação Homossexual* (Group of Homosexual Affirmation). Designations that included the word *gay* were roundly rejected because, participants argued, they imitated the movement in the United States.

The final compromise—*Somos: Grupo de Afirmaçao Homossexual*—was the name the group took to a debate held on February 6, 1979, at the Social Science Department of the University of São Paulo, Brazil's largest and most prestigious university. The debate, which was part of a four-day series of panel discussions on the topic of organizing Brazil's "minorities"—a reference to women, blacks, indigenous people, and homosexuals—became the coming-out event for the Brazilian gay and lesbian movement. The program on homosexuality featured a panel of speakers that included editors of the journal *O Lampião* and members of *Somos*. More than three hundred people packed the auditorium to attend the event. The discussion period that followed the panelists' presentations was electric, as charges and countercharges between representatives of leftist student groups and gay and lesbian speakers crisscrossed the assembly room. For the first time, lesbians spoke openly in public about the discrimination that they encountered. Gay students complained that the Brazilian Left was homophobic. Defenders of Fidel Castro and the Cuban Revolution argued that fighting against specific issues, such as sexism, racism, and homophobia, would divide the Left. Rather, they opined, people should unite in a general struggle against the dictatorship.

The first controversy in the emergent Brazilian gay-rights movement was taking shape. The lines were drawn. The rhetoric was already being spun. Within a year, tactical questions about aligning with other social movements or maintaining political and organizational autonomy would split *Somos*, by then the country's largest gay-rights group, leaving other organizations throughout the country demoralized and without direction.

Few who listened to this public debate, however, could imagine how quickly a gay and lesbian movement would explode onto the Brazilian political scene. In a little more than a year, a thousand lesbians and gay men would pack the Ruth Escobar Theater near downtown São Paulo to attend an indoor rally at the closing ceremony of the First National Gathering of Organized Homosexual Groups. A month later, on May 1, 1980, with the city surrounded by the Second Army and the zone under siege, a contingent of fifty openly gay men and lesbians marched with hundreds of thousands of other Brazilians through the downtown working-class neighborhood of São Bernardo in the nation's industrial center to commemorate International Workers' Day during a general strike. When the contingent moved into the Villa Euclides Soccer Stadium to participate in the rally at the end of the march, thousands of bystanders welcomed them with applause.[2] Six weeks later, one thousand gay men, lesbians, transvestites, and prostitutes weaved through the center of São Paulo, protesting police abuse and chanting, "Abaixo a repressão—mais amor e mais tesão" ("Down with repression—more love and more desire"). A movement had been born.[3]

Fifteen years later, in June 1995, over three hundred delegates representing gay and lesbian groups in sixty countries of Asia, Europe, North America, Central America, the Caribbean, and South America gathered in Rio de Janeiro to attend the week-long Seventeenth Annual Conference of the International Lesbian and Gay Association (ILGA). At the opening ceremony a federal congresswoman from the Workers' Party launched a national campaign for same-sex domestic partnerships and for a constitutional amendment to prohibit discrimination based on sexual orientation. At week's end, the delegates and two thousand gay and lesbian supporters ended the convention by celebrating the twenty-sixth anniversary of the Stonewall rebellion with a march along Atlantic Avenue, the boulevard that borders the shining white sands of Copacabana Beach. A 25-foot-wide yellow banner demanding "Full Citizenship for Gays, Lesbians, and Transvestites" led the parade. A contingent of women followed, carrying signs advocating "Lesbian Visibility," which drew applause from observers. Drag queens teased and flirted with onlookers from atop a pink-hued "Priscilla" school bus and two large sound trucks lent by the bank workers' union. Many participants dressed in Carnivalesque masks and costumes. A 125-meter-long rainbow flag billowed in the wind. At the end of the march, people tearfully sang the national anthem and lingered until a light rain dispersed the crowd. The movement had come of age.

Legal but Not Legal

Although Brazilian colonial law had considered sodomy a sin, punishable by burning at the stake, the 1830 Imperial Criminal Code eliminated all references to sodomy.[4] Late-nineteenth- and twentieth-century laws, however, restricted homosexual behavior. Adults engaging in sexual activities with other adults in a public setting could be charged with "public assault on decency" for "offending propriety with shameless exhibitions or obscene acts or gestures, practiced in public places or places frequented by the public, and which . . . assaults and scandalizes society."[5] This provision, a revised carryover from the earlier criminal code, provided the legal basis for controlling any public manifestations of homoerotic or homosocial behavior. With catchall wording, the police or a judge could define and punish "improper" or "indecent" actions that did not conform to heterocentric constructions. Another method for regulating public manifestations of homosexuality was to charge a person with vagrancy. The police could arrest anyone who could not prove a means of support and a fixed domicile or who "earned a living in an occupation prohibited by law or manifestly offensive to morality and propriety."[6]

These two legal provisions gave the police the power to arbitrarily incarcerate homosexuals who engaged in public displays of effeminacy, wore feminine clothing or makeup, earned a living through prostitution, or took advantage of a shadowed building to enjoy a nocturnal sexual liaison. Criminal codes with vaguely defined notions of proper morality and public decency, along with provisions that strictly controlled vagrancy, provided a legal net that could readily entangle those who transgressed socially sanctioned sexual norms. Underpaid police extorted bribes from men caught in compromising situations or without proper identification or work papers. Homosexuality, then, although not explicitly illegal, was behavior that could be easily contained and controlled by Brazilian police and courts.

Gay and Lesbian Life Prior to the 1970s

Brazil went through dramatic changes in the 1950s and 1960s. Millions of rural peasants and workers flooded the country's cities, and industrial production expanded to provide employment and many new manufactured products for the domestic market. Cities such as Recife and Salvador in the impoverished northeast, and Rio de Janeiro and São Paulo in the industrializing southeast, acted as magnets for homosexuals from rural areas who sought anonymity in large cities away from their families' control. There they mingled with the natives of Brazil's major cities and joined in urban homosexual subcultures.

At that time, Brazil's traditional gender-based construction of homosexuality was (and, to a great extent, remains) hierarchical and role based. Men who engage in same-sex activities fall into two categories: the *homem* ("real" man) and the *bicha* (fairy). This binary opposition mirrors the dominant heterosexually defined gender categories of *homem* (man) and *mulher* (woman), in which the man is considered the "active" partner in a sexual encounter and the woman, in being penetrated, is the "passive" participant.[7] As anthropologist Richard G. Parker has pointed out:

The physical reality of the body itself thus divides the sexual universe in two. Perceived anatomical differences begin to be transformed, through language, into the hierarchically related categories of socially and culturally defined gender: into the classes of masculino (masculine) and feminino (feminine) . . . Building upon the perception of anatomical difference, it is this distinction between activity and passivity that most clearly structures Brazilian notions of masculinity and femininity and that has traditionally served as the organizing principle for a much wider world of sexual classifications in day-to-day Brazilian life.[8]

Thus, in same-sex activities, the *homem* takes the "active" role of anally penetrating his partner. The *bicha* takes the "passive" role of being anally penetrated; his sexual "passivity" ascribes to him the socially inferior status of the "woman." Whereas the sexually penetrated "passive" male is socially stigmatized, the male who assumes the public (and presumably private) role of the penetrating *homem* is not. As long as he maintains the sexual role attributed to a "real" man, he may engage in sex with other men without losing social status.[9]

Similarly, women who transgress traditional notions of femininity—manifesting masculine characteristics, expressing independence, or feeling sexual desire for other women—are marginalized. Many lesbians' rejection of traditional feminine roles, including "passivity," place them outside the boundaries of the dominant gender paradigm. A common pejorative term for a lesbian, *sapatão*, literally "big shoe," reflects the social anxiety about strong, masculinized women.[10]

Until the late 1950s, there were no exclusively gay or lesbian bars in Brazil. Public homosociability centered on parks, plazas, cinemas, public restrooms, or the tenuous occupation of restaurants, sidewalk cafes, and slices of popular beaches. Because many single people lived with their families until they married, sexual encounters often took place in rooms rented by the hour or in the homes of friends. Small parties, discreet drag shows, and weekend excursions to the country or a beach house afforded space free from social censure.

Carnival was the one time during the year when gay men could express themselves freely and openly. Lesbians, although much more constricted by social norms, also appropriated Carnival to playfully express their desires in public. For four days, drag balls, cross-dressing in public, and campy behavior reigned. In the 1950s, Rio de Janeiro's *Baile das Bonecas* (Dolls' Ball) began to attract an international audience, as gay men from all over South America came to participate in the revelry and watch plumed and sequined men compete with each other to be crowned the most glamorous and beautiful goddesses of Carnival celebrations. Carnival was the unique moment during the year when *tudo e permitido* (everything is allowed).

In 1964 the Brazilian military overthrew the radical-populist government of President João Goulart and initiated twenty-one years of authoritarian rule. Backed by the United States, the Brazilian generals outlawed opposition political parties, arrested leftist leaders, purged radical unions, and imposed tight controls over the press. Except for closeted homosexual leftists who were arrested by the dictatorship, the gay and lesbian subculture of Brazil's largest cities was initially unaffected by the coup d'état. Recently opened bars with a predominantly gay or lesbian clientele continued to provide a venue for socializing. Drag shows, which originated in these bars, began to reach a wider public, and several cross-dressers became celebrities. Various social groups held private drag parties, and one group even published over one hundred issues of its newsletter, *O Snob*, between 1963 and 1969. The success of this mimeographed newsletter, with its gossip columns and glamorously drawn man in drag on the cover, inspired nearly thirty similar publications throughout Brazil, as well as the short-lived *Associação Brasileira da Imprensa Gay* (Brazilian Association of the Gay Press) founded in 1967 and dissolved a year later.[11]

By 1968, public opposition to military rule had become widespread. Workers occupied factories in two industrial centers, and over one hundred thousand students and their supporters marched through the streets of Rio de Janeiro demanding an end to the military dictatorship. In response, a group of generals carried out a coup within the coup, putting hard-liner General Emilio Garrastazü Medici in power as president. From 1968 to 1973 the government waged a campaign of state terrorism against the opposition, especially against leftist organizations. Thousands were arrested and tortured.[12]

News of the gay liberation movement that emerged after the 1969 Stonewall riots reached Latin America in the early 1970s and encouraged the formation of groups in Argentina, Mexico, and Puerto Rico. However, the military repression in Brazil dissuaded all thoughts of founding a radical gay and lesbian movement. The informal gay publication *O Snob* and its imitators soon ceased distributing their newsletters for fear of being mistaken for members of a leftist underground organization and persecuted.[13] Under the strict moralistic guidelines of military censorship, references to homosexuality and gay Carnival balls were muted in the press. Although some alternative journals occasionally reported about "gay power" in the United States, the formation of a political movement seemed impossible.

While the hard-line generals controlled the government, social and cultural transformations were taking place in Brazil that would affect notions of gender and homosexuality. Pop singers such as Caetano Veloso, Maria Bethânia, and Ney Matogrosso presented androgynous personas that blurred sexual boundaries and implied bisexual desire. Bohemian and countercultural values that emphasized individual sexual freedom began to influence intellectuals and students. A youth culture that challenged traditional notions of sexuality and gender permeated the urban middle class.

By 1974, the military dictatorship was facing serious problems. The economy, which had grown dramatically during the period of most severe repression at the expense of the poor and the working class, was faltering as a result of the international oil crisis. The official opposition political party was gaining electoral ground in regional elections. New forms of resistance began to develop. Students revived their own organizations in the universities and held protests against military rule. Rank-and-file trade unionists staged wildcat strikes. Women who had been involved in underground opposition organizations began to publicly criticize sexism in the Left and raise feminist issues.[14] The Black United Movement emerged to challenge the national ideology according to which Brazil was a racial democracy mostly devoid of institutionalized discrimination based on race.[15] In 1978, faced with a massive strike wave against its economic policies, the military decided to accelerate a process of gradual liberalization that would eventually return the government to civil control and grant amnesty to those involved in human-rights violations.

It was within this political and social climate that first the journal *O Lampião* and then *Somos* were founded. *Somos* sparked the formation of at least seven groups by the time of the First National Gathering of Organized Homosexual Groups in April 1980. Most were small and led by lower-middle-class students, workers, and intellectuals, some of whom had been members or supporters of one of various clandestine leftist organizations that survived the worst years of the dictatorship. They brought with them both their experience as organizers and misgivings about the frequent leftist critique of homosexuality as a "product of bourgeois decadence."

In May 1980, *Somos* split over participation in working-class mobilizations and the role of leftists in the gay movement. The enthusiasm of activists who had managed to organize both a successful national gathering and a mobilization against police repression dissipated. Those opposed to building alliances with labor and Left-led movements formed a new group in São Paulo, *Grupo Outra Coisa: Ação Homossexualista* (Something Else: Homosexualist Action Group). *Somos* lesbians who had already formed an autonomous collective within the larger organization also left the group to form a separate entity, *Grupo Lésbico-Feminista* (Lesbian Feminist Group), where they could pursue their agenda without having to deal with sexism in a group dominated by gay men. *Somos*-Rio de Janeiro, which had modeled itself after *Somos*-São Paulo, also divided over leadership disputes. The principal editors of *O Lampião* attacked the activist organizations as circulation of the monthly journal, which had been in the tens of thousands, plummeted. The journal folded in mid-1981, and over the next three years most of the initial gay-rights groups followed suit. From a peak of twenty groups in 1981, only seven survived in 1984, and of these only five attended the Second Gathering of Organized Homosexuals held that same year in Salvador, Bahia.[16]

A variety of factors contributed to a decline in the movement. With certain exceptions, most organizations never grew beyond several dozen members at a given time. They lacked financial resources and infrastructure. Many of the initial leaders became demoralized and left after their groups failed to grow significantly. Other activists did not have the experience to sustain their groups during the 1980s—Latin America's "Lost Decade"—when burgeoning foreign debts sparked runaway inflation and massive unemployment. Moreover, the end of the dictatorship in 1985 created a false sense that democracy had been restored and that individual rights of homosexuals and other sectors of society would expand without effort. The print press, radio, and television carried more positive coverage of homosexuality and provided a vehicle for the movement's few public leaders to articulate their viewpoints. In addition, visible gay consumerism, which included more nightclubs, saunas, bars, and discos, sustained an illusion that greater freedom had been achieved and that Brazil's gays and lesbians did not require political organization.[17]

During this lull in activism, the *Grupo Ação Lésbica-Feminista* (Lesbian Feminist Action Group), founded in 1981, successfully won the battle to participate fully in the feminist movement. The group also maintained a public profile by publishing a bulletin, *Chanacomchana*, and participating in international lesbian conferences.[18] Luiz Mott, anthropology professor and founder of *Grupo Gay da Bahia* (currently the oldest gay-rights group in Brazil), also steered the floundering movement through important campaigns that set the stage for the movement to expand in the late 1980s. The first victory of *Grupo Gay da Bahia*, located in the northeastern capital of Salvador, was to obtain legal recognition for the group. The second campaign involved convincing the Federal Council of Health to abolish the classification that categorized homosexuality as a treatable form of "sexual deviance." Spearheaded by Mott, the campaign won the endorsement of the nation's leading professional organizations and several local and state legislative bodies. Prominent intellectuals and celebrities signed a national petition calling for a repeal of the classification. The Federal Council of Health removed homosexuality from the category of treatable illnesses in February 1985.[19]

During 1987 and 1988, Brazil held a constituent assembly to rewrite the nation's constitution. With the support of the group Lambda in São Paulo and *Grupo Gay da Bahia*, João Antônio de Souza Mascarenhas, a former editor of *O Lampião* and founder of *Triangulo Rosa* (*Pink Triangle*) in Rio de Janeiro, organized a campaign to include a provision prohibiting discrimination based on sexual orientation. On January 28, 1988, 461 of 559 members of the constituent assembly voted on the measure. But with only 130 favoring a constitutional provision outlawing discrimination, the provision failed. Twenty-five of the thirty-three evangelical pastors in the constituent assembly voted against the measure. All of the leftist Workers' Party representatives backed the prohibition of discrimination based on sexual orientation.[20] Similar laws against discrimination on the basis of sexual orientation have been included in the constitutions of two Brazilian states. Important metropolises such as São Paulo, Rio de Janeiro, and Salvador, as well as eighty other municipalities, also have local codes outlawing discrimination, but they lack any legal bite.[21] During the Seventeenth Annual Conference of the International Lesbian and Gay Association, for example, owners of two sidewalk cafes in Copacabana expelled conference participants for holding hands in public.

Violence and AIDS

Although most gay men and lesbians thought political organizations unnecessary during the apparent liberalization that accompanied the return to democracy, the dramatic increase of HIV infection and a wave of violence against gay men, transvestites, and lesbians revealed how precarious their rights were, even under a democratic regime. The first case of AIDS in Brazil was diagnosed in 1982, and most Brazilians quickly began to associate HIV and AIDS with rich gay men who had the resources to travel to the United States and Europe.[22] Reality was quite different. According to Richard Parker, the director of the Brazilian Interdisciplinary AIDS Association:

> The rapid transition from predominantly homosexual and bisexual transmission to rapidly increasing heterosexual transmission after the first decade becomes even more striking when reported cases of AIDS are viewed across time. While homosexual males accounted for 46.7 percent, and bisexual males for 22.1 percent, heterosexual men and women accounted for only 4.9 percent of the national total between 1980 and 1986. During 1991, on the other hand, cases reported among homosexual men had fallen to 22.9 percent and cases among bisexual men had dropped to 11.1 percent, while cases reported among heterosexual men had risen to 20.1 percent of the national total.[23]

In the early years of the epidemic, misinformation and homophobia caused a panic, as the scandal sheets reported the arrival of the "gay pestilence." One of the first organized responses was initiated by *Grupo Outra Coisa: Ação Homossexualista*, which had split from *Somos* because of the latter's links with the Left. Its members distributed leaflets in the gay bars and cruising areas of Sao Paulo, informing the "homosexual collectivity of São Paulo" of how to obtain more information about the disease.[24] Activists also met in 1983 with representatives of the Health Department of the State of São Paulo to ensure that public health officials fighting the epidemic would not discriminate against homosexuals.[25]

Some of the activists from the first wave of the gay and lesbian rights movement of the late 1970s began working in AIDS-related organizations. In the mid-1980s, when a second generation of gay-rights organizations emerged, they integrated AIDS education into their political activity. Groups such as *Grupo Gay da Bahia*, which survived the 1980s lull in the movement, managed to do so in part because the group also took up the fight around AIDS issues.[26]

The mid-1980s also saw a marked increase in violence against gay men, transvestites, and lesbians. Luiz Mott has documented the murder of more than twelve hundred homosexual men and women and transvestites in Brazil from the mid-1980s to the mid-1990s.[27] Several cases involved women killed by relatives who had discovered that they were having a lesbian affair.[28] Many other murderers were young hustlers who picked up gay men, then robbed and killed them. In 1987 one youth killed over a dozen men whom he had met at a park near São Paulo's financial district.[29]

Most of these murders were committed by unidentified groups or individuals who were never convicted. According to *Grupo Gay da Bahia*, twelve different groups have been involved in the bashing and killing of homosexuals.[30] During the years of military rule (1964–85), paramilitary units formed; these were attached to the armed forces and to federal, state, and local police departments. Known as death squads, these groups assisted the military in extralegal activities, including the kidnapping and torture of opponents of the dictatorship. Some of these groups also carried out campaigns to "clean up" what they deemed "immoral behavior," specifically homosexuality. One such unit, the *Cruzada Anti-Homossexualista* (Antihomosexualist Crusade) sent threatening letters to *Somos* in 1981.[31] The Brazilian dictatorship passed a law in 1979 granting amnesty to all those involved in the killing and torture that had taken place during the previous fifteen years of military rule. As a result, those guilty of violations of human rights were never punished, and violence against homosexuals and transvestites continues unchecked. Death squads and similar groups still operate with impunity in Brazil. Without "subversive elements" to target with their activities, they have chosen more and more to cleanse Brazilian society of "immorality."

Of all reported killings by groups or individuals, only 10 percent lead to arrests. Toni Reis, the president of the *Associação Brasileira de Gays, Lésbicas, Bissexuais Travestis e Transexuais*, or ABGLT (Brazilian Association of Gays, Lesbians, and Transvestites), has reported that of the twenty documented murders of homosexuals and transvestites over the last ten years in his native city of Curitiba, there were only two convictions. Adauto Belarmino Alves, the 1994 winner of the Reebok Human Rights Award, documented the killing of twenty-three transvestites in Rio de Janeiro during October 1994.[32] In some Brazilian states, because murders of homosexuals and transvestites go unreported, they are not included in dossiers documenting violence against homosexuals and transvestites.[33]

The judicial system backs up these arbitrary actions against transvestites. In October 1994, the Court of Military Justice reduced the sentence of Cirineu Carlos Letang da Silva, a former soldier of the military police, who was convicted of murdering a transvestite known as Vanessa. The judge, who dropped the sentence from twelve to six years, explained that transvestites are "dangerous." Vanessa had been shot in the nose and in the back.[34]

Perhaps the most dramatic case involved the 1993 murder of Renildo José dos Santos, a local town councilor from Coqueiro Seco in the state of Alagoas. On February 2, 1993, the town council suspended dos Santos for thirty days after he declared on a radio program that he was bisexual. He was charged with "practicing acts incompatible with the decorum due his position and bringing the reputation of the Council into disrepute." When the period of his suspension expired and the council failed to reinstate him, dos Santos sought a court order to allow his return to the council. The next day he was kidnapped. His remains were discovered on March 16. His head and limbs had been separated from his body and the corpse burned. Although five men, including the mayor of the town, were arrested in the case, they were acquitted of any involvement in the murder. To date, no one has been punished for this crime.[35]

The Second Wave

The Third National Gathering of Organized Homosexual Groups, held in January 1989 in Rio de Janeiro, was attended by only six organizations. Nevertheless, there were new groups among the participants. One such organization, *Atoba*, founded in 1985 after a young man was killed in a gay bashing, brought together lesbians and gay men in working-class suburbs of Rio de Janeiro, far from the middle-class gay bars and clubs of Copacabana and Ipanema. The following four yearly national gatherings attracted more and more groups, and during the Seventh National Gathering of Organized Homosexual Groups, held in January 1995, representatives of thirty-one organizations founded the Brazilian Association of Gays, Lesbians, and Transvestites. Although most groups are still small, the formation of a national organization with affiliates from all regions of the continent-sized country foreshadows a dynamic growth of the movement.

A few developments contributed to the resurgence of gay and lesbian activism after the establishment of a democratic regime in 1985. Many different social movements, and the Workers' Party, which had emerged intact from the struggle against the military dictatorship, began raising the question of how to democratize participation in a nonmilitary civil society. Activists from the women's movement, neighborhood organizations, labor unions, and leftist groups argued that true democracy meant respect for ordinary citizens. Moreover, in 1992, millions of Brazilians demonstrated for the impeachment of President Fernando Collor de Mello, reinforcing the importance of mobilization to achieve political goals. Local experiences politicized many gay radical groups through consciousness-raising and discussion sessions. They also sought to achieve full citizenship rights for gays, lesbians, and transvestites by fighting against homophobia, violence, and discrimination. Lesbians took a leadership role in formulating the direction of the movement, waging a battle in 1993 to increase their visibility by changing the name of the yearly national meetings to Brazilian Gathering of Lesbians and Homosexuals. In September 1997, lesbian activists gathered in Salvador, Bahia, for a four-day conference—the Second National Lesbian Seminar—which focused on health and citizenship. The event brought together women from throughout the country for a wide range of discussions with such titles as "Lesbian Citizenship," "Homoeroticism in the Press," "Our Health," "Our Pleasure," "Black Lesbians in the Union Movement," and "Lesbians and Family Relationships."

At the same time, the media's increased discussion of homosexuality and the activities of the international movement affected discussions within Brazil. All the major newspapers, magazines, and television stations covered international pride marches, debates about gays in the U.S. military, and AIDS issues. Talk shows featured the few activists who were willing to come out publicly and discuss issues openly and frankly. Popular singers such as Renato Russo announced their homosexuality and supported the movement.

There was also a shift in the way people who engage in same-sex erotic relations identify themselves. Although many Brazilians still think in terms of "active" and "passive" sexual roles, gay and lesbian identities similar to those in the United States and Europe have taken hold, especially among middle-class residents of the large urban centers. Whereas in 1980, *Somos* rejected the word *gay* as too bound to the movement in the United States, the English term now has widespread use among homosexual men and women and the media. However, coming out to family members and employers, especially for noneffeminate men and nonmasculine woman, is not as common as it is in Europe and the United States. Even so, more and more activists are coming out in newspaper, magazine, and television interviews in an attempt to break the cultural code that "you can do what you want, but don't tell anyone."[36]

Additionally, organizing around AIDS issues has not only attracted individuals seeking information and support, but has also provided new resources and infrastructure for gay-rights activism generally. Groups have learned how to apply for grants from state and national ministries of health for AIDS education and prevention. In some cases an office rented with such financial support has also served as a meeting place for local gay and lesbian groups.

The growth of the Workers' Party as an umbrella organization for most social movements and leftist groups also politicized gay activists. In recent years, the Workers' Party has channeled most of the opposition to the political, economic, and social problems facing Brazil. Its elected representatives in local, state, and federal offices provided much of the support for the gay and lesbian movement's legislative and legal activities. Recall that the entire Workers' Party bloc supported the provision to include a prohibition of discrimination based on sexual orientation in the 1988 constituent assembly.[37] During the 1980s the Workers' Party was the only ballot-status political party that included gay and lesbian rights in its program. Gay and lesbian activists formed a group within the Workers' Party to educate the membership about issues of the movement. However, the Workers' Party alliance with activists in the ecclesiastical-base communities of the Catholic Church caused the party's presidential candidate and former trade union leader, Luiz Inácio Lula da Silva, to withdraw his support for same-sex civil marriages (*uniao civil*) during the 1994 presidential elections.[38] Lula's reluctance to come out in favor of full rights for gays and lesbians has been attributed to his own desire to win support from the Catholic hierarchy. His efforts proved fruitless, since on the eve of the presidential elections his ratings in the polls dropped dramatically when the government introduced a monetary plan that stabilized the economy. As a result, Lula lost his second bid for the presidency.[39] Nevertheless, in 1995, Workers' Party Congresswoman Marta Suplicy once again introduced congressional legislation to prohibit discrimination based on sexual orientation and to establish *parceria civil* (domestic partnership).

The movement has expanded in other important areas in recent years. Leaders in the bank workers', teachers', and social security workers' unions have begun to demand domestic-partner benefits for gay and lesbian members. Students at the University of São Paulo have established a center for the study of homosexuality. Activists of the Group of Homosexuals of the *Partido Socialista dos Trabalhadores Unificados* (United Socialist Workers' Party) presented resolutions in the 1995 and 1997 Congress of the National Union of Students to endorse the campaign for same-sex domestic partnership and the constitutional provision outlawing discrimination based on sexual orientation. The resolutions were approved by the congress despite the opposition of some leftist students.

Transvestites have also become active participants in the Brazilian movement. Since the 1960s, cross-dressers, many working as prostitutes, have become more visible on the streets of Brazil's major urban centers. Hormones and silicone injections have made the creation of a traditional feminine body accessible to the large numbers of men who identify as cross-dressers. Although transvestites, like men and women who identify as gay and lesbian, have been a prime target of hate crimes and murders, for many years a gulf existed between transvestites and gay and lesbian activists. In May 1993, however, the *Associação de Travestis e Liberados* (Association of Transvestites and Liberated People) organized the First National Gathering in Rio de Janeiro. Over one hundred people from Rio de Janeiro, São Paulo, and other states attended the conference. Representatives from other newly formed groups of transvestites also converged on the Seventh Brazilian Gathering of Lesbians and Homosexuals in January 1995, insisting that the movement broaden its focus to included issues facing transvestites. As a result, the name of the national organization founded at the gathering, the Brazilian Association of Gays, Lesbians, and Transvestites, reflected an expanded constituency.

Gay and lesbian guides to Brazil boast innumerable bars and clubs, popular gay beaches, openly gay Carnival celebrations, and slick new publications. Yet visibility and festivity do not necessarily produce activists. Despite the new level of organization achieved over the last few years, including annual pride parades in Rio de Janeiro and São Paulo, the movement still remains weak, involving only a fraction of the millions of Brazilian gays, lesbians, and transvestites. Currently, there are more than fifty gay and lesbian groups in Brazil and a comparable number of AIDS organizations that direct many of their efforts to gay clients, but most of them are small, numbering no more than thirty members. Only a dozen or so larger groups have accumulated enough resources and membership to sustain offices, maintain an infrastructure, and provide leadership to the national movement. Even the largest demonstration to date, at the close of the ILGA Conference, had only two thousand participants.

Moreover, a May 1993 poll, which interviewed a cross section of two thousand Brazilian men and women, revealed that anxiety over homosexuality remains rampant. While 50 percent of those polled confirmed that they had daily contact with homosexuals at work, in their neighborhoods, or in bars and clubs that they frequent, 56 percent admitted that they would change their behavior toward any colleague they discovered to be homosexual (one in five would drop all contact with the person). Asked about hiring decisions, 36 percent said they would not employ a homosexual, even if he or she were best qualified for the position. And, of those interviewed, 79 percent would not accept having a son go out with a gay friend.[40]

Dr. Arnaldo Domínguez carried out another revealing survey in São Paulo in 1991. He distributed two hundred questionnaires to clinics and psychologists and a further six hundred to homosexuals. Thirty percent of the doctors thought homosexuality deserved condemnation. Seventy percent of the doctors considered bisexuality an abnormality, and fifty percent said they would be unprepared to discuss the subject if a homosexual client came to their office.[41]

Dramatic changes in the movement have occurred since its early days in the late 1970s. It has become much more inclusive. Members of leftist currents, such as the Workers' Party and the United Socialist Workers' Party, are considered a legitimate part of a politically diverse movement. Although gay-rights organizations did not endorse candidates, most activists supported Lula and the Workers' Party in the 2002 elections. This does not mean, however, that the movement has mechanically adopted left-wing rhetoric, analysis, or methods of organization. Colorfully painted banners and rainbow-hued bunches of balloons usually distinguish gay and lesbian participation in political demonstrations, and consciousness-raising sessions—a legacy of both the international feminist movement and Brazilian pedagogist Paulo Freire—remain a key organizing tool for most groups. Lesbians, while still a numerical minority within the movement, play an equal role in the leadership of the national association. A small number of transvestites, politicized through their experiences with the police, have also assumed a place in the movement. Where once political activities were carried out by valiant individuals and isolated groups, now the movement has developed nationally coordinated campaigns around issues such as violence, same-sex domestic partnerships, and national antidiscrimination legislation.

Moreover, the amount of public discussion about homosexuality has increased, as the media gives more coverage to issues that concern gays, lesbians, and transvestites, and popular soap operas portray them more positively. The international movement has had a strong impact on Brazil, with key leaders traveling to the United States, Europe, and other countries in Latin America to participate in conferences or attend pride demonstrations. The ILGA Conference in Rio de Janeiro brought many activists in contact with international delegates, fostering a rich interchange.

In August 1964, Gigi Bryant, a member of the social group that edited the newsletter *O Snob*, concluded a six-part series on the "art of cruising." In her article, she described Maracanazinho, a large arena where events such as Holiday on Ice and the Miss Brazil beauty pageant take place: after dishing about members of the groups who had attended shows there, Gigi joked that "since the faggot top-set is converging on Maracanazinho, it is likely to become the social center of various social classes in the future." What's more, she teased, "Indeed, it is very possible that in better days the First Gay Festival will take place there with representatives from other nations converging on our country. That would generate lots of publicity and be a grand utopia."[42]

In 1964, Gigi's predictions were good for a laugh. Yet, remarkably, she was right.

Notes

I wish to thank Daniel Hurewitz and Moshe Sluhovsky for their editorial assistance in preparing this essay.

1. Maria Helena Moreira Alves, *State and Opposition in Military Brazil* (Austin: University of Texas Press, 1985); James N. Green, "Liberalization on Trial: The Brazilian Workers' Movement," *North American Congress on Latin America, Report on the Americas* 13, no. 3 (May–June 1979): 14–25; and Thomas E. Skidmore, *The Politics of Military Rule in Brazil, 1964–85* (New York: Oxford University Press, 1988).

Just like the debate in 1979, the issue of marching in the 1980 May Day rally divided the activist group *Somos* and was fiercely discussed in the pages of *O Lampião da Esquina*. Those who participated in the demonstration argued that the fight for gay and lesbian rights and the movement against the military dictatorship were intertwined. Without democracy, the goals of the gay and lesbian organizations would be difficult to obtain. Opponents of the group's participation in the May Day demonstration, who organized a picnic at the zoo that day and split from the group several weeks later, argued that the working class and many trade union leaders were homophobic. Instead of engaging in politics on international workers' day, they maintained, gay men and lesbians should enjoy the holiday with friends as did thousands of other working people who were not protesting the dictatorship's policies.

2. For a more complete account of the early gay-rights movement in São Paulo, see James N. Green, "The Emergence of the Brazilian Gay Liberation Movement: 1977–81," *Latin American Perspectives* 21, no. 1, issue 80 (Winter 1994): 38–55; Edward MacRae, "Homosexual Identities in

Transitional Brazilian Politics," in *The Making of Social Movements in Latin America: Identity, Strategy, and Democracy*, ed. Arturo Escobar and Sonia E. Alvarez (Boulder, Colo.: Westview, 1992), 185–203; and João S. Trevisan, *Perverts in Paradise*, trans. Martin Foreman (London: GMP, 1986).

3. For another overview of the gay-rights movement in Brazil, see Luiz Mott, "The Gay Movement and Human Rights in Brazil," in *Latin American Male Homosexualities*, ed. Stephen O. Murray (Albuquerque: University of New Mexico Press, 1995), 221–30.

4. Jose Henrique Pierangelli, *Códigos penais do Brasil: Evolução histórica* (Bauru, Brazil: Jalovi, 1980), 26.

5. Ibid., 301.

6. Ibid., 316.

7. Peter Fry, *Para inglés ver: Identidade e política na cultura brasileira* (Rio de Janeiro: Zahar, 1982).

8. Richard G. Parker, *Bodies, Pleasures, and Passions: Sexual Culture in Contemporary Brazil* (Boston: Beacon, 1991), 41.

9. See Michel Misse, *O estigma do passivo sexual: Um símbolo de estigma no discurso cotidiano* (Rio de Janeiro: Achiame, 1979).

10. Peter Fry and Edward MacRae, *O que e homossexualidade* (São Paulo: Brasiliense, 1983).

11. Agildo Guimarães, interview by James N. Green, tape recording, Rio de Janeiro, October 6, 1994.

12. See Alves, *State and Opposition in Military Brazil*, and Skidmore, *The Politics of Military Rule in Brazil, 1964–85*.

13. Anhuar Farad, interview by James N. Green, tape recording, Rio de Janeiro, July 25, 1995.

14. See Sonia E. Alvarez, *Engendering Democracy in Brazil: Women's Movements in Transition Politics* (Princeton: Princeton University Press, 1990).

15. See Michael George Hanchard, *Orpheus and Power: The Movimento Negro of Rio de Janeiro and São Paulo, Brazil, 1945–1988* (Princeton: Princeton University Press, 1994).

16. "*A história do 'EBHO': Encontro Brasileiro de Homosexuais (continuação II)*," *Boletim do Grupo Gay da Bahia* 13, no. 27 (August 1993): 7.

17. Mario Blander, "*Lucros do lazer gay: Os donos da noite descobrem novo filão*," *Isto é* (São Paulo), (April 27, 1983), 76–77.

18. Miriam Martinho, "Brazil," in *Unspoken Rules: Sexual Orientation and Women's Human Rights*, ed. Rachel Rosenbloom (San Francisco: International Gay and Lesbian Human Rights Commission, 1985), 22.

19. The Brazilian campaign involved modifying Code 302.0 of the World Health Organization's International Classification of Diseases, which had been incorporated into the Brazilian code. The World Health Organization struck the category from its list eight years later. Mott, "The Gay Movement and Human Rights in Brazil," 222–23.

20. João Antônio de Souza Mascarenhas, *A tríplice conexão: Machismo, conservadorismo político e falso moralismo, um ativista guei versus noventa e seis parlamentares* (Rio de Janeiro: 2AB Editora, 1997).

21. Mott, "The Gay Movement and Human Rights in Brazil," 223–24.

22. Richard Parker, "AIDS in Brazil," in *Sexuality, Politics, and AIDS in Brazil: In Another World?* ed. Herbert Daniel and Richard Parker (London: Falmer, 1993), 9.

23. Ibid., 12.

24. Grupo Outra Coisa (Ação Homossexualista), "*Informe a coletividade homossexual de São Paulo,*" mimeographed leaflet, June 1983.

25. Paulo Roberto Teixeira, "*Políticas públicas em AIDS,*" mimeographed leaflet, n.d., 2.

26. Veriano Terto, Jr., interview by James N. Green, tape recording, Rio de Janeiro, July 24, 1995.

27. Luiz Mott, *Epidemic of Hate: Violations of the Human Rights of Gay Men, Lesbians, and Transvestites in Brazil* (San Francisco: Grupo Gay da Bahia, Brazil, and the International Gay and Lesbian Human Rights Commission, 1996).

28. Martinho, "Brazil," 18.

29. "*Casos se repetem em São Paulo,*" *Folha de São Paulo,* April 17, 1990.

30. Grupo Gay da Bahia, *Grupos de exterminio de homossexuais no Brasil,* leaflet, n.d.

31. "*Um pouco de nossa história,*" *O corpo* (São Paulo), no. 0 (November 1980): 8.

32. "*Reclamando nossos direitos,*" *Jornal folha de parreira* (Curitiba) 3, no. 25 (May 1995): 2.

33. The U.S. Department of State 1993 human rights country report for Brazil includes the following statement:

> There continue to be reports of murders of homosexuals. São Paulo newspapers reported that three transvestites were murdered on March 14; other reports claimed that 17 transvestites were killed in the first three months of 1993. One military policeman was charged in the March 14 killings and was awaiting trial at year's end. Homosexual rights groups claim, however, that the vast majority of perpetrators of crimes against homosexuals go unpunished. (U.S. Department of State, *Country Reports on Human Rights Practices for 1993* [Washington, D.C.: GPO, 1994], 376.s).

34. Marcelo Godoy, "*Justiça reduz pena de matador de travesti,*" *Folha de São Paulo,* October 9, 1994, 4.

35. Amnesty International, U.S.A., *Breaking the Silence: Human Rights Violations Based on Sexual Orientation* (New York: Amnesty International Publications, 1994), 13–14.

36. This saying, "*Pode fazer o que você quiser, mas não diga nada a ninguém*" ("Do whatever you'd like, but don't tell anyone"), usually uttered in a tone that expresses reluctant tolerance, reflects the fear of shame if friends or relatives discover that a family member is a gay man or a lesbian.

37. A similar constitutional revision introduced in 1993 and voted on in 1994 received the support of 25 percent of the legislators. João Antônio de Souza Mascarenhas, *A Tríplice Conexão: Machismo, Conservadorismo Político e Falso Moralismo* (Rio de Janeiro: 2AB Editoro, 1997), 117.

38. "*Lula se reúne con presidente da CNBB e diz que reconhecimento dos direitos de homossexuais também não será tratado,*" *Folha de Sao Paulo,* April 13, 1994.

39. Wilson H. da Silva, interview by James N. Green, tape recording, São Paulo, May 5, 1995.

40. According to the poll, in the northeast the number of those refusing to accept having a son go out with a gay friend increased to 87 percent. "*O mundo gay rasga as fantasias,*" *Veja,* May 12, 1993, 52–53.

41. Ibid., 53.

42. Gigi Bryant, "*Da arte de caçar, capítulo VII 'Country Club Gay,'*" *O Snob* 2, no. 10, August 15, 1964, 6.

"Con Discriminación y Represión No Hay Democracia"

The Lesbian and Gay Movement in Argentina

Stephen Brown

LESBIAN AND gay activism now circles the globe, but it is vastly understudied. Not even the latest syntheses of contemporary social movement theory discuss lesbian and gay movements to any significant degree (see McAdam, McCarthy, and Zald 1996).[1] Even the most important works on "social theory" tend to ignore sexuality (Warner 1993, ix). A lack of activism cannot explain this deficiency, since formal lesbian and gay organizations have existed in the United States since the 1950s, and have become prominent in North America and Western Europe in the past thirty years. During the past decade, many developing countries have become the sites of burgeoning movements as well. Lesbian and gay organizations now exist in every country in Latin America, some of them dating back to the mid-1980s (Drucker 1996, 92). [...]

Argentina hosts a lesbian, gay, bisexual, and transgender movement that is sometimes quite visible and results in concrete political advances,[2] such as the inclusion in 1996 of a clause in the municipal constitution of Buenos Aires that prohibits discrimination on the basis of sexual orientation. Explaining how the lesbian and gay movement emerged and later expanded in Argentina, and why and it did so when it did, I argue that a conjunction of local and global cycles of protest, depending on the earlier diffusion of lesbian and gay identity, led to the birth of activism in the late 1960s and early 1970s. These favorable conditions were then eclipsed by constraints that were solely domestic, causing the abrupt end of activism in the mid-1970s. During the 1980s, however, lesbian and gay activists, most from a new generation, took advantage of new political opportunities—essentially the return to democratic rule, the human-rights discourse, and some international support—to form a movement. Thus, our analysis is enriched by adopting the political-opportunity-structures approach to social movements, even if the literature underestimates the significance of identity and identity formation. Clearly, activism requires the prior diffusion of lesbian and gay identity, though identity and opportunities do not in themselves automatically produce a movement. Although one cannot draw definitive conclusions from a single case study, this article suggests that social movement theorists should question more deeply the nature of identity, especially when looking at sexuality, and examine both its origins and its consequences. [. . .]

Providing historical background on lesbian and gay activism in Argentina, and describing the movement as it is organized today, I will use the political-opportunity-structures approach to explain the emergence of the movement, and demonstrate the centrality of identity to a more nuanced understanding of the movement's current structures and strategies. I will speculate about the movement's future, which will be defined by how its goals are articulated and its alliances chosen.

Historical Background and Current Situation

In November 1969, while Argentina was under military rule, the *Grupo Nuestro Mundo* (Our World Group) was founded in Buenos Aires, becoming the first gay political organization in Latin America (though informal social groups had previously existed). In 1971 the *Grupo Nuestro Mundo* and several others, including mostly male left-wing university students, anarchists, and religious organizations, joined to form the radical *Frente de Liberación Homosexual* (Homosexual Liberation Front, hereafter FLH). Even after the democratic elections in 1973 and the return to power of Juan Perón, the FLH remained an essentially clandestine group, closely associating itself with the fight for women's and workers' rights, both in Argentina and around the world. After Perón's death in 1974, during the presidency of his widow, Isabel, there was a rapid upsurge of right-wing paramilitary attacks on homosexuals. In a short period of time, the number of FLH members fell from a hundred to a dozen. Some of them were tortured or murdered after the military coup in March 1976. Several left the country, and those who remained suspended their public activities. The FLH dissolved in June of that year.[3]

Under the brutal military dictatorship, formal lesbian and gay activism disappeared. By the end of 1982, however, a few new groups had emerged and created a coordinating committee (*Coordinadora de Grupos Gays*). By that point it was increasingly recognized that military rule would not last much longer. However, between

January 1982 and November 1983, a former member of the FLH and at least seventeen other gay men were murdered, and only two of the cases were solved. In June 1982 a paramilitary group known as the Comando Cóndor declared its intent to "wipe out" homosexuals. The commission later appointed to investigate disappearances (*Comisión Nacional sobre la Desaparición de Personas,* hereafter CONADEP) does not mention in its final report, *Nunca Más,* that four hundred or more lesbians and gay men had been disappeared, according to the estimate of a former commission member (*Gays por los Derechos Civiles* 1995, 3–4).

In 1983, after the military dictatorship had collapsed and democratic elections were held, lesbian and gay life in Argentina flourished. Many bars and clubs opened, taking advantage of the liberalization. The rebirth of activism, however, was due as much to continued repression as to new freedoms. Repression had not disappeared under democratic rule, but expectations had grown. In April 1984, soon after police officers arrested approximately 200 people in the raid of a gay club, 150 activists met in the gay bar Contramano and formed the *Comunidad Homosexual Argentina* (Argentinean Homosexual Community, hereafter CHA). [...] The CHA's founding members were a politically diverse assortment of gay men and lesbians, 14 of whom were willing to acknowledge their homosexuality publicly (Jáuregui 1987, 202). The CHA opened several chapters outside the capital and for the rest of the decade remained by far the most important group. By the mid-1990s, the organization's influence had waned, but it was given a new life in 1997 when a different set of activists began to operate under the CHA banner.

In the early 1990s, under the presidency of Carlos Menem, Argentinean popular movements in general were on the decline, but lesbian and gay groups proliferated. A lesbian feminist group, *Las Lunas y las Otras* (an untranslatable pun literally meaning "The Moons and the Others"), met for the first time in July 1990. In 1991 the CHA was formally recognized by the government after a long battle, fueling much public debate over homosexuality and paving the way for the formation of other groups. Having achieved its main objective, the CHA then succumbed to an identity crisis over what its goals and strategy should be. Several members founded their own groups, such as the *Sociedad de Integración Gay-Lésbica Argentina* (Argentinean Society for Gay and Lesbian Integration, hereafter SIGLA), the *Grupo de Investigación en Sexualidad e Interacción Social* (Research Group on Sexuality and Social Interaction, hereafter *Grupo ISIS*), and *Gays y Lesbianas por los Derechos Civiles* (Gays and Lesbians for Civil Rights, known as Gays DC). In addition, when journalist Ilse Fuskova came out on national television in September 1991, she galvanized many lesbians into activism and greater visibility and led to the formation of the *Convocatoria Lesbiana.* The first among numerous transgender groups, *Transsexuales por el Derecho a la Vida y la Identidad* (Transsexuals for the Right to Life and Identity) was founded in May 1991. The first lesbian and gay pride march took place in July 1992.

Though over thirty groups have sprung up since the early 1990s, they are all quite limited in size and are directed by a very small number of leaders, while a larger group of activists do volunteer work and often participate in public activities without getting involved in policy debates. On occasion, well-planned demonstrations draw on a larger pool of participants. [. . .]

A large number of gay groups trace their roots to the CHA, having split off from it or, like Gays DC, having been founded by former CHA members a few years after leaving the original organization. Almost all but the youngest gay male activists began their involvement in the movement in the CHA. Many lesbians have had various degrees of contact and involvement with the CHA, several having left the organization over the men's sexism. The lesbian-specific groups, though, trace their origins more to the feminist movement.

Although over the years like-minded groups have formed temporary alliances (for example, the Lesbian Front), it was only in 1995 that male-dominated groups and women-only groups began to hold meetings on a regular basis and cooperate on short-term projects. Their first concrete act was to organize a national gathering of lesbian, gay, and transgender organizations, held in Rosario in March 1996 and now an annual event. (It was at that point that transgendered people were accepted into the lesbian and gay movement, at least as close allies.) Their second major undertaking was to organize the fifth annual pride march (expanding its title to include the transgendered), held on June 28, 1996. The third was the previously mentioned campaign to prohibit discrimination on the basis of sexual orientation in the new Buenos Aires municipal charter.

The Emergence of a Movement

The collapse of the ultraconservative military regime and redemocratization in 1983 provided a new space and vocabulary for the lesbian and gay movement. The conditions for organizing around sexual identity, however, rested on prior structural (sociohistorical) changes and international diffusion of ideas. As in many other countries, in Argentina the relationship between lesbians and gays and the state, notably the police, is a difficult one. The police often raid bars and clubs and use various legal provisions to harass and detain lesbians and gay men without necessarily charging them with any crime. Thousands of transgendered people are arrested every year (*Gays por los Derechos Civiles* 1995, 33). While in custody they are often verbally and physically abused with impunity. Some disappear and are later found murdered, and the cases go uninvestigated.[4]

[. . .] Though sodomitical acts were never legally prohibited in twentieth-century Argentina, lesbians and gay men do not receive equal treatment before the law. [. . .]

Not even formal laws, however, can guarantee legal protection: one can find other reasons to fire an employee, and the police can use other methods to detain someone, for instance, by planting evidence.

Historically, the Argentine state has not recognized "sexual minorities" as legitimate collective actors and members of civil society. For years, the CHA was prevented from fund-raising and taking official positions by the government's refusal to grant it legal status. The supreme court defended this position, using justifications based on the Catholic Church's position, the protection of the family, and medical opinion (Robinson 1991). Leftist political parties have on occasion spoken in favor of lesbian and gay rights and fielded openly lesbian and gay candidates, not one of whom has ever been elected. However, prejudice and/or fear of losing popular support have prevented much of the Left from allying itself with gay politics. [...] In Argentina, power historically alternates between the Radical Party and the *Justicialistas* (Peronists), neither of which has indicated much support on issues relating to sexuality. On these matters, many lesbian and gay Argentineans hope for the emergence of a third party. [...]

From the moment it was founded, the CHA adopted a strategy of working with other social movements on matters such as human rights, violence, and AIDS. The CHA wanted to forge links with other people and groups repressed by the dictatorship. This is well illustrated by the advertisement it published in the daily newspaper *Clarín* on May 28, 1984, under a headline that read, "WITH DISCRIMINATION AND REPRESSION THERE IS NO DEMOCRACY" (see Jáuregui 1987, 225). The ad argued that "no true democracy can exist if society permits the persistence of marginalization and the various means of repression that still prevail" and referred to the more than 1.5 million homosexual citizens as people "who are worried about the national situation and who, like you, went through the hard years of the dictatorship."[5] It thus invited readers, who, whatever their views on homosexuality, were almost sure at that point to be opponents of military rule, to identify with gay men and lesbians and consequently back their struggle for a democracy without discrimination or repression.

To build bridges with other human-rights organizations, the CHA adopted the motto, "Freedom to express one's sexuality is a human right,"[6] and an approach to lesbian and gay rights based on the human-rights discourse, which was popular because of its contribution to the end of the dictatorship. The government, however, subsequently made several major concessions to the military, which greatly reduced the persuasive power of a human-rights-based approach. As a result, in 1987 the CHA decided to concentrate on AIDS instead. The organization began an AIDS prevention program, and its newsletter, *Vamos a andar*, suddenly focused on HIV/AIDS. The CHA also redirected its efforts from organizing around sexual orientation toward gaining legal recognition by the government.

Argentinean activism receives important inspiration and support from abroad. From the 1970s to the present, gay publications in Argentina show a close identification with the lives, struggles, and cultural activities of lesbians and gay men around the world, especially in the United States and Europe. Argentineans likewise use the same symbols and representations (such as pink triangles and rainbow flags) and reclaimed historical figures, further diffusing a global, essentialized identity. Naturally, the meaning of being gay or lesbian can vary in different contexts. However, the lesbian and gay movement has benefited from international opportunity structures. [...]

Long-time activists commonly mention that their work is inspired by their counterparts abroad, sometimes following close interaction. [...] Lesbian and gay identity, culture, expressions, and sense of community are further disseminated by contact at international meetings (for example, the Beijing Women's Conference, the periodic Latin American Feminist Gatherings, and meetings sponsored by the International Lesbian and Gay Association), and increasingly via the Internet. One can therefore conclude that both the earlier international diffusion of lesbian and gay identity and models of activism contributed to the emergence and expansion of activism in Argentina. [...]

Bringing Identity Back In

A large part of the literature on social movements focuses on resource mobilization and obtaining policy results. This approach analyzes collective action "in terms of the logic of strategic interaction and cost benefit analysis," using "such 'objective' variables as organization, interests, resources, opportunities and strategies" (Cohen 1985, 674–75). This emphasis on the mechanics and outcomes of protest movements improves on prior grievance-based conceptions of social movements. In a wider sense, a focus on political opportunity structures is a useful way to understand case dynamics through the opportunities and constraints that the movement encounters. In the case of Argentina, this involves linking the lesbian and gay movement to democratization, the human-rights discourse, and international influences. Other analytical tools are still required, however, because this approach ignores motivation, differing understandings, beliefs, priorities, and visions, and the dynamic and sometimes contradictory relationships between individuals and groups, in which many of the contradictions relate to identity.

Since political opportunities constitute "but a necessary prerequisite to action," the current consensus in comparative social movements is to analyze the "framing process" as well. This term refers to "the conscious strategic efforts by groups of people to fashion shared understandings of the world and of themselves that legitimate and motivate collective action" (McAdam, McCarthy, and Zald 1996, 6, 8). [...] Thus, the relationship between identity formation and lesbian and gay politics in Argentina needs to be addressed.

A crest in an international protest cycle, including the 1969 Stonewall riots in New York,[7] mass student demonstrations in France and Mexico in 1968, and the growing women's liberation movement, as well as left-wing activism (galvanized by the Cuban Revolution) across Latin America and Western Europe, contributed to the timing of the emergence of gay activism in Argentina. Domestic events, including larger-scale opposition to military rule, notably the protests in Córdoba (which were known as the *Cordobazo*), burgeoning left-wing activism, and the prominent guerrilla movement, also played a large role. [...] Stated otherwise, Argentinean gay activism was born not out of concrete changes in domestic conditions, but as part of a domestic and international moment of protesting existing social relations, adapting the examples of others to local circumstances and likely inspiring other actors in turn.

In the early 1970s, a member group of the FLH proclaimed, "We don't have to liberate homosexuals, we must liberate the homosexual in everyone"[8] (inspired by a similar slogan of New York's Gay Liberation Front). The implication was that gay men and lesbians are essentially the same as everyone else; they have merely embraced a potential that all people have. This does not imply that everyone should be gay. In fact, it argues for the elimination of the categorization of sexual orientation.

Paradoxically, organizing around identity in effect strengthens the categories of identity and the boundaries that separate them (Taylor and Whittier 1992, 111). In Argentina (and elsewhere, one may assume) greater lesbian and gay visibility has also affected heterosexual identity and more clearly limited what behavior is considered appropriate for straight people. [...]

Faced with constant messages that they are inferior, abnormal, sick, perverted, or evil, gay men and lesbians argue that homosexuality is good or at least acceptable. In a society in which their existence is stigmatized, they tend not to argue, as the FLH did, for the abolition of the category. Instead, they reclaim it, reinforce it. As a result, Argentinean activists resist heterosexual encroachment on their space. An event from a June 1996 meeting to coordinate the pride march provides an excellent illustration: two members of the Marxist League and the Revolutionary Socialist League, both very small left-wing groups, offered their support, while saying that their groups did not believe that sexual orientation was an issue. They asked that in return the lesbian and gay groups support their efforts to defend two left-wing political prisoners being held in Neuquén. Gay activists responded with great anger to their dismissal of the importance of sexuality: "I am proud to be a faggot," furiously proclaimed one, to much audible support. No one supported the proposition that the lesbian and gay movement should act collectively on behalf of heterosexuals, though groups and individuals were free to show support if they wanted to. "We have our own history, saints, and martyrs," asserted another activist.[9]

The first instance of gay activism in Argentina, led by the *Frente de Liberación Homosexual* (1969–76), was radical. After a seven-year break attributable to military repression, the CHA emerged, adopting a more integrationist approach in the mid- to late 1980s. In the 1990s, however, the numerous new groups embraced widely differing approaches and strategies, some of which may be somewhat incompatible with one other. Current lesbian and gay political organizations in Argentina can be divided into three broad categories: (1) assimilationist organizations, which favor integration into the heterosexual "mainstream," arguing that prejudice (homophobia) alone keeps them apart; (2) civil-rights-based associations, which mainly advocate legal protection for sexual minorities; and (3) radical groups, which prefer to question the nature of sexual identity.[10]

Assimilationist Organizations

Assimilationist organizations like the CHA from the mid-1980s to 1997 and SIGLA seek integration into mainstream Argentinean society. They prefer to present gay men and lesbians as being similar to everyone else, showing no such visible sign of difference as gender nonconformity in clothing or behavior. (In contrast, the FLH considered effeminacy in gay men and masculinity in lesbians subversive in a positive way.) Assimilationists decry the demonization of and discrimination against gays and lesbians, taking measures that include initiating court cases. Whereas the FLH believed in sexual liberation and the creation of a new order, these groups seek recognition. Their activists accept the current construction of sexual categories. For them, fighting for lesbian and gay rights is part of a larger struggle to give civil society more autonomy from the state. In order to "normalize" homosexuality, they sometimes cooperate more with human-rights organizations and sometimes even the government than with other lesbian and gay groups. [. . .] In general, assimilationist groups are less likely to accept bisexuality, since that would weaken assumptions that people are either homo- or heterosexual (Udis-Kessler 1996). They also tend to avoid association with transgendered people, reluctant to embrace their clear differences from the mainstream in terms of appearance and gender identity, sometimes going so far as to argue that the transgendered do not have a politics (NX 1996, 28).[11]

Civil Rights-Based Groups

As do assimilationists, civil rights-oriented groups seek to "normalize" homosexuality, but they adopt a different-but-equal approach rather than a strategy predicated on sameness. Gays DC was founded in 1991 to work for gays' and lesbians' civil (not human) rights, thus situating the struggle in civil society instead of in opposition to the state. Its motto, "Our struggle originates in the desire for all types of freedom,"[12] also illustrated a strategy of forging links with other communities. While it lasted until late 1996 [...], Gays DC provided members of "sexual minorities" and HIV-positive individuals with legal aid in cases of concrete discrimination and arrest. It also campaigned for equal rights, including marriage and adoption, and led the campaign for protection under the new Buenos Aires municipal charter. It sought the repeal of discriminatory legislation, the nondiscriminatory application of existing laws, and the passage of new measures to protect lesbian, gay, and transgender individuals from discrimination. In practice, its strategy combined casework, lobbying, and demonstrations to make its case. The issue of increasing visibility, also one of the objectives of *Lesbianas a la Vista* (Lesbians on Sight), justifies the attention drawn to this community's requirements, ensuring that they are present on the public agenda. In Argentina, where being open about one's sexuality is in many ways a risk, few gay men and lesbians are publicly out. For those who are, visibility is also a means of modifying attitudes and fighting discrimination, focused on civil society. By speaking of "sexual minorities," this strategy adopts and updates the CHA's early attempt to build bridges among those who suffered from repression under military rule. [...]

While much of the literature tends to present social movements as cases of society versus the state, the Argentinean lesbian and gay movement demonstrates a more ambiguous relationship. Members of civil-rights groups normally operate in ad hoc coalitions, seeking to limit the state's reach into the private sphere while working with the state to enact new legal guarantees and mechanisms to ensure equal protection under the law. Some gay groups place much importance on recognition by the state (as in the case of the CHA's long fight for legal status), and many want to secure equal treatment in accordance with liberal democratic principles. The movement as a whole, however, is vehemently opposed to the state's repressive capacity. In fact, the 1995 pride march's theme was, "Discrimination condemns us, the police kill us, we're still standing."[13] [...]

Any campaign based on visibility requires a positive relationship with the news media. If it is not publicized, a demonstration has very little impact. The media can send images and ideas to millions of people. Argentinean civil-rights-based activists have been very adroit at ensuring media coverage of their events through good personal relations with journalists and the use of creative visual imagery. They keep the ear of influential institutions and individuals by not using violence or being seen as too radical. [...]

Radical Groups

Radical groups such as the University of Buenos Aires's *Colectivo Eros* (Eros Collective) and the now defunct *Grupo de Jóvenes Gays y Lesbianas "Construyendo Nuestra Sexualidad"* ("Building Our Sexuality" Gay and Lesbian Youth Group) can be characterized primarily by their professed rejection of the system. These groups are mixed male/female and function mainly within the university. Though both have taken part in larger political actions, the Eros Collective functions principally around issues and activities relating to the university. [. . .]

These groups reject the commonly accepted notion that sexuality is fixed as either hetero or homo (or even residually bi). Instead, they adopt a more social-constructivist approach to sexuality, seeing sexual orientation as a continuum on which individuals can move over time. As intellectual inheritors of the FLH, they place renewed importance on the goal of gay and sexual liberation. Like the FLH, they value marginality, emphasizing that the rights-based discourse does not accord any value to difference. These activists are critical of what they term the "mainstream movement" for making short-term concessions in exchange for tolerance, rather than adopting a longer-term perspective. They strongly disagree with some assimilationist groups' strategies, sometimes even considering them worse enemies than the police because, as insiders, they can do more harm (Julio Talavera, interview, Buenos Aires, June 14, 1996). The radical groups see commonalities among oppressed groups but also links among social problems under capitalism—neoliberal policies, high unemployment, poverty, alienation, anomie, discrimination, and so forth. The ultimate goal of these groups is not merely to achieve lesbian and gay equality but to transform society—to liberate the human spirit.

These groups, however, have difficulty in identifying concrete measures to be taken. Furthermore, their wide-ranging goals cause resources to be thinly spread and can cause internal conflict over priorities (McAdam, McCarthy, and Zald 1996, 15). Nonetheless, they do count some concrete achievements, such as the collective's institutionalizing a queer studies center at the university in 1997. Otherwise, to my knowledge, these groups have not yet translated their analysis into activities that differ significantly from other groups.

Transcending Identity?

Many new groups were established during the 1990s, aided by the increase in lesbian and gay visibility, and assumed roles that the CHA and later groups did not adopt. Some were born of internal splintering, others of separate lesbian organizing. Rather suddenly in 1995, many of these groups started to collaborate as a result of a number of new developments: the inclusion of issues relating to the transgendered, person-to-person contacts between groups, internal self-confidence, a newfound spirit of compromise, and international examples. Surprisingly, AIDS played little or no direct coalition-building role, despite the fact that about three-quarters of the cases of HIV infection were the result of homosexual contact—though this could be an underlying motivating factor. Nonetheless, visions of unity had vanished by late

1996 as ideological differences, based in opposing strategies and views of identity, reemerged.

The radical goal of universally abolishing sexual orientation categories would end oppression but also erase the activists' identity. This is all but impossible to imagine, since "fixed identity categories are both the basis for oppression and the basis of political power" (Gamson 1995, 391). But the Argentinean lesbian and gay movement, by including transgendered people, made an important move toward weakening the rigid, essentialized identities of *lesbian* or *gay*. The homo/hetero binary was further destabilized in June 1996, when for the first time bisexuality was addressed. The issue was forced when a male and a female activist became romantically involved. [. . .]

Except for the assimilationists, the Argentinean movement is increasingly recognizing (sometimes less than wholeheartedly) multiple categories of identity. Still, it is not enough to embrace "the postmodern celebration of diversity" (Epstein 1990, 58). [. . .] Activists must find a middle ground between assimilation and isolation, one in which diversity is harnessed as a strength. Failing that, social movements lose their potential for wider social transformation.

Talk among lesbians and gay men of a "global community" is deceptive, for it ignores differences in power based on local conditions and subject positionings such as class, gender, and race/ethnicity. In Argentina and elsewhere, individual activists and the movement in general will have to recognize that "identities cannot be frozen or lived outside of interaction with other identities" (Plotke 1990, 94). [. . .] By reducing a person's identity to one solitary defining marker, identity politics come up against natural limits. In their desire to work with groups outside the lesbian and gay community, assimilationist organizations to some extent reject identity politics. However, their strategy is one of denying rather than valuing difference. Instead of abandoning sexual orientation as an identifier, it would be more effective to surpass it, for example, by arguing for a right to "sexual dissent" (Duggan 1995).

A Look Ahead

In many ways, lesbian and gay movements epitomize the "new paradigm of politics": their actors value "personal autonomy and identity" and seek civil equality, instead of organizing around socioeconomic interests and pursuing the redistribution of wealth or the conquest of political power. (Some other demands are monetary/material, for instance, partner benefits such as pensions or insurance.) In addition, these groups are usually informal, spontaneous, with a low degree of horizontal and vertical differentiation—quite distinct from the formal, large-scale representative organizations that partake in pluralist or corporatist interest intermediation under the "old paradigm" (Offe 1985, 832).

To sum up my argument, I contend that the emergence of lesbian and gay activism in Argentina rested on the earlier creation and diffusion (through national and international opportunity structures) of lesbian and gay identities. The FLH's formation depended in larger part on a global and local protest cycle and the diffusion of ideas than on new local circumstances. Its demise, though, resulted from domestic conditions alone: a rapid surge in violent repression and the military coup of 1976 constituted insurmountable new constraints. The foundation of the CHA in 1984 and the emergence of the lesbian and gay movement were clearly results of political liberalization, which provided activists with three key assets. First, new opportunities (for example, access to the media and the possibility of holding peaceful demonstrations) allowed them to voice their opposition to the repression and discrimination that they still experienced under democratic rule. Second, a new discourse, based on human rights, enabled them to build bridges with other groups that had opposed the dictatorship. Third, greater contact with international support and models of political organizing facilitated and inspired their efforts. The growth in the number of groups after 1990 can be explained by increased visibility, fractures within the CHA over focus and ideology, and the formation of separate lesbian organizations. [. . .]

Without a closer look at identity, this analytical approach is only partial. It is impossible to comprehend the differences among lesbian and gay groups, the potential for collaboration, the nature of their dynamics, and their future prospects without examining their conceptions of identity. When studying lesbian and gay movements, one should not conceive of them as one might other so-called new social movements. For movements based on race and ethnicity, for example, identity is usually transmitted and reinforced at home, in the family or the neighborhood, or based on physical and/or cultural attributes. In contrast, lesbians' and gay men's identity results from a sexual desire, historically constructed as transgressive, that has become a basic component of personal definition. One cannot conceptualize this as a mere subculture or as one would the political identification of pacifists, for example. Analyzing the identity of lesbians and gay men provides a crucial means for understanding a complex and dynamic movement that the political-opportunity-structures approach cannot sufficiently explain on its own.

Given the incessant friction within a very diverse community and the often incompatible strategies and objectives that various groups adopt, it is likely that—at least in the short run—they will continue to collaborate on immediate issues and actions without becoming any more unified. Nonetheless, they are slowly eroding rigid boundaries by including bisexuals and transgendered people under the same umbrella as lesbians and gay men. This might presage a weaker emphasis on issues affecting a particular community, in exchange for a greater focus on issues that concern a broader and more loosely defined group of people who are not afforded equal opportunities, perhaps moving beyond the confines of sexual orientation.

What might be the best strategy for the lesbian, gay, bisexual, and transgender movement to achieve its objectives? The answer depends to a great extent on how those objectives are identified. The major goal of assimilationists—the integration of gay men and lesbians into the "mainstream"—would necessitate abandoning the discourse of difference. Considering the respective strengths of identity and prejudice, this does not seem likely to succeed, nor do these groups' strategies and activities effectively promote that goal.

Strategies organized around civil rights have proven reasonably effective in Buenos Aires, but the rest of the country is more resistant to change. Without the possibility of ever being in a majority, lesbians and gay men will require alliances with actors who are not defined by their sexual orientations in order to achieve more fundamental change, including in the cultural sphere. This will require rising above identity politics and could involve reduced cooperation with assimilationist lesbian and gay activists, who prefer acceptance to working for more basic social change.

One writer (Drucker 1996, 101) sees the key to lesbian and gay liberation in an alliance with a unified Left that supports oppressed people's self-organization. This strategy, however, is not particularly well suited to Argentina, given the Left's current weakness and its historical distance from lesbian and gay concerns. The search for allies in social change should include a range of social movements, especially those that share a broader interpretation of contemporary problems. In the past, some Mothers of the Disappeared (*Madres de Plaza de Mayo*) have symbolically participated in a few lesbian, gay, and transgender demonstrations. Some contact has recently been made with trade unions, whose activism has been very important historically in Argentina. They would make excellent partners for change, notably in the achievement of benefits for same-sex partners of members. Nonetheless, the economic situation in Argentina is extremely precarious. Since the early 1990s, social movements have been reduced to a more defensive position, fighting to retain what they have achieved since democratization rather than to obtain new concessions. Large-scale transformation might not occur anytime soon, but the lesbian and gay movement in Argentina is accumulating many small-scale victories along the way.

Notes

1. Though Hanspeter Kriesi's chapter titled "The Organizational Structure of New Social Movements in a Political Context" does discuss the existence of a gay "collective identity," it does not distinguish it from other "subcultural movements."

2. My study focuses mainly on lesbian and gay activism, though I occasionally include a discussion of transgender issues. I use the term *transgendered* to refer to individuals called *travestis* and *transsexuales* in Argentina. The terminology can appear confusing, since Argentineans use the term *travesti* to denote not a transvestite, cross-dresser, or drag queen (called a *transformista*), but what is usually known in North America as a "pre-op" transsexual. In Argentina,

however, the term *transsexual* is used solely to refer to someone who has undergone genital reassignment surgery. I also raise the issue of bisexuality when relevant, though it has only recently started to be discussed as part of the movement. I prefer not to use the term *queer* because it is not an integral part of the movement's discourse; in fact, it is disliked by many activists because it brackets important differences within a very diverse community of non-heterosexuals.

3. It is difficult to determine whether Homosexual Liberation Front (FLH) members were targeted because they were members of the organization, simply because they were gay or lesbian, because they were leftist activists, or for a combination of these reasons. For more information on the FLH, see Perlongher (1985) and Green (1994).

4. For example, the police had repeatedly threatened Mocha Celis, a thirty-four-year-old *travesti* prostitute. On August 18, 1996, she was seen getting into a police vehicle. Later that night she was found lying on the street, bleeding. She had been shot twice in the penis and died soon after. The police reported no leads on the murder (Sardá 1996b).

5. All translations are my own. The original text reads, "CON DISCRIMINACIÓN Y REPRESIÓN NO HAY DEMOCRACIA. . . No existirá democracia verdadera si la sociedad permite la subsistencia de los sectores marginados y de los diversos métodos de represión aún vigentes" and refers to "personas que . . . nos preocupamos por la realidad nacional y transitamos junto a Ud. los duros años de la dictadura."

6. In Spanish: "El libre ejercicio de la sexualidad es un derecho humano."

7. Stonewall symbolically marks the beginning of the gay liberation movement in the United States.

8. In the original: "No hay que liberar al homosexual, hay que liberar lo homosexual de cada persona."

9. The original quotes are "Soy orgulloso de ser puto" and "Tenemos nuestra propia historia, santos y mártires."

10. I have omitted from my typology of political groups archival organizations (such as the *Biblioteca Gay-Lésbica* [Gay and Lesbian Library] and *Escrita en el Cuerpo* [Written on the Body]), whose primary function is to collect documentation for public access; religious groups (such as the *Iglesia de la Comunidad Metropolitana* [Metropolitan Community Church]), which provide for the spiritual needs of the community; research organizations (for example, *Grupo ISIS*), which are more interested in scientific and social-scientific issues surrounding homosexuality; and sports groups. Membership in these types of groups does not preclude belonging to more politically oriented ones as well, and their members often do support political work and participate in demonstrations. Nor do I discuss lesbian separatist groups such as *Las Lunas y las Otras* and the now-dissolved *Madres Lesbianas* (Lesbian Mothers). These groups provide a women-only space for discussion and analysis, personal growth, and cultural expression. [. . .] The closeted nature of their activities precludes political activism in the public sphere. Finally, I have excluded the various transgender organizations, such as the *Asociación de Travestis Argentinas* (Association of Argentinean Transvestites), *Travestis Unidas* (United Transvestites), the *Organización de Travestis y Transsexuales de Argentina* (Organization of Argentinean Transvestites and Transsexuals), and the *Asociación por la Lucha de la Identidad de las Travestis* (Association for the Struggle for Transvestites' Identity), because I do not have sufficient information to distinguish them conceptually and analytically. Moreover, the struggle of transgendered people is

somewhat different from that of gay men and lesbians: they seek recognition of their personal gender identity rather than sexual orientation, a demand considered more radical by most. Nonetheless, transgender militancy is strong and visible. Since the lesbian and gay movement itself is concentrated in the Buenos Aires area, that is where I focus my attention, though some groups, notably the *Colectivo Arco-Iris en Rosario*, have formed outside the capital, including most recently in Jujuy, Lobos, Neuquén, and Mar del Plata (where the church is more influential and people tend to be more socially conservative).

11. Nonetheless, the CHA appointed a transsexual to its executive board in April 1996. She resigned in frustration before the end of the year (Lohana Berkins, author interview, Buenos Aires, February 6, 1997).

12. In Spanish: "*En el origen de nuestra lucha está el deseo de todas las libertades.*"

13. Originally: "*La discriminación nos condena, la policía nos mata, seguimos de pie.*"

References

Brown, S. 1996. *Al enemigo no lo vamos a vencer nunca* (interview with Rafael Freda). NX 3.

Cohen, J. 1985. Strategy or identity: New theoretical paradigms and contemporary social movements. *Social Research* 59: 663–717.

Drucker, P. 1996. "In the tropics there is no sin": Sexuality and gay-lesbian movements in the third world. *New Left Review* 218: 75–101.

Duggan, L. 1995. Queering the state. In *Sex Wars: Sexual Dissent and Political Culture*, eds. L. Duggan and N. D. Hunter, 179–93. New York: Routledge.

Epstein, B. 1990. Rethinking social movement theory. *Socialist Review* 20: 35–65.

Epstein, S. 1987. Gay politics, ethnic identity: The limits of social constructionism. *Socialist Review* 17: 9–54.

Gamson, J. 1995. Must identity movements self-destruct? A queer dilemma. *Social Problems* 42: 390–407.

Gays por los Derechos Civiles. 1995. *Violaciones de derechos humanos y civiles en la República Argentina basadas en la orientación sexual de las personas y de las personas viviendo con VIH/SIDA.* 3rd ed. Buenos Aires: Gays por los Derechos Civiles.

Green, J. N. 1994. Feathers and fists: A comparative analysis of the Argentine and Brazilian gay-rights movements of the 1970s. Paper presented at the Seventeenth International Congress of the Latin American Studies Association, Atlanta, Ga., March 10.

Jáuregui, C. L. 1987. *La homosexualidad en la Argentina.* Buenos Aires: Ediciones Tarso.

Julian, R. 1991. A decisive time for Argentine gays. *The Advocate*, December 17, 50–51.

MacRae, E. 1992. Homosexual identities in transitional Brazilian politics. In *The Making of Social Movements in Latin America: Identity, Strategy, and Democracy*, eds. A. Escobar and S. E. Alvarez, Boulder: Westview Press.

McAdam, D., J. D. McCarthy, and M. N. Zald, eds. 1996. *Comparative Perspectives on Social Movements: Political Opportunities, Mobilizing Structures, and Cultural Framings.* Cambridge: Cambridge University Press.

Offe, C. 1985. New social movements: Challenging the boundaries of international politics. *Social Research* 52: 817–68.

Perlongher, N. 1985. *Una historia del FLH*. In *Homosexualidad: Hacia la destrucción de los mitos*, ed. Z. Acevedo, 272–78. Buenos Aires: Ediciones del Sur.

Plotke, D. 1990. What's so new about new social movements? *Socialist Review* 20: 81–102.

Robinson, E. 1991. Argentina's gays battle attitudes. *Washington Post*, December 12.

Sardá, A. 1996a. Argentina: 1996 Report. *Escrita en el cuerpo*, December 18.

———. 1996b. *Travesti asesinada por la policía. Escrita en el cuerpo*, August 24.

Taylor, V., and N. E. Whittier. 1992. Collective identity in social movement communities: Lesbian feminist mobilization. In *Frontiers in Social Movement Theory*, eds. A. Morris and C. McClurg Mueller, 104–29. New Haven: Yale University Press.

Udis-Kessler, A. 1996. Present tense: Biphobia as a crisis of meaning. In *The Material Queer: A LesBiGay Cultural Studies Reader*, ed. D. Morton, 243–49. Boulder: Westview Press.

Vaid, U. 1995. *Virtual Equality: The Mainstreaming of Gay and Lesbian Liberation*. New York: Anchor Books.

Warner, M., ed. 1993. Introduction to *Fear of a Queer Planet: Queer Politics and Social Theory*. Minneapolis: University of Minnesota Press.

Sociability, Secrets, and Identities

Key Issues in Sexual Politics in Latin America

Mario Pecheny

In Latin America, as elsewhere, gays and lesbians have pursued political strategies to redefine their subordinate status. I will discuss the political claims of these sexual minorities, which are formulated in the name of rights as part of the struggle to include issues of sexual and intimate relationships in a broader demand for full and equal citizenship. My central hypothesis is that political practices aimed at reverting the subordination of homosexuality are not limited to the boundaries of formal politics —such as legislation and public policies—but are also carried out in intermediate realms associated with the particular forms of sociability and social relationships of homosexual individuals.

Describing the modes of sociability of homosexuals whose identities may be qualified as *discrete/discreet*,[1] I refer to both social and personal relationships among homosexuals and how they interact with nonhomosexuals. Based on previous research done in Argentina, I can affirm that these modes of sociability characterize the lives of most nonheterosexuals, especially among middle-class persons. These modes of sociability affect the political strategies of the sexual minorities' social movement.

Secrets and Identity

Homosexuality is a secret that shapes the identity and personal relationships of homosexual individuals. Here I define *homosexuality* as the tendency to seek sensual pleasure by means of physical contact with people of the same sex (Dover 1982, 13). Not every culture has the notion of homosexuality, nor do all those who have had sexual encounters with people of the same sex consider themselves homosexual. An *identitarian* homosexual individual is someone who considers that having desire for and/or sex with and/or loving relationships with people of the same sex defines his or her own identity to some degree. In principle, this identitarian dimension is acknowledged to oneself and may or may not be assumed publicly.

Homosexual identification is not always adopted autonomously. In fact, since the invention of the term *homosexual* at end of the nineteenth century, diverse specialists have attributed this identification heteronomously.[3] Numerous authors doubt that the medical categorization can define a social identity and prefer the term *gay* or none at all (Butler 1993, Foucault 1993). In this work, when I speak of *homosexuals*, I refer only to people that feel desire toward those of their same sex, without attempting to adopt the physical appearance of the opposite sex, as in the case of transgender people. The term *homosexual* as both noun and adjective is used generically, while *gay* and *lesbian* are used more precisely to refer to homosexual individuals that are somewhat open about their sexual orientation.

In our society, homosexuality is a dimension of one's personality that constitutes a basis for stigmatization, discrimination, and exclusion (Parker and Aggleton 2002). This dimension has two features that are crucial to our discussion: on one hand, homosexuality is not generally evident to others, since it can hidden relatively easily; on the other hand, it is a condition that is not shared by the core group of primary socialization formed by family, childhood friends, etc. That is, a child or adolescent who will lead a homosexual life is customarily raised in a heterosexual atmosphere.

The first feature, nonevidence, allows individuals to control information about their sexuality depending on different interlocutors, places, and times. In a context where homosexuals face discrimination, the capacity to impersonate serves as protection. People with different skin color lack this recourse in a racist context.

The second feature, the fact that the primary unit of socialization does not share the stigmatized condition, denotes a problem unique to homosexual individuals. This differentiates them from members of other discriminated-against categories that form social groups, such as Jews in an anti-Semitic context. If, for example, a Jewish boy is tormented at school, he will probably find love and material support in his family and close friends. On the other hand, an adolescent who discovers desire for people of the same sex and experiences anguish or fear, not only may not find support in family and friends, but may feel this anguish or fear precisely because of the possibility of being rejected by the primary social group.

Research conducted in Argentina (Kornblit, Pecheny, and Vujosevich 1998) and other countries shows that the process of formation of one's personal identity regarding "relevant or significant others" is closely linked to how one manages the disclosure of homosexual orientation. This dilemma appears during adolescence or early youth and will continue in life in different stages, including, for example, lesbian mothers or gay fathers with their own biological or adopted children. Although most homosexuals disclose their sexual orientation to others throughout their lives (what is known as "coming out"), my hypothesis is that homosexuality represents a constitutive secret that establishes identity and personal relationships for homosexual individuals.

A secret may have many different meanings: it is something kept quiet, unspoken, whispered about or discussed behind other people's backs, something one should not speak of or cannot speak of [. . .] What is interesting is that a secret creates specific social ties among those who share it, related to those who do not, but who may sense it or learn of it at some point. Thus a secret causes particular types of interaction and conflict. [. . .]

For Zempleni (1984),

> [A]ccording to its etymology, a secret is something which has been set aside [*secernere*]. The constituent act of a secret is an act of rejection that involves at least two parties— either individuals or groups—connected by a negative relationship: one that keeps the content apart and the addressee/audience [*destinataire*] who is singled out by the denied content [. . .] Except in theology, there is no secret per se without a target or original addressee. Once separation is accomplished, what does the substance set aside become? [. . .] [I]t becomes oppressed, restricted, restrained, that is, *loaded with tension.* Loaded with the tension of rejection that the secret has instated and which must be maintained or preserved. The linguistic analysis of secrets reveals three ways of releasing or regulating inner tension, three ways that manifest a secret's incoercible tendency to make its way toward its addressee (103).

As we will see, these ways are revelation, communication, and leaks.

In a society that discriminates against homosexuality, homosexual individuals may be identified as "stigmatizable," a term coined by Goffman (1989). Unlike people who present a visible stigma, stigmatizable persons are those whose stigmas are not evident to others, but which may become known. Sociologists have studied biographies of this category of person in terms of stigma management throughout time and within different social settings. Controlling communication and the secret is a fundamental recourse of a stigmatizable individual.

In spite of some advances, homosexuality continues to be strongly stigmatized in Argentina and the rest of Latin America. For this reason, homosexual individuals generally reserve the right to decide when to communicate their sexual identity and to whom. Studies mention a process or typical moment in a homosexual's biography, called "coming out of the closet," in which an individual ceases to hide his or her homosexuality and makes it known publicly. [. . .] Coming out of the closet can be voluntary, political, or forced by circumstance.

The question of secrecy, illustrated by the word "closet," does not stem from any universal homosexual essence but designates a common experience (Kosofsky-Sedgwick 1993). What they have in common is a historical contingency: having been born in societies hostile to homosexuality, or "homophobic," they are forced to keep their sexual activities and love lives in the closet to a greater or lesser degree. This is not a hidden/visible dichotomy, but a constant, dynamic movement along a continuum.

Possibly the biggest difficulty that arises in a homophobic society is not the purely sexual dimension of homosexual identity, but its public display as expressions of affection, love, or commitment. Indeed, even in intolerant societies or states, "sinful" sexual acts can take place in the sanctuary of darkness or behind closed doors. More problematic is the manifestation of homosexuality as a homoerotic expression or as a loving relationship whose social and political recognition, in the form of same-sex marriage, still seems distant today in Latin America. All testimonies in the research consulted mention that the influence of discrimination is experienced mostly in the restraint of public displays of affection, such as walking arm in arm or kissing in public, or even just walking down the street with someone who is obviously gay, which a lot of people experience as traumatic at a given stage. [. . .]

[. . .] As Andrew Sullivan (1995) pointed out, the predominant mode of social interaction involving homosexuality conforms to a "hypocritical" system, so denominated because it presupposes and reproduces a double standard for private and public settings. This system has existed for at least a century. However, as we will see, the foundations of this system have weakened in the last twenty or thirty years. The development of the gay and lesbian movement and communities and the onset of the AIDS epidemic contributed to bring homosexuals and homosexuality into public visibility (Pecheny 2000).

In Latin America, consensual same-sex intercourse has not been prohibited by legislation since the nineteenth century (with a few exceptions, like Chile, where it was decriminalized only in 1999). All that is asked of homosexuals is discretion, by which is meant invisibility. The Argentine National Constitution of 1853, for example, states that any act pertaining to the private domain of an individual is allowed as long as it does not affect public order. Problems arise when these private boundaries are violated and homosexuality becomes visible. [. . .]

In the nineteenth century and during most of the twentieth century, public discretion (secrecy, clandestinity) was a characteristic of most homosexual individuals, who have had to lead different lives and adopt different identities depending on circumstances and social ties. In locations other than large cities, homosexuals are in a more difficult situation. There, if homosexuals are visible, they are often forced to become scapegoats or town characters, or their double lives may lead to blackmail and/or other painful circumstances that encourage emigration to the capital.

Since the restoration of democracy in most Latin American countries in the 1980s, the situation of homosexuals has changed. Political liberalization created a favorable context for claims for new rights and the development of new actors, such as the women's and sexual minorities' movements. Transnational social movements and networks have encouraged these processes as well (Keck and Sikkink 1998).

As mentioned earlier, the order of social interaction created around homosexuality follows a double moral standard that condemns homosexual practices in public yet tolerates them provided they are hidden from view. [...]

Although tolerance means respect for another's freedom [...], it does not mean full acceptance or social recognition. That minimum acceptance has been sufficient for many homosexuals and continues to be so today. Indeed, with some discretion, a homosexual life may be led more or less happily within the limits imposed by society, in spite of the complications of a double life. Yet this system of hypocritical interactions can only work insofar as people are willing to practice it. It demarcates homosexuality into two separate worlds, public and private, and requires a society that is comfortable with this separation. Historically, homosexuals and heterosexuals have cooperated to install this mode of interaction. Seeking to protect themselves from the mockery and discrimination that comes with revealing their sexuality, some homosexuals seem content with being allowed to experience their sexual and emotional life in private. Within their families, as long as the public conventions of discretion are respected, homosexual members can have a social life without difficulty. Many nonhomosexuals allow leeway for the "excesses" of others if they agree not to perturb social peace and the public sphere.

This mode of social (spatial and temporal) organization of homosexual practices also affects the modalities of homosexual interaction with respect to courting, relationships, and sex. Studies on the risks of HIV transmission showed how discrimination and the difficulty of courting someone of the same sex encourage taking risks or dissociating sex and affection, among other typical—even cliché—social practices of homosexual relationships (Pollak 1988 and 1993; Schiltz 1994; Pecheny 2000).

As pointed out by studies from different countries (Sullivan 1995; Pollak 1993), while both groups, heterosexuals and homosexuals, respected boundaries between the private and the public, the discretion system built around homosexuality functioned relatively smoothly. The main consequences of this predominant mode of so-

cial interaction—based on discretion and hypocrisy—on the formation of spaces of
sociability and on their dynamics, are described below.

Social Bonds

Because of secrecy, social bonds are differently structured within each world—the
world of those who do not know, the world of those who do, and the world of homosexual peers—based on knowledge, or lack thereof, of the secret. Schematically,
the personal relationships of a homosexual are structured within these three inter-
locking worlds, distinguished by the presence or absence of knowledge of the person's
homosexual orientation. These worlds overlap, and also take place at different levels
of intimacy: from the most private to the most public and political.

The Group of Those Who Do Not Know

The vast world of personal relationships made up of people who are otherwise close
to a homosexual person, yet are not privy to the person's love life, can be explained
by discrimination against homosexuality. Discrimination can be exercised directly
or indirectly. It is direct when a norm or attitude targets a type of act or person directly, or when categories are arbitrarily treated as different. Discrimination is indirect
when a norm or attitude appears to be universal, yet its discriminatory effects are suffered exclusively by a certain category of person or by people who commit a particular act. According to current laws, marriage between a man and a woman is
universally accessible; the laws' effects are discriminatory only for those who love a person of their same sex. Moreover, discrimination can be real or felt (anticipated). It is
real when effectively executed, and felt when an individual preempts rejection and
discriminates against him or herself (Green 1995). For homosexual individuals, indirect discrimination and felt or anticipated discrimination are more pervasive than direct and effective discrimination (see below). Fear of being outed as a homosexual
operates as an efficient cause for self-exclusion and personal mortification. Anticipated discrimination also favors risking AIDS and other sexually transmitted diseases,
since people may not use condoms in fear of being rejected. It also deters access to
health and legal services and leads to withdrawal from loved ones.

Our empirical study (Pecheny 2001) showed that the subjective realm (formed by
an individual confronting him or herself), the intimate-private realm (formed by the
individual's loved ones), and the public-political realm are neither coherent nor homogeneous when it comes to homosexuality. Subjective attitudes are diverse. Individuals' feelings are contradictory and ambiguous, in part due to their socialization prior
to becoming aware of their homosexuality. In most cases, individuals know or sense

that homosexuality is something to be ashamed about, something to be mocked or excluded, long before they realize they are attracted to people of their same sex. Later, feelings may evolve positively during the coming-out process, but this ambiguity never completely goes away. Also, one's personal perception of actual social discrimination—the basis for anticipated discrimination—is very powerful.

Within the family, felt discrimination appears to affect people more frequently than real discrimination. Once anticipated discrimination is overcome and what was hidden is revealed, the family's attitude is generally one of acceptance or tolerance, though not always. According to testimonies, homosexuality often generates hostile reactions from members of the immediate family, mainly the father and male siblings. Expulsion from the household, the "silent treatment," and mutual accusations between the homosexual and relatives are common occurrences; thus, homosexuality often remains secret. In most cases, when the family knows the person is homosexual, the rule is not to discuss it.

As far as friends are concerned, three scenarios are typical: some homosexuals participate in a world comprised exclusively of gays and/or lesbians (in the case of male homosexuals, it may also include women who tend to befriend gay men, often called *fag hags*, although this term has become offensive to some); others lead a double life, with interactions divided between those who share the secret of homosexuality and those who do not; finally, a smaller group are completely integrated into their world of friends as gays or lesbians, regardless of the friends' sexual orientation.

Among neighbors and coworkers, the general rule is discretion and tolerance. Nevertheless, in some professions, homosexuality is perceived as taboo. The predominant idea is that public knowledge of homosexuality could bring a professional career to an end. According to testimonies, this is the case for teachers, military personnel, doctors, psychoanalysts, politicians, members of the clergy, male athletes, referees, diplomats, judges, and police officers, among others.

Relationships with doctors and health professionals deserve particular attention. For lesbians and homosexual men, there is friction in the relationship with their doctor, unless they find a doctor who specifically "understands" their situation.

Finally, beyond the individual's circle of relevant and significant others as described by Mead (1962), there are indeterminate others or "society," perceived by our interviewees as "distinctly discriminatory," "hypocritical," or "ignorant."

These brief comments show that discrimination operates differently depending on social settings and according to the interlocutors who happen to interact with an individual who is either actually discriminated against, or fears potential discrimination. This phenomenon is also noticeable in the public and political world. In the sphere of public opinion, most people declare they are in favor of tolerance, perhaps without complete conviction. The extremes of total rejection and full acceptance of homosexuality seem to be less frequent attitudes (Vujosevich, Pecheny, and Kornblit

1997). The "politically correct" language of the media, intellectuals, and other authorized voices is not uniform, even though homosexuality has been discussed with openness and acceptance for some time. Direct discrimination on the grounds of homosexuality is widely condemned. However, the now predominant idea of "nondiscrimination," which is supposed to be the opposite of direct discrimination, is still a far cry from full recognition or approval.

Finally, we must consider the law, both as a legal regulator of behavior and as a message the state conveys to society. In Latin American countries, the law (which is based on the Napoleonic Code) does not speak of homosexuals or homosexuality. Legal inequality is derived mainly from nonrecognition of same-sex couples. Nevertheless, over the last few years, the application of laws currently in effect seems, paradoxically, more favorable to homosexuals than the wording of the laws themselves. Some rulings have permitted the extension of certain rights and benefits (social protection, adoption, etc.) to homosexual individuals and couples, although these rights were originally intended for heterosexual single persons or unmarried partners.

However, given the larger social context of discrimination, real and executed or felt and anticipated, homosexuals are likely to consider it convenient to maintain their sexual and love lives shielded from potentially hostile attitudes. Testimonies gathered in our fieldwork (Kornblit, Pecheny, and Vujosevich 1998; Pecheny 2001) show that most homosexuals do not disclose their homosexual orientation to most interlocutors.

The secret of a person's own homosexuality is protected with greater zeal in homosocial environments, that is, those formed exclusively or almost exclusively by people of the same sex. Examples of this type of environment are teenage gangs, cliques, sports teams, gatherings of bar patrons, or institutions such as the armed forces and religious orders. According to research, in both the formation of the sexual identity of an individual, as well as the group identity of homosocial collectives (i.e., groups integrated by individuals of the same sex), homosexuality has become a "constitutive exterior" (Laclau and Mouffe 1987), a difference whose denial appears to be as important as its positive affirmation in defining one's identity. That is the reason why some authors affirm that for the construction of masculinity in a "macho" context, the denial of homosexuality constitutes an element as decisive as the conquest of women.

Simulation, in the passive form of discretion or the active form of impersonation (resorting to signs of "de-identification"), constitutes a recourse of protection for stigmatizable individuals. This exercise comes at a cost, as Goffman has analyzed. On one hand, homosexual individuals, when in environments where their sexual orientation remains hidden, can learn the cruel truth regarding others' beliefs about homosexuality. On the other hand, hiding builds a labyrinth that can "force the impostor to go deeper and deeper into the meanders of a lie to stop the threat of being outed" (Goffman 1989, 103).

The Group of Those Who Know

A second world is made up of "those who are in the know." These are not necessarily most people in the family or social circles of a homosexual individual. At one end, the core of those who are in the know includes people who know but don't talk about it [. . .] and at the other end, there are persons who are able to reinforce their trust and support by being included in the most intimate, private, or "real" world. [. . .]

The World of Homosexual Peers

According to studies, a more or less integrated world of homosexual peers has always existed. What has changed throughout history is the degree of its visibility (D'Emilio 1983; Chauncey 1994; Sebreli 1997). Argentinean sociologist Juan José Sebreli illustrates this phenomenon with the image of "cities under cities." This world possesses its own codes of language and behavior, including how to dress or look at each other in public. In the traditional terms of homosexual jargon, this world is called *el ambiente*, and it is formed by *los que entienden*, as opposed to *los nada que ver* (Sivori 2000).

In recent years, the existence of a "gay community" in Buenos Aires and other big cities in Latin America has been accompanied by an economic, political, and spatial organization of homosexuals. Although this community is more visible than the homosexual subcultures of the first half of the twentieth century, it still "juxtaposes" normal social life, rather than intersecting with it. [. . .]

The physical spaces of homosexual sociability are basically tied to seduction and sexual encounters: bars, pick-up joints, and bathhouses, that is, practically clandestine places. This hinders the construction of a sociopolitical movement that by definition aspires to be public. Yet sexual minorities entered politics and addressed public opinion from precisely these kinds of places: in New York City, the first militant assembly (motivated by what was then called "gay cancer") gathered at a local sauna (Bayer 1989); in Paris it took place at a gay bar (Pollak 1988); and in Buenos Aires the creation of the first homosexual public organization—the Homosexual Community of Argentina— was decided in an assembly that convened at a disco (Jáuregui 1987).

With the AIDS epidemic, the ties that had developed in the homosexual world proved to be the main source of spiritual and material support for people living with the illness—including nonhomosexuals. In countries where there were relatively strong gay communities, as well as in Latin America, where the community began to develop together with AIDS, the first reactions to the disease occurred within networks of gay friends (Altman 1994; Pecheny 2001). In the eighties and most of the nineties, when AIDS stigmatization was considerable, reticular relationships of gay friends became what Pollak (1993) calls veritable "extended families" of AIDS victims.

Boundaries between Worlds

Adopting different roles and leading a "double life" [. . .] have been facilitated by urban development. Although big cities make possible the organization of social exchanges in distinct places and times (daytime often means "straight" time, and nighttime means gay), including social exchanges based on sexual orientation, the boundaries between the worlds described above are neither fixed nor insurmountable, but are are permeable and flexible. [. . .]

The communication initiated by sharing a secret may have the effect of forging a strong but ambivalent social bond, nourished by constant tension between an inside and an outside.

Zempleni (1984) asserts that "leaking"—"to let out," "to let slip out"—is without a doubt the most common mode of regulating tension and guarding the secret. Leaks constitute a secret's "most remarkable and paradoxical property" (106). A secret seems unable to exist as such without being shown to its [excluded] addressees somehow, with hints and fragments, which is not to say that it was revealed or communicated. "Leaking serves to regulate and maintain a secret's tension . . . Because after all, a secret is as threatened by its decrease in tension as it is by its excessive increase" (106).

Maintaining the limits of the secret, which are diffuse, unstable and dynamic, requires an effort from both sides. The invisibility of homosexuality is not a state of equilibrium or inactivity, but rather involves active efforts. In fact, the current proliferation of public discourses on "gay matters" has challenged people who are reluctant to acknowledge the existence of secret sexualities and relationships, rendering this invisibility, this "don't ask-don't tell" type of interaction, much more difficult to maintain.

Personal Links among Homosexual Peers

Personal links among homosexual peers play a key role in individual development, which may result in greater access to geographic mobility, to the job market, and/or to cultural and economic circles different from those of one's origin.[. . .]

The Gay and Lesbian Movement and the Appearance of AIDS

The development of a gay and lesbian movement and the appearance of AIDS have contributed to bringing down the boundaries among these worlds: the world of those who don't know, the world of those who know, and the world of homosexual peers.

The existence of the distinct worlds described above depends on the application of a systematic double standard. As we have seen, this system is undergoing a crisis brought on by two factors: the development of a social movement of sexual minorities, and the AIDS epidemic. Also, in most Latin American countries, the movement's development accompanied the transition from an authoritarian to a democratic regime, and the spread of AIDS happened simultaneously; regime change and AIDS awareness created a favorable context for the liberalization of cultural values and practices.

Space does not permit us to describe in extenso the history, strategies, and objectives of the sexual minorities movement (Bernstein 1997; Adam, Duyvendak, and Krouwel 1999; Pecheny 2001). However, it is interesting that the movement values visibility as a political instrument and goal, rejecting the traditional discretion adopted by homosexuals. The sexual-minorities movement has redefined feelings of shame and indifference into positive feelings, making sexual difference a source of pride, as in the pride marches that now occur around the globe. The gay movement's main argument in favor of visibility is that if all homosexuals were known as such, a threshold would be crossed and the hypocritical system would be invalidated. This movement would make sexual differences trivial, bringing about the beginnings of true acceptance.

In modern societies, a set of fundamental aspects of life, including sexuality, is considered legitimately protected from the public eye, therefore belonging exclusively to the private and intimate domain. Along with other factors, the fight against AIDS helped include the discussion of some of those aspects in the political agenda which, in normal times, had remained invisible and were not discussed publicly. [...]

The politicizing movement presupposes questioning the allegedly natural character of inter- and intra-gender relationships, that is the recognition of their social and historically constructed nature,[4] and implies breaking with the hypocritical order established by fixed boundaries between the public and the private.

The AIDS epidemic brought individuals, as well as the collective sexual minorities community, out of the closet. For a variety of reasons, AIDS prompted numerous homosexuals living with HIV/AIDS to reveal their sexuality, which until then had been restricted to the confines of intimate space (Sontag 1990, 112–13). A similar phenomenon took place on a social scale: with the AIDS epidemic, homosexuality became a topic in the press and government. Due to AIDS and the light it shed on hidden forms of sexuality, several implicit and explicit boundaries of mutual protection between homosexuals and their nonhomosexual environment began to blur.

[...] Discussion of homosexuality (or simply sexuality) became not only unavoidable, but also necessary. The unprecedented visibility of homosexuality and homosexuals caused by the appearance of AIDS produced a break in the hypocritical order mentioned above, and was a catalyst for the organization of homosexuals and for the claim for rights and public debate (Roberts 1995).

Thus the AIDS experience created, paradoxically, a context that helped to redefine the subordinate status of homosexuality as a stigmatized practice that had been relegated to the private space of discretion. It precipitated the entry of issues of discrimination and sexual rights onto the public scene. Because of AIDS, different forms of sexuality were discussed in public, not simply in terms of sexual relations, but in terms of love, public displays of affection, and social and civil rights. Moreover, the AIDS epidemic accelerated the debate on the legal status and social protection of unmarried and gay couples.

Ultimately, the politicization of sexuality endeavors to guarantee respect for a freely chosen private life. If one keeps in mind that the definition of the social status of homosexuality involves recognizing individuals as autonomous beings, the analysis of the relationship between public and private enables us to situate sexual problems in the plane of citizenship.

The acceptance of homosexuality—as well as of contraception and abortion—presumes the legitimacy of the dissociation between sex and procreation. The very notion of sexual rights entails recognizing the value of sexuality for personal realization, regardless of reproductive intentions. In other words, individual autonomy, partly determined by the control of one's body, is a necessary condition for true citizenship, with all its rights and responsibilities.

The AIDS epidemic exposed the gap between formally declared "equality" and the reality of homosexual rights. The epidemic catalyzed people's will to change the state of affairs. The defense of health, a universally shared value, has helped to legitimize human rights. Just as claims for reproductive health legitimate some rights for women, the fight against AIDS does so for the rights of sexual minorities.

These notions of rights and responsibilities presuppose recognizing autonomous individuals. According to the liberal principle of citizenship, if the state demands from individuals the fulfillment of responsibilities and obligations toward the community, it guarantees each person's rights in exchange. Rights and responsibilities in sexual and reproductive issues support the idea of sexual citizenship, citizenship that recognizes sexual differences and the legitimacy of different sexual orientations.

To conclude, I will discuss the vindication of sexual minorities and the place of social change regarding sexuality and love relationships.

Political Strategies and Social Change

Gay and lesbian activists show a tendency to combine political strategies directed at the state and government institutions with other political strategies for seeking social recognition. There is growing awareness that social change in sexual matters is not confined to the state and government, to legislation and public policies. [. . .]

In the last couple of decades, the double standard is being challenged in Latin America due to at least three concurrent phenomena: first, the development of a social movement of sexual minorities; second, the onset of the AIDS epidemic and the fight against it; and third, the new cultural atmosphere of democracy that has managed to instate itself in the region. This challenge to the hypocritical system—and to the sexual order in general—breaks the distinction between public and private. Social movements may capitalize on the public/private distinction to redefine it on more equal ground. [...] When I speak of breaking and redefining the liberal distinction between public and private, I do not mean annulling it: "the personal is political" only when, dialectically, a social actor claims his/her redefinition on more equal and nondiscriminatory ground. In my view, equal sexual citizenship does not require abolition of liberal boundaries between public and private, but rather equal political and social recognition for private sexual diversity.

Hence, if homosexuality has a status of subordination within the context of a hypocritical system, what role do institutional politics and political activism play in transforming the status quo? In order to approach these questions, it is convenient to study the evolution of the sexual minorities movement in the region, even at the risk of being too schematic.

In the 1960s and 1970s, when the sexual minorities movement was still in an embryonic state, the tone of vindication was one of transgression of normality and the established order, expressed in the language of sexual liberation. In the 1980s, democratic regimes were reinstated in many Latin American countries, and the politics of sexual transgression gave way to claims of "normality." In this decade, the demands of sexual minorities were expressed in the language of human rights and in the demand for civic inclusion. These demands clamored first for protection in terms of negative rights (nondiscrimination, protection against violence and from the police), and second, analytically and historically, for the recognition of positive rights. In the 1990s, the fundamental issue was the vindication of rights and nondiscrimination, together with some important differential concerns: for gay men, it was the issue of AIDS; for lesbians, the issue of women's rights and gender oppression; for transgender people, the question of sexual identity and police harassment and violence.

After decades of activism, there is greater awareness that political strategies based on claiming rights and framed as demands to the state are limited when it comes to sexuality and emotional relationships. Parallel to the vindication of rights, new, less formal political practices are being performed "at the level of everyday life" in order to obtain social recognition of sexual diversity. Given the early, still feeble victories in sexual equality at the governmental level—namely legislation for nondiscrimination—it is becoming increasingly evident that social recognition is a material and symbolic condition of the exercise of rights.

In principle, social recognition has two basic aspects: the *factual* recognition that something exists or takes place, and the *moral* recognition that something has the right to exist or take place. Regarding homosexuality, social recognition means that society acknowledges that homosexual practices, persons, identities, and relationships exist, and it accepts the legitimacy of a person's right to be a part of these practices, people, identities, and relationships.

Political strategies aimed at obtaining social recognition cannot take place exclusively at the governmental level, but should also include other settings: for example, civil society, public opinion, and social interactions in everyday life. Processes of recognition take place through interaction among homosexual peers and with their families, friends, workmates, and relevant others. In other words, given their particular object and subjects, democratizing public policies for sexual equality have inherent limits in scope; [. . .] not all topics of sexual minority status have made it onto the political agenda or are likely to be discussed in the public sphere.

Besides the ferocious competition among all social problems struggling to be considered legitimate issues on the public and political agenda, one of the main difficulties in articulating issues of homosexuality resides in the ambiguity of its social status, given the ambivalence of heterosexual members of society. Let us consider again the nature of discrimination against homosexuality. Discrimination exists when the state, society, a social group, or an individual separates, excludes, expels, or even wishes to destroy a person or group, denying their rights or preventing the exercise of their rights, based only on the belief that they or their practices are abnormal. The ways that discrimination is actually manifested are diverse. As noted earlier, we may distinguish direct and indirect discrimination, actually practiced discrimination and discrimination anticipated by the potential victim.

Lastly, it is necessary to distinguish different levels of social interaction where discrimination or recognition takes place, from the most intimate and private to the most public, bearing in mind that there is no necessary correspondence between levels. Acceptance at one level does not imply acceptance at other levels, nor does discrimination at one level imply discrimination at the remaining levels. That is, to understand the status of certain practices or identities, all different levels must be considered: the self, the intimate circle, the level of ordinary interactions, society in general, public discourse and opinion, and the political level which materializes as law and public policy.

At the political level, the general rule in Latin America is nondiscrimination against homosexuality. Legal protection from discrimination is a sort of halfhearted acceptance, which at the ordinary interaction level is quite compatible with the discriminatory practices that affect gay and lesbian individuals' everyday lives. The problem lies in the fact that the law can provide protection only against direct and executed forms of discrimination—when it can provide any protection at all—and when effective, it is so almost exclusively at the public level.

Indeed, discrimination against homosexuality is much more prevalent in its indirect form. Indirect discrimination is explained by or derives from the social order of Latin American countries, constructed on the pattern of heterosexual marriage and family. The social and juridical order of Latin American countries relating to social protection, civil rights, social and economic rights, and their exercise is fundamentally constructed around the model of a married heterosexual couple with a family. A person seeking to form a couple with another person of the same sex is indirectly excluded from the entire social, civil, economic, and political apparatus, both legally (de jure) and effectively (de facto). Because in theory homosexuals conserve their right to constitute a heterosexual marriage, they are not excluded directly. The problem resides in the fact that they cannot form legally recognized couples with the objects of their affection and preference.

If indirect discrimination is more frequent than direct discrimination, we also find that discrimination is more frequent in the shape of anticipated or feared discrimination than as effectively executed discrimination. The effect of anticipated or feared discrimination is self-exclusion protecting both sides. [. . .] In this way, a homosexual individual can lead a more or less happy life, interacting with discretion and anticipating possible rejection or negative attitudes from others. Once discretion is broken and what was reserved becomes explicit, discrimination, exclusion, or the anticipated rejection one feared are not necessarily realized. Yet, discretion seems to continue to be the norm, as illustrated by the apparent fact that even people that are happy and well adjusted in their homosexuality rarely come out to all of their relevant others. In spite of decades of activism and some shifts in public perception, many homosexuals in Latin America still lead a double life.

In synthesis, this subordinated status of homosexual people, produced by indirect and anticipated discrimination, confirms a hypocritical order that confines homosexuality to the private sphere and impedes public expression of love relationships as well as public recognition in the form of marriage. This order has been called into question since the 1980s due to the appearance of a movement of sexual minorities, the AIDS epidemic, and new cultural climates of democracy. One such climate is globalization, which paradoxically has helped enlarge the "supply" of available lifestyles, including sexual lifestyles. Within this framework, we must wonder what roles institutional politics and political activism are to play. Since the 1980s, the debate leans towards social recognition and the idea of normality, formulated in the language of human rights and formal democracy. This has been somewhat realized in indirect access to citizenship, implicit in the political and legal recognition of sexual minority organizations.[5] Just as reproductive health activism has helped legitimize the sexual rights of women, the fight against AIDS has done its share towards legitimizing gay rights (and to some extent drug users' rights) (Pecheny 2000). The late 1990s brought about a shift in gay organizations and their claims, which were absorbed by the fight against the AIDS epidemic. While incorporating sexual minorities' organizations into citizenship, the fight against AIDS has depoliticized the demands for the full recognition of sexual diversity by reducing the broader range of sexual politics into a health issue. Concurrently, feminist and women's movements gradually are beginning to make lesbian issues more visible.

Beyond AIDS, demands for civil sexual rights appeared primarily along two axes: political and juridical. The first axis is institutionalized politics through lobbying and active networking with other organizations, politicians, and government officials. Several achievements can be attributed to this pursuit. For example, in 1996 the Buenos Aires City Constitution included provisions against discrimination based on sexual orientation and identity, and in 2003 Buenos Aires approved civil unions for both heterosexual and homosexual couples. Social movements' acceptance of institutional policies contributed to the framing of social demands almost exclusively as issues for public debate and political decision.

The second axis of these demands for civil rights has to do with lawsuits. The lawsuits in cases, for instance, of job discrimination or lack of access to health care, were generally favorable to the plaintiffs, opening new interpretations of laws already in effect and making way for new hermeneutics that benefited sexual minorities. These were scattered cases at first, but several verdicts overcame the expectations of the plaintiffs to the point of granting social protection to same-sex couples in some cases.

Yet today the trend seems to be one of regression in sexual minority organizations. This is explained by multiple factors, namely: generalized apathy regarding politics, internal disagreements within sexual minority organizations, the establishment of "fund-raising" logic (the prioritization of fund-raising over political mobilization), and co-option by the state and financial donors. These phenomena currently affect NGOs and social movements in many fields, but in the LGBT field, they have specific implications related to the tensions of making sexual difference a fundamental base of political and personal identity.

The ebb in organizational strength accompanies another ambiguous phenomenon. Although the organized social movement of sexual minorities is undergoing a reversal, we witness a steady growth in less institutionalized, nonpolitical networking around gay and lesbian interests. This phenomenon is evident in the market, civil society institutions, universities and schools, the appearance of gay neighborhoods, growing exposure in the media and cultural expressions, and the presumed expansion of less rigid emotional relationships and sexual practices.

How should we interpret these ambiguous and seemingly contradictory phenomena? What opportunities are offered to political strategy in this context of waning social movements and advancing alternative forms of the social permeability of homosexuality? This leads us again to the limits of public policy concerning homosexuality. As mentioned before, public policy implies intervention based on the state's concept of a specific controversy. A necessary condition for a public policy is an issue's inclusion in the public agenda. In Latin America, several controversies have involved "negative rights," such as protection from violence and discrimination and the right to be "left alone" by the police; some controversies have generated public scandal, such as the issue of transgender sex workers on the streets. In addition, in countries like Brazil, Colombia, Mexico, and Argentina, controversy has arisen around positive concerns: access to health care and to social protection, and the issues of same-sex civil unions and adoption.

In all these cases, the state takes a position on controversies that have entered the public and political agendas. This has seemed to be generally favorable to sexual minorities, though still within the limits of the private sphere. Direct discrimination in the public sphere, particularly in the workplace, is denounced more and more frequently, and some legal protections and public policies have been implemented. In these areas, legislation, court rulings, and their enforcement have been quite effective. Furthermore, gay activists and organizations are participating fully in communities and networks for HIV/AIDS policy.

However, no Latin American state has yet dealt with indirect discrimination, that is, discrimination derived from civil exclusion and exclusion from the social protections associated with heterosexual marriage or union. These exclusions constitute an implicit public policy that is detrimental to the gay and lesbian population because it excludes them from all rights and benefits provided by the institution of marriage.

What are the achievements, potential achievements, and limits of the claims homosexuals make at the political level? Much research has focused on the limits of repressive policies relating to homosexuality (D'Emilio 1983; Weeks 1995; Vujosevich, Pecheny, and Kornblit 1997). It is known that repressive policies neither eliminate nor diminish the frequency of homosexual practices. Similarly, we may speculate that policies that favor the acceptance of sexual diversity do not necessarily eliminate, diminish, nor increase the number of homophobic practices.

Can acceptance and social recognition of sexual minorities be regulated in strict political terms? Surely, a liberal, democratic framework will encourage debate of the issues. In spite of the perception of urgency and the seriousness of the injustice, change will most certainly take time and occur gradually. However, experience has shown we cannot demand from public policy what public policy cannot provide. Acceptance and recognition of homosexuality and the homosexual individual—or in less taxonomic terms, acceptance and experience of sexual diversity and sexual freedom—result from the work of life itself, rather than from any institutional policy. That is, acceptance and recognition imply a wider cultural project, not accessible through politics alone. Sexual minority movements should attempt to join both theoretically and practically the claims for rights at the political level with nonformal strategies of social recognition at the level of relevant others.

Notes

This chapter is taken from a lecture given at ILAS-SIPA, Columbia University, February 2004. Previous versions of this paper have been presented in several meetings in Argentina, the United States, and other countries. In previous work, I have researched issues of homosexual identity, the structure of different social worlds, and the impact of the gay movement and the AIDS epidemic (Kornblit, Pecheny, and Vujosevich 1998; Pecheny 2000, 2001). The important role played by personal links among homosexuals in social mobility surfaced in these studies, but I have no systematic empirical evidence to support the hypothesis that political practices aimed at reverting the subordination of homosexuality extend beyond politics to include sociability and social relationships.

1. In Spanish, *discreet* and *discrete* are homonyms: *discreto* and *discreto*. People who talk or act with tact or moderation, who are careful not to bother others, are considered discreet, while tactless persons who meddle into what is concealed or kept in secret are indiscreet. The label applies to people's actions. People who know how to keep a secret are discreet; those who reveal it are indiscreet. Furthermore, something that does not stand out is deemed discreet. Lastly, spaces that favor privacy and mystery are discreet: "a *discreet* corner." Discontinuous parts of a totality are discrete. In mathematics and in linguistics, discrete elements are physically distinct, disaggregated, delimited, or separate (in social sciences, would we say "alienated"?).

2. Examples of intermediate spaces are nongovernment public spaces, civil society organizations, and the spheres of social interaction with relevant or significant others. Significant others are people who are important in affection for an individual, such as family members, friends, peers, etc.

3. Homosexual identity results from the conflict between heteronomy—inherent to the imposed taxonomy—and autonomy—inherent to homosexual identity's re-appropriation and re-definition, for example, in terms of "gay" identity. Although some critics would say that all definitions set arbitrary boundaries to pure and free practices, I agree with Jeffrey Weeks (1995), according to whom sexual identities, especially those different from heterosexual hegemonic identities, are "necessary fictions" that give support and a sense of belonging, helping individuals assume a practice that clashes somewhat with the accepted values and the social models learned almost universally in childhood and adolescence.

4. The similarity between arguments that have been utilized to discriminate against women and homosexuals is remarkable: biological nature, morals, concerns for children, education of youth, preservation of the social order . . . In both cases, what is important is not the difference itself, but its being judged in the name of what society deems desirable and acceptable at a given point in time, according to its concept of normalcy. Women were only able to make strides toward equal rights when the boundaries between what was considered normal and abnormal shifted, when discrimination seemed arbitrary and no longer natural. Similarly, vindication of equal rights for all individuals regardless of sexual orientation cannot be accomplished

as long as homosexuality continues to appear as abnormal in contrast to heterosexuality, considered by many the only natural sexuality.

5. These processes are inseparable from the anti-AIDS movement and the feminist and women's movements in the region, which deserve further analysis; however, we have no space to deal with this here.

References

Adam, B., J. W. Duyvendak, and A. Krouwel, eds. 1999. *The Global Emergence of Gay and Lesbian Politics. National Imprints of a Worldwide Movement.* Philadelphia: Temple University Press.

Altman, D. 1994. *Power and Community: Organizational and Cultural Responses to AIDS.* London: Taylor and Francis.

Bayer, R. 1989. *Private Acts, Social Consequences: AIDS and the Politics of Public Health.* New York: Free Press.

Bernstein, M. 1997. Celebration and Suppression: The Strategic Uses of Identity by the Lesbian and Gay Movement. *American Journal of Sociology* 103, no. 3 (November): 531–65.

Boudieu, Pierre. 1998. *Quelques questions sur le mouvement gay et lesbian.* In *La domination masculine,* 129–34. Paris: Seuil.

Brown, S. 1999. Democracy and Sexual Difference: The Lesbian and Gay Movement in Argentina. In *The Global Emergence of Gay and Lesbian Politics. National Imprints of a Worldwide Movement,* ed. B. Adam, J. W. Duyvendak, and A. Krouwel, 110–32. Philadelphia: Temple University Press.

Chauncey, G. 1994. *Gay New York: Gender, Urban Culture, and the Making of the Gay Male World 1890–1940.* New York: Basic Books.

D'Emilio, J. 1983. *Sexual Politics, Sexual Communities: The Making of a Homosexual Minority in the United States 1940–1970.* Chicago: University of Chicago Press.

Dover, K. J. 1982. *Homosexualité grecque.* Grenoble: La Pensée Sauvage.

Feldman, S., and M. Murmis. 2000. *Algunas discusiones teórico metodológicas,* 5. Mimeo, Universidad Nacional de General Sarmiento.

Foucault, M. 1993. *Histoire de la sexualité.* Vol. 1, *La volonté de savoir.* Paris: Gallimard.

Gays por los Derechos Civiles. 1995. *Violaciones de derechos humanos y civiles en la república Argentina basadas en la orientación sexual de las personas y de las personas viviendo con VIH/SIDA.* 3rd. ed. Buenos Aires, mimeo., December.

Goffman, I. 1989. *Stigmate. Les usages sociales des handicaps.* Paris: Editions de Minuit.

Green, G. 1995. Attitudes Toward People with HIV: Are They as Stigmatizing as People with HIV Perceive Them to Be? *Social Science and Medicine* 41 (4): 557–68.

Habermas, J. 1971. *Desarrollo de la moral e identidad del yo.* In *La reconstrucción del materialismo histórico,* 57–83. Madrid: Taurus.

Jáuregui, C. L. 1987. *La homosexualidad en la Argentina.* Buenos Aires: Tarso.

Kaplan, M. B. 1997. *Sexual Justice: Democratic Citizenship and the Politics of Desire.* New York: Routledge.

Keck, M., and K. Sikkink. 1998. *Activists beyond Borders: Advocacy Networks in International Politics.* Ithaca: Cornell University Press.

Kornblit, A. L., M. Pecheny, and J. Vujosevich. 1998. *Gays y lesbianas: Formación de la identidad y derechos humanos*. Buenos Aires: La Colmena.

Kosofsky-Sedgwick, E. 1993. Epistemology of the Closet. In *The Lesbian and Gay Studies Reader*, ed. H. Abelove, M. A. Barale, and D. M. Halperin, 45–61. New York: Routledge.

Laclau, E., and C. Mouffe. 1987. *Hegemonía y estrategia socialista. Hacia una radicalización de la democracia*. Buenos Aires: Siglo XXI.

Mead, G. H. 1962. *Mind, Self, and Society*. Chicago: University of Chicago Press.

Parker, R., and P. Aggleton. 2002. HIV *and* AIDS*-Related Stigma and Discrimination: A Conceptual Framework and Implications for Action*. Rio de Janeiro: ABIA.

Pecheny, M. 2000. *La salud como vector del reconocimiento de derechos humanos: La epidemia de sida y el reconocimiento de los derechos de las minorías sexuales*. In *La salud en crisis. Una mirada desde las ciencias sociales*, ed. A. Domínguez Mon, A. Federico, L. Findling, and A. M. Mendes Diz, 199–215. Buenos Aires: Dunken.

———. 2001. *La construction de l'avortement et du sida en tant que questions politiques: le cas de l'Argentine*. Vol. 2. Lille: Presses Universitaires du Septentrión.

Perlongher, N. 1983. La represión del homosexual en Argentina. Pts. 1 and 2. *Cerdos y Peces— El Porteño*, Buenos Aires, no. 22 (October): 8–9; no. 24 (December): 16.

Plummer, K., ed. 1981. *The Making of the Modern Homosexual*. London: Hutchinson.

———. *Telling Sexual Stories. Power, Change and Social Works*. New York: Routledge, 1995.

Pollak, M. 1993. *Une identité blessée. Etudes de sociologie et d'histoire*. Paris: Métailié.

———. 1988. *Les homosexuels et le sida. Sociologie d'une épidémie*. Paris: Métailié.

Roberts, M. W. 1995. Emergence of Gay Identity and Gay Social Movements in Developing Countries: The AIDS Crisis as a Catalyst. *Alternatives* 20(2): 243–64.

Saléis, J. 1995. *Médicos maleantes y maricas. Higiene, criminología y homosexualidad en la construcción de la nación Argentina. Buenos Aires: 1871–1914*. Buenos Aires: Beatriz Viterbo.

Schiltz, M. 1994. *Les homosexuels séropositifs: Trois années d'enquêtes*. In *Les personnes atteintes: des recherches sur leur vie quotidienne et sociale*, ed. D. Michèle, 41–51. Paris: ANRS.

Sebreli, J. J. 1997. Historia secreta de los homosexuales de Buenos Aires. In *Escritos sobre escritos, ciudades bajo ciudades*, 275–370. Buenos Aires: Sudamericana.

Sivori, H. 1994. *Rehearsing morality at the margins. Contexts of gay interaction in a provincial city of Argentina*. Master of Arts thesis. Department of Anthropology, New York University, New York.

———. 2000. Locas, chongos y gays. Autoría y autoridad de género en el habla homosexual. Paper presented at the Congreso Argentino de Antropología Social, Mar del Plata, September.

Sontag, S. 1990. *Illness as Metaphor/*AIDS *and Its Metaphors*. New York: Anchor Books.

Sullivan, A. 1995. *Virtually Normal. An Argument about Homosexuality*. New York: Alfred A. Knopf.

Vujosevich, J., M. Pecheny, and A. L. Kornblit. 1997. *La homofobia en la Ciudad de Buenos Aires. Acta Psiquiátrica y Psicológica de América Latina* 43, no. 3 (September): 212–21.

Weeks, J. 1995. History, Desire and Identities. In *Conceiving Sexuality*, ed. R. Parker and H. Gagnon, 33–50. New York: Routledge.

Zempleni, A. 1984. *Secret et sujétion. Pourquoi ses "informateurs" parlent-ils à l'ethnologue? Traverses* 30–31:102–115.1.

Sexual Politics and Sexual Rights in Brazil

A Case Study

Adriana R. B. Vianna and Sérgio Carrara

FEW COUNTRIES have an image as connected with eroticism and sexuality as Brazil's. The country abounds with symbols of sexual freedom, depicted in pictures of everything from Carnival and beaches to interracial relationships, transvestites, and samba. However, this representation belies the realities of Brazilian society; beneath a feigned liberalism, the country is deeply affected by sexism, homophobia, and racism, which, when taken together with other social markers, create a reality of massive inequality. To examine the construction of sexual rights in Brazil requires analysis of this contradictory view, while recognizing its local impacts and avoiding traditional stereotypes.

The analysis of sexual politics and rights in Brazil involves going beyond a mere description of conceptions and practices associated with a single sexual culture. One must focus on the context in which these rights have developed, giving consideration to the legal structure, political process, and social actors. We will examine this context, starting with themes that are especially relevant to the very configuration of these rights in Brazil: reproduction/abortion, STDs/AIDS, and sexual diversity. We aim to provide a wide informative view, concentrating on the identification of the main actors, existing legal instruments and those still being discussed, and, finally, the public policies that have been adopted in the last two decades. We will also introduce the issues that can and must contribute to any conceptual discussion on sexual rights.

This discourse holds that the 1988 Brazilian Constitution—widely known as the Citizen's Constitution—must be considered the catalyst that inspired civil society's demands for new rights, while also generating public policies and legal instruments to satisfy those demands. The promulgation of the 1988 constitution put an end to the long period of authoritarian rule instituted by the 1964 military coup, and its contents reflect the redemocratization process that began in the late 1970s. The process brought about a convergence of left-wing political forces displaced by the military coup and new social actors who organized around issues of gender, race, and sexuality. As in other Latin American countries, the struggle to reinstate democratic political rights took place in tandem with demands for the implementation of a larger human-rights agenda; social rights were brought forward, along with women's rights and the rights of racial, ethnic, and sexual minorities.

In terms of social rights, the fact that health care was acknowledged as a fundamental right in the new constitution had crucial consequences for reproductive rights and for the Brazilian response to HIV/AIDS. According to the constitution, the right to health must be "guaranteed through social and economic policies aiming at reducing the risk of any illness and other disorders and providing universal and equalitarian access to actions and services for its promotion, protection and recovery." Moreover, health care was considered both an individual and a transindividual right.[1]

As to specific rights, the 1988 constitution reflected the configuration of forces in different social movements. In some cases achievements were impressive; the formulation of gender equality as a constitutional right and the legal acknowledgment of various kinds of family clearly reflect the power of women's and feminist groups. Gender equality—understood in the constitution as equal rights for men and women—appears both in general articles and in others more specific to family planning, which couples are free to choose and the state is required to provide. The constitution also forbids labor-market discrimination on the grounds of "sex, color, age or marital status." Many of these clauses have been expanded into specific federal laws.

But the political climate did not favor Brazil's lesbian, gay, bisexual, and transgender communities; sexual orientation is not included in the constitution. In spite of the LGBT movement's call for discrimination based on sexual orientation to be outlawed, this issue of a constitutional amendment is still debated. In fact, the constitution's general tone of respect for human rights is a useful tool for advocates seeking to consolidate new rights. For example, the state is obliged to implement international agreements it has signed, some of which offer legal protections for LGBT individuals, which provides activists wider advocacy options.

The contradiction arising is that national legal codes, such as penal laws, were not brought in line with the constitution, although more recently some civil laws have been changed.[2] In the case of penal legislation, for example, one sees terms like "crimes against *family*" or "crimes against *customs*" (our emphasis), which contradict the principles of gender equality laid down in the constitution. Moreover, even in those cases where intraconstitutional legislation was intended to implement the new constitutional principles, public policies to support this were not instituted.

Given all this, the process of affirming sexual rights in Brazil takes place in a complex and heterogeneous space, in which different types of legislation (penal, civil, labor) with different scopes (federal, state, and municipal) correspond to public policies equally varied in their formulation and range. Another important element lies in the judiciary system itself; although jurisprudence does not have the power of law in Brazil as it does in countries ruled by common law, it is noteworthy that countless judges, as they seek to interpret constitutional principles, have granted rights that are not explicitly included in the laws.

The process of building sexual rights in Brazil is marked by ambiguity. There is a very strong commitment to producing and implementing human rights, especially given international obligations, but this commitment is constantly threatened by deep social, racial, ethnic, and gender inequalities. Even as social movements have strived to redemocratize the country, conservative lobbies—especially those backed by religion-oriented political parties—have sought to prevent the advance of rights related to sexual diversity or the individual's right to sexuality and reproductive choices.

From Homosexual Rights to LGBT Rights

In Brazil, public criticism of the view that homosexuality is a mix of immorality, dishonor, sin, and disease began in the late 1970s as the redemocratization process in the country progressed.[3] Homosexuality began to emerge as a political issue and gays, lesbians, and transgendered people started to become citizens with rights. In the beginning, besides promoting political awareness among its members, the movement struggled against prejudice, endeavoring to change stigmatizing stereotypes.

In its first stages the Brazilian homosexual movement was dominated by men. Lesbians generally participated through mixed groups, and this still happens in many activist groups. It was only in the latter half of the 1990s that the lesbian movement became stronger and achieved autonomy in relation to mixed groups and the feminist movement. The First Lesbian National Seminar took place in 1996, and in 2003 a Brazilian Lesbian League was founded that had its first meeting the following year.[4] Today, the Brazilian lesbian movement even has its own calendar, celebrating the National Day of Lesbian Pride (August 19) and the National Day of Lesbian Visibility (August 29).

Transvestites were not always welcomed by the first activist groups,[5] and only began organizing independently in the early 1990s. Their first national meeting, called National Meeting of Transvestites and Liberated People, took place in 1993, and in 1995, transvestite militant groups began to participate in national gay and lesbian meetings. By 1996, transvestites had mobilized sufficiently within the arena of HIV/AIDS activism to organize a National Meeting of Transvestites and Liberated People Fighting against AIDS. Transvestite activists were now a visible force to be reckoned with.

The language used for national meetings reflected the political emergence of new sexual identities, and the inclusion of new groups in the movement: while the first six meetings (1980–92) were called Brazilian Meeting of *Homosexuals* (our emphasis), the seventh (1993) was called the Brazilian Meeting of *Lesbians and Homosexuals*, the eighth, the Brazilian Meeting of *Lesbians and Gays*, and the ninth (1997), the Brazilian Meeting of *Lesbians, Gays, and Transvestites*. After this, until the twelfth meeting in 2005, they were called Brazilian meetings of *Lesbians, Gays, and Transgenders*. The category *transgender*, an umbrella term assigned to transvestites and transsexuals, is controversial, finding great resistance among transvestites.[6] Perhaps for this reason, the twelfth national meeting was designated *Lesbian, Gays, Bisexuals, and Transgenders*; the new name included *bisexuals*, and the *T* in LGBT was seen as covering both *transvestites* and *transsexuals*, instead of just *transgendered* people.

The year 1995 must be considered a landmark in the LGBT movement's history on both the national and international levels. First, the Brazilian Gay, Lesbian, and Transvestite Association (ABGLT) was founded during the Eighth National Meeting of Lesbians and Gays.[7] And second, the state and the movement began building closer ties, as federal grants were made available to activist groups for meetings and projects.[8] The government grants (initially made through the STDS/AIDS National Program) and those provided by state and municipal governments (initially through their health-care bureaus) were directed at first to groups dealing with HIV-prevention activities or assistance to AIDS patients, and later extended to the national meetings, which began to take place simultaneously with AIDS-related national lesbian, gay, and transvestite meetings.

At the international level, it was also in 1995 that the International Lesbian and Gay Association (ILGA) meeting took place in Rio de Janeiro, with financial support from the federal government through the STDS/AIDS National Program. It was the first time that the ILGA organized its annual meeting in a South American country. During the meeting, the first LGBT pride parade in Brazil took place. Since then LGBT pride parades have been organized in different Brazilian cities with an increasing number of participants, becoming the most eloquent symbol of the enormous visibility the movement achieved in the second half of the 1990s. The one held in São Paulo in 2006 drew more than two million people, and the parade is now considered the most important tourist event of the city's annual calendar.[9] In addition to the massive visibility of the parades, the LGBT community has attracted more and more coverage in the Brazilian media, in national newspapers and magazines and on TV shows with huge audiences (especially soap operas and reality shows).

However, even though homosexuality is not a crime in Brazil, discrimination against gays, lesbians, transvestites, and transsexuals remains rife, and has thus been the movement's active focus since the beginning. Sexual minorities have achieved rights by taking action against discrimination through legal channels, and by seeking to extend the civil and social rights enjoyed by heterosexuals to these minorities. One of the fundamental roadblocks to progress has been the fact that the 1988 constitution did not directly address discrimination on the basis of sexual orientation. When the National Constitutional Assembly first began meeting, it was a period of political reorganization within the Brazilian homosexual movement.[10] Although the now defunct group *Triângulo Rosa*, from Rio de Janeiro, led a campaign for the inclusion of a measure banning discrimination based on sexual orientation, the term *sexual orientation* was withdrawn from the final text.

Since 2001, within the ambit of the UN World Conference against Racism, Racial Discrimination, Xenophobia, and Related Intolerance, Brazil has played an important role in efforts to include the expression *sexual orientation* in the idiom of human rights at the United Nations. In 2003, the Brazilian delegation put before the UN Human Rights Commission a resolution on sexual orientation discrimination as a human-rights violation. Militant groups from all over the world, as well as many governments, expressed their support for this resolution. Besides lobbying the UN's Human Rights Commission, ILGA organized an international campaign in support of the resolution, creating a Web site and collecting forty-five thousand signatures in a petition. But under strong pressure from Muslim countries and the Vatican, a vote on the resolution was postponed until 2004. When it came up again, Brazil, realizing that the resolution did not yet have enough support, requested that the discussion be postponed once more. However, Brazil did not present the resolution in 2005, due to pressure from Muslim countries related to trading concerns. Although the resolution is no longer on the commission's agenda, the debate and the international coalition created to support it have helped to consolidate the place of the LGBT movement on the human-rights international agenda.[11]

In terms of state and municipal legislation, several important antidiscrimination measures have been put in place. According to ABGLT, more than seventy municipalities have enacted laws to protect LGBT communities. Three states have prohibited sexual discrimination in their constitutions, and another five, as well as the Federal District, have sanctioned important antidiscrimination measures. However, sanctions and legislative guidelines are inconsistent. In some cases, the focus is on discrimination at the workplace and on contractual agreements like renting property, in others, on the repression of public displays of affection between people of the same sex.[12] Some of these laws are explicit about who is being protected, whether homosexuals, bisexuals, and/or transgendered people. Others are based on more general principles, such as a law recently passed in Rio Grande do Sul that "deals with the promotion and acknowledgement of the freedom of orientation, practice, manifestation, identity and preferences as regards sex," and emphasizes the relationship between such freedoms and the "uniform dignity of the human person."

The visibility of LGBT rights has also been increased due to activism for legal recognition of homosexual partnerships. A 1995 federal bill to regulate "the civil union between people of the same sex" reinforced this issue, since it was the first attempt at such legislation, and there was predictably strong public and political reaction to it. The rights to property and inheritance are central to this bill, since it intends to redress judicial injustices. After being scrutinized by a special commission in 1996, the bill was modified, including replacement of the term "union" with "partnership," and watering down the reference to "affectionate bonds" between the partners. The amendment details the property issues at stake, including those related to inheritance.

More significant than these changes, however, is the inclusion of a paragraph vetoing "any agreement on adoption, tutelage or warding of children and adolescents, even if they are the children of one of the partners." The inclusion of this paragraph in the amendment illustrates the tension around the full recognition of civil partnerships as family. Although the Partnership Bill, as it is called, emphasizes that civil partnerships are not equivalent to marriage or to stable heterosexual unions, the presence of articles dealing with the marital status of partners, or laying down a partnership's exclusivity, makes the commitment of partnership sound very similar to the commitment of marriage.[13] The bill goes halfway towards effectively accepting homosexual unions—on the legal level at least—while at the same time consigning such relationships to a subordinate status.[14]

Congressional representatives who disagree with the bill depict it as the sanctioning of gay marriage, which they deem an aberration. The bill has never been brought to a vote because congressional representatives favorable to its passing have calculated it does not have the necessary support.[15] This strong parliamentary resistance is in keeping with other initiatives taken by religious groups and institutions to block any bills they view as a threat to the family, as for example those seeking to legalize abortion.[16] Yet in spite of its limitations, the Partnership Bill has given more visibility to the rights of gays, lesbians, and transgendered people in the national media. Although there is debate, the mainstream current of the movement, headed by ABGLT, supports the bill.[17]

In an effort to challenge the forces of social conservatism in the Brazilian legislature and to support bills related to LGBT rights, the House of Deputies created the Mixed Parliamentary Front for Free Sexual Expression in October 2003. It came as a result of collaboration between activists and seventy-five deputies and nine senators from different political parties.

The judiciary has been another important arena for building up the rights of sexual minorities. In many cases, especially those involving social welfare and the rights of HIV-positive people, some actions by the judiciary have paved the way for legislative changes. For example, the public prosecutors in Rio Grande do Sul, acknowledging criticisms voiced by the activist organization *Nuances* (from Porto Alegre), successfully brought a civil action against the Brazilian Social Welfare Institution (INSS) to extend the benefits of death pensions and other rights to homosexual couples. The favorable judgment eventually forced national acknowledgment of such rights.[18]

In other areas the situation has not been as clear-cut. For example, with regard to the custody and adoption of children by same-sex couples, since the judiciary cannot acknowledge the existence of homosexual couples, judges have sometimes used the Child and Adolescent Statute and the new civil code to concede these rights to individual partners. Such rulings, however, depend very much on the views of individual judges and can be affected by the sex of the child involved.[19] Highly visible cases, such as that granting custody of the child of a famous Brazilian female singer to her female partner after her death, are important for mobilizing public opinion, but not enough to establish a clear policy.

In the criminal field, a recent case with great impact involved the murder of Edson Néris da Silva in February 2000 in the city of São Paulo. Néris was lynched by a skinhead group, for the "crime" of walking hand in hand with another man. The case was characterized as a "hate crime" by the prosecutor in charge, a term previously unused by the Brazilian judiciary. But besides this, the severe sentence handed down by the jury—about twenty years—and the emphasis placed on Néris's right to equality regardless of his sexual orientation turned the case into a landmark one in the debate around violence against homosexuals. Before this, even though some cases of homosexuals who had been murdered resulted in rigorous sentences, an examination of legal actions reveals a very stereotype-based view of homosexuality, which is often portrayed as a dangerous lifestyle or even as a kind of pathology.[20]

As the LGBT movement has been saying for decades,[21] homosexuals and transgendered people are subject to many forms of violence aside from murder. Recent data on victimization,[22] compiled from surveys conducted at LGBT gay pride parades in Rio de Janeiro, Porto Alegre, and São Paulo, have noted that 60 percent of those interviewed report having been victims of some discrimination or violence. Verbal violence (abuse, jokes, aggressive threats) is the main complaint. Situations of violence and discrimination involve strangers as well as family members, colleagues, and even sexual partners. The data, produced in 2004, in Rio, revealed that most discrimination takes place among friends and neighbors (33.5 percent), followed by family members (27 percent).[23]

In relation to media bias, the citizen rights regional attorney in São Paulo, together with LGBT and human-rights organizations, brought a successful civil suit against the TV network *Ômega Ltda.* (also known as *Rede TV*) and the presenter of a show called *Hot Afternoons* for broadcasting jokes that ridiculed and humiliated people on the basis of their sexual orientation. The action also extended to the Federal Union, which is responsible for the concession of sound and vision broadcasting services. In a preliminary order, the network's TV signal was suspended for forty-eight hours when it refused to acknowledge the guilty verdict. Under pressure, the network signed an agreement in November 2005, pledging to broadcast, in the *Hot Afternoons* slot, thirty human-rights programs presented by the organizations that brought the action. It also had to pay the Diffuse Rights Defense Fund some two hundred thousand U.S. dollars and withdraw all "insults to homosexuals, afro-descendants, women, elders, disabled persons, Indians, children and adolescents." The overall cost of the action was around ten million U.S. dollars, and the presenter was dismissed. For the first time in the country, a commercial network was obliged to change its programming for disrespecting human rights.

This case and its underlying acknowledgment of the diverse forms of violence against homosexuals led to a new initiative, the creation of Brazil without Homophobia: A Program to Combat Violence and Discrimination against LGBTs and to Promote Homosexual Citizenship, which was launched by the federal government in May 2004.[24] A commission comprising representatives from the Discrimination Combat National Council and the Ministry of Health devised the program with the participation of many activists and militant organizations, such as ABGLT. Its wide-ranging recommendations include the stipulation that state institutions, especially those concerned with education, security, law, health care, and supervision, must take steps to ensure their policies and practices are nondiscriminatory and inhibit violence. The commission also calls for incentives to encourage LGBT movement leaders to participate in different social councils and mechanisms created by the federal government; to disseminate information about homophobic violence and discrimination and about the health condition of gays, lesbians, and transgendered people; and to support Brazilian initiatives acknowledging and protecting LGBT rights at the international level, especially with regard to the creation of the Sexual and Reproductive Rights International Convention.

Some of the guidelines of Brazil without Homophobia have been executed, further strengthening the partnership between the state and civil society. In 2005, the Republican Presidency General Bureau launched a competition among public institutions and NGOs to design projects aimed at combating and preventing homophobia, to include the provision of legal and psychosocial advice for victims, guidelines on taking legal action, and conflict management and mediation. Also in 2005, the Ministry of Education launched a competition for projects to qualify education professionals to advise people on sexual orientation and gender identity.

With explicit penal sanctions against homosexuality absent from Brazil since the beginning of the nineteenth century, the critique of psychological/medical discourses on homosexuality and pathology-oriented processes became paramount. One of the movement's greatest achievements in this regard was its success, in 1985, in getting homosexuality withdrawn from the roll of diseases acknowledged by the Brazilian Medical Association (which even the World Health Organization did not do until

1993). In 1999 the Psychology Federal Council followed with a ruling that no professional could "favor pathological diagnoses of any homoerotic behavior or practice," and that psychologists "shall not adopt coercive action to direct patients to nonrequired treatments." The ruling expressly stated that professionals "shall not collaborate with events and services that propose treatment for and cure of homosexuality."

Still, the process of ending medical prejudice against homosexuality is complex, and the struggle is not over. The Psychology Federal Council's resolution has become the target of attacks from psychologists affiliated with evangelical religious groups. Arguing that homosexuality is not an innate characteristic and that those who "suffer" because of their sexual orientation have a "right to be taken care of," these groups have organized with the aim of getting the resolution annulled.[25]

The LGBT movement is considering its response, but some of its leaders have tended to adopt a naturalizing and innate conception of homosexuality (that is, what is innate cannot be cured) as a way to oppose the evangelical psychologists' efforts to annul the resolution.

There is one area in which the traditional medical/psychological discourse still dominates: the right of transgendered people to undergo sex-change surgeries and change their legal identities. Until 1997 the Brazilian Medical Association considered this kind of surgery nonethical, and it could be criminally interpreted as "bodily harm." A 1997 resolution established the conditions for legal surgery, but it stipulated that "the patient must be a trans-sexual with permanent psychological deviation of his/her sexual identity, phenotype rejection and tendencies to self-mutilation, and/or self-extermination," thereby depicting transsexuality as an extreme pathology. In addition, changes to the civil register are only allowed after surgery is completed and legal permission obtained. This mechanism not only shows the distance that separates the different disciplines involved (medicine, psychology, and law), and the concrete experiences of social individuals, but also conveys, under the pretext of "healing," that there is an inherent disconnect between sex and gender. In other words, the mechanism sets up a perverse duality.[26]

Prospects for Further Progress

Sexual rights in Brazil have advanced significantly over the last three decades. Anchored in the legal structure allowed by the constitution and in important international landmarks, like the Cairo and Beijing conferences, a plethora of organizations have won a variety of legislative and judicial rights, and new and revised public policies. The strong resistance put up by conservative groups, especially toward LGBT and abortion rights, however, should not be forgotten; as we have seen, extreme social inequality in Brazil brings into question the true extent of those victories, especially when there are no all-inclusive and effective public policies to fight the disparities.

The trajectory of social movements has resulted in real progress, especially on HIV/AIDS policies, but there are risks that must be noted. If closer ties between civil society organizations and the state can empower these organizations, they can also curb their critical potential, creating patronage and cooptation. On the other hand, as the movement for sexual rights takes steps forward, gathering social and political support, it tends to fragment into different identity groups with their own specific demands and agendas. The competition for public resources tends to exacerbate such fragmentation along sexual orientation and gender lines. It is significant that the sexual orientation antidiscrimination law passed in São Paulo was used for the first time by a transvestite group against gay nightclubs that forbid their entry or membership.[27]

Despite its potential for weakening the struggle, such fragmentation and infighting can create original ideas and unexpected opportunities for progress. Recently, for example, transgender organizations, especially those of transvestites, have approached feminist organizations, participated in some of their discussion forums, raised an important and delicate debate on the state of feminine identity, and criticized the naturalization of the category "woman." In the process of becoming progressively more autonomous and, in certain contexts, presenting itself as a dissident voice more concerned with gender than sexuality, the transgender movement seems to oscillate between belonging to the homosexual and feminine fields.

In this sense, beyond specific demands, the greatest development in the struggle for sexual rights in Brazil has been the reshaping of alliances among different groups of activists. Throughout 2005 LGBT and feminist groups, committed to building a common agenda, held a series of strategic dialogues. Though these meetings were sometimes marked by tension between transgender and feminist militants, they presented an opportunity to strengthen the commitment of gay militants to the abortion cause, and to bring sex workers and feminists together. The alliance was best summarized in two of the banners at the last LGBT gay pride parade in São Paulo; behind the main banner that read, "Homophobia is a Crime," there was another flying high: "Sexual Rights Are Human Rights."

Notes

1. Rios, R. R. 2002. *Respostas jurídicas frente à epidemia de HIV/AIDS*. In *Aprimorando o debate: Respostas sociais frente à AIDS*, ed. R. Parker, V. Terto, and C. Pimenta, 23–29. Rio de Janeiro: ABIA.

2. Although Brazilian states have their own constitutions, their independence in terms of legislative capacity is very limited. Besides respecting the constitution, they must submit to the civil and penal codes, which are within the scope of federal legislation. The current penal code dates back to 1940 and the civil code, adopted in 1916, was only revised in 2002.

3. This criticism sprung up initially in the universities, in the counterculture sphere, and, above all, among the first groups of homosexual activists. This period was marked by the rise of a politically engaged homosexual press, beginning with the launch of a newspaper, *O Lampião da Esquina*, in 1978 by intellectuals from Rio de Janeiro and São Paulo, and by the 1979 founding of the group *Somos*, which became the nucleus of homosexual activism in the country. See Fry, P. H., and E. MacRae. 1983. *O que é homossexualidade*. São Paulo: Brasiliense; MacRae, E. 1990. *A construção da igualdade: Identidade sexual e política no Brasil*. Campinas: Editora da Unicamp.

4. Almeida, G. 2005. *Da invisibilidade à vulnerabilidade: Percurso do 'corpo lésbico' na cena brasileira face à possibilidade de infecção por DST e AIDS*. PhD diss., Universidade do Estado do Rio de Janeiro.

5. The conflict between transvestites and gay/lesbian activists is evident in the rhetoric that one of the most important leaders of the movement used to argue for including prohibition against discrimination based on sexual orientation in the new constitution during the National Constitutional Assembly. In his opinion, it was fundamental to combat the tendency of the media to equate "homosexual" and "prostitute/transvestite" because this was a manifestation of prejudice and a way of "sullying" homosexuality (Câmara, C. 2002. *Cidadania e orientação sexual: A trajetória do Grupo Triângulo Rosa*. Rio de Janeiro: Academia Avançada, 116).

6. Facchini, R. 2005. *Sopa de letrinhas? Movimento homossexual e produção de identidades coletivas nos anos 90*. Rio de Janeiro: Garamond.

7. Nowadays called *Associação Brasileira de Gays, Lésbicas, Bissexuais, Travestis, e Transsexuais*, ABGLT has 144 affiliated groups in Brazil. For more information, see www.abglt.org.br.

8. For an excellent analysis of these relations, see Facchini, R. 2005. *Sopa de letrinhas? Movimento homossexual e produção de identidades coletivas nos anos 90*. Rio de Janeiro: Garamond.

9. Data collected in Brazilian parades (in Rio de Janeiro, Porto Alegre, and São Paulo) indicated that, besides an important heterosexual attendance, these social gatherings now include the participation of various groups that comprise the movement today and even of politicians aligned with the cause, as well as segments of the thriving Brazilian pink market. See Carrara, S., S. Ramos, and M. Caetano, 2003. *Políticas, direitos, violência e homossexualidade: Oitava parada do orgulho LGBT—Rio de Janeiro—2003*. Rio de Janeiro: Pallas.

10. Facchini, R. 2005. *Sopa de letrinhas?*; Câmara, C. 2002. *Cidadania e orientação sexual*.

11. For a detailed account and analysis, see also Girard, F. 2007. Negotiating sexual rights and sexual orientation at the UN. In *Sex Politics: Reports from the Front Lines*, ed. R. Parker, R. Petchesky, and R. Sember, 339–51. New York and Rio de Janeiro: Sexuality Policy Watch. http://www.sxpolitics.org/frontlines/book/pdf/sexpolitics.pdf (accessed December 3, 2009).

12. Since homoerotic manifestations of affection are not a crime—in the penal code, there is only one article dealing with "obscene acts"—the legal battle that is needed is one to criminalize repressive and violent behaviors towards such manifestations. In this spirit, there is a bill now before the federal legislative body, aimed at modifying the penal code and Law 7.716, that criminalizes color or race prejudice, including punishment for gender and sexual orientation discrimination and prejudice.

13. See Uziel, A. P. 2002. *Família e homossexualidade: Velhas questões, novos problemas*, PhD diss., IFCH/Unicamp.

14. Arguing from the constitutional definition of *family*, which includes single-parent families, Rios points out that *family* and *marriage* are not necessarily related. See Golin, C., F. A. Pocahy, and R. R. Rios. 2003. *A justiça e os direitos de gays e lésbicas: Jurisprudência comentada.* Porto Alegre: Nuances/Sulina, 180.

15. For a more multilayered analysis of the discussions on civil partnerships taking place in the House of Deputies, see Mello, L. 2005. *Novas famílias. Conjugalidade homossexual no Brasil contemporâneo.* Rio de Janeiro: Garamond.

16. According to press reports in 2001, when the Partnership Bill was ready to be voted on, the National Conference of Bishops of Brazil sent a letter to all 513 deputies on the "dangers" of "anti-natural" unions. This attitude, in turn, is perfectly in agreement with that of the Vatican (2000) in its document, *Family, Matrimony and de facto Unions.* Vatican City: Pontifical Council for the Family.

17. For some, it represents a step forward to a more comprehensive law. The defense of same-sex unions or civil partnerships has been a recurrent theme of the main gay pride parades. In 2004, in Curitiba, the slogan was, "Family, Pride and Respect"; in Rio, "Civil Union Now"; in Blumenau, "Homosexuality, A Family Subject"; and lastly, in São Paulo, "We Have Pride and Family" (Carrara, S., and S. Ramos. 2005. *Política, direitos, violência e homossexualidade: Pesquisa da Nona Parada do Orgulho LGBT—Rio, 2004.* Rio de Janeiro: CEPESC.) In 2005, the São Paulo parade, one of the largest in the world, had as its theme, "Civil Partnerships Now! Same Rights! Neither More nor Less." See more at http://www.comunidadeLGBT.com.br/.

18. For comments by the federal attorney in charge of the action, on the free expression of sexuality and the many stages in the process, see Golin, C., F. A. Pocahy, and R. R. Rios. *A justiça e os direitos de gays e lésbicas.*

19. Uziel, A. P. *Família e homossexualidade.*

20. For more about the way the Brazilian judiciary treated homosexuality in murder cases in former periods, see Carrara, S., and A. Vianna. 2004. *As vítimas do desejo: Os tribunais cariocas e a homossexualidade nos anos 80.* In *Sexualidades e saberes: Convenções e fronteiras,* ed. A. Piscitelli, M. F. Gregori, and S. Carrara, 365–83. Rio de Janeiro: Garamond.

21. Mott, L. 2000. *Violação dos direitos, humanos e assassinato de homossexuais no Brasil.* Salvador: Editora Grupo Gay da Bahia; Mott, L. and M. Cerqueira. 2001. *Causa mortis: Homofobia.* Salvador: Editora Grupo Gay da Bahia.

22. Carrara, S., and S. Ramos. 2005. *Política, direitos, violência e homossexualidade.*

23. An important initiative toward identifying and ending such forms of violence, rarely supported in an effective way by local governments, is the creation of support services. The first one, called *Disque Defensa Homosexual,* or Dial Homosexual Defense (DDH), was created in Rio de Janeiro in 1999, and others were set up later in other cities, such as Campinas, Brasília, and Salvador. The merit of such initiatives lies in forging closer relations between LGBT groups and law enforcement officers; in offering the possibility of counseling to victims; and, lastly, by establishing a quantitative information data bank—though partial—on the kinds of violence to which these groups and individuals are subjected.

24. *Brasil sem homofobia: Programa de combate à violência e à discriminação contra GLBT e de promoção da cidadania homossexual.* Brasília: Ministério da Saúde, 2004, at http://www.aids

.gov.br/data/documents/storedDocuments/%7BB8EF5DAF-23AE-4891-AD36-1903553A 3174%7D/%7B9DBDED32-FD1B-4D3C-96D0-EA64F6664EEF%7D/brasil_sem_homofobia.pdf.

25. A psychologist from the so-called *Rede Cristã da Profissionais da Saúde* (Healthcare Professionals Christian Network) is founding a movement to revoke the resolution.

26. For recent works dealing with the theme of transsexuality in Brazil, see Bento, B. 2006. *A reinvenção do corpo: Gênero e sexualidade na experiência transsexual.* Rio de Janeiro: Garamond; Zambrano, E. 2003. *Trocando os documentos: Um estudo antropológico sobre a cirurgia de troca de sexo.* Master's thesis. PPGAS/UFRGS.

27. França, I. L. 2006. *Cercas e pontes: O movimento LGBT e o Mercado GLS na cidade de São Paulo.* Master's thesis, Universidade de São Paulo.

Puerto Rico and the Caribbean

Linda Rapp

THE ISLANDS of the Caribbean are renowned for their pleasant tropical climate. The social climate for GLBTQ people, however, is not always an inviting one.

Native Americans had already been living on many of the Caribbean islands for centuries when European explorers, beginning with Christopher Columbus in 1492, arrived in the New World. The advent of the Europeans spelled doom for the native cultures. Conquerors massacred many people, and settlers enslaved others. Oppressive treatment and new diseases took a heavy toll. Some Native Americans assimilated into the Europeans' communities, but for the most part the native peoples were eliminated.

The Spanish led the way to the Caribbean with voyages of discovery and the establishment of settlements. Other nations—England, France, and the Netherlands in particular—fought for territory in the region. In many cases islands were conquered and reconquered by warring countries numerous times over the centuries. Pirate ships also sailed the Caribbean, wreaking their own havoc.

The Europeans had hoped to find gold, but the Caribbean yielded little of it, and so the settlers turned to agriculture. With the native populations virtually wiped out,

Europeans began bringing slaves from West Africa in the early sixteenth century to labor on their plantations.

Interaction between slaveholders and slaves gave rise to new languages, called creoles. The best known of these is probably the French-based Haitian creole. Others include the English-based creole of Jamaica, and Papiamentu, which includes Portuguese, Spanish, and Dutch elements and is spoken in the Netherlands Antilles.

In addition to their languages, the Europeans brought their religions. Particularly on the Spanish and British islands, these have historically played and continue to play a major role in shaping cultural prejudices against GLBTQ people.

The nineteenth century brought a major debate over slavery. Haitian slaves led by Toussaint L'Ouverture rose in revolt in 1801, leading to the country's independence in 1804. In other areas events were less dramatic. Freedom for slaves came gradually, mainly between the 1830s and midcentury.

Cuba became independent in 1902, but for the most part the Caribbean islands remained colonies or territories of European nations. In the 1960s many of the British islands opted to become independent members of the Commonwealth. Aruba became an autonomous member of the Kingdom of the Netherlands in 1986, but the rest of the Dutch islands remain politically part of Holland. Likewise, residents of the French islands are citizens of France. Puerto Rico has been under United States control since the end of the Spanish-American War. U.S. citizenship was extended to Puerto Ricans in 1917.

From the twentieth century onward, the tourism industry has been of great importance in the Caribbean. Despite aggressive marketing campaigns to lure visitors, GLBTQ travelers will not find a warm welcome in all destinations. Sasha Alyson, the owner of a gay and lesbian travel agency, commented, "Very broadly, the Dutch and French islands, just based on their heritage, are very good. The British are the worst. The Spanish islands are fine, but they are less open."

Puerto Rico

The long and pervasive influence of the Roman Catholic Church in Puerto Rico historically prevented gay men and lesbians from achieving any degree of public acceptance. Further contributing to their marginalization was the concept of machismo, which equates "manliness" with power. Various traits, such as physical strength or the ability to provide for one's family, are considered manly, but central to the image of the macho man is his sexual appeal to and prowess with women. Even a man with little power in any practical or objective sense can strive to gain the respect of others within his social circle through displays or talk of his machismo. Conversely, a man can be socially devalued for not behaving in a way considered macho.

In recent decades Pentecostal churches have been gaining ground in Puerto Rico. In a 1990 interview, activist Roberto Caballero called the Catholic and Pentecostal churches "the most influential forces in molding public opinion" against GLBTQ rights.

Nor have political parties in Puerto Rico shown much enthusiasm for advancing GLBTQ rights. Activist José Santini stated in 1991 that "historically there has been a lot of homophobia in the *independentista* movement," referring to the faction favoring independent status for Puerto Rico, an issue on which there have been nonbinding referenda in 1967, 1993, and 1998. The *independentistas*, one of the more liberal groups, have attracted many GLBTQ supporters. Santini stated that despite their contributions, "their work as lesbians and gay men hasn't been recognized."

The fight against AIDS led some GLBTQ Puerto Ricans to favor the option of statehood, arguing that this would bring more funds for health care to the island. Proponents of statehood feared that the economy of an independent Puerto Rico would not be strong enough to afford better health care services.

Pedro Julio Serrano became the first openly gay man to run for public office in Puerto Rico when he announced his candidacy for an at-large seat in the commonwealth's House of Representatives in 1998. Although he had been a lifelong worker for the New Progressive Party, its leaders failed to support him, some even claiming that they did not know him.

Serrano's independent campaign was fraught with danger; his life was threatened and his property vandalized. Although forced to abandon his campaign due to lack of funds, Serrano remains strongly committed to the cause of GLBTQ rights in Puerto Rico. The founder of *Puerto Rico para Todos* (Puerto Rico for All), he is a vigorous and courageous defender of GLBTQ Puerto Ricans.

A recent political struggle was the campaign to repeal Puerto Rico's antisodomy law, Article 103. The commonwealth's Senate finally struck it down in 2003, one week before the U.S. Supreme Court decision in *Lawrence v. Texas* voided all American laws against sodomy.

Tourist guidebooks typically refer to Puerto Rico as the most gay- and lesbian-friendly destination in the Caribbean, citing San Juan's Condado quarter with clubs, cafés, and lodgings that welcome the GLBTQ public. Other cities have smaller gay scenes. The island of Vieques (which the U.S. Navy no longer uses for target practice), with a number of gay- and lesbian-owned restaurants and guesthouses, is a favorite with GLBTQ travelers.

Despite the glowing recommendations of the travel books, in 2004 conservative Representative Miriam Ramírez de Ferrer took objection to a statement on the official tourism Web site that "Puerto Rico has a diverse product directed to satisfy many segments of the market, including the gay market," demanding that the anodyne sentence be removed.

It is clear that progress must still be made before GLBTQ people enjoy full equality in Puerto Rico. There are, however, some hopeful signs. Through the efforts of organizations like *Puerto Rico para Todos*, GLBTQ citizens are gaining greater visibility and a stronger voice.

The United States Virgin Islands

The U.S. Virgin Islands—St. Croix, St. Thomas, and St. John—are an unincorporated territory of the United States. Residents are American citizens and send one nonvoting delegate to the House of Representatives.

Sodomy was decriminalized in the Virgin Islands in 1984.

With a small population to begin with, the islands do not have much of a gay scene. St. Croix, however, has two gay-owned hotels. The Cormorant Beach Club offers packages that include commitment ceremonies. GLBTQ locals and tourists alike enjoy the resort's fine restaurant, bar, and beach.

The Dominican Republic

[. . .] Dominican law makes no distinction between same-sex and opposite-sex relations. The age of consent is eighteen for all. Article 330 of the Penal Code, however, which forbids "every violation of decorum and good behavior on public streets" and carries a penalty of up to two years in prison, is occasionally used to target gay men. In 2003 Luis Villalona-Pérez succeeded in gaining political asylum in the United States based on evidence that he had "suffered threats, beatings, harassment, and humiliation" in the Dominican Republic because of his sexual orientation.

Travel writer Richard Ammon reports that outside Santo Domingo, "There is very little identifiable LGBT life in the Dominican Republic" and that, as in most spheres of Dominican life, socioeconomic class plays an important role in the nature of the experience of GLBTQ people. Members of the more affluent classes may patronize trendy clubs without fear of harassment, but they show little solidarity with low-income GLBTQ people, and they look down upon "boogie boys," young men who do sex work (prostitution is legal in the Dominican Republic), and do not make them feel welcome in nice restaurants and clubs.

There is a small lesbian community in the capital, and younger women feel freer to make nontraditional life choices than do those of earlier generations. Nevertheless, in a culture dominated by the Catholic Church, the expectation is that girls will become wives and mothers. Both young men and young women may enter into a heterosexual marriage or simply remain in the closet rather than reveal their sexual orientation to their families.

With many gay men reluctant to be publicly recognized as such, providing education about and treatment for AIDS has been a challenge. Since the 1990s, however, nongovernment organizations, including *Amigos Siempre Amigos*, have made vigorous efforts to provide counseling and help.

The Dutch Islands

The Dutch presence in the Caribbean dates back to the 1630s. St. Maarten (the southern portion of the island shared with French St. Martin), St. Eustatius (also known as Statia) and Saba in the Leeward Islands, and Aruba, Bonaire, and Curaçao off the coast of Venezuela are part of the Kingdom of the Netherlands. Aruba has been a self-governing autonomous state within the realm since 1986. Residents of the other islands are Dutch citizens.

The Dutch islands are among the more hospitable in the region for GLBTQ people. Laws do not discriminate between same-sex and opposite-sex relations. The age of consent is sixteen for all.

Tiny Saba (only five square miles in area) has a gay tourism director and is a popular winter destination for gay men. The scene there is welcoming but often described with terms like "low-key."

German-born Boris Strehlke stated that he and his life partner, Michael Hirner, chose to open their hotel, the Delfina, on St. Maarten after encountering hostility in the British islands. On social life, Strehlke commented that "there's no gay bar scene [in St. Maarten]. It's mixed, but no one cares. You can dance with your lover, and nobody cares."

A similar situation obtains on the other Dutch islands, none of which is particularly large or very populous. Of course, not every citizen is free of homophobia, but the prevailing cultural attitude is one of acceptance.

The French Islands

The French settled Guadeloupe, Martinique, and St. Martin in the 1630s, and St. Barthélemy (also known as St. Barts) a decade later. St. Barthélemy was sold to Sweden in 1784 but reacquired in 1877. All four are now politically part of France, and so French law obtains there. The age of consent for all people is fifteen.

Tourism industry experts consistently tout the French islands as being among the more welcoming to GLBTQ travelers, but they quickly point out that none of them has much of a local gay scene.

In a recent study conducted in Martinique, anthropologist David A. B. Murray learned that gay men found it difficult to come out publicly or even to their families.

In the historically Catholic culture, there is a strong expectation that both men and women will conform to traditional gender roles.

Murray reported that gay Martinican men often resort to "masking," assuming a heterosexual public persona, not only to protect their own reputations but also those of their families, a serious concern in the small island community. "Masking" may include marrying or having a girlfriend while meeting with other gay men at private venues. Younger men, perhaps influenced by reports of progress on gay and lesbian rights in other cultures, were less likely to see this as an acceptable solution than older ones. Nevertheless, it cannot be said that the GLBTQ rights movement has yet reached Martinique.

Although the laws are relatively favorable and tourists find acceptance, the conservative culture of the French islands makes it difficult for GLBTQ citizens to live openly as such.

Haiti

The French established their first settlement in Haiti in the mid-seventeenth century, and ruled the country until it achieved independence through revolution at the dawn of the nineteenth century.

The nation's political history has been one of tumult, repression, and corruption, particularly under the rule of the Duvaliers, François "Papa Doc" and his son Jean-Claude "Baby Doc," which began when the former was elected president in 1957 and ended when the latter fled the country in 1986.

The gulf between the small wealthy elite and the impoverished majority is great. Haiti has the lowest per capita income in the western hemisphere. The country is saddled with enormous debt, much of it incurred through mismanagement and corruption during the Duvalier years. As a result little money has been available to fund important public needs such as infrastructure and health care.

A particularly serious health concern is the AIDS epidemic. As of 2003, some 6.1 percent of adult Haitians had the disease, the highest rate in the Americas. In addition to deficient health care services, lack of education has contributed to the spread of the disease. A low literacy rate has made it hard for agencies to reach people, and since many homes are without electricity, television or radio campaigns are not effective substitutes.

In Haiti, AIDS is not regarded as a "gay male disease." It affects significant numbers of bisexual men and heterosexual men and women as well. Various international organizations have instituted education and treatment programs, but the situation remains grave.

Although same-sex relations are legal and anti-gay violence is relatively rare, no real gay community exists in Haiti. In the 1980s the government of Jean-Claude Duvalier eliminated the gay bar scene, ostensibly to curb the spread of AIDS but likely doing more harm than good, since forcing gay people underground only made education efforts more difficult. The regime of Jean-Bertrand Aristide, a former Roman Catholic priest, in the 1990s and early 2000s, did nothing to improve the lot of Haiti's GLBTQ population.

The British Islands

Numerous islands in the Caribbean are part of the British Commonwealth. Many were settled in the early seventeenth century. Others were acquired later through treaty or conquest.

The Cayman Islands and Jamaica lie south of Cuba. Commonwealth islands in the Lesser Antilles include the British Virgin Islands, Anguilla, Barbuda, St. Kitts and Nevis, Antigua, Dominica, St. Lucia, St. Vincent and the Grenadines, and Grenada. The Bahamas and the Turks and Caicos Islands, north of Cuba and Hispaniola, respectively, Barbados, east of the Windward Islands, and Trinidad and Tobago, north of Venezuela, are generally considered part of the Caribbean group because of their geographical proximity.

The islands of the British Commonwealth are among the least hospitable to GLBTQ people. The cultural climate is particularly hostile in Jamaica. (Ironically, Jamaica was the place where gay playwright and actor Sir Noël Coward was able to find a peaceful haven from the 1940s until his death at his home, Firefly, in 1973. The house, donated by his life partner, Graham Payn, to the Jamaica National Heritage Trust, is now a museum.)

Homophobic violence has caused some Jamaicans, especially men, to flee to other countries for asylum. Hundreds have been attacked and beaten, sometimes fatally. Amnesty International reported in 2001 that Jamaican police were party to the harassment, participating in or permitting beatings of gay men and effecting "arrests and malicious detentions."

In a 2002 interview Michael Wynter, the head of the Jamaican Constabulary's Office of Professional Responsibility, claimed to have received no complaints from gay men about police conduct but admitted that Jamaica's law against sodomy may have discouraged them from coming forward. The Offenses of the Person Act criminalizes same-sex relations. Being in a "compromising position" can be enough to bring about arrest. Those convicted face up to ten years in prison at hard labor.

Virulent expressions of homophobia can be found in Jamaican reggae songs, some of which suggest that "batty boys" and "chi chi men"—two pejorative terms for gay men—be killed by various means. Activist Peter Tatchell protested the homphobic lyrics at the MOBO (Music of Black Origin) awards shows in London in 2002 and 2003 and was set upon by angry reggae fans. Subsequently three reggae singers defended their lyrics, claiming that "homophobia is part of Jamaican culture." The Jamaican GLBTQ-rights group The Jamaican Forum for Lesbians, All-Sexuals and Gays (J-FLAG) reported that "there has been a wave of homophobic assaults and murders coinciding with the release of anti-gay records."

J-FLAG, founded in 1998, has been working to improve the lives of GLBTQ Jamaicans by providing counseling, advocating constitutional revisions to eliminate discrimination, and helping to document the cases of people seeking asylum in other countries.

Discrimination remains alive and well in Jamaica, however. The island's popular Sandals resort chain (which also has hotels in St. Lucia, Antigua, the Turks and Caicos, and the Bahamas) unapologetically accepts only heterosexual couples as guests.

The Cayman Islands, too, have discriminated against GLBTQ travelers, in 1998 refusing a cruise ship carrying some nine hundred gay passengers permission to dock. Thomas C. Jefferson, the Cayman Islands minister of tourism, defended the action, saying, "Careful research and prior experience has [sic] led us to conclude that we cannot count on this group to uphold the standards of appropriate behavior expected of our visitors." The "prior experience" proved to be a 1987 visit by gay men from a charter cruise, some of whom publicly displayed affection, which, according to Jefferson, "offended" and "disturbed" local residents.

The scheduled arrival in 1998 of a cruise ship carrying gay tourists to the Bahamas also engendered protests led by Pentecostal Bishop Harcourt Pindar. Prime Minister Hubert Ingraham condemned the homophobic statements and said, "Homosexuality is not a contagious disease, and it is not a crime in the Bahamas"—neatly parsing his words because while consensual relations in private are legal, public activity might bring jail time.

The British government, after a decade of unsuccessful efforts to persuade Caribbean Commonwealth members to abolish laws against same-sex relations, took the unilateral step of repealing local laws in Anguilla, the British Virgin Islands, the Cayman Islands, Montserrat, and the Turks and Caicos, effective January 1, 2001, since the statutes were in violation of human-rights agreements to which Britain subscribed. Clerics in the Cayman Islands Ministers' Association denounced the action.

The consecration of Canon Gene Robinson as Episcopal bishop of New Hampshire also met with opposition from Anglican bishops in the Caribbean, who condemned his ordination at their 2003 synod. Patrick Manning, the prime minister of Trinidad and Tobago, also announced his opposition to Robinson's elevation.

It is clear that progress on GLBTQ rights in the British Caribbean will have to overcome serious obstacles before equality is achieved. [. . .]

References

Ammon, Richard. Gay Haiti, 2003. Global Gayz. www.globalgayz.com/g-haiti.html.

———. Gay Dominican Republic: New Surprises and Old Fears. Global Gayz, 2006. http://www.globalgayz.com/country/Dominican%20Republic/view/DOM/gay-dominican-republic-new-surprises-and-old-fears (accessed November 8, 2009).

Chestnut, Mark. Decision in Puerto Rico; Making Room for Lesbian and Gay Issues in a Time of Transition. *Gay Community News*, October 13, 1990, 7.

Dogget, Scott, and Joyce Connelly. *Dominican Republic and Haiti*. 2nd ed. Melbourne: Lonely Planet Publications, 2002.

Fineman, Mark. Gay Cruise Fuels Debate in Bahamas. *Toronto Star*, March 7, 1998, G25.

Gonzalez, David. As AIDS Ravages Caribbean, Governments Confront Denial. *New York Times*, May 18, 2003, 1.

Graves, Amy K. Outbound; Different Isles, Different Attitudes toward Gay Travelers. *Boston Globe*, February 23, 2003, M14.

The Guardian. Britain Scraps Islands' Anti-Gay Laws. *The Guardian*, January 6, 2001, 7.

J-FLAG Jamaica. www.jflag.org.

Lewis, Linden. Caribbean Masculinity: Unpacking the Narrative. In *The Culture of Gender and Sexuality in the Caribbean*, ed. Lewis Linden, 94–125. Gainesville: University Press of Florida, 2003.

McDowell, Edwin. Gay Cruises Draw Hostility in Caribbean. *New York Times*, May 10, 1998, 3, 5.

Murray, David A. B. Between a Rock and a Hard Place: The Power and Powerlessness of Transnational Narratives among Gay Martinican Men. *American Anthropologist* 102 (June 2002): 261–70.

Neufville, Zadie. Jamaica: Facing Violent Homophobia, Gay Men Seek Asylum Overseas. *Global Information Network*, December 2, 2002, 1.

Nkonde, Mutale. Another Gay in Paradise; Rampant Homophobia in Jamaica Led One Man to Flee His Home and Seek Asylum in the U.K.—But He Intends to Return and Fight. *The Voice*, February 24, 2003, 16.

Peffer, Randall. *Puerto Rico*. Melbourne: Lonely Planet Publications, 1999.

Porter, Darwin, and Danforth Prince. *Frommer's Caribbean 2004*. Hoboken, N. J.: Wiley Publishing, 2003.

Ramírez, Rafael L. Masculinity and Power in Puerto Rico. In *The Culture of Gender and Sexuality in the Caribbean*, ed. Linden Lewis, 234–50. Gainesville: University Press of Florida, 2003.

Rohr, Monica. U.S. Grants Asylum to Gay Man, Rules Dominican Faced Threat at Home. *Boston Globe*, September 5, 2003, B3.

Serrano, Pedro Julio. The Face of Gay Puerto Rico. *The Advocate* 905 (December 2003): 10.

Tatchell, Peter. The Reggae Lyrics of Hate. *New Statesman*, September 29, 2003, 16.

Zarcone-Pérez, Teresa. Marketing to Gay Community Heightens Ire of Legislator. *San Juan Star*, May 12, 2004, 38–39.

Identity, Revolution, and Democracy

Lesbian Movements in Central America

Millie Thayer

IN THE 1970s and 1980s, revolutionary guerrilla movements fought poverty and dictatorship throughout much of the Central American isthmus. In the late 1980s, a new kind of social movement was born in the region. In the space of five years, fledgling lesbian movements surfaced in four Central American countries: Costa Rica (1987), Honduras (1987), Nicaragua (1991), and El Salvador (1992). These movements were a product, in part, of the political and social upheaval of preceding decades; in part they were related to underlying structural changes, to the onset of AIDS in the region, and to the influence of gay and lesbian movements elsewhere.

Despite some common roots, however, there were striking differences among the movements that developed in different countries. In Costa Rica, the movement turned inward to construct its collective identity. The lesbian feminist group *Las Entendidas* combined therapeutic support for its members with efforts to create a larger lesbian community, and used an idiom of spirituality and woman-centered culture that might be familiar to students of the 1970s lesbian movement in the United States.[1]

In contrast, Nicaraguan lesbians took an assertive public stance, insisting on their right to membership in society and on the rights of all people to "sexuality free of prejudice." *Fundación Xochiquetzal*, a nonprofit organization founded by lesbians and gays, sought to remake social mores in the sexual realm. The *Nosotras* collective provided emotional support and education about sexuality and feminism to its members, but many of them also joined in a coalition effort to fight a repressive antigay law passed by the country's legislative assembly.[2]

Lesbian movements in Nicaragua and Costa Rica represent opposite ends of a continuum of social movements from a more internal to a more external orientation. At one end, there is a stress on the self-esteem and personal identity of group members that, in the case of Costa Rica, extends to efforts to construct a broader lesbian community out of existing social networks. At the most "extroverted" end, lesbians in Nicaragua sought to revolutionize how society conceives of sexuality, while simultaneously claiming a place in that society. Though both orientations were founded on a concern with identity, lesbian movements in these two Central American countries defined that identity and their goals and arenas of action in sharply divergent ways. I examine and explain these contrasting approaches to lesbian organizing [. . .][3]

Theorizing Variation in Social Movement Identities

New social movement (NSM) theorists have situated lesbian movements within a new genre of social movements that they see as a product of global shifts away from societies based on production and toward postmaterial, information societies, in which states and complex systems have come to intrude on the individual's very core. According to these scholars, the peace, feminist, ecological, community, and gay and lesbian movements of the 1970s and 1980s represented means of resisting these growing threats to personal autonomy (Escobar 1992; Habermas 1984; Melucci 1980, 1985, 1994; Offe 1985; Slater 1985; Touraine 1985, 1988).

The protagonists of these movements, according to NSM theorists, were both those sensitized to the negative effects of modernity—the new middle class—and those suffering from it; the proletariat was no longer the epic actor on the stage. Unlike traditional, class-based movements, NSM modes of action tended toward direct democracy, horizontal organization, and a rejection of hierarchical forms of representation and institutionalization. Furthermore, resistance to domination of everyday life occurred on cultural, not political ground. Rather than contesting for political power, or pressing demands on the state, these movements struggled for the right to difference. Construction and defense of identity were central concerns.[4]

Some recent analyses support the idea that certain elements shared by many contemporary movements, such as the politicization of the private and the assertion of identity as a primary goal, represent a significant departure from the past (Buechler 1995; Johnston, Larana and Gusfield 1994). But others criticize the reification of a category that does not take into account differences among collective identities (Gamson, J. 1989; Gamson, W. A. 1992).[5]

In privileging identity-based movements, NSM theory offers important insights into movements such as those analyzed here. However, its sweeping structural explanations obscure distinctions among these movements and overlook the historical specificities that might enable us to explain why, for example, Nicaraguan lesbians constructed their movement differently than their Costa Rican counterparts.

Theorists in the resource mobilization and political process traditions, on the other hand, have been more concerned with explaining variation. By situating social movements in their political and historical environments, they provide a number of useful tools for comparative analysis of the forces that shape different movements (Jenkins 1983; McAdam 1982; McCarthy and Zald 1977; Oberschall 1973; Tarrow 1988, 1994; Tilly 1978). However, much of this work rests on a definition of social movements that unduly narrows the field of inquiry to what Tarrow describes as "collective challenges by people with common purposes and solidarity in sustained interaction with elites, opponents, and authorities" (1994, 3–4). Although social networks, symbols, and collective identities sometimes are given a place in movement formation, these are usually viewed as means to an end: the moment of overt engagement with political institutions. This exclusive focus on a certain kind of social movement eliminates, as objects of study, movements for whom construction of identity is an end, rather than a means, and whose field of engagement does not (or does not primarily) include the state.

There is a growing body of scholarly literature from this perspective that compares social movements that have been considered "new" across different national contexts (della Porta and Rucht 1995; Kitschelt 1986; Kriesi 1995, 1996; Rucht 1996). However, because of their bounded view of what constitutes a social movement, these theorists tend to take the conceptualization of goals and orientation of action as given,[6] directing their attention instead to explaining mobilization, structure, degree of militancy, or political outcomes. Although it offers useful insights into variation among "political" movements, most work in the resource mobilization and political process traditions is less helpful in explaining why movements concerned with constructing identities outside the institutional political arena take fundamentally different forms in divergent national contexts.

A number of recent works, however, have begun to integrate NSM-inspired concerns with collective identity and the sociopolitical factors often cited by resource mobilization and political process theorists (Taylor 1989; Taylor and Rupp 1993; Taylor and Whittier 1992; Whittier 1995). Much of this analysis focuses on changes over time within one movement, the shift from Melucci's (1985) visible moment, when movements emerge to confront a political authority, to what he calls "latency," during which subterranean movement networks construct new "cultural models" (what Taylor [1989] calls "abeyance"). While they offer an important corrective to studies that recognize only the overt, political aspects of organizing, there is a tendency among these authors to identify a "cultural" orientation with low points in the life of a social movement, a characterization that does not apply to movements, such as that of Costa Rican lesbians, that are inwardly focused during their most active moments. Nevertheless, these temporal analyses suggest the possibility of applying political factors to explanations of differences among identity-based movements. I will continue in this spirit, seeking to extend the tools of resource mobilization and political process theories in order to explain the varying orientations of movements that assert identities beyond the space of formal politics. Rather than comparing single movements over time, I will analyze cross-national differences in the ways movements express their identities.

In Costa Rica, the lesbian movement looked inward toward definition of personal identity, creation of community, and assertion of autonomy as a sexual minority. The Nicaraguan movement took a different path, choosing instead to defend the right of lesbians (and gays) to full social integration, and to project to the society at large its vision of a free sexuality for all. I argue that these contrasts can best be understood by attention to the way three factors are expressed in a given society: (1) the impact of the particular economic structure and development model on social actors, (2) the relationship between the state and civil society, and (3) the nature of the broader sea of social movements—including political parties—within which any given movement must navigate.

Economic Structure

In their efforts to dichotomize old and new movements and declare an end to the dominion of material concerns, NSM theorists usually eschew consideration of the limits and opportunities presented by the economy in specific national contexts, preferring to remain at the level of epochal transformation.[7] Resource mobilization theory generally goes to the opposite extreme, focusing its analytic eye on the micro level of resources available to particular movements. In contrast, I argue that the class structure in a given country, while in no way determining the nature of social movements, plays a role in providing or denying a potential social base for different kinds of movement.[8] Costa Rica's more diversified economy and sizable middle class, and Nicaragua's agro-export orientation and polarized class structure, have offered distinct possibilities and limitations for social movements.

State–Civil Society Relations

NSM theory sees the growing penetration of the state into private life as key to the contemporary creation of movements that assert the right to define identities, but pays less attention to the ways distinctive state–civil society configurations influence the nature of these identities. Political process theorists have introduced the concept of "political opportunity structures," the complex of interrelations among state and party institutions, elite and oppositional strategies, as an important variable in the mobilization of social movements (della Porta and Rucht 1995; Kitschelt 1986; Kriesi 1995, 1996; Meyer and Staggenborg 1996; Rucht 1996; Tarrow 1994). However, while such an approach helps analyze the behavior of movements within the formal political sphere, it does little to explain the formation of collective identity among movements not primarily concerned with making demands on the state (cf. Rucht 1996).[9] If NSM theorists have a lens set at too wide an angle to take in variations among identity-based movements, the political process literature tends to locate movements too narrowly within the context of political institutions. It is not only these political institutions, but also their relationship with civil society, the "'private' apparatus of 'hegemony,'" which plays a key role, not only in shaping class-based movements as Gramsci argued, but in the fundamental nature of all kinds of movements (Gramsci 1971, 261). The state–civil society relationship is particularly important for movements around issues, such as sexuality, that are constructed and struggled over in a variety of arenas: the family, the community, the church, popular culture, the economy, and others, as well as the state.

In Costa Rica, where the state has exercised a stable form of hegemony through civil society, interest groups competed within a status quo that was rarely challenged, and the possibility of a unifying identity seemed either utopian or authoritarian. In Nicaragua, on the other hand, a state–civil society relationship that had seesawed [in the 1980s and 1990s], along with the heritage of a vanquished revolutionary regime, left a fragile conservative state hegemony and a cadre of activists with the memory of an inclusive form of social integration as a model.

Social Movement Field

In NSM theory, identity-based movements tend to spring fully formed from the fissures produced by structural transformation. There is little concern with conjunctural mediating influences in the environment, or, more specifically, with other movements that have left their mark on both participants and their interlocutors. Political process scholars, on the other hand, theorize the importance of previously existing organizational resources in the development of new movements (McAdam 1982), the role of "early risers" in a social movement cycle in expanding opportunities for later-emerging movements (Tarrow 1988), and the mechanisms of "spillover" from one movement to another (Meyer and Whittier 1994). From a symbolic interactionist perspective, "frame" theorists elaborate the process by which social movement "master frames" established early in a given cycle constrain and influence later conceptions of organizing (Snow and Benford 1992; see also Snow and Benford 1988; Hunt, Benford, and Snow 1994). While all of these theories offer intriguing insights about the processes by which one social movement affects others, they tend to treat intermovement relationships in isolation from a broader political and social context, failing to link the influence of particular movements to the kind of state–civil society relationship and structural environment in which they are located.

I emphasize the relationship of new movements to a broader "social movement family" with similar fundamental values (della Porta and Rucht 1995), while at the same time locating these movements in an expanded historical framework. In Costa Rica, lesbian organizing grew out of a feminist movement with a long history and strong liberal and academic feminist components; whatever small Left had once existed had long since been silenced. In Nicaragua, the feminist and lesbian movements were born simultaneously, led by women whose worldview and sense of politics was shaped by a once-strong, class-based movement.

While class structure both restricts and creates possibilities, it is an expanded political realm that shapes social movement orientations and fundamental conceptions of goals and strategy. [. . .] Economic structure and political context work together to construct the profound differences between the Nicaraguan and Costa Rican lesbian movements.

Costa Rica: Circling the Wagons

Costa Rica's first lesbian organization, founded in March 1987, appeared in some ways to be the quintessential "new social movement" described by theorists. A small group, whose activists never numbered more than twenty, *Las Entendidas* never tried to recruit on a mass scale and actually limited membership by criteria such as knowledge and acceptance of feminism. Until 1990, when its first coordinator was elected, the group had a loose structure made up of ad hoc commissions. All but one of its active members were professionals, members of the "new middle class" evoked by NSM adherents.

Theorists describe new social movements as growing out of a reaction to the failures of so-called old social movements, rather than being inspired by and allied with them. Whether the formation of a lesbian organization responded to shortcomings of the small Costa Rican Left is difficult to say; what is certain is that there were no ties between the two movements. None of the group's members came out of Left party activism and, according to its coordinator, *Las Entendidas* had no ongoing relationship to Left organizations. Most importantly, the group's goals reflected the inward turn noted by analysts of many contemporary movements. In an article summarizing their first five years of work, members of *Las Entendidas* expressed their ongoing commitment: "We continue giving soul and body to [our] lesbian identity" (*Las En-*

tendidas 1992, 8).[10] From the beginning, a primary objective was to build internal strength by promoting self-esteem, combating internalized guilt and "lesbophobia," and developing a new lesbian (and later lesbian feminist) identity. *Las Entendidas* functioned as a support and social group for its members; time was set aside at the meetings for sharing personal feelings and experiences, and members went on recreational outings together. The group sought personal liberation via intellectual practice, engaging in discussions of feminist literature and the collective elaboration of new theories.

As the organization evolved, the concept of identity came to embrace not only individuals, but a wider community. By the end of 1987, *Las Entendidas* had begun to define its ideology as feminist and set itself a second goal: to create a lesbian feminist community through outreach and consciousness raising among Costa Rican lesbians. With this in mind, the group founded a monthly "women's night" at a San José gay bar, where they offered speakers and workshops on topics such as sexuality, feminism, self-esteem, and alcoholism, as well as theater, poetry readings, and other cultural events. One historian of the movement comments: "It was an activity ... which may have made [women] feel part of a community, of a larger group with the capacity to be involved in activities outside of the ordinary, and the possibility of learning new things" (Serrano n.d., 8).

The group also conducted a survey of lesbian life, organized a therapy group for survivors of incest, and published a newsletter bearing the slogan, "For a Lesbian Solidarity." With the hope of involving and educating new local members, among other goals, *Las Entendidas* hosted the Second Latin American and Caribbean Lesbian Feminist Encounter in 1990. Despite an extremely hostile atmosphere, the event was attended by 150 women, from Costa Rica and all over the continent (see Carstensen 1992; Jiménez 1990; Madden Arias 1994; *II Encuentro Lésbico Feminista de América Latina y el Caribe* 1990).

Another goal articulated by members of *Las Entendidas* was to win space and acceptance in the broader feminist movement. But this objective was never fully realized, since most members of *Las Entendidas* were reluctant to go public about their sexual orientation, even within women's organizations.

The final set of goals claimed by *Las Entendidas* was "to conquer invisibility" vis-à-vis the rest of the popular movement and society at large, and to demand rights in a patriarchal society (*II Encuentro Lésbico Feminista de América Latina y el Caribe* 1990, l). But, while these objectives were occasionally stated, it is difficult to find their expression in the group's practices. Apart from their appearance at a women's march against violence, *Las Entendidas* seems to have entered the public eye only reluctantly.

The international Lesbian Feminist Encounter, for example, was intended more as an opportunity to strengthen the different participating groups internally and establish networks between them than as an effort to confront homophobia in Costa

Rican society. The conference was not locally advertised outside of feminist circles, and it was only when the press got wind of the event, and opposition began to escalate, that members of *Las Entendidas* agreed to meet with reporters.[11] One activist commented: "*Las Entendidas*' goal is collective visibility of lesbians, but we continue to work internally and fear coming out."

There are at least four possible arenas of struggle for lesbian movements such as *Las Entendidas*, ranging from the most intimate to the most public. Groups may focus on (1) strengthening and developing a sense of identity among their *own members*; (2) reaching and involving a wider *lesbian community*; (3) educating those active in the *women's movement*; or (4) addressing *society as a whole*. In the case of the Costa Rican movement, the emphasis was clearly on the first two arenas. Participation in the women's movement was sporadic and limited to only some members; efforts to have an impact on society at large were rare.[12]

In an editorial on the fifth anniversary of *Las Entendidas*' founding, Lila Silvestre wrote: "Today, although discrimination against lesbians continues to affect us, we have more strength to create our own spaces and new relationships because we have a support group in which we recognize and nurture each other" (Silvestre 1992, 1). In many ways, *Las Entendidas* presented the ideal type of a new social movement. Its educated, middle-class membership, loose structure, personal identity focus, and lack of involvement with traditional politics of Left or Right, as well as its efforts to create an autonomous space for difference, seemed to confirm NSM theorists' predictions about the kinds of movements that would arise in this period. Within this conception, *Las Entendidas*, even at its apogee, fell at the latent, defensive end of Melucci's continuum. That this form of development was not inevitable, however, becomes clear when we examine the lesbian movement just across the border to the north in Nicaragua.

Nicaragua: Publicizing the Private

The lesbian movement in Nicaragua in the late 1980s and early 1990s consisted of two organizations that worked directly with lesbians, and a number of other individuals and nongovernmental organizations (NGOs), which played an important role in promoting and supporting the movement. *Nosotras* and *Xochiquetzal* brought lesbians together to work on issues of sexuality and sexual preference. Though each had a different structure and functions, their memberships and goals overlapped—in fact, *Xochiquetzal* served for three years as a kind of umbrella for *Nosotras*, as well as the gay collective *Somos*—and, during this period, they can be considered complementary parts of one movement.[13]

In contrast to *Las Entendidas* in Costa Rica, the lesbian movement in Nicaragua was not an archetypal new social movement. Instead, it was a kind of hybrid, combining features of lesbian movements in Central America both "new" and "old," in the context of the construction and defense of identity. While the coordinators of *Xochiquetzal* were middle class, the membership of the *Nosotras* collective, some thirty altogether, were a mixture of urban working-class and professional women. Unlike the Costa Rican movement, Nicaraguan lesbians had close ties to the Left. Despite the history of conflict between the *Frente Sandinista Liberación Nacional* (FSLN) and the gay and lesbian movement, all the members of *Nosotras* were (or had been) Sandinista supporters and continued to identify with the party's revolutionary goals. Several activists were party members and at least one had important political and administrative responsibilities during the decade of Sandinista state power. Although *Nosotras* had a loose structure, with a rotating coordinator and no formal legal status, *Xochiquetzal*, which provided resources and support to the collective, was a staff-based institution with legal status and funding sources abroad.

Through their movement, lesbians in Nicaragua addressed a broader and somewhat different set of goals than did their sisters in Costa Rica, with *Nosotras* focusing more on internal identity and *Xochiquetzal* more on outreach beyond the lesbian community, although neither confined itself entirely to one end of the spectrum. Within the collective, members of *Nosotras* sought to build self-esteem, to strengthen their identity as women and as lesbians, and to "learn about our gender condition," as one woman put it. The group held monthly meetings dedicated to study and recreational activities. One of their main endeavors was a nine-month course coordinated by *Xochiquetzal* on feminism, sexuality, and women's health issues.

A second goal, this one articulated by *Xochiquetzal* staff, was outreach in the lesbian community and support for the formation of new collectives. Besides the training and logistical support it offered initially for lesbian and gay groups, the foundation organized a series of fiestas in an effort to reach the broader lesbian community. However, these were soon abandoned for lack of funds and because they did not succeed in drawing in new activists. Plans for *Nosotras* to do outreach at the few, newly founded lesbian social clubs were slow to get off the ground.

A third goal for the Nicaraguan lesbian movement was to support and influence the growing feminist movement. To this end, representatives of both *Xochiquetzal* and *Nosotras* participated in meetings and activities of the National Feminist Committee (CNF), a coalition of some twenty-five women's groups that conducted feminist education and organizing projects. The two lesbian organizations successfully insisted that the groups in the CNF support the right to sexual preference as a principle of their educational work and that the committee as a whole incorporate this as a plank in its platform (*La Boletina* 1992; Blandón 1993). *Xochiquetzal* offered workshops on sexuality to women's organizations, and staff members aggressively challenged homophobia in feminist meetings.

A final cluster of goals addressed the broader social arena. In their literature, leaders of *Xochiquetzal* linked personal and social change, defining their mission to promote "the integral development of people on the terrain of sexuality, through a knowledge of human sexuality free of prejudices, and the creation of social conditions which favor [such development]" (*Fundación Xochiquetzal* n.d., 2).

Organized lesbians in Nicaragua went beyond defending their existence as individual members of a sexual minority. *Xochiquetzal* made demands for rights based on lesbian membership in and identification with a range of other marginalized groups, including "equal rights to participate [politically] . . . without any kind of political, economic, or social or cultural discrimination . . . the right to peace and security" (*Fuera del clóset* 1993, 315). These were demands not just for space in society, but for a thorough transformation of the society in which lesbians wanted to be included.

These objectives required moving beyond the lesbian and feminist communities. As the *Xochiquetzal* subdirector explained: "[We] realized that if we wanted to influence the population and promote respect and tolerance for sexual preference, we couldn't do it by staying in the ghetto. [Also], gays and lesbians are not only those who are organized, but they are in all sectors; the majority are in the closet. So we broadened the groups that we worked with."

The foundation conducted workshops and produced radio programs, articles, and educational materials aimed at society at large, but in particular at students, women's groups, and medical personnel. In these forums, besides advocating lesbian and gay rights, the foundation sought to demystify the arena of sexuality and preached a doctrine of self-acceptance, liberation from the tyranny of norms, and the right of all people—gay or straight—to sexual pleasure. This social orientation was shared by members of *Nosotras* as well. Along with the foundation, *Nosotras* joined coalitions to plan gay-pride and AIDS-awareness events designed to reach heterosexual society, as well as gays and lesbians. At the first public gay and lesbian celebration in 1991, organizers were explicit about this aim, choosing to invite well-known straight intellectuals to make presentations alongside gays and lesbians. Perhaps most visibly, in 1992 the lesbian movement participated in a "Campaign for a Sexuality Free of Prejudice" to oppose a newly enacted antisodomy law and educate the Nicaraguan public about the issue (see Andersson 1993; Bolt Gonzalez 1995; *La Feminista* 1993; *Fundación Xochiquetzal* 1992. More than twenty-five organizations were involved in the campaign. When their requests to speak with President Violeta Chamorro were ignored, they held public forums and debates, presented their case in the media, gathered over four thousand signatures protesting the law, and challenged its constitutionality in court.

The goals and activities of the Nicaraguan lesbian movement extended across the spectrum of strategic arenas, from an inward focus on its own members to an outward focus on the rest of society, with much of its energy going in the latter direction.

While *Nosotras* worked to build lesbian identity among its members, *Xochiquetzal* took on the task of coordinating educational and political activities directed toward civil society and, in self-defense, toward the state. Until 1994, the two groups worked together to promote awareness in the women's movement and, to a lesser extent, to reach the unorganized sectors of the lesbian community.

In contrast to the Costa Rican experience, the Nicaraguan lesbian movement combined the concern with subjectivity stressed by NSM analysts with other features often associated with older, class-based movements. It was a movement with both a loosely structured and an institutionalized expression, with both middle-class and working-class members, and with a concern for personal identity, as well as a commitment to recreating society in an inclusive image.

If anything, this movement leaned toward the visible, political end of the continuum theorists have described. Unlike some other identity-based movements, including *Las Entendidas, Xochiquetzal* and *Nosotras* chose to enter the political sphere, not seeking to win power as "old" movements had, but to defend rights and further educational goals. They sought, not just to gain tolerance, but to reshape society's thinking about sexuality. The goal was not primarily autonomous space, but social integration. As one Nicaraguan activist told Margaret Randall, "[N]ot creating ghettos really is important. We need to defend our place in society as a whole and make society respect us for what we are, for what we do, for our work" (Randall 1992, 75).

Costa Rica: Sex and Democracy

The Costa Rican and Nicaraguan lesbian movements of the 1980s and 1990s offered a stark contrast not easily explained by current social movement theory. While one consisted primarily of middle-class professionals, the other had a strong working-class representation; while one functioned in a fairly ad hoc manner, the other had both informal and institutionalized components; while one adhered to a radical feminist ideology, focusing its attention on personal growth and building community, the other embodied revolutionary feminism, building alliances within civil society around a totalizing, liberatory vision. Three factors, one economic/structural and the other two rooted in the political domain, seem to account for these differences.

For a series of historical reasons, Costa Rica developed a significantly different class structure than Nicaragua. A relatively wealthy country with a more diversified economy, its 1992 GNP per inhabitant was more than three times that of Nicaragua. Whereas 68.7 percent of Nicaraguans lived in poverty in 1985, only 28.1 percent of Costa Ricans did. Though Costa Rica was no more urbanized than its northern neighbor, it had a larger middle class and more educated population. In 1990, higher education accounted for 11.6 percent of all Costa Rican students enrolled in school; in Nicaragua the figure was 2.6 percent. In 1980, professionals, technicians, administrators, and managers made up more than one-fifth of the economically active population in Costa Rica; these sectors in Nicaragua were less than one-tenth of those employed (FLACSO 1995: 36, 104, 113, 139, 140).

These structural conditions had important implications for lesbians and gays, particularly in the context of urbanization, which began in the 1950s and reached its peak in the 1970s. For both gays and lesbians, life in the city offered greater opportunities to interact, and a degree of anonymity, economic independence, and freedom from the constraints of the extended family.[14] While there was no real homosexual "ghetto," the number of gays in the growing middle class made possible a small gay male culture organized around bars and private parties. Though lesbian culture was much less visible and lesbians as a group were certainly much less economically independent than gay men, it is likely that urban life had some of the same effects on them, bringing them together and offering those with the means the option of a somewhat less clandestine lifestyle. From the 1950s onward, educational opportunities for women expanded, and so, to some extent, did the possibilities for financial independence for the educated middle-class woman. (Although in Nicaragua women made up a slightly greater percentage of the working population than in Costa Rica, the percentage of women in professional and technical occupations was nearly twice as high in Costa Rica [FLACSO 1995: 117, 119].) All of these factors laid the groundwork for the growth of an urban lesbian community.

This parallel culture and the availability of individual solutions meant that it was possible for some lesbians to avoid direct confrontation with the dominant society, and there was less of a sense of urgency around economic and social issues that might have linked lesbians more closely to other activist groups than in Nicaragua. Participation in a semi-autonomous community was a viable possibility for a certain group of women in Costa Rica. Furthermore, there was a significant academic community, which could support a more intellectually oriented movement than the one that developed in Nicaragua. But class structure does not determine, and cannot by itself explain, the shape social movements take in a given society. It is to the political realm —more specifically to the kind of state and its relationship to civil society—that we must turn to further understand the variation in movements.

Since 1948, Costa Rica has had a stable constitutional democracy with a pervasive discourse of individual rights and justice. Despite moves toward neoliberal retrenchment in the 1980s, Costa Rica's was a modified welfare state that offered significant social protection to at least some sectors, and actively promoted the institutionalization of interests.

This state rested firmly on a hegemony based in civil society (Gramsci 1971). While occasionally resorting to coercion, the state relied primarily on eliciting the consent of the governed through cooptation and the legitimacy of its representative political institutions (see Vilas 1995; Palma 1989). Clearly delineated and institutionalized interest groups competed within the framework of the status quo. At the same time, an internally differentiated elite maintained control of the reins of state through a long-established system of rotation of power. The overall effect, according to activists, was a political culture dominated by apathy, individualism, and a fear of conflict that went beyond the boundaries of the hegemonic consensus.

Costa Rica enjoys a reputation as a leader in the area of women's rights. In 1949, in response to local feminist demands as well as to international pressure, the country became the first in the region to guarantee political rights for women, and since then the state has continually intervened in gender politics as a champion—at least rhetorically—of women's equality (see Escalante Herrera 1990; García and Gomáriz 1989; Saint-Germain 1993; Saint-Germain and Morgan 1991). In a country with a sizable group of educated women and "femocrats"—female bureaucrats—as well as an active grass-roots women's movement, political leaders were quick to try to turn gender issues to their advantage.[15]

Regarding gender, as with other themes, challengers faced the sense of exceptionalism fostered by the state and shared by many Costa Ricans. As one feminist put it, "In Costa Rica you can't question the venerated and mythical 'equality' of all Costa Ricans without running the risk of being called a traitor to the country" (Facio 1988, 9). But the permeability of the state to women's concerns masked continuing social and economic inequalities, such as discrimination in land ownership and employment, as well as threats to women such as rape, domestic abuse, and paternal irresponsibility (Facio 1988).

For lesbians in particular, oppression was rooted in civil society rather than within the confines of law. The first line of defense of the dominant sexual order was what participants in the lesbian movement called "invisibilization." As one journalist noted, the topic of lesbianism did not appear in either university or public library catalogs, and only entered the media in relationship to the 1990 Lesbian Feminist Encounter (Mandell 1991, 9). One longtime member of *Las Entendidas* explained one aspect of social control: "Here, repression isn't carried out by the police or the army, but by your neighbor . . . It's a democratic country, but all the aggression takes place in the family." Related, but even more insidious, was what Mandell called "self-censorship." Another activist commented: "They don't have any army, because they don't need one . . . Lesbophobia is internalized; people are afraid and don't even try to come out."

In Costa Rica, the relationship between state and civil society had been stable over a long period of time. The state promoted a particular set of moral values which only became visible when sexual hegemony was under threat. Minister of Government Alvarez Desanti, reacting to the international Lesbian Feminist Encounter in Costa Rica, made this quite clear: "This is a democratic country, where the laws guarantee us the right to meet freely; nevertheless, there are ethical and moral values which the national authorities should defend. For this reason, we believe that a congress such as the one which has been announced affects our lifestyle and threatens the education and moral principles which we wish to inculcate in our youth" (*II Encuentro Lésbico Feminista de América Latina y el Caribe* 1990).

An earlier challenge to conventional mores, in the mid-1980s, when AIDS began making inroads among gays, had also produced a negative governmental response. The disease's appearance drew people together and sparked initial organizing efforts. It also made gays visible to the straight community and aroused irrational fears. The government made no efforts to respond to the medical emergency provoked by the epidemic, and instead moved to shut down gay and lesbian bars and harass their clientele. In March 1987, police raided a bar called *La Torre,* frequented by middle-class gay men, and arrested 253 people. Meanwhile, the government began requiring public employees to take AIDS tests, a move criticized by gays as blatantly discriminatory and without international precedent.

These actions were the spark that led to the birth of a movement among both lesbians and gay men.[16] By the end of 1987, four gay and lesbian organizations had formed, among them *Las Entendidas.* But these moments of overt state repression were rare, and, for the most part, the illusion of a value-free democracy was preserved. The Costa Rican state, with its largely invisible moral foundation and stable integration with civil society, offered a slippery target for transformatory challenges and discouraged a focus on politics, per se. The proliferation of interest groups also left little room for inclusive identities. Together, these conditions help account for the development of a lesbian movement that withdrew into a semi-autonomous community founded on conceptions of women's essential difference, rather than pursuing a crusade to change broader social values, as the movement did in Nicaragua. In the end, retreat may have seemed more attractive than participation in a rejecting society that offered meager sources of common identity.

The final factor shaping any given social movement is also political: the field of other movements within which it moves, particularly those that share underlying values. In Costa Rica, the virtual absence of the Left in the 1980s was a product, in part, of the mediating effects of the country's civilian welfare state, representative political institutions, and dominant liberal discourse (Solís 1989). The resulting lack of widespread experience with cross-class relations around a common political project left *Las Entendidas,* despite its attempts to reach working-class lesbians, with a professional and intellectual constituency. The unifying Left ideology and identity that shaped those who founded the lesbian movement in Nicaragua was absent in Costa Rica, opening the way for a movement that stressed difference, demanded autonomy, and retreated into self-healing and self-protection, rather than seeking to reshape society. In the end, lesbians became another interest group of sorts, struggling to carve out a niche for yet another particularized identity.

Whereas in Nicaragua, a class-based movement established a "master frame" with which other movements had to contend (Snow and Benford 1992), in Costa Rica, gender-based organizing set the stage. Perhaps in part inspired by the state's liberal democratic discourse, in the mid- to late 1970s, during the UN Decade for Women, an active women's movement emerged (see Berrón 1995; Candelaria Navas 1985; García and Gomáriz 1989; Saint-Germain and Morgan 1991). By the end of the 1980s, Costa Rica had over 150 women's groups, more than any other country in Central America (García and Gomáriz 1989, 212). Many of the women later involved in *Las Entendidas* participated in women's organizations of one kind or another, and all were shaped by the political climate this movement helped create.

The feminist movement in Costa Rica had three main strands in the 1980s: liberal (Saint- Germain 1993), academic feminist (González Suárez 1988), and popular feminist (*Colectivo Pancha Carrasco* 1994). The first—and dominant—sector consisted of mainstream institutions, political party members, government functionaries, and independent, professional women, and set its scope on legislative change, an arena where there was little room for addressing lesbian concerns. Academic feminists' efforts focused on gender and a women's studies program in each of the two principal universities. Popular feminism was the focus of several small nongovernmental organizations, staffed by middle-class women, who sought to build a movement among women of the working class. *Las Entendidas* was primarily influenced by university-based feminists, a fact that is reflected in its intellectual discourse. Some members' experience with popular feminism may have been expressed in its efforts—albeit unsuccessful—to reach working-class lesbians in the bars.

Although homophobia and fear of being identified as lesbians may have been more widespread among mainstream feminists, it was expressed in all sectors of the women's movement, reflecting the kind of internalized repression in the wider society. For the most part, *Las Entendidas'* initiatives to the feminist movement met with rejection, despite group members' long history of activism in women's organizations. Feminists not only failed to openly defend organizers of the 1990 Lesbian Feminist Encounter when the state, the church, and the media launched vicious attacks, but one group withdrew its sponsorship of the lesbians' request for a meeting space at the university.

The Encounter did force feminist recognition of lesbian existence and, subsequently, *Las Entendidas* was invited to participate in several women's events, but the reception remained chilly. After their presentation at one conference, the published version of the proceedings changed *Las Entendidas'* name to disguise the group's nature. Feminist homophobia functioned as another force pushing *Las Entendidas* back into the collective closet. If lesbians could not be confident of allies even in the feminist movement, how could they make links to broader issues of sexuality and take on the task of outreach to the larger society?

In Costa Rica, a diversified class structure, stable and hegemonic state–civil society relations, and the dominance of a particular kind of feminism with particular attitudes toward lesbianism combined to generate a lesbian movement that resisted the imposition of dominant values by reinforcing its own boundaries, rather than by seeking allies with whom to reinvent society's sexual practices.

Nicaragua: Sex and Revolution

Compared with Costa Rica, Nicaragua had a much more underdeveloped agro-export economy, with a class structure polarized between a very small, educated upper class and a large, impoverished majority. Though urbanization was no less significant in Nicaragua than in Costa Rica, the middle class was too small to provide an economic base for the kind of gay and lesbian community built around consumption that developed in San José. Most lesbians continued to live with, and depend on, their families, and there was little chance of individual autonomy for the majority who were working class. A movement based on the creation of an enclave community could have little appeal (Ferguson 1991). The structural constraints also meant that it would have been difficult to create a viable lesbian movement limited to the middle class and isolated from the broader social issues that affected the poor majority.

Turning to the political sphere, both the nature of the state and its relationship to civil society had undergone drastic shifts, passing through three distinct phases in the fifteen years prior to the movement's founding: from dictatorship, to revolutionary government, to conservative, neoliberal state. Perched for more than forty years atop a vastly unequal distribution of wealth in an agro-export export economy, the Somoza dictatorship destroyed or co-opted all organized identities independent of its own interests. In this way, the Somozas stunted the growth of civil society and polarized the populace, managing to unify a heterogeneous opposition and ultimately spelling the end of their long reign in 1979. Prior to the regime's end, as the regime grew more repressive, it invaded the sphere of personal life in dramatic ways, killing, torturing, and "disappearing" suspected opponents. In the process, new sectors, including housewives and young women, mobilized into the opposition and took on unaccustomed roles as soldiers, weapons makers, and logistical support for revolutionary forces.

After the dictatorship's defeat, the FSLN came to power in a country without a vibrant civil society or history of democratic practice and set about creating these from the top down (Vilas 1995). Throughout the 1980s, the Sandinistas built popular organizations and sought to draw society's castoffs into the political process.[17]

Both before and after the taking of power, the Sandinista movement had a profound impact on the personal lives of its followers. In effect, the revolution too invaded the personal realm, turning traditional gender and generational arrangements upside down. Young people who joined the movement exchanged the structure of patriarchal authority within the family for a newfound personal and sexual freedom. Mobilized to fight in the army, teach literacy in remote areas, pick coffee and cotton, and work far from home, Nicaragua's youth, particularly its young women, took on new roles and formed new kinds of relationships. In a social situation resembling the World War II period in the United States (D'Emilio 1983), Nicaraguan lesbians, as well as gays, found, if not social acceptance, at least greater room to maneuver amid the social turmoil. Though there was no real gay "community" to speak of and the Sandinista regime had closed down the few gay clubs that had existed during the Somoza period, gays and lesbians did begin to find one another.[18]

The Sandinista regime, which came to power in Nicaragua in 1979, sought to unite actors from various points along a broad social spectrum in the service of an interventionist political project to benefit the poor and the previously powerless, including women (see Chinchilla 1990, 1994; Criquillion 1995; Murguialday 1990; Thayer 1994). The Sandinista government spoke of women's rights to equal participation in society and made concrete advances, which alleviated some of women's burdens and allowed them more independence from oppressive family structures.[19] Beyond their new freedoms, women also won legitimation for their claims to be treated as integral, equal members of society, a lesson not lost on the lesbians among them.

However, while there seemed to be consensus within the revolutionary government on the subject of women's rights, at least at a rhetorical level, the same was not true of lesbian and gay issues. At the end of 1986, a semiclandestine gay and lesbian organization, the Nicaraguan Gay Movement, formed to offer emotional support, internal education about sexuality and AIDS, and discussion of sexual identity, as well as opportunities for social contact (see *Breakthrough* 1992; Merrett 1992; Zúñiga 1995). These activities came to an abrupt halt three months later when the group was infiltrated by Sandinista State Security. Members were taken to Security headquarters, questioned about their personal lives and collective activities, and told in no uncertain terms that such gatherings were considered counterrevolutionary, despite most of the participants having long histories of revolutionary activism.[20]

Meanwhile, other parts of the state and revolutionary leadership took an entirely different position. As in Costa Rica, AIDS served as both catalyst to and cover for gay and lesbian organization. After their organization was disbanded, Nicaraguan gay and lesbian activists formed the Popular AIDS Education Collective (CEPSIDA), which eventually grew to some two hundred people, including both men and women. The group conducted AIDS-prevention workshops in a Managua park that served as the gay cruising ground and among the prostitutes at a local shopping mall (see *Breakthrough* 1992; Merrett 1992; Nicaragua Information Center 1988; Otis 1991). Health Minister Dora Maria Téllez offered support for CEPSIDA and intervened with the revolutionary leadership to prevent harassment of group members.

Despite contradictions within the state on the issue of sexual orientation, for the most part during the Sandinista period, society was organized around an explicit moral and political consensus under the hegemony of the FSLN. The new institutions and identities were fluid and there was an ideology of makeover—the "new man" was under construction. While many lesbians questioned the absence of the "new woman," and at least some experienced rejection from party functionaries, the revolutionary process as a whole offered the basis for a social integration that had not earlier seemed possible. It also legitimated the conception of a society founded on an explicit set of values that could be articulated to reflect a broad array of interests. It is fitting that, once the Sandinistas lost state power and commitments to the FSLN began to fade, lesbians who had come of age in the 1980s should develop a movement that stressed continuities as well as differences and should pursue inclusion in a reconstructed society organized around transformed values.

With the FSLN loss at the polls in 1990, an internally divided state with a neoliberal economic plan and a conservative gender agenda came to power, and the fledgling civil society was on its own without tutelage for the first time. The new government revamped education to reflect traditional conceptions of morality: sex education was banned and new textbooks called *Morality and Civics* were distributed. An anti-abortion campaign was launched and efforts to criminalize domestic violence were defeated (Kampwirth 1992).

The incoming mayor of Managua, Arnoldo Alemán, launched a campaign to "clean up" the city and eliminate homosexual activity from public spaces (Merrett 1992). One month after he assumed office, the doors to the ruined cathedral that had served as a gay socializing and cruising area were barred, and police harassment of gays in the nearby park escalated. In June 1992, as part of its "family values" campaign, the new legislature passed what has been called the most repressive antisodomy law in the hemisphere. According to the law, anyone who "induces, promotes, propagandizes or practices cohabitation among people of the same sex in a scandalous manner" is guilty of the crime of sodomy, punishable by up to three years in prison (*Asamblea Nacional* 1992).[21]

Given the history of mobilization and popular education about rights in Nicaragua, these moves generated a sense of outrage and generalized opposition to the regime among lesbian activists, as well as others, and reinforced ties among different groups within civil society. In fact, legal attacks on gay rights only provoked a more militant opposition, which sought allies and defined the issues in ways that drew support from many sectors of the population. In general, the dramatic shift in the values being promoted by those in power seemed only to serve to make clearer the constructed nature of gender and to invite a movement dedicated to reconstructing it along different lines.

Before the elections, gays and lesbians had already made their first public appearance when a group of some fifty Nicaraguans and thirty internationalists, wearing T-shirts emblazoned with pink triangles, marched and danced together at the celebration of the tenth anniversary of the revolution (Matthews 1989). But the effect of the election results accelerated organizational efforts, and gays and lesbians increasingly claimed visibility, with a public presence at International Women's Day celebrations in 1990 and 1991, and the first open gay pride celebration in June 1991 (Merrett 1992; Quirós 1991). It was during these years that the lesbian collective *Nosotras* and the gay and lesbian nongovernmental organization *Xochiquetzal* were founded.[22]

A third factor shaping the identity of the lesbian movement and linked to these different relations between state and society was the panorama of social movements. In Nicaragua, a class-based, rather than a gender-based, movement defined the terrain. There, a revolutionary party, which held power for ten years, created a totalizing identity and culture and left behind a legacy of popular activism. This historical experience shaped the identity, the ideology, and the sense of goals and strategy of those who ultimately became lesbian activists. The drive to integrate society, and the common project around which the Sandinistas sought to organize it, were based on a revolutionary framework influenced by Marxism and liberation theology. The commitment to social justice for the majority and to collective, rather than individual, solutions left their mark on the lesbian movement that surfaced after the 1990 elections. Although the Sandinista defeat discredited use of the state as a vehicle for change, the lesbian and gay movement continued to work within the arena of civil society, and addressed the state when necessary to defend its room to maneuver.

The presence of a mass movement of the Left also created networks of people with similar ideologies and history. While in the 1980s many of these people—including those who would later become active in the gay and lesbian movement—channeled their energies through the state, in the 1990s they moved into the institutions of civil society. Whether or not the FSLN as a party continued to claim their allegiance, their shared worldview facilitated building alliances. In the concrete case of gays and lesbians, it led to a model of cross-gender collaboration, which began with the formation of the first collectives and AIDS education efforts, and continued into the 1990s.

The FSLN's strategy of cross-class alliances under middle-class leadership was also reflected in the lesbian movement. In an environment where working-class people were mobilized and active, and where there was a commitment to eliminating the exclusions of class, it was not only natural for middle-class activists to look beyond their own social class for participants, but also for working-class lesbians to respond or even take leadership.

Finally, the strong—indeed, dominant—Left presence in Nicaragua in the 1980s attracted politicized gay and lesbian fellow travelers from around the world who helped spark organizing efforts and reinforced the social orientation of the budding movement in Nicaragua.[23] It also attracted support from social democratic governments and progressive foundations who, after the 1990 elections, shifted their support to nongovernmental organizations, including those, like *Xochiquetzal*, working on issues of gender and sexuality. The requirements for aid recipients in turn had consequences visible in the kind of formal structure—so unlike that of *Las Entendidas*—that *Xochiquetzal* adopted.

By the end of the 1980s, as the unifying revolutionary identity that had prevailed earlier in the decade began to disintegrate in the face of wartime hardships and an increasingly undemocratic style of party leadership, a small but significant autonomous feminist movement had developed. Its growth was due, in large part, to the contradictions between FSLN rhetoric and action on women's issues (see Chinchilla 1990, 1994; *Colectivo las Malinches* 1993; *Comité Nacional Feminista* 1993; Criquillion 1995; Murguialday 1990; Quandt 1993; Thayer 1994).[24] This growing women's movement provided a space where lesbians could meet and interact. Participating in a movement that questioned traditional sex roles opened the possibility of challenging traditional models of sexuality as well. However, while this movement fought for women's concerns, for the most part in the 1980s, lesbians' concerns were left unspoken. For the time being, even here, lesbians remained invisible.

Ironically, the FSLN's defeat at the polls gave a further impetus to both the feminist and the lesbian and gay movements, as Sandinista activists were freed from commitments to suppress what had been seen as particularistic needs in favor of defending an embattled revolutionary project. The party leadership was exposed as fallible, and newly legitimized critiques began to proliferate, including those of women, gays, and lesbians.

While in Costa Rica the feminist movement was firmly established by the time lesbians began to organize, in Nicaragua the two movements came into their own simultaneously, after a period of semiclandestine gestation under the revolutionary government. This created a situation of mutual influence, in which it was possible to put lesbian demands on the feminist agenda. Some women's organizations actively promoted public attention to gay and lesbian issues, through Gay Pride celebrations and other means, and there were fewer complaints of feminist homophobia among Nicaraguan than among Costa Rican activists. Overall, feminist support made it possible to forge links between concerns about the right to choose sexual partners and fundamental issues about the nature of sexuality, as well as a kind of collective "coming out" around these issues to the wider society.

In contrast with the Costa Rican experience, in building their movement, Nicaraguan lesbians encountered a polarized class structure, a history of wild swings in state–civil society relationships, culminating, in the 1990s, with an unstable and only partial hegemony, and the persistent hold of revolutionary ideology on the popular psyche. Together, these produced a lesbian movement with broad ambitions to reconstruct society in a new image.

In recent decades, a new collective phenomenon—the identity-based movement—has made its appearance on the analytical stage. An examination of lesbian movements in Central America, however, makes clear that the category of new social movements is not as monolithic as it is often made to seem. NSMs manifest a wide variety of expressions, from more outwardly oriented to more internally focused. This raises questions about not only why identity comes to be a concern, but what that identity consists of in each case, and why the movements inspired by these identities take the forms that they do.

While activist lesbians in both Nicaragua and Costa Rica shared a commitment to defining and defending identity, identity itself, as well as what it took to defend it, meant something different in each country. In Costa Rica, lesbian identity was a relatively private affair, embodied in the individual and an isolated community of peers who shared a culture and worldview. *Las Entendidas* sought to fortify individuals and the group against a hostile world and, when necessary, to defend their space against incursions. In Nicaragua, lesbians involved in *Nosotras* and *Xochiquetzal* defined themselves as members of a larger polity and as messengers for a new way of thinking about sexuality. Their goals included social, as well as personal, transformation, and their arenas of action extended to include the whole society.

Economic-structural factors created possibilities and/or foreclosed options for the movements in each country. However, the influences most crucial in defining how members conceived of both their own and their movement's identity were to be found in a broadly defined political space.

Organizing lesbian movements anywhere in Central America, and many other places, requires the will to defy deeply rooted notions of sexuality and personhood, and the courage to imagine different kinds of relationships. But social movements are built, and collective identities constructed, by particular people in particular locations at particular moments in history. These movements are, as Snow and Benford argue, "signifying agents" (1992, 136). What they signify and why, what they struggle for and how—these are questions that can only be answered by looking beyond global structural shifts and the confines of formal political institutions to the sociopolitical relationships that shape the lives of the human beings who make them.

Notes

Thanks to Michael Burawoy, Laura Enriquez, and Raka Ray for repeated and thorough readings of this work; to Amy Bank, Lissa Bell, Bill Bigelow, Norma Chinchilla, Ana Criquillion, Norm Diamond, Ana Quirós, and anonymous reviewers for their thoughtful comments on earlier drafts; and to the many colleagues and friends with whom I discussed the ideas presented here along the way. Thanks also to the International Gay and Lesbian Human Rights Commission for the use of their archives, to Maxine Downs and Judy Haier for invaluable logistical support, and, most of all, to the Central American lesbian activists who shared their struggles and their stories.

My work was supported by a National Science Foundation Graduate Research Fellowship and a fellowship from the Andrew W. Mellon Foundation. Any opinions, findings, conclusions, or recommendations expressed in this publication are those of the author and do not necessarily reflect the views of either foundation. Versions of this piece were presented at the XIX International Congress of the Latin American Studies Association in Washington, D.C., in September 1995, and at the Conference on Feminism(s) in Latin America and the Caribbean at the University of California at Berkeley in April 1996.

1. On the Costa Rican lesbian movement, see Carstensen (1992); Cruz (1995); *Las Entendidas* (1992); Madden Arias (1994); Mandell (1991); *II Encuentro Lésbico Feminista de América Latina y el Caribe* (1990); and Serrano (n.d.). *Las Entendidas* roughly translates as "those in the know" and is a term often used by lesbians in Latin America to refer to themselves.

2. On the Nicaraguan movement, see Bolt González (1995); *Breakthrough* (1992); *La Feminista* (1993); *Fuera del clóset* (1993); *Fundación Xochiquetzal* (n.d., 1992); and Merrett (1992). *Nosotras* is the feminine form of *we* in Spanish; Xochiquetzal (pronounced "so-chee-ketsahl") was the Aztec goddess of flowers and patron of domestic labors, as well as the guardian of courtesans.

3. This work is based on interviews with lesbian and feminist activists from Costa Rica and Nicaragua, as well as participant observation and an analysis of newsletters and other documents from the organizations described here. The research was conducted during two trips, the first to El Salvador to the VI Latin American and Caribbean Feminist Encounter in October and November 1993, and the second to Costa Rica and Nicaragua in June and July 1995.

4. Melucci was among the first to theorize the dynamics of collective identity construction. More recently, others have addressed this issue from various perspectives (Friedman and McAdam 1992; Gamson, W. A. 1992; Taylor and Whittier 1992).

5. Other critics of NSM theory argue that its supposedly distinct features appeared in earlier movements as well (D'Anieri, Ernst, and Kier 1990), and may be no more than the product of a stage in a cycle of development (Tarrow 1988).

6. Ferree (1987) is one of the few who asks why movements—in her case women's movements —in different countries take divergent approaches to similar issues.

7. Some authors, such as Melucci (1985) and Offe (1985), analyze the particular actors attracted to new European movements, but generalize across countries.

8. Rucht (1996) identifies class structure as part of the social context that influences movement form, but does not link it to movement orientation.

9. Ferree's (1987) explanatory factors go beyond narrowly defined political opportunities to include both historical political configurations and the discourses linked to them. Nevertheless, she continues to give substantial weight to the formal political realm.

10. All translations are my own, unless otherwise noted.

11. In fact, this may have been a wise calculation, given the intensity of the opposition that developed once word was out. Conference organizers faced site cancellations, condemnation from church leaders, and a decision by the Ministry of Government to deny visas to single

women seeking to enter the country for the period surrounding the Encounter. The final night of the event, participants were terrorized by a group of drunken would-be assailants outside the secluded estate where Encounter was being held. Nevertheless, the shock apparent in conference organizer accounts of these events suggests that a particular strategic vision, rather than fear of hostility, no matter how justified, dictated their initial conceptions of the Encounter.

12. A second, fairly short-lived organization, formed by a group of lesbians in their twenties, never really went beyond the first level described here. *Las Humanas* (The Female Humans) functioned primarily as a recreation and support group for members. It fell apart in 1992 when discussions were initiated about more public political activity within the lesbian and gay community (Serrano n.d.)

13. Although *Xochiquetzal* worked on behalf of lesbians and gays, I will treat it as part of the lesbian movement. The organization was directed by lesbians and played an important role in the coordinating of lesbian organizing. The collaboration between *Xochiquetzal* and *Nosotras* lasted until 1994, when the collective became independent. This recent development, as well as the founding in 1993 of another gay and lesbian group, *Neconi,* have yet to be analyzed, but may represent shifts in orientation based on the changing political panorama of postrevolutionary Nicaragua.

14. See Schifter Sikora (1989) for a history of the Costa Rican gay male movement, including the initial formation of a homosexual community. See D'Emilio (1983) for a discussion of how similar factors operated in the United States.

15. To illustrate, in his successful election campaign in 1986, Oscar Arias promised to bring about a "government with the soul of a woman." Once in office, he launched a widely publicized "feminist offensive" to put women's issues on the agenda. In 1988, the Arias administration proposed a "Law of Real Equality for Women" aimed at increasing women's political participation, as well as their access to social and economic rights (Saint-Germain 1993; Saint-Germain and Morgan 1991).

16. A month after the raid, an open letter to the ministers of health and security, criticizing government harassment of gays and calling instead for preventive measures to fight the disease, was published in the country's largest newspaper, signed by 150 prominent intellectuals, politicians, and professionals, gay and straight. The letter made full use of the political discourse of Costa Rican exceptionalism noted earlier, ending: "To begin to distinguish among Costa Ricans with slanderous labels is an attack on all our civic and democratic traditions and opens a dangerous door to arbitrariness and State terrorism" (Open letter published in *La Nación*, April 5, 1987).

A few days later, a sympathetic editorial echoed the letter. Despite the entrenched homophobia in Costa Rican society, at this particular political moment the Arias administration was vulnerable to the claims of marginalized groups. In an effort to restore the country's image as a neutral peacemaker and to prevent regional conflicts from spilling across borders, Arias had taken the lead in Central American peace negotiations and been awarded the Nobel Peace Prize. According to Schifter Sikora (1989), Arias's role in promoting the peace plan put the focus on Costa Rica as a supposed model of democracy for the region, and raised the level of international scrutiny of its human-rights record. It was an opportune moment for the fledgling gay and lesbian movement. A week after the open letter was published, the government suspended mandatory AIDS testing.

17. It is important to note that these efforts were often paternalistic and frequently resisted by the groups targeted for integration. For my argument, however, what is important is the way inclusiveness was established as a societal goal.

18. The Sandinistas seem to have taken the same approach to gay institutions as had the Cuban revolution earlier, classifying them as part of the corruption of the defeated dictatorship, along with casinos and prostitution rings, which the new Nicaraguan government also closed down.

19. In the first few years, the government appointed women to leadership positions in state institutions, banned advertising that exploited women's bodies, instituted the principle of equal pay for equal work, granted maternity leave, and launched the first agrarian reform in the hemisphere to recognize women as potential recipients of land. Women were encouraged to organize and the new women's association, AMNLAE, fought for and won legislative victories, including laws challenging patriarchal relations in the family and mandating sharing domestic work. In addition, women, who made up 60 percent of the country's poor, benefited from increased access to state-funded health services and educational facilities, as well as new job opportunities in the growing state sector.

20. Testimony to the group's commitment to the Sandinista state was its decision not to discuss the interrogations with anyone outside the organization. It was only after the FSLN's 1990 electoral loss that the news spread in the lesbian and gay community.

21. The law went into effect in spring 1994 after a prolonged legal battle over its constitutionality.

22. Earlier, in 1989, a nongovernmental organization known as *Nimehuatzin,* which was dedicated to AIDS prevention and treatment, had been established. Although it briefly served as a center for gays and lesbians, this function was later taken on by the groups described in this article.

23. Some of these gay and lesbian internationalists came on delegations or work brigades, such as the all-gay-and-lesbian Victoria Mercado Brigade, which came to work on a construction project in a low-income Managua neighborhood in 1985, or the San Francisco AIDS workers who came down for the International Health Colloquium in 1987. Others came to stay, integrating themselves into Nicaraguan institutions and neighborhoods. Many Nicaraguan gays and lesbians later involved in organizing efforts came into contact with these visitors and learned from them about gay and lesbian movements around the world (Zúñiga 1995).

24. As the 1980s progressed, Nicaraguan feminists became increasingly critical of Sandinista gender policy. The government's auspicious beginnings in the area of women's rights soon faded under the pressures of war and the machismo of most of the party leadership. Gender-specific concerns took a backseat to national priorities, and an ambitious feminist legislative campaign was shelved as potentially divisive. As early as 1983, a few Sandinista feminists, frustrated with the party's foot-dragging, began to launch their own independent projects—women's clinics, research teams, theater groups, and legal offices—and to make inroads in the press.

References

Andersson, S. 1993. The Fight Against Penal Code Article 204: Embracing a Sexual Right. *Barricada Internacional* 365:22–23.

Asamblea Nacional. 1992. *Ley 150: Ley de reformas al código penal.* Managua: Comisión Permanente Mujer-Niñez-Juventud y Familia.

Berrón, L. 1995. *¿Feminismo en Costa Rica? Testimonios, reflexiones, ensayos*. San José: Editorial Mujeres.

Blandón, M. 1993. *¿Por qué defendemos una sexualidad libre de prejuicios? La Feminista* 3:12–13.

Bolt González, M. 1995. Nicaragua. In *Unspoken Rules: Sexual Orientation and Women's Human Rights*, ed. R. Rosenbloom, 133–37. San Francisco: IGLHRC.

Breakthrough. 1992. De Ambiente: Interviews with Members of the Nicaraguan Movement of Lesbian Feminists and Gay Men. *Breakthrough* 16:17–23.

Buechler, S. M. 1995. New Social Movement Theories. *Sociological Quarterly* 36:441–64.

Candelaria Navas, M. 1985. *Los movimientos femeninos en Centroamérica: 1970–1983*. In *Movimientos populares en Centroamérica*, ed. D. Camacho and R. Menjívar, 200–236. San José: EDUCA.

Carstensen, J. 1992. Fighting Fear in Costa Rica. *Advocate* 595:36–37.

Chinchilla, N. 1990. Revolutionary Popular Feminism in Nicaragua: Articulating Class, Gender and National Sovereignty. *Gender and Society* 4:370–97.

———. 1994. Feminism, Revolution and Democratic Transitions in Nicaragua. In *The Women's Movement in Latin America: Participation and Democracy*, ed. J. Jaquette, 177–97. Boulder: Westview.

Colectivo las Malinches. 1993. *La experiencia de Nicaragua*. Paper presented at the *VI Encuentro Feminista de Latinoamérica y el Caribe*, Costa del Sol, El Salvador, Oct. 31.

Colectivo Pancha Carrasco. 1994. *Del feminismo popular al feminismo como opción vital política*. In *Lo que siempre quisiste saber sobre feminismo en Centroamérica y no te atreviste a preguntar*, ed. C. Murguialday and N. Vázquez. San Salvador: Centro Editorial de la Mujer.

Comité Nacional Feminista. 1993. *Comité Nacional Feminista: Procesos y desafíos*. Paper presented at the VI *Encuentro Feminista de Latinoamérica y el Caribe*, Costa del Sol, El Salvador, Oct. 31.

Criquillion, A. 1995. The Nicaraguan Women's Movement: Feminist Reflections from Within. In *The New Politics of Survival: Grassroots Movements in Central America*, ed. Minor Sinclair, 209–37. New York: Monthly Review Press.

Cruz, P. 1995. The Lesbian Feminist Group *Las Entendidas*. Paper presented at the XIX International Congress of the Latin American Studies Association, Washington, D.C., Sept. 30.

D'Anieri, P., C. Ernst, and E. Kier. 1990. New Social Movements in Historical Perspective. *Comparative Politics* 22:445–58.

della Porta, D., and D. Rucht. 1995. Left-Libertarian Movements in Context: A Comparison of Italy and West Germany, 1965–1990. In *The Politics of Social Protest: Comparative Perspectives on States and Social Movements*, ed. J. C. Jenkins and B. Klandermans, 229–72. Minneapolis: University of Minnesota Press.

D'Emilio, J. 1983. Capitalism and Gay Identity. In *Powers of Desire: The Politics of Sexuality*, ed. A. Snitow, C. Stansell, and S. Thompson, 100–113. New York: Monthly Review Press.

Escalante Herrera, A. C. 1990. *El subdesarrollo, la paz y la mujer en Costa Rica*. San José: Universidad de Costa Rica.

Escobar, A. 1992. Culture, Economics and Politics in Latin American Social Movements Theory and Research. In *The Making of Social Movements in Latin America: Identity, Strategy, and Democracy*, ed. A. Escobar and S. E. Alvarez, 62–85. Boulder: Westview Press.

Facio, A. 1988. *¿Igualdad? Mujer/Fempress* 80:9–10.

Ferguson, A. 1991. Lesbianism, Feminism and Empowerment in Nicaragua. *Socialist Review* 3–4:75–97.

Ferree, M. M. 1987. Equality and Autonomy: Feminist Politics in the United States and West Germany. In *The Women's Movements of the United States and Western Europe: Consciousness, Political Opportunity, and Public Policy*, ed. M. F. Katzenstein and C. McClurg Mueller, 172–95. Philadelphia: Temple University Press.

FLACSO. 1995. *Centroamérica en cifras, 1980–1992*. San José: FLACSO.

Friedman, D., and D. McAdam. 1992. Collective Identity and Activism: Networks, Choices, and the Life of a Social Movement. In *Frontiers in Social Movement Theory*, ed. A. D. Morris and C. McClurg Mueller, 156–73. New Haven: Yale University Press.

Fuera del clóset. 1993. *Derechos de lesbianas y homosexuales*. Fuera del clóset 0:15.

Fundación Xochiquetzal. 1992. *Campaña por una sexualidad libre de prejuicios*. Pamphlet, Managua.

———. n.d. *Fundación Xochiquetzal*. Brochure, Managua.

Gamson, J. 1989. Silence, Death, and the Invisible Enemy: AIDS Activism and Social Movement "Newness." *Social Problems* 36:351–67.

Gamson, W. A. 1992. The Social Psychology of Collective Action. In *Frontiers in Social Movement Theory*, ed. A. D. Morris and C. McClurg Mueller, 53–76. New Haven: Yale University Press.

García, A. I., and E. Gomáriz. 1989. *Mujeres centroamericanas: Efectos del conflicto*, vol. 2. San José: FLACSO.

González Suárez, M. 1988. *Estudios de la mujer: Conocimiento y cambio*. San José: EDUCA.

Gramsci, A. 1971. *Selections from the Prison Notebooks*. Trans. and ed. Q. Hoare and G. Nowell Smith. New York: International Publishers.

Habermas, J. 1984. *The Theory of Communicative Action*, vol. 1. Trans. T. McCarthy. Boston: Beacon Press.

Hunt, S. A., R. D. Benford, and D. A. Snow. 1994. Identity Fields: Framing Processes and the Social Construction of Movement Identities. In *New Social Movements: From Ideology to Identity*, ed. E. Laraña, H. Johnston, and J. R. Gusfield, 185–208. Philadelphia: Temple University Press.

II Encuentro Lésbico Feminista de América Latina y el Caribe. 1990. *Memoria de un encuentro inolvidable*. Costa Rica: II Encuentro Lésbico Feminista de América Latina y el Caribe.

Jenkins, J. C. 1983. Resource Mobilization Theory and the Study of Social Movements. *Annual Review of Sociology* 9:527–53.

Jiménez, A. 1990. Despite Hostility, Latina Lesbians Gather in Costa Rica. *Outlines* (June): 28.

Johnston, H., E. Laraña, and J. R. Gusfield. 1994. Identities, Grievances, and New Social Movements. In *New Social Movements: From Ideology to Identity*, ed. E. Laraña, H. Johnston, and J. R. Gusfield, 3–35. Philadelphia: Temple University Press.

Kampwirth, K. 1992. The Revolution Continues: Nicaraguan Women's Organizations under the UNO. Paper presented at the American Political Science Association Meeting, Chicago, September 3–6.

Kitschelt, H. P. 1986. Political Opportunity Structures and Political Protest: Anti-Nuclear Movements in Four Democracies. *British Journal of Political Science* 60:57–85.

Kriesi, H. 1995. The Political Opportunity Structure of New Social Movements: Its Impact on Their Mobilization. In *The Politics of Social Protest: Comparative Perspectives on States and*

Social Movements, ed. J. C. Jenkins and B. Klandermans, 167–98. Minneapolis: University of Minnesota Press.

———. 1996. The Organizational Structure of New Social Movements in a Political Context. In *Comparative Perspectives on Social Movements: Political Opportunities, Mobilizing Structures, and Cultural Framings*, ed. D. McAdam, J. D. McCarthy, and M. N. Zald, 152–84. Cambridge: Cambridge University Press.

Las Entendidas. 1988. Nicaragua Responds to AIDS. *Bulletin of the Nicaragua Information Center* (Dec.–Jan.): 1–4.

———. 1992. *Han pasado cinco años y todavía soñamos. Confidencial* (March): 8.

La Boletina. 1992. *Aunque Ud. no lo crea. La Boletina* 6:25–26.

La Feminista. 1993. *Crónicas de la 11 Jornada por una sexualidad libre de prejuicios. La Feminista* 3:6–16.

Madden Arias, R. M. 1994. *La experiencia de un grupo lésbico feminista en Costa Rica.* In *Lo que siempre quisiste saber sobre feminismo en Centroamérica y no te atreviste a preguntar*, ed. C. Murguialday and N. Vázquez. San Salvador: Centro Editorial de la Mujer.

Mandell, Z. 1991. *La lucha por las mentes de la gente: El conflicto de baja intensidad y la liberación lésbica en Costa Rica. Iconoclasta* 2:6–15.

Matthews, T. 1989. Without the Participation of Lesbians and Gays . . . There Is No Revolution. *NICCA Bulletin*, Sept.–Oct.

McAdam, D. 1982. *Political Process and the Development of Black Insurgency 1930–1970.* Chicago: University of Chicago Press.

McCarthy, J. D., and M. N. Zald. 1977. Resource Mobilization and Social Movements: A Partial Theory. *American Journal of Sociology* 82:1212–41.

Melucci A. 1980. The New Social Movements: A Theoretical Approach. *Social Science Information* 19:199–226.

———. 1985. The Symbolic Challenge of Contemporary Movements. *Social Research* 52:789–816.

———. 1994. A Strange Kind of Newness: What's "New" in New Social Movements? In *New Social Movements: From Ideology to Identity*, ed. E. Laraña, H. Johnston, and J. R. Gusfield, 101–30. Philadelphia: Temple University Press.

Merrett, J. 1992. Nicaraguan Gays Fight New Conservatism. *Advocate* 601:42–43.

Meyer, D. S., and S. Staggenborg. 1996. Movements, Countermovements, and the Structure of Political Opportunity. *American Journal of Sociology* 101:1628–60.

Meyer, D. S., and N. E. Whittier. 1994. Social Movement Spillover. *Social Problems* 41:277–98.

Murguialday, C. 1990. *Nicaragua, revolución y feminismo (1977–1989).* Madrid: Editorial Revolución.

Oberschall, A. 1973. *Social Conflict and Social Movements.* Englewood Cliffs, N.J.: Prentice-Hall.

Offe, C. 1985. New Social Movements: Challenging the Boundaries of Institutional Politics. *Social Research* 52:817–68.

Otis, J. 1991. Fight Against AIDS Started Nicaragua's "Gay Revolution." *San Francisco Chronicle* (November 15).

Palma, D. 1989. The State and Social Co-optation in Costa Rica. In *The Costa Rica Reader*, ed. M. Edelman and J. Kenen, 132–37. New York: Grove Weidenfeld.

Quandt, M. 1993. New Directions for Nicaraguan Feminists: "No Political Daddy Needed." *Against the Current* 8:23–25.

Quirós, A. 1991. *Construyendo una sociedad sin etiquetas.* Paper presented at the Gay Pride Day celebration, Managua, June 23.

Randall, M. 1992. *Gathering Rage: The Failure of Twentieth Century Revolutions to Develop a Feminist Agenda.* New York: Monthly Review Press.

Rucht, D. 1996. The Impact of National Contexts on Social Movement Structures: A Cross-Movement and Cross-National Comparison. In *Comparative Perspectives on Social Movements: Political Opportunities, Mobilizing Structures, and Cultural Framings,* ed. D. McAdam, J. D. McCarthy, and M. N. Zald, 152–84. Cambridge: Cambridge University Press.

Saint-Germain, M. A. 1993. Paths to Power of Women Legislators in Costa Rica and Nicaragua. *Women's Studies International Forum* 16:119–38.

Saint-Germain, M. A., and M. I. Morgan. 1991. Equality: Costa Rican Women Demand "The Real Thing." *Women and Politics* 2/3:23–75.

Schifter Sikora, J. 1989. *La formación de una contracultura: Homosexualismo y SIDA en Costa Rica.* San José: Guayacán.

Serrano Madrigal, E. 1994. Breve historia de las organizaciones formales de mujeres lesbianas en Costa Rica. Unpublished manuscript.

Silvestre, L. 1992. Editorial. *Las Entendidas* 14:1.

Slater, D. 1985. *New Social Movements and the State in Latin America.* Amsterdam: CEDLA.

Snow, D. A., and R. D. Benford. 1988. Ideology, Frame Resonance, and Participant Mobilization. In *From Structure to Action: Social Movement Participation Across Cultures,* ed. B. Klandermans, H. Kriesi, and S. Tarrow, 197–217. Greenwich, Conn.: JAI Press.

———. 1992. Master Frames and Cycles of Protest. In *Frontiers in Social Movement Theory,* ed. A. D. Morris and Carol McClurg Mueller, 133–55. New Haven: Yale University Press.

Solís, M. 1989. The Fragmentation and Disappearance of the Costa Rican Left. In *The Costa Rica Reader,* ed. M. Edelman and J. Kenen, 309–13. New York: Grove Weidenfeld.

Tarrow, S. 1988. Old Movements in New Cycles of Protest: The Career of an Italian Religious Community. In *From Structure to Action: Social Movement Participation Across Cultures,* ed. B. Klandermans, H. Kriesi, and S. Tarrow, 281–304. Greenwich, Conn.: JAI Press.

———. 1994. *Power in Movement: Social Movements, Collective Action and Politics.* Cambridge: Cambridge University Press.

Taylor, V. 1989. Social Movement Continuity: The Women's Movement in Abeyance. *American Sociological Review* 54:761–75.

Taylor, V., and L. J. Rupp. 1993. Women's Culture and Lesbian Feminist Activism: A Reconsideration of Cultural Feminism. *Signs* 19:32–61.

Taylor, V., and N. E. Whittier. 1992. Collective Identity in Social Movement Communities: Lesbian Feminist Mobilization. In *Frontiers in Social Movement Theory,* ed. A. D. Morris and C. McClurg Mueller, 104–29. New Haven: Yale University Press.

Thayer, M. 1994. After the Fall: The Nicaraguan Women's Movement in the 1990s. Paper presented at the XVIII International Congress of the Latin American Studies Association, Atlanta, March 10.

Tilly, C. 1978. *From Mobilization to Revolution.* Reading, Mass.: Addison-Wesley.

Touraine, A. 1985. An Introduction to the Study of Social Movements. *Social Research* 52:749–87.

———. 1988. *Return of the Actor: Social Theory in Postindustrial Society.* Trans. M. Godzich. Minneapolis: University of Minnesota Press.

Vilas, C. 1995. *Between Earthquakes and Volcanoes: Market, State and Revolutions in Central America.* Trans. T. Kuster. New York: Monthly Review Press.

Whittier, N. E. 1995. *Feminist Generations: The Persistence of the Radical Women's Movement.* Philadelphia: Temple University Press.

Zúñiga, J. 1995. La casa cincuenta. Unpublished Manuscript.

PART 3

LGBT Movements' Relations with
Political Parties and Legislators

Global Communities and Hybrid Cultures

Early Gay and Lesbian Electoral Activism in Brazil and Mexico

Rafael de la Dehesa

In 1982, gay and lesbian activists approached the electoral arena for the first time in Latin America's two most populous countries, Brazil and Mexico. Both elections took place under authoritarian regimes during protracted transitions to formal democracy. While parallel disputes over partisan alliances had bitterly split both movements, two quite different electoral strategies ultimately coalesced. In Mexico's presidential and congressional races, activists mobilized around gay and lesbian candidates, forging a tight electoral alliance with the Revolutionary Workers' Party (PRT), a small Trotskyist party that, while electorally insignificant, played an important role in both homosexual liberation and feminist movements at the time. In Brazil's gubernatorial and legislative elections, on the other hand, most activists ultimately eschewed such a close alignment with any single party, approaching candidates and parties across the ideological spectrum with a set of demands they pursued in legislatures after the race. Both movements' entry into the electoral arena reflected their embeddedness in broader movements for democratic change. Both also reflected certain activists' participation in the international arena, although in very different ways. This article does not seek to provide a full account of the conditions—both national and global—that permitted each electoral path to coalesce. Rather, it focuses on prevailing electoral strategies in 1982 as a window to explore how activists variably engaged in the global system, responding to national-level imperatives and constraints.[1]

Social movement theorists have paid growing attention to how international forces shape activism at the national level. Some scholars have argued that transnational institutions and norms regulating statecraft support national-level activists by expanding a repertoire of available tactics or providing the symbolic weight of precedent for particular demands (Keck and Sikkink 1998; Petchesky 2000; Ramirez, Soysal, and Shanaham 1997). Others have underscored how the changing global system—and specifically, in Latin America, a broad regional convergence on liberal democratic institutions and liberalized markets—has fundamentally transformed social movements, fostering their reconfiguration as narrowly defined interest groups or professionalized nongovernmental organizations (Alvarez 1997; Oxhorn 1998; Chalmers, Martin, and Piester 1997). I build on these insights while challenging two common if often tacit assumptions about processes of globalization: that the global system can be understood in the singular—after all, there is only one world—and that symbolic and political practices appropriated from transnational repertoires are directly translatable at the national level (Tarrow 1998; McAdam and Rucht 1993).

To this end, I draw on the work of anthropologist Néstor García Canclini and postcolonial theorists to suggest two alternative understandings of activists' engagement with the international arena (Appadurai 1996; Chatterjee 1993, 1998; García Canclini 1995a, 1995b). First, without denying the growing weight of international norms in regulating tactics of governance across countries, I argue that beneath the level of state and international institutions, there is a much more heterogeneous and contested terrain, populated by various "global communities" participating in the transnational arena in different ways, though those ways often overlap and compete. Second, I suggest that political and symbolic practices appropriated from this arena—whether at the level of social movement strategies or at the level of liberal democratic institutions, writ large—should not be read at face value, as uniform reproductions transplanted across national boundaries, but as embedded in societal settings; attention must therefore be paid to processes of selection and to how such practices respond to contextual needs, often through hybrid reinvention.

Specifically, I argue that in both Brazil and Mexico, the electoral strategies that coalesced in 1982 emerged not as the response of so-called unitary rational actors, but within internally heterogeneous "social movement fields" through processes marked as much by conflict as by consensus (Armstrong 2002). Ultimately, prevailing strategies reflected both their principal advocates' relative strength and influence within these fields and their variable articulations with global communities internationally. These advocates' positions, however, were not fortuitous, but rather were shaped by broader transitions from authoritarian rule and the nature of progressive coalitions mobilizing against that rule in each country. In effect, these national factors also constituted a process of selection at work, determining the relative salience and use of particular transnational practices.

The argument in this piece proceeds in four sections. In the first, I briefly discuss the emergence of organized movements, the 1982 elections, and gay and lesbian electoral participation in more detail. The second section maps debates on partisan alliances within both social movement fields and discusses their embeddedness in broader movements for democratic change. The third section draws on García Canclini's notions of global communities and hybrid cultures to examine how the principal advocates of each electoral path participated in the international arena in different ways, selectively appropriating, reinventing, and redeploying specific transnational practices to appeal to particular audiences at the national level. The conclusion draws theoretical implications for broader debates on transnationalism and democratization.

This piece draws on a broader comparative research project focusing on the relationship that gay, lesbian, bisexual, and transgender activists in each country have established with political parties. This work involved approximately fourteen months of fieldwork in each country, which included over one hundred interviews with activists, political party and state actors, movement allies, and opponents, again in each country, as well as extensive research in movement, state, and party archives. I should note that my use of the terminology *gay and lesbian* and *homosexual* is based on the political identities most activists used at the time, particularly in their state-directed efforts. This distinction is important to make in light of the literature on sexuality in Brazil and Mexico that emphasizes certain limitations of these categories and of identities structured around sexual object choice, a point to which I briefly return below (Carrillo 2002; Nuñez Noriega 1999; Carrier 1995; Parker 1999; Green 1999).

Coming Out and Into Elections

In both Brazil and Mexico, homosexual liberation movements emerged as public actors in the course of the 1970s. In Mexico City, a few intellectuals led by theater director Nancy Cárdenas founded the first group in the country, the Homosexual Liberation Front (FLH), in 1971 after a Sears Roebuck employee in the city was fired for his homosexuality. Like other groups to emerge in the decade (SexPol in 1974, Lesbos in 1977), the FLH met primarily as a consciousness-raising group, maintaining a limited public presence. It was only in 1978 that gay and lesbian activists participated in their first public marches in the country. On July 26, the Homosexual Revolutionary Action Front (FHAR), a new group largely comprising gay men and transvestites, named for a French homosexual liberation group known for its radical politics, participated in a march commemorating the Cuban Revolution. On October 2, it was joined by Lambda, a group of gay men and lesbians, and the lesbian group Oikabeth in a second march marking the tenth anniversary of the government massacre of student protestors in Mexico City's Tlatelolco Plaza. In both cases, activists thus marked not only a new public presence but a clear identification with the Left. The three new groups that emerged that year would spearhead an early wave of activism that would last until the mid-1980s.

The year 1978 also saw the emergence of an organized movement in Brazil. That year, a group of intellectuals and academics from Rio de Janeiro and São Paulo who had been brought together to collaborate on an anthology of Latin American gay fiction with San Francisco's Gay Sunshine Press, founded *Lampião da Esquina*, an alternative newspaper that sought to cover topics of interest to gays and lesbians in particular as well as other "minorities." The same year, activists in São Paulo founded *Somos*, the country's first homosexual liberation group. Two years later, most of the women in it split to form the country's first independent lesbian organization, the Autonomous Lesbian Feminist Group (GALF). By this time, the movement had reached an early peak, with over twenty groups throughout the country, though the Brazilian movement, like the Mexican movement, would suffer a decline by the mid-1980s. Between both movements' emergence as public actors in 1978 and activists' first broad-based efforts to approach the electoral arena four years later, the question of alliances with political parties had provoked quite heated debates.[2]

In both countries, the 1982 elections marked a significant moment not only for the movements but for a broader democratic opposition to authoritarian regimes. In Brazil, it was the first election to be held under the multiparty system with which the military government had replaced the earlier bipartisan system (which it too had installed) in an effort to divide an increasingly effective opposition. The deceptively renamed Social Democratic Party (PDS), which supported the military government, and the Party of the Brazilian Democratic Movement (PMDB), once the only opposition party, faced three other parties for the first time, including the Workers' Party (PT), created in 1980.

Along the lines of the gradual process of democratization taking place in Brazil, the Mexican government responded to social upheavals in the 1960s and 1970s through a combination of repression and piecemeal tinkering with electoral institutions to channel discontent. A series of electoral reforms, most notably the Federal Law for Political Organizations and Electoral Processes of 1977, had paved the way for the legal registration of a number of new political parties on the Left and their entry into electoral politics. By 1982, the United Socialist Party of Mexico (PSUM), the product of an alliance led by the former Communist Party, had resolutely embarked on the Left's electoral and parliamentary turn, becoming the second-largest opposition party. To the left, it faced the radical challenge of the recently registered Revolutionary Workers Party, PRT, whose presidential candidate that year, Rosario Ibarra de Piedra, the founder of the country's first human-rights organization, whose own son had been "disappeared" in the government's dirty war against the Left, captured some attention in the press as a symbolic challenge to the democratic ritual being enacted in the race. For broad opposition movements to authoritarian regimes, the elections revolved primarily around democratization. For many on the Left and in civil society, the challenge was to expand this political project beyond the narrowly institutional and into social, economic, and in this case, sexual terrain. The question for gay and lesbian activists was how.

In Mexico, activists' principal electoral vehicle was an alliance with the PRT and the creation of a gay and lesbian commission to support the party and its gay and lesbian candidates. In January 1982, activists from Mexico City's main groups held a press conference declaring their support for Rosario Ibarra and urging gay and lesbian citizens to vote. On February 20, the newly founded Rosario Ibarra Lesbian and Homosexual Support Committee (CLHARI) organized a meeting to discuss the election, attended by about 150 activists, at the Hotel Galeria Plaza.[3] CLHARI would launch six activists for federal deputy: three for the post and three as running mates. Two tickets ran in Mexico City and the other in Guadalajara, with one man and one woman on each.[4]

Participants in CLHARI approached the election not as a doorway into the state but as a stage for political theater to increase the movement's visibility and mobilize support. As candidate and Lambda activist Claudia Hinojosa declared at the fourth gay and lesbian pride march that year: "The CLHARI campaign is not a manual of electoral illusions because we never believed in the parliament as a liberatory space for gays and lesbians. We used the electoral arena to talk about ourselves, about the need to organize and participate."[5] Electoral activities thus focused largely on campaign rallies and public protests. In a subsequent assessment of the effort, one of its principal architects and another candidate, Max Mejia—a dual militant in Lambda and the PRT—cited among its achievements the establishment of new gay and lesbian groups in Nogales and Monclova, as well as in Mexico City; the organization of the first gay and lesbian public marches and the first Gay Cultural Week in Guadalajara; and activists' first experiment in mobilizing a nationwide campaign.[6]

The story was quite different in Brazil, where—despite most groups' relatively weak institutionalization and limited financial resources—activists approached the electoral arena more along the lines of an interest group (Rucht 1996). In this regard, most activists throughout the country rejected close alignment with any single party and approached candidates regardless, almost, of party affiliation or sexual orientation. While visibility was certainly a desired windfall, the strategy also sought political leaders' commitment to the movement's agenda after the race. Activists pursued this course through both local initiatives and what essentially became an informal, loosely coordinated nationwide network.

At the local level, for instance, the three main groups in São Paulo—the Autonomous Lesbian Feminist Group, or GALF, *Somos* São Paulo, and *Outra Coisa*— approved a joint strategy, resolving: (1) not to support any candidate or party for the election, to preserve the movement's autonomy; and (2) to present all the parties with a list of demands. Later, these three groups jointly organized a debate on homosexuality and feminism, attended by candidates across party lines. Activists from Rio de Janeiro's two main groups, *Auê* and *Somos* Rio de Janeiro , likewise presented a list of demands to candidates, regardless of party affiliation (Míccolis 1983).

Two tools became particularly important in coordinating local efforts. First, activists directed a questionnaire to all the political parties, calling on them to take a stand on homosexuality. Ultimately, only the Workers' Party, the PT, responded, having repudiated discrimination against homosexuals in its first national program. The second was a petition that the *Grupo Gay da Bahia* (GGB) had begun circulating the previous year at the annual conference of the Brazilian Society for Scientific Progress, and activists around the country circulated among candidates before the election. The petition called on the federal government to suspend the application in Brazil of Paragraph 302.0 of the World Health Organization's International Classification of Diseases (ICD), which at the time still categorized homosexuality under the rubric of "Deviance and Sexual Disorders." It also called for a constitutional guarantee to protect citizens from discrimination based on sexual orientation. In fact, the petition thus laid the foundation for activists' two principal legislative campaigns of the 1980s.

In short, while activists in Mexico pursued a New Left strategy of community organizing and visibility in the public square, Brazilian activists approached the election like an interest group, presenting a list of demands to candidates across party lines that they pursued through legislatures after the race. In one way or another, each strategy reflected its principal advocates' variable engagement with the international arena in response to local imperatives. Before considering the transnational dimension, therefore, I turn to how each strategy coalesced at the national level.

Mapping Social Movement Fields

The analytic category *social movement* can be deceptively unifying, obscuring organizational, strategic, and ideological differences, as well as differential access to resources and relations of power (Melucci 1996; Rucht 1996; Chalmers, Martin, and Piester 1997). The concept *field* offers one useful way to take this internal heterogeneity into account (Armstrong 2002). Setting aside the simplifying assumptions of rationalist approaches, which generally assume the identities and interests of social movements to be unitary and given, such an approach permits a closer understanding of the processes and tensions giving rise to particular strategies, including national actors' variable articulations with the global communities. After contextualizing the prevailing electoral strategies discussed above within social movement fields—fields within which what was "rational" was contested—I contend that national factors shaped not only the course of these debates but ultimately the salience and use of particular transnational practices.

The question of party alliances became, along with tensions between gay men and lesbians, the primary contention dividing both movements in the early 1980s. In both countries, the dispute pitted, on the one hand, "dual militants" linked to tiny Trotskyist parties—the Revolutionary Workers Party Homosexual Work Commission (CTH) in Mexico and the Gay Faction of the Socialist Convergence in Brazil—and, on the other, activists rallying around the banner of movement autonomy, variously defined. Within both social movement fields, dual militants advocated a socialist orientation and a broader commitment to the "general [i.e., class] struggle." More specifically, they pressed for the creation of nationwide umbrella organizations among activists, and alliances with other progressive sectors. Such parallel proposals in some sense reflected a united-front strategy borrowed from the partisan Left as well as the sector's vanguardist orientation, with its emphasis on consciousness raising through community organizing, both nationally and transnationally.

In Mexico City, for instance, CTH dual militants, most of whom were active in Lambda, promoted gay and lesbian activists' incorporation into progressive umbrella organizations like the National Front for the Liberation and Rights of Women, a feminist coalition, and the National Front Against Repression, Mexico's first human-rights coalition, led by Rosario Ibarra—both created in 1979. Within the movement, activists fostered alliances through the creation of umbrella organizations like the short-lived Front for Lesbian and Homosexual Civil and Political Rights. In a 1983 document, the CTH called the Front its top priority within the movement, "Precisely because it is through this Front . . . that we can intercede for the adoption of a feminist-socialist perspective in the HLM [Homosexual Liberation Movement]."[7] Of course, the Rosario Ibarra Lesbian and Homosexual Support Committee, or CLHARI, itself was perhaps the most extensive effort to encourage ties both among activists and across progressive sectors.

Broadly speaking, autonomists' rejection of dual militants in both countries revolved around the style and substance of what they advocated; in other words, around the closely related questions of *how* and *what* the homosexual liberation movement should represent. Regarding *how* it should represent, many activists who emphasized a disruption of social disciplines as a strategy for liberation saw leftist activists' proposals as a bureaucratization and containment of liberation politics that undermined this effort. Drawing on feminist critiques, many lesbian activists in particular regarded party politics as merely an extension of the state, inevitably tainted by its hierarchical structures of patriarchal authority. Regarding *what* it represents, the debate revolved largely around the trade-offs entailed by alliances: the degree to which activists should establish commitments to issues that many did not see as directly relevant to gays and lesbians, as well as the sometimes extensive sacrifices that potential allies often demanded in the movement's own agenda, particularly in terms of visibility. In Mexico City and São Paulo in particular (where the Socialist Convergence and the Workers' Party, the PT, were the strongest), the conflict between Trotskyist dual militants and autonomists bitterly divided movements in the early 1980s. Indeed, in Mexico City, the Rosario Ibarra Lesbian and Homosexual Support Committee, or CLHARI, produced a split that resulted in two gay and lesbian pride marches in 1982.

Despite these disputes, however, there were certain underlying assumptions on which both sectors agreed. First, both tended to prioritize a politics of visibility in the public square over state-directed efforts, although differences arose over the content of that politics. In essence, this reflected a common skepticism about the efficacy of existing state institutions in changing the relations of power structured around sexual stigma at the level of everyday life. Second, while autonomists generally resisted a close alliance with the partisan Left, most were nonetheless relatively sympathetic with its broader goals and tenets and suspicious of parties of the right and center.

In Brazil, a few activists who challenged both of these assumptions emerged. On the one hand, they underscored the importance of approaching the state and political elite, particularly given the limited resources of a relatively small movement. On the other, they regarded partisan alliances more instrumentally than ideologically, as a vehicle to press a narrowly defined, identity-specific, state-directed agenda. Two activists in particular played a significant role in advancing this approach. One was anthropologist Luiz Mott, who founded the *Grupo Gay da Bahia* in Salvador in 1980: today the GGB is Brazil's oldest surviving gay group and one of its most important. The second was João Antônio Mascarenhas, a lawyer and independent activist originally from Rio Grande do Sul but residing in Rio de Janeiro, who played a major role coordinating efforts among activists nationwide during the election and following up on them in legislatures afterward. Indeed, he became one of the principal architects of the movement's state-directed strategy during the 1980s.

Embedded Fields in Democratic Transitions

To understand the processes of conflict and alliance-building among these sectors that ultimately produced two different electoral paths in 1982, each movement's embeddedness within a broader polity and movement for democratic change must be taken into account. One crucial difference shaping the course of these debates was in the electoral arenas themselves. Most important, while formal democratization in both countries would proceed through piecemeal tinkering with electoral institutions in response to opposition gains, in 1982 this process had clearly proceeded further in Brazil. The military government had replaced the bipartisan system in response to the opposition's mounting effectiveness in eroding its hold on power through electoral gains. While a gradual electoral opening had already begun in Mexico, it would only gain significant momentum after the challenge by the National Democratic Front, led by Cuauhtémoc Cárdenas, in 1988. In 1982, the hegemonic party system dominated by the Institutional Revolutionary Party (PRI) was only beginning to erode, and beyond the rotation of elites linked to the ruling party, the function of elections was still largely a ritual performance of the regime's claims to democratic standing.[8]

Despite the undeniably tighter constraints in Mexico, it is important to keep in mind that alternative paths were not only thinkable but discussed in the country at the time. Beyond the debates mentioned above, one might ask more pointedly why the movement made little effort to approach the most important party on the Left that year—the United Socialist Party of Mexico, or PSUM—particularly in light of activists' inroads into the Mexican Communist Party, the PSUM's predecessor, which adopted a resolution on sexuality at its nineteenth congress in 1981 that was unprecedented for any communist party in the region, and that the PSUM retained in its program. Indeed, this very question was raised at the Gay and Lesbian Cultural Week in Mexico City that year, prompting considerable debate among activists on their relations with political parties.[9]

Similarly, in Brazil, alternative strategies were not only thinkable but tried. Indeed, a few gay candidates ran that year. While most steered clear of the movement and did not run as openly gay, São Paulo State Assemblyman João Baptista Breda (Workers' Party, or PT), formerly of the Brazilian Democratic Movement, was running for reelection. After being "outed" during his term, Breda had proven a public ally for activists by, for instance, calling for unprecedented public hearings on a wave of massive police raids targeting homosexuals. His campaign could certainly have proven an effective vehicle for the kind of symbolic politics taking place in Mexico, and indeed, a few activists linked to the PT did participate in it, suggesting that alternatives were possible. The campaign, however, never fostered the kind of broad-based mobilization represented by the Rosario Ibarra Lesbian and Homosexual Support Committee, or CLHARI, as reflected in the resolution by the city's principal groups refusing to endorse any candidate or party in order to preserve movement autonomy.

The different political opportunities opened by electoral institutions in each country undeniably shaped gay and lesbian electoral participation that year. Clearly, for instance, activists in Brazil would not have embraced a strategy of approaching candidates across party lines were there not candidates across party lines who could be approached. For the purposes of this discussion, however, I would highlight these arrangements' impacts less in terms of the electoral opportunities they opened and more in terms of how they shaped the political culture of the broader progressive alliances pressing for democratic change, alliances within which gay and lesbian social movement fields in each country emerged and participated.

In Mexico, the ruling party's authoritarian hold on power was opposed on the Right by the National Action Party (PAN) and on the Left by a relatively small community of social movement activists, progressive journalists and intellectuals, and leftist party militants. The PAN's roots in the Catholic Church and socially conservative base made it an unlikely ally for activists, and the divided opposition only reinforced the tight-knit though internally diverse ideological community on the left of the ruling party, within which debates on sexuality and gender emerged in the country, particularly in the capital, in the 1970s. In Brazil, on the other hand, the right-wing military regime was opposed by a broader, more ideologically diverse though more politically unified democratic front encompassing sectors ranging from Marxists to centrist liberals and even old-line political bosses, and although many gay and lesbian activists, including many autonomists, identified with the Left, the movement overall reflected this relatively greater ideological heterogeneity. In both cases, social movement fields' embeddedness within these variably constituted democratic alliances implied that the former to some extent shared the terms of debate and ideological range of the latter.

For dual militants in Mexico, this meant their audience was more receptive to a proposed electoral alliance with the Revolutionary Workers Party, or PRT, even among autonomists participating in the Rosario Ibarra Lesbian and Homosexual Support Committee, or CLHARI. In other words, dual militants retained a relatively greater influence in 1982. This responsiveness in part reflected the greater salience of Marxist discourse in the movement overall, and the relative prioritization of a symbolic logic of representation that was more about "presenting who we really are" (or would like to be) for the purposes of community organizing than about gaining a foothold in the state. Indeed, I would argue not only that this shared logic of symbolic representation reflected the movement's embeddedness within the Left, but also that it helps to explain activists' embrace of the PRT, even to the exclusion of other leftist parties less forthcoming in their support, as alliances had to be thick with ideological consistency, not thin with conjunctural strategy.

In contrast, while in Brazil dual militants linked to the Socialist Convergence had played a prominent role in the early years of the movement in São Paulo, their participation and influence had declined substantially by 1982. This decline in influence was partly due to the tiny party's reorientation away from the student sector and toward workers after it entered the PT as an organized current, but it also reflected the fallout of rancorous divisions surrounding the question of autonomy, culminating at the First Meeting of Brazilian Homosexuals in São Paulo in 1980. By 1981, the movement in that city had fractured into eight to ten tiny groups, some of which formed an umbrella collective called the Autonomous Homosexual Movement (MHA). The broader political fallout of the split was that the question of autonomy, which for many had become a standard against which to gauge activism, became even more significant. Indeed, Mascarenhas strongly criticized São Paulo activists' resolution on autonomy, arguing that their refusal to make any endorsements reflected a basic misunderstanding of the tit-for-tat nature of electoral politics under representative democracies: this division, again, underscores the heterogeneous perspectives of activists working together during that election.[10]

In short, the different electoral paths taken in 1982 grew out of processes of conflict and coalition building within heterogeneous social movement fields. In Brazil, many autonomists, while somewhat skeptical about the efficacy of state-directed efforts, worked together with activists advocating the importance of a state-directed agenda, giving these efforts geographic scope. In Mexico, the Homosexual Work Commission, or CTH—and the Left more broadly—retained a greater influence within the movement, garnering the support of many autonomists who participated in CLHARI.

I should note that the literature on social movements in the region has focused some attention on the question of autonomy (Vargas 2002; Ray and Korteweg 1999). While this literature has certainly contributed to our understanding of tensions within social movements and the potential pitfalls of alliances with parties or the state, it has often echoed debates among activists themselves on whether or under what circumstances autonomy is good or bad. The discussion above suggests that such qualifications may obscure a level of politics by presuming and naturalizing a unitary rationality that should itself be regarded as a political outcome. On the one hand, Brazilian and Mexican gay and lesbian activism in the early 1980s reveals *autonomy* as a contested category, even among its advocates. On the other, a review of this activism links the fate of competing "rationalities" to broader processes of formal democratization—processes with a transnational dimension that should likewise not be regarded as politically neutral. Prevailing electoral strategies in 1982 reflected their principal advocates' variable engagements with the international arena, and their conflicts produced variable imprints on globalization.

Global Communities and Hybrid Cultures

Focusing on the global market, García Canclini (1995a) posits an international system populated by multiple global communities of "interpretive consumers" of symbolic practices. He imagines one community consuming a given set of cultural products—Brahms, Cortázar, and Sting, for instance—and another consuming another set: Julio Iglesias, Alejandra Guzmán, and Venezuelan soap operas. Drawing on Pierre Bourdieu, such patterns of consumption can be linked to the variable constitution of these communities' status or identity. The implication is a certain identification of communities across national boundaries, constituted by the consumption of shared repertoires.

By noting the interpretive dimension of this consumption, however, García Canclini cautions against reading national actors as passive recipients of "foreign ideas." In this regard, he underscores not only a process of selection at work in the appropriation of particular practices, but also their reinvention in national settings. In these settings, "culture" is consequently understood as a hybrid terrain, where particular actors combine transnational practices with local ones, reinventing them to suit their needs. While blurring the line between the national and the foreign, this approach does not imply that either hybrid cultures or global communities are free of power asymmetries, exclusions, or conflicts. Rather, it provides an analytic approach that frames globalization as a contested and polyvalent process, focusing attention on what practices are appropriated, by whom, and to what effect.

From Social Movement Fields to Global Communities

Reading *consumption* broadly and expanding the notion of community to encompass production and political participation, we can imagine different sectors in social movement fields participating in the global system in different ways, though overlapping and competing. The electoral strategies that came to prevail in each country reflected their principal advocates' variable participation.

In Brazil, Mascarenhas and Mott, in particular, established early contacts with activists abroad that had a significant impact on the overall movements' subsequent trajectory. Particularly important on the eve of the election were contacts with European activists linked to the International Gay Association, or IGA (today, the International Lesbian and Gay Association [ILGA]). At the time, for instance, several groups in Brazil had established "twinning" partnerships with European counterparts, who provided information and, on rare occasions, limited funding.[11]

In a 1982 letter to an activist in Norway, Mascarenhas described his efforts to coordinate an informal nationwide network of activists, drawing on these contacts:

> I elaborated a very ambitious and time-consuming plan that I am carrying out. First, I translate the most important news I find in the newspapers I receive (*Gay News*, *Le Gai Pied*, *Fuori!*, the *Body Politic*), and I forward them to the eight [most active] gay groups, as some material I receive from European friends. Second, in long letters and long-distance calls, I discuss the goals I think most meaningful for the Brazilian Gay Liberation [sic] and I say how I suppose they can be attained, and what I imagine [are] the best tactics to employ. Third, I try to act as a cheerleader and a catalyst also to infuse them [with] hope and enthusiasm. Fourth, I strive to form a national gay circuit. To do this, the bits of news I receive from a group I send to others to foster a sense of belonging; besides, when I write to a group, I mail copies of my letter to the others, so all examine the same subject almost simultaneously.[12]

Interestingly, the letter went on to cite winning the support of the centrist Party of the Brazilian Democratic Movement, the PMDB, as a central goal that election year, one that more left-leaning activists clearly did not share. In another letter, for instance, Mascarenhas responded to a *Somos* São Paulo leader's repudiation of a fellow activist's joining the (reformist) party:

> As I see it, even for tactical reasons, we should hope that Brazilian *bichas* [queens] vote for more than one party, as we would thus have more congressmen seeking to please us. This, in fact, is what happens in the United States (where there are gay associations in the Democratic Party and gay associations in the Republican Party); in Great Britain (Labour and Conservative Parties); and in Holland, Denmark, Sweden, Norway, and Spain.[13]

The statement is noteworthy not only because it justifies a strategy of crossing party lines against more left-leaning sectors of the movement, but because it does so by citing a specific transnational model, in effect affirming the narrowly identitarian, rights-based approach of a liberal interest group.

Such linkages with the transnational arena were reflected more specifically in the two main tools used to coordinate electoral efforts that year among activists around the country: the survey sent to political parties, and the petition against the World Health Organization's ICD Paragraph 302.0. Mascarenhas received the former from the Scottish Homosexual Rights Group, which was linked to IGA, adapting it from a global survey of parties promoted by the association.[14] Mott began circulating the latter the same year that the Council of Europe approved Resolution 756, calling on the WHO to eliminate the reference. When the Federal Medical Council finally suspended the paragraph's application in the country in 1985, Mascarenhas noted that Brazil followed Denmark, Finland, Norway, and Sweden in this ruling.[15]

If the electoral strategy that came to prevail in Brazil reflected its principal advocates' participation in a global community in very specific ways, CLHARI, reflected its proponents' parallel participation in a different global community. Broadly, such a strategy cannot be understood without taking into account the transformation of the Marxist Left internationally, and the participation of the Revolutionary Workers Party, or PRT (and thus the Homosexual Work Commission, or CTH) within it. More specifically, in the late 1970s, the United Secretariat of the Fourth International, the Trotskyist current to which the PRT belonged, promoted a global discussion of women's liberation among its sections, leading to the adoption of a resolution on the issue in 1979. The resolution challenged many dogmas of the Marxist Left prevailing in Mexico (and internationally) at the time, notably the privileging of class as the engine driving history to the exclusion of the so-called specific struggles. The resolution instead framed the fight against sexism as a necessary component of a broader revolutionary project, concluded that women's liberation could not be reduced to class, and called for the elimination of laws criminalizing homosexuality and discrimination more broadly.[16]

Within the PRT, the resolution and the international debates that led up to it served as a major reference point for militants raising questions of gender and sexuality.

Hence in 1978, when a tiny group of militants first raised the idea of organizing the CTH, their founding document stated: "We have taken the initiative of this political work, departing from the experiences—of which, incidentally, we know little—of the Fourth International."[17] Likewise in 1983, when the party's Central Committee approved a resolution on homosexual liberation, unprecedented at the time for any party in Latin America, it rooted this position in the crisis of Marxism of the 1960s and the subsequent development of the Fourth International as "the first [international] Marxist organization not only to understand but to adopt the liberation of women and sexual liberation as an intrinsic part of the socialist revolution."[18] To the extent, therefore, that an international current incorporated issues of gender and sexuality as issues meriting attention on their own terms, albeit within a broader project of social transformation, national actors could draw on these developments to bolster their position at home.

From Global Communities to Hybrid Cultures

But the deployment of transnational practices should not be read as a mere replication of "foreign" ideas. Rather, attention must be paid not only to the selection of particular practices but to their specific applications and possible reinventions at the national level. Moreover, the dynamics of "globalization" at work in the early 1980s were occurring at two significant and interrelated levels. If on the one hand, we find certain tools for social-movement activism crossing national boundaries, these developments must be read in the context of a broader regional convergence on liberal democratic institutional norms as "the only game in town" (Linz and Stepan 1996). At both levels, one should be attentive to the uses, transformations, and limitations of transnational practices in national settings.

Again, gay and lesbian activism emerged in the course of formal democratic transitions in both countries. In different ways, the electoral processes under way in 1982 were thus constrained not just by institutional shortfalls—electoral fraud, for instance—but by the relatively shallow penetration of liberal democratic institutions more generally, given their embeddedness in highly skewed arrangements of power in the private sphere. Indeed, perhaps one of the most remarkable aspects of early gay and lesbian activism in both countries was that activists were fully aware of these limitations but were nonetheless able to take advantage of the institutional opportunities available to them, if at times for strictly symbolic ends.

Interestingly, the possibilities and limitations of the liberal democratic institutions being implanted in Brazil were addressed quite explicitly by one of the chief architects of the movement's state-directed efforts. At around the time of the election, Mascarenhas directly responded to the assertion that the experiences of gay and lesbian movements in advanced industrial countries were irrelevant to Brazil, given its vastly different socioeconomic reality. He countered that those making such arguments were forgetting the crucial reality of class in Brazil, which made these experiences relevant, at least for some. Specifically, recalling historic arguments about "dual societies" in the country, Mascarenhas mentioned two important distinctions between the roughly 10 percent of the population comprising the middle and upper class and the rest of society.

First, he noted differences at the level of sexual identity itself. In an article entitled "The Third World and the Gay Liberation Movement" that he prepared for the Third Annual IGA Conference in 1981, Mascarenhas discussed differences in the organization of sexual practices in the country and the variable identities, prohibitions, and permissions attached to homosexuals across class lines:

> Prejudices against homosexuals are a middle-class phenomenon in Brazil. The upper class does not care about them, and the working class's sexual behavior, at least in large cities, is completely different. Very often, single urban workers are bisexual, and maintain a very masculine demeanor. When they have homosexual relations, with some frequency, they play both roles, but they do not think that this way of behaving makes them homosexuals. For them, homosexuals are those who have an effeminate demeanor. I would say that Brazilian workers have a truly revolutionary lifestyle . . . For them, sex is something that you do and appreciate; not something to discuss. It therefore makes no sense for them to join gay liberation . . . The only people in Brazil who might therefore be interested in the movement come from the middle class, those who suffer deeply from stigma and whose income allows them to face the problem politically.[19]

The Brazilian middle class, he went on to argue, shared more in common with the European middle class than the regions' respective working classes, and it was precisely consumption of this shared cultural repertoire that made the latter's experiences relevant. But class divisions cut across more than sexual identity. Indeed, in Mascarenhas's view, they cut across the very model of liberal democracy taking root in the nation, where the specter of a dual society again emerged. The 90 percent of Brazilians who were working class and poor, he wrote an activist in England, "do not bother with existing laws, as they [see] them—and correctly—as products of a world they do not share. Sad but true."[20]

The middle and upper classes' participation in the project of liberal modernity, whatever its limitations, also explained the strategic relevance of an international tool kit in 1982. Noting the elite origins of the country's political leaders, Mascarenhas underscored two strategic uses of this shared repertoire in appealing to them. First, it offered politicians the symbolic security of precedent: "For Brazilian politicians, homosexuality is at best a delicate matter; at worse, a burning one. They fear mainly to be ridiculed for endorsing gay rights, and they feel relieved when they see they are not supposed to do anything new, as before them, Oslo, Strasbourg, and Paris took the initiative." Second, he argued, Brazilian political elites' participation, albeit subordinate participation, in a transnational liberal project laid the groundwork for an effective counterstigmatizing discourse: "These people are quite aware of human rights, even when they do not like to hear about them, and they do not like to be considered backward. For this bracket, Europe is very important as they suffer what we call 'cultural colonialism,' and of course Brazilian gays must take advantage of this."[21]

Many activists at the time would no doubt have balked at such an assessment of the movement's limitations, and indeed, a number of questions can be raised about Mascarenhas's arguments. Undoubtedly, for instance, he underestimated the sexual stigma experienced outside the middle class, though that sigma was sometimes organized around different constructions of sexual identities, and indeed class differences were reflected within the movement itself at the time. The two main groups in Rio de Janeiro, *Auê* and *Somos* Rio de Janeiro, for instance, met in the northern and southern zones of the city, respectively, and reflected the mostly working- and middle-class populations of each. Likewise, whatever the undeniable limitations of the country's formal democratic institutions, the results of the movement's state-directed efforts (like other aspects of Brazilian democracy) have in some instances penetrated beyond the 10 percent Mascarenhas envisioned. Still, it is worth underscoring that one of the principal architects of the movement's state-directed strategy in the 1980s understood, on the one hand, the contextual limitations of the formal democratic model being implanted in the country and thus of his own efforts, and on the other, this model's symbolic appeal as rooted in a transnational project of liberal modernity, an appeal that could be turned to the movement's advantage by playing on the political elite's aspirations to the status it conferred.

With regard to Mexico, the salient difference in each movement's relationship with the transnational arena has less to do with the question of access to international repertoires, which at least some activists in both countries had, and more to do with what was selectively drawn from these repertoires and how it was transformed and applied. In this regard, one former PRT Central Committee member who spearheaded early debates on gender in the party recalls the importance of the Fourth International in pressing for an opening in Mexico:

> The International was a very important factor in our achieving a feminist position in the party as a party [and in] achieving a position in favor of gay liberation as a party. And this has to do with two things. It is not only the ideological strength of the International, and its importance as a reference point, but the fact that large sections of the International ... had mass women's movements going on [in their countries], which we did not have ... We didn't have that bottom up push that said: look, you asshole, you might think this isn't important but we have 50 women outside screaming, so you better listen. We didn't have that. We had the International, which the [Communist Party] didn't have.[22]

Again, activists turned to a transnational repertoire for a stock of symbolic capital to support their claims. But here too, this use was selective, responding to national actors' specific needs in appealing to particular audiences, and must be read in this light. After all, while the United Secretariat had a number of sections around the world, not all of them broached discussions on gender and sexuality. One factor that made the PRT different was that—not unlike other radical Left parties around the world, including the Socialist Convergence—it reflected a generational shift within the Left and the growing importance of students as leftist cadres. While certainly not without differences, students and youth activists would become particularly important allies for gay and lesbian activists within the Mexican Left during the decade, in part because both sectors were primary targets of the massive police raids and official abuses commonplace throughout the country at the time. In this context, the Fourth International became an important tool because it responded to the specific needs of a current within the PRT that was appealing to a new and more receptive audience. Given the absence of a mass movement, its salience as a legitimizing frame was further magnified.

Finally, while the Communist Party lacked the Fourth International as a reference, it is perhaps worth noting that a parallel story can be told regarding its own, more limited opening to homosexual liberation, which similarly drew on changes in the international Marxist Left. The question was initially raised in the new party magazine *El Machete.* Its first issue, appearing in May 1980, included an interview on feminism and homosexuality with the noted public intellectual Carlos Monsiváis, who had already played a central role in raising debates on sexual politics in the country, particularly within the Left. The militants linked to *El Machete* comprised a sector of the party associated with Eurocommunism and backed by longtime general secretary, Arnoldo Martínez Verdugo. They later published several other stories on homosexual liberation and successfully pressed for a number of important changes at the party's nineteenth congress, including its resolution on sexuality. In Eurocommunism, they found tools to press for the party's electoral and parliamentary turn and for a concomitant opening to "specific struggles," contrary to more orthodox currents. In short, while Brazilian activists found tools in advanced capitalist countries they could use to appeal to the aspirations of a political elite across party lines, Mexican activists participated within a tight-knit community, more narrowly identified with the international Left, which made relevant an entirely different set of tools and discourses.

The Broader Implications

Politically, the electoral strategies that came to prevail in 1982 established significant precedents for both movements. In Mexico, while activists have certainly tried other tactics in subsequent races, they have continued to rely more heavily on launching often symbolic candidacies with small Left parties. In 1997, this symbolic-candidacy strategy took a new turn when Patria Jiménez was elected the first openly lesbian federal deputy in Latin America, running with the Party of the Democratic Revolution (PRD). Notably, Jiménez had been a CLHARI candidate, and she attained her position on the PRD candidate list through its electoral alliance with the PRT. In Brazil, at least fifteen candidates elected in 1982 had indicated some degree of support for the movement during the race.[23] Activists soon began approaching these candidates as early doorways into the state, initiating a long trajectory of legislative activism. They have tried other tactics in later races, but, like their Mexican counterparts, they have continued to rely more on building networks of sympathizers, approaching candidates across party lines and regardless of sexual orientation.

This consideration of Brazilian and Mexican activism contributes to broader debates on transnationalism and social movement activism in the context of democratization. Activists can participate in the transnational arena in different and even competing ways, and national-level factors can determine the relative salience and use of particular transnational practices. Departing from approaches that frame the global system in the singular, we can imagine a transnational arena that includes a number of competing, though overlapping, global communities and processes of selection and adaptation at the national level, forming variable imprints on globalization. This understanding of the global system, moreover, opens new possibilities for a critical understanding of Latin America's participation in a project of liberal modernity and of social movement activism in democratic transitions. Two final points can be made in this regard.

First, drawing on García Canclini's suggestion that participation in global communities can be constitutive of status or identity, the two electoral strategies that prevailed in 1982 ultimately framed the collective political identity of gays and lesbians in two very different ways: in Mexico, as a potentially revolutionary agent with a necessary commitment to broader structural change; in Brazil, as a rights-bearing minority group meriting representation in the liberal state. The point is worth making in light of the relationship sometimes drawn between the transition from Keynesian to neoliberal economic models and the transition from class-based, corporatist to more atomized forms of representation, including social movements, in the region (Oxhorn 1998; Chalmers, Martin, and Piester 1997). Thinking of Brazil in particular, the discussion above suggests that representation through the liberal formula of "rights-bearing individuals" preceded neoliberalism, and is more closely associated with political rather than economic transformations. Needless to say, in the context of broader regime transitions and with the growing weight of transnational state regimes, the positions of global communities too have changed, both internationally and nationally, but an understanding of these processes as occurring in a plural and contested terrain avoids reification of their effects as politically neutral or "rational."

Second, extending the notion of cultural hybridity to the political arena allows us to consider liberal democratic institutions' embeddedness in variably constituted relations of power in the private sphere. Optimistically, this discussion suggests a role for formal democratic institutions, even when ineffective in terms of their own purported ends. It is a symbolic role that the partisan opposition in both countries clearly used to advantage in gradually eroding the "legitimacy" of authoritarian regimes, as the literature on democratization in the region has widely documented. A consideration of homosexual liberation activism in Mexico and Brazil points to a parallel and embedded process at the level of social movement activism and a fledgling gay and lesbian politics: to the extent that elections in regime transitions defined the symbolic boundaries of "legitimate" public debate, these boundaries could still be contested.

Pessimistically, however, the discussion points not only to possibilities but more importantly to limitations. In this regard, whatever qualifications one might make to Mascarenhas's arguments about class constraints limiting the rule of law and the effective application of human rights standards in Brazil, a sizeable literature suggests that these arguments contain more than a grain of truth. Along these lines, for instance, political scientist Guillermo O'Donnell (1999) has argued that the penetration of democracy in the region (and outside it) can itself be "mapped" on a sort of symbolic field through the institutional prism of citizenship, with areas marked in one color on this topography implying the full enjoyment of the rights of citizenship, and those marked in another, that these rights exist only on paper. Extending this discussion to social movement activism, an examination of Brazilian and Mexican activism thus suggests how activists' state-directed efforts might, perhaps not surprisingly, be conditioned by these maps.

Notes

I would like to thank Jorge Domínguez, Grace Mitchell, Jean Halley, and Salvador Vidal-Ortiz for their very helpful suggestions on earlier incarnations of this work.

1. As social movement activists approach the electoral arena, they can draw on a repertoire of tactics, including running for office, seeking commitments from candidates or party leaders, organizing debates between candidates, and participating in campaigns. Here, I refer to the variable use of such tactics as "electoral strategies" or "electoral activism" (McCarthy, Smith, and Zald 1996).

2. While 1982 marked the first time broad-based movements engaged in electoral activism in Brazil or Mexico, it was not the first election in which the question of homosexuality was raised. In 1978, a single candidate ran unsuccessfully for federal deputy in Pernambuco, Brazil, on a platform of homosexual rights. In Mexico, Víctor Amezcua Fragoso, the manager of a

transvestite theater troupe, unsuccessfully sought a candidacy for federal deputy with the ruling PRI (Institutional Revolutionary Party) in 1979, with actress Verónica Castro as his running mate.

3. J. Martín Moreno Durán, "*Apoyo del 'tercer sexo' a la candidata del PRT*," *La Prensa*, January 28, 1982; Leslie Serna, "*'Estaré donde sea que haya un oprimido': RIP*," *Bandera Socialista*, no. 220, March 1, 1982.

4. Another gay candidate also ran for federal deputy that year, with the newly created Social Democratic Party, also Trotskyist, but failed to mobilize much support within the movement.

5. Jorge Aguilera, "*Cuarta marcha: 'Estamos en todas partes,'*" *La cultura en México*, July 21, 1982.

6. Max Mejia, "*Un primer balance de CLHARI*," *Bandera Socialista*, no. 236, August 30, 1982.

7. PRT (Comisión de Trabajo Homosexual), "*La línea del PRT en el movimiento de liberación homosexual y su instrumentación*," PRT (Comisión de Trabajo Homosexual), 1983.

8. In Brazil's elections for the Federal Chamber of Deputies, for instance, the military's PDS and the opposition, PMDB, would capture 43.2 percent and 43 percent of the valid votes, respectively, with the rest going to the populist Democratic Labor Party (PDT, 5.8 percent); the resurrected Brazilian Labor Party (PTB, 4.5 percent); and the PT (3.6 percent). By the admittedly questionable official results in Mexico, the PRI and the PAN (National Action Party) captured 69.3 percent and 17.5 percent of the votes for the federal chamber, respectively. The PSUM became the second-largest opposition party, garnering 4.4 percent of the votes, with remaining votes distributed among several smaller parties, including 1.3 percent for the PRT (Brazil: 1982 Legislative Election, http://www.georgetown.edu; and Mexico: Resultados Electorales para la Cámara de Diputados, 1961–91 http://www.georgetown.edu/pdba/Elecdata/Mexico/mex61-91.html. *Political Database of the Americas,* Georgetown University.)

9. Braulio Peralta, "*José Ramón Enríquez: Debe ser autónomo el movimiento homosexual*," *Uno más uno*, June 24, 1982.

10. João Antônio Mascarenhas, Rio de Janeiro, to Antonio Carlos Tosta, São Paulo, 6 July 1982, no. 228/82, Edgard Leuenroth Archive, University of Campinas (hereafter referred to as AEL-UNICAMP).

11. João Antônio Mascarenhas, Rio de Janeiro, to gay and lesbian groups, 26 December 1981, AEL-UNICAMP.

12. João Antônio Mascarenhas, Rio de Janeiro, to Karen-Christine Friele, Oslo, Norway, 29 March 1982, no. 160/82, AEL-UNICAMP.

13. João Antônio Mascarenhas, Rio de Janeiro, to Luzenário Cruz, São Paulo, 21 December 1981, AEL/UNICAMP.

14. International Gay Association (IGA), "Political Parties: World Survey 1981," AEL-UNICAMP; João Antônio Mascarenhas, Rio de Janeiro, to Peter Ashman, Essex, England, 26 January 1982, no. 51/82, AEL-UNICAMP.

15. João Antônio Mascarenhas, "*Comunicado no. 1/85 do Triângulo Rosa: A campanha contra o código 302.0, histórico e consequências*," Rio de Janeiro, 25 March 1985, AEL-UNICAMP.

16. "*Resolución del Secretario Unificado de la IVa: Revolución socialista y la lucha por la liberación de la mujer*," Special Issue, *Folletos Bandera Socialista* 59 (April 1978).

17. PRT and Lamda members, untitled document, 1978, mimeo, in author's possession.

18. Partido Revolucionario de los Trabajadores. 1983. *"Liberación homosexual: Un análisis marxista."* Special issue, *Folletos Bandera Socialista* 91.

19. João Antônio Mascarenhas, *"O terceiro mundo e o movimento de liberação gay,"* paper presented at the IGA Third Annual Conference; IGA Newsletter 81–1, Original manuscript, Grupo Gay da Bahia Archive, Salvador, Bahia.

20. João Antônio Mascarenhas, Rio de Janeiro, to Peter Ashman, Essex, England, 5 April 1982, no. 169/82, AEL-UNICAMP.

21. Ibid.

22. Heather Dashner (former PRT Central Committee member), in interview with author, Mexico City, July 11, 2000.

23. João Antônio Mascarenhas, Rio de Janeiro, Circular, 8 December 1982, no. 380/82, AEL-UNICAMP.

References

Alvarez, S. E. 1997. *Articulación y transnacionalización de los feminismos latinoamericanos. Debate feminista* 15:146–70.

Appadurai, A. 1996. *Modernity at Large: Cultural Dimensions of Globalization.* Minneapolis: University of Minnesota Press.

Armstrong, E. A. 2002. *Forging Gay Identities: Organizing Sexuality in San Francisco, 1950–1994.* Chicago: University of Chicago Press.

Carrier, J. 1995. *De los Otros: Intimacy and Homosexuality among Mexican Men.* New York: Columbia University Press.

Carrillo, H. 2002. *The Night Is Young: Sexuality in Mexico in the Time of AIDS.* Chicago: Chicago University Press.

Chalmers, D. A., S. B. Martin, and K. Piester. 1997. Associative Networks: New Structures of Representation for the Popular Sectors? In *The New Politics of Inequality in Latin America: Rethinking Participation and Representation,* ed. D. A. Chalmers, C. M. Vilas, K. Hite, S. B. Martin, K. Piester, and M. Segarra, 543–82. Oxford: Oxford University Press.

Chatterjee, P. 1993. *The Nation and Its Fragments: Colonial and Postcolonial Histories.* Princeton: Princeton University Press.

———. 1998. Beyond the Nation? Or within? *Social Text* 16(3):57–69.

García Canclini, N. 1995a. *Consumidores y ciudadanos: Conflictos multiculturales de la globalización.* Mexico City: Editorial Grijalbo, S. A. de C. V.

———. 1995b. *Hybrid Cultures: Strategies for Entering and Leaving Modernity.* Trans. C. Chiappari and S. L. López. Minneapolis: University of Minnesota Press.

Green, J. N. 1999. *Beyond Carnival: Male Homosexuality in Twentieth Century Brazil.* Chicago: University of Chicago Press.

Keck, M., and K. Sikkink. 1998. *Activists beyond Borders: Advocacy Networks in International Politics.* Ithaca, N.Y.: Cornell University Press.

Linz, J., and A. Stepan. 1996. *Problems of Democratic Transitions and Consolidations: Southern Europe, South America, and Post-Communist Europe.* Baltimore: Johns Hopkins University Press.

McAdam, D., and D. Rucht. 1993. The Cross-National Diffusion of Movement Ideas. *The Annals of the American Academy of Political and Social Science* 528:56–74.

McCarthy, J., J. Smith, and M. N. Zald. 1996. Accessing Public, Media, Electoral, and Governmental Agendas. In *Comparative Perspectives on Social Movements: Political Opportunities, Mobilizing Structures, and Cultural Framings*, ed. D. McAdam, J. D. McCarthy, and M. N. Zald, 291–311. New York: Cambridge University Press.

Melucci, A. 1996. *Challenging Codes: Collective Action in the Information Age*. New York: Cambridge University Press.

Míccolis, L. 1983. *Prazer, gênero de primeira necesidade*. In *Jacarés e Lobisomens: Dois ensaios sobre a homossexualidade*, ed. L. Míccolis and H. Daniel, 69–133. Rio de Janeiro: Achiamé.

Núñez Noriega, G. 1999. *Sexo entre varones: Poder y resistencia en el campo sexual*. Mexico City: Universidad Autónoma Metropolitana de México.

O'Donnell, G. 1999. On the State, Democratization, and Some Conceptual Problems: A Latin American View with Glances at Some Postcommunist Countries. In *Counterpoints: Selected Essays on Authoritarianism and Democratization*, ed. G. O'Donnell, 133–57. Notre Dame: University of Notre Dame Press.

Oxhorn, P. D. 1998. Is the Century of Corporatism Over?: Neoliberalism and the Rise of Neopluralism. In *What Kind of Democracy? What Kind of Market?: Latin America in the Age of Neoliberalism*, ed. P. D. Oxhorn and G. Ducatenzeiler, 195–217. University Park, Pa.: Penn State University Press.

Parker, R. 1999. *Beneath the Equator: Cultures of Desire, Male Homosexuality, and Emerging Gay Communities in Brazil*. New York: Routledge.

Petchesky, R. 2000. Sexual Rights: Inventing a Concept, Mapping an International Practice. In *Framing the Sexual Subject: The Politics of Gender, Sexuality, and Power*, ed. R. Parker, M. R. Barbosa, and P. Aggleton, 81–103. Berkeley: University of California Press.

Ramirez, F. O., Y. Soysal, and S. Shanaham. 1997. The Changing Logic of Political Citizenship: Cross-National Acquisition of Women's Suffrage Rights, 1890 to 1990. *American Sociological Review* 65(5):735–45.

Ray, R., and A. C. Korteweg. 1999. Women's Movements in the Third World: Identity, Mobilization, and Autonomy. *Annual Review of Sociology* 25:47–71.

Rucht, D. 1996. The Impact of National Contexts on Social Movement Structures: A Cross-Movement and Cross-National Comparison. In *Comparative Perspectives on Social Movements: Political Opportunities, Mobilizing Structures, and Cultural Framings*, ed. D. McAdam, J. D. McCarthy, and M. N. Zald, 185–204. New York: Cambridge University Press.

Tarrow, S. 1998. Fishnets, Internets, and Catnets: Globalization and Transnational Collective Action. In *Challenging Authority: The Historical Study of Contentious Politics*, ed. M. P. Hanagan, L. P. Moch, and W. T. Brake, 228–44. Minneapolis: University of Minnesota Press.

Vargas, V. 2002. The Struggle by Latin American Feminisms for Rights and Autonomy. In *Gender and the Politics of Rights and Democracy in Latin America*, ed. N. Craske and M. Molyneux, 199–221. Houndsmills, Basingstoke, Hampshire: Palgrave.

Social Movements and Political Parties

Gays, Lesbians, and *Travestis* and the Struggle for Inclusion in Brazil

Juan P. Marsiaj

THE QUESTION of how social movements affect political institutions and, more broadly, promote social and political change has received significant scholarly attention in the recent past. The relationship between social movements, political parties, and the state is a complex one, working in multiple directions and across different dimensions simultaneously. As outlined in political opportunity and political process models, while social movements can have an impact on other mainstream political institutions through protest action or more direct engagement with these institutions, change in the configuration of the institutional framework may also generate new opportunities for those social movements (and perhaps their opponents) (Tarrow 1993; Tarrow 1996; Tarrow 1998; Kitschelt 1986; Tilly 1978; Engel 2001). [...]

The democratization process in Brazil, as in other Latin American countries, brought about a liberalization of the political party system. Since political parties are key actors in the struggle for state power and in struggles for the representation of groups in society, examining their relationship with social movements provides a more thorough comprehension of the opportunities the democratization process makes available to marginalized groups.[1] As Scott Mainwaring (1999) points out, even in cases where parties are weak, as he believes to be the case in Brazil, their study is important for a proper analysis of the prospects for democratization. [...]

Political parties are also important for analyzing which groups have influence over and are included in the decision-making processes that define public policy and legislation. These policies and laws, in turn, are key to the protection of marginalized groups against discrimination and abuses and to the guarantee of their human rights. Other paths to inclusion are also available to social movements representing marginalized groups. [...] Nevertheless, as the development of the women's movement in Brazil indicates (Alvarez 1990), political parties should not be dismissed as a vehicle for change.

I address these issues by asking how political parties matter for the struggle for inclusion of gays, lesbians, and *travestis* (GLTs) in the political decision-making process in Brazil.[2] Are parties an effective vehicle for social and political change for sexual minorities? How is support for GLT rights distributed along the Left–Right spectrum, and what are the main reasons behind this pattern of support? While political parties are not the sole or main avenue for change open to GLTs in Brazil, they play a significant role in the recognition and visibility of sexual minorities as political actors in the political field and in promoting policy and legislative change in favor of GLTs.

Leftist parties show a greater level of support for GLT rights, while right-wing parties tend to be opposed to them, with centrist parties falling somewhere in between, adopting a more ambiguous position. Institutional factors (the existence of institutional spaces for GLTs in leftist parties) and the progressive attitudes of individual party members are key in explaining leftist support. This position, however, is neither completely stable nor unanimously accepted within the Left. Religion (the historical presence of the Catholic Left in these circles) and discriminatory attitudes help explain such limitations to the support from the Left. Moreover, religion, electoral incentives, and, to a lesser extent, progressive attitudes also help qualify the general opposition to GLT rights found among right-wing parties.

The Brazilian GLT movement emerged in the late 1970s and has addressed pressing issues affecting the GLT population, such as homophobic discrimination and violence, and the AIDS epidemic. The activity of federal deputies in the Chamber of Deputies provides a privileged vantage point from which to explore the relationship between the GLT movement and political parties. It is particularly the complex relationship between GLT activists and the *Partido dos Trabalhadores* (Workers' Party, PT), that reveals both the sources and limitations of the support for sexual minorities among leftist parties. In spite of opposition to GLT rights in right-wing parties, opportunities remain for occupying political spaces within those parties. While alliance with political parties is an important tool in the GLT movement's struggle, other venues and strategies are also available; many parallels exist in the way different social movements and political parties relate to each other in Brazil, a point highlighted by a comparison between the GLT and feminist movements.

The Emergence of the GLT Movement and the Violent Reality of Sexual Minorities

The gay and lesbian movement was born during the period of political liberalization in the late 1970s, at a time when a number of other social movements, such as the Afro-Brazilian and feminist movements, were becoming increasingly visible in the public sphere.[3] [...]

By the beginning of the 1980s, approximately twenty gay and lesbian groups had formed throughout the country, but by 1984, only seven still existed (*Grupo Gay da Bahia* 1993). The weakness and small size of many groups, the growing economic crisis, and the onset of the AIDS epidemic, which took the lives of many in the gay community and became a priority for many activists, contributed to this decline (Green 1999).

During the second half of the 1980s, some gay groups, such as *Grupo Gay da Bahia* in Salvador and *Grupo Atobá* in Rio de Janeiro, started working with AIDS-prevention programs, which would later become central to most GLT organizations. It was only in the early- to mid-1990s that a new wave of mobilization arose in the GLT movement. [...] In 1995, this increase in organization led to the creation of a national umbrella organization, the *Associação Brasileira de Gays, Lésbicas e Travestis* (Brazilian Association of Gays, Lesbians and *Travestis*, ABGLT). By 2003, over 100 GLT organizations, spread across all 27 states in the country, had joined the ABGLT. The size and diversity of the Brazilian GLT movement make it the largest and one of the strongest of its kind in Latin America.

In addition to AIDS, violence and discrimination have been central concerns of the GLT movement.[4] [...] A recent report by the *Grupo Gay da Bahia* indicates that, on average, since 1990, about 126 gays, lesbians, or *travestis* are murdered in Brazil every year, allegedly because of their sexual orientation. This is the most violent and visible part of a more widespread problem, as made evident by the numerous other instances of nonfatal acts of violence and discrimination listed in the report (Mott and Cerqueira 2003).

Sexual Orientation and the 1988 Constitution

From the early years of the gay and lesbian movement in the late 1970s and early 1980s, those activists who sought a greater engagement with political parties and state institutions, though historically linked to the Left, remained open, at least in principle, to broader partisan alliances (Green 1994; Green 1999; Green 2000; Trevisan 2000, 353–64; *Grupo Gay da Bahia* 1993). [...] In 1986, elections were held for a new Federal Congress that was entrusted with the drafting of a new constitution. At that time,

GLT organizations mobilized to pressure the Constituent Assembly to include *sexual orientation* in the new constitution as one of the grounds for protection against discrimination. This mobilization was headed by João Antônio Mascarenhas, president of the group *Triângulo Rosa*, from Rio de Janeiro, but received support from other groups from São Paulo and Bahia (Câmara 2002, 110). [. . .] Despite Mascarenhas's best efforts until the last stages of the drafting of the constitutional text, and the support of a number of leftist politicians, the campaign was unsuccessful, highlighting what Mascarenhas saw as key factors behind the opposition to the rights of sexual minorities in the federal legislature: conservatism, machismo, homophobia, and religion (Câmara 2002, 107–29; Mascarenhas 1997).

The distribution of support for the amendment including *sexual orientation* in the constitution among parties in the Chamber of Deputies highlights some of the main patterns of support across parties for the rights of sexual minorities. Parties on the left end of the spectrum—the PT, the *Partido Comunista do Brasil* (Communist Party of Brazil, PC do B), the *Partido Comunista Brasileiro* (Brazilian Communist Party, PCB), and the *Partido Socialista Brasileiro* (Brazilian Socialist Party, PSB)—voted unanimously in favor of the amendment. Members of the *Partido Democrático Trabalhista* (Democratic Labor Party, PDT) also demonstrated significant support, with 60 percent in favor. As we move toward the center and the right end of the spectrum, support drops precipitously, albeit not completely: 25 percent of centrist deputies and 5 percent of right-wing ones supported the amendment. Therefore, already in the late 1980s, we can see that legislators from leftist parties provided significantly greater access to sexual minorities and supported their demands more clearly than centrist and right-wing politicians.

The Activity of Legislative Allies

In the 1990s, since the failed attempt to include *sexual orientation* in the 1988 Constitution, a number of pro-GLT legislative bills and constitutional amendments have been presented in the federal Congress. [. . .] A closer look at this body of bills confirms the general distribution of support across parties mentioned above: most of the proponents of pro-GLT legislation come from leftist parties, particularly the PT. It is important to note, however, that some of these bills were put forward by centrist and right-wing politicians from the *Partido Trabalhista Brasileiro* (Brazilian Labor Party, PTB), *Partido da Frente Liberal* (Liberal Front Party, PFL), and *Partido Liberal* (Liberal Party, PL). In a number of cases, both within the Left and the Right, legislative bills emerged out of the close interaction between GLT activists and parliamentary aides, who often provide a bridge between the movement and deputies. Despite these various attempts, however, only one of these bills or constitutional amendment proposals has been put to a vote on the floor of the Chamber of Deputies (as of late 2009). In November 2006, after two years of intense negotiation between GLT activists and allied leftist legislators, on one side, and right-wing and centrist leaders, on the other, an antidiscrimination bill was put to a vote and approved by the Chamber of Deputies. The bill has stalled in the Senate ever since. One of the main reasons for the failure of parties in producing legislative change is exogenous to them: the relative weakness of the legislature vis-à-vis the executive, which has extensive powers that restrict the legislature's ability to set its own agenda (Power 1998; Mainwaring 1997).

In late June 2003, in response to pressure from the GLT movement and negotiation with elected officials and public bureaucrats, a National Seminar on Affirmative Policies and Rights of the Gay, Lesbian, Bisexual, *Travesti*, and Transsexual Community was held in the Chamber of Deputies, bringing together the GLT movement, federal deputies, and bureaucrats. [...] Out of discussions held during the seminar emerged the idea to create a Parliamentary Front for the Freedom of Sexual Expression, which subsequently came into existence in October 2003. The main function of the Parliamentary Front, as seen by its members, is to defend the interests and rights of sexual minorities in Congress, proposing legislation and pushing for the effective implementation of existing policies and protective mechanisms for the GLT community. While deputies in the Front have not yet managed to pass explicitly pro-GLT legislation, they were successful in allocating 3 million reais (approximately $1.2 million U.S.) in the 2005 federal budget for programs aimed at combating homophobia (Lugullo 2005).

A more detailed examination of the membership of the Parliamentary Front highlights where support for sexual minorities lies. As of August 2005, of the 85 members of the Parliamentary Front (76 federal deputies and 9 senators, out of a total of 513 deputies and 81 senators),[5] 56 percent were from the PT.[6] Members from leftist parties (PT, PC do B, PSOL, PPS, PDT, PSB, and PV) accounted for 81 percent of the Parliamentary Front, much above their combined proportion of seats in Congress (32 percent). Reflecting the pattern witnessed in the 1980s, the centrist and right-wing party clusters also contribute to the Front, with 8 members each (9.5 percent of the total). Another interesting pattern emerges from an analysis of the membership in this Parliamentary Front: a disproportionate number of members are women. While women fill only about 10 percent of seats in Congress, about 30 percent of the Parliamentary Front's members are female, which means that slightly less than half of all congresswomen are in the Front. [...]

A number of factors contribute to the support for GLT rights among federal [...] deputies.[7] As can be seen by the composition of the Parliamentary Front in the federal Congress, gender is a factor: female deputies are more likely to support the struggle of sexual minorities than males. [...] A number of women supportive of the rights of GLTs have been involved in the feminist movement, and are thus sensitive to questions of machismo and homophobia. Some politicians were involved in the countercultural movements in the 1960s and 1970s under the dictatorship or in exile, which contributed to their open attitude toward sexual diversity. Given the history of the creation of leftist parties since the early 1980s and their linkages to progressive social movements, most of these cases are found among leftist deputies, which helps to account for the greater degree of support among those parties. In other cases, however, a less ideological motivation is behind the support granted to GLTs: some politicians, witnessing the growth of GLBT pride parades and the increasing visibility of sexual minorities in Brazilian society, have sought to gain electoral support from that community. This motivation, according to some activists, can be found on both the Left and the Right. Finally, individual attitudes are not necessarily conducive to support for GLTs, but often form the basis for opposition to GLT rights, as in the case of politicians with strong religious beliefs.

The PT and Sexual Diversity Politics

The existence of institutional spaces for sexual minorities in the PT is one of the key reasons why the party has been open to these issues. There are important limitations to this openness, however. The strong presence of the Catholic Church within the party's ranks has created significant obstacles to the deepening of the relationship between the PT and sexual minorities. In addition, the difficulty of traditional leftist ideology in dealing with issues of identity politics, the persistence of discrimination among a number of party members, and organizational and resource constraints have also prevented the development of a stronger and firmer party positioning in support of gays, lesbians, and *travestis*.

During the period of democratic transition in the late 1970s in São Paulo, a diverse group of social movements joined other groups in the Left, including unionized workers, the Catholic Left, and leftist intellectuals, to form the PT. From its early days, the party expressed its openness to the struggle of sexual minorities, as demonstrated by the speech of the party leader, Luiz Inácio Lula da Silva, at the First National Convention of the PT in 1981. [. . .] Since then, a number of official party documents, including resolutions from national meetings, plans for political action, and electoral government plans and directives, have included the fight against discrimination based on sexual orientation as part of the party's general struggle for the inclusion of minorities. [. . .]

This early support created a propitious environment for a widening of institutional space for the debate of sexual diversity issues within the party. In 1992, a group of PT activists formed the Group of Gays and Lesbians of the PT in São Paulo in order to increase the visibility of gays and lesbians within the party.[8] The group started pressuring PT parliamentarians across the country to push for pro-GLT legislation, and these GLT activists also participated in electoral campaigns for the party (Green 2000, 65). Slowly, GLT groups from the PT started emerging at the state level across the country. From 2001 until 2003, these various regional GLT groups managed to hold three National Plenary Meetings of Gays, Lesbians, *Travestis* and Transsexuals of the PT. [. . .] These GLT groups of the PT have undoubtedly provided a good mechanism for accessing and pressuring PT politicians. This access and pressure, in turn, have resulted in legislative and policy initiatives from a number of politicians.

Many of these GLT groups, however, face serious constraints to their effective functioning. Divisions, strategic and other, among activists, infrastructural constraints, lack of funding, and difficulty in mobilizing activists contribute to this problem. Consequently, a number of groups experience an unstable existence. [. . .]

Recent scholarship has highlighted the democratizing reforms implemented by the PT in a number of municipalities, especially the participatory budget, first implemented in Porto Alegre in 1989 (Abers 2000; Baiocchi 2005; Nylen 2003), whereby the municipal government allows direct participation of citizens in the allocation and spending of part of the city's budget. In a few cities where the participatory budget was implemented, such as Campinas, São Paulo, and Porto Alegre, gays, lesbians and *travestis* joined other organized groups in society to take part in this process (Wampler 2004, 379). Concrete results have emerged from this experience, such as the creation of the Homosexual Reference Center in Campinas. [. . .]

The PT's openness to and support for GLTs has limits, however. One of the main obstacles to the promotion of the interests and rights of sexual minorities lies in the important presence of the Catholic Left within the party. Many of the social movement activists and workers who founded the PT were also closely involved with the Catholic Church (Follmann 2000; Keck 1992). The strong historical presence of the Catholic Left in the PT has naturally been a source of tension in regard to gender and sexuality issues. In a telling example, as Lula trailed behind PSDB candidate Fernando Henrique Cardoso in the 1994 presidential campaign, the PT sought to strengthen support for the party among some key constituencies where it felt it was losing ground— notably those active in the Catholic Church. In order to accommodate its numerous potential Catholic voters, the party dropped support for abortion from its platform in that campaign (Burdick 2004, 88). For similar reasons, support for full rights for GLTs was put on the back burner (Green 2000, 66).[9] [. . .]

Gay and lesbian rights are still seen as secondary and unimportant by many PT activists and politicians.[10] According to a PSB state deputy in Bahia, the Left in general often has difficulty understanding and accepting identity politics ("the struggle of minorities"), since the class struggle ("the struggle of the majority") is seen as primary.[11] Many GLT activists from the PT have reported having met with discrimination from other party activists, party officials and politicians, and from social movement activists linked to the PT.[12] Consequently, discussion of gay rights within the party has at times been stifled. [. . .] A deeper incorporation of sexual diversity concerns into the PT's political agenda is thus made difficult by persistent homophobia within the party, in addition to the traditional difficulty of leftist ideology in dealing with the issue.

What are some of the main factors that help explain the greater level of opposition to GLT rights among right-wing parties? As seen earlier, activists do find some support among a minority of politicians from these parties. What explains these cracks in the opposition to the rights of sexual minorities?

Sexual Diversity and Right-Wing Parties

The main source of right-wing opposition to GLT rights is religious conservatism. Conservative attitudes toward gender and sexuality are prevalent among politicians from these parties, many of whom have strong links to churches, both Catholic and Protestant. In addition, the elitist bias of most right-wing parties makes them unlikely allies in the struggle for the inclusion of marginalized groups. As is the case on the Left, however, this position is not unanimous. Electoral and clientelistic dynamics can also generate opportunities for GLTs, as illustrated by the cases of right-wing GLT candidates. Moreover, individual attitudes also help explain the presence of GLT supporters within the right-wing party cluster. [. . .]

The turning point for the political activism of Protestant churches and, more specifically, Pentecostal ones, was the return to civilian rule and the 1986 elections for the federal Congress. A number of these churches started openly campaigning for "their" candidates, contributing to the election success of a growing number of politicians (Oro 2003). From 1933 to 1987, of the 50 members of Congress from Protestant churches, only 6 percent came from Pentecostal ones. From 1987 to 2000, in contrast, of the 104 Protestant members of Congress, 61 percent were affiliated with Pentecostal denominations (Freston 2001, 19). A significant number of these politicians have migrated to smaller right-wing parties (Freston 1994, 47).

The participation of Pentecostal politicians since the time of the Constituent Assembly has featured a strong defense of the "traditional" family. At the time of the drafting of the constitution, Pentecostals broke ranks with "historical" Protestants to align with Catholics in support of an antidivorce bill. Abortion was strongly opposed by virtually all Protestants, with Pentecostals being more outspoken and visible in their opposition. Protestant politicians have also demonstrated staunch opposition to GLT rights. This opposition has been the most vocal among Pentecostals and other charismatic denominations (Freston 1994; Freston 2001).[13]

While the growing presence of Pentecostal churches on the Right represents a barrier to the support for GLTs from those parties, there are a limited number of spaces open to sexual minorities in right-wing parties. Electoral and clientelistic dynamics are behind the emergence of a small but noticeable number of right-wing GLT candidates. [...] The majority of openly GLT candidates have run for office under leftist parties, but a few, especially in municipal elections, have done so under right-wing ones. [...]

Despite numerous attempts at the ballot box, right-wing GLT candidates have been overwhelmingly unsuccessful. To my knowledge, only two have succeeded since the first GLT candidates emerged on the political scene (until late 2009). Two successful cases are at the municipal level [...] it was simply something that "people knew about" (Ranieri 2004; Fidalgo 2001). The third successful openly gay candidate was the late Clodovil Hernandez—a famous fashion designer and television celebrity who ran for office under the right-wing *Partido Trabalhista Cristão* (Christian Labor Party, PTC)—who was elected federal deputy in 2006. In March 2009, he died of complications following a stroke.

The first interesting characteristic of many of these right-wing GLT candidates is their dissociation from the GLT movement. A number of them do not promote their public identity based on their sexual orientation. [...]

Secondly, in some cases, a right-wing candidacy may have a strategic goal. In regions of the country more strongly characterized by patrimonial politics, where *coronelismo* (rule by local strongmen) is predominant, running for a right-wing, clientelistic party may be the only path available for advancements, or the only means by which to attain some level of power. [...]

Indeed, most of these candidates had previously built a strong local electoral base, in a manner typical of local clientelistic networks. In some cases, they are linked to powerful traditional families. More often, they have built a reputation through significant levels of community work, typically in the areas of greatest need for marginalized populations, such as health, employment, poverty alleviation, basic infrastructure, or in providing support for vulnerable groups in the community, such as youth and the elderly. Electoral support is then sought based on the promise of or [...] the actual delivery of some of these goods.

These characteristics of right-wing GLT candidates highlight the fact that the political dynamics typical of the Right in Brazil can, under certain circumstances, overpower opposition to a candidate's "alternative sexuality." [...] Given the characteristics of these right-wing candidates, however, it becomes clear that these spaces are qualitatively different from those in the PT. GLT identity is not emphasized in right-wing parties, while it is the driving force in the GLT groups within the PT. Support for GLT rights is thus more likely to be incorporated into leftist party agendas than into those of right-wing parties.

The diversity of individual attitudes among right-wing politicians also helps account for the existence of a small group of supporters for GLT rights within their ranks. While religion has been identified as a major factor contributing to the opposition to GLT rights, not all politicians allow their religious affiliation and beliefs to influence their political behavior. [...] Moreover, while many right-wing politicians may function within a more elitist conservative worldview, whereby rights are granted based on social status (DaMatta 1997, 179–248), some are more tolerant of marginalized groups in society, including GLTs.

Social Movements and Political Parties

Political parties matter for the struggle of sexual minorities in Brazil. While they are neither the sole nor the main vehicle for change used by GLTs, they have contributed significantly to the increasing recognition and visibility of gays, lesbians, and *travestis* as political actors in the public sphere and in state institutions. [...] Under certain circumstances, parties have also proven to be an effective tool for policy change and legislative reform, especially at the local level. Moreover, the higher level of support for GLT rights found among leftist parties, as well as the few opportunities within centrist and right-wing parties, were based on both institutional factors and individual attitudes. [...]

These findings are not inconsistent with the literature that views political parties in Brazil as weakly institutionalized, fragmented, fragile, and inchoate, showing low levels of discipline and weak programmatic bases, with politicians focused on supplying patronage rather than building ideological support for their parties (Mainwaring 1995; Lamounier and Meneguello 1986; Ames 2001). While painting a negative picture of the Brazilian party system as a whole, the scholars who have produced this literature point out that this diagnosis does not apply to most leftist parties, especially the PT.[14] [...] The pattern of support for GLT rights across the left-right spectrum and the reasons behind it confirm these differences among party clusters (leftist, centrist, and right-wing). In analyzing the relationship between social movements and political parties in Brazil, therefore, we should beware of overgeneralizations and pay close attention to individual cases. [...]

In the Brazilian case, as analyzed in the discussion of the activity of legislative allies, the impact of the broader institutional framework sets clear limits on the impact parties can have through their deputies. Even though the PT was elected to the presidency with Lula in 2002, the incapacity of the federal Congress to set its own legislative agenda has resulted in the inability of allied deputies to pass pro-GLT legislation. In addition, the relative marginality of sexual diversity issues in the political sphere and the absence of clear and strong support for GLT rights from the PT administration help explain why the executive did not initiate such legislative change, either.

While parties are part of the puzzle, the GLT movement in Brazil also uses other vehicles for the advancement of the rights and interests of sexual minorities. In addition to working with parties and deputies in legislative houses, GLT activists have success-fully pushed for change within the public bureaucracy. The establishment of a gov-ernmental response to the AIDS epidemic, for example, grew out of an engagement of the GLT movement with health officials at the state level (Teixeira 1997). [. . .] An increase in pressure exerted by the movement on bureaucrats linked to human-rights agencies since the turn of the century has also led to important gains, such as the creation of the Brazil without Homophobia program, a set of initiatives aimed at combating discrimination against sexual minorities, launched in May 2004 by the Special Human Rights Secretariat. [. . .]

Some interesting comparisons can also be made with other social movements, in particular the women's movement. The women's movement's level of engagement with political parties since the early 1980s has been significantly higher than that of gays and lesbians. The work of women activists with deputies and politicians of the PMDB and the PT led to significant gains in public policies and legislation (Alvarez 1990). The level of organization and influence of women (and feminists more speci-fically) within the PT has been quite substantial, even though, as with GLTs, some is-sues are still contentious, such as abortion and sexuality (Godinho 1998). Since both the feminist and the GLT movement target gender oppression as central to their strug-gle, the wider inroads of women in the party have undoubtedly opened up spaces for sexual minorities as well. As seen in the composition of the Parliamentary Front for the Freedom of Sexual Expression, leftist women tend to be highly supportive of GLT rights.

Another parallel between GLT struggles and the women's movement is in the way in which right-wing parties dealt with women's issues during the transition to dem-ocratic rule. Female militants in conservative parties conceptualized women's partic-ipation as an extension of their role in the private sphere, and what were considered more radical feminist demands were disregarded (Alvarez 1990, 162–65). In the case of GLTs, while some individuals have found space within right-wing parties, they tend to shy away from asserting their gay, lesbian, or *travesti* identity or incorporating rights for sexual minorities into their platforms. Finally, the fact that success in leg-islative or policy change can take place even in the absence of openly GLT politicians underlines the importance of allies and the fact that under certain conditions, their actions can be effective. Similarly, despite the limited effect of electoral quotas on the number of female deputies elected, the women's movement has managed to achieve a significant impact on legal reform in Brazil (Htun 2002).

The relationship between social movements and political parties is multidimen-sional. In the case of sexual diversity politics in Brazil, contradictions and limitations are part of the complex relationship between the GLT movement and political parties; nevertheless, parties, especially on the Left, represent an important vehicle for the construction of a more inclusive society.

Notes

I would like to thank [. . .] David Rayside for insightful comments and advice as this work took shape. An earlier version of this essay was presented at the 2005 Annual Meeting for the American Political Science Association in Washington, D.C., and received generous and helpful comments from participants, especially Martha Ackelsberg. Thanks also to Erica Frederiksen, who provided many comments on earlier drafts of this work.

1. Social movements are not monolithic entities, and activists and organizations in the gay and lesbian rights movement frequently avoid engagement with political parties and state institutions. Nevertheless, as social movements grow and stabilize, some degree of involvement with partisan politics is virtually unavoidable.

2. I use the initialism GLT (gays, lesbians, and *travestis*) to refer to individuals who are part of that group, and to the organized social movement fighting for the rights of sexual minorities. [. . .]

3. For more information on the rise of the Brazilian gay and lesbian movement, and a discussion of the late 1970s, see MacRae 1990, Green 1994, Trevisan 2000, and Facchini 2005.

4. Since the presentation of a bill for the legalization of civil unions between same-sex partners in the federal Chamber of Deputies in 1995, same-sex relationship recognition has also been part of the movement's agenda.

5. Information as of early August 2005 (Julian Rodrigues, e-mail to GLTBS mailing list, August 9, 2005).

6. The members of the Parliamentary Front are distributed as follows: forty-eight from the PT, five from the PC do B, four from the *Partido Popular Socialista* (Popular Socialist Party, PPS, formerly *Partido Comunista Brasileiro*, PCB), four from the PDT, three from the *Partido Socialismo e Liberdade* (Socialism and Liberty Party, PSOL, formed in 2004 by leftist politicians who left the PT), three from the PSB, three from the *Partido da Social Democracia Brasileira* (Party of the Brazilian Social Democracy, PSDB), three from the PTB, three from the PFL, three from the PL, two from the *Partido Verde* (Green Party, PV), two from the *Partido do Movimento Democrático Brasileiro* (Party of the Brazilian Democratic Movement, PMDB), and two from the *Partido Progressista* (Progressive Party, PP).

7. These factors were mentioned to me repeatedly in anonymous interviews with GLT activists and federal deputies conducted in 2003.

8. Interview with PT gay activist, Brasília, D.F., February 13, 2003.

9. The strong presence of the Catholic Church in the PT should not be taken as an insurmountable barrier, however. Some cases indicate that political support from the Church or even strong religious beliefs and the defense of rights for GLTs can be reconciled. Federal Deputy Maria José Maninha (PT/Distrito Federal) and Bahia State Deputy Yulo Oiticica (PT/Bahia) fall into this category. Interestingly, given the important role of the Catholic Left in the human-rights movement, the discourse of human rights is often used to defuse this tension.

10. Interview with PT activist and two PT federal deputies, Brasília, Distrito Federal, February 13 and March 17, 2003, Rio de Janeiro, September 1, 2003, respectively.

11. Interview with Bahia State Deputy, Salvador, Bahia, October 30, 2003.

12. This point was raised by some participants of the Third National Plenary Meeting of GLTs of the PT, held in June 2003 in São Paulo.

13. As in the case of the Catholic presence within the PT, there are instances of progressive-ness towards sexual minorities among politicians linked to these churches. Interestingly, most of them are part of a small group of leftist Protestant politicians, sincluding Lysâneas Maciel (PDT), Benedita da Silva (PT), Jurema Batista (PT), and Rose de Souza (PT). Some of these politicians, however, mute their support for GLTs when pressure from their church increases.

14. The wave of corruption scandals under the Lula administration that emerged in 2005 cast some doubt on the PT's degree of exceptionalism.

References

Abers, R. 2000. *Inventing Local Democracy: Grassroots Politics in Brazil*. Boulder, Colo.: Lynne Rienner.

Alvarez, S. 1990. *Engendering Democracy in Brazil: Women's Movements in Transition Politics*. Princeton, N.J.: Princeton University Press.

Ames, B. 2001. *The Deadlock of Democracy in Brazil*. Ann Arbor: University of Michigan Press.

Baiocchi, G. 2005. *Militants and Citizens: The Politics of Participatory Democracy in Porto Alegre*. Palo Alto, Calif.: Stanford University Press.

Burdick, J. 2004. *Legacies of Liberation: The Progressive Catholic Church in Brazil at the Start of a New Millennium*. Burlington, Vt.: Ashgate.

Câmara, C. 2002. *Cidadania e orientação sexual: A Trajetória do Grupo Triângulo Rosa*. Rio de Janeiro: Academia Avançada.

DaMatta, R. 1997. *Carnavais, malandros e heróis: Para uma sociologia do dilema brasileiro*. 6th ed. Rio de Janeiro: Rocco.

Diretório Nacional do PT. Secretaria Nacional de Formação Política, and Fundação Perseu Abramo, Projeto Memória. 1998. *Partido dos Trabalhadores: resoluções de encontros e congressos*. São Paulo: Editora Fundação Perseu Abramo.

Engel, S. 2001. *The Unfinished Revolution: Social Movement Theory and the Gay and Lesbian Movement*. New York: Cambridge University Press.

Facchini, R. 2005. *Sopa de letrinhas? Movimento homossexual e produção de identidades coletivas nos anos 90*. Rio de Janeiro: Garamond.

Fidalgo, J. 2001. *Parati troca estrelas por peixes em hotéis e cria selo GLS*. *Folha Online*, May 21. http://www1.folha.uol.com.br/folha/turismo/noticias/ult338u707.shtml.

Follmann, J. I. 2000. Progressive Catholicism and Left-Wing Politics in Brazil. In *The Church at the Grassroots in Latin America: Perspectives on Thirty Years of Activism*, ed. J. Burdick and W. E. Hewitt, 53–67. Westport, Conn: Praeger.

Freston, P. 1994. *Evangélicos na política brasileira: História ambígua e desafio ético*. Curitiba: Encontrão Editora.

———. 2001. *Evangelicals and Politics in Asia, Africa and Latin America*. Cambridge: Cambridge University Press.

Godinho, T. 1998. *O PT e o feminismo*. In *Mulher e política: Gênero e feminismo no Partido dos Trabalhadores*, ed. Â. Borba, N. Faria, and T. Godinho, 15–32. São Paulo: Editora Fundação Perseu Abramo.

Green, J. N. 1994. The Emergence of the Brazilian Gay Liberation Movement, 1977–1981. *Latin American Perspectives* 21.1: 38–55.

————. 1999. "More Love and More Desire": The Building of a Brazilian Movement. In *The Global Emergence of Gay and Lesbian Politics: National Imprints of a Worldwide Movement*, ed. B. Adam, J. Duyvendak, and A. Krouwel, 91–109. Philadelphia: Temple University Press.

————. 2000. Desire and Militancy: Lesbians, Gays, and the Brazilian Workers' Party. In *Different Rainbow: Same-Sex Sexuality and Popular Struggle in the Third World*, ed. P. Drucker, 57–70. London: Gay Men's Press.

Grupo Gay da Bahia. 1993. *Boletim do Grupo Gay da Bahia* 27. Salvador: Grupo Gay da Bahia.

Htun, M. 2002. Puzzles of Women's Rights in Brazil. *Social Research* 69.3: 733–51.

Keck, M. 1992. *The Workers' Party and Democratization in Brazil*. New Haven: Yale University Press.

Kitschelt, H. 1986. Political Opportunity Structures and Political Protest: Anti-Nuclear Movements in Four Democracies. *British Journal of Political Science* 16.1: 57–85.

Lamounier, B., and R. Meneguello. 1986. *Partidos políticos e consolidação democrática: O Caso brasileiro*. São Paulo: Editora Brasiliense.

Lugullo, M. 2005. *Gays pedirão recursos do orçamento para a causa*. Agência Câmara, November 8. http://www2.camara.gov.br/homeagencia/materias.html?pk=78291.

MacRae, E. 1990. *A Construção da igualdade: Identidade sexual e política no Brasil da "abertura."* Campinas: Editora da UNICAMP.

Mainwaring, S. 1995. Brazil: Weak Parties, Feckless Democracy. In *Building Democratic Institutions: Party Systems in Latin America*, ed. S. Mainwaring and T. Scully, 354–98. Stanford, Calif.: Stanford University Press.

————. 1997. Multipartism, Robust Federalism and Presidentialism in Brazil. In *Presidentialism and Democracy in Latin America*, ed. S. Mainwaring and M. Soberg Shugart, 55–109. New York: Cambridge University Press.

————. 1999. *Rethinking Party Systems in the Third Wave of Democratization: The Case of Brazil*. Stanford, Calif.: Stanford University Press.

Mascarenhas, J. A. 1997. *Machismo, conservadorismo político e falso moralismo: A Tríplice conexão:Um ativista guei versus 96 parlamentares*. Rio de Janeiro: 2A Editora.

Mott, L. and M. Cerquiera. 2003. *Matei porque odeio gay*. Salvador: Editora Grupo Gay da Bahia.

Nylen, W. 2003. *Participatory Democracy versus Elitist Democracy: Lessons from Brazil*. New York: Palgrave Macmillan.

Oro, A. P. 2003. *A política da Igreja Universal e seus reflexos nos campos religioso e político brasileiros*. Revista Brasileira de Ciências Sociais 18.53: 53–69.

Power, T. 1998. The Pen Is Mightier than the Congress: Presidential Decree Power in Brazil. In *Executive Decree Authority*, ed. J. Carey and M. Soberg Shugart, 197–230. New York: Cambridge University Press.

Ranieri, G. 2004. "*O respeito tem que vir pela pessoa, sem importar o sexo.*" G Online. http://gonline.uol.com.br/livre/eleicoes_2004/Katia_tapety.shtml (accessed March 5, 2005).

Tarrow, S. 1993. Social Protest and Policy Reform: May 1968 and the *Loi d'Orientation* in France. *Comparative Political Studies* 25.4: 579–607.

————. 1996. States and Opportunities: The Political Structuring of Social Movements. In *Comparative Perspectives on Social Movements: Political Opportunities, Mobilizing Structures, and Cultural Framings*, ed. D. McAdam, J. McCarthy, and M. Zald, 41–61. New York: Cambridge University Press.

————. 1998. *Power in Movement: Social Movements and Contentious Politics.* 2nd ed. New York: Cambridge University Press.

Teixeira, P. R. 1997. *Políticas públicas em* AIDS. In *Políticas, instituições e* AIDS: *Enfrentando a epidemia no Brasil,* ed. R. Parker, 43–68. Rio de Janeiro: Jorge Zahar Editor/ABIA.

Tilly, C. 1978. *From Mobilization to Revolution.* Reading, Mass.: Addison-Wesley.

Trevisan, J. S. 2000. *Devassos no paraíso: A Homossexualidade no Brasil, da colônia à atualidade.* 3rd ed. Rio de Janeiro: Editora Record.

Wampler, B. 2004. *Instituições, associações e interesses no orçamento participativo de São Paulo.* In *A Participação em São Paulo,* ed. L. Avritzer, 371–407. São Paulo: Editora UNESP.

The Civil Union Law in Buenos Aires

Notes on the Arguments by the Opposition

Renata Hiller

Translated by Christina Martínez

DURING ITS 2002 legislative session, the City of Buenos Aires approved the legalization of civil unions, becoming the first city in South America to grant same- and opposite-sex couples treatment similar to that afforded to married couples,[1] and conferring upon them some social benefits. [...] The parliamentary debate that accompanied the sanction of the law offers some keys to understanding the nature of the discourse concerning sexual diversity, the family, citizenship, and the role of the state in politics. [...]

Discourses

[...] We can distinguish different discourses, variously employed by opponents and advocates of this change. One discourse appeals to particularistic demands, emphasizing the disadvantageous condition of a segregated social group. Another argument is articulated in terms of human rights, [...] and a third set of arguments coming from gay, lesbian, transsexual, transvestite, bisexual, and intersex (GLTTBI) groups opposes the legislation of same-sex unions because their proponents oppose the institution of marriage and/or want to preserve an anarchic-autonomist position vis-à-vis the state.

Thus, encompassing more than a single discourse, the debate about and among GLTTBI citizens over [. . .] the Buenos Aires Civil Union Law must be thought of as [. . .] a dispute among heterogeneous organizations (in terms of their arguments, practices, and strategies). [. . .] Furthermore, it is also [. . .] important to analyze hostile arguments in order to better understand the arguments of GLTTBI organizations. [. . .] I draw from legislative documents (commission dispatches, observations of representatives, and transcripts of parliamentary debate) to make my analysis. [. . .]

The Context

The debate over the Civil Union Law can be thought of as an instance of state-society interaction over themes related to sexuality. [. . .] [T]his debate [. . .] is part of a prior dialogue: the entry into the legislative arena of demands by the GLTTBI community and the organizations. Arguably, these groups became political actors in the legislative institutions of Buenos Aires in 1996, when the new Constitution of the city was approved.[2] [. . .] Legislators from various parties created a channel of communication with GLTTBI organizations, which made it possible to propose a Civil Union Law in August 2001. [. . .] The bill was introduced by leaders of these organizations and was sponsored by two legislators. The bill was debated, voted on, and approved in December of 2002, and with it came the creation of new state organ: the Public Register of Civil Unions.

First Argument Against Civil Unions: Definitions

[. . .] The Argentine legal system [. . .] accepts the possibility of giving every province (or the autonomous city of Buenos Aires) its own laws, provided that they do not contravene fundamental national legislation. Consequently, one of the arguments against the change was that the local Buenos Aires legislature did not have the right to address an issue that would fall under the scope of the National Civil Code, and thus, the matter ought to have been left to the National Congress. [. . .]

This discussion at first appears to be a technicality, argued to postpone the question or transfer it to the national arena, in which the correlation of forces would be different. However, this argument was more than a pretext. It addresses the issue of definitions, which are always critical in any debate over public policy. [. . .] Most policy debates come burdened with a prior dispute over the definitions of the terms on which the problem will be formulated; the definition of the question determines the relevant actors of the debate as much as the range of possible state responses. [. . .]

In this case, the opponents of the Civil Union bill wanted to frame the question as a "family issue" in order to make any ruling dependant on the National Civil Code, so that the ruling would fall under the authority of the National Congress rather than the local legislature. Their position forced advocates of the Civil Union bill to frame the issue not as a family issue, but as a matter of "affection" (Rep. Ripoll, Legislature of the City of Buenos Aires 2002, 465) "love," "sexuality," and even of "rules of relationship" (Rep. Campolongo, Legislature of the City of Buenos Aires 2002, 436). [. . .]

[T]hose representatives that raised the discussion of the law as a family matter [. . .], arguing that nonheterosexual couples are "another type of family" and highlighting the historic and variable character of this institution, found themselves in a bind. [. . .] GLTTBI organizations advocate the recognition of types of families other than those based on heterosexual union, but this tactic had the potential to play into the hands of the opposition, which argued that a substantive change to family law was not under the purview of the local legislature.

Following Nancy Fraser's (1997) terminology, we can conceptualize the Civil Union bill as responding to dual imperatives: a need for redistribution as well as recognition. These dual imperatives would frame the concept of Civil Unions as a way to respond to two types of injustices suffered by gays and lesbians. First, it would permit, in terms of "redistribution," a betterment of the material conditions of the lives of same-sex couples, permitting them both to gain access to the social benefits conferred upon one of the members of the couple, giving them the ability, for instance, to make joint purchases (such as houses or cars) and receive pensions for deceased partners.[3] [. . .]

A second imperative, cast in terms of "recognition," attempted to foster a greater sociocultural acceptance of the affective, erotic bonds between people of the same sex and their potential roles as parents. This entailed revising, and maybe even challenging, a hegemonic notion of "family" to permit not only the legitimization of those relationships already in existence, but also new modes of family formation. [. . .]

However, the institutional structure of the state, which creates juridical hierarchies between the nation and the provinces/autonomous cities, limited the scope of possible definitions, thereby precluding the concept of Civil Union from fulfilling this dual imperative. The [. . .] impossibility of raising a more open discussion about the concept of family means that one cannot claim that the goal of achieving sociocultural recognition was achieved or even fully debated.

Second Opposing Argument: Render unto Caesar (Only) What Is Caesar's

A second opposing argument focused on the "error" of attempting to modify in some degree that which is recognized as an ostensibly "family-based" bond. Not only was the local legislative arena inappropriate for approaching this topic (according to the previous argument), but also the debate itself lacked merit, because both matrimony and family precede (temporally and logically) the law. One cannot legislate these matters; all that is left (as in contractualist theories that recognize natural rights) is to take that which preexists and adapt and reformat it into positive law. [...]

This is not to say that a "reproductive end" is present in every marriage [...] rather, it is that the idea of procreation forms part of the definition of the notion of matrimony: its principal function is the "transmission of life" (Rep. López de Castro, Legislature of the City of Buenos Aires 2002, 470). [...]

The most important thing to come from this debate is the notion that marriage and the family were "always [...] prior to the law." [...] Here, marriage is associated with the reproduction of human life. [...]

The denial of the performative character of the naming (i.e., the discursive construction of the objects) invalidates any intent of reformulation. Marriage and family, according to this discourse, have been always (or perhaps since the moment of the first baptism in human history) a determined type of union organized around reproduction, which is why any other type of affective alliance ought to be construed in a different manner.

Third Opposing Argument: Private Matters

A third argument against the Civil Union Law (that also arises in many other debates on sexuality) was that the whole issue pertained to private matters, which are protected by article 19 of the National Constitution.[4] Identities or sexual practices that deviate from the heterosexual norm are "preferences, lifestyles" (Rep. Enríquez, Legislature of the City of Buenos Aires 2002, 402). Consequently, these practices fall outside legislation and public concern, in contrast to the family institution, which is recognized as having a "social function" as the "primary unit of society" (Representative Enríquez, Legislature of the City of Buenos Aires 2002, 417), a function that the state ought to preserve.

"People with a sexual orientation towards the same sex should be treated with respect and consideration, but that does not imply *approval of the externalization* of the issue by means of a juridical order that leads to conceptual, philosophical, biological, legal, and social errors" (Representative López de Castro, Legislature of the City of Buenos Aires 2002, 471, emphasis added).

The split between an intimate sphere of permissiveness (so long as it stays private) and the public sphere has enabled some GLTTBI groups to fight against discrimination based on policies of tolerance. [...]

Confining questions related to sexuality (and more specifically, questions related to those who separate themselves from the reproductive norm of heterosexuality) to the private sphere supposes a certain artificial or superficial way of understanding nonheterosexual orientation. The discourse that insults any practice or identity that goes against heterosexual norms not only anchors itself in a characterization of homosexuality as a disease (in which the subject is the "victim of this evil") or as an unnatural crime (in which the sinners may be sinners against either the divine law or the natural law), but also supposes a form of "light" identity-based construction that is purely self-referential.[5] To characterize homosexuality as a lifestyle places identity once again at the level of the individual. [...]

This discourse alerts us to the fact that today not all criticisms or expressions of contempt regarding minority identities need to be cast in essentialist terms. It has nothing to do anymore with either model: neither biological determinism (the cultural domination that finds its final origin in the genetic-biological composition), nor what Linda Nicholson (in thinking within feminine identity) christened "biological foundationalism." Under this line of thought, the term *woman* [...] is defined as "the result of a *common condition* that, despite the variations of degree, is an experience of all human beings that are *born* women" (Nicholson 2000, 24, emphasis added). [...]

Fourth Opposition Argument: Criteria for Pertinence

The last of the arguments against the Civil Union Law is not typically salient in European and North American debates: the denial of the social relevance of legislation of this type.

In the Latin American context, the high rates of unemployment, marginalization, and poverty in the region are arguably the result of policies implemented by certain sectors. At times, the enormous social inequalities that ensue are utilized by these same sectors in an argument against the relevance or urgency of matters such as the Civil Union Law.

The Civil Union Law debate took place in the context of the grave institutional and economic crisis of 2002. [...] Most actors were primarily worried about other social problems, which led many to dismiss the case as lacking pertinence for the time being, under the argument that the greatest necessity was to find "greatest common denominators" of society and "not broach themes that are not our own" (Representative De Estrada, 430).

In addition, the image of the GLTTBI community that the media disseminates is based on the stereotype of the white gay man from the upper middle class. This image operates to discredit the demands of the GLTTBI group, since it creates the impression that this is a privileged minority. [...]

[...]This analysis of opposing arguments is of paramount importance. First, because [...] they are not static and thus restructure themselves according to their counter-arguments. [...]

Second, because all political arguments are formulated on the basis of, or in response to, an adversary argument, these opposing arguments are the ones that confront GLTTBI organizations and influence the types of arguments, tools, and strategies that these organizations must employ. [...]

Finally, it is important to analyze both sides because doing so permits us to discern models that operate in other contexts, under different circumstances, and for different cases (including even those that at first sight would hardly seem related). In particular, we gain understanding when we consider that the opposition conceives of the family as associated with the concept of reproduction (argument 2). It understands all types of nonreproductive sexuality as superfluous, erroneous, artificial (argument 3), and therefore unworthy of treatment in a public space (argument 4).

What emerges is a model that, by tying sexuality to reproduction, associates sex, gender, and desire in a coherent and necessary fashion (Butler 1999): there are two mutually exclusive sexes (defined by their roles in reproduction), which correspond to two social roles (or genders) that have the opposite sex/gender as an object of desire. Hence, heterocentric thought creates a dichotomy between the sexes and genders and imposes a reproductive tendency on sexuality. This model can be considered one of many nuclei—if not the principal nucleus—of the oppressions suffered by numerous groups, from women who do not want to fulfill the mandate of maternity, to transsexuals who see their rights, and even the very conditions of their citizenship, systematically violated. [...]

Consequently, building alliances and agreeing on an agenda among the different groups that comprise the GLTTBI camp may be possible based on common experiences as citizens living within a culture of heterocentric thought. [...] Similarly, recognizing the matrix of the opposition permits the formation of more solid ties with other groups, such as feminists, who, in their struggle for abortion rights, also attempt to disassociate sexuality and reproduction.

Notes

1. Law 1004 of the Civil Union of the Autonomous City of Buenos Aires. http://www.cedom.gov.ar/

2. Until 1994, according to the National Constitution, the City of Buenos Aires was governed by a major appointed by the president. In 1994, the reform of the Constitution (article 129) al-

lowed the city to enjoy greater legislative and jurisdictional autonomy, including the election of its major (Sconza, Perotti, and Mengoni 2003, 52). It's in the framework of the debates regarding the city's Constitution that [. . .] article 11 emerges, which calls for the elimination of discrimination on the basis of sexual orientation.

3. The Civil Union Law does not encompass inheritance rights, unlike the case of marriage. It also does not refer to adoption rights [. . .]

4. "The private acts of men that in no way disrupt public order or morality, or harm a third party, are reserved to God and are exempt from the jurisdiction of the magistrates. No inhabitant of the Nation will be obliged to carry out what the law does not demand, nor deprived of what the law does not ban" (*Constitución Nacional*).

5. I take "'light' identity-based construction" from Catanzaro (2002, 82) to refer to theoretical statements that treat identity as mere self-description that changes and fluctuates according to what the person wills.

References

Aguilar Villanueva, L. 1993. *Problemas públicos y agenda de gobierno.* Mexico City: Porrúa.

Austin, J. 1982. *Cómo hacer cosas con palabras.* Barcelona: Paidós.

Butler, J. 1999. *Gender Trouble.* New York: Routledge.

Catanzaro, G. 2002. *Materia e identidad: el objeto perdido. Apuntes para una problematización materialista de la identidad.* In *Identidades, sujetos y subjetividades,* ed. L. Arfuch, 57–84. Buenos Aires: Prometeo Libros.

Cobb, R., and C. Elder. 1984. Agenda-Building and the Politics of Aging. *Policy Science Journal* 13, no. 1 (September): 115–29.

Constitución Nacional. Buenos Aires: Bregna.

De Beauvoir, S. 1999. *El segundo sexo.* Trans. Juan G. Puente. Buenos Aires: Sudamericana.

Dirección General Centro Documental de Información y Archivo Legislativo. 2007. *Proyectos de la Legislatura (April 24).* http://cedom.gov.ar/

Fraser, N. 1997. *Iustitia interrupta: Reflexiones críticas sobre la posición postsocialista.* Bogotá: Siglo del Hombre.

Jones, D., M. Libson, and R. Hiller, eds. 2006. *Sexualidades, política y violencia: La marcha del orgullo GLTTBI Buenos Aires, 2005.* Buenos Aires: Antropofagia.

Legislature of the City of Buenos Aires. 2002. Minutes of the Thirty-third Ordinary Session of the Legislature of the Autonomous City of Buenos Aires. Transcript version 55 (December 12). http://www.legislatura.gov.ar/

Meccia, E. 2006. *La Cuestión Gay: Un enfoque sociológico.* Buenos Aires: Gran Aldea.

Nicholson, L. 2000. *Interpretando o gênero. Revista Estudos Feministas, Santa Catarina, Centro de Filosofia e Ciências Humanas, e Centro de Comunicação e Expressão da Unisersidade Federal de Santa Catarina* 8, no. 2: 9–41.

Oszlak, O., and G. O'Donnell. 1995. *Estado y políticas estatales en América Latina: Hacia una estrategia de investigación.* REDES *Revista del Centro de Estudios e Investigaciones de la Universidad Nacional de Quilmes* 2, no. 4 (September): 99–128.

Sconza, O., R. Perotti, and B. Mengoni. 2003. *La nueva justicia social en la constitución de la Ciudad Autónoma de Buenos Aires: Relevamiento de políticas sociales que implementa el Gobierno de la Ciudad.* In *La (in)justicia social en el marco de políticas públicas y modelos de desarrollo,* ed. E. M. Armiñana, 45–74. Buenos Aires: Proyecto Editorial.

Verón, E. 1987. *El discurso político: Lenguajes y acontecimientos.* Buenos Aires: Hachette.

Gay Rights in Venezuela under Hugo Chávez, 1999–2009

José Ramón Merentes

In 1999, when the Constituent Assembly met to debate and draft Venezuela's current constitution, delegates considered a provision that would prohibit discrimination on the basis of sexual orientation. This provision, however, never made it into the final document.

The decision not to go forward with the provision seems to have been made almost overnight. According to press reports, representatives of the Catholic Church and other Christian denominations held a meeting with the president of the Constitutional Commission, Herman Escarrá, a well-known Opus Dei member. Escarrá was in charge of revising the final text of the constitution. Following this meeting, the provision to prevent discrimination on the basis of sexual orientation unexpectedly disappeared.[1]

During the actual debate on the floor, the relevant article was read quickly and without mention of sexual orientation. Instantly, assembly member Vladimir Villegas asked to speak out against the exclusion of same-sex rights, but he was ruled out of order by the president of the Constituent Assembly.[2]

There is reason to believe, therefore, that religious groups intervened to prevent the inclusion of equality and human rights for homosexual individuals in the constitution.

Nevertheless, the Constituent Assembly did include in the constitution the principle of "*numerus apertus*" (open list) on human rights. This principle ensures the recognition of any rights, even if they do not explicitly appear in the text (this is equivalent to the Ninth Amendment of the U.S. Constitution). This principle was carried over from the previous constitution of 1961. Another article in the 1999 constitution granted constitutional status to international treaties on human rights. These two articles could open the door for gay rights in the future.

In October 2003, our nongovernmental organization, Affirmative Union, submitted an Appeal of Interpretation of the Constitution to Venezuela's Supreme Court. Our aim was to obtain state recognition of economic rights for homosexual couples. We based our demand on the decisions by the United Nations Human Rights Committee (UNHRC) in *Young v. Australia* and *X v. Colombia*. In each case, the UNHRC ruled that the government in question breached human rights by refusing to grant federal benefits to surviving partners of same-sex couples. Our appeal aimed to recover the provision against discrimination on the basis of sexual orientation that had been lost during the debates over the new constitution, and to get the state to grant same-sex partnerships the same rights as married couples.

Ethical Views on Human Rights Reflected in the Appeal

Our appeal was based on an ethical, neo-Kantian interpretation of human rights as a set of universal, cross-cultural values that are fundamental to Venezuela's legal order and, therefore, binding to the Venezuelan state. In its preamble, the 1999 Venezuelan Constitution notes the progressivity, interrelatedness, and indivisibility of human rights, and orders these rights to be interpreted in a manner that is progressive or expansive, rather than reductive.

The Ruling

The Supreme Court's decision came in 2008. It stated that "homosexual individuals have all their rights protected by the constitution, but homosexual couples may not claim those rights before the state." The ruling indicated that same-sex couples' rights could nonetheless be recognized through laws drafted by the legislature.[3]

On the one hand, the decision is restrictive and contrary to the spirit of our constitution and international treaties on human rights because it explicitly indicates that same-sex couples have no constitutional standing. On the other, however, the decision leaves open the possibility of obtaining such rights through legislative action. The court's position thus both violated and recognized our argument that "countries where homosexual marriage is not recognized must confer such rights upon homosexual partners if they want to fully comply with international standards on human rights."

One of the justices, Carmen Zuleta, wrote a dissenting opinion:

> The interpretation held by the majority, from my point of view, is based on a false premise. While it neither prohibits nor condemns de facto unions between same-sex partners . . . it neglects the juridical implications of the right to the free development of the personality. It implies a constitutional model of binding heterosexuality that neglects the values of a pluralist state on which the social rule of law and justice was founded.

Furthermore, Justice Zuleta decried the incongruence between the court's ruling and the constitutional principles enshrined in the Constitution's preamble. Justice Zuleta fully understood the aims and content of our appeal.[4]

A Failed Effort

Efforts to use the current legal environment to enact pro-LGBT legislation have proven futile. The latest failed effort was a bill on "gender equality and equity" introduced in the National Assembly in 2005. The bill included articles protecting sexual diversity and seeking to "eradicate gender and sexual preference discrimination," especially in health services and the media (i.e., banning the broadcasting of discriminatory messages). The bill languished in the Parliament until late November 2008, when some legislators finally decided to consider it. After the first parliamentary discussion, a pro-government deputy, Romelia Matute, proposed inserting the possibility of sex change surgery (which was removed from the bill after the first discussion) and protections for homosexual partners through a "cohabitation partnership" article.

However, these provisions were immediately rejected by Marelys Pérez, the president of the Commission on Family, Woman and Youth. Pérez is a pro-government conservative Christian.

In protest against this legislative setback, several pro-LGBT groups organized a march before the National Assembly on August 14, 2009, the day before the closing of parliamentary sessions. The march gathered more than one hundred participants. However, the march was hardly covered by the press; other larger marches—against the government's new education law—attracted all the attention, eclipsing the LGBT march.

Nevertheless, three members of the Commission on Family, Woman and Youth, Romelia Matute, Flor Ríos, and Marelys Pérez, did meet with march representatives. But once again, the effort went nowhere. Deputy Pérez argued that nothing could be done until a "frame law" covering gay rights is passed. Pérez's argument seemed unnecessary and conveniently dilatory. The February 2008 Supreme Court's ruling on Affirmative Union's appeal states clearly that the National Assembly is already empowered "to draft legislation to recognize and protect sexual orientation against discrimination including protections to homosexual partners, according to civil law."[5]

Despite the fact that Venezuela enjoys presumably one of the most advanced constitutions on human-rights protections and a leftist ruling party, the political culture within the ruling party remains imbued with hard-to-overcome prejudices. In addition, for both the government and the opposition, other issues continue to be far more important. These prejudices and alternative priorities continue to block pro-LGBT legislation in Venezuela.

Notes

1. José Peña Solís, *Análisis crítico de la sentencia de la Sala Constitucional de fecha 28 febrero de 2008; interpretación de los artículos 21 y 77 constitucionales: derecho a la igualdad, uniones estables de hecho y extensión de los efectos del matrimonio a 'uniones concubinarias,'* Revista de Derecho 27, 299, Tribunal Supremo de Justicia, Caracas, Venezuela, 2008.

2. Vladimir Villegas was a member of the leftist political group that supported the constitutional change through a Constitutional Assembly, and a liberal in social matters such as sexual rights. He also supported the first pride march, in Caracas in 2001.

3. Tribunal Supremo de Justicia, Ruling No. 190, Case 03-2630, Caso Unión Afirmativa, Caracas, February 2, 2008.

4. Ibid.

5. See the full text of Ruling No. 190 by the Supreme Justice Tribunal in response to Appeal No. 00-2630 by Affirmative Union: http://www.tsj.gov.ve/decisiones/consulta_sala.asp?etiqueta =001&sala=005&dia=28/2/2008&nombre=Sala%20Constitucional&pagina=3

LGBT Rights in Ecuador's 2008 Constitution

Victories and Setbacks

Selena Xie and Javier Corrales

In 2008, Ecuador approved a new constitution granting civil union rights for LGBT people.[1] This constitution replaced the 1998 constitution, which was the first constitution in the Western Hemisphere to ban discrimination on the basis of sexuality. Many LGBT activists called the 2008 constitution a "major step forward."[2] Others, however, wonder if the new constitution is more restrictive than the previous one. Both positions are tenable. The 2008 constitution represents both a step forward and a step backward for LGBT rights. The duality of the 2008 Ecuadoran constitution shows, once again, the perils of compromise for advancing LGBT rights. On the one hand, compromise is the hallmark of democratic politics and an essential political practice to sustain governments and coalitions. On the other hand, compromise on questions of civil rights can lead to inconsistent legal codes. For the sake of compromise, rights can be extended to please a particular constituency while simultaneously injecting a restriction to please another one. This is what happened with the 2008 constitution.

In Ecuador, LGBT activism mostly began in the mid-1990s. In June 1997, police arrested a group of fourteen gay men in a Cuenca bar, invoking article 516 of the Penal Code, which penalized homosexual sex with the possibility of four to eight years of imprisonment.[3] Reports surfaced of police torture of many other homosexuals.[4] After a campaign led by LGBT activists, the Constitutional Court of Ecuador in 1997 declared imprisonment imposed on "consenting persons engaging in homosexual activities" unconstitutional.[5] This political-legal achievement galvanized the LGBT community to become involved in efforts to influence the drafting of the 1998 constitution.

The 1998 constitution represented a clear victory for LGBT groups. Article 23, section 3 states:[6]

> Equality before law: All persons are considered equal and shall enjoy the same rights, freedoms and opportunities without discrimination on grounds of birth, age, sex, ethnicity, color, social origin, language, religion, political affiliation, economic status, sexual orientation, status of health, disability or any other difference.

This antidiscrimination section made Ecuador the third country in the world to constitutionally ban discrimination on the basis of sexuality. Some activists attribute this victory to the low-profile, "very quiet lobbying" of LGBT groups in the 1990s.[7]

Thereafter, the LGBT community became less silent, forming organizations like *Fundación Causana*. While these organizations never became too strong or stable, with some groups like ASOEGT and FEMIS Y CRISALYS expiring quickly, Ecuadorean LGBT organizations and leaders developed an international presence, participating in the World Conference against Racism, Racial Discrimination, Xenophobia, and Related Intolerance in Durban, South Africa. They also became more involved in domestic lobbying. In July 2004, for instance, they presented a proposal to the National Congress to revise the Penal Code by introducing penalties against homophobia-based hate crimes. While this proposal was defeated in Congress, LGBT activists did not feel defeated, carried on with their efforts, and actually achieved successes elsewhere. For example, they lobbied the municipality of Quito to accept proposals to recognize sexual diversity in its policies and raise awareness of these issues.[8] When the time came to negotiate the 2008 constitution, LGBT activists pushed for more extensive gay rights than were included in the 1998 constitution.

However, because LGBT organizations were still marginalized and small in 2008, they decided to join forces with a variety of feminist groups, which had a stronger, more legitimate presence in Ecuadorean politics. The feminist movement embraced gay rights under the umbrella of human rights.[9] The feminist movement coordinated efforts to protest at Montecristi, the location of the Constitutional Assembly. It held forums and demonstrations right outside the assembly chambers, demanding antidiscrimination language and the right to gay marriage, adoption, and abortion.

This joint effort between feminists and LGBT groups paid off. The 2008 constitution is more explicit and farther reaching than the 1998 constitution. For instance, article 11, section 2 states:

No one shall be discriminated against on grounds of ethnicity, place of birth, age, sex, gender identity, cultural identity, marital status, language, religion, ideology, political affiliation, past judicial, socio-economic status, immigration status, sexual orientation, health status, HIV status, disability, physical difference, or any other distinction, personal or collective, temporary or permanent, which has the purpose or effect of impairing or nullifying the recognition, enjoyment or exercise of rights. The law shall punish any discrimination. The State shall take affirmative action to promote equality in favor of rights holders who are in a situation of inequality.

This article goes farther than the 1998 constitution by banning discrimination based on HIV status and gender identity, pushing for affirmative action, and explicitly stipulating punishment for discrimination. These provisions alone, which were absent in the 1998 constitution, are evidence of progress.

An even more celebrated feature is the right to civil union. Article 68 states that civil unions do not differ from marriages in anything besides name:

The stable and monogamous union between two persons, free of matrimonial bond, who form a de facto couple, since the time and under the conditions and circumstances specified by law, will have the same rights and obligations that families, built through marriage, have.

However, this feature is also the most controversial. Article 67 explicitly states that "marriage is the union between a man and a woman." In effect, this article creates a constitutional ban on gay marriage, while granting to gay couples all the same rights a marriage affords. Furthermore, this article states that "only two people of the opposite sex can adopt," which the LGBT community concedes is a disappointing loss.

The nature of the controversy is clear. On one hand, gay men and lesbians obtained the right to form civil unions, which are effectively treated like marriages, except in name. On the other hand, the constitution restricts potential interpretations that could expand gay rights in the future. Before the 2008 constitution, LGBT people could have asked the courts to interpret a blanket no-discrimination law to include discrimination in cases of adoption. With the new constitution, adoption by same-sex parents seems legally unimaginable.

How can we explain the dual character of the treatment of LGBT rights in the 2008 Ecuadorean constitution? The answer has to do with the bargaining leverage and preferences of the actors who negotiated the new constitution. In his presidential campaign, Rafael Correa, the president of Ecuador, promised a new constitution, aligning himself with a broad array of progressive and leftist movements, including environmental organizations, indigenous people, and feminist organizations. The feminist movement, in particular, strongly advocated for expanding gay rights.

However, throughout his campaign and during the early part of his administration, Correa made homophobic remarks, raising serious questions about his true commitment to LGBT rights. Likewise, Correa's party, Alianza PAIS, seems to have been split as well. The majority of PAIS delegates at the assembly supported progressive rights, such as the right to an abortion.[10] But they seem to have been more split on the question of gay rights. Feminists like María Paula Roma, a member of PAIS, fought for gay rights under the umbrella of human rights. Yet other PAIS assembly members, most notably Rossana Queirolo, publicly declared that they wanted to eliminate the progay protections from the constitution.[11] Queirolo was supported by other PAIS members, like Baerico Estacio and Teresa Benavides, and people unaffiliated with PAIS. For example, Pastor Francisco Loor Mendoza coordinated a campaign against abortion and gay marriage on behalf of the Evangelical Christian Church. This opposition campaigned in various media outlets, calling homosexuality an "abnormality" and depicting abortion as sucking or tearing children out of the womb.[12] This issue created much debate on the assembly floor.

Ultimately, PAIS in general and Correa in particular took the middle ground. On the one hand, PAIS tried to take attention away from these polemical issues—like gay marriage, abortion, and the invocation of God—arguing that they were a distraction from the larger task of drafting the 2008 constitution.[13] Correa himself publicly supported rights for the LGBT community, especially the antidiscrimination clauses. He stated, "Let it be clear that the profoundly humanistic position of this government is to respect the intrinsic dignity of everyone, of every human being, independent of their creed, race, sexual preference, and that [the government] will seek to grant certain guarantees to stable same-sex unions, but without ever arriving at the point of marriage."[14] However, as a concession to homophobic sentiment (outside and inside the assembly, outside and inside his party, and possibly within Correa himself), Correa endorsed the ban on gay marriage (in name) and the rejection of adoption rights for LGBT people.

After the Constituent Assembly concluded its work, Correa did campaign heavily on behalf of the constitution's ratification. The Roman Catholic Church, however, openly rejected the constitution, claiming it was "incompatible with the faith."[15] Through a series of radio addresses, Correa responded by reiterating that the new constitution did not grant marriage and adoption rights for gay people. In other words, he did not challenge the Church's homophobia. He simply challenged the Church's interpretation of the constitution as being too accommodating of LGBT rights.

LGBT activists were in a bind. On the one hand, they encouraged people to vote for the constitution, recognizing that this was a case of progress, albeit with serious caveats. But because they did not want to stimulate a homophobic electoral reaction, they tried to keep a low profile during the campaign. They were helped by other progressive movements, including many progressive priests, who denounced the Church's rhetoric, calling it a result of "powerful sectors' political interests."

In short, since the mid-1990s, LGBT activists in Ecuador have made great strides. This is surprising in many ways, because Ecuador seems to be a very unlikely case. Ecuador remains a socially conservative country with one of the highest rates of church attendance in Latin America. Furthermore, the country is consumed by other pressing issues, such as a high degree of political and economic instability and enduring poverty. Yet LGBT movements have been able to persuade leading politicians to concede on an issue that would seem less urgent to some groups or objectionable to so many others. On the other hand, the Ecuadorean case also suggests that the legal progress of LGBT rights can come with legal and political setbacks, even side by side. Political compromise can open one new door and close another for LGBT citizens.

On September 28, 2009, 63.93 percent of Ecuadorians voters approved the new constitution. President Correa proclaimed "We're making history! Onward!" As far as gay rights are concerned, he was partly right.

Notes

We are grateful to Manuela Picq for her comments and contacts in Ecuador. We are also grateful to Amherst College, especially the Center for Community Engagement, the office of the president, the dean of the faculty, and the dean of students for providing funding for a field research trip in January 2009. Thank you also to Professor Farith Simon at the Universidad San Francisco de Quito, Sonia Estrella at the *Consejo Nacional de las Mujeres*, Patricio Aguirre of *Fundación Causana*, and Daniel Denvir. Many thanks to the students who came on the trip: Brooke Berman, Rhea Ghosh, Carlos Sabatino González, Sam Grausz, Elspeth Hansen, David Reinhardt, Eric Schultz, and Tara Shabahang.

1. 365 Gay, "New Ecuador Constitution Includes Gay Rights Guarantees," *365 Gay*, September 29, 2008, http://www.365gay.com/news/new-ecuador-constitution-includes-gay-rights-guarantees/ (accessed December 9, 2009).

2. Daniel Denvir, "Ecuador's Proposed Constitution Causes Rift between Left and Right," *The Advocate*, September 27, 2008, http://advocate.com/exclusive_detail_ektid62297.asp

3. International Gay and Lesbian Human Rights Commission, "Ecuador: Men Arrested During Gay Bar Raid in Cuenca; One is Raped by Other Inmates in Police Custody," International Gay and Lesbian Human Rights Commission, August 1, 1997.

4. Sofia Argüello Pazmiño, "*Ciudadanías sexuales en Ecuador: Breves aproximaciones históricas*," *Centro Latinoamericano de Sexualidad y Derechos Humanos* (2008), http://www.clam.org.br/publique/media/Ecuador%5B1%5D.pdf (accessed April 23, 2009).

5. The UN Refugee Agency, Office of the United Nations High Commission for Refugees.

6. Constitución del Ecuador, www.asambleanacional.gov.ec/documentos/constitucion_de_bolsillo.pdf (accessed December 9, 2009).

7. See Arüello Pazmiño, "*Ciudadanías sexuales.*"

8. Coalición Ecuatoriana de Iniciativa GLBTI, "*Reseña histórica del movimiento GLBTI en el Ecuador*," February 10, 2008, http://ceiglbti.blogspot.com/2008/02/resea-histrica-del-movimiento -glbti-en.html

9. Sonia Estrella, *Consejo Nacional de las Mujeres*, in discussion with the authors, Quito, Ecuador, January 12, 2009.

10. Flavia Freidenberg, "*¿Renovación o Continuismo? Actitudes, valores y trayectoria de la clase política ecuatoriana*," Instituto de Iberoamérica, Universidad de Salamanca, 2008.

11. Rossana Queirolo, "*Mis principios son inclaudicables,*" El Universo, March 25, 2008, http://archivo.eluniverso.com/2008/03/25/0001/8/C7EEDEDCF5014652AB292FC6A0911B01.aspx

12. Argüello Pazmiño, "*Ciudadanías sexuales.*"

13. *El Universo,* "*Dios, aborto y gays no irán en Constitución, según bloque de PAIS,*" El Universo, March 26, 2008, http://archivo.eluniverso.com/2008/03/26/0001/8/1E0B916A5E174931952AB 4200776F5DE.aspx

14. Rex Wockner, "Ecuadorean President Supports Same-Sex Partnerships," *San Francisco Times,* April 10, 2008, http://www.sfbaytimes.com/index.php?sec=article&article_id=7899

15. 365 Gay, "Catholic Church Blasts Ecuador's New Gay-Positive Constitution," *365 Gay,* July 31, 2008, http://www.365gay.com/news/073108-ecuador-constitutio/

PART 4

The State and Public Policies

Friendly Government, Cruel Society

AIDS and the Politics of Homosexual Strategic Mobilization in Brazil

Eduardo J. Gómez

BRAZIL HAS been repeatedly noted as perhaps the best example of how a government should respond to HIV/AIDS. Since the outbreak of the epidemic in 1981, political elites have been unwaveringly committed to insuring equal access to AIDS treatment and prevention programs while working closely with civil society to insure that services are delivered efficiently. Notwithstanding the recent burgeoning of writings explaining the politics of Brazil's success story (Gauri and Lieberman 2004; Teixeira 1997; Gómez 2006b; Parker, Galvão, and Bessa 1999), few scholars have considered the vital role that the homosexual community played during this process. The gay community contributed to these policy reforms, and offers broader lessons that we can learn from these experiences.

In contrast to recent studies explaining the contemporary politics of government response to AIDS, understanding the Brazilian success story requires that we delve back into history in order to unravel the political and social contexts facilitating—and challenging—the gay community's ability to subsequently achieve its goals. There were three historical antecedent conditions leading to the government's continued support of the gay community's needs and successful gay mobilization for policy reform: the rich government tradition of antidiscriminatory legislation toward

233

homosexuals, the absence of sexual-orientation discourse and nonheterosexual identity in the public sphere, and the persistence of violent social discrimination against gays.

While the government's historical toleration of homosexual rights and the absence of sexual-orientation discourse in the public sphere engendered an unwavering federal-government commitment to homosexual rights, the concomitant, somewhat hidden existence of indirect government repression (mainly through the police) and social hatred contributed to the emergence of what I call a conflicting double movement within the gay community. That is, a situation in which the federal government was consistently "friendly" and receptive to homosexuals' needs, while civil society was often cruel, discriminatory, and intolerant of them. Needless to say, this made it difficult for the homosexual community to immediately respond to the AIDS crisis.

I argue that these conditions generated incentives for gay NGOs to devise a unique, strategic response to the AIDS problem: indirectly lobbying the federal government while mobilizing in a manner that would avoid continued social repression—in essence, a clandestine, somewhat sneaky mobilization tactic. They achieved this by strategically aligning themselves with well-established NGOs that were simultaneously fighting for human rights and universal access to medicine at the height of the redemocratization process in 1985, while at the same time refraining from openly marketing their movement as a new, original civic movement. Creating a new gay movement for access to AIDS treatment would have instigated too much social hostility, with the inevitable consequence of discouraging further mobilization. (Keep in mind that Brazilian society initially attributed the AIDS crisis to affluent gay lifestyles.) Thus, since the AIDS outbreak, the gay community has been caught up in a double-movement dilemma, whereby it wants to approach the federal government while simultaneously realizing that it must avoid doing so directly, in order to avoid further social repression.

The dependent variable of interest is the gay community's ability to secure equal access to AIDS prevention and treatment programs. This has been achieved, and gay activists were also successful at influencing the implementation of new federal prevention campaigns that are helping to increase awareness of the social stigma of homosexuality and the need to help those living with HIV. These programs have, moreover, highlighted the government's continued toleration and support of the gay community, efforts that many nations should learn from.

Friendly Government, Cruel Society

The history of the politics of homosexuality in Brazil illustrates how the conflict between a receptive, friendly government and a repressive, cruel society emerged. Shortly after political independence, the political elite sponsored a backlash against Portuguese condemnatory actions towards homosexuals, and instituted laws that safeguarded homosexual rights; this, in turn, lead to the absence of any form of legal discrimination. At the same time, however, civil society and certain segments of the government, such as the police, continued to repress homosexuals. Explaining the emergence of this duality is important for our understanding of the political and social dilemmas that the gay community faced shortly after the AIDS outbreak, as activists coordinated a strategic yet somewhat clandestine response to a very friendly government, while maintaining a low profile and working through other human-rights NGOs in order to avoid discrimination from a very cruel society.

In the early nineteenth century, Brazil entered a critical transition period in the politics of gay rights. Until political independence in 1821, homosexuals were violently suppressed by the government and civil society. Public lynchings were typical, while employers, civil society, and families openly rejected gays. Nevertheless, shortly after independence in 1821, in an effort to establish the democratic legitimacy of the new Republican regime, political elites reacted against this movement and instituted several laws protecting the rights of homosexuals. Homosexuality was no longer a crime (Mott 1995). Indeed, as James Green (1999) notes in his seminal contribution, *Beyond Carnival*, the new Republican regime instituted new laws that banned any form of discrimination against gays. Employers, both public and private, were no longer allowed to discriminate based on sexual orientation (Green 1999). Nor were the federal police allowed to arrest homosexuals for "immoral" practices, as had been the case under the Portuguese. Thus, shortly after political independence, a regime that was friendly and receptive to the homosexual community emerged; what is more, this tradition persisted even under subsequent military regimes (Mott 1995).

These impressive policies notwithstanding, as Green notes, various informal political and social discriminatory actions against gays emerged. While public law mandated absolutely no discrimination against homosexuals, several aspects of the law were still quite vague and open to broad interpretation. The police took advantage of these ambiguities, often abusing and humiliating homosexuals, especially in jailhouses (Green 1999). These actions set the tone for continued social and familial repression. That is, social awareness of these actions made it socially acceptable to discriminate against homosexuals —and even encouraged such discrimination. The level of violence rose. Gay homicides were reported all over the country. Yet the police very rarely did anything about it (Green 1999). Homosexuality in early Brazil was still perceived—as under the colonial regime—as an immoral sin (Mott 2003).

Family violence committed against gays was also quite typical. Given Roman Catholicism's predominance, coupled with its unwavering condemnatory stance towards homosexuality, family members were inclined to incessantly chastise and in some cases even disown gay family members. Often, gay family members, especially children, would have to live two lives: to be openly gay—and proud—in public, among lovers and friends, but remain straight and "piously" obedient at home (Likosky 1992).

This conflict between a friendly, receptive government and a cruel, discriminatory society continued throughout Brazil's cycles of military-democratic transitions. Under the military, the state retained its historical commitment to safeguarding homosexual rights. Any form of discrimination was still banned by law, while, interestingly, the generals were very tolerant of homosexual prostitution, pornography, and festivals, such as the gay pride parades (Mott 1995). In fact, it was under the military in 1976 that the first gay journal was allowed to be published and circulated, that is, the journal *O Lampião da Esquina*. Some scholars are of the opinion that the generals allowed this to occur because the gay lifestyle was the "trendy, fashionable" thing to do, a true, vivid sign of modernity (Likosky 1992). This was considered a form of social "window dressing," if you will, such that the stylish gay lifestyle was socially accepted as long as it did not *directly* affect another individual and/or family member. Military support for homosexual rights was also interpreted as an effective way of maintaining political legitimacy. This contrasted sharply with the more conservative authoritarian regimes of Argentina and Chile, where homosexuals were banned from society.

Since the transition away from military rule in 1985, this duality has continued. Because of the widespread belief in the early 1980s that AIDS was a direct result of the affluent lifestyles of homosexuals, social discrimination and violence against them increased and continue to do so. According to *Grupo Gay da Bahia* (GGB), within the last 20 years, 1,661 homosexuals were murdered, with an average of 80 homosexuals killed per year in the 1980s, rising to 120 per year in the 1990s (International Lesbian and Gay Association [ILGA] 1998). In 1998, 116 homosexuals were murdered, of whom 73 were gay men, 36 transvestites, and 7 lesbians (ILGA 1998). On average, moreover, GGB reported that one gay male was murdered every three days. Consequently, by 1998, Brazil ranked first in the world—followed by Iraq, Sudan, and Zimbabwe—for the total number of homosexual homicides and violent acts against gays each year. Such violence continues (see table 16.1).

In addition to homicides and violent acts, homosexuals continue to face an enormous amount of social discrimination. Not only do they continue to be randomly accosted on the street (Goering 1997), but even local political officials have discriminated against them. Indeed, in the state of Porto Alegre, it is illegal for gay men to donate blood at hospitals because of the fear (or rather, presumption) that they are HIV positive (Glock 1999); this has incensed the homosexual community and constrained its relations with the government (Terto, Jr. 2000). Further, in December 2003, Mayor Elcio Berti of Bocaiúva do Sul, in the state of Paraná, issued a decree prohibiting homosexuals from living in his town. Several state prosecutors immediately filed charges against the mayor for violation of state and federal antidiscrimination laws, which carries a charge of two to four years in prison. These efforts notwithstanding, it is sad

Table 16.1. Homicides of gays, bisexuals, lesbians, and transvestites in Brazil					
	Gays	Bisexuals	Lesbians	Transvestites	Total
2004	81	No data	8	36	125
2005	118	1	4	35	158

Source: Luiz Mott 2005.

to note that even to this day some locally elected officials have gone so far as to issue laws that blatantly discriminate against homosexuals.

As in the past, yet another component of the state, the police force, has been accused of participating in violent acts against homosexuals. A recent report issued by the U.S. Department of State notes that several municipal police officers were members of neo-Nazi gangs and/or "*machista*" gangs committing violent acts against homosexuals (U.S. Department of State 2004). The police have also been accused of harassing homosexuals in prison, calling them, in one famous case in Porto Calvo, in the state of Alagoas, "crazy fagots," while physically assaulting them and making them wait long hours in jail (Global Justice Center 2002). Often the police have failed to respond to eyewitness accounts and testimonies of homicides and other assaults. What is more, some police officers even consider murdering homosexuals an acceptable "defense of one's honor" (Goering 1997). In short, as in the past, the police are at times equally—if not more—hostile toward homosexuals than any other segment of civil society. Violence and hostility extend beyond the jailhouse, however. For even within close-knit family circles, hostility and hatred abound. Especially within the more conservative (often Roman Catholic) households, gays are seen as outcasts and treated harshly—yelled at, publicly accosted, at times even thrown out of the house. Some have been disowned. This is debilitating, especially for young people. While more families are aware of and open to homosexuality than in the past, fully embracing homosexuality within the family is still quite challenging. The government has realized this and has responded by creating a new federal campaign to help increase toleration and acceptance within families.

Given Brazil's notoriety for open displays of sexuality and the "exotic," it is perplexing to see the continuity and growth of societal discrimination and violence against gays. The problem, as always, is that most Brazilians pride themselves on openness to the sexually exotic, yet remain highly disenchanted with the gay lifestyle when it is applied to everyday life. That is, as long as homosexuality, bisexuality, and lesbianism remain within the distant "exotic" sphere, such as on Rio's beaches, gay nightclubs, and parades during Carnival, it's "ok," accepted—and for the most part, Brazilians are, hypocritically, proud of it. But the problem is when the "exotic" crosses over into the private sphere: that is, when it affects personal family and friends. An even bigger problem presents itself when a family member is gay but seems to behave "normally"—dresses well, pays taxes, loves soccer, has *cafezinho* with family and friends, and goes to church; the distant exotic is perceived to have "poisoned" or "possessed" a seemingly normal son or daughter who should not, according to the family, be gay. This is even worse than having a more feminine (or masculine), obviously gay personality. These individuals are sorely punished and at times even disowned by family and friends.

On a more positive note, it is relieving to see that the federal government has still not tried to punish the gay community. Rather, since the early 1990s, it has created several new institutions and programs designed specifically to meet their needs. By far the most impressive reforms were undertaken under the Fernando H. Cardoso administration (1994–2001). In addition to working with the gay community by granting them full membership on the National AIDS Commission, in 2001 Cardoso created the *Conselho Nacional de Combate á Discriminação* (CNCD). This organization was created with the express intent of ending discrimination and violence against the gay community. It was composed of several NGOs, homosexual men, lesbians, transvestites, and bisexuals. It was the first of its kind and became a priority for the subsequent Luiz Inácio Lula da Silva administration.

Indeed, in 2003, Lula took yet another step in this direction by creating a technical commission to aid the CNCD in monitoring and reporting violence and discrimination against gays. Furthermore, in November 2003, the CNCD took the initiative under Lula to create a *Grupo de Trabalho* to work with the new *Programa Brasileiro de Combata á Violencia e á Discriminação a Gays, Lésbicas, Travestis, Transgêneros e Bissexuais*, which was also created in 2003. All these programs and institutions were created in order to demonstrate the government's unwavering commitment to support the rights of the gay community and to ensure that they are protected as much as possible from lingering cruelty in society.

Lastly, it is important to note the recent program created by the *Secretaria Especial dos Direitos Humanos* (SEDH) and the *Conselho Nacional de Combate á Discriminacão: Brasil sem Homofobia* (BSH), which was written by Tancredo Neves, the minister of justice, on May 25, 2003. Perhaps more than any other initiative to date, this program seeks to build a horizontal coalition among various federal and subnational ministries, such as education, health, and the judiciary, to reduce social stigma and discrimination against homosexuals while educating the masses on the various types of sexuality. The primary goal is, of course, to end discrimination and violence, but *Brasil sem Homofobia* goes beyond this to propose new funding programs to support NGOs working for gay rights, to increase the representation of the gay community within government (through various commissions), and to disseminate information and educate the masses about gay rights (Brazil 2004). The government also set aside new funding for technical monitoring programs in order to map out and report the gay community's needs (especially in the area of health care), and to work with gay-based NGOs and civil society for greater incorporation and representation in government (Brazil 2004). In short, through this new initiative, the Lula administration has shown an unwavering, open commitment to reaching out and working with the gay community, both within the health sector and across other social policy areas.

Things are not as peaceful as they seem, however. For although new programs and initiatives have been proposed, the government has not been entirely committed to funding programs in a timely manner. One year after BSH's inception, various NGOs reported that they had not received one dime from the federal government (Silva 2005). As in other areas of social policy, pundits argue that Lula has done a great job of proposing new initiatives, but has not been as eager to follow through with BSH and other related projects (Silva 2005). The current administration will need to do better if it's going to ensure that these new programs work effectively.

These shortcomings notwithstanding, since the AIDS outbreak there is no question that the federal government has been enthusiastic about supporting the rights of homosexuals while increasing their representation in government. This contrasts sharply with the response of other parts of the state, such as the behavior of local government officials and the police, as well as the cruel elements of civil society. It is interesting to note, moreover, that the government's recent efforts comport with its long history (even under the military) of protecting gay rights through various programs and institutions. While the states and municipalities have been responsible for creating and enforcing all antidiscrimination laws, the government has maintained its open, supportive stance towards homosexuals. Nowhere is this more evident than in the government's institutional and policy response to AIDS, which has provided a big window of opportunity and incentives for the gay community to mobilize.

Sexual Identities, Forbidden Pleasures, and Secularism in the Moral Sphere

Unique sexual identities, activities, and secularism in the moral sphere also contributed significantly to the social backdrop necessary for expanding the identities and collective capacity of the homosexual community. These preconditions eventually helped this community collectivize and approach the government when seeking to influence AIDS policy. With regard to sexual identities, it is important to note that until very recently, these identities were never associated with Brazilians' commonly held notions of "homosexuality," "bisexuality," or "lesbianism,"[1] but rather with physical *acts*. This way of distinguishing sexual identities is known as the "folk model" of Brazilian sexuality. As Richard Parker explains, individuals often identified themselves as being either the aggressive sexual partner, *com actividade* (with action), or the passive partner, *com passividade* (with passivity); further, he explains that

> the man who obstructs his masculinity is seen as a failure, coming to be known as *viado* (from *veado*, deer) or *bicha* (literally, worm or intestinal parasite, but also, instructively, the feminine form of *bichoi*, or female animal), due to his inappropriate femininity, while the inadequate *mulher* is known as a *sapatão* (big shoe) or even *coturno* (army boot), due to her unacceptable masculinity (Parker 2009, 244).

Historically, moreover, male youths were often expected to experiment with other males through various games, such as *troca-troca* (turn taking), where two or more boys would take turns inserting their penises into each other's anuses. As Parker notes, *troca-troca* is perhaps best captured in the expression—"*Homen, para ser homen, tem que dar primeiro*"—A man, to be a man, first has to give.

These acts had several ramifications. First, they lessened the degree of social awareness about homosexuality, since individual—and thus collective—sexual identities were not labeled as clearly *homosexual*, but rather specific kinds of acts were labeled *homosexual.* Therefore, labeling someone either as *actividade* or *passividade* did not immediately suggest that the person was gay. Because it was difficult to assign a person's sexual preference based on an individual act, the labeling of *acts*, vs. *orientations*, permitted these activities to continue, further expanding and consolidating what we would now call the homosexual community. Second, these activities allowed for the emergence of an open sexual culture that *expected* people to engage in sexual taboos. Because they were forbidden pleasures, homosexual taboos, such as experimentation through games or other types of *felacio*, generated even more incentive to take part in them. This, in turn, allowed for the expansion of what we now call the homosexual community, allowing for a growing collective identity, even in the face of social discrimination.

Other traditions of Brazilian politics have allowed for the concomitant rise of a responsive government and homosexual community. A major issue has been the absence of the institutionalization of a Christian, puritanical moral outlook toward sexuality, akin to the Victorian impulse that shaped the antigay, antidrug, and prohibition legislations of early America (Morone 2004). To better understand this, one must first understand that sexual activity was socially constructed into something socially and scientifically acceptable to discuss. In his book *Bodies, Pleasures, and Passions*, Richard Parker (2009) notes that Portuguese Catholicism was rich with what he called "hidden morals," that is, Catholic ideals that were understood to be present in the family and the community, while never surfacing in the political and economic sphere. Portuguese-style Catholicism, moreover, was very open to sexuality, to the point were followers believed in saints that gave spiritual advice about good and proper sex (Parker 1991, 68; Freyre 1956). Parker argues that this led to the discovery of the personal self and individual bodily pleasures, unmasking the truth about what sex actually meant for the person, sans *any* fear of social and political repercussion. This backdrop aided political modernizers of the twentieth century and allowed for the concomitant transformation of economy, society, and sexuality. That is, the European movement toward the scientification of sexual activity, the movement toward discussing and analyzing sex in a scientifically objective manner, was embraced by government and civil society (Parker 1991, 86).

A social activity that deepened homosexual identities and political acceptance was Carnival. In *Sex, Drugs, and HIV/AIDS in Brazil*, James Inciardi (2000) writes that the yearly Carnival festivities held in Rio helped to suppress any potential movement towards sexuality as a social—and hence, political—taboo:

> Carnival, an annual three day pre-Lenten festival, is a ritual reversal in that every form of pleasure is possible—there are no prohibitions that temper sexual practice or desire. It is a time when Brazilians momentarily suspend their moral categories and undertake "dangerous," prohibited practices. In this way, Carnival momentarily serves to both suspend and challenge dominant social structures like religion and the gender hierarchy (Inciardi, Surratt, and Telles 2000, 35).

Thus in Brazil, colonial history, modernization, and contemporary activities all contributed towards sustaining the anti-Victorian drive that kept stern, potentially sexually discriminatory Christian moral principles at bay. This, in turn, influenced the government's view about who was responsible for HIV/AIDS. But more importantly, it would also omit any possibility of any openly discriminatory discourse or action on the part of the federal government toward the gay community.

Strategic Mobilization

Even though a flurry of civic associations and organizations emerged to pressure the seemingly apathetic Collor administration (1990–92), the gay community's strategy of mobilizing for policy reform was quite innovative. Gay activists believed that they could accomplish more, not by immediately claiming their association with AIDS and their right to medicine, but rather by, initially, modestly lobbying the government while joining and working through well-established civil and human-rights NGOs that were already well established and pressuring the government for human rights and universal rights to medicine. The burgeoning expectation and civil societal demands for human rights and equality that emerged prior to and throughout the democratic transition had led to a myriad of well-organized NGOs fighting for this cause.

The conditions could not be any more propitious. Gay-rights organizations picked up on the success of these NGOs and viewed a partnership with them as a strategic and effective way to successfully voice their concern within government. The beauty of this strategy was that it would not draw much social awareness and contention. Indeed, Barros (1999) notes that the

> fight for citizenship in a country that was emerging from an authoritarian government provided a larger, better umbrella for homosexual anti-AIDS organizations than what a new, independent, public homosexual movement might have provided. At the time, homosexuals believed that they would be more effective at influencing policy by working with other groups that were already quite successful in mobilizing support for policy reform, such as pro-women's rights and drug user's organizations, rather than with their own (Barros 1999, 176).

The possibility of working through well-established human-rights NGOs, coupled with the new opportunities (and need) for gay-rights organizations, led to the emergence (and re-emergence) of several homosexual NGOs. The *Somos* and *Lampã* gay-rights associations, which were created in the 1970s, reemerged to campaign against AIDS, while the *Atobá* in Rio and the *Grupo Gay da Bahia* (GGB) in the city of Salvador, Bahia, emerged as well. New groups, such as *Grupo de Apoio à Prevencãò à AIDS* (Support Group of AIDS Prevention), also formed in more than a dozen major urban centers, led by a diverse group of social workers, health professionals, gay activists, and individuals concerned with providing social and psychological support for AIDS victims. *Grupo Pela VIDAA* (Group for Life) was also formed in Rio at this time. This was the first publicized organization committed to fighting for the rights of gays and challenging the justice system for equal access to medicine. *Pela VIDAA* was also the first organization to address the issue of "living with AIDS," which was vital for uplifting those struggling with the virus on a daily basis. Other formal institutions emerged, such as ABIA (Brazilian Interdisciplinary AIDS Association), formed by influential intellectuals and scientists, and ARCA (Religious Support Group against AIDS), an ecumenical group formed by liberal religious leaders (Parker 2009).

The re-emergence and growth of gay NGOs notwithstanding, even during the early 1990s, these organizations refrained from ardently lobbying the government in an open, highly publicized manner. The stigma and fear of being gay was still very much present. Lingering rumors of AIDS being attributed to the fancy, liberal lifestyles of white upper-middle-class men in Rio and São Paulo were still very much present. Society was still quick to point the finger.

Although they feared continued social repression, gay rights NGOs nevertheless began to openly express their views and need for better treatment. The arrival of the more liberal presidency of Fernando H. Cardoso in 1994 certainly provided more opportunities to do this. More than any prior administration, Cardoso's was very open to working with the gay community. NGOs picked up on this and tailored their lobbying strategies accordingly.

Despite the new impulse for open gay activism and lobbying campaigns, social repression continued and has even increased. Throughout the 1990s, Brazil ranked among the top 10 nations in the world for violence towards gays. And as table 16.1 illustrates, homicidal acts towards homosexuals increased from 81 in 2004 to 118 in 2005. Most deaths were attributed to firearms and knifings, while the main motives cited were homophobia and passion (Mott 2005).

This recent violence notwithstanding, it is important to note that with time, the gay community would gradually spring forth with its own publicized agenda. This began to occur especially during the more liberal and receptive Cardoso administration (1994–2001). Such pressures from activists were vital for pushing the Cardoso administration to do more on AIDS. The gay community's efforts slowly but surely began to pay off.

Government Response to AIDS and the Homosexual Community

Since the outbreak of the HIV/AIDS epidemic in 1982, the government has responded quite aggressively. Within three years, it created a brand new federal agency, the National AIDS Program (NAP), which was—and still is—an independent bureaucratic agency *not* falling under the purview of the Ministry of Health; it has been staffed by highly competent directors, and it has had a very low turnover rate (Serra 2004; Galváo 2000). The NAP staff has been highly trained, while periodically coordinating with other branches to ensure that there is no overlap in policy responsibility (Galváo 2000). At the same time, the government has implemented a host of anti-AIDS prevention and treatment programs, using the decentralized *Sistema Único de Saúde* (SUS) (universal) health care system to disseminate services. With regard to prevention, the government has continued to provide antiviral medication for all of its citizens, free of charge, while incessantly bargaining with multinational corporations for a steady reduction in price. Moreover, it has provided a host of federally sponsored HIV-prevention programs, such as the free distribution of condoms, federal- and state-sponsored sex-education programs, and the incessant use of the media to increase citizen awareness of HIV. As table 16.2 indicates, in 2005 most of Brazil's citizens knew how HIV is transmitted.

The overall decline in cases of HIV and AIDS, especially cases of death from HIV/AIDS, has been astounding. Since 2000, Brazil has seen a faster decline in the number of HIV and AIDS cases than the United States. These impressive aggregate results notwithstanding, the years between 1996 and 2001 saw an increase in cases of HIV, mainly among young homosexual men. During this time period, the rate of in-

Table 16.2. Brazilian population's understanding of HIV transmission

	N (%)	NE (%)	SE (%)	S (%)	CW (%)	Average (%)
Understand how HIV is transmitted	57.6	57.5	71.8	73.5	70	67.1
Believe HIV can be transmitted through insect bites	4.3	7.3	3.4	4.1	3.3	4.6
Believe HIV can be transmitted by using public toilets	16.4	19.9	11.5	11.5	13.3	14.2
Believe HIV can be transmitted by sharing cutlery, glasses and dishes	22.6	20.3	12.8	10.8	12.6	15.2
Believe HIV can be transmitted by sharing syringe needles	85.7	89.6	92.9	94.8	90.7	91.6
Believe HIV can be transmitted by having unprotected sex	97.1	96.5	95.4	95.7	96	95.9

Source: Berquó (2000) and the National AIDS Program Web site, Ministry of Health, Brazil, 2005.

fection among gay men between the ages of 15 and 24 grew approximately 8.7 percent, and for men between the ages of 25 to 34, grew 3.4 percent.

Perhaps the main reason there was—and continues to be—an increase in HIV/AIDS prevalence among young homosexual men has been the paradoxically negative consequence of a universal health care system that provides antiretroviral therapy (ARV) medication free of charge. This has, in combination with the fact that life expectancy for the HIV-positive has steadily increased through AV usage, generated few incentives for the young homosexual community to take the necessary precautionary measures before having sex.

In addition to the host of general prevention and treatment programs implemented throughout the 1990s, the government has been equally as committed to working with the homosexual community to combat AIDS. These efforts started under Cardoso and have continued under the Lula administration. Recently, Lula has openly stated that he remains firmly committed to helping the HIV-positive homosexual community (Mott 2005). And this has occurred in the presence of consistently high levels of social violence and stigma against the gay community. As in the past, the government continues to reveal an open, secular commitment to insuring that *all* segments of society are treated equally.

The obvious next question to ask is, why? Why would the government remain so committed to reaching out to a segment of society that has been repeatedly discriminated against? If most of civil society, that is, voters (including some local politicians and police officers), are still hostile to the gay community, then why do nationally elected legislators and the president continue to respond by openly supporting the gay community through the creation of new programs and policies? The answer to this question is rather complex.

The answer appears to lie amid the intricate combination of the perennial, unwavering commitment of political and medical elites to sustain their deep tradition of responding to *all* segments of society, regardless of sexual orientation, for medical treatment in response to epidemics, and, on the other hand, the relentless efforts of the homosexual community, both through their own (now prosperous) NGOs and others, to tactfully lobby the government. Indeed, just before the Cardoso administration's new anti-AIDS policies for the gay community were implemented, the director of the National AIDS Program openly stated in a BBC interview that protecting homosexuals from AIDS was just as important as any of their other prevention programs: "Respecting differences is as important as using condoms," said Paulo Teixeira, NAP director (Murray 2002). This showed that the Cardoso administration was willing to stick its neck out and support a highly contentious position within civil society. This, in turn, reaffirmed the government's long-held tradition of supporting the gay community—and other minorities—even before the transition to democracy.

In addition to maintaining its tradition of equality in public health treatment, responding to the homosexual community has also been medically necessary. Recently, of all the gender and age classes in Brazil, the rate in increase of HIV prevalence has been highest among young homosexual males between the ages of fifteen and twenty-five. Since it has become widely known that the NAP and state governments continue to provide free antiretroviral medication for all, the tendency has been for homosexuals and other groups to become less protective of themselves than before. Naturally, the consequences have included a steady increase in infection among those groups that are less cautious, and this tends to include the younger population.

To curb the further spread of HIV among homosexual youth, in June 2002 the NAP created a new prevention program that was aimed at the gay community. The biggest, arguably most important component of this program is TV propaganda. Through public service announcements, the government has tried to not only educate young men on the importance of using condoms, but it has also tried to increase familial and social acceptance of gays. Hoping to reduce stigma within the family, wherein the social stigma of homosexuality causes problems between family members, between those who are gay and those who are not, leading to incessant abuse and violence, the government televised a commercial in which a father and a son are hugging each other; in it, they are openly talking about the son's sexual orientation, and the father is supporting the son. In another commercial, a mother consoles and supports her son by stating, "It's OK, son. You'll find a guy who deserves you—who'll use a condom" (Murray 2002).

The social ramifications of these public service announcements are quite powerful, for three key reasons. First, they reveal to civil society that the federal government is wholeheartedly committed to helping the homosexual community, especially young men. Second, these programs help educate families about the importance of respecting their sons' sexual orientation. Hopefully, this will have the effect of motivating fathers and mothers to question and talk about the sexual orientation of their children, which is the first step to trust, acceptance, and healing. And third, this information will help keep the rate of gay people living on the "down-low" really, really low, down to near nonexistence: that is, by increasing openness and support within families, homosexuals (especially youth) may refrain from engaging in clandestine sexual activities and thus refrain from having unprotected sex. Instead, family members can be more open and supportive, in turn leading to more advice and pressure to practice safe sex.

These prevention programs are part of a larger federal campaign to not only insure the medical treatment of the homosexual community (which is, like every other community, currently guaranteed through universal health insurance), but to further increase prevention by continually working with gay NGOs, and increasing social awareness of this issue. Recently, Bargas Negri, the minister of health, and the director of NAP, Paulo Teixeira, created a new federal campaign called *Homens que fazem Sexo com Homens* (HSH). Costing the government more than three million reais, it is a federal program designed to increase social awareness and, especially, tolerance of homosexuals. Further, through this program, both the Ministry of Health and the NAP work with gay NGOs for greater intervention in disseminating information about HIV transmission among homosexuals, and the proper precautionary measures to take. Government financing for those NGOs engaged in these activities has been critical for reaching out to the homosexual community.

Realizing the ongoing stigma within families and the professional community, through this program the government has also provided information for family members (in part through the public service announcements discussed above) while distributing packets to university professors (both within and outside of the medical schools), and even giving information tapes to the alumni of these schools (National AIDS Program 2006). Through these initiatives, the goal has been to educate families and the professional community in order to increase awareness of the ongoing HIV problem, reduce social stigma, and to permanently transform social conceptions of this disease (National AIDS Program 2006).

This type of government response is sui generis, in that no other government in the world has created a separate program for the gay community. However effective this program has been, the simple fact that this program was passed in the legislature and adopted as a federal program sends a huge signal that the government is unwaveringly committed to helping the gay community. Only time will tell how effective these efforts are. Yet, when considering the continued stigma and discrimination against homosexuals in Brazil, this program further warns that that the federal government will not tolerate any sort of social or, especially, medical harassment or discrimination against this community. This is vital not only for domestic security, but also for maintaining the peace and safeguarding democracy.

Lessons for Democracies

Several key lessons emerge from the consideration of Brazil's National AIDS Program. First, it is essential that there be a receptive government willing to working with the gay community in response to the AIDS epidemic while securing access to prevention programs. Despite the continued presence of a hostile society, the federal government has always been committed to serving the gay community's social welfare needs. This is emblematic of the rich history of the military and democratic elite's commitment to viewing sexually transmitted diseases through a nonmoral, objectively scientific lens.

Second, not only has the presence of a receptive government been necessary for protecting homosexuals from AIDS, but it has been vital for kindling strategic collective mobilization tactics with this community. Facing a cruel civil society, during the initial AIDS outbreak, the gay community had to work around these constraints by strategically aligning themselves with well-established, nongay NGOs fighting for human rights prior to and throughout the redemocratization process. Thus the key lesson here is that when responding to epidemics that instigate negative reactions within society, stigmatized communities may have to engage in collaborative relationships with other NGOs that have well-established traditions of working with the government. This may be needed in order to temporarily avoid social—and even familial—repression while being able to effectively lobby the government. While governments —such as Brazil's—may be friendly and receptive to the homosexual community's needs, fear of continued social repression within society may generate sufficient pressures that activists choose not to lobby the state.

This intriguing finding suggests that we should revisit other schools of thought emphasizing the importance of domestic institutions as necessary and sufficient conditions for effective civic mobilization. Take for instance the seminal work of Theda Skocpol in *Protecting Soldiers and Mothers* (1995). Looking at the contributions that unemployed mothers (especially widows) played in the development of America's first social welfare policies, Skocpol shows that their capacity to mobilize and influence the creation of new unemployment pension policies for widowed mothers was facilitated by the presence of federal institutions encouraging mothers to mobilize by guaranteeing their representation at the national level. (Others have labeled these institutions as "open ended," since they both represent and bolster the influence of interest groups; see Montero 2001; Gómez 2003). While mothers were certainly motivated to collectivize, guaranteed institutional representation through national committees and the unwavering support of legislative members and the bureaucracy decreased the costs typically associated with collective action. This occurred because all mothers were essentially guaranteed that their voices would be heard and that they could, consequently, influence social policy.

Similarly, recent research by Renee Loewenson (2003) shows that policy practitioners are now realizing that what determines the success of civil societal mobilization in response to epidemics—such as AIDS—is the presence of federal institutional structures guaranteeing interest-group representation. She thus encourages us to look at the factors "within the state" that influence the capacity and willingness of civil society to mobilize. These factors are institutional guarantees, such as contracts, laws, and committees, designed by political elites to encourage civil societal mobilization and lobbying (Loewenson 2003).

What this Brazilian case study has shown, however, is that the presence of "open-ended" institutions will not guarantee that afflicted groups within civil society will mobilize in response to an epidemic. As we saw in Brazil, notwithstanding the unwavering support of a "friendly" government throughout history—even under the military— the gay community could not *directly* approach the state. The presence of supportive institutions did not guarantee that civil society would not retaliate against public demonstrations of homosexual needs in response to AIDS. Rather, in order to take advantage of the government's institutional receptivity, the gay community had to *indirectly* approach the state through other NGOs, which had preexisting connections with the military and new democratic administrations. Thus, the mere presence of supportive federal institutions may not be necessary and sufficient for successful mobilization within civil society.

Lastly, the mere transition to democracy, free market reforms, and the provision of progressive social welfare programs may not guarantee peace, equality, and progress within civil society. Homosexuals and other stigmatized groups afflicted with HIV, such as prostitutes and drug users, may continue to face social repression. As seen in other nations, such as Russia, the United States, and China, this, in turn, may continue to generate few incentives for collective mobilization for more effective anti-AIDS policies. Further, Brazil's case shows that what is necessary but, of course, insufficient for successful mobilization is the presence of a friendly government, one that devises institutions that are amenable to and supportive of the needs of the homosexual community.

Indeed, perhaps more than anything else, future democracies will need to ensure that political elites are wholeheartedly committed to creating public health institutions and policies that meet the needs of socially stigmatized groups. Moreover, elites will need to periodically modernize these institutions by creating new programs that evolve along with the medical needs of these stigmatized groups—as modeled by the recent federal campaign for homosexuals under the Ministry of Health and the National AIDS Program in Brazil. If and when this is achieved, especially within those nations that do not currently have this type of arrangement in place, for example, Russia, China, India, and, arguably, even the United States, nations may be able to further consolidate their democracies by guaranteeing the protection of human rights—regardless of sexual orientation—while safeguarding their citizenry from the ongoing devastation of AIDS and other ongoing and newly emergent health epidemics.

Note

1. Believe it or not, it was not until the 1980s that the term *homosexual* was adopted as a category of sexual identity. This definition was, as Parker notes, adopted from the United States by Brazilian medical scientists and quickly adopted by upper-class intellectuals, gradually trickling down to the masses (Parker 1999).

References

Bastos, C. 1999. *Global Responses to AIDS: Science in Emergency.* Bloomington: Indiana University Press.

Berquó, E. 2000. Com portamento sexual da população brasileira e percepções do HIV/AIDS. Série Avaliaçao 4. Brasília: Ministério de Saúde.

Feldman, D. A., ed. *Global AIDS Policy.* South Hadley, Mass.: Bergin & Gravey Press.

Freyre, G. 1956. *The Masters and the Slaves: A Study in the Development of Brazilian Civilization.* New York: Alfred Knopf Press.

Galváo, J. 2000. *AIDS no Brasil: A agenda de construção de uma epidemia.* São Paulo: ABIA Publishers.

Gauri, V., and E. Lieberman. 2004. AIDS and the State: The Politics of Government Responses to the Epidemic in Brazil and South Africa. Paper presented at the Annual Meeting of the American Political Science Association, Chicago, September 2–5.

Global Justice Center. 2002. *Human Rights in Brazil—2002: The Global Justice Center Annual Report.* http://www.global.org.br/english/arquivos/annual_report.pdf (accessed December 9, 2009).

Glock, C. 1999. Brazil: HIV-Carriers—10 Years Fighting for Their Lives. *Inter-Press Service,* April 26. http://www.aegis.com/news/ips/1999/IP990403.html (accessed October 8, 2009).

Goering, L. 1997. Brazil's Gay Men Appear Singled Out, Attacked for Living Ordinary Lives. *Chicago Tribune,* April 4. http://www.aegis.com/news/ct/1997/ct970402.html (accessed December 9, 2009).

Gómez, E. J. 2003. Decentralization and Municipal Governance: Suggested Approaches for Cross-Regional Analysis. *Studies in Comparative International Development* 38 (3): 57–80.

———. 2006a. The Politics of Government Response to HIV/AIDS in Russia and Brazil. Working Paper 4, Harvard Initiative for Global Health.

———. 2006b. Lessons from the Past: State Building and the Politics of HIV/AIDS Policy Reform in Brazil. *Whitehead Journal of Diplomacy and International Relations*.

Green, J. N. 1999. *Beyond Carnival: Male Homosexuality in Twenty-first Century Brazil*. Hyde Park: University of Chicago Press.

Inciardi, J., H. Surratt, and P. R. Telles, eds. 2000. *Sex, Drugs, and HIV/AIDS in Brazil*. Washington, D.C.: National Academy Press.

International Lesbian and Gay Association. 1998. Brazil—World Champion in the Murder of Homosexuals. http://www.pangea.org/~cogailes/ilga/repilga99text.html

Likosky, S., ed. 1992. *Coming Out: An Anthology of International Gay and Lesbian Writings*. New York: Pantheon Books.

Loewenson, R. 2003. Civil Society-State. Interactions in National Health Systems. Civil Society Institute, Working paper, World Health Organization.

Ministério de Saúde/Conselho Nacional de Combate á Discriminação, Brasília. 2004. *Brasil sem homofobia: Programa de combate à violencia e à discriminação contra GLTB e de promocão da cidadania homossexual*.

Morone, J. A. 2004. *Hellfire Nation: The Politics of Sin in American History*. New Haven: Yale University Press.

Mott, L. 1995. The Gay Movement and Human Rights in Brazil. In *Latin American Male Homosexualities*, ed. Stephen O. Murray, 221–30. Albuquerque: University of New Mexico Press.

———. 2003. *Homossexualidade: Mitos e verdades*. Salvador: Editora Grupo Gay da Bahia.

———. 2005. *O Presidente Lula e os gays. Grupo Gay da Bahia*, http://www.ggb.org.br/presidente-lula.html (accessed December 9, 2009).

Murray, I. 2002. Brazil AIDS Campaign Causes Stir. BBC News, 8/8/02.

National AIDS Program. 2006. *Campanha para homens que fazem sexo com homens (HSH)*. Official federal campaign Web site. www.aids.gov.br.

Parker, R. 1999. *Public Policy, Political Activism, and AIDS in Brazil*. In *Global AIDS Policy*, ed. D. A. Feldman, 28–46. Westport, Conn.: Bergan and Garvey Press.

———. 2009. *Bodies, Pleasures, and Passions: Sexual Culture in Contemporary Brazil*, 2nd ed. Nashville: Vanderbilt University Press.

Parker, R., J. Galvão, and M. S. Bessa, eds. 1999. *Saúde, desenvolvimento e política: Respostas frente á AIDS no Brasil*. São Paulo: ABIA Publishers.

Serra, J. 2004. The Political Economy of the Brazilian Struggle against AIDS. Working Paper 17, Institute for Advanced Study Friends' Forum, Princeton University.

Silva, W. H. 2005. *Brasil sem homophobia, só com muita luta! Partido Socialista dos Trabalhadores Unificado*, May 31.

Skocpol, T. 1995. *Protecting Soldiers and Mothers: The Political Origins of Social Policy in the United States*. Cambridge: Harvard University Press.

Teixeira, P. R. 1997. *Políticas públicas em AIDS*. In *Políticas, instituicões e AIDS: Enfrantando a AIDS no Brasil*, ed. R. Parker. Rio de Janeiro: ABIA Publishers.

Terto, V., Jr. 2002. Homosexualidade e saúde: Desafios pra a terceira década de epidemia de HIV/AIDS. *Horizontes Antropológicos* 8 (17): 147–58.

U.S. Department of State. Bureau of Democracy, Human Rights, and Labor. 2004. *Brazil Country Report on Human Rights Practices*.

Sexual Rights of Gays, Lesbians, and Transgender Persons in Latin America

A Judge's View

Roger Raupp Rios

THE CURRENT situation concerning the rights of gays, lesbians, and transgender persons (hereinafter referred to as "LGBT sexual rights") in Latin America can be examined from various perspectives. These include analyses of the successes and failures, the limits and possibilities, and the levels of formal recognition of these rights by Latin American national states, in an approach pertaining more to political science. Adopting a more sociological perspective, studies can also be proposed to examine the effectiveness of existing rights, based on the degree of commitment by various government institutions involved in their enforcement. Anthropological research can also point to the impacts that formal recognition of these rights can have on the social representations concerning these groups, both inside and outside the groups themselves.

We may also examine the current situation regarding the rights of gays, lesbians, and transgender persons from a legal perspective. What does such an analysis entail? What is the relevance of a legal approach to this issue? One should begin by distinguishing between a legal analysis and a mere inventory of legislation and case law on the topic. A legal analysis involves more than compiling data; on the contrary, it requires a critical examination of the prevailing legislation and its potential and limits for dealing with these rights, whether or not the legislation is explicit in relation to sexual rights. A legal analysis should also cover the trends regarding and challenges to the recognition and enforcement of these rights, serving as important material for a more adequate understanding of reality, to be incorporated by researchers and activists. To the extent that the law (whether in its official wording or its enforcement by legal bodies) is also a fact of social reality, we must both understand and analyze it in order to adequately reflect on and practice it. Hence the relevance of a legal approach to the sexual rights of gays, lesbians, and transgender persons.

Typology of Legal Frameworks Concerning LGBT Rights

The relationship between the law, viewed as a legal framework (that is, the set of normative state instruments prevailing at a given moment in a given country, encompassing both legislative acts and court decisions), and sexuality is not new. Traditionally, state law was produced as an instrument to reinforce and preserve the majority and dominant sexual moral norms. In other words, state law acts to confirm hegemonic sexual relations and practices. Examples include the consecration of the petit bourgeois nuclear family, the attribution of sexual rights and duties between spouses, and the criminalization of homosexual acts.

With the emergence of social movements vindicating the acceptance of practices and relations divorced from this model, the issue of sexual rights, and especially that of LGBT rights, was shifted into the political arena and thus into the legal debate. The emergence of these demands and the recognition of some rights (albeit slowly and unevenly) launched a new modality in the relationship between these legal frameworks and sexuality. Historically, and concentrating on modernity, one observes the emergence of these rights in the 1980s, when a landmark decision by the European Court of Human Rights overruled a law criminalizing sodomy, on the grounds that said legislation violated a basic human right, namely the right to privacy.

Since then it has been possible to speak of various levels of protection for the sexual rights of gays, lesbians, and transgender persons, and hence the following proposed typology of legal frameworks:

1. legal frameworks with a minimal degree of protection: those that have revoked the traditional prohibition of sexual practices that depart from hegemonic standards (especially linked to penal law);

2. legal frameworks with an intermediate level of protection: those which besides not criminalizing such sexual practices also institute measures to penalize discriminatory acts, especially by prohibiting discrimination on grounds of sexual orientation;

3. legal frameworks with a maximum degree of protection: those which besides not criminalizing the above-mentioned practices and penalizing discriminatory acts

also establish positive measures for the protection and recognition of the sexual practices and identities of gays, lesbians, and transgender persons.

In the Latin American context, the application of this typology of legal frameworks vis-à-vis the degree of protection of LGBT rights allows one to evaluate the situation regarding such rights in the region. To map the situation in each individual country would require a joint effort by numerous researchers and detailed data collection, not to mention keeping pace with the dynamism characterizing the legislative and juridical output in such a broad area. However, it is instructive to identify the most salient elements in this scenario, allowing an analysis of the trends and challenges for these rights in Latin America.

An overview of the Latin American situation, considering the available data, shows that (1) there is no legal framework in Latin America that criminalizes homosexual sexual practices, except in specific contexts such as military establishments; (2) most legal frameworks in Latin America penalize acts of discrimination on grounds of expressions of sexuality (Argentina, Brazil, Colombia, Ecuador, Mexico, and Peru, for example); and (3) few legal frameworks establish positive measures for the protection and recognition of these sexual rights (Argentina and Brazil).

In fact, as for the division between repressive and protective frameworks (the latter in their various degrees), only Cuban law explicitly establishes punishment for public homosexual manifestations (Penal Code, article 303). Although legal frameworks such as that of Chile cannot now be considered repressive (having revoked legislation that criminalized relations between persons of the same sex), in some cases such relations were still considered a crime until very recently (1998, in the Chilean case).

Meanwhile, in the sphere of protective frameworks, Brazil, Argentina, and Colombia are examples of countries that not only prohibit discrimination, but also institutionally recognize unions between persons of the same sex (in Brazil and Colombia based on court rulings, while in Argentina there is explicit legislation). The degree of protection varies from country to country. Brazil has shown a high degree of institutional protection, at least formally, since the country launched the Second National Human Rights Program and the "Brazil without Homophobia" government plan, not to mention the government support (especially through the Ministry of Health) for visibility campaigns and specific attention to gay and lesbian groups.

In the context of protective frameworks, Ecuador should be highlighted for its constitutional provision explicitly prohibiting discrimination on grounds of sexual orientation, with the following wording:

Equality before the law. All persons shall be considered equal and shall enjoy the same rights, freedoms, and opportunities, without discrimination on grounds of birth, age, sex, ethnicity, color, social origin, language, religion, political affiliation, economic position, sexual orientation, health status, disability, or difference of any other nature.

A broader survey of the situation with LGBT rights in Latin America (that is, without a detailed analysis of each national juridical framework, a task beyond the scope of this study) also shows in practice the absence of legal regulation based on a human-rights perspective in dealing with the specific situation of transsexualism or that of transvestites. On these fronts, the biomedical approaches usually prevail, especially in relation to transsexualism. As for treatment towards transvestites, even in countries where cross-dressing is not considered illegal, a repressive approach prevails, based on the criminalization of what are considered obscene acts in public byways and the repression of prostitution.

Trends in the Development of LGBT Rights

Several trends can be extracted from the emergence and development of LGBT rights in Latin America. Among them are (1) recognition of these rights within an overall context of redemocratization in Latin America, (2) the impact of the HIV/AIDS epidemic, (3) the link in public discourse between these rights and public health concerns, and (4) the affirmation of these rights within demands for social rights.

Since the mid-1980s Latin America has undergone a process of redemocratization resulting from the exhaustion of various military dictatorships and changes related to the international order, and stemming from the dismantling of the former Soviet Union and the subsequent détente in East-West relations. Within the broader context of social concerns, there emerged spaces for the strengthening of civil society and various social movements, among which the feminist and gay movements have played outstanding roles in demanding LGBT rights vis-à-vis the state.

More specifically, this dynamic reached the legislative and judiciary branches, not only by the gradual establishment of alliances and dialogue with progressive congressional forces, but also by the strengthening of judicial bodies. The latter, encouraged by post–World War II Continental European constitutionalism, were opened to the possibility of human-rights protection, consecrated not only in the international order but also in the respective national constitutions.

Constitutional change was an important factor for the development of LGBT rights in Latin America. Constitutional courts in various countries such as Brazil, Colombia, and Peru handed down rulings that penalized acts of discrimination on grounds of sexual orientation.

Another important factor in the development of LGBT sexual rights has been their increased impetus since the emergence of the HIV/AIDS epidemic. Although the epidemic was initially a factor in the stigmatization of gays and transvestites, eventually the responses developed to fight the epidemic provided greater reflection and networking among such groups. This in turn helped raise awareness concerning discrimination and has demanded reflection on the relationship between the law and sexuality, highlighting the need to adopt a human-rights paradigm in this area.

Along this same line, another important trend in the development of LGBT rights has been their relationship to issues of health services access. Countries with public health services, and especially those that intend to increase the population's access to such services, are faced with multiple demands in this area. This emphasizes the need to provide health services that consider the specific situations of groups claiming sexual rights, such as transvestites.

To conclude this inventory of trends in the development of LGBT rights in Latin America, one should not overlook a Latin American specificity when comparing the issue's evolution here and in Europe and North America.

From the legal point of view, in Europe and North America the recognition of LGBT sexual rights began (and continues to develop) on the basis of demands invoking the right to privacy and the right to nondiscrimination. This involves so-called negative rights, that is, demands for nonintrusion by either the state or third parties in individual choices and practices. For example, case law history in Europe and the United States has always emphasized privacy as the principal constitutional premise for the affirmation of LGBT individual and group rights.

Meanwhile, the Latin American experience has revealed other alternatives. Demands for social rights have fueled the discussion on LGBT rights. An example is the demand for social security rights and health plan entitlement, which has been the pioneering (and most successful) legal strategy for the recognition of these rights in Brazil.

Challenges to the Development of LGBT Rights

Although recent, the history of the development of LGBT rights in Latin America has included several challenges, such as (1) the difficulty in developing a specific field related to sexual rights, not necessarily linked to the idea of reproductive rights; (2) the need to base sexual rights on a human-rights paradigm rather than merely cultivating sexual health; (3) the conservative religious backlash against the recognition of LGBT sexual rights, and the difficulty in affirming a lay state; (4) the persistence of cultural realities that are incompatible with the development of LGBT sexual rights; and (5) socioeconomic conditions of poverty affecting huge population contingents in the region.

As demonstrated by the history of international human-rights instruments, sexual rights were not originally conceived as autonomous in relation to reproductive rights. On the contrary, they were seen as a kind of appendix to the idea of reproductive rights. In fact, historically speaking, the main underlying concern in the expression "reproductive and sexual rights" has been to weigh against the injustice contained in gender relations and the denial of reproductive autonomy. There is no denying the importance of the struggle against reproductive and gender-based injustice.

Still, as LGBT rights make quite clear, the sphere of sexuality extends far beyond these limits. It encompasses freedom of sexual expression and gay, lesbian, transsexual, and transvestite issues. In addition, the affirmation of sexual rights even reaches sexual practices not associated with identities, with sadomasochism offering one good example.

Another important challenge for the affirmation of LGBT sexual rights is the tendency towards a biomedical justification of such rights. To assess this challenge it is necessary to focus on the underlying tenets in the demand for such rights. While it is true that sexual health concerns are important for the achievement of sexual rights, it is equally true that the recognition of sexual rights stems from a broader perspective than merely preserving and cultivating health. Sexual rights in general, and especially LGBT sexual rights, are informed by a human-rights perspective, one that may clash with narrower biomedical views. An arena where this conflict is particularly evident is the situation of transvestites.

A highly important aspect of this same challenge is the widespread resistance to the very idea of human rights in our Latin American countries. For a considerable share of our population, the very notion of human rights is perceived in a twisted and prejudiced way, as if human rights were devoted exclusively to protecting criminals. This mindset, the result of a long history of authoritarianism, permeates many institutions and groups both inside and outside the state, thus further hindering demands for LGBT rights based on human-rights principles.

The emergence of fundamentalist religious movements poses another major challenge for the development of LGBT rights in Latin America. This trend is seen not only among many of the so-called neo-Pentecostal churches, but also in the heart of the Catholic Church, where conservative currents in relation to sexual conduct have gained force. Together, these groups react to the empowerment of the LGBT movement by proposing, for example, legislation aimed at "converting" homosexuals into heterosexuals, even proposing making use of the public health system for this purpose.

Along this line, the difficulty in affirming the lay nature of the state in the young and immature Latin American democracies is a crucial obstacle, to the extent that our societies bear a historical experience of a strong, centuries-old institutional association between the Catholic Church and the civil state.

Persistent representations of female inferiority and gender subordination, as expressed in such cultural formulations as machismo, pose another cultural challenge to the development of LGBT sexual rights in Latin America. We are dealing with a cultural context divorced from human-rights principles, reaching such extreme examples as the assassination of gays and transvestites and the widespread rape of women.

Finally, the precarious socioeconomic conditions affecting a major portion of the Latin American population pose a huge challenge for the enforcement of LGBT sexual rights. Poverty and destitution are real barriers that prevent access to various benefits such as knowledge, information, and services related to sexuality. They limit the perception of risks related to unsafe sex. They maintain a barrier to formal schooling and have nefarious consequences for attempts to establish a social life free of prejudices.

Persistent Challenges

Considering the above discussion and especially the analysis of the principal trends and challenges related to the development of sexual rights in Latin America, one can reach a conclusion which is both positive and worrisome.

While it is true that in recent years the rights of gays, lesbians, and transgender persons have received greater institutional attention and have even achieved legislative and legal gains at various moments, it is also true that persistent factors challenging such rights still leave their affirmation and consolidation in jeopardy. In addition, if this situation is true for the countries in which these sexual rights have already reached some degree of recognition, all the more so in those countries where such rights have scarcely been achieved.

References

Alpízar, L., and M. Bernal. 2004. Youth, sexuality, and human rights: Some reflections from experience in Mexico. Special issue, *Health and Human Rights: Sexuality, Human Rights, and Health* 7 (2): 217–30.

Cabal, L., M. Roa, and J. Lemaitre, eds. 2001. *Cuerpo y derecho—legislación y jurisprudencia en América Latina*. Bogotá: Editorial Temis.

Cáceres, C., M. Pecheny, and V. Terto, Jr. 2002. *SIDA y sexo entre hombres en América Latina: Vulnerabilidades, fortalezas y propuestas para la acción*. Lima: Universidad Peruana Cayetano Heredia.

The Center for Reproductive Rights and University of Toronto International Programme on Reproductive and Sexual Health Law. 2003. Bringing rights to bear—An analysis of the work of UN Treaty Monitoring Bodies on Reproductive and Sexual Rights.

Golin, C., F. Pocahy, and R. Rios. 2003. *A justiça e os direitos de gays e lésbicas—jurisprudência comentada*. Porto Alegre: Editora Sulina.

Guesmez, A. 2004. *Estado laico, sociedad laica: un debate pendiente. Ciudadanía Sexual en América Latina: Abriendo el debate*. Lima: Universidad Peruana Cayetano Heredia.

Heinze, E. 1995. *Sexual Orientation: A Human Right*. The Hague: Martinus Nijhoff Publishers.

León, M. 1999. *Derechos sexuales y reproductivos. Avances constitucionales y perspectivas en Ecuador.* Quito: FEDAEPS.

Parker, R., and S. Correa, eds. 2003. *Sexualidade e política na América Latina.* Rio de Janeiro: ABIA.

Rios, R. R. 2004. *Apuntes para un derecho democrático de la sexualidad. Ciudadanía sexual en América Latina: Abriendo el debate.* Lima: Universidad Peruana Cayetano Heredia.

Vásquez, R., and I. Romero. 2003. *Diagnóstico sobre la situación de los derechos sexuales y los derechos reproductivos, 1995–2002.* Lima: CLADEM.

Vianna, A. 2004. *Direitos e políticas sexuais no Brasil: Mapeamento e diagnóstico.* Rio de Janeiro: CEPESC.

Villanueva Flores, R. 2006. *Protección constitucional de los derechos sexuales y reproductivos. Revista Instituto Interamericano de Derechos Sexuales* 43 (June): 391–450.

Chile

Seizing Empowerment

Tim Frasca

IN CHILE in the late 1980s, as in many other countries, approaches to homosexual empowerment sprang from differences of strategic vision. Those more interested in gay emancipation created a sexual-rights workshop and eventually formed their own organization, known as MOVILH, the Homosexual Liberation Movement, in 1991. After a period of consolidation, it went public and caused a sensation, both in public opinion and among homosexuals themselves. Interested gays and lesbians flocked to their new offices [...]; fifty people sometimes attended their planning meetings, and several times that number their parties.

Despite its decision to shun the AIDS issue in favor of overtly gay politics, MOVILH promptly inaugurated an AIDS program of its own, and the conflict over mission that had marked our Chile AIDS Prevention Association's early years shifted over to theirs. But it didn't disappear. One public spokesman was particularly adamant about eliminating AIDS as an issue for gay politics and campaigned relentlessly to suppress the group's AIDS activities, finally forcing yet another split.

Chilean author Juan Pablo Sutherland was among MOVILH's founders and supported its decision to distance itself from the AIDS issue—a position he criticizes today. A lanky and kindly man who was pilloried by the right-wing press when the government gave him an arts grant for one of his gay-themed books, Sutherland tries to promote cultural activities around sexuality and eroticism. He keeps a hand in gay politics but considers it too influenced by the left-wing habits of the 1980s.

Sutherland says MOVILH quickly decided to move beyond AIDS and tolerated little internal dissent.

> Eventually, we realized the impact of the epidemic among our own people, but even then there wasn't really much reflection, just, Hey, this is affecting us. And then that one, and that one, and that one. We came from a fairly uniform political style, and that led to big mistakes, which we realized later because our people were getting hit by what was happening.

As a result, the two groups, the AIDS Prevention Association and MOVILH, constructed their independent but symbiotic prevention strategies directed at gay men despite their ongoing conflicts; these eventually included gay magazines, a permanent presence in the nightclubs and cruising areas, HIV testing, workshops of all sorts, alliance building, lobbying, and participation in public debates. Thousands of men received basic information about AIDS, and condoms gradually began to be part of Chilean gay sexuality.

At the same time, AIDS forced a public debate on homosexuality, and MOVILH took advantage of the opening to loosen things up. Opinion surveys confirm that social attitudes have shifted markedly in Chile during the last decade, and a nineteenth-century antisodomy law finally was eliminated from criminal statutes in 1999.

But participants on both sides of the issue today wonder why the two currents, gay politics and AIDS prevention, could not have evolved in a more cooperative spirit. Alejandro Guajardo was a teenager when he first participated in both organizations, and later joined *Vivo Positivo* (for HIV-positive persons) where he ran a drug-adherence program until 2003. He recalls trying to convince his colleagues at MOVILH not to dismiss AIDS.

> The gay movement pushed aside the people with HIV because supposedly that wasn't part of the political fight. So today you have a gay movement working on AIDS and living off it, applying every month for survival through AIDS work. The gay radio program wouldn't have any funds without the AIDS subsidy . . .
>
> The two issues should never have been separated. Had there been [unity] from the beginning, I think the homo-bisexual population would have lowered the HIV curve a lot more because the intervention strategies would have been more similar, rather than two different things.

By the late 1990s, as the numbers of people living with HIV continued to grow, the centrifugal forces became even greater. Having been in all three camps—gay rights,

AIDS prevention, and HIV-positive advocacy—Guajardo saw little collaboration and synergy among the different activist currents.

> Next we're going to have the homosexuals of the La Pintana district, the PWAS [People Living with AIDS] of La Pintana, then the women of La Pintana, the non-homosexuals of La Pintana. Identity is essential, but it's clearly the collaborative, collective fight that can bring about positive changes.

It would be easy to pin the blame for this fragmentation, the splits and the subsplits, the carving out of political territory, on personality conflicts or the misplaced desires for the spotlight of a few individuals. But keeping issues like homosexuality, AIDS, and HIV seropositivity together as a set of integrated phenomena probably was doomed from the beginning. The appeal of identity brought people together and in fact forms the basis of much HIV prevention and solidarity work relying on "peer educators," on people who can bring the message to others defined as somehow "like themselves."

These initiatives make no sense detached from a focused, slightly selfish perspective. Gay men woke up to AIDS and gathered to take action not as public health educators but as gays. Once people with HIV found their voice, they did the same thing.

Universalist appeals make good rhetoric, but lousy institutional glue. Any nuanced, integrated approach is destined to be overshadowed by an unapologetic interest-group discourse that interprets the fight for "empowerment" in narrower, but more attractive ways. Articulating this essentially self-interested approach in the most seductive and emphatic fashion may not be particularly generous or statesmanlike, but as politicians know, it works.

Just like the gay-emancipationists five years before, groups of people living with HIV and AIDS ("PWAS" in the old terminology) felt more comfortable operating from their particular identities and addressing public opinion from those standpoints—certainly a legitimate choice in both cases and in any case a brilliant public relations strategy. Like the early organizers of MOVILH, who saw other gay groups as a bit lily-livered for not "coming out," people with HIV could not understand why AIDS-related organizations had not dedicated more of their institutional energies and resources to meeting the needs of those affected, that is, to them.

Both of these criticisms had merit; both were also slightly demagogic. Neither offered any guarantee that their representation of the groups mentioned in their titles would be more consistent, democratic, or altruistic than that which had gone before.

César Herrera, fifty, is a store owner in the northern zone of Santiago served by the San José Hospital, and the president of *Vida Optima*, representing the eight hundred registered HIV patients at San José. The group concentrates on direct aid and provides lunch for forty people daily, plus home visits and other types of assistance. Herrera was a founder of the *Vivo Positivo* coalition that led the drug-access fight, and applauds its handling of that lengthy struggle, which meant the difference between life and death for many.

At the same time, Herrera laments the transformation of the PWA coalition into a super-NGO that concentrates power in its own hands. His criticism echoes the same resentment that the nascent PWA groups felt towards the first-generation AIDS groups.

> We formed it to provide help to people and not for what it has become, a business with paid employees that has never given the hospital groups a sheet of paper. To feed forty people every day, I go to the produce market to beg. We live off charity, week after week. It's tiring.

Writer Juan Pablo Sutherland has worked with hospital-based PWA groups, and perceived the single-minded focus of the drug-access battle led by their national leadership.

> I did a writing workshop in six hospitals with people from the organizations, and I was struck by how instrumental the whole relationship was, how focused it was on direct aid. People came to see what help they could get, and of course they had a lot of needs.

Ironically, Herrera's criticism of his own movement is precisely that the focus of PWA organizing was too narrowly concerned with members' immediate needs.

> Now that the ARV [antiretroviral] drugs are available, the (hospital-based) groups are dying, they're disintegrating. Most people, what were they looking for in an organization? Access to the drugs. Once they get it, they go back to their lives or back to work and leave the organizations.

Those living with HIV/AIDS were the only individuals that could turn stigma and discrimination on end and express their demand to live and receive treatment. They had a unique voice that echoed with concrete experience and direct, personal interest, and they used it with enormous skill to obtain their demands. At the same time, the PWA leadership's domination of the scenario encouraged people—including their own people—to redefine AIDS activism strictly in terms of clinical care.

The original social movement around AIDS responded to other concerns; it had arisen from people not directly affected, who had joined in without receiving a diagnosis, out of concerns over people's rights to be informed, to live their sexual and intimate lives as they chose, to receive services and to be treated humanely and properly when sick. These sidelined actors are now expected to fulfill a supporting, backup role, and in large measure, they do.

~

The early success of grassroots groups that sprang up to address AIDS and homosexual emancipation have obscured their structural weaknesses. Raquel Child, who directed Chile's national AIDS program for a decade until 2003, says the new actors who arose to grapple with these issues were a welcome development. But she sees stagnation setting in as well.

> The response in Chile has fallen off; the initiatives and creativity have declined. I would have expected a stronger public presence, more development, more growth, more capacity to mobilize people, and this hasn't happened. I think that the organizations have become entropic entities that aren't visible. I suppose they are doing things, but you don't see what we had at the beginning of the 1990s. I won't say it doesn't exist, but I don't see it.

I left my job as the director of the Chile AIDS Prevention Association in 2000 over differences about strategy and internal practices. Inevitably, these divergences became personalized, and our long cohabitation and friendship came to an end. Paradoxically, this happened despite our historical attempt to empower the weak and rein in the strong.

Although our group had started out with few university-educated collaborators, some of the staff and volunteers pursued their studies over the years, in some cases with our assistance. We tracked down and funded English courses to expand their access to research and conferences, and encouraged people to accumulate the all-important credentials, even when not taking them too seriously. But the increase of university degrees did not lead to greater internal democracy.

Is prevention education on AIDS for gay and homosexually active men in Santiago effective today? Our own 1997 study suggested that condom use was common, although inconsistent, among at least half of self-identified gays at that time. HIV seroprevalence rates are hard to estimate, but some 12 percent of men who report homosexual practices turn up HIV-positive at the city's STD clinics. The figure hasn't risen in recent years, but it doesn't have to; at those rates, any sexually active, unattached gay man who is not extremely careful has a good chance of acquiring the infection over the course of his life.

Some close observers fear that the momentum is now being lost and that members of the younger generation of gays are less likely to take precautions than their older peers. Vicky Braga is a bar owner who says she lost an entire generation of clients in the first wave of AIDS.

> The young kids don't go to the organizations, they disdain them. Their attitude is that nobody is going to tell them what to do, they're grown up and know what they're about

[. . .] Nobody is surprised at the death of the next guy, he just died, and that's that. It doesn't mean a thing.

Just as the lengthy treatment-access debate shifted public attention away from sexuality issues to clinical ones, the government's decision to shift funds to drug purchases and away from public information lowered the general level of awareness about the continued risk. Dr Child thinks the society is generally more comfortable with a more traditional, doctor-patient approach to the whole business.

> The viewpoint has changed, and you can see it in the way the issue is handled by the news media. Preventive behaviors and probably the whole AIDS phenomenon in all its dimensions are less important. Treatments exist, so what are we worried about? You see how society medicalizes every subject. It's the easiest way out and furthermore a solution that is not up to me . . . I take a pill, and that's that.

Child suggests that in AIDS and in many other areas, the promise of the post-Pinochet period and the enthusiasm of the populace to make meaningful changes has dissipated, that Chilean society has settled back into much more traditional patterns. Her argument is a familiar one: that the country's age-old power brokers—the armed forces, the business elite, the right-wing press, the Catholic bishops—although a minority, have neutralized the weak, liberal state and forced it to administer, rather than solve, social problems. The forms of popular sovereignty are respected, but the underlying reality is glacial change, if any. Meanwhile, those who have no choice but to survive under this system look for ways to empower themselves as best they can.

Speech of the President of the Brazilian Republic at the Opening of the First National Conference of Gays, Lesbians, Bisexuals, Transvestites, and Transsexuals

Convention Center, Brasília, D.F., June 5, 2008

Luiz Inácio Lula da Silva

Translated by Nicole Panico

MY DEAR colleague Paulo Vannuchi, special secretary of human rights; my dear colleague José Gomes Temporão, minister of health; my dear Carlos Eduardo Gabas, interim minister of social welfare; my dear colleague Luiz Dulci, minister in chief of the secretary-general of the presidency of the republic; my dear colleague José Antônio Toffoli, general lawyer of the union; my dear colleague Elói Ferreira de Araújo, interim minister in chief of the special secretary for the promotion of racial equality; our dear colleague Nilcéa Freire, special secretary of politics for women; my colleague Marisa; my dear colleague Cida Diogo, president of the GLBT Citizens' Parliamentary Front, in whose name I welcome all my parliamentary colleagues that are present here; my dear colleagues Tony Reis, Fernanda Benvenuti, and Negra Cris, through whom I would like to welcome all the delegates present at this First National Conference of Gays, Lesbians, Transvestites, and Transsexuals; invited guests; my dear colleague Sérgio Mamberti; my dear colleague Arlete; my dear colleagues representing the foreign delegations present here—I know that there are fourteen countries represented in this first conference; colleagues from the press; my friends; colleagues,

First, Paulinho, I would like to thank you for this moment. Paulinho, last year, sought me out to tell me that of all the conferences, of the many we have organized

... There have already been forty-nine conferences that we have organized. Certainly we have already involved, in total, more than three and a half million Brazilians, from all over the country. This year we organized the conference, and Paulinho said, "Lula, it's important"—he did not call me *Lula*, he called me *Mr. President*, despite forty years of friendship—"we need to have this conference. And I would like to know if the president will give the opening address by decree." I said, "Paulinho, prepare the decree because we will open with it."

And why did I begin by complimenting Paulinho? Paulinho, I think that Temporão said something here that, if nobody has recorded it, is important to record, because I think that it is memorable. Those that give a lot of speeches have days when they get it right and days when they get it wrong.

You record texts, don't you, Serginho? There are days when you go there, record a text in thirty seconds, and then go home; and there are days when that thirty-second text takes three hours to record. I remember that one time we stayed with Suplicy from nine at night until three o'clock in the morning to record a text that was I believe thirty-five seconds long.

Well, my colleagues, I want to thank you for being here today. It is not easy for a president of a republic, not here in Brazil nor in any other country in the world, to participate in events that involve a segment so large, so heterogeneous, and so motivated to eliminate prejudices as yourselves. It is not easy.

And so, when Tony Reis says that never in the history of the planet has a president ever opened a conference like this one, I am proud because we are living in Brazil in an era of reform.

I have said, Paulinho, that when I inaugurate PAC [Programa de Aceleração do Crecimento, or Growth Accelerating Programs] projects in the shantytowns, that what we are doing is repairing the damage caused by irresponsible governments that, over fifty or sixty years, have allowed the poor to establish themselves in places where they should not be established. Truthfully, if when these first groups of the poor showed up, the mayor and the councilmen had been there and had taken care of them and put them in a more adequate place, they would have prevented these in-adequate places from becoming cities; they would have prevented the large numbers of people that are living in degradation in this country. There have been moments of irresponsibility. And so, I have said that we are making an effort to reform. And Brazil needs a process of reform.

When I received, at the Planalto Palace, our dear colleagues that have played several roles, a colleague from São Paulo made a speech and said, "Mr. President, if we don't achieve anything else in life, just the fact that we are putting our foot in the door of the Planalto Palace will already be worth it, because we never imagined we would ever even get close to the Planalto Palace."

I participated, with my colleague Nilcéa in Rio de Janeiro two years ago, in—I think it was the Day Against AIDS, if my memory serves me correctly—and I said to

Nilcéa: We need to create in Brazil a Day Against Hypocrisy. I know that this infuriates some people and leaves others distressed, but the concrete fact remains that, if I can't create it, somebody will create it, Nilcéa. Do you know why it is necessary to create a Day Against Hypocrisy? Because when it comes to preconceptions, I know it in my gut, I know what prejudice is. It may be the most perverse disease impregnated into the head of man. It is a disease that we do not combat simply through laws. The law helps, the Constitution helps, building advisories helps, Tony, everything helps, but it is a cultural process. It is a process that undergoes a cultural revolution where people will begin to understand that we need to like ourselves as we are, that we do not have to want everyone to be unequal. Even within this platform, it is very possible that there are differences, that there are prejudices, some people who think "I can do this, but he can't do that." If we do not air out our heads and clear the pollution of prejudices from our minds, we will not accomplish what Paulinho has asked of us here, which is unity about the things voted on at the National Congress.

I will say to all of you the same thing I said at the meeting we had at the Racial Equality Conference. We have a great project to establish a Racial Equality Statute inside the National Congress. I was very clear with my delegate companions: if you do not agree, for whatever reason, someone will have to come up with something to construct a consensus for the National Congress to vote on. If you are divided within the Congress, there will not be a Racial Equality Statute today or ever.

You will have three days at this conference and, without a doubt, will argue, speak, write, retract, and present a proposal to the government. I can tell you: the treatment that you will receive, with the document that you present, will be equal to the treatment that we gave to the forty-nine conferences that happened before you. If it is not like this, we would be making only a half democracy, that democracy that can appear when I want it, when I need it, but that is not complete, that will not preside over our heads twenty-four hours a day, over the heads of those that, through prejudice, do not want to understand what makes each of us who we are.

Obviously we will also be honest, just as we were honest with the other conferences. What cannot be done we will say with the same camaraderie: comrades, this here doesn't work, this here won't do, this here isn't right. If we do not establish this friendly relationship between us, the conference will be over and we will go back to the distrust we had before coming here.

I said thank you for being here today, because one time I said that every politician is filled with certainties, that every politician is filled with very precise convictions. People were scared when I would say: "Look, I am the walking metamorphosis." In my life, I think that I have everything defined. The next day, I learn that there is something that I am not sure of, and that I need to define; that there is something I was against, that now I am in favor of; that there is something I disagreed with, that now I agree with. This is the way to govern a family with 190 million children. There is no only child, we do not have only one religion, we do not have only one sexual option.

They said it well, all of those who have spoken here, from Paulinho to our colleague Temporão: nobody questions your sexual orientation when you go to pay your income tax, nobody questions it when you pay any tribute in this country. Why discriminate at the moment when you, freely, choose what you want to do with your body? It is easier to talk than to transform words into concrete actions, because then it becomes necessary to measure the correlation of forces in society. But you did accomplish something sacred: you were able to break the shell of the egg, you were able to shout out to Brazil that you exist and that you want nothing more or less than anybody else. You want to be Brazilians, to be respected as you work and live, as everyone in the world wants to be respected.

Because of this I want to say to you that, when we sign the decree, people will begin to ask, "But will you, Mr. President?" You know what I felt when I put this hat on my head, Tony? The same prejudice I felt against me when I put on the Homeless Movement hat. I have never been scolded so harshly. I was the newly elected president of the republic, and I put the Homeless Movement hat on my head. I was scolded in the press for I think a month. I could have put on the Bank of Brazil hat, the Real Bank hat, the Bradesco hat, the Vale do Rio Doce hat, the Petrobras hat, the Corinthians hat, the Flamengo hat, the Vasco hat, I could have chosen any of them . . . Now, I could not put on the Homeless [Movement] hat, and I saw a light: I will put them all on, because only like this can I break the prejudices that people have of thinking what you can and cannot do.

It is gratifying to come here because we leave with a lesson learned, the lesson of the political maturity of the movement, the lesson of understanding that there is only one way for, step by step, society to recognize the movement: each time we must fight more, walk with our heads held high, fight harder against prejudice, denounce more firmly arbitrariness. Only like this will we be able to win over the entire citizenship so that everybody can walk the street with their heads held high, without anybody wanting to know who we are, only that we are Brazilians and that we want to build this country without prejudices.

I know important leaders. During my life, I have met very important world figures, who do not have the courage to take up homosexuality in their countries. It gives the impression that it doesn't exist, because people always think, "In my country we don't have this, in my house that doesn't exist, I'll never get this, I'll never get that." We are always passing things over to others, when truthfully, it would be so much more simple, and the world would be so much happier, if we were less rigid with the taboos that were placed in our paths over time.

I want to say to all of you, colleagues and friends: God illuminate you, and present here the proposal that you understand here to be the best and that you can guarantee . . . I can say to you: for what depends on the support of the government, for what depends on the support of the executive power of the ministry, we will work so that the National Congress will approve what needs to be approved in this country.

I remember, Paulinho . . . I don't think I ever told you, because it is still not of your time. You know that one time, I discovered that here in Brasília—Paulinho was already a minister—there was the problem of a law that did not permit a handicapped person—primarily a person with vision problems—to take public transportation with a seeing-eye dog, to take the metro, to enter a supermarket, to enter a church. Then I said, "Paulinho, we are going to have a meeting inside the Planalto Palace, because, in reality, the dogs are an extension of that handicapped person."

I think it is examples like these that we will have to keep working towards, more and more, until one day it will be possible to walk down the street without noticing anybody giving us strange looks, judging looks, or skeptical looks.

And so, I think that this day is, in reality, historical. I think that you have not even realized the possible dimensions of what might be accomplished here today, an exponentially increasing effect of breaking down prejudices and gaining rights.

It is a shame, my dear deputies—I want to thank you for your presence here—that more deputies and senators are not here. It is a shame because, upon seeing you, they would be surprised, and would make the exclamation: "They are the same as me." Who knows, they might have returned to their activities with less racism and less prejudice.

Good luck, and good conference. May God bless all of you.

Interview with Mariela Castro on the Future of Sex and Socialism in Cuba

Anastasia Haydulina

*Mariela Castro is Director of the National Center
for Sex Education in Cuba,
daughter of President Raúl Castro,
and niece of former president Fidel Castro.*

Anastasia Haydulina: One day your uncle Fidel Castro . . . is going to die. Do you think his death will change the status quo of your Cuba?

Mariela Castro: First of all, the death of Fidel will bring great suffering for the Cuban people, and it will be an enormous loss. But as far as I can see, the Cubans are willing to continue on the path of socialism even when our Comandante is no longer with us, even when my father and other forefathers of the revolution are not. Our people want socialism. Of course, we're very self-critical, so what we need is a better and rich social reform that will resolve most of the existing contradictions. People themselves are proposing actions necessary for the survival of our socialist society, a society that should always guarantee social justice, equality, and solidarity within the nation, as well as in relations with others. We want welfare, but not as exaggerated as that of consumer societies. I think that socialism in Cuba will survive and become what we have considered to be a utopia.

Anastasia Haydulina: Same-sex unions in a communist, originally Catholic, state?

Mariela Castro: Yes, I believe that, in societies like ours, same-sex unions are possible. It's true that, in the history of countries that have tried to create socialism, sexuality-related prejudices from the capitalist past have persisted. But in the Cuban version of socialism it will surely be possible to make fundamental changes in the lives of men and women according to their sexual orientation and other elements of their sexuality that haven't been contemplated by other socialist nations to date. Of course there are very strong influences of religions predominant in our cultures, but they are not going to become obstacles to achieving the aim of guaranteeing human rights socialism must guarantee. That is why we proposed a bill to legalize same-sex unions to parliament.

Anastasia Haydulina: What makes you feel you can overcome the stigma within the Communist Party and legislative barriers to pass it as well?

Mariela Castro: As head of the National Center for Sex Education, not as daughter of the president, I presented an educational strategy strongly based on the mass media to bring the attention of the Cuban society to various expressions of sexuality within it.

Anastasia Haydulina: Realistically, when do you think we are going to see this bill passed here in Cuba?

Mariela Castro: We've already accomplished a lot. For example, we've achieved a resolution by the public health ministry that guarantees transsexuals specialized attention, including sex change surgeries. The first of these types of operation are about to begin. They were first performed in 1988 but were interrupted due to people's incomprehension. We're proposing important changes to the family code that include the right of people of the same sex to legalize their unions. We're also working on a gender identity decree law that will make it easier for transsexuals to change their sex and identity papers, regardless of the sex change surgery. Because not all of them are automatically eligible for this operation, but nevertheless people do need society to recognize them in accordance with their gender identity, not by biological sex.

Anastasia Haydulina: Tell us more about the history of homophobia in this country.

Mariela Castro: Just like many other patriarchal societies in the world, Cuban society is homophobic. In the 1960s and 1970s, it expressed itself as a political decision that discriminated against homosexuals, especially men. That was a general criterion coming from not only religions but even from sciences. Psychiatry classified homosexuality as a mental disorder. There were even therapists to change homosexuals into heterosexuals, since that's what was considered normal and healthy. So, the Cuban politicians, educationalists, and doctors acted in accordance with the scientific precepts of the time as well. Neither teachers nor doctors could be gay. Today, no military person can be gay either. But there are homosexuals everywhere, whether out in the open or not. So we attend to them in our center, because humanity is about diversity. The most important thing here is that there have been discussions and changes ever since. And in order to avoid this [homophobia] in the future, we've got to be explicit in our laws and policies. Homosexuality is a reality to be taken into account, not got rid of.

Anastasia Haydulina: Two thirds of Cubans with HIV/AIDS are homosexual men. Are they provided due treatment? Are the Cubans with HIV provided the treatments they need?

Mariela Castro: In 1983, when Fidel learned about the existence of AIDS, he asked the doctors of the Pedro Kourí Institute of Tropical Medicine to carry out research to avoid the tragedy on our island. Since then the state began designing its policies for HIV/AIDS treatment and prevention. Each patient infected with the virus is provided with all the medical assistance at the cost of the state. Although the medicines are very expensive, as [are] prevention [measures], these are fundamental to avoid the spreading of the epidemic. Even though Cuba maintains the lowest level [of infection] in the region and in the world, it keeps rising, so we need much more effective prevention and treatment. For example, the island buys condoms for the pharmacies, but many are donated and distributed free of charge as part of the center's educational activities across the country. Thanks to this efficient work, [HIV] infection hardly occurs among adolescents. Unfortunately, the existing prejudices impede us from many of the educational activities planned for the homosexual male population.

Anastasia Haydulina: Is your father supportive of your work?

Mariela Castro: Yes, he's supportive of my work, thanks to the past influence of my mother on sexual education, and mine. Of course, from time to time we have discussions meant to convince him of the need for quicker solutions. He's also influenced by other people that disagree with my work, and it's those people who create obstacles. But I believe that dialogue is fundamental to progress, so whenever I have a chance to sit down and talk with my father to convince him, I do so.

Anastasia Haydulina: Your mother was an internationally recognized champion of women's rights. What challenges remain for women in Cuba?

Mariela Castro: There are still the remains of machismo and inequality between men and women. Although there are few women in top governmental positions, we observe rising percentages of women technicians, lawmakers, vice ministers, ministers, as well as [more women] among the regional party leadership. Besides, in the last two hurricanes that hit the island, the actions of the women governing the two worst affected provinces made Cubans, and especially women, very proud.

In troubled families, women keep returning to household chores and the upbringing of children, because most of them still think that is our job, that "nobody can do it better than us." But men's participation in all these household duties is no less fundamental, especially in a time of crisis.

Anastasia Haydulina: What other changes would you like to see in Cuba?

Mariela Castro: I would like the U.S. government to lift the financial, economic, and commercial blockade that it has imposed on our island for fifty years against the Cuban people, and that has considerably prevented us from achieving our development goals. It has affected our economy, commercial relations, and financial mechanisms. Cuba doesn't receive credit from any bank, and it's very difficult for us to survive in the field of the international economy. The companies that trade with Cuba are being penalized. We have big problems with the Internet without the access to optical fiber. It would be fundamental for life in Cuba to change, for its economy to grow, the salaries to rise. Then, we'd be able to produce, obtain more materials, and use the latest technologies. For example, I'd like to see improvements in democratic participation mechanisms on the island, so that our government could function more fluently. It has a very peculiar and good structure, like no other in the world, and we like its maturity. That's why we need to cultivate mechanisms for people's participation. It's one of the things that preoccupy me most and will bring about a whole range of other changes.

Note

This interview was broadcast by *Russia Today* on January 1, 2009. The text above is a partial transcript of the interview.

Out in Public

Gay and Lesbian Activism in Nicaragua

Florence E. Babb

2000: I return to Nicaragua after being away for two years to find the capital city transformed with a new city center boasting hotels, shopping malls, and multiplex cinemas. The movie *Boys Don't Cry* is playing, and its story of sexual transgression in the U.S. Midwest is meeting a favorable response, at least among those I talk to in the progressive community. Rita, a longtime AIDS activist and self-proclaimed "dyke," tells me she wishes all the legislators in the country would see it and expand their notion of citizen rights to include sexual minorities.

2002: "I'm neither in the closet nor on the balcony," is the way that Carlos, a Nicaraguan in his early thirties, describes himself to me during Gay Pride Week in June. We are sitting with a couple of other men in the local gay bar they run, waiting for a panel discussion to begin on HIV and safer sex practices. While Carlos is quite comfortable with his sexuality as a gay man, and has a middle-class awareness of the globalized identity that *gay* confers, like many others in Managua's LGBT (lesbian, gay, bisexual, transgender) population, he does not feel a need to proclaim his identity loudly.

2003: At a weekly Sunday service of the gay Metropolitan Church in Managua, the young pastor named Alberto speaks of "God's love for everyone, rich and poor, gay, straight, lesbian, and bisexual." The dozen assembled men—including several I know as renowned drag queens, here wearing street clothes—and a couple of women pass a candle from one person to the next, saying "God loves you as you are." They take communion and Alberto gives thanks to the *jornada*, in reference to Gay Pride Week, for allowing the LGBT community to speak out about human rights. They conclude their mass with guitar music and flirtatious dancing on the patio. A few days later, some of these same individuals are present when I give a talk based on my research on lesbian and gay politics and culture in Nicaragua. The venue is *Puntos de Encuentro* (Gathering Points), Nicaragua's largest feminist nongovernmental organization (NGO), and I am addressing the small community of activists and their allies. The audience includes women and men who work in other NGOs, such as Xochiquetzal, which offers services relating to health, sexuality, and AIDS. After I finish, a lively conversation ensues about whether there is truly something that can be called a "movement" in the country. Later, a reporter asks whether I would say that it is "normal" to be homosexual and whether human rights should extend to the homosexual population. I don my anthropological hat for the occasion and assure the well-meaning man that homosexuals are normal and deserving of full rights to social inclusion.

∾

These are a few of the many private and public responses to an increasingly vocal and visible gay and lesbian presence that I have encountered in Nicaragua since 1989. As a foreign researcher and observer of the public emergence of an LGBT community and social movement since the Sandinistas lost the 1990 elections, I had expected to find some resistance to my participation in the charged discussion. What I have found, to my surprise, is a passion for debating the local, national, and transnational aspects of gay culture and politics with as broad and international a group as possible.

To understand the current context, however, one needs to look back at the changes that have occurred over the last twenty-five years. The revolutionary Sandinista National Liberation Front (FSLN) government (1979–1990) provided an opportunity for disenfranchised women and men to become players in the social drama transforming much of the country in the 1980s. Along with agrarian, health, education, and legal reform, gender equality became part of the agenda. And the new constitution of 1987 included women's rights under the rubric of protecting the family as the basic unit of society.

The inclusive vision of the Sandinistas did not extend, however, to a nonheteronormative conception of the Nicaraguan family and society. When lesbians and gay men began organizing in the second half of the 1980s, the Sandinistas were not prepared to extend their revolutionary vision to this new constituency by supporting their call for social recognition and civil rights. As in other socialist-oriented societies, homosexuality was regarded as part of the "decadent" bourgeois past, and it met a chilly response from party militants, despite the fact that well-regarded Sandinistas were among those quietly organizing in Managua. Although same-sex relations, particularly among men, were well known in urban Nicaragua, in 1987, FSLN security agents called in and detained a number of gay men and lesbians whose more political sexual identification was viewed as a deviation.

If the silencing of the nascent gay movement in Nicaragua was effective at first, this had changed by 1989, when some fifty Nicaraguan gay-rights activists and their international supporters marched openly to the Plaza de la Revolución for the tenth anniversary celebration of the Sandinista victory, capturing national and international attention. They wore black T-shirts with hand-painted pink triangles, symbolic of gay pride internationally. Although the FSLN initially clamped down on gay organizing, this public appearance of activists who were both Sandinista and gay marked the beginning of a more open and outspoken movement, along with a more tolerant public reception.

The Sandinista loss in the 1990 election signaled the entry of a centrist government eager to reclaim U.S. support, peacetime relations, and an end to the economic embargo. The consequent neoliberal climate favored the return of some Nicaraguans who had left the country during the years of revolutionary government. Among these were a number of gay "Miami boys" who established businesses that included gay-friendly bars and cultural venues. At the same time, Nicaraguan and internationalist activists began establishing NGOs to meet needs the state was no longer willing or able to address. Whereas the Sandinista Health Ministry was by the end of the 1980s promoting AIDS education and making condoms widely available, such proactive services became the provenance of NGOs in the subsequent decade. Centers operated by lesbian and gay activists, often feminist in orientation, provided not only services but also a base for a gay community to form.

Not coincidentally, the NGOs were catalyzing agents for the first gay pride celebrations in the country. The year 1991 marked the separation of many feminists from the Nicaraguan Women's Association (AMNLAE) and also the first public gay pride event. Several hundred people, both gay and straight, gathered at a popular cultural center for a film showing of the gay-themed *Torch Song Trilogy*, followed by a panel discussion of homosexuality and human rights. The audience responded with passionate testimonies of experiences in family and society, endorsing a call for greater tolerance and understanding. In the years since then, gay pride has received more attention, with weeks of activities for its commemoration.

Lesbian and gay activism was galvanized the following year by the reactivation of a draconian sodomy law. The government of Violeta Barrios de Chamorro set out to regulate sexual behavior, sanctioning as "natural" and legal only those sexual practices related to procreation. The law criminalized sexual activity "between persons of the same sex" conducted in a "scandalous way." More than twenty-five groups joined together to launch the Campaign for a Sexuality Free of Prejudice. Despite years of protest, however, the law remains on the books. Although it is rarely enforced, many believe that the law fuels continuing intolerance.

Throughout the 1990s, gay activism continued to find expression in small groups of individuals and in NGOs, health clinics, and cultural venues. The Central American University offered its first course in sexuality studies, and gay bars and clubs offered space for same-sex individuals to socialize. The NGO Xochiquetzal began publishing the magazine *Fuera del clóset* (*Out of the Closet*) in 1993, which offers a mix of poetry, art, and informative articles. Women were often the ones putting a public face on lesbian and gay issues, notably when Mary Bolt Gonzalez wrote the first book on gay identity in Nicaragua, *Sencillamente diferentes* (*Simply Different*), published in 1996, focusing on lesbian self-esteem.

Lesbians are certainly prominent in the organized activity of the fledgling movement, but they are far less in evidence in the social spaces that are by and large available to gay men in the larger society. This is not surprising given the continued separation of genders in *la casa* and on *la calle* (at home and on the street). The neoliberal turn has presented new opportunities for men, particularly those of the middle class, who have the economic means to enjoy gay bars and other venues. Women, in contrast, are scarce until gay pride brings together more diverse crowds for a host of events ranging from academic panels to readings of erotic poetry. Annual gatherings, such as a contest to select the Goddess Xochiquetzal, are intended to help democratize the social space, but the majority of those who compete are men in drag. The 2003 competition saw the first woman contestant to enter and win.

A former pastor of the Metropolitan Church, Armando, related to me places where gay men regularly meet in Managua, including bars, movie theaters, house parties, and even the Metrocentro Mall, which he called "Metro Gay." In contrast, he said lesbians have few places to meet and socialize, and he described their parties as *fiestas de traje* (potluck dinners). Lesbians themselves frequently cite their family responsibilities, including care of children, and lack of financial resources to enter what they perceive as male spaces. A number of those lesbians working in NGOs also have very full professional lives and close circles of friendship, but little available time to spare. As a result, there is occasional tension between gay men and lesbians over the women's perceived dominance in NGOs and men's perceived advantages as consumers under the new market conditions of globalization.

The transnationalization of lesbian and gay politics and culture is on display in Nicaragua. The adoption of the gay pride annual celebration on or around June 28, in honor of the 1969 Stonewall rebellion in New York City, as practiced in the United

States and other countries, is one sign of global connection. Other material, ideological, and linguistic markers also suggest Nicaraguans' desire to affiliate with the international gay movement. Pink triangles, red ribbons, rainbows and the acronym LGBT—or LGBTT, which not only recognizes lesbians, gay men, bisexuals, and transgendered individuals, but also transvestites—are all in evidence. The tropes of the "closet" and "coming out" are widespread now, as many lesbians and gay men seek greater public visibility.

In contrast to the past, when male same-sex partners were often described as "active" (penetrative) and "passive" (penetrated), with the latter category being stigmatized, today the terms *gay* and *lesbian* are heard more frequently and in a more positive light. Also common is more open discussion of AIDS and human rights, as Nicaraguans participate actively in the global discourse surrounding these issues. On the cultural front, the popular television program *Sexto Sentido* (*Sixth Sense*) brings a sympathetic gay character to viewers throughout the country. In all these ways, lesbian and gay issues have received growing public attention in recent years. Although not always favorable, this attention contributes to an increasing awareness of sexual diversity among the broader Nicaraguan population.

In a similar way to the women's movement of a decade or two ago, the gay and lesbian movement today reveals how far some nations are willing to go in accommodating cultural difference and extending citizenship rights to all. In Nicaragua, the mass women's movement produced a feminist leadership that became instrumental in charting the direction of lesbian and gay culture and politics. This has been one of the most striking aspects of the nascent movement—the degree to which women have assumed prominent roles through participation in NGOs and social activism. Indeed, to understand contemporary sexual politics in the country, it is crucial to consider women's stake in the course of local and national change. Moreover, the association of Nicaraguan gay politics with transnational currents is most clearly apparent through the involvement of women, as well as men, in a host of projects across Central America and beyond.

During gay pride week in 2002, the lesbian-feminist leadership of Xochiquetzal called together thirteen lesbians and thirteen gay men for a daylong meeting held in a lesbian-owned bar. They formed a Managua "cell" in hope of inspiring more cells to organize around the country, which could eventually coalesce into a national movement. Among the advances were agreements to endorse lesbian and gay rights, to support others to "come out," and to move cautiously toward forming alliances internationally. While the initiative to build a national lesbian and gay movement has yet to bear fruit, the event stimulated a good deal of productive discussion. The participants took the collective thinking of the group back to their various individual organizations and put it to practical use.

For now, lesbian and gay groups and NGOs often find that more is gained by creating and claiming ties with international counterparts and movements than by remaining focused at local or national levels. In the face of continued homophobia and internal political differences, identification and solidarity with international groups may be desirable. Furthermore, most organizations depend on international financial support, often from Europe, and funding agencies expect to find programs and services that mirror the activities of their own countries' gay-rights movements. As a result, competition over scarce funding is often fierce among feminist and gay organizations. Arguably, the competition for resources among NGOs and other groups substantially impedes the formation of stronger ties of solidarity at the national level. Even those who are the beneficiaries of such international support are often harsh critics of the consequences of the state relinquishing responsibility for many social projects now taken on by NGOs. As Nicaraguan feminist and Left intellectual Sofía Montenegro put it, "NGOs are cheap for the state and good for capitalism, but the social movements have become NGO-ized."

While globalization presents opportunities for individuals and social movements to expand sexual expression and sexual rights, neoliberalism has benefited some far more than others as sexual subjects and citizens, particularly men and cultural elites. Women and members of the popular classes in general have experienced diminished possibilities and greater hardship in the post-Sandinista years, even if they have also found new ways of organizing collectively.

The mass mobilization of the population brought about by the Nicaraguan Revolution provided an opportunity for young women and men to explore and redefine their sexuality. During their years in power, the Sandinistas began to provide a space for more open discussion of gender and sexual relations and of personal life and politics, though they were ambivalent about the new desires expressed as a result of those spaces. In the post-Sandinista neoliberal era, the FSLN leadership has faced its own crisis, signaling that there is much left unresolved in Nicaragua's *machista* political culture. Thus, it is all the more remarkable that lesbians and gay men in this small Central American nation have been at the forefront of charting a politics of sexuality in Latin America.

PART 5

Intrasociety Relations

The Rationale of Collective Action within Sexual-Rights Movements

An Abstract Analysis of Very Concrete Experiences

Mario Pecheny

Translated by Mariana Alcañiz

IN ANALYZING the ways in which actors intervene in the field of sexual citizenship, two perspectives of political analysis, which at first appear inadequate for this object, turn out to be quite revealing: game theory and communicative action theory.

In previous studies, I have approached the topic of political claims for sexual rights and HIV/AIDS prevention and treatment within the context of claims for equal citizenship [. . .] (Pecheny 2003).

The ways in which the identity and sociability of nonheterosexual persons are structured [. . .] have implications on the political strategies of sexual minority movements. These modes of sociability—some exclusive of nonheterosexuals, others common to our contemporary market-driven world—install logics of political construction, actions and debates, often invisible, which boycott the collective objectives. Because of these rationales, individuals and groups who pursue an interest or a collective or individual good in a seemingly rational way (according to the terms of game theory) are made to arrive at results which are not the best, and may even be the worst possible for one and all. For this reason they are known as "perverse rationales."

An Empiric Source of Reflections: Some Hints

I will not describe here the experiences that originated these reflections, but point out a constant I have detected in them, which is the tendency of all the participant actors to make use of energy in a direction that turns out to be a self-inflicted boycott of the collective project.

It would be very interesting to measure empirically, that is to count and compare, the number of hours spent in playing a game of argument and counterargument regarding issues that have to do with spaces of political and personal power, and to compare that number with the number of hours spent fighting what is outside and pursuing common goals. We could do the same with the intensity and passion put into them. Thus economists and political scientists would be able to measure the cost-effectiveness of such efforts, exactly as they do in other areas of human activity. Of course, I am not seriously suggesting counting hours in this way, but the impression shared by many actors is that the hours lost in futile arguments and retaliation are excessively high in relation to the hours dedicated to the vital problems that trouble implicated actors.

An abstract approach will call attention to a few clues that explain the self-boycott phenomenon. Firstly, these clues describe how the rationale of interaction among actors is established, how it impedes the achievement of collective goals, and how this rationale is difficult to escape. Within certain contexts, what is important is not the attitude of each actor, but the rationale that governs the interaction. The rationale implied in the interaction does not only have to do with the search for individual and common interests (an instrumental logic), but with a certain idea of the common good (a normative logic), and the idea of sincerity (a rationale of veracity or authenticity), which, according to Habermas (1989), defines any type of social interaction.

First Source of Analytic Reflections: Game Theory

Game theory has a central characteristic that makes it as useful as it is limited: it simplifies ("models") human qualities, courses and alternatives of action, and decisions to the extreme. This is quite useful, since it allows us to schematically visualize the alternatives offered to the actors in a given situation (a "game"), and understand what they do, or predict what these actors will do when behaving "rationally," which in this theory means pursuing their own interests. It is quite limited because rarely are actors perfectly aware of available alternatives, because courses of action do not often constitute clear and defined alternatives, and because admittedly, people hardly ever behave only "rationally," if that is what "defending their own interests" means.

When certain rationales—which this theory labels "perverse"—are installed, if actors (individuals or groups) pursue their own interests rationally, the results attained are not the best, either from the actor's point of view or from that of the group.

Basically, games formalize situations that have rewards and punishments, whose value is determined based on the interdependent or strategic decisions that actors-players make. That is, the results of the decisions and actions of each actor-player will depend on his or her own decisions and actions, as well as on the decisions and actions of the rest. [...] When analysts are able to detect the underlying rationale of the main social interaction or conflict (namely, what interests are pursued and what calculations the actors are making), they may understand why the actors chose the path that they did and what results they will achieve. [...]

The interaction among participants of sexual rights movements and other movements often seems guided by a rationale similar to the "prisoners' dilemma": a game in which selfishness appears as the dominant rational strategy, and yields a collective and individual result which, while not the worst possible result, is not the best either.

Within sexual rights movements, conflicts among participants of the same game, following a "zero-sum" logic (if one person wins, another must lose)—the logic of the prisoners—are created around issues and conflicts between identities:

- Friends of *x* vs. friends of *y* (former partner of *x*)
- Capital city vs. provinces
- Gay rights vs. HIV/AIDS activism
- Gays vs. lesbians
- GLTTB vs. MSM (men who have sex with men)
- Older generations vs. newcomers
- Activists vs. researchers
- Grassroots activists vs. international activists
- "Those who are always traveling" vs. "those who never travel"
- Those who have or receive money vs. those who neither have money nor receive it
- Women's movements vs. feminist movements
- Nongovernment organizations vs. government organizations
- People living with HIV/AIDS vs. people not living with HIV/AIDS
- Network or group *a* vs. network or group *b*

[...] What draws the attention of observers and those directly interested is not the existence of conflicts, but their perception and treatment as if they were zero-sum games in which if somebody wins, then somebody loses, and in which it appears to be more rational for all to lose than for each to win in turn and collectively.

Certainly, these phenomena relate to more complex processes and genealogies, to history, and to meaning and identities—in other words, to anthropology and psychology. Here I simply wish to highlight that for whatever cause or reason, there are rationales that trap the actors within interactions that are harmful to each and everyone.

The Game of Chicken

This is a game with no rational solution. No calculations are possible—all calculations are recurrent, becoming a vicious circle. The interaction based on this rationale is definitively perverse, as it leads to the destruction of the game. Unfortunately, it is not uncommon that social movements and collective efforts to forward sexual rights are governed by the chicken rationale. Examples abound, in different countries and in Latin America, in which a chicken logic leads to the self-destruction of organizations, networks, demonstrations, magazines, and so on.

In synthesis: although the Catholic Church, conservatives, homophobes, and sexists have done much to obstruct advances in sexual and reproductive rights and in fighting HIV/AIDS, at some point we should stop and reflect on what part we have played in constructing obstructions ourselves, not in a penitent spirit, but in order to be more efficient in pursuing common goals.

Second Source of Analytic Reflections: The Theory of Communicative Action

In the *Theory of Communicative Action*, Jürgen Habermas (1989) states that in every act of enunciating, in every act of speech, there is an enounced and an enunciation (Schuster and Pecheny 2002). The enounced is the immediate content, the significant content of the act of speech. The enunciation is the act of affirming, of sustaining that which is enounced. Whenever we speak, we not only produce an enounced, but we also sustain what we enunciate. We may not understand what is enounced, not because of the meaning itself, but because of the discursive context in which it is affirmed, because of its enunciation. According to Habermas, the idea of the enunciation relates to the concept of the validity claim. For Habermas, inherent in every enunciation is a claim to that statement's validity. Its speaker asserts, either implicitly or explicitly, that what he has said is valid. In response, the listener can only reject, accept, or leave unchallenged this underlying claim. In the very act of enouncing, the speaker asserts the validity of the enounced.

Why do I say *valid* and not *true*? Because truth is but one validity claim among many. Indeed, there are different validity claims or criteria that help us judge what we say and do: claims to be saying something true, to be doing something effectively and/or efficiently, to be doing or saying something correct from a moral point of view, or that we are being sincere in what we are expressing. Thus, it is erroneous to evaluate, for example, an action that claims to be good from an ethical point of view as if it were an instrumental action, that is, one that claims to be an effective means to an end. Disagreement about validity claims is what hinders the coordination of actions and communication among different actors and speakers.

Certainly, not only linguistic manifestations, but all social actions have validity claims, that is, criteria with which one can evaluate them as "better" or "worse." Within this framework, [. . .] Habermas (1989) makes an analytical distinction between four types of actions. Each action supposes a concept of rationality, a particular relationship between the actor and the world, and a specific validity claim. [. . .] The first type of action is the teleological or instrumental, which is the means selected or used to reach a particular end. The validity claim of this type of action is efficacy and the propositional truth that evaluates judgments of the "objective world," that is, the world considered as a means or an obstacle to reaching the outcomes the actor wishes to achieve. According to Habermas, efficacy is a legitimate validity claim in reference to instrumental action, for instance, work. Problems arise when this claim, which is characteristic of work or the implementation of a technology, is applied to politics and other types of activities and social bonds.

The second type of action is normative action, whose validity claim is the correctness or the righteousness of an action as compared to the norms (norms, values, moral principles, or ethical convictions) that make up the "social world" in which actors are placed. When someone acts normatively, the action's validity claim is neither truth nor efficacy: one can be normatively correct and yet be ineffective. The concept of an action regulated by norms presumes relationships between an actor and two worlds: the social world exists in tandem with the objective world, which consists of entities and facts. This social world provides a normative context for actions, because it dictates what are and what are not legitimate interpersonal relationships (Habermas 1989, 127–28). At this level, the criteria for evaluation refer to a correspondence of actions to the notion of "common good" shared by the actors in interaction.

Following the sociologist Erving Goffman (Habermas 1989), the third type of action is dramaturgical action: it is the expressive action of the actor's "subjective world" and the validity claim is authenticity. In dramaturgical action, the actor must reference a subjective world in order to convey the weight or validity of his thought or emotion (Habermas 1989, 131–32). If a person says, "I feel very sad," and someone responds, "There is no reason to be sad," that person may reply, "I am sad, that is what I truly feel." In this case the validity claim is not the efficacy (or inefficacy) of being sad, nor is it the truth conceived as a correspondence between the sadness one felt and objective reasons for being sad. Nor is it about ascertaining the moral appropriateness of being sad because that is the way "it should be" in a given situation. The validity claim of an expressive action is authenticity, the sincerity with which subjective states are manifested. What is invalid from the point of view of expression is the lack of authenticity, that is—in our example—when someone expresses sadness and such a feeling does not exist.

This is the domain of veracity or sincerity—that is, the domain of the belief in sincerely stating the truth—and not the domain of propositional truth, which corresponds to the first type of action. It does not make sense to evaluate certain interpersonal bonds—for example, those of friendship—in strategic-instrumental terms or in moral terms, but it does make sense to evaluate them in terms of the authenticity, sincerity, or veracity of the reciprocal expressions.

Finally, we find a fourth type of action, which for Habermas is simultaneously a condition of possibility for the first three: communicative action. Communicative action is defined as an action oriented to understanding in the sense that participants reach a consensus on their perspectives, on how they see the world, which allows them to act in harmony. Reaching an agreement is based on interaction and argumentative dialogue. In communicative action, the validity claim is a rational agreement—that is, actually or potentially supported by reasons—about the validity claims of all parties involved. When someone speaks with claims of truth, what the speaker expects is that the other party recognize that what she affirms is true. If the other party rejects the truth of her utterance, they both should provide arguments regarding the validity claim. Something similar occurs with normative rightness and veracity (Habermas 1989, 143). In communicative action, coparticipants are basically on equal footing regarding their competence and the validity claims at stake, since both should be able to offer reasons if asked. [...]

Within sexual minorities organizations and AIDS organizations [...], there are heated theoretical, methodological, and policy discussions on short-, mid-, and long-term goals, or on what are the best strategies to achieve community building and full integration to citizenship. Frequently, this process takes on the appearance of a veritable civil war. However, such discussions contribute to the wealth and diversity of the movement and to an argumentative and organizational position for the struggle, which is increasingly strengthened in the face of the rest of society and the state. [...]

Regardless of ideological and strategic conflicts, within social movements for sexual rights lie substantial disagreements in the domains of ethical-normative and expressive validity claims. It is these disagreements that often explain the conflictive interactions that occur under the guise of dissent in the strategic domain.

Observers [...] of the aforementioned social movements cannot but be surprised by the degree of virulence and entrenchment of the existing distrust among different actors of the same "movement." [...] The expectations that "one" has of "the other" define the fate of the relationship. [...] In the Argentine social movement at least, the general rule is distrust, an assumption of insincerity, the idea that others do not genuinely seek the ends that they say they do, but rather have a hidden agenda, usually a personal one that determines their interaction with other actors. This becomes particularly evident when real or presumed privileges and rewards enter into play, such as in conflicts concerning spaces of political representation, trips, and subsidies.

To determine the causes and reasons that have created this context of disagreement on instrumental, normative, and expressive claims far exceeds the expectations of this brief essay. However, in concluding, I wish to assert that explanations should aim at instituting, in the social movement and the sociability of its members, a rationale derived from neoliberal values and practices, even when most of the current discourse is allegedly positioned in opposition to this vision. The process of transformation of militant groups into NGOs and foundations whose survival is determined by governmental and international subsidies, does nothing if not materialize this state of things (Jelin 1998). [...]

References

Habermas, J. 1989. *Teoría de la acción comunicativa*, vol. 2. Buenos Aires: Taurus.

Jelin, E. 1998. Toward a Culture of Participation and Citizenship. In *Cultures of Politics, Politics of Cultures: Re-Visioning Latin American Social Movements*, ed. S. E. Alvarez, E. Dagnino, and A. Escobar, 405–11. Boulder: Westview Press.

Pecheny, M. 2003. *Identidades discretas*. In *Identidades, sujetos y subjetividades: Narrativas de la diferencia*, ed. L. Arfuch, 125–48. Buenos Aires: Prometeo.

Schuster, F., and M. Pecheny. 2002. *Objetividad sin neutralidad valorativa según Jürgen Habermas*. In *Filosofía y métodos de las ciencias sociales*, ed. Federico Schuster, 286–310. Buenos Aires: Manantial.

Sexual Orientation and Human Rights in the Americas

Andrew Reding

[...]

Methodological Cautions

LGBT RIGHTS groups occasionally fall into the methodological trap of assuming that all violence directed toward members of sexual minorities is motivated by those persons' sexual orientation. But like any other persons, LGBT individuals also fall victim to crimes that have nothing to do with their sexuality. In countries with high overall crime rates, one would expect a comparably high crime rate against homosexuals even in the absence of societal prejudice. The only point that can validly be made from aggregate crime statistics, in the absence of specific evidence indicating intent for each crime, is that higher crime *rates* against homosexuals—as opposed to the population at large—point to the effects of social stigma and hatred.

In its first annual report on human rights in Chile (covering the year 2002), the Movement for Homosexual Integration and Liberation (*Movimiento de Integración y Liberación Homosexual*, MOVILH) cautioned:

That a homosexual is murdered does not necessarily mean that it is the result of homo-phobia, since other phenomena can lead to homicide, such as common crime, drug trafficking, amorous disputes between partners, etc. Simply put, homosexuals, like other persons, are assaulted, robbed, and murdered by criminals, and not necessarily because they are gay, lesbian, transvestite, transgendered, or transsexual.

Our organization does not wish to commit the error, which is quite frequent among homosexual organizations in various parts of the world, to explain any tragedy or prob-lem that affects a member of a sexual minority as being motivated by homophobia. Be-sides being immoral, such an approach is sensationalist and irresponsible.[1]

In the late 1990s, two reports by a Mexican group raised serious concerns about killings of homosexuals. At the May 6, 1998, launching of the Citizen's Commission against Homophobic Hate Crimes (*Comisión Ciudadana contra los Crímenes de Odio por Homofobia*, CCCCOH), conveners presented a report alleging a national epidemic of homicidal hate crimes. The report listed 125 murders throughout Mexico over a three-year period from February 1995 through April 1998, with 65 occurring in the Federal District, 24 in the adjoining state of Mexico, 12 in Veracruz, and a lesser num-ber in other states.

Though the report raised troubling questions, it suffered from methodological shortcomings. Its sole source was the Mexico City daily newspaper *La Prensa*, a tabloid (*nota roja*) that focuses on the police beat.[2] Second, many of the victims were listed as "unknown," with brief descriptions—"beaten and strangled," "hung," "stabbed," "asphyxiated with a plastic bag and shot in the head"—insufficient to corroborate ei-ther their homosexuality or allegations of a hate crime. Third, no effort was made to verify any of the newspaper accounts, or find corroborating sources.[3]

Rodolfo Millán, the attorney who was the report's chief author, explained that human-rights investigators face serious challenges in trying to obtain the facts needed to find out what really happened in such murders. The first problem is legal. Mexican law restricts access to police files to those who have a material interest in the case, such as family members. That leads to a second problem. Relatives are often reluctant to allow public disclosure of information that could expose the sexual orientation of the deceased, and thereby embarrass the family. For these reasons, he said, it had been virtually impossible to obtain further information about the cases.[4]

Mexican criminologist Rafael Ruiz, on the other hand, cautioned that the overall numbers did not point to a higher homicide rate for homosexuals than for the general population. There were 3,257 reported homicides in the Federal District (*Distrito Fede-ral*, D.F.) in the years 1995 through 1997. The 57 reported killings of homosexuals in the D.F. during that period represented only 1.75 percent of total reported homicides.[5] That figure is, if anything, smaller than most estimates of the percentage of the pop-ulation thought to be homosexual. It is likely, however, that homicides of homosex-uals were underreported, to avoid unwanted publicity for their families.

In the summer of 1999, the Citizen's Commission against Homophobic Hate Crimes issued a second report, claiming a total of 495 hate-motivated "executions" of homosexuals in the four years beginning in 1995 and culminating in 1998. The much higher reported number of killings attracted sensational coverage in some news media.[6] Yet careful examination of the report revealed little that was different from the first report. The only new information was a figure of 47 alleged "homophobic hatred executions" in Mexico in the year 1998. The same tabloid—*La Prensa*—was the sole source, and the report suffered from the same methodological limitations as its predecessor. Moreover, the figure of 495 was obtained by arbitrarily multiplying the total number of alleged murders over four years (164) by three, ostensibly to compensate for underreporting.[7]

There is another reason to question even the base figure of 164 hate-inspired murders over four years. Several influential Mexican periodicals—including the Mexico City daily *La Jornada*, and the national weekly *Proceso*—are left-leaning and sympathetic to the movement to secure equal treatment for all persons regardless of sexual orientation. It was *Proceso* that exposed the killings of transvestites in Chiapas in the early 1990s, and *La Jornada* that focused attention on an antihomosexual hate crime in Mexico City in 1995.[8] Both publish the columns of Carlos Monsiváis, a writer who is among Mexico's most prominent gay men. Neither has reported any widespread pattern of hate-inspired homicides since 1995.

Another example of statistical sleight of hand was an assertion by the Jesuit-run Miguel Agustín Pro Juárez Human Rights Center that Mexico ranked second only to Brazil in the number of homicides of homosexuals in Latin America. Though true, the statement was misleading, because it implied that hate was the cause, when such an outcome would be expected from relative population sizes alone.[9] Brazil's total population was then 166 million, the highest in Latin America; Mexico's was in second place at 96 million, well above Colombia, which was third with 41 million.[10] All other things being equal, one would have expected Mexico to have the second highest number of homicides, whether of homosexuals or heterosexuals.

The methodological cautions cut both ways, though. As pointed out by MOVILH in its 2002 report on human rights for sexual minorities in Chile, many crimes against LGBT individuals are never reported.[11] In homophobic societies, such individuals and their families often do not want sexual orientations exposed to the public. In many countries, LGBT individuals also have legitimate reasons to expect anything from indifference to abuse if they report a crime to the police, as documented in country profiles in this report. Police all too frequently dismiss murders of homosexuals as "crimes of passion" instead of conducting a proper investigation. It is true, as discussed further on, that societal stigmas against "unmanliness" contribute to pathologies in which some men, feeling their masculine image impaired by having sex with other men, attack and kill or beat casual sexual partners or sex workers. And true crimes of passion occur in homosexual liaisons just as they do in heterosexual ones. Yet in much of Latin America and the Caribbean, it is all too common for the police to affix the label "crime of passion" without supporting evidence, thereby eliminating any possibility of uncovering hate crimes. [. . .]

Machismo and Gay Men

[. . .] Machismo has important implications for how most Latin Americans view homosexuality. Unlike the United States, where homophobia tends to be directed against all individuals who are attracted to other persons of the same sex, in Latin America it is primarily directed against those who violate norms of male and female conduct. That is especially pronounced among men, where effeminate behavior elicits far greater levels of social disapproval than does homosexuality per se. In the *machista* perspective, a man's greatest offense against the norm is to not act like a man. Effeminacy and cross-dressing are serious violations of the masculine ideal. But the greatest transgression is for a man to assume the sexual role of a woman in intercourse. The man who penetrates another man remains masculine. The man who is penetrated loses his masculinity, and incurs by far the greater social stigma.

In the words of Mexican Nobel laureate Octavio Paz,

> It is likewise significant that masculine homosexuality is regarded with a certain indulgence insofar as the active agent is concerned. The passive agent is an abject, degraded being. This ambiguous conception is made very clear in the word games or battles—full of obscene allusions and double meanings—that are so popular in Mexico City. Each of the speakers tries to humiliate his adversary with verbal traps and ingenious linguistic combinations, and the loser is the person who cannot think of a comeback, who has to swallow his opponent's jibes. These jibes are full of aggressive sexual allusions; the loser is possessed, is violated, by the winner, and the spectators laugh and sneer at him. Masculine homosexuality is tolerated, then, on condition that it consists in violating a passive agent. As with heterosexual relationships, the important thing is not to open oneself up and at the same time to break open one's opponent.[12]

[. . .] According to Brazilian anthropologist Luiz Mott, "[I]n the ideology common to other Mediterranean-derived cultures, only the *pasivo* is homosexual, while the *activo* is not."[13]

So ingrained are these distinctions that they are reflected in the popular vocabulary. In everyday speech, Latin Americans distinguish male homosexuals by their degree of masculinity and their sexual roles. Writing about Nicaragua, anthropologist Roger Lancaster says:

Thus "to give" (*dar, meter, poner*) is to be masculine; "to receive" (*recibir, aceptar, tomar*) is to be feminine ... This relationship holds as the ideal in all spheres of transaction between the genders. It is symbolised by the popular interpretation of the male sexual organ as active in intercourse and the female sexual organ (or male anus) as passive.

Cochones [passive homosexuals] are, therefore feminine men, or, more accurately, feminized men, not fully male men. They are men who are "used" by other men. Their stigma flows from this concept of use. Used by other men, the *cochón* is not a complete man. His "passive" acquiescence to the active drive of other men's sexual desires both defines and stigmatizes his status. Consequently, when one "uses" a *cochón*, one acquires masculinity; when one is "used" as a *cochón*, one expends it. The nature of the homosexual transaction, then, is that the act makes one man a *machista* and the other a *cochón*. The *machista*'s honour and the *cochón*'s shame are opposite sides of the same coin. The line that this transaction draws is not between those who practice homosexual intercourse and those who do not (for this is not a meaningful distinction at all in Nicaragua's popular classes) but between two standardized roles in that intercourse. *Machistas* make *cochones* out of other men, and each is necessary to the definition of the other in a dynamic sense that is very different from the way North American categories of the heterosexual and homosexual define each other.[14]

Joseph Carrier describes a similar pattern in Mexico:

From early childhood on, Mexican males are made aware of the labels used to denote homosexual males—*puto, joto, maricón*—with the clear understanding that these homosexual males are guilty of unmanly, effeminate behavior. It is important to note that *homosexual* and *afeminado* are synonymous with the more often used colloquial terms *puto, joto, and maricón*. Since all these terms apply only to those males who play the anal-receptive sex role in a homosexual encounter, the implication is that the anal-insertive masculine male is not homosexual—and separate terms exist to describe him (*mayate, chichifo*, and *picador*). Thus, from an early age Mexican males are likely to be aware of same-sex contacts and of the *activo-pasivo* dichotomy that exists between males having sexual contact, and that there is a stigma associated with the *pasivo* but not the *activo* sex role.[15]

It is commonplace to think of men who consistently take the "active," "top," or "dominant" role in intercourse as still being "manly," and not really "homosexual." Though the particular labels used often vary from country to country, the essential meaning remains the same. According to Robert Francoeur,

Brazilian sexual culture is centered on the distinction between masculine activity (eating [*comer*], conquering and vanquishing [*vencer*], owning and possessing [*possuir*], and feminine passivity (giving, being penetrated, dominated, subjugated, and submissive). In keeping with the overriding importance of every male considering himself macho, the Brazilian male considers himself heterosexual, man, *homem* as long as his dominant mode of sexual expression involves active phallic penetration, regardless of the gender of the partner being possessed and penetrated.

If the category of "men," or *homens*, seems clear, its counterpart is less so. Those who *dão* (give or submit) include biological women or *mulheres*, and others, the biologically male *veado* (deer), *bicha* (worm, intestinal parasite), and the feminine form of *bicho* (best translated as queer or faggot). Though endowed with male anatomy, the *veado* or *bicha* is linked with the fundamentally passive social role of *mulher*, not *homem*. Within these categories, a male can have sexual relations with *mulheres*, *veado*, and *bicha* and maintain his masculine (heterosexual) identity provided he exercises phallic dominance.[16]

For men who are able to project a masculine image, there is a degree of tolerance, corresponding to the society's tolerance of extramarital dalliances by heterosexual men:

Although Mexican society generally disapproves of homosexuality, it seems to recognize the inevitability of homosexual contacts between men. There seems to be acceptance in Mexico of the reality that most males have multiple sexual outlets both when single and when married. A man's sexual outlets other than his wife are not socially approved, but are nevertheless put up with so long as they are carried out discreetly.[17]

Sofia Kamenetzky notes a similar pattern in Argentina:

To be gay or lesbian in a repressive environment whose stereotypes are the macho man and the submissive reproductive woman is not an easy task indeed. Anyone who deviates from a strict heterosexual behavior is ridiculed: a gay is not a man, a lesbian is a degenerate woman. However, to be bisexual is not so annoying, as long as one's same-gender behavior is kept very private.[18]

In Costa Rica, anthropologist Paul Kutsche found the same basic imperative to protect one's public image as a "real man":

[S]traight men find it convenient from time to time to have sex with other men, and those who are *de ambiente* [self-identified as homosexual] find it exciting to have sex with those they can regard as *hombres de verdad* [real men] . . . In return, the latter tolerate and at times protect gays, so long as gays don't object when straights utter homophobic remarks in public, and so long as gays stay deeply in the closet and act as straight as they are able in non-sexual situations.[19]

Socialization into machismo begins in early childhood, making it very difficult to change later in life. It also teaches young men that they can demonstrate their masculinity by denigrating that of their peers. Writing about Nicaragua, Roger Lancaster says:

[T]he taunting and provocation of young boys begins while they are still babies and continues in some form or other throughout childhood. All boys are constantly disciplined by their elders—by parents and siblings alike—with the humiliating phrase *No sea cochón!* (Don't be a faggot!) when their demeanor falls short of the assertive, aggressive, masculine ideal. Any show of sensitivity, weakness, reticence—or whatever else is judged to be a feminine characteristic—is swiftly identified and ridiculed. By adolescence, boys enter a competitive arena where the signs of masculinity are actively struggled for and can be won only by wresting them away from other boys around them.[20]

The emphasis on hypermasculinity has serious consequences. It means that most Latin American gay or bisexual males, regardless of the sexual roles they assume in private, are at pains to project a manly image in public. The relative few who are unable to do so are therefore highly exposed and subject to ridicule and harassment, to say nothing of discrimination in employment.

A further hazard arises when social stigmas become internalized. The fear of losing one's masculinity, or the public image of masculinity, is so strong that it can lead to hatred of one's self and one's partners for indulging in stigmatized behavior. E. A. Lacey describes this tortured dynamic among men who try at all costs to reconcile their sexual orientation with the stern demands of the *machista* code:

Influenced by the social reality he inhabits, he has accepted and bowed to the *macho* ethic . . . by completely internalizing and assimilating its code of rules, and attempting to live by them. He is no closet case: he openly pursues and beds down boys, and he appears to recognize and condone, even to trumpet, his own homosexuality, but only to the extent that he is the active partner. He is unable psychologically to abandon his cherished masculine orientation. Intimately, moreover, he despises his sexual tendencies, despises all other gays, especially effeminate ones, despises his own sexual partners and despises himself.[21]

Such insecurities often lead to violence against effeminate males, prostitutes, and casual sex partners. Occasionally, they culminate in murder, as described by Joseph Carrier:

Gilberto talked at length about his belief that in small-town Mexico it is very important to play *only* one sexual role in anal intercourse. The consequences of fucking a *mayate* [a man who has a reputation of being dominant in sex] when he is drunk may be severe. As an example he related the details of a murder late in 1986 of a relatively young queen (about twenty-eight or twenty-nine) across the river from Tuxpan in San Vicente. "She" was found shot in the head. Gilberto thinks the murder might be the result of a vendetta by a *mayate* the queen had fucked. Gilberto said that though he personally was *internacional* while living in California (that is, he played both sex roles), he is *puro pasivo* (only anal receptive) with men in Tuxpan.[22]

So strong is the stigma against effeminacy that the suggestion that a man is effeminate can lead to murderous retaliation by male relatives, in order to defend the family's honor. Rodrigo fled his home town in Veracruz after hacking to death a buddy —Carmelo—who insulted his brother. The two young men had been drinking when Rodrigo's brother showed up to try to coax Rodrigo home. Carmelo, inebriated, said, "Hey Rodrigo, your brother seems like a fag, the way he moves, and when I look at him he smiles; they say in town that he likes to go out at night in your sister's clothes in search of a husband." Rodrigo immediately punched Carmelo in the mouth. But townspeople continued to gossip that his brother was a *marica* (an effeminate homosexual). One night, at a bar, a group of friends teased him to the point where he snapped. In a drunken stupor, Rodrigo assaulted Carmelo outside the latter's home, slashing him to death with a machete. He then fled to Mexico City, where he joined a suburban police force in order to avoid being pursued for the murder. The last he had heard, his brother had moved to Guadalajara, where he was working in a transvestite bar.[23] [. . .]

The stigma against effeminacy and receptive male behavior also means that transvestites are particularly subject to hatred, harassment, and police abuse. Police abuse stems not only from popular prejudice, but from the fact that sex work is often illegal. Police officers, whose wages tend to be very low, are notorious for corruption in many Latin American countries. In Mexico, the bribes they extort from citizens and foreigners alike are commonly known as *mordidas* (little bites). Male and female sex workers are particularly vulnerable. Police officers frequently lie in wait for them to complete a transaction, then emerge to demand payment. Should the sex worker not comply, he or she may face detention and physical abuse. Also, when sex workers are mistreated or killed by their patrons, the police generally show little interest in pursuing investigations. [. . .]

In Brazil, where sex work is not a criminal offense, police have used "charges of vagrancy, disturbing the public peace, or conducting obscene acts in public to control prostitution by cross-dressers."[24] [. . .]

Another manifestation of the desire to keep homosexuality out of public view is a bit more bizarre. It is commonplace for Latin American men—particularly younger men—to be seen in public with their arms around each other, an act that would generally be interpreted in the United States as a sign of homosexual affection (and that is thus a frequent cause of confusion for American visitors to Latin America). In most Latin American countries, such behavior is universally accepted, and assumed to signal no more than friendship. Peruvian anthropologist Manuel Arboleda Grieve, for instance, says that "masculine Peruvians generally show considerable physical affection for other men without this being viewed as suspect (as it would be in Anglo America)."[25] Yet if two men should *hold hands*, it is commonly seen as homosexual and as an affront to community values. According to Joseph Carrier, police often invoke municipal ordinances against public morals (*por faltas a la moral*) against men who hold hands.[26] [...]

This cultural obsession with keeping up appearances—with covering up all visible indications of male effeminacy and homosexuality—has implications for finding employment. In most of Latin America, there are no laws protecting homosexuals against job discrimination. Even where such laws exist, they are difficult to enforce. Employers in most trades, conscious of the impression their businesses make on the public, seek to avoid the embarrassment of having obviously effeminate or homosexual men on their payrolls.

In recent research in São Paulo, it was found that homosexuals, especially those with exaggeratedly effeminate behavior, were usually rejected for employment following interviews with the company psychologists, although these same psychologists deny being prejudiced against homosexuals. In some areas, such as sales, there are minimal chances for an overt homosexual to find employment.[27]

That tends to constrain such individuals to trades that have traditionally been considered fit for women and (by association) homosexuals, such as cooking, the arts, hairdressing, and, unfortunately, sex work.

Annick Prieur, a female Norwegian doctoral student who lived for extended periods among male transvestite sex workers in Mexico, has provided a rare glimpse of that subculture from within. She stayed in the two-bedroom home of Mema, a sex worker in his thirties who provides a sort of sanctuary and way station for young effeminate boys with nowhere else to go. Typically, the boys had been molested by male relatives such as uncles or brothers, beaten by family members or peers, and expelled from their households. For most of these boys, the only two options for making a living were hairdressing and sex work.[28]

Reinforcing attitudes toward homosexuality in Latin American culture is the stance of the Roman Catholic Church. Cardinal Juan Luis Cipriani, archbishop of Lima, has mandated the distribution of pamphlets by the Pontifical Catholic University of Peru that describe homosexuality as an illness that can be "cured."[29]

Mexico City's Cardinal Norberto Rivera has denounced "euphemisms" that contribute to "moral disorientation": "The arguments expressed by those who sympathize with this current that favors sexual libertinism, often appear under humanist banners, although at root they manifest materialist ideologies that deny the transcendent nature of the human person, as well as the supernatural calling of the individual." The complementary union of man and woman, he says, is the only relationship capable of generating "true conjugal love."[30]

The new Catholic catechism describes homosexual acts as a "grave depravity" and "intrinsically disordered." It states that lesbian and gay relationships are "contrary to natural law ... They do not proceed from a genuine affective and sexual complementarity. Under no circumstances can they be approved." Recognizing that "the number of men and women who have deep-seated homosexual tendencies is not negligible," it specifies that "they must be accepted with respect, compassion, and sensitivity," avoiding "every sign of unjust discrimination." Yet it mandates that "homosexual persons are called to chastity."[31]

Despite the inherent conservatism of Latin American culture, change is nevertheless emerging from international contact in the context of globalization. Increased trade, tourism, the Internet, and satellite television are bringing to bear an infusion of European and North American influences, particularly from the United States and from Spain. Not surprisingly, that influence is being felt most strongly in large metropolises, such as Mexico City, Buenos Aires, São Paulo, and Rio de Janeiro; in areas frequented by North American and European gay tourists, such as Acapulco, Puerto Vallarta, and Cancún; and on the U.S.-Mexican border, especially in Tijuana. In all these places, a semantic change is signaling new perspectives among youth. Anthropologist Marta Lamas describes that change among the homosexual youth of Mexico City, where

[columnist Carlos] Monsiváis finds that an overwhelming majority have reached a certain level of acceptance of "normality" with the term gay. Monsiváis suggests that the semantic space of the word "gay" is becoming transformed into the social space of tolerance: to become gay is to become part of an international movement, to go from a problematic position to an extravagant, yet "modern," lifestyle.[32]

Machismo and Lesbians

Because machismo is by definition male oriented, and is premised on male dominance in relations between the sexes, lesbian relationships are generally perceived as less threatening to society. That is to the extent that they are perceived at all, because to a great degree they remain invisible in a cultural context that scarcely recognizes female sexuality. [. . .]

That helps explain the view often expressed among Latin American men that lesbians are women who have not experienced real sex with a real man. If women lack their own sexuality, what could possibly fulfill them other than a man? Such attitudes easily lead to justifications for sexual harassment and rape, on the premise that a woman who resists sexual advances from men does so only because she has not yet experienced her true sexual nature.

Rape is a widespread but severely underreported problem in Latin America, according to Marta Donayre, a Brazilian immigrant to the United States who is public education director of the National Center for Lesbian Rights in San Francisco:

The most common crime against lesbians is rape. Rapists, including police officers, usually tell the victims they are doing it to "show them what is good for them." In addition, most crimes against lesbians occur at the hands of family members, turning the crime into a domestic issue. Gay men, on the other hand, tend to be victimized by strangers, making it easier to report. If a crime against a lesbian is ever reported, it would usually be reported as a rape or as domestic violence, not as a homophobic attack. This blends the crime with overall crimes against women, effectively hiding lesbophobia.[33]

Married women are expected to model themselves after the Virgin [Mary] by bearing and raising children without concern for sexual gratification, thereby remaining "pure." Men, on the other hand, are expected to seek sexual gratification, but primarily outside the bounds of the marriage. [...] In this dichotomy, married women are idolized in an asexual way, while unmarried women are typically seen as fair game for sexual advances and conquest by men. Because they are not claimed by another man, lesbians suffer much the same treatment as other unmarried women in a society that subordinates women to the perceived needs of men.

Overt lesbians are, in addition, subject to discrimination. [...] In the few places in Latin America where lesbians are beginning to come out of the closet, that process often brings new hazards. [...]

Notes

1. *Movimiento de Integración y Liberación Homosexual, Informe 2002: Primer informe anual sobre los principales hechos que involucran a las minorías sexuales chilenas* (Santiago: MOVILH, 2003), 5.

2. *La Prensa* is not a newspaper of record. If one were to make an analogy to New York City, it would be to the *Daily News*, not the *New York Times*.

3. Rodolfo Millán, Angela Aguayo, and Antonio Candelas, *Reporte de crímenes cometidos por odio homofóbico: Investigación hemerográfica* (Mexico City: *Comisión Ciudadana contra los Crímenes de Odio por Homofobia*, May 6, 1998).

4. Rodolfo Millán, telephone interview with the author, May 27, 1999.

5. Telephone interview, February 5, 1999, in "Mexico: Treatment of Sexual Minorities," Research Directorate, Immigration and Refugee Board, Ottawa, Canada, April 1999.

6. Diego Cevallos, "Rights—Mexico: 495 Murders of Gays Go Unpunished," Inter-Press Service, August 13, 1999.

7. Citizen's Commission Against Homophobic Crimes, *1998 Crime Report*, (Mexico City: Citizen's Commission Against Homophobic Crimes, undated [issued Summer 1999]), 8. Careless errors are commonplace. For example, the anonymous authors assume that "for every registered case of execution, there may be at least three more cases." That would suggest multiplying by four to reach an estimate, but they instead multiplied by three. Even so, multiplying 164 alleged cases by 3 yields 492, not 494. The error occurred when a 0 was multiplied by 3 to get 3 in one cell of the spreadsheet.

8. "*Psicosis en Chiapas por la cacería de homosexuales,*" *Proceso* 852 (1993): 26; "*Atacaron a grupo de homosexuales en la calzada de Tlalpan; uno murió,*" *La Jornada,* June 28, 1995.

9. "*México, segundo lugar en asesinatos de homosexuales en América Latina,*" *Servicio Diario de Derechos Humanos en México, Centro de Derechos Humanos Miguel Agustín Pro Juárez,* May 7, 1998, VI.

10. Rounded off from United Nations 1998 revision of the World Population Estimates and Projections.

11. *Movimiento de Integración y Liberación Homosexual, Informe 2002: Primer informe anual sobre los principales hechos que involucran a las minorías sexuales chilenas* (Santiago: MOVILH, 2003), 5.

12. Octavio Paz, *The Labyrinth of Solitude: Life and Thought in Mexico* (N.Y.: Grove Press, 1961), 39–40. Originally published in Spanish as *El Laberinto de la soledad* (Mexico City: Fondo de Cultura Económica, 1950).

13. Luiz Mott, "The Gay Movement and Human Rights in Brazil," in *Latin American Male Homosexualities*, ed. Stephen O. Murray (Albuquerque: University of New Mexico Press, 1995), 224.

14. Roger N. Lancaster, *Life Is Hard: Machismo, Danger, and the Intimacy of Power in Nicaragua* (Berkeley: University of California Press, 1992), 242–43.

15. Joseph Carrier, *De Los Otros: Intimacy and Homosexuality Among Mexican Men* (N.Y.: Columbia University Press, 1995), 17. See also "Hispanic Homosexuals: A Spanish Lexicon," in *Latin American Male Homosexualities*, ed. Stephen O. Murray (Albuquerque: University of New Mexico Press, 1995), 184–88.

16. Robert T. Francoeur, "Brazil," in *The International Encyclopedia of Sexuality*, ed. Robert T. Francoeur (N.Y.: Continuum Publishing Company, 1997), vol. 1.

17. Joseph Carrier, *De los Otros: Intimacy and Homosexuality Among Mexican Men* (N.Y.: Columbia University Press, 1995), 16.

18. Sofia Kamenetzky, "Argentina," in *The International Encyclopedia of Sexuality*, ed. Robert T. Francoeur (N.Y.: Continuum Publishing Company, 1997), vol. 1.

19. Paul Kutsche, "Two Truths about Costa Rica," in *Latin American Male Homosexualities*, ed. Stephen O. Murray (Albuquerque: University of New Mexico Press, 1995), 113.

20. Roger N. Lancaster, *Life Is Hard: Machismo, Danger, and the Intimacy of Power in Nicaragua* (Berkeley: University of California Press, 1992), 42–43.

21. E. A. Lacey, introduction to *My Deep Dark Pain Is Love: A Collection of Latin American Fiction*, ed. Winston Leyland (San Francisco: Gay Sunshine Press, 1983), 10.

22. Joseph Carrier, *De los Otros: Intimacy and Homosexuality Among Mexican Men* (N.Y.: Columbia University Press, 1995), 83–84.

23. Nelson Arteaga Botello and Adrián López Rivera, "*Viaje al interior de la policía: El caso de un municipio de México,*" *Nexos*, April 1998, 73.

24. James N. Green, *Beyond Carnival: Male Homosexuality in Twentieth-Century Brazil* (Chicago: University of Chicago Press, 1999), 252.

25. Manuel Arboleda Grieve, "Social Attitudes and Sexual Variance in Lima," in *De los Otros: Intimacy and Homosexuality Among Mexican Men*, by Joseph Carrier (N.Y.: Columbia University Press, 1995), 105.

26. Joseph Carrier, telephone interview with the author, July 7, 1999.

27. Gonçalves de Freitas, Sérgio Luiz, with Elí Fernandes de Oliveira and Lourenço Stélio Rega, "Brazil," in *The International Encyclopedia of Sexuality*, ed. Robert T. Francoeur (N.Y.: Continuum Publishing Company, 1997), vol. 1.

28. Annick Prieur, *Mema's House, Mexico City: On Transvestites, Queens, and Machos* (Chicago: University of Chicago, 1998).

29. Lucien Chauvin, "Lima Students Decry Homosexuality Tract," *The Chronicle of Higher Education*, October 4, 2002, 55.

30. "*La Iglesia, contra la marcha lésbico-gay*," *La Jornada*, September 24, 1999, 58.

31. *Catechism of the Catholic Church*, 1994 English edition, articles 2357–59. The new Catechism stated in article 2358 that "They [homosexuals] do not choose their homosexual condition; for most of them it is a trial." That language was altered in 1997 to read, "This inclination, which is objectively disordered, constitutes for most of them a trial." Ontario Center for Religious Tolerance, "Roman Catholic Church and Homosexuality," www.religioustolerance.org /hom_rom8.htm.

32. [. . .] See Marta Lamas, "*Escenas de un campo de batalla: la política sexual en México*," *Letra S*, supplement to *La Jornada*, January 7, 1999.

33. Marta Donayre, e-mail message to the author, June 12, 2003.

Desire, TV, Panic, and Violence Surrounding the Transgendered in Argentina

The Metamorphoses of 1998

Alejandro Modarelli

Translated by Mariana Alcañiz

THE YEAR that concerns us is 1998. Presidential elections are coming up, and the current administration is beginning to withdraw from institutional power, a move that it assumes will last for a strategically short period. Now autonomous, the city of Buenos Aires has just been won by an opposition which represented itself as progressive, and has designs on the Argentine presidential palace in national elections. Within this political context, some social and cultural debates take place for the first time, some of which concern sexuality. First, the city-province's new constitution made discrimination based on sexual orientation illegal. [. . .] Then, the city eliminated some police edicts that had been used as instruments of repression to take young people, transients, and beggars, and in a very deliberate manner, sexual divergents, into custody at police stations. The purpose was to check for a police record, and enabled the police to reach the quota of bureaucratic detentions the police chiefs demanded. The reality was that above all, by controlling zones of transit for homosexuals and the transgendered—or where prostitution and illegal gambling took place—police edicts generated illegal income in different police jurisdictions. There was no transgendered person in prostitution who did not leave a tithe at the customs office of the keepers of the order. They sometimes were made to leave an even higher percentage, often facing violence, torture, and threats if payment was delayed or resisted. Territories of exchange were diversified: their variable location was negotiated through a criminal surveillance system that [...] was tolerated—at times even supported—by the administration in office.

It must be made clear that, nevertheless, Buenos Aires's gay and lesbian community had been enjoying considerable freedom to circulate and meet for years. The old edicts had modified their gay-lesbian target and focused on hunting down the transgendered. [...]

In 1988, a new Code of Coexistence in Buenos Aires came to replace the old regulations on misdemeanors, among them police edicts. Supposedly, the objective was to democratize interurban relationships, thus diminishing the submissive relationship between the so-called residents and the institutions of power. Promoted by the local government, neighborhood organizations began to form—which of course did not make city life any more democratic. The people who more fervently met for the debate on how to tackle coexistence were the very same for whom coexistence had always signified surveillance and exclusion. They immediately reported that the new code said nothing regarding the practice of prostitution (whether on the streets or indoors), and as a result whatever was not explicitly forbidden was allowed. The truth is that with the implicit permission for the supply and demand of sex, both the pimps and their police-officer confidants were attacked for the money. It was around this issue that the transgendered appeared publicly at the center of a sociopolitical battle. The war also emerged as an issue in the electoral campaign. The discourse of panic and public security used by the federal government against its opponents in the city, and especially by those who were losing part of the booty, drove the residents of the red zones to focus their time and efforts against the marginalized populations. Some even formed combat groups.

The transgendered, [...] who had previously been shifted around by the police's strategy of distribution and segregation of spaces, were forced to deal with unsolicited overexposure. [...] The areas of sex trade constituted unstable territories, with the population of workers controlled by the police in terms of number, movement, and earnings. Spending some time in one area, they were suddenly pushed toward other corners or neighborhoods by patrolling police cars. Suddenly, the most exclusive of these areas, the bourgeois neighborhood Palermo Viejo, became overpopulated by the police and the attention of the media. What had been a secretive, restricted, specific space for the supply and demand of sex became a gallery of noisy drivers-by and candid news cameras. For middle-class youths, it became an all-night party, cruising to view the multiplicity of monumental breasts and buttocks that were also being featured on television talk shows. Female prostitutes could not emulate the exorbitant bodies that technology had produced; they were minor characters in this urban drama. Additionally, for the common Argentine, they represented the traditional role of a biblical Mary Magdalene, worthy of compassion rather than punishment. They were assumed to be abandoned wives, mothers forced to work out of necessity, the opposite of virgins, denied any true pleasure. Their appearance after sundown had always been tolerated. For this reason, it was the transgendered who took center stage in the media's treatment of the new code. Only a few human-rights organizations and gay and lesbian organizations came to support the transgendered. These organizations played a decisive role in bringing together the transgendered as a political collective, despite some early reluctance to incorporate them into the liberation movement. We must not forget that the ascent of the gay model relied somewhat on an exile of femininity; it was necessary to be discerning and differentiate the modern gay man from the old queen and, needless to say, from the transgendered. To the coalition of groups was added a community of nuns devout to the Christ of the marginalized, the *Oblatas del Santísimo Sacramento*, whose pastoral mission was to aid victims of prostitution. These holy women witnessed firsthand all the physical and moral abuse suffered by the transgendered. [. . .]

Alliances formed within the gangster-like state—that is, between the police institution that benefited from the prohibition against prostitution and the ubiquitous apparatus of the regime—as well as between the state and the traditional, masculine middle-class family. The mass media played an ambiguous role in the days of anti-transgender panic. This panic broke out around individuals who, by their mere presence, produced fascination, desire, and anger: transfugitives from gender and family, hyperbolic women marked by social injustice and the need for survival. In the construction of the transgendered as monsters to be sacrificed, the goal was to preserve a violent, corrupt order in opposition to a few attempts at political liberalism, as well as to define the geographical and symbolic spaces of acceptance and tolerance for the sexually divergent.

Disturbing Metamorphoses

In the spring of that year, a resident of Palermo Viejo, a former judge and militant against the new Code of Coexistence, declared, "I wish to return to the old police edicts, because all the degenerates of Buenos Aires flock here, and I do not mean only the transgendered, but also young males and dirty old men looking for adventure. Legislators want us to take justice into our own hands." Thus spoke a former judge. Similarly harsh remarks were enunciated, somewhat more carefully, at the Friday rallies of the self-convened Palermo residents. These groups called themselves self-convened, but they were secretly advised by the police precinct. Many of these protesters wanted to "take justice" into their own hands. [. . .] "We also are residents of the neighborhood," the transgendered stated in their defense. However, their residence is always on the periphery. The monster always comes from the exterior, even when becoming visible in increasing proximity. Alien to democratic benefits, their habitat concentrates around a red zone; they do not own property and are not residents in a strict sense: by no means are they citizens. Caesar Aryans, a top official in the Menem administration and a representative of the ruling party, barks on a talk show: "These men should not be included in the concept of human rights." Deprived of everything, even of their humanity, they cram into miserable hotels like the *Gondolín*, which the police sporadically raid just to remind them of their boundaries. These officers are the same ones who demand sexual favors. [...] And here comes the second part of the alleged problem the judge mentioned: the young guys—police officers—and dirty old men, with whom the transgendered normally associate. [...]

Homosociability and homosexuality as a practice are two concepts in permanent tension. A fraternal hug may become sexual. Family, religion, and the state often see themselves as charged with preventing this step. The boundary that separates homosociability from homosexuality is conflict itself. Irigaray says that homosociality is concerned with fraternal relationships among peers, within which a woman operates as a mere instrument of exchange and guarantees the passage of males into the social order, and into the symbolic order. There is no exchange with women, but of women. [...] Banned everywhere, homosexuality is played out through the bodies of women. Lovers, daughters, sisters serve as offerings facilitating relationships among men. The passage toward homosexual practices is culturally perceived as a situation of deep anxiety and crisis. It jeopardizes the social order, the symbolic order. In that sense, it implicates the nation itself, as the nation represents the primal community of fellow men. In a patriarchal society such as Argentina's in 1998, are the sexual connections between a male identified as heterosexual and a transgendered person perceived as a disturbing threat? [...] The rise in the number of territories where these erotic exchanges take place is relevant data, against which the traditional family crosses itself and builds alliances.

The question would be whether sexual dealings with the transgendered endanger the homosocial pact, pushing it towards the sordid, or rather strengthen it, given that a transgendered person is a woman, merchandise for exchange, and not a fellow man. [...] But if the heterosexual male does not consider sexual dealings with a transgendered person as a loss of his virtue within the homosocial pact, a kiss between them, on the other hand, will always be censured. It would mean a male's resigning his identity and breaking through the veil of latent homosexuality. [...] The hierarchical model would be broken, and also the secrecy that hid its inconsistency from view. [...]

In a stalwartly masculine society, maps are plotted around the body-frontier of the transgendered, on which spaces of normality and abnormality are distributed: feminine and masculine, health and disease, the haves and the have-nots, the interior and the exterior. Yet the frontier is always porous: the vision of an invented monster is terrifying, but at the same time seductive, immobilizing. Almost a woman, a transgendered person has an anatomical bonus that denotes the weirdness of the gender, and this extra feature may prove charming and disconcerting. The suspicion that this bonus is occasionally used to penetrate doubles up the inversion of gender roles: what is at first perceived as a pardonable deception becomes much more disturbing later. A male that has mostly transformed into a woman threatens to effeminize those who approach her sexually. This inversion is not circumscribed only by anatomy and gender. The accent and manner of the transgendered are also of the periphery, though sometimes ostentatious and glamorous. They do not pay taxes, but are laterally made to pay more than anyone else. It used to be homosexuals who threatened the interior of the community: there was a need for a confrontation in order to define an "us" in opposition to "them," and even a "that" rather than a "them." But in what bastion could that "us" now feel sheltered, when it encompasses a multitude of "young guys and dirty old men" awestruck by "bodies of strange metamorphosis?" (in the words of an outraged resident of Palermo on television). That is, the "degenerates" the judge spoke of are recruited from among males of mostly heterosexual behavior of various social classes and ages. It is the same reality that a female resident referred to when she admitted she fears her husband might get mixed with "one of them" under the pretense of walking the dog. There seems to be a multiform desire that pulls away from binary classifications of male/female, heterosexual/homosexual. [. . .]

With exceptions, the mass media played a decisive role in this triumph of paranoia. Television captured the figure of the transgendered as a novel piece in the identity museum. Gays and lesbians no longer constituted the threat to be investigated and exposed: they had fallen by the wayside. [. . .] What was left was "that other thing." On the question of the peddling of prostitution, a crusade on the distribution of meanings and values was introduced, declaring what was right, what was wrong, and eliminating any nuances that would deconstruct ideological discourse. In order to formulate binary spaces, the talk-show circuit attempted to extract a positive tone of humanity from some charismatic transgendered and transsexual characters. Their humanization was contingent upon their not defending streetwalking, and therefore they were unable to denounce the police abuse linked to prohibition. They were unwanted as militants, but rather as testimonies, laboratory rats telling their personal stories and displaying their exemplary suffering. [. . .]

In addition to the suffering transgendered, television produced glamorous ones. By this time TV had made famous two young, beautiful transgendered persons who became the objects of desire of the Argentines. [. . .] Thanks to their being on screen and on stage, they were able to rise above the rigors of the wandering sex trade and offer a stellar representation of the transgendered, but with certain limitations. They too were forced to endure countless jibes about their hidden male attributes—their mouths never quite allowed to reach for a man's kiss. Once there were even tears when a troglodyte TV host called one of them, who soon after died of AIDS, a "fag." It was at these times when the new media characters perceived that phobias about sexual and gender divergence also concerned them, that in the long run, the desire that they caused was inseparable, in their cultural context, from some form of violence. The truth is that the battle of Palermo again placed the transgendered in the enemy camp. It put them in their place. No glamour, no artifice. These violent beings, with a five o'clock shadow hanging over their collagen lips, were the ones shouting at the doors of the legislature, which was considering the possibility of making the Code of Coexistence harsher. Prohibitionist residents, speaking in the voice of the settled family, as well as the police, the media, and the federal government, through calculation and harassment, unraveled the inner contradictions of thorny bourgeois liberalism. Its legislators, evoking some European legislation, ended up passing a code that, in terms of the urban supply and demand of sex, became the most repressive in history. [. . .]

The liberalism of Buenos Aires in 1998 was unable to inspire a single public act of solidarity when the transgendered charged the police with treatment [resembling that under the Brazilian dictatorship]. Some legislators merely proposed creating boundaries for red zones, to be patrolled by an unspecified security force—perhaps the same operatives that beat and rob transgendered sex workers—far from the urban perimeter where they can come across neighborhood residents, but where they may feel more protected from violence.

The transgender question became a political issue for the city of Buenos Aires. [. . .] Those who had believed in democratizing social relations had already lost the battle. After a few months, the legislature passed a midway solution: it penalized the supply and demand of sex near residences, schools, and places of worship, or when the public peace was being disrupted due to their congregating, noise, interruption of traffic, or exposure of their bodies in undergarments or in the nude. The very same legislators who months earlier had condemned criminal connections between the federal police department and prostitution—as well as the violence brought about by illegality—had handed back to the police a power of persecution that was very similar to that of the formerly repealed edicts.

The prohibition of bodily exposure, which is ambiguous in its scope, seemed to be directed towards the silicone spheres of the transgendered, always popping out, conspicuous even under their clothes. Not in vain is this mount of artifice the anatomical feature that police in action target the most, as seen in the Brazilian case and as denounced by the Argentine transgendered. [. . .]

The chief editor of the *Perfil* newspaper, supposedly a liberal, [. . .] wondered if "perhaps a judge will turn up in the shadows one late night to restore the order between two men in blonde wigs threatening each other with broken bottles" or "whether a legislative representative of the city of Buenos Aires will arrive to put a stop to the racket from a transgendered whose honor has been offended, and to avoid the emotional outburst of a resident heartbroken by what his teenage children are forced to witness when coming home from clubbing in the early hours of the morning." [. . .] While the transgendered smash bottles, the residents' hearts break; and they are pure heart, even when they throw water and excrement on the unmentionable spectacle offered their teenage children. Children are torn between looking and not looking. The truth is that judging by the testimonies and admitted fears of neighborhood inhabitants, when children look, they desire. If they do not, they also desire. This is why these figures of unnerving metamorphosis must be "made to disappear," within all boundaries, in every season. [. . .]

While the physical disappearance of the transgendered was unlikely, the legislative body improvised a measure to annihilate the trade that sustains them, passing a law— unseen before in this region of the world—that punished consumers in their role as "perpetuators of the exploitation of another's body." Extending the punishment to those who pay to sin naturally confronted feminists with the issue of prostitutes and transgendered sex workers as never before, given that feminists preferred to speak of free contracts rather than of the categories of oppressed and oppressor. Obviously, the police detected a new way of reestablishing their extralegal income, by means of hounding the clients. [. . .]

What prohibitionist legislators had failed to mention was that in the areas they referred to, along with the persecution of clients, a series of relief programs for sex workers were set into motion, including facilitating low-interest loans for them to get off the streets and become involved in less carnal micro-endeavors. The argument favoring prohibition based on the desire to eliminate sexual servitude—mostly justified on the basis of the relationships of power instituted between the male user and the exploited—thus vanishes because the state actually never had any other goal in mind than that of making the evidence disappear. [. . .]

Thus the Code of Coexistence lost most of its political and ideological support by returning the underground regulation of so many of the contradictions and antagonisms inherent to relations with residents to the public forces, which happened to be suspect in all sorts of crimes. This reinforced the perception that every single progressive attempt—besides being detrimental to the efficient functioning of the community—sooner or later ended up betraying its own principles. [. . .]

Once order was restored, those who "went too far" were punished in the public discourse, laying bare the return to violence. The Rosario chief of police, Rosario being the second largest city in Argentina, called homosexuals and the transgendered "AIDS faces" on a local radio station and was later forced to resign. Before he did, as an apology, he argued in his defense that he considered a top police official "who is gay" "a most respected and effective man." Perhaps unknowingly he was drawing boundaries between a declared homosexual—homosexuality becoming increasingly accepted in the constellation of social individuals—and the transgendered. [. . .]

Vanesa Ledesma and Nadia Echazú: Signs of Reality

Amnesty International authored a report on the situation of human rights in Argentina called "Argentina, Death of a Transgendered in Custody" in April 2000. It centered its condemnation on the case of Vanesa Ledesma, who was arrested and held incommunicado in a local police station after an unclear episode in a Córdoba city bar. Her five-day detention culminated in her funeral. Her friends photographed her damaged body, which showed clear signs of having been tortured and slashed. The police had gone too far, as on so many other occasions that had not been made public in the media or acknowledged by human-rights organizations. It must be said that none of these organizations had ever made an effort to bring forward charges on criminal acts of this nature. In this sense, there was a political gain that must be highlighted, and which was the result of efforts between the Córdoba movement and the *Comunidad Homosexual Argentina*. With respect to Vanesa Ledesma, the police contended that she had died of heart failure.

The Amnesty report, written in moderate, cautious language, listed international agreements endorsed by Argentina, and ignored by the repressive practices of its institutions. It held that police edicts and codes of misdemeanors served to persecute the transgendered and transsexuals, and that their incarceration was "cruel, inhumane and degrading." It mentioned the sexual harassment, beatings, and extortion to which they were subjected. It also found that Vanesa Ledesma, who was living with HIV/AIDS, was denied regular medication, which would have kept her healthy. Her face was covered in bruises. The police chief referred to this as her "AIDS face." The death of "AIDS face" seemed, from this point of view, a logical and perfect act.

The assassination of Vanesa Ledesma did not produce the penal consequences that the case's media exposure would seem to have warranted. [. . .] As in any other criminal fatality, the police seemed to operate with the same impunity as they do in the case of the atrocities committed against the collective transgendered, as often happens in Palermo. [. . .]

To conclude, I would like to reproduce several paragraphs from the statement given to the court by Nadia Echazú—a transgendered person who resides in Palermo and is the president of a human-rights defense organization. The statement summarizes the return to reality, after the failure of the Code of Coexistence in late 1998:

At approximately two in the morning on October 7 I was working on an AIDS-prevention campaign, for which I give out condoms, lubricant, and flyers with information on how to prevent the disease and the rights that the transgendered are entitled to. At that moment from an unmarked automobile going down Godoy Cruz Street . . . three people insulted and threatened me, demanding that I stop . . . I recognized two of them as members of the Police Headquarters 25 Brigade who had severely beaten me on March 11 and whom I had never been able to identify. The officers demanded my ID and when I offered it, they snatched it from me. One spit at me and threatened to "mess me up" if I ever passed through "his" jurisdiction again (which was whichever he happened to be at the time). At that point the deputy commissioner pulled up in a squad car wearing civilian clothing, accompanied by an unidentified uniformed officer. I demanded an explanation for what was happening while pointing out that they were retaining my ID. When I tried to get it back, the brigade officer punched me in the stomach, and, winded, I began to scream. His partner grabbed me by the hair and pushed me over. When I landed on the ground he kicked me, while the other hit me in the face. I kept screaming and they hit me harder, twisting my arms; they handcuffed me and sprayed mace in my face, they took my purse and hurled my things on the ground, the condoms, the flyers . . . "I'll show you rights, you degenerate queer" they said and picked me up by the handcuffs, twisting my arms around. They shoved me into the unmarked car, where they again threatened me, this time at gunpoint. They took me to the police station, beating me the whole way there and I never got to make a phone call . . . After a number of other humiliations, they released me without my money and forbade me from showing up in their jurisdiction.

A year later, when she appeared on a television show, [. . .] the host reprimanded Nadia for being "so paranoid." Whether giving testimony or harboring political aspirations, a transgendered person must check the truth in her suffering if she is to be allowed into the democratic arena.

Lesbians in (Cyber)Space

The Politics of the Internet in Latin American On- and Off-line Communities

Elisabeth Jay Friedman

TWO WOMEN, heads close together, beam at the camera, with a caption in Portuguese that reads, "Stable Union: Luciana and Kátia made their declaration with us! You do it too!"[1] A magenta book cover, illustrated with one Renaissance woman gazing at another, proclaims in Spanish, "Compilation of the Third Competition of Lesbian Erotic Poetry." Two rainbow-striped, rotating women's symbols draw attention to announcements about lesbian publications and organizations, separated by rainbow ribbons. In Spanish, the name "GALF: Group of Feminist Lesbian Activists" head-lines a page swirling with pastel colors, evocative paintings of women, and twined women's symbols.

These images represent lesbian political and social action in Latin America: out, proud, and visible, in cities from São Paulo, Brazil, to Lima, Peru. But though the events, publications, and organizations described above are from specific places, their impact reaches far beyond their locales: their images appear on Web sites that Latin American lesbian feminists have created to celebrate their identities, build their com-munities, and demand equality. The global tool of the Internet offers this marginal-ized, yet resolute, group of women new opportunities for making social change.

Although Latin American lesbians have achieved greater visibility and, in some countries, increased equality since the mid-1990s, they are routinely discriminated against—as are gay men, bisexuals, transsexuals, transvestites, and transgendered people. This discrimination all too often takes the form of social denigration and physical violence. Recent reports reveal the vicious murders of lovers who dared to hold hands in public; legislators considering public funding for "conversion therapy" for homosexuals; the arrest of lesbian activists for producing television programs on sexual rights; "promasculinity" and right-wing counterdemonstrations at lesbian marches; heavy-handed Catholic Church opposition to LGBT (lesbian, gay, bisexual, and transgender) organizations in schools;[2] and law after law restricting a panoply of social benefits to heterosexuals.

Living in societies that use law, mainstream media, and social opprobrium to deny their enjoyment of basic rights—and sometimes their very existence—Latin American lesbians have long relied on alternative ways of expressing and associating themselves. They created spaces for community building and political organizing that existed largely outside the public view. Then, in the 1990s, they adopted a powerful new tool that is also a "virtual" space: the Internet, or cyberspace.

Cyberspace—the dense web of information and communication created by e-mail, chat rooms, distribution lists, and Web sites—is a virtual public sphere especially useful for Latin American lesbian communities. The Internet addresses the central problems impeding the effectiveness of lesbian organizing: isolation, repression, resource restriction, and lack of community cohesion. Lesbians can find each other via the Internet even if they are isolated in their daily lives, and if they can find a reasonably private place to go online, they can be out without fear of stigma or violence. Compared to the often-transient spaces of "women's nights" at bars or cafés, or the expense of keeping up an office, Web sites offer a more stable and inexpensive platform for socializing and activism. E-mail, distribution lists, and Web sites are relatively accessible sources of alternative information, crucial for communities ignored or criticized in the mass media. Finally, the Internet cannot end contentious regional debates over political practice, but it provides new possibilities for communication within and across national boundaries.

Despite the opportunities cyberspace offers, it also presents new challenges for organizers. Women who maintain distribution lists or update Web sites have a new set of demanding responsibilities. Although activists have celebrated the potential of the Internet to unite people across cultural and geographical borders, social and linguistic barriers impede even virtual border crossing. And Internet-based communication, whether by e-mail or through Web sites, can erode the delicate politics of accountability lesbian communities have struggled to develop. Nevertheless, the contributions of the Internet far outweigh its complications.

This study brings together insight gathered from three sources: secondary material on the history of Latin American lesbian organizing and the impact of the Internet on LGBT communities; original interviews with members of six lesbian feminist organizations in Argentina and Mexico; and analysis of a representative sample of lesbian feminist Web sites from Mexico, Chile, Argentina, Peru, and Brazil. The sites are:[3]

- Les voz (Les[bian] VOICE; www.lesvoz.org.mx/): This Web site, started in 2000, is the online counterpart of *Les voz* magazine, a Mexico City-based publication dedicated to "lesbian feminist culture," from arts to politics. Run by a volunteer staff of eight, the organization is funded by magazine sales, as well as grants from two U.S. foundations. Les voz also sponsors artistic competitions and other events and distributes an electronic bulletin. The Web site is amateur, and only the magazine and other published works are updated regularly.

- *Rompiendo el Silencio* (Breaking the Silence; www.rompiendoelsilencio.cl/): Begun in 2002 in Santiago, Chile, this Web site is an Internet-only lesbian magazine that supports "whatever group, creation or idea that wants to develop through the internet and has as its goal the respect and dignity of lesbian women." A staff of five manages the site, aided by seven Chilean and nine international collaborators. Its funding sources are unclear, but it does host a few ads for lesbian-friendly businesses. The Web site has a professional look, and staff update it very regularly. Besides the wide-ranging magazine contents, the site offers several interactive elements, including a chat room, letters to the editor, and a list of discussion forums.

- *Safo Piensa* (Sappho Thinks; http://www.rimaweb.com.ar/safopiensa/): This "Lesbian Feminist Network" is a page of the Web site for RIMA: Information Network of Argentine Women. Begun in 2001, its main function is hosting a discussion list. Two women run RIMA, an Internet-based project that relies heavily on many volunteer contributors. *Safo Piensa* has received funding for one meeting and publication from the Global Fund for Women. The page is updated sporadically, and has an amateur design.

- *Grupo de Activistas Lesbianas Feministas* (Group of Feminist Lesbian Activists or GALF; www.galf.org/): This Peruvian organization's goal is "to struggle for the construction of inclusive societies with social justice and gender equality, based in a culture of peace and exercise of human rights for everyone and, in particular, for lesbians." GALF developed its Web site as part of its 2004–05 plan to construct "spaces for the diffusion and exchange of information and projects on lesbian themes," and provides electronic copies of the group's magazine, *Labia*, as well as a document center of downloadable articles. GALF provides no information on staffing. The Global Fund for Women underwrites the Web site, which is professionally designed; its updating focuses on the magazine and documents.

- *Um Outro Olhar* (An Other Look; http://www.umoutroolhar.com.br/): This Web site, started in 2004, forms part of the lesbian feminist documentation center of this Brazilian organization, which also publishes a print magazine. The Web site covers a wide range of subjects, ranging from activism to horoscopes, and hosts an interactive bulletin board and a personals section. Funded by magazine sales, donations, and some government grants, the organization has a staff of eight, six of whom are volunteers. The Web site has a professional look, and is updated regularly.

Latin American lesbian movements face a unique set of challenges, as the brief history below suggests. Considering whether cyberspace has the potential to address these challenges, scholars such as Edward Stein and Jonathan Alexander have proposed that it is a "virtual lifeline" for socially isolated individuals, and has the potential to build national and transnational communities. My research supports these findings, showing that Latin American lesbian organizing helps to ameliorate isolation and build community, which is central to developing and sustaining efforts for social change. As a relatively inexpensive source of information, the Internet allows individuals with few resources to affirm their identities and connect to larger communities; it also is a vehicle for promoting lesbian visibility and solidarity. However, it can also exacerbate ongoing issues of accountability and representation. I conclude that cyberspace is a place where, and a means through which, Latin American lesbians can connect with each other and develop regional solidarity.

Come Out, Come Out? The Delights and Dangers of Real-Time Community Building

Publicly proclaiming same-sex love and seeking social toleration and legal status for LGBT people are revolutionary acts in the Latin American region. Strong Catholic social norms, particularly the tenet that the heterosexual family is the "building block" of society, as well as social rejection and violence, have made LGBT life generally difficult. But pervasive male dominance has made the assertion of female life lived without primary reference to men nearly impossible to imagine. As regional activist Alejandra Sardá (2002, 108) has written, before lesbians began to mobilize on their own behalf, in the Latin American "social imaginary the homosexual was male and the lesbian was practically inconceivable." Nevertheless, over the last three decades, lesbian movements have expanded across the region.

The emergence of independent lesbian activism can be traced to four influences: macrolevel politics, the Left, mixed gay/ lesbian movements, and women's liberation movements. Given the tumultuous political history of the region, including long periods of authoritarian repression as well as drawn-out democratization processes, LGBT organizing has been marked by the political contexts of different countries (Mongrovejo 2000, 63). Region-wide political liberalization in the 1980s allowed more room for LGBT social movement activity (Green and Babb 2002), but democratic politics have been no guarantee of LGBT rights.

Many early lesbian activists came out of communist, socialist, or anarchist parties, through which they struggled for national (socialist) and sexual liberation. Nevertheless, Left parties and movements often rejected homosexuality as contrary to revolutionary morality. Revolutionary regimes in Cuba and Nicaragua were actively hostile to homosexuals. Castro promoted reeducation until the 1990s, and the revolutionary Nicaraguan Sandinistas forbade even stalwart cadres from forming an LGBT organization (Babb 2003; Mongrovejo 2000).

Initially, lesbians identified as part of mixed gay/lesbian and/or women's liberation movements. The development of the former was slowed by political repression, but the movement grew clandestinely and with increasing inspiration from the United States and Europe. Women joined men in the early groups, but some became disillusioned by the predominance of male leadership and gay issues. Meanwhile, both the international and regional development of feminist movements attracted lesbian participants. Throughout the 1970s, many lesbians directed their energies to feminist demands for reproductive rights and an end to violence against women. But many straight feminists ignored or actively repressed lesbian-specific issues for fear of realizing society's suspicions that feminism was indeed the work of "man-hating" lesbians. It would take years before the feminist demand for women's control over their own bodies and the lesbian demand for women's control over their own sexuality would be seen as part of the same struggle.

In response to misogyny from gay men and homophobia from straight feminists, lesbians began to found autonomous groups in the early 1980s. Several credit a "miniworkshop" on lesbianism that drew an audience of three hundred at the 1982 regional feminist meeting as the inspiration to form groups back home (Jitsuya and Sevilla 2004). The development of an autonomous movement—one with its own forms of organization and goals—has allowed lesbians to explore new forms of expression and new arenas for encounter and organizing (Mongrovejo 2000).

In particular, lesbian activists can now focus more directly on their own interests, without having to subordinate them to the larger gay or feminist agenda. Independent lesbian activism has created a more vigorous sense of community and enabled greater visibility. Lesbian-only spaces offer women the opportunity to meet others for friendship or intimate relationships, as well as political solidarity. In some large urban centers in Latin America, it has become easier to assert lesbian identity, whether registering as a domestic partner in Rio de Janeiro, Brazil or Buenos Aires, Argentina, or playing in the lesbian indoor soccer tournament in Mexico City. And several out women have been elected to municipal, and even national, office. But challenges remain: besides the social stigma attached to lesbian identity—which makes coming out difficult, if not dangerous—resource restrictions, political repression, and internal divisions characterize the contemporary situation.

It is hard for women to procure information about lesbianism, let alone attend meetings, given the lack of resources groups have to communicate about their existence and efforts. Most rely on word of mouth to publicize issues and events. Some groups have published a newsletter or journal in order to share information and political, literary, and artistic work, but the publications have had limited circulation. In the 1980s, for example, the handmade Peruvian bulletin, *Al Margen* (*On the Margin*) was passed out in discotheques and in a few women's centers (Jitsuya and Sevilla 2004; Mongrovejo 2000, 309).

Lesbian groups, whether social or political, have found it almost impossible to maintain physical spaces. In one telling example, lesbians meeting at a regional feminist gathering in 1999 told story after story of closed bars, cafés, and other meeting spaces. Clearly, establishing gathering places has been an ongoing problem. A Peruvian lesbian feminist group lost its meeting place when a local café closed. Having a permanent space helped one group in Mexico in terms of visibility and attracting supporters, but its upkeep fell to a few people with little money, and it too closed down. Finally, when members of a Chilean group revealed in an interview that they used a feminist organization's headquarters for their meetings, their group was denounced (and renounced) by the organization, whose members were frightened to be associated with a then-illegal activity under the Pinochet dictatorship (Mongrovejo 2000).

The repression of lesbians and their organizing efforts, sometimes sanctioned by the state, has not been limited to authoritarian governments. In one notorious incident, during the preparations for the 1990 Second Latin American Lesbian Feminist Encounter in democratic Costa Rica, a major newspaper published the names of the organizers and the themes for discussion. In response, the Costa Rican secretary of state announced that all border police were to question single women headed into Costa Rica on suspicion that they might be attendees, and that all Costa Rican consulates were to deny visas to single women during the meeting dates. Threatened and frightened, the organizers found a secret location for the meeting, at which they assembled all the attendees who had succeeded in entering the country or had already been in it. With a regular "patrol" outside, the meeting took place over the next four days without incident, until the last night when a group of drunken men attacked the site, shouting obscenities, hammering on the doors, and throwing rocks. Only in the early hours of the morning were the women able to evacuate (Mongrovejo 2000, 340–44). As Alejandra Sardá argues, even in democracies, lesbians' degree of citizenship is "tenuous, limited and fragile," considering their nonexistent protection from discrimination; their overall lack of legal recognition as parents or partners; and their risk of physical attack if they come out, particularly outside the major cities (Sardá 1998, 2002).

Some challenges are internal. Lesbians disagree, sometimes bitterly, over the meaning of political autonomy and what it implies for political practice. Initially autonomy was a decision to undertake work on lesbians' behalf, since their interests were not prioritized by feminist women and gay men. But questions of who determines these interests, and how they should be promoted, quickly emerged. Activists now debate how to ensure accountability (responsiveness to the community), and/or its mirror concept of representation (the political claim of accountability), along with the issue of how completely to separate from sometime allies. These allies are no longer restricted to the Left and other national social movements. The growth of international lesbian networking and (limited) external funding from international foundations, and even some governments, have further complicated internal politics. Are leaders and groups responsive to the government or international foundations' and networks' agendas, or to local demands?[4] International intervention, while a key source of resources and ideas, intensifies the already-complex politics of autonomous lesbian organizing.

Clearly, Latin American lesbian organizations face a host of challenges. They struggle to reach out to (isolated) others in a situation of resource restriction. They endeavor to organize while facing social denigration, governmental repression, and internal divisions. And they seek to balance the benefits of international networking with the complications external influences bring to local groups. Can the Internet help activists face these challenges? A brief survey of the literature reveals a very positive answer.

Cyberspace: A "Virtual Lifeline" for the LGBT Community

The relatively inexpensive medium of the Internet offers a unique virtual public sphere open to a wide range of actors and expressions (Dilevko 2002; Leon, Burch, and Tamayo 2001; Warkentin 2001). This range is clearly restricted by traditional sources of exclusion, such as race/ethnicity, gender, class, and geographical location (Ebo 1998; Hafkin and Taggart 2001). But the increasing accessibility of travel within cyberspace, whether from public locales such as community telecenters, or private means such as wired (or WiFi) cafés, helps to mediate restrictions. As a result, the Internet "may be of particular importance to small or marginal groups with limited finances or expectation of mainstream support for their views" (Friedman 2005, 5).

Studies from various countries demonstrate that the Internet is being used to end the "social isolation of homosexuals," since online they can "try out behavior that is socially labeled as deviant and . . . fulfill personal and political needs" (Burke 2000, 593; see also Haag and Chang 1997; Koch and Schockman 1998; Weinrich 1997). One comparison of LGBT Web sites in the United States, Germany, China, and Japan claimed that "there is no other forum in which so many people of so many different backgrounds have safely disclosed, and felt comfortable disclosing, their sexual identities" (Heinz et al. 2002, 109). Cyberspace is crucial for "sexual minorities," according to legal scholar Edward Stein (2003), because of social and legal discrimination that either compels them to be closeted or punishes them should they emerge. In sharp contrast to mainstream society, cyberspace is "an ideal environment and a 'virtual lifeline'" (Stein 2003, 183).

According to some, the benefits of cyberspace include the expansion of queer communities within and across national boundaries (Alexander 2002b). Whereas homophobia and political subjugation have isolated LGBT individuals from others in their own societies, and geography and politics have kept them separated from others elsewhere, "cyberspace promises, at least in theory, an emancipatory and community-building realm that transcends intra-national boundaries and international borders" (Heinz et al. 2002, 108). This potential globalization of communication and connection may allow a virtual escape from the repression and rejection of real-time interactions into a place of acceptance and solidarity.

Still, some observers worry about the end result of virtual community building. The construction of specifically LGBT (or L, G, B, or T) spaces online may further entrench participants' separation from the heterosexual world (or from each other). In the LBGT community, the "replication of ghettos in online spaces may serve only to reinforce differences as opposed to fostering communication across those differences" (Alexander 2002a, 99). As Cass Sunstein (2001) argues more generally, an individual's ability to tailor what she sees online and screen out other viewpoints or lifestyles may well result in a narrowing, rather than an expansion, of public discourse via the Internet.

The fact of the Internet's (potential) existence in all space, and thus, in some way, no place, may also exacerbate issues of accountability and representation in LGBT communities. One study of the relationship between a real-time lesbian organization and the virtual community it created revealed that the off- and online communities had very different goals. Online discussions tended to be oriented toward personal expression and relationship development, rather than the educational and political purposes for which the off-line group had been established (Nip 2004). While personal interaction is a key benefit of the Internet for isolated lesbians, the lack of control that the organizers had over the direction of the online "arm" of the group meant they had trouble establishing members' accountability to stated goals.

Finally, the very global nature of Internet-mediated communication carries with it the risks inherent in boundary crossing. Transnational organizing efforts have made excellent use of the Internet, but the speed and range made possible by virtual communication can also jeopardize or compromise carefully negotiated local or national strategies and discourses (Friedman 2005). Reaching across geographical expanses does not guarantee cross-cultural understanding, and the presence of ever-larger audiences available for "transmission" does not promise appreciation for the reality of grounded experiences. As Nina Wakeford reminds us, "There is a risk that . . . geographically located experiences and the local politics of boundary markers become lost in the rush to claim the Internet as a vehicle of a global (lesbian) community"

(1998, 190). Internet-based community building may well trample over local problems and politics.

Lesbian Internet use in Latin America largely reflects findings from the literature on LGBT experiences of cyberspace. Online interaction mitigates social isolation, and a Web presence eases resource restrictions for organizations. The Internet does act as a "virtual lifeline" in the face of widespread oppression, allowing lesbians to connect, express their ideas, broadcast news, and mobilize. Although inherently transnational virtual reality complicates the politics of local lesbian communities, it also permits more voices to participate in regional discussions. Establishing regional connections through the Internet is more vital to these communities than achieving international ones. Rather than creating virtual ghettos, lesbian feminist Web sites and individuals are busy strengthening their identities and traversing (some) borders.

Safe (Cyber)Space: Out Online

"Why have a website? To show that a group of lesbian mothers exists here in Argentina. In the interior [of the country] there are women who are mothers who have feelings for other women . . . how are they going to know who they are?"[5]

The role of the Internet in ending—or at least alleviating—the isolation of lesbians is undeniable. The nonterritorial nature of the community, and the threat of violence that isolated members face at home, make the refuge provided by online exchange critical. Because lesbian organizations concentrate in the major cities, and rural areas tend to be much more traditional, women living in the "interior" of countries such as Argentina and Mexico depend on the Internet to make contact. But even in Buenos Aires and Mexico City, cyberspace is an essential resource for closeted women, those who cannot easily attend meetings, and those who may not be interested in a bar scene. Lesbian organizations with a Web presence have recognized the potential of virtual relations, offering personal ads and electronic discussion lists for personal and movement development.

Interviews and messages to Web sites confirm the significance of putting lesbians in touch with each other, or providing them with hard-to-come-by information. When I spoke with Martha Patricia Cuevas Armas, the cocoordinator of the Mexico City-based New Generation of Young Lesbians, she reported receiving regular e-mail messages from lesbians from different states seeking information about local groups.[6] According to Mariana Pérez Ocaña, editor of the *Les voz* lesbian magazine and Web site, also based in the capital, there may not have been much to tell them: "We get a lot of email from women from the provinces because in the provinces there is nothing! No magazines, nowhere to go . . . but if there are groups, we publish what they are doing."[7] The founders of the Argentine Autonomous Feminist Lesbian Mothers group, located in Buenos Aires, have been active distributing information via the Internet to reach isolated women "not only in our country, but also to countries such as Paraguay, Mexico—to women who don't belong to a group, but are lesbian mothers."[8] E-mail allows those who are wary of revealing their identities to remain anonymous when making contact, and facilitates the sharing of crucial information such as the location of local lesbian organizations. Gabriela de Cicco and Irene Ocampo, cofounders of *Safo Piensa*, note that in Argentina, the Internet is "quite a resource for women who have trouble finding each other"[9]—wherever they live. The safe space provided by Web sites is at once local, national, and regional, as revealed by recent posts to *Safo Piensa*'s "guest book." A Buenos Aires woman reflected on the importance of the Web site for community creation and political change:

> It seems really important to have a place to go when we are eager for information. Society is quite hard and makes an effort to make difficult a life that, particularly, I think is beautiful. In this way I can learn, socialize, try to change situations and share moments and ideas. Simply for that, THANK YOU.

An Argentine woman outside the capital city affirmed this appreciation: "Thank you very much for existing and helping us, I live in a city where we don't have any help like you offer." Another woman wrote in because there was nowhere to turn with her coming-out process in her home country of the Dominican Republic: "Two years ago I realized I am a lesbian it affected me a lot but I didn't accept it; now I need help I don't know if it's alright." While this area of the Web page may not be a place to find support, the fact that a Dominican woman posted her distress on an Argentine site reveals how the Internet can create at least tangential connections across vast distances.

Although the provision of Internet personal ads may seem to be peripheral to creating social change, this Web-based service is an integral part of creating community (Burke 2000). Placing or answering a personal ad is a direct affirmation of lesbian identity; simply reading them can also foster a sense of belonging. The realization that others are "out" there is particularly significant for women who are struggling to accept their own identities in a hostile environment. Of the Web sites I examine here, personal contacts are fostered by four, and are in high demand. *Safo Piensa* runs a discussion list in which around 70 lesbian, lesbian feminist, bisexual, and bisexual feminist women participate. Les voz accepts personal ads via e-mail (which are then printed in their print magazine). *Um Outro Olhar* has about 500 personals listed. *Rompiendo el Silencio* hosts 13 different discussion forums, the largest of which (with nearly 3,500 messages) is for "contacts," and provides a chat service for instant interaction. It also offers psychological counseling, a boon for women unable to discuss issues related to their sexuality elsewhere.

The lines between personal contact, community development, and political mobilization can easily blur. *Rompiendo el Silencio* provides a page for the public denunciation of acts of discrimination "so that others might know about the injustices that continue to be committed in our country and in the world because of our sexual orientation." One entry on the Denouncing Silences page presents a pointed and poignant example of the importance of online contact in the face of off-line abuse:

> I'm a faithful visitor of this page, and I wanted to tell you my story: last year through chat I met the person that I love the most in my life (along with my son), and I started on an adventure, I never thought that I would meet the most beautiful person in the world . . . I had her live with me without thinking that I would make her suffer so much, thanks to the people that are around me, my family, my work and friends, in general, they have humiliated us, they have singled us out, it is an immense sorrow what is happening to us, they are threatening to take my son away, we've been beaten, we've been threatened with death in general it is a forbidden love. MY CITY IS A HELL. I ask myself what is wrong with our loving each other. I love you, *negra*, my greatest joy was meeting you, you were the most important person, I will fight for you even if they've mistreated us, if they've told us that we are the most horrible and sinful people, if loving you is a sin I want to die sinning, I will endure the beatings for you only for you . . .

As this message reveals, not only did this woman meet her partner in cyberspace, but the Internet offers a way for her to denounce their mistreatment—and to proclaim her love. This personal testimony serves as a potential spur for others to get involved in social action, or at the very least reassures readers that they are part of a larger community that continues to love despite societal sanction. This level of visibility for lesbian reality would be impossible in Latin America without virtual reality.

Building Community Online

> Lesbian Kiss Becomes Police Case in USP East: Two girls, 22 and 18 years old, who kissed, on October 7, in the cafeteria of the University of São Paulo in the East Zone, had their kiss registered, as an obscene act, in the [local police station], where they were detained for three hours to give "explanations." The complaint was filed by a military policeman who argued that the University is a place for mothers and serious people who do not condone that kind of activity. (*Um Outro Olhar* 2005)

As inexpensive platforms for expression and exchange comparatively free from censorship, Latin American lesbian Web sites and distribution lists address ongoing problems with resources and repression. They distribute distinct kinds of information —political, social, even artistic—that promote community and frame individual actions as part of the fight for lesbian human rights. News about LGBT politics reminds lesbians that they face common problems along with other LGBT people, and offers ways to get involved; scholarly articles and personal testimonies enable deeper reflection on what it means to be a lesbian; interviews, reviews, and artistic presentations reflect other facets of lesbian life; and erotic images and lesbian symbols stand as visual rebukes to the repression of lesbian desire and existence.

Although the Internet cannot erase—and may even exacerbate—ongoing tensions around accountability and representation within lesbian communities, it also serves to expand participation in region-wide debates. But this global tool does not eliminate every boundary. While it does seem to be creating the "emancipatory and community-building realm that transcends intranational boundaries" envisioned by Heinz et al., it does not fully traverse "international borders" (2002, 108). Judging by the intended audience of the Web sites, as well as information available about Web site use, the communities woven together by this virtual web are national and regional. Latin American lesbians are largely reaching out to each other.

Of course, "digital divides" exist along the region's deep divisions of class, race, and geographical position (Hilbert 2001). Internet cafés provide commercial access for those who cannot go online at home, school, or work. Nevertheless, the majority of the population has neither regular entry into cyberspace, nor the "digital literacy" to facilitate navigation. This means that lesbians from lower-middle-class, working-class, and poor backgrounds, whose class position may already limit their exposure to lesbian feminist organizations, also have difficulty entering virtual community spaces. Some may be helped by community organizations that run telecenters and offer basic Internet skills training for lower-income people. But outing oneself in the real world while seeking information in the virtual one, given the public nature of many access points, remains a problem. Even these seemingly enormous barriers may be breached, as "chains of access" connect those who can travel into cyberspace to those who cannot, facilitating information transmission in real time in real communities (Friedman 2005). While the most isolated women cannot take advantage of others' access, those who have trusted contacts who can go online may not need direct access to take advantage of digital resources.

Getting the Word/s Out

Supplying readers with current information about LGBT politics is a key feature of all the Web sites. *Rompiendo el Silencio* republishes articles from other news sources about international LGBT news, and offers original articles and editorials. *Um Outro Olhar* posts Brazilian lesbian groups' events and gives readers information on their rights and how to protect them. *Safo Piensa* publishes reports on the lesbian and feminist movements in Argentina and pertinent legislative initiatives. Les voz also advertises political and cultural events on their Web site.

GALF goes farthest by providing in-depth, often scholarly, articles in a convenient format: its Web site hosts a virtual documentation center with .pdf versions of a wide range of analytical and provocative articles. The Web site is also the home of GALF's online lesbian feminist magazine, *Labia*. While the offerings of GALF's "virtual library" are quite impressive, the diverse array of information available from different Web sites also informs and enriches lesbian community.

Each Web site finds other ways to present material that increases lesbian visibility and solidarity. In October 2005, *Um Outro Olhar* began a column where lesbian couples can announce their registration as a "stable [civil] union," complete with happy photo. The Web site also features sections on the LGBT symbols, culture and leisure, tourism, and even horoscopes "with a lesbian perspective." In a particularly Brazilian touch, the advertisement for the group's T-shirt promises that buying one guarantees a spot on their *trio eléctrico* in the gay-rights parade.[10] *Safo Piensa* has a small database of "saffic [Sapphic] writings" by women from their distribution list and more well-known writers, such as Adrienne Rich (in translation). Les voz uses its Web site to solicit participation in erotic poetry, story, drawing, and indoor soccer competitions; the winners of the first three are published in their magazine, while the final contest presumably leads to real-time encounters on the soccer field. Across the different pages, the ever-present double women's symbols—rainbow hued, golden, rotating— and erotic stories and pictures invoke a common identity daring to speak its name. The Web sites' names themselves evoke this identity: An *Other* Look; Sappho Thinks: Network of Lesbian Feminists; Breaking the Silence: Lesbian Online Magazine; Les(bian) VOICE: Lesbian Feminist Culture; and Group of Lesbian Feminist Activists. These images and ideas are now available to women in even remote areas, an opportunity almost unthinkable prior to the Internet.

Several of these Web sites, as well as many other lesbian organizations, also use electronic distribution lists as a potent tool for political work. While Web sites reach a greater audience than the hand-distributed bulletins of earlier organizing periods, a largely anonymous audience makes information hard to target. Distribution lists— a regular transmission of news and events of interest sent directly to subscribers— enable organizations to reach out directly to many people in a timely fashion. Les voz sends its bimonthly electronic bulletin to 900 subscribers; *Rompiendo el Silencio*'s list has nearly 700 subscribers. Other lesbian organizations, faced with severe political and/or resource restrictions, rely on distribution lists to reach supporters. The Mexico City-based, all-volunteer Lesbians in Collective group believed agents of the federal government were spying on their e-mail account because of the group's involvement with radical political movements. Despite this disturbing setback, which forced them to close one account and open another, anonymous account on a free server, in 2002 the collective distributed information to 150 contacts, half in Mexico and half international.[11] Gloria Carreaga Pérez, a founding member of Mexico City-based The Closet of Sor Juana—which has served as the women's secretariat of the International Lesbian and Gay Association—explained that the group's lack of resources led to the use of the Internet, since it is inexpensive, and "allows us to be in contact with people at all levels, in practically the whole world."[12] Carreaga Pérez herself distributes several lists on lesbian and gay issues at the national, regional, and international levels, which reach up to 100 people. These groups do not only send out information; distribution lists also incorporate them into larger networks of progressive action. *Safo Piensa*'s coordinators easily named nearly 40 lists to which they subscribed.

As Carreaga Pérez's efforts attest, one of the benefits of Web sites and distribution lists for lesbian organizations is that a few individuals can provide many others with space for reflection, connection, education, and mobilization. The *Safo Piensa* list is run by two volunteers, yet they spur discussion among seventy women. If successful, of course, a small staff can easily find itself overwhelmed; as Pérez Ocaña reflected about the Les voz Web site, "it's almost doubled the work, but with the same people, and the same amount of money." While they cannot respond fully to demand, she still insists that "it's been great, because it's opened up the field" of lesbian action to many people through the work of a few (interview, 2002).

The importance of the Internet in getting broad content into circulation is clear to Pérez Ocaña. She explained that the Web site and distribution list reached far more people than the relatively small run of the magazine. While it was hard to get magazine stands to carry the *Les voz* magazine, and many lesbians could not afford a subscription, the Web site had a very different life:

> It's very good, because we've really developed, lots of people know us, the magnificent thing of having a permanent page there, it's a communications media that everyone can access, that is very economical, whereas other media are very expensive, or even blocked. [And] it's always there! So for us it's magnificent, and we can put whatever we want. Nobody's going to censor us, to tell us what we can and can't put on it. There it is, because we want it. (Interview, 2002)

Escaping censorship to present a rich array of resources to a wide audience—in Latin America, only the Internet can make this possible. Cyberspace presents lesbians with opportunities to break free from social, economic, and political constraints on their freedom of expression and action to foster community building and political change.

Tensions between the Virtual and the Real

Community building online does not solve the long-term conflicts over accountability and representation, and the distributional power and anonymity of the Internet add new levels of complexity to these issues. However, the openness of cyberspace means that different points of view—not just those of established groups or well-connected leaders—can find wide audiences. In addition, some organizations are implementing mechanisms of "virtual" accountability so that the Internet can be a more transparent and responsible tool for activism. Wakeford's concern about losing "the local politics of boundary markers" in using the Internet to build (supranational) community is evident in some instances—although this loss may also be a gain. In a 2001 interview, members of the Argentine Autonomous Feminist Lesbian Mothers claimed that a virtual presence sometimes represented no one on the national level. They referenced groups that were known to Dutch funders

> . . . that aren't known here. They exist online but don't know people in the next block. [It's] a fantasy image. They can use the Web, they can use English, write projects, but they don't exist as groups. Except they exist on the Web so they exist for the rest of the world. (Interview, 2001)

In a community that fiercely values accountability, the Web can exacerbate the already-loaded politics of international funding when newcomers change the boundary markers of the community itself. What one organization sees as a "fantasy image" with no local interlocutors could well be an online group that is building community among its Internet-based interlocutors. Given the difficulty of face-to-face meetings, virtual interaction is a crucial resource for lesbians located down the block—or elsewhere in the region.

In some cases, the Web has exposed difficult internal debates to a much wider audience, exacerbating local tensions. Several lesbian groups in Mexico described how a national debate over the representational legitimacy of a lesbian who won a seat in Congress became known throughout Latin American lesbian feminist networks. When some organizations felt shut out of the representative's nomination process, they circulated an e-mail message around the region declaring that they did not consider this woman their representative. Another group responded via an e-mail message, also aired regionally, denouncing what they saw as a personal attack against the woman, who had a long history of activism. A second acute disagreement between Mexican activists over the ownership of a set of archives achieved regional notoriety after one side posted its claims on a Web page. Although the other side saw this action as defamation, they were unable to persuade the server to take down the page.

Fierce national debates reached regional audiences prior to the use of e-mail and Web sites, but the transmission was slower and more limited. Rapid regional spread can have serious national fallout; for example, the exchange over the Mexican representative had such negative repercussions within the Mexican lesbian feminist community that at least one organization swore off using the Web politically. Still, there is no denying the communicative power that Web sites give to voices that might otherwise lack a platform, as they can now offer whole Web sites detailing their particular positions.

Attempts to restore or create mechanisms of accountability have begun to surface in cyberspace. *Rompiendo el Silencio* posts "Principles" that clarify it "is not an organization and only acts as a medium of truthful communication within the Internet." It maintains its independence from any political, religious, or occupational organization (and refuses to publish political candidates' platforms, no matter how lesbian-friendly). While its collaborators may use the space to share information about their organizations, the Web site offers only the director's editorials. The moderators of *Safo Piensa*'s distribution list responded to some subscribers' anger at being "observed" by other subscribers who "wouldn't show their 'faces'" (i.e., never wrote in, only read) by instituting a more inquisitive registration process. They ask potential subscribers to provide their names; how they heard about the list; why they want to subscribe to a list of lesbian feminists; how they self-identify; what they think the list will offer them—or what they can offer the list; and whether they are interested in face-to-face meetings. Through this process the coordinators of *Safo Piensa* attempt to infuse their online community with some of the personal relations and responsibility off-line communities can more easily demand.

The Regionality of Virtual Reality

Much has been made of the potential for global community building in cyberspace, and certainly Latin American lesbians use the Internet to establish and nourish connections outside their home countries and regions. The International Gay and Lesbian Human Rights Commission's Web site, for example, regularly posts information and action alerts about LGBT status in the region. International solidarity via e-mail has also been credited with positive intervention during incidents of flagrant discrimination. But analysis of the Web sites' intended audiences and actual use reveals a national and regional perspective rather than a focus on international concerns. This perspective could be seen as somehow limiting the "inherently" global nature of cyberspace. But this "global nature" has been premised, if implicitly, on the use of English—still the leading language of the Internet—and the primacy of U.S.-based Web sites and organizations. Thus, defiance of the U.S. and English-language domination of the Internet shows the potential of this "global" tool to foster Latin American and Spanish-speaking solidarity.

Hyperlinks are a central mechanism through which Web sites foster solidarity. Hyperlinks out of each Web site indicate where it locates itself with respect to others within cyberspace—a type of travel recommendation—making links a telling element for analysis. Hyperlinks into each Web site indicate which other guidebooks include that destination. The hyperlink maps created by the Web sites under study illuminate the largely national and regional communities—lesbian, LGBT, feminist, progressive—within which the organizations situate themselves and are located by others. Hyperlinks are virtual pathways for readers, helping them find organizations they may not have been aware of.

Extraregional hyperlinks account for only a small percentage of all the hyperlinks from the Web sites, with most to and from Spain and Puerto Rico. When these Web sites link to international human-rights, gay-rights, and women's-rights Web sites, they usually select sites that have Spanish translations available. U.S. representation is confined to funders, magazines, one portal, and two universities, with the Mexican Web site responsible for a majority of these links. These Web sites collect and then publish information that their regional readers can use, rather than working to speak to a global audience. A combination of language and politics trumps a complete internationalization of the lesbian community.

An examination of the individual Web sites attests to a national, and to some extent regional, use of online connections. Written in Portuguese, *Um Outro Olhar* is definitively directed at Brazilian lesbians. The Web site designers are so sure that users will be Brazilians that the site registration offers a pull-down menu of Brazilian states rather than other countries. Nearly all of its links are to Brazilian LGBT organizations. Not surprisingly, the links into the site are Brazilian or Portuguese-language LGBT sites. *Um Outro Olhar's* privileging of national community no doubt reflects its decades of publication and activism in Brazil, but it also indicates the sheer size of the country and, of course, its use of Portuguese rather than Spanish.

Like *Um Outro Olhar,* Les voz assumes a national audience, though not for language reasons. It provides an annotated list of Mexican LGBT and feminist organizations, a majority of which do not exist in cyberspace, making them useful only to Mexicans. While its electronic bulletin claims to be "for lesbians all over the world," content is limited to news from the organization, activities for the Mexican lesbian community, and editorials about Mexican politics and culture. However, in 2002, the editor noted that among their subscribers were people or organizations in three other Latin American countries, Puerto Rico, and the United States. The Web site links to as many U.S. organizations, including its U.S. funders and two U.S. lesbian magazines, as those from Latin America, and almost no regional lesbian organizations link to the organization. While their proximity to the United States results in a relatively high number of links to and from U.S. Web sites, as a whole this Web site reflects Les voz's identity as a lesbian magazine and its deep roots in a Mexican community. It is a mark of the Internet's reach, as well as a sign of the paucity of real-time opportunities for lesbian community, that readers from outside Mexico use the organization's resources.

The information on the *Safo Piensa* page focuses mainly on Argentina, though it includes coverage of regional issues and general lesbian themes. Its hyperlinks are to Argentine and Latin American lesbian organizations, as well as a gay Argentine news source. It also links to international foundations that give grants to lesbian organizations. *Safo Piensa* posts its connection statistics, and the countries of their visitors break down as follows: 46.4 percent Argentina; 13.2 percent Spain; 9.2 percent Mexico; 5.3 percent Chile; 4 percent Peru; 3.6 percent United States; 2.7 percent Uruguay; 2.6 percent Colombia; 2.5 percent Venezuela; and 0.7 percent Brazil. Because the founders are Argentine and the organization is physically located in Argentina, it focuses on national issues. But since it was created online with its primary mission to build virtual community, that community can easily cross intraregional boundaries.

Rompiendo el Silencio takes a different approach. While designed for Chilean lesbians, its news and resources encompass all of Latin America and beyond. It has international collaborators from Argentina, Canada, Mexico, Spain, and the United States, and covers events of regional interest, such as the third annual lesbian march in Mexico, as well as offering international LGBT news. Its neatly organized list of links includes many Chilean lesbian organizations and blogs, and other Latin American, Spanish, and international lesbian and progressive organizations. Since it provides connection statistics, it is possible to see the countries of users accessing the Web site. Users from Chile make up 55.9 percent; Spain, 9 percent; Mexico, 6.8 percent; Argentina, 4.4 percent; Colombia, 3.4 percent; the United States, 3.2 percent; and Australia, Peru, Uruguay, and Venezuela all near 2 percent. *Rompiendo el Silencio* clearly positions itself as an online news outlet that reports on local, regional, and international news for the region. Its investment in regional community building is evident in its extensive and regularly updated hyperlinks section.

More than the other Web sites, GALF has a regional, if not an international, audience in mind. While the events page focuses on Peru, the article database offers work from Latin America and elsewhere (in Spanish translation), and the electronic journal *Labia* (published in Spanish and, recently, Portuguese) is intended for the entire region and possibly elsewhere. According to its first edition, it seeks "to reach large numbers of lesbians, already organized or not, from the region of the Americas, and if possible, lesbians from around the world; to communicate, debate and develop regional/global strategies [for the recognition of lesbian rights as human rights]." GALF links include Peruvian groups but also many from Latin America, Spain, and Puerto Rico. Although the majority of the links are to lesbian organizations, there are plenty that focus more generally on the LGBT community, as well as some progressive and human rights organizations. Although the Web site builds on GALF's more than twenty years of political and social activism in Peru, its online presence seems largely intended as a regional resource for reflection on the lesbian condition.

Though created as a national resource, each Web site also serves to link lesbians across the region—with some notable exceptions. Most markedly, the language division between Brazil and the rest of Latin America is a near-complete barrier. Given Brazil's considerable size, *Um Outro Olhar*'s national focus is understandable, but the barrier does show a limitation of regional networks. Indeed, *Um Outro Olhar* neither links to, nor is linked by, any of the other Web sites under study here. Given the language division, GALF's effort to translate *Labia* into Portuguese is a worthy bridging attempt.

The regional connections created by the sites are largely South American and Mexican, with Central American countries completely absent, and Andean countries, with the exception of Peru, scarcely represented. Of course these "omissions" may reflect the absence of online lesbian organizing in those areas. But absences are worth considering. For example, the four non-Brazilian Web sites under study here do not all link to each other: *Rompiendo el Silencio*, GALF, and *Safo Piensa* link to each other, and *Safo Piensa* additionally links to Les voz, but Les voz only connects to (a previous version of) *Safo Piensa*. Although there is a risk of overinterpreting the meaning of links, this pattern may well reflect off-line political differences, as well as Les voz's choice to focus on national issues. When these sites decide which Web sites to list as additional resources, they are creating—and circumscribing—paths for their readers to follow.

Although divisions and omissions exist, the potential for the Internet to create "ghettos" does not seem to be realized in this case. In societies where it is often dangerous to assert lesbian identity, the Internet can hardly be the primary reason for lesbian isolation. Moreover, given the difficulty of lesbian organizing in the region, having online spaces dedicated to the community is vital. All the Web sites do provide links to nonlesbian sites within Latin America, a sign that they see their demands for lesbian rights and their efforts at community building as a part of a larger progressive effort. If any ghettoization is in process, it seems to be driven more by the outside world. Given the extensive resources provided on these sites, the fact that there are few hyperlinks into them attests to the continuing marginalization that lesbians experience.

The geography of the Latin American lesbian community in cyberspace is one that reflects regional realities. Largely circumscribed by the shared language of Spanish, with Portuguese marking a distinct border, the territory also reflects uneven distribution of resources and organizational capacity. It encompasses a long history of interregional interactions with Spain and the United States, as well as intraregional interactions and their consequences. The organizations may be country-focused, but Latin Ameri-can (and other Spanish-speaking) lesbians eager for information clearly surf multiple Spanish-language sites, particularly women who do not have prominent Web sites available in their own countries.

Latin American Lesbians: Weaving a Homespun Web

Like other LGBT communities, lesbians in the Latin American region have found the Internet to be a kind of (cyber)shelter, distant enough from the difficulties of their off-line existence to enable their own and their communities' development and visibility.

The relatively safe arena of cyberspace counters a sense of social isolation, including from family, and the sometimes dangerous consequences of coming out. Lesbians who are not able, for social or geographic reasons, to make connections with others in real time can make those connections online. Through submitting personal ads or posting to discussion lists, or simply reading about lesbian identity and looking at images celebrating lesbian life, women can explore their sexuality and its social context.

Cyberspace also provides a vital place for lesbians to build their community and carry out political action. Web sites transmit news, events, ideas, and whole publications of general interest to lesbians, making them less dependent on an oblivious or biased mass media, or the more narrowly circulated alternative print media, for information. Distribution lists allow political organizers to target audiences for pertinent and timely updates on issues of concern. The rapid and extensive distribution of information and opinion by more and less established activists complicates the question of who represents lesbian communities to themselves and outsiders, but this complication is the result of a democratization of communication—including increased visibility of divergent and minority views—enabled by the Internet.

Latin American lesbians have used this global tool to assert the centrality of the region to their identity and political practice. Although hyperlinks, users, and information flow over regional boundaries, the Web sites and lists target national and regional audiences, often filtering international information on their behalf. The text basis of the Internet is doubtless partially responsible for this finding, as well as for the intraregional division along language lines. But, overall, Latin American lesbians are weaving a homespun web.

Notes

The field research for this chapter was made possible by a Fulbright-Hays Faculty Research Abroad Fellowship. I want to thank the interviewees and Web sites for their contributions and inspirational work, Kathryn Hochstetler for her astute commentary, and Kathryn Jay for her tireless editorial efforts. This chapter was enriched by participants at the 2005 Western Political Science Association Annual Meeting and the DeWitt Wallace Center for Media and Democracy at Duke University.

1. All translations are by the author.

2. In Latin American organizing, both LGBT and GLBT are used widely; however, some movements and organizations opt for variations, including the addition of "Transsexual," "Transvestite," "Intersex," and/or "Queer" into their respective initials.

3. The information from these Web sites was collected in January 2006, and may have changed since.

4. Babb (2003) explains that in Nicaragua, lesbian organizing was stimulated by international influences: those with experience abroad, or international solidarity workers themselves, founded local nonprofits. But competition over international funding may be contributing to the current decline in LGBT visibility.

5. Interview with a founder of Argentine Autonomous Feminist Lesbian Mothers, Buenos Aires, October 25, 2001.

6. Interview with Martha Patricia Cuevas Armas, Mexico City, June 9, 2002.

7. Interview with Mariana Pérez Ocaña, Mexico City, May 31, 2002.

8. Interview with a founder of Argentine Autonomous Feminist Lesbian Mothers, Buenos Aires, October 25, 2001.

9. Interview with Gabriela de Cicco and Irene Ocampo, Rosario, Argentina, September 27, 2002.

10. A *trio eléctrico* is the float vehicle usually used in the Carnival parades in Brazil; the LGBT-rights community has adopted the *trio* for their own, very Brazilian, yearly march.

11. Interview with Corona Tinoco, Mexico City, May 24, 2002.

12. Interview with Carreaga Pérez, Mexico City, June 5, 2002.

References

Alexander, J. 2002a. Homo-pages and Queer Sites: Studying the Construction and Representation of Queer Identities on the World Wide Web. *International Journal of Sexuality and Gender Studies* 7 (2/3): 85–106.

———. 2002b. Queer Webs: Representation of LGBT People and Communities on the World Wide Web. *International Journal of Sexuality and Gender Studies* 7 (2/3): 77–84.

Babb, F. E. 2003. Out in Nicaragua: Local and Transnational Desires after the Revolution. *Cultural Anthropology* 18 (3): 304–28.

Burke, S. K. 2000. In Search of Lesbian Community in an Electronic World. *CyberPsychology & Behavior* 3 (4): 591–604.

Dilevko, J. 2002. The Working Life of Southern NGOs: Juggling the Promise of Information and Communications Technologies and the Perils of Relationships with International NGOs. In *Civil Society in the Information Age*, ed. P. I. Hajnal, 67–94. Burlington, Vt.: Ashgate.

Ebo, B., ed. 1998. *Cyberghetto or Cybertopia? Race, Class, and Gender on the Internet.* Westport, Conn.: Praeger.

Friedman, E. J. 2005. The Reality of Virtual Reality: The Internet and Gender Equality Advocacy in Latin America. *Latin American Politics and Society* 47 (3): 1–34.

Green, J. N., and F. E. Babb. 2002. Introduction to *Latin American Perspectives* 29 (123): 3–23.

Haag, A. M., and F. K. Chang. 1997. The Impact of Electronic Networking on the Lesbian and Gay Community. *Journal of Gay & Lesbian Social Services* 7 (3): 83–94.

Hafkin, N., and N. Taggart. 2001. *Gender, Information Technology, and Developing Countries: An Analytic Study.* Washington, D.C.: Office of Women in Development Bureau for Global Programs, Field Support, and Research, U.S. Agency for International Development.

Heinz, B., L. Gu, A. Inuzuka, and R. Zender. 2002. Under the Rainbow Flag: Webbing Global Gay Identities. *International Journal of Sexuality and Gender Studies* 7 (2/3): 107–24.

Hilbert, M. R. 2001. *Latin America on Its Path into the Digital Age: Where Are We?* Santiago: CEPAL/ECLAC.

Jitsuya, N., and R. Sevilla. 2004. All the Bridges that We Build: Lesbophobia and Sexism Within the Women's and Gay Movements in Peru. *Journal of Gay and Lesbian Social Services* 16 (1): 1–28.

Koch, N. S., and H. E. Schockman. 1998. Democratizing Internet Access in the Lesbian, Gay, and Bisexual Communities. In *Cyberghetto or Cybertopia? Race, Class, and Gender on the Internet*, ed. B. Ebo, 171–84. Westport, Conn.: Praeger.

Leon, O., S. Burch, and E. Tamayo. 2001. *Social Movements on the Net*. Quito: Agencia Latinoamericana de Información.

Mongrovejo, N. 2000. *Un amor que se atrevió a decir su nombre: La lucha de las lesbianas y su relación con los movimientos homosexual y feminista en América Latina*. México, D.F.: Plaza y Valdés Editores/CDHAL.

Nip, J. Y. M. 2004. The Relationship between Online and Offline Communities: The Case of the Queer Sisters. *Media, Culture & Society* 26 (3): 409–28.

Sardá, A. 1998. Lesbians and the Gay Movement in Argentina. NACLA 31 (4): 40–42.

———. 2002. *Avances y retrocesos en el reconocimiento de los derechos de lesbianas y mujeres bisexuales. Cuadernos Mujer Salud* 5:107–12. http://www.reddesalud.org/espanol/datos/ftp/sarda.pdf (accessed January 2006).

Stein, E. 2003. Queers Anonymous: Lesbians, Gay Men, Free Speech, and Cyberspace. *Harvard Civil Rights-Civil Liberties Law Review* 38 (1): 159–213.

Sunstein, C. 2001. *republic.com*. Princeton, N.J.: Princeton University Press.

Um Outro Olhar. 2005. Lesbian Kiss Becomes Police Case in USP East. *Um Outro Olhar*, October 25, http://www.umoutroolhar.com.br/ (accessed January 8, 2006).

Wakeford, N. 1998. Urban Culture for Virtual Bodies: Comments on Lesbian "Identity" and "Community" in San Francisco Bay Area Cyberspace. In *New Frontiers of Space, Bodies, and Gender*, ed. R. Ainley. London: Routledge.

Warkentin, C. 2001. *Reshaping World Politics: NGOs, the Internet, and Global Civil Society*. Lanham, Md.: Rowman and Littlefield.

Weinrich, J. D. 1997. Strange Bedfellows: Homosexuality, Gay Liberation and the Internet. *Journal of Sex Education & Therapy* 22 (1): 58–66.

Gay Space in Havana

Scott Larson

FOR DECADES homosexuals have been viewed as social undesirables in revolutionary Cuba,[1] and even today certain aspects of homosexual behavior can be construed as criminal.[2] In the past, those who were found "guilty" of being gay were ostracized, stripped of their jobs or social positions, and at times even imprisoned or sent to forced-labor camps.[3] Such treatment ultimately led thousands of Cuban gays to flee the country.

No longer officially demonized for their sexual orientation, homosexuals in Cuba are ostensibly free to live as they wish, and an estimated 4 percent to 6 percent of the country's 11.2 million inhabitants are gay.[4] Still, the gay community in Cuba is more tolerated than accepted, and a powerful cultural tradition of machismo contributes to an overall environment of male homosexual marginalization. Consider the words of Tomás Gutiérrez Alea, whose 1993 film *Fresa y chocolate* focused international attention on the issue of repression and discrimination of homosexuals in contemporary Cuba:

> Even today, it's still there at the social level—I won't say the official level, but at the social and individual levels. The macho tradition of our country, as in many other, especially

Latin American, countries, is very strong, and the rejection of homosexuals is visible in all of them (Chanan 2002, 48).

Yet within that environment, male homosexuals in Cuba's capital city, Havana, have managed to claim a number of the city's public places as spaces of their own. It is through these spaces—where homosexuals meet to socialize, make new acquaintances, and exchange information—that the community has gained a share of societal visibility and viability.

This study aims to explore the role space plays in the lives of Havana's homosexuals, to investigate how gay-tolerant spaces there are constructed, defined, and defended. It focuses on three main geographic spaces: *Calle 23*, also known as *La Rampa*, in *Vedado*, where a string of bars and cafés functions as a magnet for gays; a stretch of the *Malecón*, the broad avenue that runs along Havana's oceanfront, where gays gather to socialize at night; and *Parque Central* in *La Habana Vieja*, a traditional meeting point for homosexuals that continues to serve as a prime, modern-day homosexual cruising spot. Together these spaces form part of what has come to be known in Havana as "*el mundo bajo*," literally "the lower world."

Why Homosexual Space? Why Havana?

Contemporary Cuba and its ever-evolving, ever-controversial relationship with the outside world remain fertile areas of interest, particularly in regard to political freedoms, social constraints, and human rights. Within that context, much attention has already has been focused on the lives of homosexuals in Cuba, in large part because a significant number of immigrant gay artists, writers, and filmmakers have contributed their stories to the voluminous and oft-politicized discourse on life on the communist island. At the same time, a plethora of geographic research has investigated the general issue of homosexuality and space in relation to society, especially as it relates to the creation of gay or socially marginalized space and the role that process plays in the formation of group identity (Elder 1995; Knopp 1987; Mitchell 1995; Rothenberg 1995; Myslik 1996; Valentine 1993; Visser 2003).

Yet as a number of researchers have pointed out, the bulk of the body of work on homosexuals and space revolves around North American and European experiences, particularly urban ones. As a result, in the past, when geographers studied sexuality and space, there was "a total lack of questions focusing on how sexualities are constructed and negotiated in peripheral economies" (Visser 2003, 124), and a bias toward "categorizations informed by Anglo-industrialized experience" (Elder 1995, 58).

It is within this context that Havana's homosexual community offers particularly compelling insight into how socially marginalized groups can and do claim a certain degree of visibility and acceptance, even within a largely restrictive society, through the use of physical space.

While Havana itself is one of Latin America's least densely populated major cities, with 2,849 people per square kilometer, perpetual subdivision of houses and apartments has left families crowded into tiny spaces. In addition, in many cases throughout the city, family living arrangements are fluid, with various relatives and friends —often unemployed and officially not allowed to live in Havana—bedding down in whatever space is available in already-compact apartments and houses. Such cramped and often dismal surroundings offer little in the form of relative comfort or entertainment, not to mention privacy. As a result residents of Havana often opt, if one considers that they have much choice, to live a large amount of their private lives in public places. They flock to parts of the city that offer escape, and this interplay between Havana's residents and its public spaces is a fundamental element of the city's character.

Private Uses of Public Spaces

The primary role of Havana's public spaces—parks, plazas, museums, and certain streets and avenues—flows from the socialist imperative to provide for the needs of the collective whole before those of private individuals (Curtis 1993, 66). Of all of Havana's landmarks, the *Malecón* is perhaps is the most famous. Described by Scarpaci and colleagues as "Havana's social living room" (Scarpaci, Segre, and Coyula 2002, 277), this broad, oceanfront boulevard is active twenty-four hours a day and attracts all sorts of visitors: lovers, street musicians, and those out for a walk along Havana's rugged northern shore. Here *habaneros* gather to socialize or just to hang out, and only during storms, when waves crash over the bulwark and flood nearby streets, is the *Malecón* empty. During the day, enterprising boys and men fish off the rocky seawall, entrepreneurs sell copies of pirated compact discs, and hustlers of all stripes work the strolling tourists. Late at night the seafront becomes an open-air party with various groups staking out space all along its length. Despite the ever-present police, the *Malecón* has also become a place for Cubans to voice discontent, though usually in subtle, self-edited ways.

Parque Central and *La Rampa* serve similar roles. There, couples, families, and groups gather to relax and socialize, free from the restrictive environments of the home. In *Parque Central, béisbol* aficionados gather daily to debate the goings-on of the *Liga Nacional,* while *La Rampa* is home to the popular movie house *Cine Yara, Parque Coppelia,* with its world-famous ice cream emporium, and various cafés.

These three spaces have also become important to *habaneros* in another vital sense: as spaces for sexual expression. Given the lack of privacy available in the typical Cuban household, it should come as no surprise that a significant amount of interaction between couples of all ages and persuasions takes place away from the home, and that public spaces such as the *Malecón, La Rampa,* and *Parque Central* would become active sexual spaces. This is particularly true in terms of male homosexuals, who at certain times claim at least parts of these spaces as their own. Historically it has been through this use of public spaces that Cuba's gays have asserted their right to participate in public society.

Gay Havana: Then and Now

As mentioned above, the story of homosexual life in revolutionary Cuba is a complicated one, and several writers have tackled the topic from a scholarly perspective. One of the most current and comprehensive works is that produced by scholar Ian Lumsden (1996), who speaks of an institutionalized homophobia that stems from a Cuban strain of machismo. Lumsden notes how five hundred years of entrenched social attitudes left over from Spanish colonialism have left their mark on Cuban society. He details how, in Cuba, typical modern definitions, terminologies, and perceptions of homosexuality cannot always be applied to Cuban males who have sex with other males. "Before 1959," Lumsden notes, "masculine, ostensibly heterosexual males were able to satisfy some of their sexual needs with 'nonmasculine' males" (28), and such *activos* ("inserters," according to Lumsden) were considered "'real men' who passed as *hombres* but who used *maricones* (the equivalent of the English "faggot") as occasional or even regular outlets to satisfy their sexual appetites" (30). *Entendidos,* or discreet gays who at least outwardly appeared to be heterosexual males, were tolerated if still "despised" within Cuban society. Those less inclined to submit to such self-oppressive behavior, however, faced complete rejection. Not surprisingly, such conditions forced many of Havana's prerevolutionary gays to adopt double lives, hiding their homosexuality from friends, family members, and coworkers, while privately enjoying intimate relationships with other males. Still, in spite of such societal pressures and prejudices, the city's gay community actively sought to establish places where its members could meet and be themselves. As Lumsden writes:

> There were countless bars, such as Dirty Dick, Johnny's Bar, and the Barrilito, where they could hang out day and night. The ambiente of the Colón barrio in Centro Habana attracted some American tourists just as it did gente decente from the middle-class neighborhoods on the other side of town ... Male brothels such as the Lucero, which catered to tourists, were the exception, and unlike female brothels were not really part of the ambiente of the barrio Colón. There were many cinemas like the Rialto, the Verdun, and the Campoamor to which, according to an old homosexual, "you could go and immediately pick up a young guy. Many had their first experience there. There was a lot of sex in those cinemas." There was also a rich street life in which you could always find someone with whom to pass the time of day. (Lumsden 1996, 33–34)

With the Communist Revolution of 1959, life changed dramatically for Cuba's homosexuals.

> Cuba was also led by Fidel Castro, whose public persona was the incarnation of machismo. Revolutionary Cuba, he said, "needed strong men to fight wars, sportsmen, men who had no psychological weaknesses." The traditional Cuban image of homosexuals hardly fit this paradigm of revolutionary attributes. (Lumsden 1996, 61)

Far from providing new freedoms and space for homosexuals, then, the Revolution only heightened the sense of outsiderness among Cuba's gays, at times even institutionalizing what until then had been homophobic cultural traditions. Through its efforts to transform Cuban society by asserting absolute control over the population and discouraging all manner of antisocial activity, the revolutionary government deemed the gay community deviant and began to close or alter many of its traditional social spaces. Again according to Lumsden:

> [T]he ambiente available to [gays]—also began to diminish. For example, bars patronized by homosexuals began to close because of state intervention, emigration of their owners, or unprofitability due to declining patronage. Cruising and sex became more difficult in traditional venues such as the Campoamor, Negrete, and Duplex cinemas on account of increased police surveillance. There was less room for homosexuals to socialize or even to "pass" and therefore all the more reason for entendidos to be protective of their private lives. (Lumsden 1996, 62)

While the situation for gays has improved dramatically since the early years of the Revolution, being gay in Cuba still carries a significant stigma, and finding spaces for the free expression of one's sexuality is a challenge. As a result, as Lumsden points out, few contemporary Cuban homosexuals are "out," at least in the Western sense, and most lead hidden lives, much as their predecessors did for the better part of four centuries. Revolutionary Havana, unlike cities in the capitalist West, contains no permanent or overtly gay spaces, and while interviewees for this study identified the aforementioned gay-friendly places, many other onetime meeting places—such as in front of the Fiat car dealership on the *Malecón*, and two cafés, *Bin Bom* and *Arcada*, along *La Rampa*—have been closed or otherwise restricted by the authorities.

Even those places where gays have found some material space in which to gather are marked by a conspicuous police presence, and the character of these spaces varies over time. Not only do they become increasingly gay late at night, but accessibility to them can ebb and flow along with the prevailing mood of Cuban authorities.

> "We go to [*Cine*] *Yara* or the *Malecón*. We used to go to *Arcada*, *Bin Bom*, but they [the authorities] are closing them down," said one interviewee, a twenty-six-year-old, in late

May 2003. "Now I go to my house with my partner because there is no longer a place for us. Now the only [public] place we can go is the *Malecón*."[5]

Aside from the outright shutting down of a location, one favored tactic of the government is to restrict gatherings, not just of LGBT folks, but of any Cubans, by imposing per-person *consumos*—or minimum orders—at restaurants and bars, which under Cuba's socialist system are controlled by the state; another is for the police to descend, whistles blowing, whenever a crowd begins to congregate in a chosen public place. Ostensibly, the police are merely ensuring public safety and order by keeping a tight reign on groups gathering in public, but their presence in gay-friendly spaces is particularly ubiquitous. The need to stamp out drugs and prostitution is often used as the rationale for such patrols. "But sometimes there is no explanation, just a power play," said Kristian, a straight street musician, who along with his musical partner, Orleydis, plays songs for money along the same section of the *Malecón* as the gay community meets.[6]

At other times there have been broader, more sweeping clampdowns on spaces frequented by homosexuals. Often these crackdowns are in response to larger events that have occurred elsewhere, or have no direct relation to the gay community. These, it can be presumed, are designed to send the message to the entire Cuban population that the authorities are in complete control. Still, these actions have a decidedly disproportionate impact on the gay and other marginalized communities, because of the limited and tightly controlled spaces where those groups are allowed to congregate. In late March 2003, for instance, some seventy-five Cuban dissidents were arrested and sentenced to long jail terms for criticizing the Castro regime's record on human rights and calling for a referendum on increased civil liberties. In an unrelated incident within days of the arrests, three men hijacked a ferry and attempted to sail across the Florida Strait to the United States. Forced back to Cuban waters by lack of fuel, the hijackers were captured, and nine days later they were executed following expedited court proceedings that were deemed little more than show trials in the West.

Fearing an increase in dissident activity, a backlash against the executions, and additional hijack attempts, the Cuban government moved quickly to head off potential problems by reasserting its control over Havana's public spaces. The number of police patrolling public places such as the *Malecón*, the long stretch of *Calle 23* that leads to it, and *Parque Central* increased noticeably. "It got much worse in March and April, in the sense that the police were around more," noted Kristian, the musician.[7] The authorities, he and other interviewees maintained, became much quicker to confront Cubans for seemingly trivial things such as talking to foreigners or simply hanging out.

Also, within days of the arrests, the gay-friendly café *Arcada*, located just off *La Rampa*, was shut down. "One day it was just closed," said Marco, a thirty-two-year-old who had visited the café nightly and often augmented his income as a model at an art school by surreptitiously selling clothes and jewelry to those sitting at the café's tables.[8]

Until the day in early April when it was closed, the café, which is marked by a red-and-white awning and floor-to-ceiling windows offering a clear view of the goings-on inside, had served as a vital communication hub for the gay community. By day it was one of the hundreds of nondescript government-owned cafes in Havana that serve an uninspiring menu of ham and cheese *bocaditos* (sandwiches), pizza, and juice, soda, or beer. At night, however, it metamorphosed into an unofficial gay social house. Its location made it an accessible way station on the way to the *Malecón*, a convenient place for *pingueros*, male prostitutes, to bring their foreign friends for coffee or a beer, and for members of Havana's gay community to trade gossip and find out about parties or what their friends were planning for the night. By 9 PM, pairs or groups of men—often two or three young Cubans and an older foreigner—began to occupy the tables, and by 11 PM, the place would be bustling with male activity. Among *Arcada*'s regular clientele were dozens of transvestites, but on most nights the only women around were either in the café with gay friends, or were merely stopping by to use the restroom.

A month after it was shuttered, *Arcada* reopened, but with changes that reduced its accessibility and attractiveness to the gay community. A three-dollar (U.S.) minimum *consumo* was established, which effectively meant that only those with money and the intent to spend it were allowed inside. Since most Cubans have little discretionary income, many of the former clientele were effectively locked out. Similarly, the sale of alcohol was prohibited, and the frequency of police patrols outside increased. Taken together, these measures insured that large numbers of gays could no longer meet there for a leisurely night of conversation over a soda or beer. By first closing *Arcada*, then allowing it to reopen, but with the new regulations in place, the government had effectively cut off one of the few public spaces in Havana where the homosexual community had felt free to congregate.

Illegal in Their Own Land

Revolutionary ideology and an invasive government have had additional impacts on gay spaces as well. In the capitalist West, the location of marginalized groups—including gay residential communities, with their attendant businesses and services—can often be attributed to economic factors (Winchester and White 1988; Knopp 1990; Adler and Brenner 1992; Binnie 1995; Kirby and Hay 1997; Visser 2003). But with the adoption of socialist policies that have affected every aspect of life—from the theoretical elimination of social classes to government ownership of all property and enterprise and state control of housing—the Castro regime has insured, whether it purposefully intended to or not, that Cuba's cities have no concentrations of homosexual residences, no gay neighborhoods, no explicitly gay clubs, bars, or businesses, and none of the gentrification so often associated with male homosexual communities in developed countries.

Instead, Havana's gay spaces are impermanent, contested sites typically converted into temporary gay social spaces by stealth. The process, as described by members of the community, is a fluid, ongoing one: a homosexual pair finds a place—a public park or street, bar, restaurant, or café—that isn't too crowded and where the atmosphere is to their liking. They begin to frequent the place, then tell friends who tell other friends and so on in a process similar to that described by Rothenberg (1995) in her study of the creation of lesbian social space. As the number of gays gathering increases, heterosexuals stop coming, presumably uncomfortable with or fearing the stigma of frequenting a spot popular with homosexuals. Soon, the location has become a de facto gay space, a place where homosexuals feel comfortable because they are surrounded by others like them.

But much as the *Arcada* example illustrates, such places offer relatively provisional havens. Once a location becomes overwhelmingly gay, the authorities take note, beef up the police presence, and keep close tabs on whatever activity goes on. Eventually such spaces are closed, restricted, or the authorities make being there so uncomfortable that the group moves on, and the cycle starts over again.

Another example of the government's conspicuous impact on gay social space is the effort to control migration to Havana. As one might expect, homosexuals say they face greater discrimination outside of the relatively cosmopolitan capital. Elsewhere, they maintain, life is much more conservative and social traits such as machismo often manifest themselves more fully. Such constraints have led hundreds of predominately young homosexuals to leave the countryside and Cuba's smaller cities for Havana, where, despite the capital's own oppressive atmosphere, the sheer size of the gay community offers some degree of anonymity and escape. But because of the strict laws governing where Cubans can travel, work, and live, a gay migrant's mere presence in Havana can make him a criminal.[9]

Police patrol high-profile public areas such as parks and main streets, asking those who frequent them for their national identification cards, or *los carnets*. Those without a *carnet* or the proper permission to be in Havana are taken to a nearby police station, where they are held for several hours before being released with a fine, or *multa*.

"If they discover you are illegal they give you a five-hundred-peso [roughly fifty-dollar] *multa*," explained one twenty-one-year-old gay émigré from Holguín.[10] While the amount of the fine is not so much by foreign standards, it is a crippling amount in a country where doctors and teachers can make the equivalent of twelve U.S. dollars a month. Equally punishing, if not more so, is the reminder that in Cuba, where one lives, works, and plays is subject to government approval.

"Imagine," said the twenty-one-year-old. "In your own country you are illegal."

The Primacy of Space

Of course, gays are not the only Cubans who face such overt government intrusion into their lives. Indeed, all Cubans deal with such conditions on a daily basis. For those who frequent spaces associated with homosexuals and other marginalized groups, however, the likelihood of being asked to produce a *carnet* is much greater. The term *el mundo bajo* is used equally by those who frequent these spaces and the city's mainstream citizens. Depending on who is speaking, however, it carries far different connotations. To the marginalized, *el mundo bajo* represents temporarily appropriated space where, to a degree, all are free to be themselves. Among average citizens, however, the perception runs that this "world" is a place for drugs, illegal or immoral conduct, and antisocial activities. To many *habaneros*, only people of dubious character would enter these spaces. To be sure, *el mundo bajo* attracts a certain amount of illegal activity. But in keeping with the theory of Winchester and White (1988), the widely held but not entirely accurate negative view of this world only contributes to the marginalization of those who gather there.

Ironically, virtually all of the spaces that make up *el mundo bajo* are public places that at other times of day or in other ways serve much more socially accepted purposes. Indeed, it is their very nature as places where, theoretically at least, everyone is free to assemble, that makes them attractive to gays and members of other marginalized groups in the first place. Additionally, the fact that many of Havana's traditional homosexual spaces (the *Malecón* and *Parque Central*, for instance) remain important to the contemporary gay community is a testament to the central role these places have played and continue to play—geographically, symbolically, and emotionally—in the public life of the city. In many ways both the *Malecón* and *Parque Central* serve as Havana's version of the traditional Latin American central plaza, a place of "primacy within the urban landscape" that can offer "daily interaction between friends and strangers and provide important sites for the public life of the city" (Rosenthal, 50). In addition, much like the classic plaza, they provide a point of contact between different classes and types of people. It should come as no surprise that in seeking greater social access, Havana's gays would gravitate to them.

Parque Central also sits at the heart of the government's efforts to develop a robust tourism industry, which gives it additional geographic significance. The park—which covers two city blocks on the border between *Habana Vieja* and *Centro Habana*—is ringed by upmarket hotels like the *Inglaterra*, *Telégrafo*, *Parque Central*, and *Plaza*, and is near popular tourist attractions such as the *Capitolio*, the *Gran Teatro*, and Ernest Hemingway's old haunts, the *El Floridita* bar and the *Hotel Ambos Mundo*s. It is also within walking distance of numerous museums and *Habana Vieja*'s collection of colonial buildings, churches, and plazas.

As a consequence, the park is especially important to Havana's male homosexual prostitutes, because of its proximity to potential clients—the relatively wealthy foreign tourists who visit these sites and stay in these hotels. For many gays, the park serves as a sort of headquarters. During the day many *pingueros* stroll the shady paths looking for likely customers, while others simply sit in groups on stone benches passing the time until nightfall, when they move on to *La Rampa* or the *Malecón*.

For Havana's male homosexual community, the *Malecón* is a default destination, a place where one can always find friends, foreigners, and escape from the drudgery of daily life. At night Havana's gays can be found all along the boulevard, but the greatest numbers congregate along the seawall just west of the intersection with *La Rampa*, in the shadow of the grand hotel *El Nacional*. On a typical evening, scores of gays meet there, often splitting off into smaller groups to talk, drink rum, or listen to music. They move up and down *Calle 23* to buy cigarettes or rum at a nearby gas station (in Cuba, one can invariably find alcohol, snacks, and ice cream being sold alongside spare parts and motor oil), or something to eat in the nearby cafés, bars, and clubs. Much like *Parque Central*, this stretch of *Calle 23* and the *Malecón* is near a number of high-profile hotels such as the *Habana Libre* and the *Hotel Vedado*, making it a prime place to encounter and mix with foreign tourists.

One's choice of space, or more accurately the places one chooses to frequent, can also serve as a vital means of expressing one's sexual preference. Single men, for instance, know that by going to places such as *Parque Central*, or certain parts of the *Malecón* and *La Rampa* at specific times of day, they will not only find but be found by other gays. Of course, one's presence in such spaces sends the same message to the authorities and homophobic Cubans. As such, one's dress, behavior, and choice of where to spend free time can constitute unmistakable—and inherently "antisocial" —statements about one's inclinations.

"It's not possible to live an open life," said one interviewee, a twenty-six-year-old gay mechanic originally from the city of Holguín, who was interviewed late one night in June 2003 on his way to the *Malecón*. "The police hassle us all the time," he added, grasping his wrist in a motion akin to being handcuffed, a reference to being hauled off to the police station for some violation or another.[11] As if on cue, just minutes after being interviewed, the man was stopped by the police on *Calle 23* and asked to produce his *carnet*.

"*D'acuerdo?*" he shouted across the street. "You see?"

"Here in Cuba we're very discriminated against," added a sixteen-year-old transvestite, an unemployed English student who lives with her male partner but works as a prostitute at night.

"The police bother us constantly, asking for our papers. They know who we [gays] are and that's why they continually bother us. Now, every so often they round us [transvestites, or *travesti* in Spanish] up and lock us up [*nos encieran*] for three or four days and fine us."

"Why?" I ask.

"Because we're not allowed to dress like women."[12]

Despite the oft-stated opinion that gays are harassed purely because of their sexual orientation or manner, it is unclear whether this is the sole explanation for the mistreatment of Havana's homosexuals and transvestites. Being outwardly gay or dressing like women certainly marginalizes them, makes them easier to identify, and stigmatizes them. But neither professing one's (homo)sexuality nor being a transvestite is specifically prohibited by law. And while many of those interviewed for this study believe their lifestyle alone is to blame for police harassment, observation suggests that whether a person is gay or not, or is a transvestite, can be a partial, perhaps even secondary explanation. Cuba's is an oppressive society, one where all sorts of freedoms—not just the freedom to publicly announce one's sexuality—are limited. Gays undoubtedly experience police harassment more because as gays they are forced to the fringe of society, but all Cubans deal with this lack of freedom to some degree.

Indeed, there is also plenty of observational evidence to support Lumsden's (1996) view that the police in and around recognized homosexual spaces are more focused on maintaining order and control rather than on hassling gays. Most of the places where gays congregate, after all, are occupied by nongays as well, and straight groups and individuals appear to be just as likely to attract police attention. In fact, the argument could be made that homosexuals are targets for police harassment not so much because of their sexual orientation, but because as homosexuals they inhabit marginalized and contested spaces. Much as Winchester and White (1988) theorize, the homosexual spaces discussed in this study exist on the margins of acceptable society. As a result, a person's mere presence in such places—whether that person is gay or not—makes him or her a candidate for police suspicion, and homosexuality has become "criminalized" precisely because homosexuals choose to occupy such public locations. A related explanation is that Cuban authorities equate homosexuality with prostitution, and that an ongoing crackdown on the selling of sex, particularly when it involves tourists and other foreigners, leads to increased harassment of gays.

While Cuba has no laws that explicitly prohibit homosexuality, there are numerous broadly defined offenses that can be used to criminalize homosexual behavior. For instance, public displays of even innocent affection among homosexuals can bring *multas* of up to four hundred pesos. "If the police see us holding hands they take [arrest] us for causing a public scandal," said one twenty-one-year-old baker.[13] As a result, one rarely sees Havana's homosexuals holding hands, kissing, or touching each other in public.

That does not mean there is not a sexual component to Havana's male homosexual spaces. Clearly, the spaces identified in this study are vital for all manner of homosexual activity, leading up to actual sexual relations. These spaces are where male homosexuals meet other gay men, go on dates, find sexual partners, and learn of and arrange for safe spaces in which to be intimate. Due to the lack of privacy inherent in Havana's housing situation, and the very real possibility that one's neighbors, friends, or coworkers might discover one's sexual persuasion, many of Havana's gay men—even those with long-term partners—prefer to visit *alquileres*, houses where rooms can be rented by the night or the hour, to have sex. Such rooms—which usually offer little more than a toilet and a metal-frame bed topped by a tattered mattress—are scattered throughout the city's neighborhoods, and typically rent for twenty-five pesos a night.

Desperation also forces Cubans of all sexual persuasions to steal private moments in public spaces. For Havana's homosexuals, there are two parks—*Parque de la Fraternidad*, situated just south of the *Capitolio*, and *Parque el Curita*—where once the sun goes down, many among Havana's gay community go in search of casual sex. Even within the marginalized world of *el mundo bajo*, however, these two parks have a somewhat notorious reputation.

For Havana's homosexuals, then, the search for "safe" space in which to live a gay lifestyle and pursue gay relationships is never-ending. While outright violence is rare, homophobic traditions, vague laws, and the confines of contemporary Cuban life all conspire to push Havana's homosexuals to the margins of society, both culturally and physically. Gay spaces, to the degree that they exist, are secure only as long as the authorities allow them to be, and the ongoing process of finding new spaces remains fraught with risk.

A Serious Game

Clearly, Cuba does not fit many of the descriptive frameworks from which geographers have looked at gay communities in Western, free-market democracies. And it should come as no surprise that the forces that have helped shape gay spaces across Europe and North America often fail to describe the dynamics at work in Cuba. While the situation for gays has improved markedly since the openly homophobic rhetoric of the early Revolution, being gay in Cuba still carries a significant stigma, and finding spaces for the free expression of one's sexuality remains a challenge. This is especially true in public spaces. Today, those among Havana's homosexual community who wish to live public lives have been forced by a powerful mix of societal disapproval and official antagonism to create their own spaces when and where they can, often in the face of official antagonism.

In spite of this limited and contentious access to space, Havana's gays have managed to establish a number of gay-tolerant sites within which they are able to lead some semblance of an open life. Three in particular—the *Malecón*, *Parque Central*, and *La Rampa*—have long and established traditions as gay meeting places. These spaces continue to form physical focal points for the gay community. Still, as the stories of these spaces illustrate, they are temporary and temporally specific havens, their accessibility subject to the whims of the authorities.

For Havana's more public homosexuals, then, their very presence in specific public spaces becomes simultaneously a declaration of their sexuality and a challenge to existing homophobic traditions and societal mores. By frequenting high-profile public spaces, Havana's gays, in effect, are publicizing their homosexuality and putting themselves in the precarious position of confronting Cuban authority. Still, that there are spaces in which Havana's homosexuals have found relative havens suggests a willingness among certain gays to expose themselves to the resulting harassment and abuse in exchange for physical locations to call their own. Consider the words of a twenty-six-year-old gay mechanic originally from Holguín: "The police bother us because we're gay, and they know we're gay because we concentrate in groups in these places. Every day we go to the *Malecón*, and every day the police come and hassle us, so it's sort of a game. A serious game, but a still a game."[14]

In the end, had certain homosexuals not persevered in, in fact insisted on, creating and publicizing these locations, no gay-tolerant spaces, no matter how temporary, would exist in Havana.

Notes

Research for this project was supported by a grant from the *Centro de Estudios Puertorriqueños* at Hunter College of the City University of New York.

1. Any discussion of homosexuality in contemporary Cuba raises the question of terminology (Lumsden 1996, xxiv), especially as homosexual spaces often are shared by a multitude of diverse individuals who, for the sake of convenience, fall under the collective heading of *homosexual* (i.e., queers, transgendered people, and transvestites, not to mention the finer Cuban distinctions of *pasivo, completo, maricón, bugarrón, loca*, etc.). Lumsden argues for use of the term *homosexual* (as opposed to *gay* or *queer*), since he claims it is the more readily recognizable and meaningful term to the community in Cuba. Since I have found many among Havana's homosexual community to also use and relate to the term *gay*, I use *gay* and *homosexual* interchangeably throughout the study.

2. In 1971 the first National Congress on Education and Culture declared homosexuality to be antisocial and queers "sociopaths." The Congress determined that known gays—"notorious homosexuals" was the phrase used—shouldn't be allowed to infect others with their deviant ways by holding down jobs where they might come in contact with the nation's youth. Even after consensual homosexual sex in private was decriminalized in the late 1970s, official prejudice continued. It took a revision of the Penal Code in 1987 before "ostentatious" homosexual behavior in public, and private homosexual acts witnessed by a third party, were no longer considered crimes. Still today, homosexuals who kiss or touch in public run the risk of being accused of "creating a public scandal," an act which can bring a stiff fine.

3. In 1965 the Communist government of Fidel Castro established forced-labor camps, dubbed Military Units to Aid Production, as a means of rehabilitating citizens who didn't ex-

hibit socialism's requisite conformist attitude. Slackards, counterrevolutionaries, and others whose "immoral" behavior was considered anathema to the new Cuba were sentenced to labor in rural sugarcane fields. Known by their initials, UMAP, the camps became notorious for their brutal conditions, and gays and effeminate males were among those put to work there as a means of molding them into "real" men. The camps existed for three years before internal and international pressure led Castro to close them in 1968.

4. International Lesbian and Gay Association, www.ilga.org (accessed September 19, 2003).

5. Interview by author, May 25, 2003.

6. Interview by author, June 1, 2003.

7. Interview by author, June 1, 2003.

8. Interview by author, May 25, 2003.

9. Citing concerns about security, public health, overcrowding, and public order, Cuban president Fidel Castro signed Decree 217 on April 22, 1997. The decree prohibits persons residing in other provinces from moving to Havana. To enforce the law, police frequently check the identifications (*los carnets*) of people on the streets of the city. Those found in violation are fined between three hundred and one thousand pesos (between twelve and forty U.S. dollars) and sent home. If violators are unable to pay the fine, they are jailed. (Human Rights Watch, http://www.hrw.org/legacy/reports/1999/cuba/Cuba996-03.htm [accessed December 10, 2009]).

10. Interview by author, May 26, 2003.

11. Interview by author, June 1, 2003.

12. Interview by author, May 26, 2003.

13. Interview by author, June 1, 2003.

14. Interview by author, August 19, 2003.

References

Adler, S., and J. Brenner. 1992. Gender and Space: Lesbians and Gay Men in the City. *International Journal of Urban and Regional Research* 16 (1): 24–34.

Binnie, J. 1995. Trading Places: Consumption, Sexuality and the Production of Queer Space. In *Mapping Desire: Geographies of Sexualities*, ed. D. Bell and G. Valentine, 182–99. London: Routledge.

Chanan, M. 2002. We Are Losing Our Values: An Interview with Tomás Gutiérrez Alea. *Boundary* 2, no. 29 (3): 47–53.

Curtis, J. 1993. Havana's Parque Coppelia: Public Space Traditions in Socialist Cuba. *Places* 8 (3): 62–67.

Elder, G. 1995. Of Moffies, Kaffirs and Perverts: Male Homosexuality and the Discourse of Moral Order in the Apartheid State. In *Mapping Desire: Geographies of Sexualities*, ed. D. Bell and G. Valentine, 56–65. London: Routledge.

Kirby, S., and I. Hay. 1997. (Hetero)sexing Space: Gay Men and "Straight" Space in Adelaide, South Australia. *Professional Geographer* 49 (3): 295–305.

Knopp, L. 1987. Social Theory, Social Movements and Public Policy: Recent Accomplishments of the Gay and Lesbian Movements in Minneapolis, Minn. *International Journal of Urban and Regional Research* 11:243–61.

————. 1990. Some Theoretical Implications of Gay Involvement in an Urban Land Market. *Political Geography Quarterly* 9:337–52.

Lumsden, I. 1996. *Machos, Maricones and Gays: Cuba and Homosexuality.* Philadelphia: Temple University Press.

Mitchell, D. 1995. The End of Public Space? People's Park, Definitions of the Public, and Democracy. *Annals of the Association of American Geographers* 85 (1): 108–33.

Myslik, W. 1996. Renegotiating the Social/Sexual Identities of Places: Gay Communities as Safe Havens or Sites of Resistance? In *Bodyspace: Destabilizing Geographies of Gender and Sexuality*, ed. N. Duncan, 156–69. London: Routledge.

Rothenberg, T. 1995. "And She Told Two Friends": Lesbians Creating Urban Social Space. In *Mapping Desire: Geographies of Sexualities*, ed. D. Bell and G. Valentine, 165–81. London: Routledge.

Scarpaci, J., R. Segre, and M. Coyula. 2002. *Havana: Two Faces of the Antillean Metropolis.* New York: John Wiley and Sons.

Valentine, G. 1993. Negotiating and Managing Multiple Sexual Identities: Lesbian Time-Space Strategies. *Transactions of the Institute of British Geographers* 18 (2): 237–48.

Visser, G. 2003. Gay Men, Leisure Space and South African Cities. *Geoforum* 34 (1): 123–37.

Winchester, H. P. M., and P. E. White. 1988. The Location of Marginalized Groups in the Inner City. *Environment and Planning D: Society and Space* 6 (1): 37–54.

Divergence between LGBTI Legal, Political, and Social Progress in the Caribbean and Latin America

Jim Wilets

RECENT HISTORY in much of Latin America and the Caribbean has been marked by high levels of anti-LGBTI animus, including very high levels of anti-LGBTI violence.[1] Both regions have been characterized by a *machista* culture in which gender nonconformity has been widely suppressed, often violently. Nevertheless, there has been a growing divergence between the implementation of LGBTI rights in English-speaking Caribbean countries and Latin American countries. It is difficult to make broad generalizations about a region as diverse and large as Latin America and the Caribbean, but it can nonetheless be generally stated that, with some notable exceptions (El Salvador and Honduras deserve special mention in this regard), Latin America has made sporadic, but substantial, progress in implementing LGBTI rights (Wikipedia 2009; Ottosson 2006), while the English-speaking Caribbean is still characterized by extraordinarily high levels of anti-LGBTI social animosity and repressive legislation (Ottosson 2006; Amnesty International 2009). The progress in Latin America is most notable the further the countries in the region are from the United States.

The reasons for this general divergence include: (1) the role of religion; (2) the role of women with regard to the two regions' respective religions; (3) the effects of colonialism; (4) the effects of slavery; (5) approaches to domestic incorporation of international human-rights norms; and (6) geopolitical perspectives and locations, and the effects of U.S. hegemony.

The Role of Religion

At the risk of stating the obvious, the evidence is overwhelming that religion is a determining factor in almost all countries with respect to determining societal attitudes toward homosexuality. For example, there is a high correlation between religious attendance and animosity toward LGBTI rights (Reinhardt 1997). However, it is not simply a question of differing theological approaches to homosexuality that is critical, since the principal religions in both regions, Catholicism (in Latin America) and Fundamentalist Protestantism (in the Caribbean) share a theological perspective that is strongly anti-LGBTI. Moreover, religion itself is frequently simply an expression of underlying societal attitudes that may exist independently of the theological tenets of the particular religion itself.

From an empirical perspective, there is little contemporary correlation between the degree of Catholic affiliation per se in a particular country and that country's implementation of LGBTI rights. Belgium, Spain, and Quebec were among the first jurisdictions in the world to legally recognize same-sex unions, and Spain and Belgium even preceded the traditionally tolerant and overwhelmingly Protestant countries of Scandinavia in recognizing same-sex marriage. The Catholic Church has frequently taken a strong stance against pro-LGBTI legislation in various Latin American countries, but has been less successful in such efforts than Protestant churches have been in similar efforts in the English-speaking Caribbean.

This divergence can at least partially be explained by the degree to which adherents of the different religions consider the theological positions of their respective religions determinative of their own personal approaches to those issues. It should not be surprising that Fundamentalist or Evangelical Protestantism should have greater success in shaping individuals' personal approaches to social issues than does Catholicism, since Evangelical Protestantism is predicated upon a much closer relationship between an individual's acceptance of the religion's specific tenets and personal salvation. Catholicism, in contrast, is often treated by its adherents as more of a cultural institution. As the default religion for much of Latin America's history, Catholicism did not require the same degree of personal affirmation of the religion's specific tenets, or active attendance at religious services by Catholic parishioners. Thus, Catholic religious affiliation in many countries is not necessarily correlated with consistent church attendance, which is more closely correlated to anti-LGBTI attitudes (Reinhardt 1997). Moreover, the phenomenon of latitudinarianism in Catholic belief has been well documented, although repeatedly condemned by the Catholic Church itself.

Latitudinarianism does not, however, fully explain the gender-based divergence in approaches to homosexuality between the predominantly Fundamentalist Protestant Caribbean and Catholic Latin America. One of the distinguishing characteristics between the two regions is the markedly more hostile view of homosexuality between women in the Caribbean. To understand this phenomenon more completely, it is helpful to understand the role of women within the religious institutions of the Caribbean and Latin America.

The Role of Women

Women have a vested interest in their religious communities throughout much of the Caribbean. The Evangelical Protestant churches in the Caribbean play a critical role in holding families together. Unlike in Latin America, women are deeply involved in churches in the Caribbean, and view the strong moral tenets of their religions as a critical social glue. In Latin America, on the other hand, women have relatively little vested interest in the Catholic Church, and have been marginalized within the power structure of the Church. A socioeconomically "successful" woman in Latin America will frequently distance herself from the Church and its strictest mores, whereas many "successful" women in the Caribbean remain closely tied to their churches and their religious and social mores. This is, admittedly, somewhat counterintuitive, since many Evangelical Protestant denominations theologically subscribe to a gender-conformist view of societal relations. Thus, the greater involvement by women in the churches in the Caribbean does not, once again, provide a complete explanation for this gender divergence on the issue of homosexuality.

In a society where women, quite apart from religion, often are the primary breadwinners and heads of households, gender nonconformity, particularly by males, is frequently viewed as harmful by diminishing, from a heterosexual female perspective, a primary social utility of males as participants in the family unit. As one government minister in The Bahamas explained to me, "Life is hard enough for women in the Caribbean and a male who is not a 'strong' male is but one more burden."[2] Needless to say, this phenomenon is also present in Catholic Latin America, but in the more patriarchal society of Latin America, a "weakened" male has fewer negative repercussions for the female population.

Religion, of course, is but one part of the puzzle. Other explanations for the divergence of attitudes can be found in the effects of colonialism and slavery, the resistance of the English-speaking Caribbean to incorporation of international human-rights norms, and the location of the two regions in an area deeply affected by U.S. hegemony.

The Effects of Colonialism

The first thing to note about the effects of colonialism and societal and legal perspectives on LGBTI individuals is the well-documented different consequences of British colonialism, on the one hand, and Spanish and Portuguese colonialism, on the other. As an empirical and legal matter, British law was historically much more severe in its treatment of homosexuality than Spanish or Portuguese law in the colonies (Wilets 1994; Tielman and Hammelburg 1993).[3] A review of anti-sodomy laws, for example, demonstrates that the incidence of such laws in former British colonies is substantially greater than the incidence of such laws in former Spanish or Portuguese colonies (Gay and Lesbian Archives of the Pacific Northwest 2007).

However, the effects of slavery cannot be viewed simply as a consequence of laws imposed by the colonial masters, but also as a consequence of the greater impact of slavery accompanying colonialism in the Caribbean.

Effects of Slavery in the Caribbean

Under the slave system, a man was frequently powerless to protect family members from assaults against their bodily integrity and dignity by the white overlords (David 2007, 324–45). This history has resulted in a much more pronounced expression of revulsion by black society in response to perceptions of male "subservience" or male gender nonconformity. Extensive literature on the effect of this phenomenon in the African American community in the United States helps explain the elevated levels of anti-LGBTI attitudes and hostility to male gender nonconformity in the African American community.[4] Although there does not appear to be much literature that specifically discusses this phenomenon in the Caribbean, there is every reason to suppose that the consequences of slavery in the United States have their parallels in the postslavery and postcolonial societies of the Caribbean.

It must be noted here that the traditional historiography critiquing the alleged dysfunctionality of slave families has been subject to widespread criticism; however, the alleged effects of male powerlessness in the face of the white power structure have been much less contested.

Approaches to Domestic Incorporation of International Human-Rights Norms

Whereas much of Latin America has witnessed a growing and inexorable legal acceptance of LGBTI rights and other internationally accepted human-rights norms, the English-speaking Caribbean has been far more reluctant to incorporate such international norms. One of the more visible manifestations of this reluctance can be seen in the bitter resistance of much of the English-speaking Caribbean to the growing international movement for banning capital punishment. Indeed, this resistance to the abolishment of the death penalty provided much of the support for the creation by the Caribbean Community (CARICOM) of the Caribbean Court of Justice to replace the Commonwealth's Privy Council in London as a court of last appeal.[5]

Similarly, much of the Caribbean resistance to decriminalization of homosexuality has been articulated as a resistance to the imposition of European colonial norms on the Caribbean, particularly in light of the United Kingdom's quantum leap in the recognition of internationally recognized norms of nondiscrimination and privacy in the context of sexual orientation. The irony in such a reaction, also witnessed in former British colonies in Africa and Asia, is that the original source for those anti-LGBTI laws was British colonialism itself, not indigenous precolonial antipathy to homosexuality (Wilets 1994, 989–1050; Tielman and Hammelburg 1993, 249–342).

Part of the reason for this resistance to internationally recognized human-rights norms, frequently perceived as "European" norms, in the Caribbean as opposed to Latin America, is that the political elites in Latin America themselves much more closely identify with the culture and legal norms of continental Europe. Many of the political elites in Latin America trace their lineage to Europe, as the political elites in the English-speaking Caribbean do not. It is notable that this phenomenon is much more pronounced in South America than Central America. This greater receptiveness to the expansive pro-LGBTI jurisprudence developing in Europe by South American elites can be explained partly by the greater tendency among South American elites to culturally identify with Europe, and partly by South America's greater distance from the United States, with its traditionally more anti-LGBTI legal tradition. It is therefore helpful to explore the effects of location in terms of a geopolitical perspective, and the effects of U.S. hegemony in the Caribbean and Central America.

Geopolitical Perspectives and Location, and the Effects of U.S. Hegemony

The proximity of the United States to the regions of the Caribbean and Central America has had a mixed effect on the realization of LGBTI rights. On the one hand, the proximity and influence of the United States, with its history of repressing LGBTI rights, have served to diminish the progress of LGBTI rights in both Central America and the Caribbean, particularly to the extent that the United States serves as an alternative legal model to the European model.

On the other hand, one can witness a marginally greater tolerance for LGBTI individuals in The Bahamas than in many of the other islands of the Caribbean, largely because of the intense commercial and personal ties between The Bahamas and the United States. Although the United States has historically been less receptive to LGBTI rights than Europe, the exposure of the Bahamian population to the relatively open LGBTI communities of southern Florida and other U.S. metropolises has had an ameliorative effect on the otherwise hostile attitudes of the population to LGBTI rights.

The effect of U.S. hegemony in Central America has been somewhat less positive, particularly with respect to El Salvador, Honduras, and, to some extent, Guatemala. Historically, ongoing U.S. support for repressively conservative military regimes in much of Central America, versus the relatively shorter duration of the U.S.-supported military regimes in South America (collectively referred to as "Operation Condor"), has also contributed to greater social and political polarization in Central America. This process has led to enormous economic and political polarization in many Central American societies, with dire consequences for LGBTI communities in those countries.[6]

First, human-rights abuses against sexual minorities occur in a context of relatively recently ended civil wars, conflicts, or prolonged oligarchic dictatorships that deeply polarized Central American societies and created a perception that any challenge to the social order was a political threat as well. Because LGBTI individuals challenge the deeply felt assumptions of many individuals in those countries about the proper gender roles of men and women, sexual minorities have frequently been considered a threat to the stability of those societies. As such, LGBTI identity, which would in most Latin American countries be considered a largely social transgression, takes on a political dimension, vastly augmenting the danger of violent persecution beyond the kinds of antigay violence otherwise documented in Latin America.

Second, as a result of these social upheavals and political polarization, *rule of law* has become severely compromised. Rule of law is usually defined as the existence and implementation of law independent of corruption, political partisanship, or irrelevant biases. However, social conflicts and the resulting polarization meant that law and security became less important than political concerns and the goal of subordinating nonconforming sections of society. Without rule of law, societal groups that are subject to societal or other persecution have little or no recourse to the state for protection, particularly when state actors share the same prejudices as the society at large, and may in fact hold those prejudices more strongly.

Third, the breakdown of rule of law has greater implications for sexual minorities than simply making them more vulnerable to antigay violence. For example, many Salvadorans, Hondurans, and Guatemalans, gay and heterosexual, experience a real threat from physical violence at the hands of organized gangs for various motives. For gay individuals, however, that risk is exponentially greater, since perpetrators of that violence understand that sexual minorities can be physically assaulted and even killed with near-impunity from state prosecution. The widespread social acceptance of anti-gay discrimination and antigay violence, which is particularly prevalent in organized gangs, aggravates this already-deadly situation.[7] From a practical perspective, it is not difficult to appreciate that a person who can be robbed, assaulted, or killed with impunity is much more likely to be a victim of such crimes than a citizen who has recourse to state security forces to protect her or him.

The United States has essentially operated as a processing center for gang members, as Hondurans and Salvadorans come to the United States, join gangs, and return to those countries to form their own gangs. Many of those returning gang expatriates are even primarily English speaking. In a sense, the United States has exported the most nocent aspects of its criminal gang culture to these countries of Central America.

Inexorable Progress

Although, as a generalization, the divergence between Latin America and the English-speaking Caribbean is real, this does not mean that the prognosis for progress in LGBTI rights in the Caribbean is entirely bleak. Although the relative difference in progress between Latin America and the Caribbean is likely to persist in the near future, some progress in acceptance of LGBTI individuals can nevertheless be witnessed in some English-speaking Caribbean countries. What is notably lacking in the English-speaking Caribbean is any significant progress in the realization of legal rights for LGBTI individuals. However, there has been more discussion of LGBTI rights in the Caribbean press, even though such discussion has frequently been highly controversial.

The progress in Latin America is largely due to the same trends affecting much of the rest of the world community. That the English-speaking Caribbean is less receptive to such trends does not mean that such trends have had no impact on the Caribbean at all. Indeed, the political elites are subject to some of the same transnational legal and cultural influences contributing to greater LGBTI tolerance in other countries, even if these influences are being met with greater resistance by the general populace. Nevertheless, history has demonstrated that the first steps toward legal recognition of LGBTI equality result from a complicated dialectic between elite norm creation and popular sentiment. The obstacles to that successful dialectic in the English-speaking Caribbean are greater than in Latin America, but the beginnings of that dialectic can be found in public discussions among the political and academic elites. History has also shown that once the dialectic has begun, its effect in ultimately realizing fundamental human rights for LGBTI individuals is inexorable.

Notes

1. For example, the high number of people from Latin American and Caribbean countries granted asylum by various other countries attests to the documented, historically high level of violence in the great majority of Latin American and Caribbean countries (see Political Asylum and Research Documentation Service 2006).

2. Interview by the author, Nassau, February 4, 2002.

3. Tielman and Hammelburg argue,

> From a historical perspective, the English legislation against homosexuality has had (and unfortunately still has) appalling consequences for the legal position of homosexual men, and, to a lesser extent, lesbians in the former British colonies. The effects of the former French, Dutch, Spanish, and Portuguese colonial legislation against homosexuality are less severe. In general, nevertheless, Christian-based homophobia has damaged many cultures in which sexual contacts and relationships between men and between women used to be tolerated or even accepted. Recently, Christian Puritanism from the West, mixed with Islamic fundamentalism, has attacked homosexuality, even in countries where same-sex contacts had usually been tolerated. (Tielman and Hammelburg 1993, 249, 251)

4. Devon Carbado (1997), in "The Construction of O. J. Simpson as a Racial Victim," writes critically of the role the belief in black male emasculation plays in the black community, but notes that "this sense of Black male emasculation is very real in the Black community" (*Harvard Civil Rights–Civil Liberties Law Review* 32, no. 1: 83). See also Darren Hutchinson, 1999, "Ignoring the Sexualization of Race: Heteronormativity, Critical Race Theory, and Anti-Racist Politics," *Buffalo Law Review* 47, no. 1: 40–41.

5. CARICOM is a relatively advanced example of an integrated common market with efforts at free movement of people, goods, and services throughout the Caribbean region. Also, another rationale for the creation of the Caribbean Court of Justice resided in a perception of the Privy Council's role as a remnant of British colonialism. Nevertheless, the rationale of creating the Court of Justice as a means of permitting the death penalty presented a dilemma for those jurists who agreed with the rationale for the replacement of the Privy Council as an expression of regional sovereignty, but were opposed to the death penalty.

6. Of course, the United States has also participated in the overthrow of democratically elected regimes in South America, but U.S. involvement there was somewhat more indirect, the dictatorships were of shorter duration, and the dictatorships did not create socioeconomically polarized societies to the same extent as in Central America, where the purpose of the U.S. intervention was essentially to preserve a plantation economy.

7. Documentation by the U.S. government and human-rights organizations demonstrates the record of antigay persecution by state actors, and the very close nexus between "vigilante" groups that target gays and lesbians and members of the police force. As just one example, the traditionally very circumspect and cautious U.S. Department of State Country Report on Human Rights Practices for El Salvador, released on March 11, 2008, documents that "[t]here

were reports of violence and discrimination by public and private actors against persons with HIV/AIDS, and against homosexual, lesbian, and transgender persons, including denial of legal registration for a homosexual rights advocacy group" (U.S. Department of State 2008, section 2.b).

References

Amnesty International U.S.A. 2009. LGBT Legal Status Around the World. http://www.amnestyusa .org/lgbt-human-rights/country-information/page.do?id=1106576 (accessed April 1, 2009).

David, J. C. 2007. The Politics of Emasculation: The Caning of Charles Sumner and Elite Ideologies of Manhood in the Mid-Nineteenth-Century United States. *Gender & History* 19:324–45.

Gay and Lesbian Archives of the Pacific Northwest. 2007. Sodomy Laws Around the World. http://www.sodomylaws.org/ (accessed March 29, 2009).

Ottosson, D. 2006. LGBT World Legal Wrap Up Survey. http://www.ilga-europe.org/europe/ issues/international/lgbt_world_legal_wrap_up_survey_november_2006 (accessed October 13, 2009).

Political Asylum Research and Documentation Service. 2006. Country-Specific Meritorious Asylum Claims. http://pards.org/meritorious.html (accessed April 3, 2009).

Reinhardt, B. 1997. Examining Correlates of Homophobia in Heterosexual College Students. Paper presented at the Annual Meeting of the American Psychological Association, Chicago, August 15–19, 1997. http://www.eric.ed.gov/ERICWebPortal/custom/portlets/recordDetails/ detailmini.jsp?_nfpb=true&_&ERICExtSearch_SearchValue_0=ED412445&ERICExtSearch _SearchType_0=no&accno=ED412445 (accessed October 13, 2009).

Tielman, R., and H. Hammelburg. 1993. World Survey on the Social and Legal Position of Gays and Lesbians. In *The Third Pink Book: A Global View of Lesbian and Gay Liberation and Oppression*, ed. A. Hendriks, R. Tielman, and E. van der Veen, 249–342. Buffalo, N.Y.: Prometheus Books.

U.S. Department of State. 2008. *2007 Country Reports on Human Rights Practices: El Salvador.* http://www.state.gov/g/drl/rls/hrrpt/2007/100639.htm (accessed October 13, 2009).

Wikipedia. 2009. LGBT Rights by Country or Territory. http://en.wikipedia.org/wiki/ Homosexuality_laws_of_the_world (accessed April 2, 2009).

Wilets, J. 1994. Conceptualizing Private Violence against Sexual Minorities as Gendered Violence: An International and Comparative Law Perspective. *Albany Law Review* 60:989–1050.

The Fight and Flight of Reinaldo Arenas

Rafael Ocasio

BEGINNING ON April 20, 1980, thousands of Cuban emigrants began sailing in hundreds of small boats from Cuba, to seek greater freedom in Florida. Among them were significant numbers of what the Castro regime labeled "social misfits," including people with criminal backgrounds and with records of mental hospitalization. The refugees' major crime, however, seems to have been their desire to leave Cuba for the United States, as shown by the high number of refugees given immediate entry upon their arrival. At the end of a rather chaotic and highly controversial relocation process, Victor H. Palmieri, U.S. coordinator for refugee affairs for President Carter, indicated in a memo that 119,252 emigrants had sailed in small boats from the port city of Mariel, some twenty miles from Havana. By the end of the boatlift on September 29, 1980, according to media reports, out of 124,779 refugees, 121,000 had been released to family, friends, or sponsors (Preston 1980).

Among the "social misfits" expelled from their country were gays and lesbians, including the renowned novelist, short story writer, poet, and playwright Reinaldo Arenas (1943–1990). He was released within one day, perhaps because he was sponsored by an aunt who was living in Miami. He was lucky; many other single gays who arrived without families in the United States were held in relocation centers and released only after gay associations served as sponsors.

Arenas arrived on May 5, 1980, in Key West, where he was processed at the Truman Annex of the U.S. naval facilities. He was penniless and, like all of his fellow travelers, he had been stripped of his material possessions, including his literary work in progress. In spite of his strong international reputation—particularly in France, where three of his novels published in French had received high critical praise—Arenas arrived, not as an intellectual seeking freedom of expression, but as a homosexual with a criminal record. The American reporter Marlise Simons (1980), writing from Havana for the *Washington Post* on May 12, reported Arenas's arrival in the United States as the arrival of a writer with "a jail sentence for a homosexual offense."

Simons also stated that Arenas barely escaped the Cuban authorities once it was discovered that he had attempted to leave the island under a pseudonym. That incident would become one of Arenas's most frequently narrated episodes of his hellish escape. According to his version, Arenas had changed the name on his passport to read *Arinas*, and, as his good friend Roberto Valero joked, like *harina* (the Spanish word for flour), Arenas flowed away from the island.

Documents available at the Carter Presidential Library do not estimate the numbers of *Marielito* homosexual refugees. The reason, as indicated in a press release dated September 9, 1980, was that:

> The Department of Justice has concluded it has the legal obligation to exclude homosexuals from entering the United States, but it will be done solely upon voluntary admission by the alien that he or she is a homosexual . . . To ensure a uniform and fair enforcement policy and to prevent invasion of privacy, INS inspectors have been directed not to ask aliens questions concerning their sexual preference during the initial inspection process. However, if an alien makes an unsolicited, unambiguous admission of homosexuality he or she will undergo a secondary inspection.

According to that statement, this policy had been in effect since August 2, 1979, after the Public Health Service "announced it would no longer certify that homosexuality is a mental disease or defect" (records of the Cuban-Haitian Task Force-RG 220, Public Affairs File, box 22). One assumes that no queer refugee volunteered that information. Even today there is no known concrete number of gay refugees, but the numbers were often characterized as "thousands."

Who was Reinaldo Arenas, and why did he choose to become one of the most vocal figures among activists in exile opposed to the Castro regime, to the detriment of his literary reputation? Arenas was born in 1943 in a rural village in the remote eastern *Provincia de Oriente*. He became for a short period of time proof that the Cuban government's literacy campaign, among the nation's first openly socialist projects, could produce literary jewels. Among the first generation of trained socialist students, the so-called Young Communists, Arenas witnessed in 1961 one of the most controversial socialist projects of the Cuban Revolution: the nationalization of private lands. Against his wishes, Arenas eventually became a farm manager. His heart was set, however, upon becoming a writer.

When Arenas wrote *Hallucinations; or, The Ill-Fated Peregrinations of Fray Servando*, his second novel, at the age of twenty-four, Havana was still the glitzy city that had enchanted Ernest Hemingway and Hollywood stars, and would soon become Arenas's favorite literary setting and his preferred sexual playground. The book was a way to contest the revolutionary political code of the so-called new man, of which the iconic representation was the macho rebel Che Guevara. The concept of the new man did not allow space for gays, who were kept away from revolutionary projects by means of national campaigns in which they were rounded up in police raids and sent to work camps that were established after 1963. Those camps also housed other people considered "antisocial elements," most particularly young people who refused to participate in revolutionary projects, and people with strong religious convictions, mainly Protestants such as Jehovah's Witnesses, and Catholic priests (Alonso 1985).

Arenas avoided apprehension for quite some time, even though he had a rather open homosexual life, including sexual acts at public beaches, an activity well known to his friends. Perhaps he was testing the limits of his ability to escape police raids, a skill that he often bragged about. But Arenas was not so lucky in his capacity as a writer. Although *Hallucinations* won a national literary contest in Cuba in 1967, the official publishing house stalled publication of the novel, perhaps because of its open allusions to homosexuality. Always fearless, in 1967 Arenas did not hesitate to smuggle the novel to Paris. Publishing abroad without permission from Cuban cultural institutions was then, and still is, a violation of Cuban revolutionary regulations. With the publication in 1968 of the French translation of *Hallucinations*, Arenas became an instant celebrity. The French press declared it one of the best novels published in French translation that year, an honor that it shared with Gabriel García Márquez's *One Hundred Years of Solitude*. Arenas became a cause celebre as one of the few underground writers in Cuba who dared to publish his smuggled works abroad. That fame would lead to his incarceration in 1973 for "ideological deviation."

When his third novel, *The Palace of the White Skunks*, appeared, first in French translation in 1975, Arenas was in prison after his arrest in 1973 at a Havana beach, where he'd been charged with the corruption of minors. His reputation as a sexual outlaw, almost at the level of that of French novelist Jean Genet, a writer Arenas admired, had finally caught up with him. As Arenas would vehemently claim, his arrest was carefully orchestrated, with the help of some of his "friends" acting as police informants. The local police set up an entrapment sting using two adult men who claimed at the trial to be minors.

Arenas's conviction led to his incarceration in the Morro prison, a four-hundred-year-old castle built for defense in Havana, which in the 1970s was still functioning as one of the most horrific of Cuban prisons. There he endured torture, such as isolation in perpetually illuminated cells so small that the prisoners called them "drawers." The interrogation sessions eventually paid off: Arenas broke down and signed a document in which he agreed that his work published abroad had a counterrevolutionary intention. Bravely, however, he did not reveal the names of any of the Cuban friends who had helped him to hide the manuscripts or to smuggle them abroad.

Arenas's criminal record as a felon, a homosexual pederast charged with corruption of minors, was to become his "ticket" out of Cuba. Arenas considered his arrest and the period during which he became a fugitive as political persecution. Perhaps the most debatable accusation was the charge of corruption of minors.

Soon after his arrival in the United States, Arenas took on the role of the outlaw in his numerous interviews with literary critics and reporters for Spanish-language newspapers, promoting himself as both a *Marielito* and a homosexual. From these two positions he became a political and a sexual outlaw. His increasingly graphic discussions of his gay sexual activity became part of his political activism against the Castro regime. He soon became known as the most vocal and most feared of antirevolutionary Cuban writers exiled in the United States or abroad. He maintained close ties with Cubans and *Marielitos* who had criminal records. He wrote personal letters to jailed *Marielitos*, and in 1987 went to Atlanta as a volunteer to serve as a mediator during the riots at the federal prison.

During his ten years in exile, he remained active as an organizer in national boycotts against the Castro regime, and he often underwrote their promotion. This was an economic sacrifice, because he was living in poverty in New York's Hell's Kitchen district and receiving care through Medicaid. One example of Arenas's work against the Castro regime was his open letter to Castro, which demanded that a plebiscite be held in Cuba, modeled on an earlier election in Chile. Published in France in 1989 with his good friend and exiled Cuban painter, Jorge Camacho, it was signed by 163 international figures, including Camilo José Cela, Ernesto Sábato, Federico Fellini, Juan Goytisolo, Manuel Puig, Susan Sontag, and Octavio Paz (Ojito 1989).

A self-made, clumsy activist, Arenas often vacillated between the gay and the antirevolutionary aspects of his message. Unlike other Latin American writers, particularly those living in the United States, Arenas began fairly soon after his arrival in 1980 a gradual coming-out process, which involved revealing select details about his criminal case and, controversially, outing fellow Cuban intellectuals, whether residing on the island or abroad. In the restrained climate of the early 1980s, he became one of the first Latin American writers to speak openly about his personal life as a gay man, always linked to his fierce attacks upon the Castro regime. As an out-of-the-closet writer, his gay activism was considerably less robust than his antirevolutionary work. Even so, unlike many other gay Cuban refugees, he took increasingly strong progay stances, and dared to explore in his writing a gay sexual aesthetic that often included autobiographical anecdotes and expressions of his own concerns about particular sexual practices.

Was Arenas too hot to handle for the mainstream press and the literary journals? He certainly was. An example would be his first self-outing interview, which took place in 1980 in conversation with Cuban American scholar Ana Roca. According to a letter from Dr. Roca to Arenas, in that interview they had spoken about "Cuba, politics, and gays." The interview was not published in its original form, however. Dr. Roca apologized that the journal that had accepted the interview for publication, *Americas: The Official Publication of the Organization of American States*, had edited out certain sections from the published version. [. . .] The following quotation is one of several statements that reflect Arenas's extremist positions concerning homosexuality and its marginal, criminal status in revolutionary Cuba. It is a plea for acceptance that even today might fail to gain acceptance in traditional U.S. society:

> There is a reality of which I have always spoken in regard to the homosexual world in Cuba. A totalitarian state is always going to persecute the world called gay, the homosexual world, simply because one needs a broader margin of liberty than does the person, let's say, conventionally established among the traditional canons of bourgeois morality. A reactionary system in Cuba, because we cannot speak of a revolutionary system in Cuba, because it is an absolutely reactionary and fascist system, has to persecute all those manifestations of liberty and rebellion, and every manifestation of liberty and rebellion, as much sexual as political and intellectual, indisputably bears implicitly manifestation opposed to tradition, to totalitarianism. A totalitarian system cannot permit itself the luxury of having in its country and in its jail people who do not avail themselves of that completely stupid morality.

In retrospect, it is understandable that in 1980 an American publisher might have been reluctant to deal openly with Arenas's charges of Cuban revolutionary homophobia, with his charges of severe human-rights violations. Furthermore, elsewhere in the interview, Arenas left some of his most serious accusations unsubstantiated, and mentioned the names of alleged victims. A publisher would have hesitated to print the specific charges or to reveal the identities of people still living in Cuba.

In his 1992 autobiography, *Antes que anochezca*, published as *Before Night Falls* in the following year, Arenas continued his political outing practices, which he intended as part of his campaign against Castro's revolutionary homophobia. The book was produced with the clear intention to shock its reader with revelations of extreme sexual practices. Not only was Arenas a pioneer gay activist—both in the Latino and in mainstream gay circles—but even today he's among a handful of gay Latin American writers who have been willing to discuss their sexual orientation. Arenas knew the publication of the autobiography would be posthumous, a fact that may explain his willingness to be explicit and even crude in many of its sexual descriptions. His raging behavior, whether in real life—he had many confrontations with dissenting critics, such as the Nobel Prize winner Gabriel García Márquez—or in his highly erotic literary explorations, provided him the outlaw status that he seemed to thrive on.

Arenas's memoirs are organized around specific episodes that seem to define his gay self, particularly ones that reveal homophobic attitudes in Cuba, and later in mainstream Latino communities in the United States. In his autobiography, for example, he makes an effort to recall his earliest memories of gay sex, which are more important to him than his Cuban ethnicity. An affection for Cuban culture does show itself, such as his happiness in remembering how Cuban peasants celebrate Christmas. Arenas's interest in Cuban identity is largely confined to the times when Cuban culture helped shape his gay identity or limited the development of his gay sensibility by restraining his literary and sexual freedom.

Although Arenas's autobiography deals with his life in Cuba, he was also writing as an out-of-the-closet Cuban ten years after his arrival in the United States. In documenting his sexual past, Arenas was writing as an outlaw, and not only in terms of engaging in sexual relations against revolutionary ideology or against sodomy laws in the United States. He engaged in sexual activities in public places, both in Cuba and in the United States, and his preference for unprotected sex is fully documented in his autobiography and in his private correspondence. Perhaps Arenas's most contentious statement in the autobiography is that his sexual dealings with minors were both numerous and consensual. His encounters with teenage boys, which he labeled as "exceptional adventures," became connected to a fixed process, a mandatory routine prior to his sitting down to write. Critics have ignored this side of Arenas's sexual makeup, a motif that appears in various forms in his writings.

Because of advanced AIDS, Arenas committed suicide on December 7, 1990. As a self-made personality, albeit one rather rough around the edges, Arenas became an activist and a gay advocate of national and international notoriety, and he did this despite knowing that his self-promoted identity as a gay man would result in rejection by his Latino and Latin American readers. This was the fearless Arenas that many people remember today, risking the consequences of saying in public and writing down in books things that promote outrage in those bound by cultural constraints and personal conventionality.

Note

All documentation and data about the Mariel boatlift come from the Carter Center in Atlanta, Georgia. Citations for items referenced in this article are available upon request. I would like to thank Dr. Ana Roca for her permission to quote from the unpublished manuscript of her interview, which she made public at the Cuban Research Institute (CRI) Conference at Florida International University, February 8, 2006.

References

Alonso, P. M. C. 1985. *Cuba, Castro y los católicos del humanismo revolucionario al marxismo totalitario.* Miami: Hispamerican.

Arenas, R. 1990. *The Palace of the White Skunks.* Trans. A. Hurley. N.Y.: Viking.

———. 1993. *Before Night Falls.* Trans. D. M. Koch. N.Y.: Viking.

———. 2002. *Hallucinations; or, The Ill-Fated Peregrinations of Fray Servando.* Trans. A. Hurley. N.Y.: Penguin.

Ojito, M. 1989. *Intelectuales piden apoyo a llamado pro libertad. El Nuevo Herald,* Dec. 2.

Preston, J. 1980. The Cuban Refugees: Escape to Captivity. *Village Voice,* Dec. 10–16.

Simons, M. 1980. Letter from Cuba. *Washington Post,* May 12.

Valero, R. *El mundo alucinante de Reinaldo Arenas* (The Hallucinatory World of Reinaldo Arenas). Reinaldo Arenas Collection (CO 232), Princeton University Library.

From Invisible Subjects to Citizens

A Report on Human Rights and Lesbians in Paraguay, 2006

Rosa M. Posa Guinea, Carolina Robledo Desh, and Camila Zabala Peroni,
on behalf of Aireana, *Group for Lesbian Rights*

Translated by Sarah Harper

CONSIDERING LESBIANS within the framework of women's rights will make visible the diversity among women, who represent half of the population. Analyzing the degree of compliance with international pacts and conventions on human rights ratified by Paraguay demands a reflection on the guarantee (or lack thereof) of these same rights for lesbians.

A proper consideration of lesbian rights requires addressing, in our current Paraguayan context, not only what are considered "specific" rights—for example, the recognition of civil unions and the right to adoption—but also the obstacles that lesbians face in exercising their human rights within a framework outlined by a state that, in its Magna Carta, is committed to removing these obstacles, but still fails to recognize discrimination against this particular sector.

If human rights mean "the affirmation of the dignity of the citizen with respect to the State,"[1] what we can emphasize is, on the one hand, the inaction of the state, exemplified by the complete lack of public policy or government response, but also in the encouragement of discrimination as a norm; and, on the other hand, the impossibility of communicating with the state, due to the inexistence of proper mechanisms of denouncement, and the stigma surrounding the act of denouncement caused by cultural pressures that condemn sexual practices that deviate from the heterosexual norm. Consequently, looking at 2006, as in other years, we encounter cases of the violation of the human rights of lesbians that go undenounced.

While contemplating various basic rights, the examples presented in this report demonstrate how women's sexual orientation influences the practice of their economic, social, and cultural rights, as well as civil and political rights, and how the stigma against homosexuality impedes, for lesbians, the fulfillment of the measures identified by the Convention Concerning the Elimination of All Forms of Discrimination against Women CEDAW and the Convention of Belém do Pará.

Labor Rights

Convention Concerning the Elimination of All Forms of Discrimination against Women, article 11: "States will adopt all necessary methods to eradicate discrimination against women in the realm of employment."

We maintain that discrimination against women is not limited to heterosexual women. The case of one lesbian who was pressured to resign while working for a private company is an example of how discrimination based on sexual orientation prevents the exercise of economic rights, and how discrimination operates as an impediment to acts of denouncement.[2] Discrimination against lesbians in the labor environment is evidence of this problem,[3] but the existing public policies that seek to eliminate discrimination against women do not include specifications for lesbians.[4]

One sixteen-year-old girl in the city of Itá was a victim of domestic discrimination, as well as discrimination in her workplace and discrimination in housing, for having publicly identified herself as a lesbian. After the news was released that her girlfriend had committed suicide, the girl was thrown out of her home and fired from the mechanic shop where she worked. She tried to acquire a lease for a place to live, but the landlords did not want to lease to a publicly open lesbian.[5] This case exemplifies the series of limitations that may be placed on a lesbian's economic, social, and cultural rights, such as the right to work and the right to shelter, simply for having "outed" herself. This instance of discrimination, and in reality all discrimination, impedes the fair practice of human rights.

The Right to Education and the Right to a Nonsexist Education

Convention Concerning the Elimination of All Forms of Discrimination against Women, article 10: "States will adopt all necessary measures to eradicate discrimination against

women, with the intention of ensuring equal rights for women and men in education
spheres . . . Subparagraph c) The elimination of all stereotyped concepts of masculine and
feminine roles at every level and in every form of teaching . . . Subparagraph f) The re-
duction of the female dropout rate . . ."

The pressure to conform to obligatory heterosexuality as the only valid gender norm
for women (and men) is one of the reasons that adolescent and young lesbians do not
get to fully exercise their right to education.

In a private high school in Asunción, an adolescent was victimized because of her
sexual orientation.[6] Two female peers entered into a relationship. When the parents
of the other students in the school found out, they petitioned for the expulsion of one
of the girls from the institution. The social sanction was concentrated on this girl
because she was perceived to be more masculine. Parents threatened to withdraw
their sons and daughters from the school. The young girl could not bear the pressure,
and left the educational institution halfway through the school year.

"The elimination of all stereotyped concepts of masculine and feminine roles," as
the CEDAW states in article 10 (above), not only demands reconsideration of the sexual
division of labor and the attribution of traditional roles to particular genders, but
also demands the elimination of obligatory heterosexuality as a gender imperative
and as the only model deemed acceptable in educational environments.

To our knowledge, concern over this category of dropouts or expulsions as the
result of discrimination against sexual orientation does not yet exist within the Ministry of Education, due to the fact that the Ministry does not consider these instances
to be acts of discrimination.

The Right to Health

[. . .] Instances of discrimination against lesbians in both public and private gynecol-
ogy practices begin with the simple presumption of heterosexuality—in other words,
bombarding the patient with questions about the existence of her sexual relations,
and on receiving a positive answer, asking if the patient uses contraceptives. When the
answer is "No, I don't use them," "I don't need them," or "I have sex with women," the
reaction is in the majority of cases discriminatory: "Ah! And what you do guys do?
What do you insert into each other?" Discriminatory instances range from these assumptions and questions to outright malpractice, often resulting in the delivery of
misinformation based on prejudice. One gynecologist advised a lesbian patient that
homosexuality was caused by the mother's use of contraceptives. Who can have faith
in the professionalism of someone who says that? How can one denounce misinformation based on the prejudice of a medical professional?

The state is obligated to provide nondiscriminatory health care, in accordance with the National Plan of Sexual and Reproductive Health 2003–2008 that establishes,[7] as a basic principle, nondiscrimination on the grounds of sexual orientation.[8]

The Right to Freedom of Expression

The right to freedom of expression can be defined as a citizen's right to express publicly and externally their opinions, beliefs, and all aspects of their personality.[9]

At a Multiplaza shopping center,[10] a young lesbian couple was held by private security for more than a half hour and abusively held "to look for drugs" after having kissed in public.

The incident began when these young women realized that a female worker at the mall was following them and "was watching them with distrust." On the terrace, the couple kissed, and some guards that were observing them took pictures of the women and then proceeded to ask them for identification. One of the girls did not have her ID, and the other refused to give hers. The guards left them waiting for thirty minutes. One of the guards abusively examined the young women; they were made to undress in order "to check for drugs." The guards threatened them with "community service" and forbade them to ever reenter the shopping center. They told the women that they were detained for not having proper identification. The couple did not want to report the incident for fear of involving their families.

Prejudice often clumsily connects homosexuality and the suspicion of a crime: rather than accusing the victims of homosexuality, they are are accused of some other crime. Once again, the difficulties of denouncement show us the distance we have left to travel, legislatively and culturally; to the struggle to achieve state mechanisms we must add the promotion of a culture of human rights.

The Right to a Life Free of Violence

The inter-American convention to prevent, condemn, and eradicate violence against Women, "Convention of Belém do Pará," article 3: "Every woman has the right to a life free of violence, in the public sphere as well as in the private sphere." Article 6: "The right of every woman to a life free of violence includes, but is not limited to, the following: (a) the woman's right to be free of all forms of discrimination, and (b) the woman's right to be valued and educated free of stereotypes of behavioral, social, and cultural practices based on concepts of inferiority or subordination."

One activist for lesbian rights, just moments before appearing on television to promote her group's activities, was insulted and beaten in the street by a member of her own family who asked her how she could do "that" to the family. The victim did not want to denounce the relative,[11] being aware of the difficulties that it would cause in her personal life. It still is very difficult, even when we define ourselves as subjects who deserve rights, and as victims of discrimination, to denounce our personal relations, because in the private sphere, barriers are erected as a result of a culture that espouses ideas such as "family honor" that are based on the control of women's sexuality. These situations are very painful and often connected with violence in the domestic environment.

The Right to Liberty and Personal Security

> *International Pact on Civil and Political Rights, article 9: "No person may be submitted to arbitrary detention or imprisonment. No person may be deprived of their liberty except in a case where the cause is clearly grounded in the law, in accordance with the established procedure of that law."*

In October of this year, a twenty-six-year-old woman was a victim of arbitrary detention in the Ayolas police station. The victim was at home with her partner when two police officers arrived by motorcycle and wanted to enter the house to see if they "had no drugs." She did not allow them to enter and demanded that they present a warrant. The police left and in ten minutes, returned with a patrol car and more officers; they entered the house, surveyed everything, and detained the woman for not having documentation at that time. Two hours later, a male friend went to the police station and brought the woman's identification card. The officers still would not let her leave until the following day. The chief asked her what relationship she had with the girl that was in her house, and the victim responded that it was her girlfriend. Then the chief began to taunt her, saying, "What do two women do in bed; who is the man between you two?" And the victim, fed up, responded, "What do you care?" Then the agent said, "What you need is someone to teach you a lesson so that you learn to like it." After that, she ceased to reply, for fear that the officers would abuse her. During the whole time that she was held, she was harassed by the chief. She spent the entire night in a cell, without a phone call, and the police never wrote up a report. The chief, when he finally let her leave, told her that they kept her overnight so that she would learn a lesson, "Because no one should talk back to me, especially not in front of my subordinates." Moreover, he told her to go to Asunción and "Don't come back to Ayolas." Even now, as we write this report, we are attempting to publicly denounce this case.

The report of the working group on arbitrary detention of the UN Commission on Human Rights devotes the fifth chapter of their report to "The arbitrary—and discriminatory—nature of detentions motivated by sexual orientation."[12] The group based their opinion on the declaration of the Committee on Human Rights, and stipulated that the reference to "sex" that occurs in paragraph 1 of article 2 and in article 26 of the International Pact on Civil and Political Rights should include "sexual preference."[13]

Recommendations

The recommendations of Aireana include:

- Include lesbians in national plans for equal opportunity between women and men.
- Implement mechanisms that guarantee the fulfillment of the CEDAW and the recommendations of the Paraguayan State Committee.
- Implement mechanisms that guarantee the fulfillment of the Convention of Belém do Pará, expanding Law 1600 to include a clause against domestic violence.
- Require municipalities to issue proclamations of nondiscrimination on the basis of sexual orientation in public and commercial places, among others.
- Pass a law that utilizes article 46 of the National Constitution against all forms of discrimination, and that includes mechanisms for denouncing instances of discrimination.

Notes

1. Nikken, P. 1994. *El concepto de derechos humanos*. In *Estudios básicos de derechos humanos* vol. 1, 15. San José, Costa Rica: IIDH Instituto Interamericano de Derechos Humanos.

2. Case recorded in Aireana, Group for Lesbian Rights. 2006.

3. See the report published by IGLHRC (International Commission on Human Rights for Gays and Lesbians), "Lesbians and Labor Discrimination in Latin America." Available at www.iglhrc.org.

4. Proposals to include lesbians in the Plan for Equal Opportunities between Men and Women 2003–2007 were presented by Aireana to the secretary for women in 2005.

5. *Crónica*, Wednesday, October 4, 2006.

6. Case recorded in Aireana, Group for Lesbian Rights. 2006.

7. National Plan of Reproductive and Sexual Health 2003–2008. Ministry of Public Health and Social Wellness. Asunción 2003. Available at http://www.unfpa.org.py/subprogramas/salud/index.php (accessed December 10, 2009).

8. There have been private initiatives this year [. . .] such as the agreement signed between Aireana and CEPEP (Paraguayan Center of Population Studies) regarding an investigation about

sexual health, HIV, and lesbians (financed by ONUSIDA, UNIFEM, and Mama CASH), in which awareness of nondiscrimination against lesbians was raised for the benefit of persons working within this center. Information is available at http://www.cepep.org.py/noti-cepep.

9. IEPALA Institute of Political Studies for Latin American and Africa. www.iepala.es.

10. Case recorded in Aireana, Group for Lesbian Rights. 2006.

11. Ibid.

12. December 16, 2002. Commission on Human Rights, 59th session.

13. Human Rights Committee, 1994, *Toonen v. Australia,* para. 8.7, U.N. Doc. CCPR/C/50/D/488/1992, March 31.

The LGBT Organizational Density of World Cities

Javier Corrales

THIS REPORT presents the first-ever index of LGBT organizational density of world cities. The index ranks leading cities according to how many LGBT-owned or LGBT-friendly organizations exist in the most important cities in the world. The data is extracted from *Spartacus: International Gay Guide 2007* (Gmünder 2007), a publication that for the past 39 years has been producing a directory of LGBT businesses and organizations in cities worldwide. Billed as the world's best "international gay guide," *Spartacus* is, at one level, a mere travel guide. But it could also be considered one of the few annual directories of LGBT-friendly business and organizations in the main cities of approximately 160 countries, for a total of almost 22,000 addresses. Precisely because its mission is to help gay travelers find gay-friendly establishments and resources abroad, *Spartacus* is a useful source for measuring the LGBT organizational density of world cities.

To construct this index, we counted the number of LGBT-friendly businesses (bars, clubs, discos, coffee shops, restaurants, hotels, bookshops, sex shops, saunas/baths, leather clubs, publications, media outlets) and organizations (centers, liberation groups, religious groups, health services, help organizations, switchboards, help lines) as listed in *Spartacus*. For each country, we listed its top 3 most populous cities. We then corrected for population, since smaller cities are expected to have fewer LGBT establishments, by dividing the total number of LGBT businesses and organizations by each city's population. This yielded the number of LGBT establishments per 1 million inhabitants.

Choosing the appropriate population data for each city was tricky. Some cities report 3 levels of urban population data: population for the inner city, for the urban area, and for the metro area. We chose the metro area mostly because "city" and "urban" data are missing for many cities. Consequently, our index is biased against very large cities: since *Spartacus* focuses mostly on gay businesses and organizations in the inner city, those cities with large "metro" populations will rank relatively lower.

With that caveat in mind, several features stand out in the ranking (see table 29.1):

1. There is a wide spectrum of LGBT organizational density, ranging from cities with no data (meaning that the editors of *Spartacus* do not identify or report LGBT-friendly businesses and organizations) to very gay-friendly cities (see figure 1). Rome tops the list with 61 LGBT establishments for every 1 million inhabitants.
2. The top 10 cities in the index, not surprisingly, are all among the world's richest cities.[1]
3. Most Latin American cities are located in intermediate positions—not quite at the bottom (score of 0 to 0.99), not quite at the top of the list (the 30 to 61 range). Only 2 of 33 Latin American cities have scores of 0 (Port-au-Prince and Tegucigalpa).
4. Some Latin American cities do quite well, with per-capita scores that are higher than New York City's: Montevideo, San José, Quito (remember, it is a per-capita index that favors cities with small metro populations).
5. Most Latin American cities do much better than the majority of cities in the developing world (the majority of which are at the very bottom of the list in the 0 to 0.99 range).

This gay-friendliness index must be treated with extreme caution, for a number of reasons. First, as mentioned, the index is biased *against* cities with larger metro populations. In the index, a city such as Asunción, with only 13 LGBT establishments, appears higher on the ranking than New York City, with 140 establishments; this is because Asunción's population (2 million) is so much smaller than New York's (21.8 million). Second, it is fair to assume that in larger cities, there is a greater chance of missing data, since it is harder for researchers to find all LGBT establishments in large environments. Third, this missing data probably does not occur randomly: it is a problem that is most likely to occur in the least wealthy parts of the cities; thus, the index says nothing about the number of gay-friendly organizations and businesses in the most populous and possibly poorest portions of most cities in developing coun-

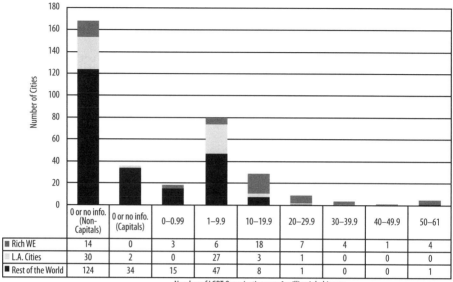

	0 or no info. (Non-Capitals)	0 or no info. (Capitals)	0–0.99	1–9.9	10–19.9	20–29.9	30–39.9	40–49.9	50–61
■ Rich WE	14	0	3	6	18	7	4	1	4
░ L.A. Cities	30	2	0	27	3	1	0	0	0
■ Rest of the World	124	34	15	47	8	1	0	0	1

Number of LGBT Organizations per 1 million inhabitants

Figure 1. LGBT organizational density index by world city

tries. Fourth, the source used, *Spartacus,* was not created by scholars, but by an organization that is trying to explore the tourism-friendliness of cities. It is thus somewhat biased towards more touristy destinations—mostly in Europe and North America—the regions of the world that in fact receive the largest influx of tourists. Fifth, the lack of *open* LGBT establishments does not mean that the city's gay *underground* life is nonvibrant or unsafe. The index thus underreports an important component of LGBT life—that which occurs in private or undisclosed domains, which affects the gay-friendliness of any city. Sixth, the index treats all organizations equally, regardless of each organization's relative strength. One well-functioning organization is more significant than multiple poorly run or weak organizations, but our index does not account for this variation in quality of organizations. Seventh, the index makes no mention of the legal and illegal forms of discrimination, which affect the gay-friendliness of any city. Eighth, the index does not take into consideration risk factors such as the incidence of hate crime or gender-based crimes, the impact of sexual epidemics, or the gay-friendliness of health services in each city, all of which affect the quality of life of LGBT persons.

Yet the index does provide the best account we have of the density of LGBT organizations in world cities. It follows the same methodology throughout, which makes it preferable to relying on comparisons of locally produced directories.

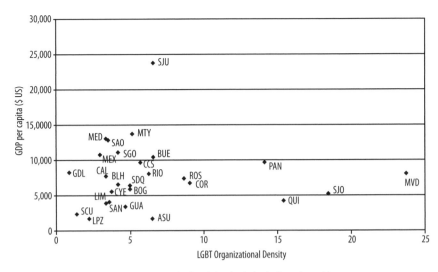

Figure 2. GDP per capita and LGBT organizational density in Latin American cities

The index shows clearly that Latin American major cities, on a per-capita basis, are not gay deserts. They are not as dense with LGBT organizations as European capitals such as Rome, Amsterdam, and Berlin, but they are not as empty as the vast majority of cities in the developing world continue to be, or as those very same cities were in the recent past.

In addition, the index reveals a number of interesting puzzles for future researchers to unravel. First, the ranking cannot be explained by income levels, which are usually considered to be a strong predictor of a vibrant associational life. Figure 2 plots the relation between the index scores for Latin American cities and each city's per-capita income, calculated by the magazine *América Economía*. There is virtually no correlation.

A better predictor of LGBT organizational density is "regime type." Figure 3 shows the correlation between the LGBT-friendliness index and levels of democracy in the country where the city is located. The measure of regime type used is the "Freedom in the World Index" produced by Freedom House.[2] This freedom index assigns two scores per country: one for political liberties (ranging from 1, freest, to 7, least free), and one for civil liberties (same scoring). Figure 3 adds both the civil and political liberties scores, creating a scale ranging from freest countries (2 points, one for political liberties plus one for civil liberties) to least-free countries (14 points, 7 for political liberties plus 7 for civil liberties). Figure 3 shows, not surprisingly, that the cities in mostly authoritarian regimes (those scoring 7–15) tend to have low gay-friendliness scores,

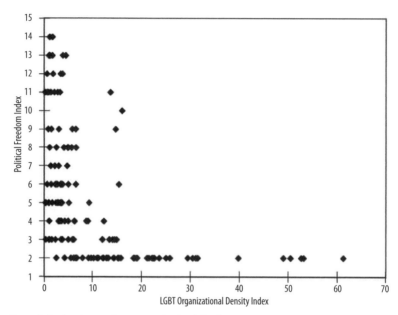

Figure 3. Regime type and LGBT organizational density

suggesting that regime features matter: authoritarianism tends to block a city's gay-friendliness.

However, even this predictor is imperfect. It is not correct to say that higher levels of democracy always yield high LGBT organizational density. Within the 2 score for regime type, there is far more variation in LGBT organizational density values. Levels of democracy seem to be a necessary but not a sufficient condition for a healthy density of LGBT-friendly spaces.

Notes

I would like to thank Lee Badgett for her comments, and Sarah Harper and Rachel Meketon for their research assistance.

1. These are cities in the richest countries in the world, including Western Europe, the United States, Canada, Australia, New Zealand, and Japan.

2. Freedom House, www.freedomhouse.org/template.cfm?page=439 (accessed December 10, 2009).

Reference

Gmünder, B., ed. 2007. *Spartacus: International Gay Guide*, 36 ed. Berlin: Bruno Gmünder Verlag GmbH.

Table 29.1. Ranking of cities according to LGBT organizational density (number of LGBT organizations per 1 million inhabitants)

City	Density	City	Density	City	Density	City	Density	City	Density
Rome	61.29032	Thessaloniki	14.88834	Singapore	6.492147	Kaohsiung	3.418803	Amman	1.415929
Amsterdam	53.15789	Beirut	14.70588	Lodz	6.422018	Ho Chi Minh City	3.392857	Santa Cruz	1.35135
Prague	52.67176	Riga	14.45466	New York	6.422018	Medellín	3.380282	Dubai	1.342282
Antwerp	50.45045	Stuttgart	14.33962	Rio de Janeiro	6.229508	**Cali**	3.333333	Nairobi	1.290323
Zurich	50.45045	Marseille	14.28571	Zagreb	6.227758	San Salvador	3.333333	Shanghai	1.156069
Berlin	48.99408	**Panama City**	14.0625	Naples	6.060606	Donetsk	3.320421	Yangon	1.08108
Brussels	39.79058	Phnom Penh	13.66906	Taipei	6.043165	Kharkiv	3.278689	Damascus	1.071429
Montreal	31.46667	Athens	13.42857	Tel Aviv-Jaffa	5.806452	Durban	3.259259	Valencia	1.058201
Barcelona	31.08434	Rhine-Ruhr North	13.21739	Yerevan	5.785124	Almaty	3.252033	Tokyo	0.988024
Copenhagen	30.43478	Melbourne	12.88591	Caracas	5.625	Johannesburg	2.987013	Homs	0.970874
Vienna	29.44162	Rotterdam	12.83784	Birmingham	5.490196	Kathmandu	2.985075	Ulaan Baatar	0.970874
Stockholm	25.78947	Cape Town	12.30769	Monterrey	5.063291	Lusaka	2.941176	Seoul	0.948276
Helsinki	25	London	12.25	**Bogotá**	4.970414	Mexico City	2.941176	Jakarta	0.939597
Montevideo	23.63636	Toronto	12.07547	Tbilisi	4.958678	Bucharest	2.926829	Harare	0.91954
Auckland	22.65625	Sofia	12	Haifa	4.950495	Surabaya	2.735043	Osaka	0.903614
Dublin	22.42991	Göteborg	11.20797	Santo Domingo	4.918033	Saint Petersburg	2.722513	Cairo	0.880503
Valencia	22.1519	Porto	10.94891	Colombo	4.8	Managua	2.678571	Casablanca	0.774194
Budapest	21.53846	The Hague	10.21898	Guatemala City	4.705882	Kuala Lumpur	2.47191	Alexandria	0.594059
Madrid	21.17647	Warsaw	9.684211	Minsk	4.444444	Izmir	2.45614	Nizhniy Novgorod	0.588235
Lisbon	19.1453	Belgrade	9.271523	Belo Horizonte	4.210526	Katowice	2.45614	Hai Phong	0.551268
Sydney	18.97143	Brisbane	9.139785	**Santiago**	4.201681	Dakar	2.376238	Ankara	0.522876
Oslo	18.58736	Guadalajara	9.033203	Maracaibo	4.044944	Busan	2.237762	Delhi	0.28436
Paris	18.49246	Córdoba	9.032258	Aleppo	3.826087	La Paz	2.222222	Nagoya	0.242424
Milan	18.43972	Rosario	8.661417	Hanoi	3.764706	Manila	2.142857	Calcutta	0.193548
San José, C. R.	18.38235	Chicago	7.897436	**Guayaquil**	3.75	Moscow	2.089552	Bombay	0.187793
Bangkok	16.02339	Los Angeles	6.703911	Taichung	3.71134	Tunis	1.777778	Lahore	0.127389
Manchester	15.75758	Buenos Aires	6.592593	Kiev	3.609023	Havana	1.684211		
Quito	15.38462	San Juan	6.545455	Lima	3.536585	Beijing	1.653543		
Lyon	15.38462	Johor Baharu	6.542056	**São Paulo**	3.529412	Bandung	1.587302		
Vancouver	15.17241	**Asunción**	6.5	Istanbul	3.504274	Daegu	1.495327		

Note: Of the top three most populous cities per country, only cities scoring higher than zero are reported.

PART 6

Diversities Within

Political Practices and Alliance Strategies of the Chilean GLBTT Movement

Héctor Núñez González

Translated by Sarah Harper

> If we accept that they see us, we also accept that they are watching us.
>
> Leo Bersani, *Hornos*

[...] I CANNOT begin this essay without recalling, briefly, the thirty years that have passed since the military coup in Chile that overtook the democratic government of Salvador Allende. That September 11, 1973, democracy was repressed, leading the way to a long and painful sixteen years of bloody military dictatorship. Years have passed since the restoration of democracy, but impunity for crimes committed by the dictatorship persists, and memory of Chile's repressive past seems to fade. It is necessary, now more than ever, to continue striving for and demanding truth and justice. The words "*Dónde están?*" ("Where are they?"), referring to those who were "disappeared" under the repressive regime, will remain etched in the history of the Chilean and Latin American people for those who fought and continue to fight against fascist oppression. [...]

In 1991, the *Movimiento de Liberación Homosexual* (Homosexual Liberation Movement) erupted onto the Chilean sociopolitical scene. After years of discussion, debate, and alliance making that incited a dialogue about sexual minorities and broke the boundaries of exclusion, the *Movimiento de Liberación Sexual* presented itself as a force of social and cultural change that reclaimed its *derecho de diferencia* (right to be different) against the repressive uniformity of the majority identity. The groundbreaking cultural and performative interventions of the group *Yeguas del Apocalipsis* (lead by artists Pedro Lemebel and Francisco Casas) are also significant. The first organization of *Lesbianas Chilenas* (Chilean Lesbians), within the group *Ayuquelen*, was formed after the homophobic murder of activist Mónica Briones in 1984.

The nascence of the *Movimiento de Liberación Homosexual*, in 1991, was accentuated by the demand for justice and truth raised [. . .] by the *Agrupación de Familiares de Detenidos Desaparecidos en Chile* (Collective of Relatives of Victims of "Disappearance" in Chile). Homosexuals, lesbians, and transvestites adopted this dialogue of human rights as their own, in order to petition for respect for diversity of sexual orientation. One morning in 1992, as part of the march, mottoes promoting sexual diversity were spread across placards, banners, and flags. Writer Pedro Lemebel remembers this event in his tribute to the deceased founder of *Agrupación de Familiares de Detenidos Desaparecidos*, Sola Sierra:

> The drag queens of the processional have painted and adorned themselves as if it were Carnival; all of gay culture is present, loud and proud, to march through the *Alameda* neighborhood and scream: "Justice! Justice! We want justice!" [. . .] The next day all of the papers covered the march that topped off its scandalous performance by denouncing impunity.

Sola Sierra could not have understood why the multitudes of homosexuals participated in that particular march, demanding respect. She was, for a long time, disgusted with the gay movement and did not share the desire to unite the gay front with its human-rights counterpart. In time, coalitions were formed and the presence of gays, lesbians, and transvestites in human-rights marches was applauded. [. . .]

Following international precedent and complicit with the feminists of the *Casa de la Mujer* (Women's House), *La Morada*, and other sectors tied to the national Left, gay-lesbian visibility converged within a political group founded by multiple leftist activists.

The birth of this group was spurred by a tragic event. On September 4, 1993, sixteen homosexuals burned to death in the nightclub Divine in Valparaíso. Ten years have passed since this voracious fire, believed to be motivated by homophobia, and the arsonists are yet to be found, leaving behind a shadow of doubt. Accusations surrounding this homophobic incident continue to circulate; a decade later, this tragedy has become the focal point of the desire for the vindication of the rights of sexual minorities in Chile, as well as a historical reference point for the activities of the GLBTT pride movement.

This milestone, which undoubtedly impacted public opinion at the time, inspired the new pride movement to lobby for the abolition of the law against sodomy—article 365 of the Chilean Penal Code—that prohibited, under penalty of imprisonment, homosexual practices. This demand was fundamental for the gay struggle during the first half of the 1990s.

Feminists, as well as other social and cultural players, supported this political objective within transitional Chile; they saw in the penalization of sodomy an outdated and paralyzing "custom" carried over from an oppressive period.

But the initiative was not immune to criticism, even from groups within its own ranks. Lesbians, suspecting gay chauvinism, denounced the institutionalization of the homosexual movement and distanced themselves from the foundling alliance. [. . .] This disjuncture continues today and worsens with the new arrivals of gay men to the national political arena. During the 1990s, the feminist movement dealt with its own divisions, fomented by the Chilean state and its discriminatory policies toward women. The *Servicio Nacional de la Mujer* (SERNAM)—a group that, with ministerial rank, controlled the dialogue between the state and feminist representatives—with time, diluted feminist power. [. . .] In addition, a political consensus imposed by *Concertación por la Democracia* (Alliance for Democracy), a government alliance, began to be felt by women's movements and unraveled the network formed by feminists in the 1980s.

On the other hand, gay men had to develop their own plan of attack in the wake of the AIDS epidemic and its sad homosexual obituary. For many, it was necessary to distinguish, on one side, the fight for civil liberties, in which homosexuals would not let themselves be associated with the pandemic, and, on the other, the urgent need to prevent the spread of HIV/AIDS, because queens were dying.

This debate created yet another division in the gay movement—one that at that time lacked many lesbian followers. The decadence of the incipient organization was owing to its inability to generate clear political projects that revitalized previously failed objectives, such as cultural and legal change during the beginning of Penal Code reform. Therefore, the organizations *Movimiento de Integración y Liberación Homosexual* (MOVILH), Lambda, and the *Coordinadora Lésbica* created the basis from which the new *Movimiento Unificado de Minorías Sexuales* (MUMS, United Front of Sexual Minorities) originated, whose birth was marked by the overturning, in 1998, of Penal Code article 365. This milestone would represent one of the most important achievements of the gay movement. However, the victory was not celebrated equally by lesbian groups, who believed that the situation limited their sexual rights, which up to this time, had not been mentioned in the Penal Code.

Battling the HIV/AIDS crisis [. . .] continues to be, even today, the fundamental aim of MUMS activists, but without lesbian participation. However, these women would begin to create their own spaces of political dialogue. They involved themselves in HIV/AIDS-prevention work with the *Comisión Nacional del SIDA* (CONASIDA, National AIDS Commission), part of the *Ministerio de Salud Chileno* (Chilean Ministry of Health). [. . .] At this time, it was vital to intervene politically and advocate for change in the current models of AIDS prevention, specifically those models directed at homosexuals. These men and women, invisible to the public and stigmatized by the Catholic Church and conservative parties, were, paradoxically, the group most affected by the pandemic.

Undoubtedly, this alliance gave the homosexual movement an invaluable political turnaround. The crisis situation demanded it, and soon, their fierce activism succeeded in developing abilities and expertise to mediate between the state and the gay population in the fight against AIDS.

Thus, a close relationship developed with the state through CONASIDA and other nongovernmental organizations that sought strategic alliances for the benefit of AIDS prevention and the civil liberties of sexual minorities. With the arrival of the socialist government, headed by Ricardo Lagos, in 2000, regular conversations and round-tables were held for many types of civil conflict, from "disappeared" persons, to indigenous claims, confrontations between businesses and workers, and even the demands of homosexuals. This system, along with the efforts of civil society organizations, brought forth a public debate over "discriminated minorities." The first meeting took place in the basement of the *Palacio de la Moneda* in 2000 (literally, in the basement of the president's office). One can see the importance that the socialist government was giving the issue. As a result, the *Oficina de Tolerancia y no Discriminación* (Office of Tolerance and Nondiscrimination) was established, but, with a low profile and barely enough capacity to execute its objectives. Today, it remains a small bureaucratic office that supports an array of minority groups who are supporters of the state. [. . .]

Within this office, MUMS began to integrate and make alliances, creating the *Foro por los Derechos Sexuales y Reproductivos* (Forum for Sexual and Reproductive Rights), as well as the *Foro de la Sociedad Civil* (Civil Society Forum), both of which still operate today. [. . .] MUMS continued its coalition building and began to distance itself from leftist groups that were outside of the government alliance, creating, in its wake, the *Comité de Izquierda por la Diversidad Sexual* (Committee of the Left for Sexual Diversity). This organization, led by the Communist Party, proposed a gay candidate for the 2000 parliamentary elections—who received hardly any support from homosexual activists, directly causing the severance of this group from other pride movements. The *Comité de Izquierda por Diversidad Sexual*, in collaboration with popular assemblies, contributed to the creation of the *Primer Sindicato de Trabajadoras y Trabajadores* LGBTT (First Union of LGBTT Workers). [. . .] The Communist Party's alliance with gays was highly criticized, both publicly and privately, by other activists and militants of diverse groups, who accused the leftist party of institutionalizing the homosexual movement. The situation was taken advantage of by progovernment gays, in order to discredit the labor directors who supported the alliance, as well as to back a political discourse clouded with lesbophobia and travestophobia, purporting that "scandalous transvestites" and "unnatural lesbians" hindered the gay movement.

Amid all this alliance making and criticism, the organization *Travestis y Transgénero de Chile*, or *Traves Chile* for short (Transvestites and Transgenders of Chile), was born. With the help of MUMS and state-sponsored AIDS-prevention projects, *Traves Chile* organized and later became autonomous. Then transgender activists would have another political success, taking advantage of the collaborative environment, when they burst onto the national public scene in early 2000, piquing media interest and inspiring debate within the government, political parties, and civil society. These acts demonstrate the discrimination faced by the transgendered at the hands of the state (especially those working in the sex industry) as a result of article 373 of the Penal Code, which castigates "immorality" and "bad practices." These actors also denounced the mysterious and unresolved murders of street workers. These outcries, surprisingly, were answered by the mayor—leader of the most reactionary conservative faction and a strong supporter of the president—Joaquín Lavín. The transgender activist Silvia Parada commented on the unlikely partnership in an interview with the *Revista de Crítica Cultural*: "We have a very good relationship with Mayor Lavín. He is the only person, the only politician, despite his affiliation with *Opus Dei*, despite the fact that he is a conservative of the extreme right, that has supported us. Not even President Lagos, a socialist, did the same."[1]

The political Right's involvement, made permanent by the Catholic Church's offering of sewing classes for transvestites and the subsequent renovation of a sewing school (still in use today), alarmed and upset other gay-pride organizations that felt more represented, historically, by the *concertacionista* government and the communist Left.

Although Joaquín Lavín's involvement was celebrated by the Catholic Church, the major media corporations had a field day with this new "alliance," underscoring the "conversion" of sinful transvestites into repenting Christians. The precarious situation of Chilean transgender people and their historic social marginalization led them to value the Right's initiative and to criticize mainstream gay pride movements that, in their passion for "more modern" recognition, have begun—like other neighboring countries—to debate about civil unions. This debate was fomented by the success, in this arena, of the gay citizens of Buenos Aires, Argentina. [. . .]

Conservative involvement in the birth of transgender organizations does not have, in my opinion, any other result than to reinforce stereotypes about Catholics and conservatives who appropriate the transvestite body—a symbol of the transgressor because of its superimposed and peripheral identity—in order to neutralize controversial political discourse and to assuage transvestite demands.

The *homonormalization* of gay/lesbian discourse, propagated by political parties and financial benefactors of gay projects, requires leaders of GLBTT groups (bound by their alliance with *concertacionista* officials) to succumb to the linguistic schematic of the patriarchy in power, yet it places important demands of sexual diversity on legislative and governmental agendas. Ironically, the sly hands of the political Right and the Catholic Church disrupt transvestite discourse to develop their own justification of their support for "lost souls."

This transvestite/conservative alliance is known within gay and lesbian movements as the "*traición travesti*" ("transvestite treason") to the country's historical political process—a betrayal that strengthens the discourse that recasts the gay man into a more masculine being, as well as damages the vitality of the pride movement's political fight. This unique transvestite-conservative partnership, that the *concertacionista* government does not trouble itself to dismantle, continues to shut doors in the faces of transgender citizens, who, by responding to the offer of alliance by Mayor Lavín, clash publicly with other gay activist groups. [...]

The events that have marked the evolution of GLBTT activism and its ties to party practices that generate disagreements and estrangements along the way reveal the conflicting discourses of sexual diversity and minority subjectivities within traditional political parties. These important events have yet to precipitate a debate at the highest level of party directorship, or in the offices of policymakers; if it has not happened in the *concertacionista* parties, much less is to be expected of the far Right. The election of a bisexual to the central committee of the Chilean Communist Party is one deserving exception.

Without doubt, political parties, the new government, and cynical LGBT movement leaders—whose lust for political power overcomes their sense of public duty—have hindered the circulation of a more revolutionary discourse against the political-cultural structure of heterosexuals. Effectively, they are responsible for continually recasting sexual minority movements as agents to be domesticated with minimal access to power.

Note

1. Parada, Silvia, interview by Sebastián Reyes, *Revista de Crítica Cultural* 25, November 2002, 72.

"The Gay Pride March? They're Not Talking About Me"

The Politicization of Differences in the Argentine GLTTTB Movement

Aluminé Moreno

Translated by Sarah Harper

[...] WHO ARE the subjects of sexual diversity that constitute the GLTTTB movement of the city of Buenos Aires?[1] Differentiation among participants is based on disputes over the definitions of identity posited by this social movement (based on gender, on sexuality, on social class), and on diverse understandings of the state's role in the perpetuation of and the fight against the oppression of these subjects. [...]

Existing literature about social movements associates the GLTTTB movement with identity politics (Adam, Duyvendak, and Krouwel 1999, 4–5). This notion refers to a series of struggles during the twentieth century whose protagonists have mobilized in the name of race, gender, ethnicity, sexuality, nationality, and religion. This type of mobilization contrasts conceptually with other types, in which political intervention is tied to the common interests of a group relative to its position in the social relations of production, or in which the principal differences are considered a question of political postures, the "politics of ideas" according to the definition given by Phillips (1995, 1–2). [...]

In interviews I conducted,[2] the protagonists of the Buenos Aires GLTTTB movement discuss the concept of identity politics, question its effectiveness, and resist including their practices under this umbrella category. However, for the majority of those interviewed,[3] this label serves as a starting point for a criticism of political identities constructed around experiences connected with sexuality and gender, for a consideration of the consequences of the differences derived from social class, and for the formulation of diverse political programs associated with the sexual-diversity movement.

The Politicization of the Body, of Gender, and of Desire

> I can't go out and fight for an identity that I don't have. In the name of what?
>
> Patricia, lesbian activist, *Desalambrando*

> The problem with identities is a very serious one, you see, identity is a thing. . . . It's just a thing. So, it has a static nature.
>
> Laura, lesbian activist, *Izquierda* GLTTB

Political strategies that resort to sexuality- and gender-based identities have been criticized in different contexts, because identities that are invoked for the mobilization of sexual diversity are founded on "the dichotomies produced by society (homosexual/heterosexual, man/woman) [that] are the base of oppression; the fluid and unstable experiences of the self are fixed to serve as mechanisms of social control" (Gamson 2002, 143). Identity politics are questioned because they simply resort to the same perspective on social relations that produces the subordination of nonheterosexual subjects: that is, to the idea that marginal social groups exist in accordance with their sexual orientations, sexual practices, or gender identities that are far from heteronormative. From this point of view, identity politics is an example of symbolic violence (Bourdieu 2003, 49, 146–47), because it reinforces the same classifications that produce the subordination of subjects of sexual diversity. [. . .]

Although the aforementioned analysis is based on a sociohistorical context different from that of contemporary Argentina, some of its elements prove useful for understanding the disputes about identities articulated by the local GLTTB movement.

To begin with, lesbian, gay, and bisexual identities are often grounds for controversy among participants in the sexual-diversity movement. A large portion of those interviewed question the very idea of identity, and emphasize the restrictive effects that this label can have with regard to experiences and subjectivities. Contention arises from the consequences (intentional or not) of the definitions of sexual identities and gender understood by the GLTTB movement that ultimately regulate experiences, and exclude those who do not subscribe to these characterizations:

> Sometimes it was bad to be too feminine, sometimes to be too macho . . . Sometimes it was bad to be too much of anything, but, having an identity like that, so cut and dry, there's a very clear limit, and that is really messed up because there are a lot of people

that get left out, because they're not part of the dominant society but they're also excluded from those other spaces, you know? (Laura, lesbian activist, *Izquierda* GLTTB)

One finding that emerged was that many interviewees expressed a general criticism of the supremacy of gay identity in the social movement. Within the GLTTB movement, gay middle-class men seem to occupy a position of privilege to which others are subordinate. Even interviewees who presented themselves as gays attempted to draw limits within their identity's attributes by employing differentiation strategies.

Diatribes against the role of the activists and organizations representing gay interests signal a monopoly of political representation and privileged access to symbolic and material resources. Various lesbian activists, transvestites, and bisexuals explain the issue by pointing to the notion of subordination of gender: the values within which men have been socialized constitute an advantage in the competition intrinsic to political activity (Moreno 2007).

Lesbians, in particular, have called attention to the fact that the movement's agenda does not reflect their demands. The words used by one interviewee refer both to critical situations, such as the AIDS epidemic, and institutional violence against transvestites and transsexuals, as well as to the subjectivity and the construction of the lesbian collective as possible elements of an explanation of their difficulties in integrating themselves into the GLTTB movement under conditions of equality:

No because finally, I mean, lesbians have been, I imagine that some of my peers have already told you this, but it's a feeling that I have, that within the GLTTB movement, we've been losing ground. First, with the AIDS struggle. All of us lesbians allied with the boys, asserting that we had to take care of them, more or less a maternal thing that society imposes on you. Well, we were sort of pseudomothers. After that, with the transvestite case, poor transvestites, they're being killed. They suffered more than we did, right? So, there was that. Let's ally with the transvestites, let's support their cause, because it's a good one, I mean, I did it . . . And we couldn't sit down, ground ourselves and say, "Well, we're here, and we have this list, these are our problems, and this is a list of our demands." It's like at that point we always lose our footing; I don't know if it has to do with questions of socialization or what. It seems to me that lately, in the last few years, this tendency is reversing a little, but even so, it's still costing us a lot. (Patricia, lesbian activist, *Desalambrando*)

Just as some gay activists try to differentiate themselves from the privileged masculine identity, one female interviewee affirms her interest in deconstructing the association between the categories *lesbian* and *woman*. This activist participates in feminist spaces that try to include lesbian needs and demands, and she constitutes an example of the dual militancy that is common among lesbian activists who simultaneously participate in the sexual diversity and feminist movements:

From that point on, I began to participate in a feminist group that was called *Las histéri-cas, las mufas y las otras*. Sometimes I feel a little socially marginalized, but I don't know, it's as if you just get used to it. It was really funny when at the last meeting of *Las histéri-cas y las mufas* we were asked: "How many are in the group?" "Well, we're eleven." Then I said: "No. We have to be able to say that we're ten and one lesbian." "Ah, you're right" . . . It's not just a question of visibility but also, in terms of identity, the lesbian question is very strong, not just an expression of difference of sexuality. For me, talking about identity, it's already a question about a different gender. And that's the way I live it and feel it. I mean, it's not just a good thing politically to say, "I'm lesbian." If you say *woman*, I don't absolutely identify with that word, which doesn't mean that I can't work for women's rights; in a way that's what we were talking about, they're one and the same. We have common agendas with gay men and common agendas with heterosexual women and each one just depends on how we do. (Patricia, lesbian activist, *Desalambrando*)

Bisexuality destabilizes gay and lesbian identities when they are defined exclusively in terms of eroticism between persons of the same sex. Activists who present themselves as bisexual often relate situations in which they were questioned about the supposed ease with which bisexuals are integrated into heteronormative spaces. For bisexuals, participation in homosocial spaces is not exempt from difficulties. For example, one interviewee confesses that he feels "diluted in a collective of gays and lesbians" and that it becomes difficult to find conditions under which he can politicize his bisexuality.

In the interviews, there are references to the low visibility of bisexuality as actually being an advantage for bisexuals. Some interviewed activists interpreted the absence of issues concerning bisexuality on the agendas of sexual-diversity movements as a consequence of bisexual privileges, which would explain the inexistence of a specifically bisexual activism:

If politically we think that it's strategic to join with other identities of gays, transvestites, transgenders, etc., in order to form a common agenda, there are many other things that are . . . I don't know, I would love it if there was a bisexual organization in which both male and female bisexuals could participate—there are also male bisexuals—so that they could have their agenda and identify their specific issues. But that organization doesn't exist. So, my response is this: if that organization doesn't exist that means that they don't have any claim to make to society. I can't, as a lesbian, assume an identity that isn't claiming anything, what they need is to assume that . . . But I can't go out and fight for an identity that I don't have. In the name of what? (Patricia, lesbian activist, *Desalambrando*)

More frequent among the interviewed activists than reflections on bisexuality are considerations of transgender identities. The differences with respect to this question constitute a key point in comprehending many of the alliances and confrontations within the GLTTTB movement. The interviewees refer to the irruption onto the political scene of transvestites and transsexuals during the mid-1990s as a turning point in the way in which nonheteronormative experiences and subjectivities are conceptualized.

In accordance with Gamson's approach, one can state that the controversy surrounding identities articulated by the sexual-diversity movement is intensified by the participation of transvestites, transsexuals, and transgenders in activist spaces where the relationships between *gay* and *male* and *lesbian* and *female* identities serve to define group borders. Trans- identities call into question the supposed biological base of gender identity, a supposition left intact by a politics based on the notion of sexual orientation.

This challenge has two dimensions. First, the participation of activists who resist being identified as women or men, on the one hand, demonstrates that the terms *man* and *woman* can have multiple meanings. On the other hand, their efforts to join sexuality-oriented organizations—which do not necessarily prioritize issues of gender—may inadvertently end up reifying the terms *man* and *woman*, or at least, allowing them to remain too easily accepted. Accordingly, one transgender lesbian activist narrates the way in which her presence brought about the redefinition of the criteria of participation in an activist lesbian space, and coincided with the subjective redefinition of some members:

> But, afterward, there were other women of *Lesbianas en Lucha* that left because they said, contrary to what I believe, that the lesbian NGO didn't suit them, that they felt more trans . . . That was funny because in one instance one of them said: "Because I don't feel lesbian, I feel trans." So I said: "Well, if that makes you feel better"—I told the others that did feel lesbian—"I feel more lesbian than trans, so I'll stick with you." That was surprising; no one thought that I would come out like that. (Dora, transgender activist, *Lesbianas en Lucha*)

Secondly, the demand for inclusion by transvestites, transsexuals, and transgenders in some activist environments attests to the fact that there are certain requirements for participation in organizations, or for the configuration of coalitions founded on the classification of subjects according to the "authenticity" of their gender or sexual identities:

> We, for example, always worked within what was, at that time, the GLTTB movement and not as much within the women's movement, something that *Las Lunas* did, for example. *Las Lunas* and the *Otras* were separatists, so they only worked with women and didn't want to know anything about transvestites or gays, and the transvestites, for them and for many feminists, were men disguised as women that profaned the feminine identity and things like that. It wasn't like that for us. We used to work with gays, with transvestites; we worked with them a lot. (Laura, lesbian activist, *Izquierda* GLTTB)

One important aspect of the transformations spurred by the participation of transvestites, transsexuals, and transgenders in the GLTTTB movement is the way in which new issues were prioritized and incorporated into demands on the agenda of sexuality-based political groups. First, there are some who attempt to combine the claims of these subjects with gay, lesbian, and bisexual demands. Then, there are those who argue that the situation of transvestites, transsexuals, and transgenders should be privileged because, as a population, they find themselves living in critical conditions based on their lack of access to basic social politics. A final group maintains that the questioning of the relationship among sex, gender, and desire that constitutes transvestite identity should top the list of priorities of the sexual-diversity movement. Several interviewees posited this idea, but their arguments varied. While some noticed a type of intrinsic radicalism in the presence of transvestites, transsexuals, and transgenders within sexuality-based political groups, others opted for a type of domino theory applied to the social valorization of nonheteronormative subjectivities. In the following fragment of an interview, many of the aforementioned opinions mix, and moreover, the interviewee hypothesizes that if social acceptance of an identity that destabilizes the gender order is achieved, gay and lesbian identities (implicitly less controversial) would simultaneously be positively affected:

> Because of this, I sometimes believe that the transvestite question is much more important than the gay-lesbian one, because I believe that if we achieve the acceptance of transvestites, the acceptance of gays and lesbians will be something much more digestible, for lack of a better term. I think that many radical things are presented within . . . like the sex-gender system for one, sometimes it seems to me that it's much more important to fight for transvestite problems than gay and lesbian ones . . . Because in general the movement often takes the opposite approach, am I right? (Marcelo, gay activist, Alliance of Activists against Social and Sexual Marginalization and Oppression [AGAMOSS])

In addition, the incorporation of transvestites, transsexuals, and transgenders in the sexual diversity collective calls into question demands that used to be considered part of a consensus. While one group of activists considers the claim for antidiscriminatory methods to be a glue holding together the social movement, one transvestite activist questions the notion that the inclusion of sexual orientation and gender in the antidiscriminatory clause of the city constitution, an inclusion called for by gay/lesbian and feminist organizations, constitutes a step forward for transvestites, transsexuals, and transgenders. In reference to the article in question,[4] this activist upholds that while seemingly a step forward, this clause silences the specificity of transgender identities and, furthermore, that part of the blame rests with gay and lesbian organizations that fought for the change:

We defended tooth and nail that article [article number 11] that in reality, didn't even consider us . . . It just mentioned sexual orientation, it said gender but in reference to women . . . So, it seems to me that trans persons interpret this in specific themes, supporting an agenda that not only erases the possibility of our establishing an agenda, but instead, further complicates our cause . . . Who's going to go back to reform the constitution now in order to add gender identity? Don't reform it again! And if they do reform it, Macri will do it.[5] And he'll take out sexual orientation! . . . I mean, they are making themselves more visible and establishing a political agenda in concrete terms that's all messed up with dichotomies and social guidelines. (Marisa, transvestite activist, Association for the Struggle for Transvestite and Transsexual Identity, ALITT)

Lastly, a portion of the interviewees thought that the participation of transvestites, transsexuals, and transgenders in the GLTTTB movement obligated the group to rethink the question of the interests of sexual diversity subjects within the context of social class differences.

The Sexualization of Social Class

[. . .] Nancy Fraser affirms that the identity-based conflicts take place in a world of exacerbated material inequality. These conflicts involve demands for recognition that feed the mobilization of subjects grouped around national, ethnic, sexual, and gender identities. She maintains that the political grammar that underlies these demands often implies that "group identity replaces class interest as the principal motive of the political mobilization. Cultural domination replaces exploitation as a fundamental injustice. And sociocultural recognition displaces economic redistribution as the remedy for that injustice and the ultimate goal of political struggles" (Fraser 1997, 11).

The dilemma posited by Fraser is dealt with in different ways by the interviewees. Some indicated their agreement with the preeminence of demands for recognition by the state; others believed that the GLTTTB movement should concentrate its efforts on modifying norms of access to consumption and property as the key to reversing the subordination of subjects of sexual diversity. Some also upheld the idea that the types of claims should be evaluated according to their individual sociopolitical contexts.

If the participants of the social movement in general use complex definitions of gender and sexual identities, the same does not occur with respect to social classes. The first issue that presents itself is the intimate association among subjects of the social movement and certain social classes. While the majority of the interviewees argue that interests expressed by gay and lesbian activists are middle-class demands, transvestites, transsexuals, and transgenders emerge as "natural" spokespersons of the interests of the popular and marginal sector.

For some of those interviewed, this aforementioned association explains the fluctuation of the social movement between the demand for special rights (gay-lesbian movement) and the demands for universal policies (transvestite, transsexual, and transgender movement). From this perspective, this divide is reflected in the way in which groups and leaders prioritize either the fight for civil rights (gay-lesbian movement) or claims for economic and social rights (transvestite, transsexual, and transgender movement). In terms of concrete demands, the interviewees consider that recognition of same-sex partners and their rights to adoption are primarily gay-lesbian demands that reflect middle-class interests, and are methods that ultimately seek recognition of subjects. Meanwhile, the right to work, home ownership, health, and education are perceived as demands prioritized by transvestites, transsexuals, and transgenders, and are connected with the necessities of popular sectors and function essentially as redistribution measures. [...]

Another aspect worth mentioning concerns the stereotypes involved in these arguments over special rights vs. universal policies. These stereotypes can be placed on a continuum: at one end we find extreme gay men, undeniably of the middle-class and generators of an assimilationist agenda, and at the opposite extreme transvestites, transsexuals, and transgenders, unavoidably radical in their demands and belonging to popular sectors. Lesbians and bisexuals are located somewhere in the middle. When it comes to the class origins of transsexuals and transgenders:

> Here there's not only the gender dynamic, there's also the social class dynamic ... For me, here lesbians are better than middle-class gay men, who are mostly professionals, who have big salaries, who take vacations ... I don't have anything in common with them ... And what's more, they have ideas that aren't very progressive. With those people, I don't have ... With the gays in general, I don't have affinity, I don't have anything in common ... With the lesbians, yes, because it's a female thing, a gender thing ... Me, in a gay space, it's obvious that I'm not going to militate ... It's an identity that I don't understand. (Dora, transgender activist, *Lesbianas en Lucha*)

In some activist discourses, social class is almost as destabilizing for the movement of sexual diversity as transgender identities themselves. For some interviewees, mobilization surrounding social class interests would structure an agenda of demands radically different from the one constructed by the sexual-diversity movement from the 1980s to the present. [...]

Sex and the State

[...] Some activists argue that identity politics correspond to a specific historical moment in the alliance between the GLTTTB movement, the state, and other political actors. From this point of view, identity politics is understood in a hostile context, in which there is no political opportunity for demanding more than just "negative rights" (Meccia 2006, 56), such as protection against institutional and social violence. In other words, the strategies of this moment in time were primarily defensive ones. [. . .]

Bernstein (1997) affirms that the exhibition of identities that emphasizes differences among subjects of sexual diversity and other social groups is more common in contexts where there are no channels of transmission for open demands by these subjects. These circumstances promote emphasis on particularities as a medium for constructing solidarity and facilitating political mobilization (Bernstein 1997, 541). This reading is similar to that developed by a participant in the GLTTB movement who considers that identity politics fit within a historical period that began with the return to democracy during the mid-1990s, and that it became obsolete in the years to come:

> I think that at the beginning of the '90s, the middle of the '90s, the context was one thing, where there wasn't as much GLTTB visibility, there was a much higher level of prejudice and discrimination, there were many more elemental things to be achieved, let's say, from the political and social standpoint . . . and in that moment, I don't know if we were thirty, forty, fifty activists with all the fury and we defended ourselves strongly in terms of identity politics. We were people with very marked differences, very different. (Laura, lesbian activist, *Izquierda* GLTTB)

This interviewee depicts the hostile panorama that the sexual-diversity movement faced by citing institutional violence, the lack of public policy, the consequences of the AIDS epidemic, the severity of police edicts in Buenos Aires, and the isolation from other social movements, like the human-rights movement and feminism. In such an arduous context for the expression of nonheteronormative experiences, it makes sense to abandon differences between subjects of sexual diversity, such as ideological and partisan differences, and those derived from different experiences of eroticism and gender.

However, once the possibilities of impact on public policy and alliances with other social movements are generated, the development of identity politics is no longer a viable strategy for promoting rights. The argument developed in the previously quoted interview is taken up again by other participants, who also believe that participants of sexual-diversity movements should integrate with other activist spaces structured around social class, from which they can demand universal rights from the state. [. . .]

For some, the objective is to obtain a room of their own in the state, by way of a process that recalls one developed by women's movements in the 1980s and 1990s (Guzmán 2001; Archenti and Moreno 2004). One interviewee posits this development in pseudoevolutionary terms, as if its trajectory were almost inevitable:

On one side someone will want to be progressive and they'll introduce the word *sexual preference* or *sexual orientation* or *sexual choice*, and it all begins there. But I think that the issue now and in the future is culture. Culture and politics, not influencing the state but fomenting change from within, becoming part of the state. One of the first terrible discussions that I had with Jáuregui in the Farolito assembly, terrible, because I remember that in that moment I said, "We'll continue on this way and one day we'll have our very own office that reads 'Office of Gay Rights' in some ministry" . . . and Jáuregui lost it and said to me: "I'm not going to fight for some office!" But, well, that was just the beginning. (Rodolfo, gay activist, Society for the Integration of Gays and Lesbians in Argentina [SIGLA])

Others believe strongly that they must thoroughly consider the national political climate in order to evaluate the likelihood of being able to promote sexual diversity rights from within state institutions. One transvestite activist underscores the fact that more than considering the intricacies of each government department, it is also necessary to consider the heterogeneity that characterizes public bureaucracies, and evaluate which areas of the state would be more welcoming of this kind of group effort:

It would be necessary to begin to disarticulate this idea of the state as a unique entity that is inherently against its social counterpart . . . In this sense, I think that the claims and social changes at the institutional level . . . have a lot to do with an attentive and demanding society with respect to rights; and on the other hand, I think that there is no better way to mine state ideology than from within. I think that this is part of the same movement . . . I don't know if it will continue now, because everything is *aggiornando* the *K* era [reference to the presidency of Néstor Kirchner between 2003 and 2007], but with Menem there was a strong resistance from activists to become involved with institutions, and now these state institutions are much more permeable because they think that effectively there is a discourse that looks legitimate, a discourse of human rights fomented by Kirchner. And, in this sense, I think that it's very possible, I don't see it as an annoyance. It doesn't bother me that today an activist is getting involved with the state, because I think that above all there are practices. (Clara, transvestite activist, *Hotel Gondolín*)

The issue does not end with possible cooperation with the state, or with the option of some participants of the social movement integrating with public departments. There still remains to be explored the question of which type of public policy is necessary for counteracting subordinations associated with heteronormativity. On one hand, the interviews include allusions to the need for the existence of state agencies and special protection programs for subjects of sexual diversity. While some consider that these methods are necessary and positive, others criticize these strategies and consider them to be based on the notion of a minority that reinforces the same sexual and gender classifications that generate discrimination against nonheteronormative experiences.

On the other hand, for some activists the central issue becomes modifying the logic of state interventions by transforming the definitions of the beneficiaries of public policy.

> For example, when we won the debate with the *Instituto de la Vivienda* [Housing], we insisted that they include single persons, for example. Not even that, not even that . . . No, [we transvestites] aren't the *physique du role*, just like a single person isn't. But maybe a single person has an advantage, because [a single person] is, I don't know, hypertense [suffering from hypertension]. But we don't fit in this stuff of being hypertense or disabled, or abandoned, something like that . . . We don't fit in, absolutely not, and it still happens today in the state. (Marisa, transvestite activist, ALITT)

The recipients' characterization of state interventions is intimately connected with the construction of the figure of the ideal citizen (Bacchi and Beasley 2002; Moreno 2002). Some activists believe that the central objective when attempting to influence the state is to make possible the basic exercise of citizens' rights on behalf of subjects of sexual diversity. This type of strategy distances itself from those that privilege the creation of agencies and specific programs. Instead, the objective is to transcend the viewpoints of sexual diversity to effectively transform public policies into tools of inclusion for gays, lesbians, transvestites, transsexuals, transgenders, and bisexuals.

Finally, another set of voices demands the concentration of efforts in modifying cultural conceptions and stereotypes of "common interest," and considers full citizenship for subjects of sexual diversity to be a consequence of these modifications. Those who adhere to this platform advocate the deprioritizing of interlocution with the state via legislative proposals and public-policy initiatives, and instead embrace projects of understanding and the diffusion of positive values associated with nonheteronormative experiences and subjectivities. Exemplifying this perspective, one interviewee suggests that strategies centered on the state and the legal system can become counterproductive with respect to the day-to-day exercise of rights by subjects of sexual diversity.

> So I think that the most important change proves to be a cultural one, laws don't even come close, we can have five hundred thousand laws that don't come close to what we need. [Former national legislator and ex-president] de la Rúa succeeded in passing the [anti]discriminatory law three hundred years ago and it doesn't serve any purpose because people weren't empowered by the law . . . We have to change people's mindsets, and that can't be done with a law. With a law, the only thing you do is keep the government satisfied; they say, "Well, we're very politically correct and we don't discriminate," and so the international human-rights organizations give them a "Very good," because "You guys follow the laws and keep your word," and these organizations give the government more money, you know? But we keep on having the same problems. (Patricia, lesbian activist, *Desalambrando*)

[. . .] This panorama does not purport to be definitive. The GLTTTB movement is characterized by instability and variation in terms of its participating subjects, perhaps because this political space is under constant construction, and because the conflicts that constitute this space span a vast array of experiences of subjectivity that exceed the voices currently representing those implicated in GLTTTB politics.

Finally, the history of the sexual-diversity movement and the state strategies for confronting this question mutually affect one another. The state should not be conceived of as a monolithic entity, but rather as a meeting place for different social forces in conflict for the purpose of setting criteria that condition the inclusion/exclusion of citizens and the corresponding access to symbolic and material goods. [. . .]

Notes

1. The acronym GLTTTB refers to gays, lesbians, transvestites, transsexuals, transgenders, and bisexuals, and its uses are grounds for debate within different sectors of the social movement investigated in this essay. There are many controversies among the movement's participants about how best to label the movement. One major controversy has to do with which subjects are represented (or not) by the acronym and its uses in different contexts. The form most frequently used by activists to allude to the social movement is the "GLTTTB Movement" or "GLTTTBI Movement." The mention or omission of the *I* refers to the inclusion or exclusion of intersexuals as protagonists of the same political space. "Sexual-diversity movement" is an alternative way to refer to the same social movement. This formula is also used by activists, although it is not used as commonly as "GLTTTB Movement." Although GLTTTB and *sexual-diversity movement* have different connotations, in this work both terms are used interchangeably.

2. In this essay I present part of my analysis of sixteen in-depth interviews I conducted in 2005 and 2006 with participants of the sexual-diversity movement of Buenos Aires for an investigation regarding the construction of subjects, demands, and political incidence strategies of this social movement. In the following list of interviews, names were changed to protect anonymity: Ariana, *Futuro Transgenérico* (Transgeneric Future), Buenos Aires, July 25, 2005; Alejandro, former member of Alliance of Activists against Social and Sexual Marginalization and Oppression (AGAMOSS), Buenos Aires, August 1, 2005; Pedro, former member of Alliance of Activists against Social and Sexual Marginalization and Oppression (AGAMOSS), Buenos Aires, August 1, 2005; Susana, Association for the Struggle for Transvestite and Transsexual Identity (ALITT), Buenos Aires, August 23, 2005; Dora, *Lesbianas en Lucha* (Lesbians at Fight), La Plata City, August 24, 2005; Marcelo, former member of Homosexual Community of Argentina CHA, former member of Alliance of Activists against Social and Sexual Marginalization and Oppression (AGAMOSS), Buenos Aires, August 25, 2005; Marisa, Association for the Struggle for Transvestite and Transsexual Identity (ALITT), Buenos Aires, August 27, 2005; Fabián, former member of Homosexual Community of Argentina CHA, member of *Area Queer*,

Buenos Aires, August 31, 2005; Julio, *Area Queer*, Buenos Aires, September 2, 2005; Mariela, former member of the Society for the Integration of Gays and Lesbians in Argentina (SIGLA), member of *Asociación Docentes* GLTTTBI (GLTTTBI Teachers' Association), Buenos Aires, September 10, 2005; Laura, former member of *Lesbianas a la Vista* (Lesbians at Sight), member of *Acción Política* GLTTB (GLTTB Political Action), and of *Izquierda* GLTTB (GLTTB Left), Buenos Aires, September 21, 2005; Juana, *La Fulana* (A Place for Women Who Love Women), Buenos Aires, August 17, 2006; Rodolfo, the Society for the Integration of Gays and Lesbians in Argentina (SIGLA), Buenos Aires, August 17, 2006; Clara, *Hotel Gondolín*, Buenos Aires, August 18, 2006; Isadora, *Mulabi*, Buenos Aires, September 18, 2006; Patricia, *Desalambrando*, Buenos Aires, November 25, 2006.

3. I have left out of my analysis those groups congregated around what Figari (2006) calls aesthetic-expressive affinities, whose ends are associated with sociability, like the Bears Club of Buenos Aires.

4. Article number 11 of the Constitution of the Autonomous City of Buenos Aires protects citizens against discrimination based on sex, gender, or sexual orientation, among other sources of prejudice. It is available online at http://www.cedom.gov.ar/.

5. Current head of state of the City of Buenos Aires, leader of the center-right political party *Propuesta Republicana* (PRO).

References

Adam, B. D., J. W. Duyvendak, and A. Krouwel, eds. 1999. *The Global Emergence of Gay and Lesbian Politics. National Imprints of a Worldwide Movement.* Philadelphia: Temple University Press.

Archenti, N., and A. Moreno. 2004. *Las mujeres en la política. Estrategias institucionales y sus lógicas. Trayectorias, revista de ciencias sociales de la Universidad Autónoma de Nuevo León* 6, no. 15 (May–August): 32–49.

Bacchi, C. L., and C. Beasley. 2002. Citizen Bodies: Is Embodied Citizenship a Contradiction in Terms? *Critical Social Policy* 22 (2): 324–52.

Bernstein, M. 1997. Celebration and Suppression: The Strategic Uses of Identity by the Lesbian and Gay Movement. *American Journal of Sociology* 103, no. 3 (November): 531–65.

Bourdieu, P. 2003. *La dominación masculina.* Barcelona: Editorial Anagrama.

Figari, C. 2006. *Política y sexualidad abajo del Ecuador: Normalización y conflicto en las políticas GLTTTBI de América Latina. Orientaciones: Revista de homosexualidades* 11:27–46.

Fraser, N. 1997. *Justice Interruptus. Critical Reflections on the 'Postsocialist' Condition.* N.Y.: Routledge.

Gamson, J. 2002. *¿Deben autodestruirse los movimientos identitarios? Un extraño dilema.* In *Sexualidades transgresoras. Una antología de estudios queer,* ed. R. Mérida Jiménez, 141–72. Barcelona: Icaria.

Guzmán, V. 2001. *La institucionalidad de género en el estado: Nuevas perspectivas de análisis.* Santiago, Chile: Naciones Unidas.

Meccia, E. 2006. *La cuestión gay. Un enfoque sociológico.* Buenos Aires: Gran Aldea Editores.

Moreno, A. 2002. *Políticas sociales, ciudadanía y corporalidad: Vínculos y tensiones. Feminaria* 28/29 (July): 16–24.

———. 2007. *Participación de mujeres.* In *Diccionario de estudios de género y feminismos,* ed. S. B. Gamba, 248–51. Buenos Aires: Editorial Biblos.

Phillips A. 1995. *The Politics of Presence: The Political Representation of Gender, Ethnicity and Race.* Oxford: Oxford University Press.

The Feminism-Lesbianism Relationship in Latin America: A Necessary Link

Yuderkys Espinosa Miñoso

Translated by Joan Flores

A Personal Journey of Feminism and Lesbianism

WITH APOLOGIES to my colleagues who have always tried to deny the relationship between feminism and lesbianism, I must confess a real inability to subscribe to any political concept of feminism that dispenses with this link. This is [...] perhaps [...] personal [...] because [...] the politics of feminism to which I have subscribed since the beginning, and in which I still believe today, even at this point in the dissolution of the movement, cannot be thought of without the existence of lesbians; in the same way, the lesbian politics that interest me [...] cannot be thought of outside of feminist theory and practice. To deny or hide the link between these would be to deny my own history, my own foundation.

The feminist theory and practice that I encountered in the late 1980s [...] created a series of unexpected cataclysmic consequences in me. A familiarization with the theory, coupled with deep reflection about my own attachments [...] sparked an inquisitiveness [...] that led me to question my own desire. From there, dissident love was only a step away. In that moment, and still today, I felt that the path I had chosen could not have been another. For me, the reinscribing of desire itself was the biggest challenge, the ultimate liberation.

Mitilene [...] was the most radically feminist group that existed in the Dominican Republic in the 1980s. It was thanks to its existence that I nourished myself with that idea of feminism that I call an "experience of subjectivation" (2005) [...] And it was thanks to this feminism that I found and developed a lesbian desire as a sexual politics, and took pleasure in resistance. I sincerely believe that radical feminist politics and practice unavoidably lead you to "a choice for women," which tends to have as one of its consequences the development of a not at all insignificant lesbian erotic, and therein lies one of the problems faced by feminists who oppose the lesbianization of the movement. I have the sense that this experience of feminism as a journey to another place, as a resubjectivation, is an experience through which many of us have recovered our love for other women, once lost in our first infancy.

In the early 1990s, we began to perceive a change. [...]

Feminism was not the same, and now there was no space for the countercultural politics in which lesbians [...] became a standard, though marginal, of discourse and practice.

A new agenda of human and sexual rights began to appear on the international stage, heralding a space of articulation for the so-called sexual minorities. It was called the lesbian, gay, transvestite, transgender, and bisexual movement. In a time when lesbians ceased to be embraced by an increasingly heterocentric feminism, which, in a search for legitimization, kept pointing out the difference between being a feminist and being a lesbian, the GLBT movement was the new site of affiliation for many lesbians.

Though the first groups of homosexuals began to mobilize throughout the continent starting in the late 1970s, it wasn't until the 1980s and late 1990s that the movement began to have an international outlook. This movement, which aggregated different sexual identities and focused on the demand for recognition raised by Nancy Fraser (1995), had formalized as such in the U.S. and began to gestate in Latin America. [...]

With a strong push from financing agents, a new agenda was defined for lesbians, homogenized and diluted into that of other groups of dissident sexuality. Lesbians, driven by and contained in an increasingly fragmented discourse that considered different oppressions separately, particularly patriarchal oppression and heterosexist sexual oppression, were placed in the common fight for the right to inclusion through access to health and health care (the fight against HIV/AIDS), antidiscriminatory legislation, and the right to marry and to maternity and paternity.

Encounters, congresses, and seminars kept calling [...] the movement a "community." My ever-increasing closeness to theory and my subscription to feminist lesbian politics led me to venture into these spaces, as well as into the new institutionalized feminist space, where I have always been a type of dissonant voice, a kind of "problem." [...] Along with the pain at what is practically the disappearance of the lesbian figure from the feminist ambit, it has been a dagger to the heart to observe the evolution of the GLBTTI movement, through which, once again, the lesbian, *become* woman, has come to be forgotten, much like in any of the ancient patriarchal orders. [...]

Nonetheless, I can't fail to mention the gap opened in the mid-1990s by the autonomous feminism current in Latin America, in which many lesbian feminists, including myself, found an active space of resistance. I also cannot fail to mention the particular case of Argentina, where, thanks to a dictatorship extending to 1983, social movements, particularly the feminist movement and others enabled by it, were still in development throughout the mid-1990s. For example, the *Casa de las Lunas*, a feminist lesbian space in Buenos Aires, existed in a time of rupture when in almost every other place feminist lesbian politics had been canceled, discarded, and accused of separatism.[1]

In Chile, a self-denominated autonomous current, fundamentally articulated by feminist lesbians, managed, for a brief moment, to call attention to the loss of radicalism in feminism, with slogans and a vision of the movement impregnated with the spirit of a "women's community." They called for a reimagination of other ways of being in the world, as articulated in the writings and actions of Margarita Pisano (1996) of Chile, of Ximena Bedregal (1997) of Mexico, of the *Mujeres Creando* of Bolivia, of the journals and publications of the publishing house ATEM in Argentina, as well as of the *Chinchetas*, a group I formed along with Ochy Curiel in the Dominican Republic.

Though this movement did not identify with the feminist lesbian movement, I maintain [...] that it was the last collective resistance of note to the progression of a feminism that, emptied of its more radical stances, forwent the analysis of obligatory sexuality as a founding institution of the patriarchy, and of lesbians as a standard and imaginary of liberty and independence, available for all women, not only for [other] lesbians.

What autonomous feminism brought to the fore was the assurance that many had possessed in the 1970s and 1980s that removing the grounds that perpetuate the existence of women as a group in the service of males cannot succeed without a deep struggle with our own selves and our places in the world, with all that which sustains the normative ideas of gender and desire.

The Trajectory of Lesbian Feminism in Latin America

There is a vital link between feminism and lesbianism that,[2] I believe, has to do with an understanding of obligatory heterosexuality as a social institution responsible for the production of a feminine subject whose desire and identity ensure dependency on the male.[3] [...]

A feminist practice that goes beyond the demand for equality, identity, and rights risks upsetting the assumed unity of sex, gender, and desire [...] In this way, it points the way to self-questioning and personal experimentation, in which lesbianism appears as a conscious action and a desire to unite politics and life. In fact, there are many documented experiences of feminists who did not find, did not perceive, or did not confront their lesbian desires until they joined the movement. What I want to say with this is that enough historical proof supports the affirmation that a path of freedom for women is linked to a revision of the relationship with males on all levels, and that this has led many women to develop forms of sexuality and relationships that exclude or marginalize the presence of men in their lives.

Affirming this reality has been fundamentally difficult for a feminism whose struggle for inclusion made the lesbian figure problematic. [...]

A feminism given over to demands [for legitimization] resulted in the near disappearance of the political and symbolic force of lesbians in the movement. Feminist lesbians themselves had something to do with this, since in the 1990s many of them supported a human-rights agenda that they had the possibility of sharing with the rest of womankind. State feminism did its own strategic reading of the treatment of the lesbian figure in the least conflictive way, ergo, the most devoid of content. This was how, from questioning obligatory sexuality as a patriarchal institution oppressive to all women, a shift occurred towards a politics of respect for sexual diversity and/or sexual and reproductive rights. These initiatives coincided with the politics of recognition driven by the international GLBTT agenda.[4]

In turn, lesbianism, in frank opposition to a feminism oppressive to lesbians, transformed its proposal into a mere addendum to a gay politics focused on the demand for rights and recognition, attractive to financing agents. With the consolidation of an international agenda stripped of a complex analysis of the interrelation among the different oppressions of gender-class-race-heterosexism, focused on AIDS prevention and the demand for the legalization of homosexual couples, lesbians were relegated to second tier, made invisible by the gay advance and later, by the inclusion of transvestites.

Though lesbians have been the active producers of conceptual and theoretical arguments that have served as sustenance to sociosexual movements, it is gays and transvestites who, to date, have obtained the most benefit from these theories. I ask myself how a concept such as obligatory heterosexuality, incomprehensible outside of a critique of patriarchy, can end up being less beneficial for lesbians. This question deserves careful thought.

Notes

1. In addition to the *Casa de las Lunas*, Buenos Aires was home to many other lesbian spaces, such as *Lesbianas a la Vista*. I do not mention them because these spaces did not refer to themselves as feminist. [...]

2. For more on the trajectory of lesbian feminism in Latin America, see Hinojosa 2003 and Mogrovejo 2000.

3. See Butler 2001a and 2001b, and De Lauretis 2002.

4. [. . .] See Fraser 1995 and 1997 [. . .] and Butler 2000. [. . .]

References

Bedregal, X. 1997. *Permanencia voluntaria en la utopía.* Mexico City: CICAM.

Butler, J. 2000. *El marxismo y lo meramente cultural. New Left Review* 2 (May–June): 109–21. Originally published in 1998. Merely Cultural. *New Left Review* 1, 227 (January–February): 33–44.

———. 2001a. *El género en disputa. El feminismo y la subversión de la identidad.* Trans. M. Monasur and L. Manríquez. Mexico City: Paidós.

———. 2001b. *Mecanismos psíquicos del poder. Teorías sobre la sujección.* Madrid: Cátedra.

De Lauretis, T. 2002. *Diferencias: Etapas de un camino a través del feminismos.* Madrid: Horas y horas.

Espinosa Miñoso, Y. 2005. *Sobre el feminismo hoy: A la búsqueda de un otro sentido del ser y el hacer feminista en este tiempo.* In *Miradas desencadenantes: Los estudios de género en la República Dominicana al inicio del tercer milenio,* ed. G. Candelario, 99–119. Santo Domingo: Centro de Estudios de Género, INTEC Universidad.

Fraser, N. 1995. From Redistribution to Recognition? Dilemmas of Justice in a "Post-Socialist" Age. *New Left Review* 1, 212 (July–August): 68–93.

———. 1997. *Justicia interrupta: Reflexiones críticas desde la posición postsocialista.* Bogotá: El Siglo del Hombre Editores.

———. 1998. Heterosexism, Misrecognition and Capitalism: A Response to Judith Butler. *New Left Review* 1, 228 (March–April): 123–34.

Hinojosa, C. 2003. *Historia sobre la presencia pública de las feministas lesbianas.* Sentidog, May 16, http://www.sentidog.com/lat/?p=4188 (accessed December 15, 2009).

Mogrovejo, N. 2000. *Un amor que se atrevió a decir su nombre: La lucha de las lesbianas y su relación con los movimientos homosexual y feminista en América Latina.* Mexico City: Plaza y Valdés.

Pisano, M. 1996. *Un cierto desparpajo.* Santiago, Chile: Número Crítico.

Transvestism and Public Space

Transvestism and the Lesbian, Gay, Bisexual, Transvestite, and Transsexual Movement

Josefina Fernández

Translated by Zoe Fenson

> The principle of our struggle is the desire for all freedoms.
>
> Carlos Jáuregui, gay-rights activist, died 1995

THE POLITICAL organization of transvestites in Argentina is relatively recent, in comparison to that of other sociosexual groups, like gays and lesbians. By the 1970s and 1980s, some gay-rights groups already had their own modes of communication on which to rely, albeit in restricted circulation, and in the 1980s a gay-rights group received legal recognition for the first time.[1] Associations of lesbian women, many of whom started their organizational careers within the feminist movement, made their first public appearance in 1987.

Paradoxically, this history refers to the 1990s, a period in which Argentine society was immobilized, with weak or fractured social-change organizations. The social movements that, during the previous decade, with the opening of democracy, had possessed an important capacity to oppose and resist on different social, political, and economic fronts, began to unravel. Citizen participation in protests and petitions diminished notably during these same years in which, linked to gays and lesbians, transvestites began to organize. The first group to do so was the Association of Argentine Transvestites (ATA), formed in 1991. Within a short period of time, as a result of internal differences, ATA divided and formed two new organizations: the Organization of Transvestites and Transsexuals of Argentina (OTTRA), and the Association to Fight for Transvestite and Transsexual Identity (ALITT).

The Fundamental Milestone

At the tail end of a confrontation over a neighborhood denunciation of prostitution, a contingent of transvestite women approached the association Gays for Civil Rights, which agreed to assume legal defense of the case. In the process of interacting with this group, the women learned the first steps toward self-organization and formed ATA. A little ways down the road, initial differences in the core of the organization surfaced over whether transvestite groups should accept the practice of prostitution. Some felt that the issue should not be defended from an institutional standpoint; for others, collectively denying prostitution among transvestites amounted to little more than a lie:

> We separated because we thought differently. I was not in favor of prostitution, nor did I defend it, but I support it as a way to make a living for the person who chooses it. N. was in favor of prostitution, she defended it and flew the flag of prostitution, and L. stayed in the middle, in the sense that she supported both positions. From this base, N. formed OTTRA for the girls who were prostitutes in Palermo. At the same time, L. formed ALITT, so that our identity could take whatever form, including that of prostitutes. Those were three ways of thinking.

[. . .] At the same time that these organizations formed, transvestites began discussing different ways to be recognized in their identity. Without a doubt, their visibility as prostitutes was one of the cruxes of the dispute within the interior of these groups. For some, the transition towards social acceptance maintained transformism (whereby men wear feminine clothes for shows or special occasions, but still preserve a masculine daily appearance) as a party line, with transsexuality as the final destination and transvestitism as an intermediate point; for others, this proposition constituted a deception in the same vein as denying prostitution. A different project altogether was promoted by a third group, who warned of a need for self-examination of a socially situated identity that fell on the side of abject self-hatred, examination that sought acceptance not on the part of society, but on the part of the questioners themselves. [. . .] The impetus that they embodied seemed to impugn symbolic violence, to question those dominant schemata that had driven them to perceive and appreciate themselves according a devalued image, and so to subscribe to the views of a system of domination (Bourdieu 2000).

The impact that organized participation has had on the personal lives of transvestite individuals is an aspect that deserves to be highlighted. In the vast majority of cases, these collective spaces constituted spheres for sharing experiences and, in the discovery of similarities, to find relief from suffering. But the associations were also valued as places where rights were recognized, and where erroneous ideas about transvestite identity could be dismantled, places where, according to Bourdieu (1993) and as illustrated in the following testimonial, the point of view of the dominated class became the point of view of the dominant class:

> I grew a lot as a person (militating), I felt beyond personal abuse, I learned that I was far superior to them. Before, I didn't know if I was in the right or not. Now I know that the others are abusing us and that they're doing it deliberately, that they're committing a crime and that they do it consciously. And the greatest satisfaction is the friends I have made, that we feel proud of what we are, that we can walk freely, with our heads high, that we learned that we don't have to go out to fight in the streets, that we have to go out to convince, to start dialogues, that we have the right to enjoy the sun, the beach and all spaces, that each time we place ourselves more directly opposite those who mistreat us, that each time we overturn more and more of the myth of the violent, marginal, delinquent transvestite . . .

The organizations created an opportunity for transvestite individuals to clarify for themselves a past in which violence and crime formed part of their self-image. Through these groups they interacted with other groups and people whose solidarity and compromise were presented as "new weapons" with which they could confront their lives, and this contributed, in its turn, to the eradication of those images that subjected them to crime. [. . .] In addition, through these organizations, transvestite members found acceptance of bodies that subverted the "natural" order and caused them problems. In this case, one of them recalled, participation in collective spaces permitted her to extricate herself from a discussion of her body as "worthless."

> The most beautiful thing that ever happened to me in my life was thanks to ALITT; it was the day that I made peace with my body, when I looked at myself in the mirror and I said to myself: L. has tits, she has a dick, she's chubby, that's how it is and they can all go to hell.

The reflection initiated in these organizations did not turn them into therapy groups committed to working out problems of self-esteem; on the contrary, these organizations cast themselves as political entities and were valued by their members as places of struggle and confrontation against a society that deprived them of their most elemental rights. [. . .]

Even with differences among them, the transvestite organizations had a project in common to fight for; they collectivized concerns and discovered new worlds. In the plurality of dialogues that the organizational experience established among them, as well as among transvestite organizations and other groups and people, group members began processes of self-recognition that permitted them to distance themselves from those social constructs under which they had grown up, which they learned to consider damaging. Along the way, the characteristics that had burdened them in the past, and that were now determined by the positions that they assigned themselves in diverse social spaces, were points in question, thanks to the advent of new practices and new symbolic advantages. [...]

Even when transvestite organizations were born from gay-rights associations, the relationships between them were not, in the beginning, terribly pacific. In the words of an interviewee, the process of recognition of transvestites on the part of gays took time, during which they had to overcome their denial of transvestism:

> When we started in the lesbian and gay movement, there were few organizations that allied with us, and there was a lot of transvestitephobia. Even today, many gay people will not attend pride marches because we are there. They continue to think of us as men. They continue to trivialize our situation.

This denial of transvestism is remembered as being more pronounced in dealings with lesbian feminists:

> Back then [1993] we were rejected by the lesbians. They said we were men. Even then we were fighting so that they would put the word "transvestite" in the march, which was only gay and lesbian. The lesbians said that we should be happy that they let us participate, and I answered that I very much lamented being discriminated against by a discriminated group. That phrase prompted one group of the gays to take a stand on our side, while the lesbians and other gays remained on the other side. If you make note of the newspaper notices of that time, they ask readers to come together for the Third Gay and Lesbian Pride March, and below, in tiny print, it says: "lesbians, gays, bisexuals, transvestites, and transsexuals." The agreement was otherwise, but they changed it at the last minute when they were making the flyers, they made it tiny. The flyer was large, and below there was a white square that said, "Endorse..." in case anyone wanted to endorse it. So, we bought a stamp and we put it in the box, and those were the flyers that we distributed. For the fourth march we were prepared to put up a fight, but the same thing happened as at the third, they changed the flyers at the last minute. But still we had a greater presence at the march than before, with sequins and feathers, and in the media there were headlines like "March of Transvestites," "Transvestites in the Streets," "Colorful Transvestites," etc. At the fifth march they had agreed to call it the "Gay, Lesbian, Transvestite, and Transsexual Pride March." And they had to put the lesbians in front because they were the ones who were made invisible, so the march was called "Lesbian, Gay, Transvestite and Transsexual."

Gays and lesbians assigned a masculine identity to transvestite women, one that these last opposed without renouncing the place that they felt belonged to them in the movement towards sexual diversity. Incorporating the term with which they labeled themselves was the first gambit in the political opposition that transvestites were compelled to face in their relationships with gays and lesbians, in order to gain visibility as *transvestites*. Before this visibility was entirely recognized within the core of the movement, it was granted halfway in the Fourth LGBTT Pride March, where the participation of gays and lesbians was eclipsed by the corresponding transvestite presence. This strategy of self-presentation, chosen by a study group—"sequins and feathers"—was imposed in that instant over all discussions of gender.

Despite this, the struggle for acceptance by lesbians took years, and transvestite women would have to pass even more tests before lesbians would consider them part of the gay and lesbian movement, not just a group authorized to participate exclusively on occasion of the annual marches. [. . .]

Today transvestism is integrated into the LGBTT movement, and its strongest relationships within the movement are with gay organizations. Ties to lesbian women present greater difficulties and are almost always individual; with feminist activism these ties are even more problematic. Nevertheless, alliances have been built, and some feminists, like some gays and lesbians, stand by transvestite activists in their struggles and demands.

LGBTT Pride Marches

The precedent for marches celebrating lesbian, gay, bisexual, transvestite, and transsexual pride was set in 1991. The chosen month for the staging of these marches is November, to commemorate the date on which the first press medium of the movement was put into circulation in Argentina and Latin America. The newsletter *Nuestro Mundo* (*Our World*) appeared in print on November 1, 1967.

Preparation for the Eighth LGBTT Pride March

Preparation for the pride marches begins several months in advance, with weekly work meetings open to the entire lesbian, gay, bisexual, transvestite, and transsexual community. Community members may opt to participate through organizations or on their own.[2] As a matter of habit, these preparatory encounters begin with an agenda for the day, the themes of which are discussed and approved by consensus, a method deemed more democratic and conducive to debate than a simple vote. On the occasion of the Eighth LGBTT Pride March, which took place in 1999, the principal debates revolved around the acquisition of resources, the establishment of a unifying mission statement for the march, the placement of each participating group within the march, the selection of activities for LGBTT Pride Week, and the choice of speeches to read at the celebration.

The evaluation of possible sources of economic support focused on two theaters of action. On one hand, the implications and political costs of seeking resources outside the LGBTT movement were analyzed, especially the implications of seeking funding from the city government of Buenos Aires, whose position in the debate over the Code of Urban Coexistence had few positive consequences for the LGBTT community. On the other hand, the group discussed the role of gay bars that had supported previous marches with monetary contributions and loans of sound equipment, but which expressed a clear and explicit denial of transvestite and transsexual issues.

With respect to the city government of Buenos Aires, which would be asked to provide backdrops and sound, the majority of the participants, with the exception of the transvestites, indicated that it would only be necessary to explain the motivation for the request and that, once this was established, the government would not impose any kind of conditions. The transvestite participants, for their part, emphasized the right of citizens to use public resources without having their actions enter into the argument in any way.

> There is no need to give any explanation, we take what is ours and we're set. There's no reason why the box should have some sort of placard saying "Municipality"; if it has one, we'll take it off. I say we don't spend hours discussing this, let's move on. (OTTRA)

With equal conviction, they voiced a negative response to receiving economic support from those bars and gay dance halls that discriminated openly against transvestites. [...]

As if enacting a civil right that guaranteed citizens the ability to act without any sort of mediation, the transvestite organizers proposed avoiding the loss of visibility by erasing the identifying markers of the two conflicting groups: the city government of Buenos Aires would not be allowed to put up a poster advertising its contributions as such, and the gay bars would not be able to bring their own music.

As far as the underlying mission statement which would unify the march, the voices of the LGBTT community separated and developed proposals on their own, in some cases without regard to boundaries of identity. Nonetheless, the most pronounced differences occurred between gays and transvestites. In effect, the proposals of the gay community, for the most part, emphasized the necessity of creating a mission statement alluding to article 71 and decree 150/99 of the Code of Urban Coexistence; the rest expressed hope that the march and its mission statement would be a place to advocate for antidiscrimination laws like those protecting the right to marriage, adoption of children, and inheritance. This was not the case among transvestites, who roundly disagreed, arguing that a mission statement like the one proposed did not include them:

> We do not subscribe to the idea of laws. We must make an open break with all these concerns. We already know what the laws are; they are used however the one who uses them wishes. I do not agree with the idea of calling for laws. Call a rebellion, say that we will not live as we have lived all these years. Do not ask for more laws, marriages and all those things. (OTTRA)

On this theme, as on others that we will see later, the voice of transvestites and the voice of the lesbian community came together. Albeit with a more precise proposal, the lesbians understood that the mission statement of the march should not be directed to legislators or to governing bodies, nor should it refer to laws, but rather to the community, which must be mobilized. [...]

Toward the end of the decision-making process for the order of groups in the march, the participants evaluated questions regarding the national political climate, indicating whether it would be more or less convenient to "show off" one group before the others, in accordance with the visibility afforded each participating organization. Even giving weight to the fact that, during the preparations for the Eighth LGBTT Pride March, its organizers admitted that the problem of group visibility seemed resolved, the order in which groups should march provoked a long discussion. It was, above all, for the benefit of the lesbian groups, whose participation in previous marches, in contrast to that of gays and transvestites, received little media attention. Even if gays and transvestites did not fully agree, the lesbians addressed the need to resolve the economic differences that allowed certain groups to take advantage of more resources for their participation in the event—using music, costumes, fireworks—and, as such, to become more visible than other groups with fewer resources. The gay organizations quickly abandoned their place in the march and offered even to bring up the rear of the parade. The transvestite groups, whose visibility was guaranteed through the interest that they generated, as much among the media as the general public, proposed that they not claim a predetermined location. Assuming responsibility as the group with the greatest visibility, they offered themselves as "fishhooks" to a public that was always eager to see them.

"If the lesbians do not have their own visibility, then have them come along with transvestites, to whom the whole world looks. March at our side, and everyone will see them (ATA)."

Nudity, flaunting the body, was one of the elements that distinguished transvestites from the rest of the LGBTT community over the course of the marches, and for the celebration of this, the eighth, they petitioned the Organizing Committee for the opportunity to participate without clothing. [...]

Visibility, in the context of these celebrations, is a resource that tranvestites community has in excess, one they are able to distribute and share with others. This greater visibility did not stem from their being an economically advantaged contingent in relation to gays and lesbians. Street displays are a talent that had "found a home" among transvestites; it even became their way of life. [. . .]

The symbolic value attributed to the pride march is different for each of the lesbian, gay, transvestite, and transsexual groups that participate. It would seem that, while for gays it is an opportunity to appeal to public influence and request legal improvements, for lesbians it represents a moment of inclusion in the LGBTT community. For the transvestite community, it is a space for the denunciation of their living conditions, but it is also a space for celebration, nudity, and festivity.

As had happened with the decision of the marching order, the dispute over the visibility of diverse groups appeared again when deciding on the speeches to be read at the celebration and the posters and flyers that would be printed for promotion. The dispute over these speeches hinged on a single issue: addresses to a single identity group versus generally directed addresses. The former were speeches, grouped by identity, written by the distinct LGBTT organizations that made up the Organizing Committee. They were agreed upon within each group and then discussed and brought to consensus in committee; this constituted an occasion for each identity group to speak to its partners, distinguishing its members from what was called the "general discourse." This discourse was developed by the Organizing Committee itself and read at the end of the march, and its subject matter is habitually referred to as examples of problems on the national scale that affect the combined LGBTT community.

The majority of the gay participants involved in the organizing of the eighth march took on the responsibility of reading a single general address, in which they suggested that dividing speeches by identity group meant vindicating the "corporativist" character of identity itself. On this point, transvestite and lesbian groups united in their positions, dissenting with their gay colleagues. Both collectives proposed that there continue to be speeches from each identity group. These constituted, in the words of the transvestite organizations, an opportunity to instill in the transvestite community new vocabulary with which to identify itself, new worlds of possibility distanced from those in which they presently lived, shot through with violence and with laws that penalized them. This could only be achieved if these words were spoken by transvestite individuals themselves. [. . .]

The position of the gay participants in favor of a single address was, moreover, interpreted by lesbians and transvestite marchers as an attempt to render them invisible. [. . .]

But transvestites also sought visibility in the eyes of their own community in the flyers that they distributed in the process of recruitment for the march. They asked that mail and e-mail addresses of each participating organization be printed on the flyers. To the struggle of the transvestite community to avoid "erasures," a need was added to eliminate stereotypical images of transvestites for which the LGBTT community itself was responsible. [. . .]

The process of transforming the images that transvestites had of themselves, a process whose beginning the transvestite community attributed to organizational activity, continues within the LGBTT community, where transvestite groups fight to be recognized with new attributes.

As I have already indicated, the marches were traditionally preceded by what was known as "LGBTT Pride Week." In 1999 workshops were developed with the objective of promoting communication among diverse social institutions. When deciding which of these to invite to debate, divergent interests were expressed in the interior of the Organizing Committee. For most of the gay organizations, the workshops constituted a strategy to deepen alliances with groups of people who, like the LGBTT community, had combative relationships with institutional powers; for transvestites and lesbians, it was an opportunity for debate and discussion with those who existed outside of a defined community or who were not involved with one. [. . .]

This interest in taking advantage of the workshops to make clear to society the degrees of compromise assumed in important references to human rights was repeated when it came time to choose representatives for meetings with the media. The idea was to choose dissident voices, not allies. Perhaps because the debate that the LGBTT community had had with legislators was still recent, differences surfaced in defining this workshop. In the minds of the lesbian participants, the community had already heard too much of legislators.

For gay individuals, the officials' compromises had been beside the point and insufficient. Transvestite organizers deepened their opposition to meeting with legislators because of the uncertainty in politics that they promoted, even when, through politics, they wanted to favor the group in question. [. . .]

Over the course of the meetings organized on the occasion of the Eighth LGBTT Pride March, transvestite activists confronted the rest of the sexual-diversity groups over their eagerness over and favoring of forms of public presentation, of themselves and of the LGBTT community, designed to avoid any kind of association with the city government or with institutions like family and marriage, just as they avoided involvement with the law and those responsible for its development. Their position was clear: having been persuaded to be direct victims of the hypocrisy and deception that corroded all these institutions, and also, surely, as a result of feeling differently affected—compared to gays and lesbians—by the defeat that they had suffered only a few months before in the debate over the Code of Urban Coexistence, they were not inclined toward any sort of dialogue with those who held any kind of power; instead of petitioning for the exercise of civil rights, they suggested exercising them without further twists and turns. They renewed their efforts to fortify the possibility of dialogue that joined transvestite leaders with other transvestites who would participate publicly in the march. The argument hinged on the urgent necessity of constructing a different visibility, stripped of all the signs of marginalization that had always accompanied the images of transvestism: laws, articles, violence, denunciation. The images with which the march was promoted were a space to work in order to develop this other visibility, which sought to be removed as well from the transvestite stereotype of the exuberant body and the solitary life. The transvestite members of the Organizing Committee declared their intention of discouraging the carnivalesque attitude that the group might assume in the march. Nevertheless, during the preparation activities, the efforts made to create a consciousness of the need to eradicate stereotypes like the creation of murgas (popular dance teams) and floats, or the display of feathers and nudity, were considerably dwarfed by those involved in other projects—for example, the design of promotional posters for the march. It is necessary to clarify, nonetheless, that the leaders themselves, apart from the discourse they promoted, considered the idea of renouncing the display of their naked bodies during the march as a lost cause—perhaps because, in the end, the only firsthand visibility that would always be granted them was prompted by the transvestite body and its adornments.

Discourse by Identity Groups

At the Eighth LGBTT Pride March, three speeches were finally read, corresponding to gay, lesbian, and transvestite identity. The order established in which to read the speeches was: first the transvestites, then the lesbians, and, finally, the gays. In making the decision, the main criterion was the fact that transvestism had been, among the collective LGBTT community, the most beaten down by recent interventions by public officials in their initiatives against prostitution. That the transvestite voice was the first heard in the march was a sign of the legitimacy and proof of the consensus that they had managed to establish within the sociosexual LGBTT movement itself.

The three speeches presented many of the characteristics attributed to the discursive territory of politics, as defined by Eliseo Verón (1987). According to the author, this territory implies confrontation with an enemy and, in that sense, can be defined as a struggle between speakers. Political articulation seems inseparable from the construction of an adversary, and its specificity resides in the structural dissociation that is assumed by the simultaneous creation of a positive and negative addressee.

The three addresses, separated by identity, established polemical relations with an adversary or "anti-addressee," reinforced relationships with a positive audience or "pro-addressee," and also persuasive relationships with what Verón (1987) calls the "for-addressee."[3]

The presentational strategies chosen by gays and lesbians were marked by the use of a collective "we" that, through its inclusive character, brought together from the start the speaker and the pro-addressee in a collective of identification extended to all sociosexual diversity groups. For example, the lesbians indicated:

> We, lesbian women, have much to say to you and to each other. The transvestites have much to say to lesbians and gays. The gays have much to say to lesbians and to transvestites. And we have much to say to each other and to them.

In contrast to gays and lesbians, and as had been announced in the preparatory meetings for the march, the transvestite group chose as their pro-addressees only their own constituency, using as operators of identification nominative forms that were easily understood by that group:[4] "Hello, vicious little black girls; hello, exhibitionists; hello, AIDS-ridden masks; hello, men dressed as women." This sentence was reinforced immediately afterwards by the use of an inclusive "us": "[...] These words (*vicious little black girls, exhibitionists*, etc.) are very familiar to us, they resonate still and will for many years in our memory." [...]

Distinguished so from the rest of the LGBTT community, after the first greeting, the transvestite group's speech followed up with a description through which an anti-addressee was constructed, one that would be identified as responsible not only for the scorn of society towards transvestites, but also for the problems that affected other groups excluded by the system or murdered by it.

> *Vicious little black girls*, AIDS-*ridden masks*, *men dressed as women*, and *exhibitionists* are the disqualifiers most often used by a bourgeois class that sees their hypocrisy challenged by the shine of our incandescent silicone; by the corrupt politicians who don't hesitate to enrich themselves at the cost of [our] hunger and social exclusion; by the hostile Church; but the sensible of Palermo come clear when it comes time to choose between the barrio and gold, between marble and gypsum, between silver and tin—a sensibility that is certainly not terribly clear when working for the police, who are the sustainers of violence, [responsible for] the death of eighty-two transvestite comrades and thirty thousand disappearances. [...]

Originating in a negative valuation of the voice of the anti-addressee, the nominal forms chosen by the transvestite group were, nonetheless, received positively. In the voice of the transvestite speaker:

> But these little black girls, these exhibitionists, these masks, arrive after struggling for a long time to lift the veil from the eyes of a society that only sees the world in terms of male or female, losing in that view the infinite richness of difference. [...]

This recuperation was also present in the gay group's speech. At that time, the head of the armed forces had declared publicly that gays would be accepted into the army. Simultaneously, in the face of the reaction provoked by this proposal in diverse sectors of Argentine society, the same military head explained that this would not turn the army into "a group of little seamstresses." In the gay group's speech, the collective would express that, as opposed to the alternative of participating in a military corps known throughout the country for its genocidal practices, they "celebrated" dedicating themselves to the art of sewing. Appropriating deprecatory terms emerging from the anti-addressee and granting them a positive worth was the strategy that gay and transvestite activists found to nullify their original negative content and put another meaning in its place. [. . .]

The gay group's speech and the transvestite group's speech shared certain adversaries: the Church and the police. However, while the Church of which the transvestite presenter spoke was an institution that acted according to its own economic interests, the Church that the gay speaker addressed was criticized for pathologizing his community's sexual preferences. In both cases, however, the police presented the same characteristics in the eyes of the group. [. . .]

Not only families and workplaces, but also the institutions that regulated the bodies and desires of each group, were anti-addressees shared by gays and lesbians.

One aspect to emphasize in this first description of the three speeches is that only in the address corresponding to the transvestite contingent were there references that suggested a perspective of class in the construction and characterization of the anti-addressee. Three actors, absent in the other two speeches, seemed to indicate this. These were: the "bourgeois class," which felt itself menaced by the transvestite community; the "corrupt politicians," enriched by social exclusion; and the institution of religion and its economic interests. This observation drove me to think that the transvestite community understood, as a cornerstone of the discrimination to which it fell victim, not only an abject identity, but also that identity's arising from class.

The three addresses also account for what Verón (1987) calls "singular meta-collectives." Of great importance in political discourse, these are more inclusive entities than the properly political collectives that form the identity of the speakers, while at the same time they admit neither fragmentation nor quantification. In these three speeches, the role of "singular meta-collectives" was occupied by society, but the references, at the same time, are different among identity groups. While, for the lesbians, society appeared as an anti-addressee, and moreover, discriminates against and oppresses them not only for being lesbians, but for being women, in the gay and transvestite speeches, society was constructed as a for-addressee, which must be persuaded in order to learn to coexist with diversity.

In the transvestite group's speech, this persuasion consisted of informing society about the richness that exists in accepting more than two sexual identities. [. . .]

The lesbians issued a warning to that society that oppressed and discriminated against them, and that finds ways of doing so in its own institutions, that it not renounce an identity that provides a motive for pride. [. . .]

From a descriptive point of view, according to which the political speaker makes a balance of the situation, the peculiarity of the transvestite speech seems to be dictated by social class. In contrast to the other two identity groups, the transvestite speaker did not talk of family, did not speak of work or employment, nor of health. This should cause no surprise if the following is taken into account: that where family is concerned, kinships are often abandoned by transvestite individuals, in many cases definitively, at a very early age. In dealing with work, opportunities for employment are found to be as or more distant than family on the horizon of possibilities for the transvestite. Lastly, the health-care system is a resource of which the transvestite community does not take advantage—except when affected by acute or even terminal symptoms—because they are treated as men, placed in hospital rooms for men, and called by doctors and nurses by their male names. In none of these three spaces are the transvestites recognized as individuals in their own right, which is an indispensable condition in order to integrate into society.

From a didactic perspective, through which the speaker may form a universal truth, a general principle that is articulated in an atemporal order, the specificity of the transvestite resides, in Bordieu's (1993) terms, in questioning the principle of organization—and division—of social space in gender relations, proposing a new vision of the world which is imposed over the other, in which there is room for only two genders. The didactic content of the discourse surrounding lesbian identity is the search for an authentic life, and for gays, it is the search for coexistence with people who are different. The refusal by lesbians to be "twisted" in their search for an authentic life, as with the search for acceptance of difference in the case of the gay community, seems to be an expression of a desire to be part of a society that resists granting them a place. [. . .]

Ten years have passed since those first transvestite organizational experiences, and since the first efforts to participate with their voices and their names in the collective of minority groups that integrated in the lesbian, gay, bisexual, transvestite, and transsexual movement. In this space of time, organized transvestism has become conscious of a symbolic struggle, oriented toward the idea that their cultural practices be perceived and recognized as legitimate in a space of gender relations organized according to principles of classification and differentiation that did not consider them. The actions of organized transvestism, in order to become visible from within the LGBTT movement, an objective aspect—according to Bordieu (1993)—of all symbolic struggles, involved the display of diverse strategies of presentation through which the group was finally recognized. Paraphrasing an informant who evaluated the first years of the relationship between the transvestite community and the LGBTT movement, and the changes that she lived through, transvestites left off existing as part of the "large etcetera" with which they were named—"gays, lesbians, etc."—and managed to interject their name, the word that they had chosen to call themselves. And this is only one of the expressions of the other aspect of symbolic struggles, which Bordieu defines as subjective, and which understands those actions as designed to

> [. . .] change the perception and appreciation of the social world among cognitive and evaluative structures: the categories of perception, the systems of classification, is to say, essentially, the words, the names that create a social reality as they express it. (1993, 138)

Placing at the beginning, as the only proper capital, their interest in participating in the mobilization of sociosexual groups, among them the pride marches, the only space that was conceded to them was a stamp with their name—transvestites—and that they would be included in the margins of the promotional flyers for the third pride march. Gradually, the transvestite body, with its decorations and its exhibitionist gestures, along with certain activities that apparently sensitized the LGBTT community [. . .] added up to the original capital, and the members of the transvestite community managed to move themselves from those margins, to which they would not return, at least not the margins of the LGBTT movement. I will develop this affirmation by referring to the distinction made by Jacques Rancière, in his *El desacuerdo. Política y filosofía* (*Disagreement: Politics and Philosophy*, 1996), between two logics of existing together as humans.

Retaking the Foucauldian difference between police and politics, Rancière (1996) calls this "police order," or simply, police acting in conjunction with processes through which they effect the aggregation and consent of groups, the organization of powers, the distribution of places and functions, and the systems of legitimization of this distribution. [. . .]

On the other hand, "politics" is a well-determined activity, antagonistic to police order, which displaces an entity from its assigned place, and makes visible that which has no reason to be seen. Political activity is a mode of manifestation that unmakes the sensible divisions of police order; [. . .] political subjectivization wrenches issues from their own context and drives them to a new stage, now politicized.

From this perspective, then, it can be affirmed that the transvestite struggle within the LGBTT movement was a process of de-inscription of its participants from the place to which the police ("natural") order had assigned them, a process which, along the way, facilitated the creation of a new political stage, in which the knots restored by this police order where untied. If we attribute a police order to that which regulates gender identity, then the actions of transvestites in the LGBTT movement amounted to bringing that order into question, and fracturing it.

Notes

1. As mentioned by Jorge Salessi (1995), in May 1984 the Argentina Homosexual Community (*Comunidad Homosexual Argentina,* CHA), founded in April of that year, published a letter in a widely circulated newspaper demanding the condemnation of laws and police edicts that breached the personal liberties of homosexuals. Five years afterward, CHA would solicit legal recognition. Recognition was first denied by the Supreme Court of Justice, and finally granted by the president of the nation at the end of the year.

2. The following groups participated in the organization of the eighth march: the three major transvestite organizations, ATA, OTTRA, and ALITT; the Alliance of Activists against Social and Sexual Marginalization and Oppression AGAMOSS; a lesbian association called *La Fulana:* A Place for Women Who Love Women; the Argentina Homosexual Community (CHA); and individuals not enrolled in a particular organization. The presence of transsexuals was practically nil and there was no organized participation by bisexuals that year.

3. At the same time that the pro-addressee is a position that corresponds to a listener who subscribes to the same ideas, who possesses the same values and seeks the same objectives as the speaker, the anti-addressee is linked to him in the hypothesis of an inversion of belief. That is, what is true for the speaker is false for the anti-addressee and vice versa; or better said, what is good for the speaker is bad for the anti-addressee; or what is sincere for the speaker is insincere for the anti-addressee, etc.

4. The chosen operators of identification were the terms that, referring exclusively to transvestites, were used by the Cooperative Association of Neighbors of the Desert Company Plaza —better known as the Neighbors' Association of Palermo—and by certain police authorities in the debates over the Code of Urban Coexistence. The Neighbors' Association of Palermo was formed at the same time that the Code of Urban Coexistence replaced the old police edicts, depenalizing street-corner prostitution. Their activities constituted a kind of "moral crusade" designed to appeal to the legislative authorities to reestablish the old edicts.

References

Bourdieu, P. 1993. *Cosas dichas.* Barcelona: Gedisa.

———. 2000. *La dominación masculina.* Barcelona: Anagrama.

Rancière, J. 1996. *El desacuerdo. Política y filosofía.* Buenos Aires: Nueva Visión.

Salessi, J. 1995. *Médicos, maleantes y maricas. Higiene, criminología y homosexualidad en la construcción de la Nación Argentina (Buenos Aires: 1871–1914).* Rosario: Beatriz Viterbo.

Verón, E. 1987. *El discurso político. Lenguajes y acontecimientos.* Buenos Aires: Hachette.

"Every Jack to His Trade?"

Power Arrangements, Policies of Identity, and Market Segmentation within the Homosexual Movement

Isadora Lins França

Translated by Nicole Panico

THERE ARE several possible ways to understand the identity-segregated consumption market whose target public includes homosexuals in São Paulo.[1] Transvestites within the LGBT movement, through a protest action directed at gaining access to a sauna that had exclusively catered to the gay male segment of this population, destabilized the foundation on which the homosexual movement in Brazil is based. These events raise questions related to the understanding of the contemporary homosexual movement. [...]

The Brazilian homosexual movement began in 1978 with the creation of the group *Somos* in São Paulo (MacRae 1990). The group followed a political strategy of strengthening the homosexual identity and positive valuation of the *bicha* and lesbian categories,[2] associated by deeply antiauthoritarian politics that were critical of the state and the hierarchy of roles among same-sex couples (MacRae 1990; Fry 1982). As early as the 1980s, there was a rearticulation of the movement, which sought cooperation with the state in the fight against AIDS, and slackened its criticism of authoritarianism, still attributing positive value to the category of *homosexual* (Facchini 2005).

A different context emerged in the 1990s: the panic connected to AIDS abated, making it possible for homosexual activism to become more strongly based on different discourses and strategies. Categories that focused on the subjects of the movement as political increased. [. . .]

Besides the expansion of this circuit—now also known as GLS[3]—the 1990s brought about a configuration that was different from the former homosexual ghetto: in a way, spaces of consumption and sociability began to incorporate the political discourse of pride and visibility, making it clear that this discourse was directed to a community of a certain sexual orientation, and incorporating symbols popularized by activists, such as the rainbow flag. [. . .] Actors that in fact would constitute the segmented market also began to be seen [. . .] as articulators of political action, stimulating the "self-esteem of homosexuals" and the formation of a "positive identity" —through initiatives like film festivals, publications, and even spaces of leisure and sociability—as well as circulating information within the community through Web sites and specialized magazines. Tensions within the movement still remained, but much more ambiguously than before.

Another innovation the decade brought was the segmentation of consumption spaces for each subgroup of that community. [. . .] Within the spectrum of the GLS circuit, there are dozens of saunas designed for sexual interchange among men, one of which is the scene of the case discussed below. The vindication of transvestites carried out by the Transgenders' Office of the São Paulo Association of the LGBT Pride Parade—which demanded access to one of these saunas—originated the social drama analyzed in the third part of this report. This was an occasion when tensions among categories included in the LGBT movement and the segmented consumption market became explicit.

Collective Identities Associated for Political Action: Structures in the Movement

The building of collective identities associated for political action reveals the central problem of the processes by which certain social actors emerge as political subjects. [. . .] The appearance of new actors demanding to be considered as political subjects of the movement—as attested by the recent organization of transvestites, transsexuals, and bisexuals—evidences the fragility of theoretical perspectives that defy collective identities conceived as stable, internally homogeneous elements. These processes should be understood as part of a wider context of the movement in general, and of the segmented market. Their understanding demands an approach to power arrangements that shows the dynamics within which positions of "superiority" and "inferiority" alternate, and the possibility that the same social actors participate in relationships where they appear simultaneously "dominant" or "subordinate." [. . .]

Joshua Gamson (1998) has outlined some of the debates now present in the homosexual movement in the United States—and it would not be difficult to extract some points of correlation between processes in North America and Brazil. [...] The author approaches the idea of *queerness*:[4] an umbrella term that attempts to desta-bilize the identities of *gay* and *lesbian* and even those of *man* and *woman*, blurring group boundaries in frank opposition to what Gamson calls an ethnic-essentialist policy (Gamson 1998, 589). [...]

Gamson is dedicated to the very controversy caused by the active presence of bi-sexual and transgender people in the North American movement, reaching the con-clusion that both the policy of asserting essentialist identities and the policy of constant criticism and destabilization of these identities are important to the move-ment; they have different benefits, depending on the situation in which each strategy is used. According to the author, the movement worked simultaneously with two sources of oppression: cultural and institutional. In order to fight the former, a strat-egy that destabilizes borders and identities would be more appropriate; the fight against the oppression coming from institutional elements that would generate dis-crimination against all sexual minorities must insist on establishing fixed categories and safe limits. [...]

In a way, the subjects I will analyze in the case discussed below resemble Gamson's observations, but introduce new elements, since it is a situation in which institutional discrimination resulted from the movement's own dynamics and from the segmented market with which it is connected.

Dispute over Consumption Spaces: Transvestites' Role in the Game of Positioning the Categories that Make Up the LGBT Movement

[...] In November 2003, the Transgenders' Office of the São Paulo Association of the LGBT Pride Parade conducted a series of visits to venues in the city of São Paulo, a campaign they named "Blitz Trans." The visits were always made by transvestites, mostly from the Transgenders' Office, along with a militant of the Association of the Pride Parade acting as an attorney.

The idea of the name adopted for these visits was part of a play on words [...] that reversed the idea of police blitzes, which frequently target transvestites on the streets. [...] Taking this idea seriously provoked an inverse effect that removed transvestites from the category of victims, placing them as agents against the very prejudice they suffer from.

One of the few establishments that refused to allow the transvestites to enter after a legal presentation and brief negotiation was a sauna catering to the masculine ho-mosexual public, which generated a great mobilization around the subject, raising, in the homosexual movement in general and among users of the site *MixBrasil*, heated debates that are the focus of the present analysis.[5] [...] Owners and patrons of gay saunas (some of whom are militants of the movement), the direct interlocutors to which the transvestite claim is addressed, belong to a very close circle. The exclusion on the part of an establishment for the homosexual public, naturally understood as an ally of transvestites, intensified the transvestites' perplexity regarding the case. [...]

The market catering to homosexuals has answered, and motivated, a multiplicity of identities within the umbrella category *homosexual*, through the segregation of spaces of sociability. [...] Within this logic, saunas operate as a specific space of sexual interaction among men that have sex with men, maintaining the divisions between masculine and feminine, and excluding transvestites, who belong to a group other than that of *real men*. There are no leisure places specially destined for transvestites, so they commonly patronize "gay" or "GLS" spaces, recognizing them as the most appropriate for them, being that they share the same "community." [...]

However, even within the movement, the use of the acronym LGBT does not weaken differentiation, conflict, and hierarchy among constituting groups. The political articulation of the letters in the LGBT acronym was constructed by means of the idea that all four categories undergo discrimination and social exclusion. This was the starting point for demanding solidarity among such categories for the construction of a political subject that could demand rights for all segments; the conquest of rights for each would be understood as a conquest for all the rest. This is the relationship idealized by the movement's militants, but far from being the ideal formula, it ends up expressing conflicts among compartmentalized identities.

In the midst of those disputes, the LGBT pride parade appears as an occurrence of the massive visibility of the movement's demands and promotes, intentionally or not, [...] the dilution of these LGBT categories through the diverse crowd that takes to the streets (Facchini 2005). The Association of the Pride Parade is also one of the few organizations in the movement that keep groups that represent all four letters in *LGBT* constantly in operation. [...]

The perspective in favor of blurring the borders between gays, lesbians, bisexuals, and transgenders, when joining forces for political action, appears also on other occasions, constituting the main focus of argument for those who supported the transvestites in the episode concerning access to the gay sauna. The conflict occurs, then, between those who accept that perspective, and those who support segregation and the affirmation of each category. [...]

The perspective in favor of diluting the boundaries between gays, lesbians, bisexuals, and transgenders when it comes to joining forces for political action [...] constitutes the major focus of argument for those activists who have supported the transvestites in their efforts to gain access to the sauna. Therefore, the conflict occurs between those who adopt this discourse and those who base their reasoning on segregation and the separate affirmation of each one of the categories. [...]

Our problem becomes more complex when, within the same LGBT movement, we see segmentation acting in similar ways to the market, weakening the transvestites' claim and reducing it to the particularism of a marked group invading gay spaces. This position can be seen as a strategy reinforcing a hegemony threatened by the transvestites' demands, even when it is not consciously articulated in those terms. [...]

One of the issues serving as subtext to those who criticize transvestites is the question of what can or cannot be demanded, what is legitimate as political action. It is important to recall that, for instance, transvestites' protests against police violence are almost unquestioningly welcomed by the homosexual movement. Unlike protests against lack of access to saunas—which militants qualify as "populist"—protests against violence are seen as a serious subject, perhaps because they emphasize that transvestites are "victims of homophobia," and these protests are directed against the state (a more traditional field of political struggle than the market), and, finally, because they establish an opposition between "heterosexual homophobia" and the "human rights of homosexuals/transvestites," unlike protests against lack of access to saunas, which question the potential for inclusion within the gay scene. [...]

Initially, questioning the political validity of the transvestites' claim appears as a peaceful point among homosexual activists: the idea that a sauna frequented by homosexuals is a space of masculine sexual interchange is seen in a positive way by militants, who feel it should be preserved as such. [...] A sauna is understood as a space capable of strengthening the identity affirmation of men who like to have sex exclusively with other men, and this would make the transvestites' presence "invasive" in this space destined to male homoerotism. [...]

As soon as transvestites demand to enter commercial establishments intended for sex among men, with the justification that there should not be exclusive spaces within the homosexual scene, the gay militants that criticize this demand go into a diametrically opposite direction: it is necessary to establish limits, identities, and spaces. Starting from the definition of these terms, another recurring sentence in the messages forums on the *MixBrasil* Web site becomes possible: "Every Jack to his trade!" [...]

The socially established, rigid spaces of feminine and masculine, demarcated by the heterosexual matrix, are used by homosexual activists to attempt to place transvestites in one area or another, and determine the spaces where their presence would be legitimate. [...]

We may perceive that the question of body configuration and appearance, related to gender convention, is also essential for transvestites, but they made strategically destabilizing and provocative use of these norms. The panic this destabilization could cause and its politically strategic use were shown very clearly in their discourse.

Demands in Context

In the case of transvestites seeking access to a gay male sauna, the logic of a group of transvestites who demanded the right to use establishments catering to the homosexual public overlapped with that of actors of the prosegregation market who refused their presence, with the intention of preserving a consumer niche; the transvestites' logic overlapped also with that of a group of gays, activists and nonactivists, who were in favor of the transvestites' demand, who adopted the discourse of sexual diversity and nonsegregation; and the transvestites' logic overlapped with that of another part of the movement, which defended exclusive establishments for interaction among men, as a way of stating homosexual identity. [. . .] If we keep in mind that these relationships are not static, but dynamic and intercommunicating, it is possible to understand that, in different contexts, the demands of transvestites are interpreted in different ways, also acquiring different political meanings.

This approach also extends to the building of a political subject that has conventionally been called the LGBT movement, in the sense that it is articulated within the logic of negotiation among different identities. The situation of political dispute has not been restricted to changes of position between given and defined subjects, but expresses the contingent character of alliances established by certain political subjects. [. . .]

On the one hand, the transvestites' desires can be understood as a reiteration of the norm, demanding rights through consumption and the recurrence of a position as "women"; on the other hand, their claims adopt a subversive nature when they take a questioning and critical attitude toward the LGBT movement, and destabilize the movement's normative structures. When a socially marginalized group vindicates its rights through a specific practice, this becomes more complex when those demanding must negotiate conflicts with "natural allies."

In their efforts to gain access to the contested space of the sauna, transvestites were able to establish an internal questioning of the norms that rule the movement's political action, using the discourse of equality and sexual diversity propagated by activists, and a strategy that destabilized the structures that linked gender identities with sexual identities by means of bodily markers. By doing so, they created a situation that strained the limits of the movement, promoting discussions and articulating forces that could be considered subversive of the previously established relationship of dominance. [. . .]

Notes

1. It is important to emphasize that what we used to call the *homosexual movement* is, nowadays, a very complex political subject, comprised by multiple identity categories, not always driven by the same discourses. Without considering this problematic aspect, it becomes difficult to understand many of the positions within the movement on what concerns the segregated market, or even the relation with other social actors that integrate the movement's field of activity.

2. *Bicha* is a term used in an offensive way, to expose homosexuals to shame, but it was used in the movement in a positive way, as a strategy of inverting its prejudicial meaning. It is a process that resembles the positive use of the term *queer* in the United States.

3. GLS means gays, lesbians, and sympathizers. The initialism was created in the mid-1990s. While mainly used to qualify the city leisure circuit, today it applies to other services, even to a certain GLS spirit. For further information, see Facchini (2005).

4. The English word *queer* may be interpreted to mean both "weird" and something close to the Brazilian terms *viado* or *bicha* (fag, faggot), and has been used by part of the North American and European movement, attempting to include all who consider themselves as outside of the heterosexual norm.

5. The sources used for this analysis are messages sent to a virtual discussion list. [. . .]

References

Facchini, R. 2005. *Sopa de letrinhas? Movimento homossexual e construção de identidades coletivas nos anos 90: Um estudo a partir da cidade de São Paulo.* Rio de Janeiro: Garamond.

Fry, P. 1982. *Para inglês ver: Identidade e política na cultura brasileira.* Rio de Janeiro: Zahar.

Gamson, J. 1998. Must Identity Movements Self-Destruct? A Queer Dilemma. In *Social Perspectives in Lesbian and Gay Studies*, ed. P. M. Nardi, and B. E. Schneider, 589–604. London: Routledge.

MacRae, E. 1990. *O militante homossexual no Brasil da "abertura."* Campinas: Editora da Unicamp.

APPENDIX

TIMELINE OF LGBT POLITICAL LANDMARKS IN THE AMERICAS

Javier Corrales

1821— Brazil. A newly independent Brazil creates laws that decriminalize homosexuality and effectively ban other forms of discrimination, the first to do so in Latin America.

1871— Mexico. Homosexual acts between adults are decriminalized, making Mexico the second country in Hispanic America to do so.

1880s—Argentina, El Salvador, Guatemala. Homosexual acts are decriminalized in Argentina in 1889, and in El Salvador and Guatemala around 1880.

1924— Peru. Homosexual acts between adults are decriminalized.

1932— Chile. The founding father of Chile's Evangelical Church, the U.S.-born Willis Hoover, is outed, triggering a major schism within the church.

1934— Uruguay. Homosexual acts between adults are decriminalized.

1959— Mexico. Mexico City's Mayor Uruchurtu closes every gay bar under the guise of "cleaning up vice" (or at least reducing its visibility).

1965— Cuba. Military Units for the Aid of Production (UMAP) forced-labor camps are created. Gay men and others deemed "counterrevolutionary" are incarcerated.

1967— Cuba. Government closes UMAPs.

1969— Argentina. The first gay political organization in Latin America, Our World Group, is founded in Buenos Aires.

United States. New York City police raid the Stonewall Inn, a bar frequented by LGBT patrons, prompting spontaneous resistance and a series of clashes between the local LGBT community and the police, marking the beginning of the modern gay-rights movement in the United States.

1971— Costa Rica. José Luis Sánchez publishes *La Isla de los hombres* (*The Isle of Lonely Men*), a novel about life in a male-only penitentiary where homosexuality is rampant.

Cuba. The country's First National Congress on Education and Culture decrees that homosexuals are "pathological" and must "be rejected" from any job where they might influence youth; anti-gay purges follow.

Mexico. Homosexual Liberation Front (FLH) founded as Mexico's first gay-liberation group.

1976— Argentina/Brazil. Argentine author Manuel Puig publishes *El Beso de la mujer araña* (*The Kiss of the Spider Woman*), a novel about a political prisoner and an out gay man sharing a prison cell.

1978— Brazil. Founding of *Somos*, the country's first gay-liberation group.

Mexico. Director Arturo Ripstein releases *El lugar sin límites* (*Place without Limits*), a film based on a José Donoso novel; the film features a gay, cross-dressing sex worker in a small Mexican town.

1979— Brazil. On February 6, a debate on homosexuality at the University of São Paulo marks the first public event in the Brazilian gay-liberation movement.

Cuba. Homosexual acts between adults are decriminalized.

Mexico. First gay pride march.

1980— Cuba. Mariel Boatlift: Fidel Castro opens the port of Mariel Harbor to allow citizens to leave for the United States. Castro uses the opportunity to rid Cuba of "antisocials." A Cuban claiming homosexuality had a higher chance of being allowed to leave.

1981— Brazil. Writer and director Héctor Babenco releases *Pixote: A lei do mais fraco*, a film depicting a ten-year-old runaway boy in São Paulo, with scenes of male prostitution and transvestism.

Colombia. Homosexual acts between adults are decriminalized.

1982— Brazil/Mexico. Gay-liberation groups use high-profile elections to gain visibility for their movement, becoming politically involved for the first time.

United States. The Center for Disease Control coins the term AIDS (SIDA in Spanish and Portuguese), replacing the original term, GRID (gay-related immune deficiency).

1984— Argentina. Police raid a gay night club in Buenos Aires, arresting two hundred people.

Cuba/U.S. *Conducta Impropia* is released, one of the world's first documentaries to explore human-rights abuses in Cuba, with a special focus on LGBT discrimination and persecution.

1985— Brazil. *Grupo Gay da Bahia* succeeds in having *homosexuality* removed from the Federal Council of Health's list of treatable diseases.

Brazil. National AIDS Program is created, separate from the Ministry of Health.

Mexico. Writer and director Jaime Humberto Hermosillo releases *Doña Herlinda y su hijo*, a film about a closeted gay relationship in which one partner's mother acts as the couple's protector.

1986— Vatican City. The Church issues "Letter to Bishops of the Catholic Church on the Pastoral Care of Homosexual Persons," reaffirming the Church's condemnation of homosexual acts, but also condemning "violent malice in speech and action" against homosexuals. Letter signed by Cardinal Joseph Ratzinger (Pope Benedict XVI, 2005–present).

1987— Chile. The AIDS Prevention Association is founded, becoming the country's first AIDS-prevention and gay-activist organization, preceding the 1991 creation of MOVILH, an offshoot dedicated exclusively to gay emancipation.

Costa Rica. In the wake of government harassment and discrimination, the country's first four lesbian and gay organizations are founded.

1988— Brazil. LGBT groups demand that sexual orientation be protected in the new constitution, but ultimately their efforts fail.

Spain/Latin America. Spanish pop group Mecano releases "*Mujer contra mujer*," a ballad about lesbianism that becomes a hit throughout the Spanish-speaking world and, in translation, in several European countries.

1989— Argentina. The government denies legal recognition to the *Comunidad Homosexual Argentina*, one of the country's oldest gay organizations, founded in 1984.

Brazil. The states of Sergipe and Mato Grosso pass new constitutions that forbid discrimination on the basis of sexual orientation.

1990— Chile. First democratic government after Pinochet forms the National AIDS Commission.

Costa Rica. Government forbids unmarried women to enter the country, in an attempt to stop the Second Latin American Lesbian Feminist Encounter.

1991— Chile. *Movimiento de Liberación Homosexual* founded.

Nicaragua. Gay and lesbian groups organize the country's first pride celebrations and symposia on gay issues. Nicaragua's legislature passes one of the hemisphere's most severe antigay, antisodomy laws.

1993— Brazil. First National Meeting of *Travestis* and the Liberated Acting in the Fight against AIDS takes place in the country.

Chile. A fire in a Valparaíso gay nightclub kills thirteen patrons. Hate crime is suspected.

United States. "Don't Ask, Don't Tell" becomes official policy in the military.

1994— Cuba. Director Tomás Gutiérrez Alea releases *Fresa y chocolate* (*Strawberry and Chocolate*), a film addressing political and social homophobia in late-1970s Cuba.

United States. Cable music channel MTV's reality show, *The Real World: San Francisco*, features the Cuban-born Pedro Zamora, the first-ever openly gay, HIV-positive main character on TV. Zamora died shortly after the end of the show.

1995— Brazil. The Brazilian Association of Gays, Lesbians, and Transgenders, the country's first national gay-rights umbrella organization, is founded. Later, the organization incorporates the word *travesti* into its official name.

Brazil. Deputy Marta Suplicy of the *Partido dos Trabalhadores* tables a bill for the legalization of civil unions for same-sex partners.

Brazil. The International Lesbian and Gay Association holds its annual meeting in Rio de Janeiro, with financial support from the government, culminating in the country's first gay pride parade.

Ecuador. Police arrest approximately one hundred patrons of Bar Abanicos, a LGBT club in the city of Cuenca, on charges of homosexuality, penalized by article 516 of the Penal Code with a maximum sentence of four to eight years in prison.

1997— Brazil. First National Congress of Transsexuals takes place.

Brazil. São Paulo hosts its first gay pride parade.

Mexico. Patria Jiménez, of the Party of the Democratic Revolution, becomes the first openly lesbian member of the legislature in all of Latin America.

United States. Comedienne Ellen DeGeneres comes out on the cover of *Time* magazine.

1998— Argentina. The city of Buenos Aires adopts the Code of Contraventions (*Código de Convivencia*), stripping the police of unconstitutional powers (police edicts) that had been arbitrarily abused. However, the code still imposed restrictions on sex workers, triggering protests by transvestites.

Ecuador. New constitution includes protections for sexual orientation.

Peru. Director Francisco Lombardi releases *No se lo digas a nadie,* a film about a gay teenager in an upper-class family struggling to survive in Lima and South Beach, Florida.

Spain/Latin America. Spanish pop group Mecano releases "Stereosexual," a pop anthem to sexual ambiguity.

1999— Chile and Venezuela. Homosexual acts are officially decriminalized.

Columbia. The Inter-American Commission on Human Rights agrees to hear *Marta Lucía Álvarez Giraldo v. Colombia,* challenging Colombia's decision to disallow a woman to have an intimate homosexual visit with her imprisoned partner. The case was settled before the Commission issued a ruling.

Venezuela. A proposal to insert an article in the constitution explicitly banning discrimination against gays and lesbians is rejected by the Constituent Assembly. The approved constitution states that marriage is between man and woman.

2000— Argentina. Director Marcelo Piñero releases *Plata Quemada,* a film about a same-sex couple involved in crime.

Brazil. *Grupo Nuances* from Porto Alegre and the *Ministério Público* launch a successful class-action suit against the *Instituto Nacional do Seguro Social* (National Social Security Institute, INSS) requesting the recognition of same-sex partners for the purposes of granting pensions to partners of deceased or imprisoned individuals.

Brazil. Rio de Janeiro state legislature passes a law penalizing sexual-orientation discrimination in public and private establishments.

Brazil. A São Paulo court condemns to twenty years in prison a group of eighteen skinheads, including two women, for murdering Edson Néris; a prosecutor uses the term *hate crime.* Over the next two and a half years, seven more suspects are convicted.

Colombia. Director Barbet Schroeder releases *La Virgen de los sicarios,* a film that interweaves a gay relationship and the plight of living in drug- and violence-infested Medellín.

2001— Brazil. President Cardoso creates the *Conselho Nacional de Combate à Discriminação* (National Council for the Struggle against Discrimination), the country's first government commission to end violence against LGBT citizens, among other goals.

Honduras. The United States Special Rapporteur on extrajudicial, summary, or arbitrary executions receives information about the killings of over two hundred members of the LGBT community since 1991.

Mexico. The video music network Telehit launches *Desde Gayola,* a sketch comedy show frequently discussing issues of homosexuality, featuring famous LGBT characters such as Alejandra Bogue. The show is broadcast to sixty countries, becoming one of the network's hit series.

2002— Argentina. The city of Buenos Aires passes Law 1004, guaranteeing all couples, regardless of gender or sexual orientation, the right to register their unions with the Public Registry for Civil Unions.

United States. The *New York Times* begins to publish same-sex wedding announcements.

2003— Argentina. Province of Rio Negro extends the same rights and obligations to same-sex couples already enjoyed by heterosexual couples.

Bolivia. Director Rodrigo Bellot releases *Dependencia Sexual*, a film about five teenagers in Bolivia and the United States, with scenes of homosexuality and autoeroticism.

Brazil. The country's delegation to the United Nations Human Rights Committee puts forward a resolution declaring sexual discrimination a human-rights violation.

Mexico. The documentary *Juchitán Queer Paradise* is released, showing a city near Guatemala where homosexual individuals are accepted, considered to have a third gender.

Mexico. Government enacts a federal antidiscrimination law that includes sexual orientation.

United States. The Massachusetts Supreme Judicial Court rules 4-3 that the state's ban on same-sex marriage is unconstitutional and gives the state legislature 180 days to change the law (*Goodridge v. Department of Public Health*).

United States. The Supreme Court invalidates antihomosexual antisodomy laws in *Lawrence v. Texas*.

2004— Brazil. Following a court ruling in the state of Rio Grande do Sul, legislators pass legislation establishing gay civil unions, including joint custody of children and property and pension benefits.

Brazil. Government initiates *Brasil sem Homofobia*, a comprehensive program working with NGOs and government agencies to change social attitudes towards LGBT people.

Chile. In a 3-2 decision, the Supreme Court forces Karen Atala, a lesbian, to surrender custody of her three daughters to her ex-husband. The court argues: "The absence from the home of a male father and his replacement by another person of the female gender poses a risk to the integral development of the children."

Chile. Supreme Court removes Judge Daniel Calvo from the Santiago Court of Appeals after media reports that he visited saunas frequented by gay men.

Peru. Congress enacts Law 28.237, which prohibits discrimination based on sexual orientation and recognizes sexual minorities as a protected group.

United States. President George W. Bush endorses an amendment to the Constitution banning same-sex marriage.

2005— Brazil. After filming a scene of a gay kiss for *América*, a widely watched soap opera, the TV network Globo decides not to run the scene, leading to a number of protests.

United States. Miami-born Cuban-American Perez Hilton (né Mario Armando Lavandeira) becomes one of the most famous celebrity bloggers in the United States. Perez Hilton, who is open about his homosexuality, is often celebrated and criticized for outing celebrities, musicians, and actors.

Venezuela. Two openly gay men, Heisler Vaamonde and José Ramón Merentes, run for office unsuccessfully in the National Assembly elections.

2006— Brazil. São Paulo's pride event brings out three million, becoming the world's largest.

Chile. Legislation in favor of civil unions is introduced in the National Congress, but no action is taken.

Dominican Republic. Cardinal Nicolás de Jesús López Rodríguez asks authorities to remove gays, whom he called "social scum" (*lacras*), from the capital's colonial zone to prevent its becoming a patrimony of "perverted foreigners and Dominicans."

El Salvador. President Antonio Saca endorses a proposal to amend the constitution to outlaw gay marriage and adoptions. The opposition party, the *Frente Farabundo Martí para la Liberación Nacional* (FMLN) opposes the measure and the amendment is not ratified.

Mexico. Mexico City approves the Cohabitation Law, granting same-sex couples marital rights identical to those established for common-law relationships between men and women, including pensions, inheritance, and guardianship rights.

Mexico. Openly gay David Sánchez Camacho, of the Party for the Democratic Revolution, is elected to the Chamber of Deputies.

2007— Argentina. Congress approves a new military law (Law No. 26.394), repealing a 1951 military code, which decriminalizes homosexual acts and homosexual orientation in the armed forces. Law enters into effect in February 2009.

Argentina. Lucía Puenzo releases the film XXY, depicting the story of an intersexual teenager.

Colombia. The Constitutional Tribunal officially recognizes that same-sex unions are eligible for constitutional protection and deserve the same "patrimonial" rights as any married couple (Ruling C-075).

Colombia. A landmark gay-rights bill that would have effectively created civil partnerships akin to common-law marriages for same-sex partners is defeated at the last minute by a group of conservative senators.

Colombia/United Nations. In *X v. Colombia,* the United Nations Human Rights Committee rules in favor of a Colombian man who sought his deceased partner's pension, initially denied by the Colombian state.

Mexico. The state of Coahuila issues Decree 209, stating that adults of the same or different sexes are recognized as "civil companions." Adoptions by same-sex couples remain unlawful.

United Nations. Various nations, including three Latin American countries, Argentina, Brazil, and Uruguay, promote the launch of the Yogyakarta Principles at the United Nations. These are a set of principles, drawn from international law, that specify how states must treat issues of sexual orientation and gender identity.

Uruguay. A new law granting access to health benefits, inheritance, parenting and pension rights to all couples cohabiting at least five years passes in the legislature, the first such national law in Latin America.

Vatican City. Pope Benedict XVI reiterates the Catholic Church's opposition to gay marriage, declaring that heterosexual marriage is a "nonnegotiable" value.

2008— Brazil. Police estimate that more three million people participated in the twelfth annual gay pride march; both the São Paulo government and the company Petrobras sponsored the march.

Brazil. President Luiz Inácio Lula da Silva launches the "First National Conference of Gays, Lesbians, Bisexuals, Transvestites and Transsexuals" in Brasília.

Colombia. LGBT rights defender Fredy Pineda is killed in Apartado, a city in north-western Colombia.

Cuba. New president Raúl Castro authorizes offering free sex-change operations for qualifying citizens, a policy change advocated by Cuba's National Center for Sex Education (presided over by President Raúl Castro's daughter, Mariela Castro).

Cuba. Police ban a gay pride march in Havana and temporarily detain two march leaders.

Ecuador. Voters approve the country's twentieth constitution. Article 11 bans discrimination on the basis of "gender identity," "sexual orientation," and "HIV status" (but still defines marriage as the "union between man and woman" in article 68).

Nicaragua. A reform of the Penal Code legalizes same-sex relations and ends an anti-sodomy law.

Organization of American States. The General Assembly unanimously adopts a resolution condemning human-rights violations based on sexual orientation and gender identity.

Panama. Government repeals a 1949 law criminalizing gay sex.

United Nations. The United Nations General Assembly affirms that international human-rights protections include sexual orientation and gender identity. The statement is read to the Assembly by Argentina; twelve of the sixty-six countries that signed on were Latin American.

United States. In a referendum, 52.24 percent of California voters approve Proposition 8, banning same-sex marriages. California Latinos, representing 18 percent of the voters, approve the ban by 53 percent (but only 41 percent of Latinos aged 18–29 approve). In Florida, 63 percent of Latinos, representing 14 percent of the electorate, vote yes on Amendment 2, also banning same sex marriage.

United States. A study by the Williams Institute at UCLA finds that nearly 1 in 4 individuals in same-sex couples in California, or 52,192 people, are Latino/a (the ratio for the entire country is 1 in 10). Almost 50 percent of Latinas and 43 percent of Latinos within same-sex couples in California are raising children. These individuals are raising over 24,948 children in California.

Venezuela. The Constitutional Branch of the Supreme Court issues a ruling that, on the one hand, recognizes that discrimination based on sexual orientation is unconstitutional, but on the other hand, states that there does not exist constitutional protection for same-sex partnerships; only the legislature can confer such protections.

Venezuela. The Supreme Tribunal rejects the possibility of legalizing gay marriages, arguing that the government is not required to protect any partnerships other than marriages.

2009— Argentina. Buenos Aires city judge Gabriela Seijas ruled that banning a same-sex marriage license (petitioned for by José María Di Bello and Alex Freyre) was unconstitutional, triggering heated debates on TV, marches, and hostile billboards across the city. The archbishop of Buenos Aires, Jorge Bergoglio, publicly criticized the city's mayor, Mauricio Macri, for not appealing the ruling. Weeks later, national court judge Marta Gómez Alsina blocked the wedding, arguing that a Supreme Court ruling was necessary. The couple decided to marry in Tiera del Fuego, becoming the first same-sex marriage in Latin America.

Bolivia. New constitution bans discrimination on the basis of "sexual orientation" and "gender identity" (but only recognizes "marriage" and "free unions" as occurring "between a woman and a man").

Brazil. President Luiz Inácio Lula da Silva creates the *Coordenação Geral de Promoção dos Direitos de Lésbicas, Gays, Bissexuais, Travestis e Transexuais* as a unit within the Special Human Rights Secretariat.

Chile. Pedro Pablo Zegers, head of archives at the national library, publishes *Niña Errada*, documenting that world-renowned Chilean poet Gabriela Mistral was a lesbian. The book contains 230 love letters between Mistral and her secretary in the United States, Doris Dana, between 1948 and the time of Mistral's death in 1957.

Chile. The Unified Movement for Sexual Minorities (MUMS) organizes the first-ever mass wedding for sexual minorities in front of the Metropolitan Cathedral.

Colombia. Álvaro Miguel Rivera, a human-rights defender and a representative of the LGBT organization Tinku, is assassinated in Cali.

Colombia. The Constitutional Court upholds a lower court opinion that same-sex couples must be accorded the same benefits as heterosexual couples in common-law marriages. This ruling grants same-sex couples equal pension, survivor, immigration, and property rights.

Honduras. Human Rights Watch publishes "Not Worth a Penny," a report on human rights abuses against transgendered people, reporting that at least seventeen *travestis* have been killed since 2004, and calling for legal changes.

Mexico. In a unanimous vote, the Supreme Court rules in favor of a man-to-woman transsexual requesting the reissuing of a new birth certificate that would not reveal the change in her sexual identity.

Mexico. In a 39–20 vote with 5 abstentions, Mexico City's legislative assembly approves marriage rights for same-sex couples. In a separate vote, the assembly also approves adoption rights by a 31–24 vote with 9 abstentions.

Peru. America TV broadcasts footage of members of a neighborhood watch beating and forcibly undressing a transgender street worker.

Peru. Interior Minister Mercedes Cabanillas announces that Peru will ban homosexuals from the police force.

Uruguay. In a 17-6 vote, the legislature approves a bill that ends restricting adoptions to married couples, which many interpret as paving the way for adoptions by same-sex couples. Earlier, Montevideo Archbishop Nicolás Cotugno condemned the bill as going "against human nature itself, and consequently . . . against the fundamental rights of the human being as a person."

CREDITS FOR ORIGINAL PUBLICATIONS

Babb, Florence. 2004. Out in Public: Gay and Lesbian Activism in Nicaragua. NACLA *Report on the Americas* 37(6): 27–30.

Bejel, Emilio. 2000. Cuban CondemNation of Queer Bodies. In *Cuba, the Elusive Nation: Interpretations of National Identity*, ed. Damián J. Fernández and Madeline Cámara Betancourt, 155–74. Gainesville: University Press of Florida.

Ben, Pablo. 2009. Male Sexuality, the Popular Classes and the State: Buenos Aires, 1880–1955. PhD diss., University of Chicago.

Brown, Stephen. 2002. "*Con discriminación y represión no hay democracia*": The Lesbian and Gay Movement in Argentina. *Latin American Perspectives* 29, no. 2: 119–38

de la Dehesa, Rafael. 2007. Global Communities and Hybrid Cultures: Early Gay and Lesbian Electoral Activism in Brazil and Mexico. *Latin American Research Review* 42(1): 29–51.

da Silva, Luiz Inácio Lula. 2008. Speech of the President of the Brazilian Republic at the Opening of the First National Conference of Gays, Lesbians, Bisexuals, Transvestites, and Transsexuals, Brasília. June 5.

Espinosa Miñoso, Yuderkys. 2007. *La relación feminismo-lesbianismo en América Latina*. In *Escritos de una lesbiana oscura: Reflexiones críticas sobre feminismo y política de identidad en América Latina*, 125–37. Buenos Aires: En la Frontera Editorial.

Fernández, Josefina. 2004. *Travestismo y espacio público*. In *Cuerpos desobedientes: Travestismo e identidad de género*, 115–43. Buenos Aires: Edhasa.

França, Isadora Lins. 2006. "*Cada macaco no seu galho?*": *Arranjos de poder, políticas de identidade, e segmentação de mercado no movimento homossexual. Revista Brasileira de ciências sociais* 21, no. 60 (February): 103–15.

Frasca, Tim. 2005. Chile: Seizing Empowerment. In *AIDS in Latin America*, 213–51. New York: Palgrave Macmillan.

Friedman, Elisabeth Jay. 2007. Lesbians in (Cyber)space: The Politics of the Internet in Latin American On- and Off-line Communities. *Media, Culture and Society* 29(5): 790–811.

Green, James N. 1994. More Love and More Desire: The Building of a Brazilian Movement. In *The Global Emergence of Gay and Lesbian Politics, National Imprints of a Worldwide Movement*, ed. Barry D. Adam, Jan Willem Duyvendak, and André Krouwel, 91–109. Philadelphia: Temple University Press.

Haydulina, Anastasia, 2009. Interview with Mariela Castro on the Future of Sex and Socialism in Cuba. *MRZine,* March 1. http://mrzine.monthlyreview.org/2009/castro030109.html (accessed February 10, 2010).

Larson, Scott. 2004. Gay Space in Havana. In *Cuba Today: Continuity and Change since the "Special Period,"* ed. Mauricio Font, 63–77. Bildner Center: The City University of New York Press.

Marsiaj, Juan P. 2006. Social Movements and Political Parties: Gays, Lesbians, and *Travestis* and the Struggle for Inclusion in Brazil. *Canadian Journal of LAC Studies,* 31(62): 167–96.

Modarelli, Alejandro. 2004. *1998: Unas Metamorfosis que ciegan y embriagan: Deseo, TV, pánico y violencia en torno de las personas travestis en Argentina.* In *Ciudadanía sexual en América Latina: Abriendo el debate,* ed Carlos F. Cáceres, Timothy Frasca, Mario Pecheny, and Veriano Terto, Jr., 275–86. Lima: Universidad Peruana Cayetano Heredia.

Murray, Stephen O. 2004. Mexico. GLBTQ: *An Encyclopedia of Gay, Lesbian, Bisexual, Transgender, and Queer Culture,* http://www.glbtq.com/social-sciences/mexico.html (accessed October 15, 2009).

Núñez González, Héctor. 2005. *Prácticas políticas y estrategias de alianza del movimiento GLBTT en Chile.* In *Cuerpos ineludibles: Un diálogo a partir de las sexualidades en América Latina,* ed. Josefina Fernández, Mónica D'Uva, and Paula Viturro, 25–31. Buenos Aires: Ají de Pollo.

Ocasio, Rafael. 2008. The Fight and Flight of Reinaldo Arenas. *The Gay and Lesbian Review Worldwide* 15, no. 2 (March–April): 29–32.

Pecheny, Mario. 2004. *Lógicas de acción colectiva de los movimientos por los derechos sexuales: Un análisis con aires abstractos de experiencias bien concretas.* In *Ciudadanía sexual en América Latina: Abriendo el debate,* ed. Carlos Cáceres, Tim Frasca, Mario Pecheny, and Veriano Terto, Jr., 203–15. Lima: Universidad Peruana Cayetano Heredia.

Posa Guinea, Rosa M., Carolina Robledo Desh, and Camila Zabala Peroni, on behalf of Aireana, Grupo por los Derechos de las Lesbianas. 2006. *Anexo: Mujeres lesbianas: De invisibles a sujetas de derechos.* In *Derechos humanos en Paraguay, informe DDHH 2006,* 120–25. Asunción: Coordinadora de Derechos Humanos del Paraguay, CODEHUPY, and Editora Litocolor.

Rapp, Linda. 2004. Puerto Rico and the Caribbean. GLBTQ: *An Encyclopedia of Gay, Lesbian, Bisexual, Transgender, and Queer Culture,* http://www.glbtq.com/social-sciences/puerto_rico.html (accessed October 15, 2009).

Reding, Andrew. 2003. Sexual Orientation and Human Rights in the Americas. World Policy Reports, World Policy Institute, December, http://www.worldpolicy.org/projects/globalrights/sexorient/2003-LGBT-Americas.pdf.

Thayer, Millie. 1997. Identity, Revolution, and Democracy: Lesbian Movements in Central America. *Social Problems* 44(3): 386–406.

Vianna, Adriana R. B., and Sérgio Carrara. 2007. Sexual Politics and Sexual Rights in Brazil: A Case Study. In *SexPolitics: Reports from the Front Lines,* ed. Richard Parker, Rosalind Petchesky, and Robert Sember, 27–51. New York and Rio de Janeiro: Sexuality Policy Watch.

INDEX

Note: page references in italics refer to figures; those followed by t refer to tables; those followed by n refer to notes, with note number.

Briones, Mónica, 382
British Caribbean, attitudes toward LGBT persons in, 141–43
British colonialism, legacies of, 352
Bryant, Gigi, 83
Buenos Aires: antidiscrimination legislation, 86, 117; as LGBT-friendly city, 11; police edicts in, 36–37, 39–40, 41n12, 303–4; sodomy laws in, 34, 37–39, 42n19
Buenos Aires civil union law, 10, 22, 117; arguments against, 212–16; passage of, 212, 213
Buenos Aires Code of Coexistence: city government position in debate on, 411; failure of, 309, 310; modifications of, 308, 309; opposition to, 305–6, 308–9; and public attention to trans-gendered prostitutes, 304–5; purposes of, 304; transvestite disappointment with, 414
Buenos Aires gay pride poll (2005), 12, 13, 20

Caballero, Roberto, 137
Campaign for a Sexuality Free of Prejudice, 153, 277
capitalism: in Cuba, and origin of homophobic discourse, 47–48; and redefinition of family unit, 47–48
capital punishment, English Caribbean's support for, 353
Carbado, Devon, 356n4
Cárdenas, Cuauhtémoc, 182
Cárdenas, Nancy, 177
Cardoso, Fernando Henrique, 203, 238, 242–43, 244
Caribbean Community (CARICOM), 353, 356n5
Caribbean Court of Justice, 353, 356n5
Caribbean nations: history of, 135–36; views on homosexuality, 21, 138–43
Caribbean nations, English-speaking: acceptance of LGBT rights, factors in, 349–54; prognosis for progress in LGBT rights, 355–56
CARICOM. See Caribbean Community
Carnival, in Brazil, 73, 241
Carreaga Pérez. Gloria, 324–25
Carrier, Joseph, 65, 294, 296, 297–98
Carrillo, Héctor, 65
Casa de la Mujer (Woman's House), 382
Casa de las Lunas, 403
Casas, Francisco, 382
Castro, Fidel, 270, 316
Castro, Mariela, 270–73
Castro, Raúl, 10
Catholic Church: and family discrimination in Brazil, 235, 237; as obstacle to LGBT rights, 220, 256; opposition to abortion, 227; opposition to gay marriage, 227; and Portuguese openness to sexuality, 240–41; and "transvestite treason" in Chile, 385–86; views on civil unions, 133n16; views on homosexuality, 298–99, 302n31; views on LGBT issues, 20–22, 136–37, 350–51
Catholic left, Brazilian Workers' Party and, 202, 203
Cayman Islands, attitudes toward LGBT persons in, 142
CCCOH. See Citizen's Commission against Homophobic Hate Crimes

CEDAW. See Convention on the Elimination of All Forms of Discrimination against Women
CEM. See Centro de Estudios de la Mujer
Central America: acceptance of human rights norms in, 353; effects of U.S. hegemony in, 354; lesbian movements in, 144–49; politicization of LGBT identity in, 354
centrist parties, position on homosexual rights, in Brazil, 198, 200, 201
Centro de Estudios de la Mujer (CEM), xi
CEPSIDA. See Popular AIDS Education Collective
Céspedes, Benjamin de, 50–52, 53
Chamorro, Violeta Barrios de, 276–77
CHA. See Comunidad Homosexual Argentina
Chanacomchana, 76
Child, Raquel, 263
child labor laws, introduction of, 38, 42n23
Chile: Divine nightclub arson, 382–83; feminist movement in, x–xii, 383, 403; history of LGBT rights in, 10; lesbian movement in, 382–84; lesbian Web sites based in, 314; military dictatorship, demands for justice for, 381; purging of universities, x–xi; and the 2007 Santiago gay pride march, 12–14; youth household exodus in, 14
Chile AIDS Prevention Association, 259, 260, 263
Chilean homosexual rights organizations: establishment of, 257, 381–83; HIV/AIDS and, 259–61, 263–64; structural weaknesses in, 263. See also LGBT movement in Chile
Chinchetas, 403
Cicco, Gabriela de, 321
Cipriani, Juan Luis, 298
cities: and homosexual freedom, 155; Latin American, as gay friendly, 11
Citizen's Commission against Homophobic Hate Crimes (Comisión Ciudadana contra los Crímenes de Odio por Homofobia; CCCOH), 291, 292
citizenship: autonomy as prerequisite for, 113; rights, activism for, in Brazil, 79–80; sexual, 113
civil rights-based homosexual rights groups, in Argentina, 93–94, 98
civil rights issues, danger of compromise on, 224
civil unions: in Argentina, 117, 253; in Brazil, 81, 127, 221, 253; in Colombia, 253; in Cuba, possibility of, 270–71; in Ecuadorean constitution of 2008, 224, 226; goals of, 214; in Venezuela, 220–23. See also Buenos Aires civil union law; marriage, same-sex
CLHARI. See Rosario Ibarra Lesbian and Homosexual Support Committee
closet. See homosexual identity, hiding of; LGBT identity, hiding of
Closet of Sor Juana, The, 324–25
CNCD. See Conselho Nacional de Combate à Discriminação
CNF. See National Feminist Committee
cochones, as term, 294
Code of Coexistence. See Buenos Aires Code of Coexistence

homosexual space in Havana (*cont.*), impact of socialist doctrines on, 340–41; lack of privacy, and need for public homosexual space, 336–37, 344–45; police harassment of LGBT persons in, 338–39, 341, 343–44; reputation of, among general public, 342; as temporary, contested spaces, 341, 342, 345–46

Homosexual Work Commission (CTH), 185, 187–88

homosociability, sites of: in Brazil, 73, 74, 76, 82; characteristics of, 110; in Costa Rica, harassment of, 157; gay saunas, denial of entrance to transvestites, in São Paulo, 423–26; and hiding of homosexuality, 109; in Mexico, 63; in Nicaragua, 277. *See also* homosexual space in Havana; Internet

Honduras: disconnected street youth in, 15–16; effects of U.S. hegemony in, 354; lesbian movement in, 144

household discrimination. *See* family discrimination

HSH. See *Homens que fazem Sexo com Homens*

Las Humanas (The Female Humans), 165n12

human rights, definition of, 365

human rights, international norms of: acceptance of, in Central America, 353; acceptance of, in English Caribbean, 353; acceptance of, in Latin America, 353; constitutional status of, in Venezuela, 221; as opportunity to leverage national LGBT rights, 221; Paraguay's failure to adhere to, 365–70; resistance to, in Latin America, 256, 353

human rights movement, alliance with LGBT rights movement, in Chile, 382

Ibarra de Piedra, Rosario, 178–79, 181

identitarian homosexual persons, 103

identity, LGBT. *See* homosexual identity; lesbian identity; LGBT identity

identity-based movements, variety of, 164

identity of social movements: Central American lesbian groups, 145; in Costa Rica, 149–51, 154–59, 164; dynamics of, 422–23; fluid *vs.* stable, benefits of, 423; in Nicaragua, 151–54, 159–63; theorizing of, 145–49

identity politics, views of LGBT activists in Buenos Aires on, 387–98

IGA. *See* International Gay Association

ILGA. *See* International Lesbian and Gay Association

Inciardi, James, 241

income levels, national, and LGBT movement, 18–19

Information Network of Argentine Women, 314

Ingraham, Hubert, 142

Inquisition, persecution of homosexuals in, 62

Institutional Revolutionary Party (PRI), 182

instrumental actions: disagreements on validity claims, as source of conflict within LGBT organizations, 288; validity claims of, 287

internalization of social stigma, and self-hatred, 292, 296

International Gay and Lesbian Human Rights Commission, 327

International Gay Association (IGA), 186

international groups, activist's engagement with: activists' selection process, 175, 192; global communities and, 175, 185–86, 192; Internet and, 319, 323, 326; in Mexican and Brazilian elections of 1982, 186–88; recasting of influences at national level, 188–91; selection process for, 185–88; social movement theory on, 175

international human rights norms. *See* human rights, international norms

International Lesbian and Gay Association (ILGA): associated organizations, 325; and Brazilian election of 1982, 186; lobbying of UN, 126; report on violence against homosexuals, 20; Seventeenth Annual Conference (Rio de Janeiro, 1995), 71, 77, 83, 125

Internet: access to, 318, 323; accountability issues, 319, 325–27; distribution lists, 324–25, 331; effectiveness as vehicle for change, xiii; and increased interaction among activists, xiii; and international engagement, 319, 323, 326; and narrowing of public discourse, 319; personal ads on, 321–22; phantom organizations on, 326; as safe site of homosociability, 313; as source of strategies for LGBT movement, 25–26; undermining of local organizations and politics, 319–20, 326

Internet, and lesbian organization: access issues, 318, 323; accountability issues, 319, 325–27; benefits of Internet, 313, 315, 318–19, 320–25, 330–31; challenges of Internet, 313, 319–20; exposure of debates to wide audience, effects of, 326–27; historical challenges facing lesbian community building, 315–18; hyperlinks, 327–30; international funding, 326; lesbian Internet presence, 312, 314–15; regionality of organization, 323, 327–30

intersex individuals: definition of, 6–7; desires, practices, identities and expressions of, 4t; "normalizing" surgery and, 7

"invisibilization," of lesbians in Costa Rica, 156

Isis International, x

isolation of homosexuals, Internet and, 313, 318–19, 320–22, 331

Jamaica, attitudes toward LGBT persons in, 141–42

Jamaican Forum for Lesbians, All-Sexuals and Gays (J-FLAG), 142

Jefferson, Thomas C., 142

J-FLAG. *See* Jamaican Forum for Lesbians, All-Sexuals and Gays

Jiménez, Patria, 192

judicial bodies, and human rights protection, 254

judiciary in Brazil: extension of rights to LGBT persons, 124, 128; and LGBT activism, 127–28

juridical activism by LGBT movement, 117

Kamenetzky, Sofia, 295

Kirchner, Néstor, 394–98

Kirkwood, Julieta, xi

Kiss of the Spider Woman (1985 film), 23

Kutsche, Paul, 295

Mariposas en el andamio (*Butterflies on the Scaffold*; film), 55

marriage: heteronormative conception of, 217; as prior to law, 214; as strategy to hide homosexual practices, 17

marriage, same-sex: nations recognizing, 350; prohibition on, as indirect discrimination, 107, 118. *See also* civil unions

Martí, Jose, 50–51, 53–54

Martínez Verdugo, Arnoldo, 191

Mascarenhas, João Antonio de Souza, 76–77, 182, 184, 186–87, 188–90, 193, 200

masculine women: desires, practices, identities and expressions of, 4t; harassment and discrimination against, 6; marginalization of, in Brazil, 73

Matogrosso, Ney, 74

Matute, Romelia, 222

Mead, G. H., 108

media: in Argentina, coverage of homosexual events and issues, 94; in Brazil, and perception of LGBT rights, 216; in Brazil, coverage of homosexual events and issues, 76, 80, 83, 125; fascination with transgended prostitutes in Brazil, 304, 307–8; on HIV/AIDS, and visibility of homosexuality, 112–13; homosexual, in Brazil, 132n3; international, and acceptance of LGBT persons, 299; LGBT characters on TV, 278; punishment of anti-gay programming, in Brazil, 128–29

medical approach to sexual rights, 256

medical classification of homosexuality, as treatable sexual deviance, 76, 84n19, 129–30, 180, 298, 359

Medici, Emilio Garrastazü, 74

Mediterranean culture, constructions of homosexuality in, 293

Mejia, Max, 179

Melucci, A., 146, 151

Mema's House, Mexico City: On Transvestites, Queens, and Machos (Prieur), 19

Mendoza, Francisco Loor, 227

Menem, Carlos, 88

Mestizo culture, homosexuality in, 62

Mexican Communist Party, 183, 191

Mexican election of 1978, homosexuality as issue in, 193n2

Mexican election of 1982: issue of party alliances in, 181–82; issues and contending parties, 178–79; leftist dual activists in, 181, 184; and LGBT identity, 192; shallow penetration of democratic institutions in, 188

Mexican election of 1982, LGBT movement strategy in, 175, 179; factors affecting selection process, 183–85; international influences and, 187–88, 190–91; precedent set by, 191–92; selection process for, 176–77, 181–82

Mexicas, homosexuality in, 60–61

Mexico: acceptance of LGBT persons in, 299; anti-homosexual violence, statistics on, 291–92; colonial, homosexuality in, 61–62; constructions of homosexuality in, 63, 64–65, 293, 294, 295; demographics, 60; drag ball raid (1901),

63; increasing acceptance of lesbians, 316; lesbian Web sites based in, 314; LGBT rights, history of, 10; national character of, Paz on, 62; police corruption in, 297; postcolonial, homosexuality in, 62–64; preconquest, homosexuality in, 60–61; public decency standards in, 63; seventeenth-century purge of homosexuals, 62; sodomy, decriminalization of, 34; stereotypes of gays in, 63; transvestite sex workers in, 298; youth household exodus in, 14. *See also* LGBT movement in Mexico

Mexico City, homosexual bars and baths, 63

MHA. *See* Autonomous Homosexual Movement migration, and introduction of new ideas, 26

Miguel Agustín Pro Juárez Human Rights Center, 292

Milanés, Pablo, 55

Millán, Rodolfo, 291

Mitilene, 402

MixBrasil (Web site), 423, 425

Mixed Parliamentary Front for Free Sexual Expression, 127

Monsiváis, Carlos, 191, 292

Montenegro, Sofia, 279

La Morada, xii, 382

Moreno Franginals, Manuel, 47

Mott, Luiz, 76, 182, 186, 187, 293

MOVILH. *See Movimiento de lntegración y Liberación Homosexual*

Movimiento de lntegración y Liberación Homosexual (Movement for Homosexual Integration and Liberation; MOVILH), ix, 259–60, 290–91, 292, 383

Movimiento Unificado de Minorías Sexuales (United Front of Sexual Minorities; MUMS), 383, 384, 385

Mujeres Creando, 403

MUMS. *See Movimiento Unificado de Minorías Sexuales*

Mundo de mujer: continuidad y cambio (CEM), xi–xii

Murray, David A. B., 139

Murray, S. O., 64

Musto, Michael, 17

NAP. *See* National AIDS Program

Napoleonic Code, sodomy in, 34, 40n1

National Action Party (PAN), 183–84

National AIDS Program (NAP), 243

National Democratic Front (Mexico) 3, 182

National Feminist Committee (CNF), 152

National Front Against Repression, 181

National Front for the Liberation and Rights of Women, 181

National Gathering of Organized Homosexual Groups, 71, 75, 79

national ideology, production of, 44–45

nationalism, Cuban: discursive precariousness of, 44–45; on homosexuality as threat, 51–54

National Lesbian Seminar (Brazil), 80

National Meeting of Transvestites and Liberated People, 124

National Meeting of Transvestites and Liberated People Fighting against AIDS, 125
National Plan of Sexual and Reproductive Health (Paraguay), 368
National Plenary Meetings of Gays, Lesbians, *Travestis* and Transsexuals of the PT, 203
National Seminar on Affirmative Policies and Rights of the Gay, Lesbian, Bisexual, *Travesti*, and Transsexual Community (Brazil), 201
Neconi, 166
Negri, Bargas, 246
Neighbors' Association of Palermo, 420
neoliberal regime in Nicaragua: impact on women and lower classes, 279; LGBT rights under, 276
networking among homosexuals, increase in, 117
New Generation of Young Lesbians, 320
newletters, role in mobilization, x
new social movement theory (NSM), 145–46, 148, 149, 151, 164
Nicaragua: constitution of 1987, 275; constructions of homosexuality in, 293–94; disconnected street youth in, 15–16; economy of, 154–55, 159–63; feminist movement in, 152, 163, 167n24; gay-lesbian tensions in, 277; gay life in, 274–75; and globalization, impact of, 279; identity of social movements in, 151–54, 159–63; lesbian identity in, 164; LGBT rights in, 10, 159–61, 167n18, 275–76, 279, 316; machismo in, 295–96; sodomy laws in, 276–77; women's rights in, 275; women's rights movement in, 278. *See also* lesbian movement in Nicaragua
Nicaraguan Gay Movement, 160
Nicaraguan homosexual rights organizations: activism of, 275, 276, 277, 278; competition between, 279; establishment of, 276; international LGBT politics, connections to, 277–78, 278–79; lesbian leadership in, 277, 278
Nicaraguan Women's Association (AMNLAE), 276
Nicholson, Linda, 216
Nimehuatzin, 167n22
normative actions: disagreements on validity claims, as source of conflict within LGBT organizations, 288; validity claims of, 287
North America, LGBT rights, legal basis of, 255
No se lo digas a nadie (Don't Tell Anyone; 1998 film), 16, 17, 19
Nosotras: characteristics of, 144–45, 151–52; founding of, 162; and lesbian identity, 164; objectives of, 152–53; strategies of, 153–54
Novo, S., 62
Nuances, 127–28
Nucleo de Ação pelos Direitos dos Homossexuais (Action Nucleus for Homosexuals' Rights), 69–70
Nuestro Mundo (Our World; periodical), 410

Ocampo, Irene, 321
O'Donnell, Guillermo, 193
Oficina de Tolerancia y No Discriminación (Office of Tolerance and Nondiscrimination, Chile), 384
Oikabeth, 177–78

O Lampião da Esquina, 70, 75, 83n1, 132n3, 178, 236
Olson, Mancur, 9
Ômega Ltda. (Rede TV), 128–29
Organization of American States, anti-violence resolution, ix
Organization of Transvestites and Transsexuals of Argentina (OTTRA), 407
O Snob (periodical), 74, 83
Otra vez el mar (The Sea Again; Arenas), 56
OTTRA. *See* Organization of Transvestites and Transsexuals of Argentina
outing, fear of, as effective check on behavior, 107–8, 116, 156
Outra Coisa, 179–80

Palace of the White Skunks, The (Arenas), 360
Palmieri, Victor H., 358
Parada, Silvia, 385
Paraguay, failure to adhere to international agreements on lesbian rights, 365–70
paramilitary death squads: in Argentina, 87–88; in Brazil, 78
Parker, Richard G., 72–73, 77, 239–40
Parliamentary Front for the Freedom of Sexual Expression, 201, 207, 208n6
Partido Comunista Brasileiro (Brazilian Communist Party; PCB), 200, 201
Partido Comunista do Brasil (Communist Party of Brazil; PC do B), 200, 201
Partido da Frente Liberal (Liberal Front Party; PFL), 200
Partido Democrático Trabalhista (Democratic Labor Party; PDT), 200, 201
Partido dos Trabalhadores (Workers' Party; PT): democratizing reforms by, 203; establishment of, 178; history of, 202; LGBT support for, 82; support of LGBT rights, 80–81, 180, 198, 200, 201, 202–4
Partido Liberal (Liberal Party; PL), 200
Partido Socialista Brasileiro (Brazilian Socialist Party; PSB), 200, 201
Partido Socialista dos Trabalhadores Unificados (United Socialist Workers' Party), 81
Partido Trabalhista Brasileiro (Brazilian Labor Party; PTB), 200
Partido Trabalhista Cristão (Christian Labor Party; PTC), 205
Partnership Bill (Brazil), 127
Party of the Brazilian Democratic Movement (PMDB), 178, 186
Party of the Democratic Revolution (PRD), 192
patlacheh, 61
Paz, Octavio, 62
PCB. *See* Partido Comunista Brasileiro
PC do B. *See* Partido Comunista do Brasil
PDS. *See* Social Democratic Party
PDT. *See* Partido Democrático Trabalhista
Peniston, William, 35, 36
Pentecostal churches, views on LGBT issues, 137, 204, 209n13
Pérez, Marelys, 222–23
Pérez Ocaña, Mariana, 320, 325

Perón, Juan Domingo, 38
personal security, right to, in Paraguay, 369–70
PFL. See *Partido da Frente Liberal*
Philadelphia Manufacturer (newspaper), 49–50
Pindar, Harcourt, 142
Pisano, Margarita, xii, 403
Pixote (1981 film), 16
PL. See *Partido Liberal*
PMDB. *See* Party of the Brazilian Democratic
    Movement
police: corruption in, 297; crimes against homo-
    sexuals, lack of interest in, 292; policy on ho-
    mosexuality, in Mexico, 63; transvestites, abuse
    of, 297; unmaking of police order by political
    activity, 419
police abuse of LGBT persons: in Argentina, 36–37,
    40, 41n9, 41n12, 89–90, 99n4; in Brazil, 35–36,
    72, 235, 236, 297, 303–4, 306, 308, 310–11; in
    Cuba, 338–39, 341, 343–44, 360; in Equador,
    224–25; in Mexico, 63, 297; in Nicaragua, 276;
    in Paraguay, 369–70
police edicts on homosexuality: in France, 35–36;
    in Latin America, 35–37, 40; *vs.* penal codes,
    41n10
political-opportunity-structures analysis, 87, 91,
    97, 147–48. *See also* political process tradition
political parties: importance to LGBT movement,
    198, 206; LGBT activists' reluctance to engage
    with, 208n1; and party-movement divide,
    22–27; weakness of, in Brazil, 206. *See also* cen-
    trist parties; leftist parties; right-wing parties
political process tradition, 146, 147–48
politics, new paradigm of, and LGBT rights, 96
Pollak, M., 110
pop music, 55, 74, 80
Popular AIDS Education Collective (CEPSIDA), 160
Portuguese colonialism, 352
Posada, Guadalupe, 63
postmaterial information society, threats to per-
    sonal autonomy in, 18, 25, 145
PRD. *See* Party of the Democratic Revolution
PRI. *See* Institutional Revolutionary Party
Prieur, Annick, 64, 298
*Primer Sindicato de Trabajadoras y Trabajadores
    LGBTT* (First Union of LGBTT Workers), 384
privacy: civil union legislation as threat to, 215–16;
    HIV/AIDS and, 112; lack of in Havana, and pub-
    lic sexual spaces, 336–37; and overruling of
    sodomy laws, 252; redefining of public/private
    distinction, 114; respect for, as necessary condi-
    tion for homosexual discretion, 106–7; theory
    of, as offensive to LGBT persons, 215–16
*Programa Brasileiro de Combate à Violencia e à
    Discriminação a Gays, Lésbicas, Travestis,
    Transgêneros e Bisexuals*, 238
prostitution, male homosexual: in Cuba, 342–43,
    344; employment discrimination, 298; as issue,
    in transvestite movement, 407; police abuse of
    sex workers, 297, 303–4, 306, 308; suppression
    of, as repression, 254. *See also* Buenos Aires
    Code of Coexistence; transgendered prosti-
    tutes in Brazil

La prostitctión en la ciudad de la Habana
    (*Prostitution in the City of Havava*;
    Céspedes), 51
Protecting Soldiers and Mothers (Skocpol), 247
Protestant churches, views on LGBT issues, 20–21,
    204, 209n13
Protestantism, fundamentalist, views on LGBT is-
    sues, 350–51
PRT. *See* Revolutionary Workers' Party
PSB. See *Partido Socialista Brasileiro*
PSUM. *See* United Socialist Party of Mexico
PT. See *Partido dos Trabalhadores*
PTB. See *Partido Trabalhista Brasileiro*
PTC. See *Partido Trabalhista Cristão*
public decency standards, 297–98; in Brazil, 71–72,
    77, 123–24, 126, 132n12, 308–9; in Cayman Is-
    lands, 142; in Cuba, 344, 346n2; in Dominican
    Republic, 138; hiding of homosexuality to
    meet, 105–7; in Mexico, 63; transvestites and,
    254. *See also* police edicts on homosexuality
public opinion on homosexuality: in Brazil, 82; in
    Latin America, 108–9. *See also* Buenos Aires
    gay pride poll (2005); Santiago gay pride
    march poll (2007)
Puerto Rico: attitudes toward LGBT persons in,
    136–37; independence movement in, 137
Puerto Rico para Todos (Puerto Rico for All), 137
Puig, Manuel, 23
Puntos de Encuentro (Gathering Points), ix, 275

queer, as term, 99n2, 423
queer approach to gender, 5–6
Queirolo, Rossana, 227

Ramírez de Ferrer, Miriam, 137
Rancière, Jacques, 419
Randall, Margaret, 153
rape, of lesbians, 299–300
Rede TV. See *Ômega Ltda.*
Reis, Toni, 78
religion, as impediment to gay rights, 20–22; in
    Brazil, 198, 204; in Caribbean, 136; in English
    Caribbean *vs.* Latin America, 350–51, 356n3
religion, suppression of in Cuba, 360
Religious Support Group against AIDS (ARCA), 242
reproduction, association of sexuality with, 217
reproductive rights, separating from sexual rights,
    255–56
resource mobilization tradition, 146
Revolutionary Workers' Party (PRT): alliance with
    LGBT movement, 175, 179, 181, 184, 190–91; in-
    ternational influences on, 187–88, 190–91; and
    1982 election, 178–79
right-wing parties: LGBT persons in, 204–5, 207;
    and "transvestite treason" in Chile, 385–86;
    views on homosexual rights, in Brazil, 198,
    200, 201, 204–6
Rios, Flor, 222
Rivera, Norberto, 298
Robinson, Gene, 142
Roca, Ana, 362
Roma, María Paula, 227

Rompiendo el Silencio (Breaking the Silence) Web site, 314, 321, 322, 323, 324, 327, 329, 330
Roosevelt, Theodore "Teddy," 49
Rosario Ibarra Lesbian and Homosexual Support Committee (CLHARI), 179, 181, 182, 183, 184, 187
Rothenberg, T., 340–41
Ruiz, Rafael, 291
rule of law, breakdown of, and violence against LGBT persons, 354–55
Russo, Renato, 80

sadomasochism, 256
Safo Piensa (Sappho Thinks) Web site, 314, 321, 323, 324, 325, 327, 328–29, 330
St. Croix, attitudes toward LGBT persons in, 138
St. John, attitudes toward LGBT persons in, 138
St. Thomas, attitudes toward LGBT persons in, 138
Salessi, Jorge, 37
Samizdat literature, role in mobilization, x
Sandals resorts, discrimination against LGBT persons, 142
Sandinistas. See *Frente Sandinista Liberación Nacional*
Santiago gay pride march poll (2007), 12, *13*, 14, 20
Santini, José, 137
São Paulo, LGBT pride parade in, 125
Sardá, Alejandra, 315, 317
Scarpaci, J., 336
Sebreli, Juan José, 110
Second National Human Rights Program (Brazil), 253
secrets, social ties between those sharing, 104
self-hatred: in homosexuals, as source of violence, 292, 296–97; in transvestites, debate on within transvestite community, 407–8
Sencillamente diferentes (*Simply Different*; Gonzalez), 277
SERNAM. See *Servicio Nacional de la Mujer*
Ser política en Chile (Kirkwood), xi
Serrano, Pedro Julio, 137
Servicio Nacional de la Mujer (SERNAM), 383
sex, dissociation from affection, in closeted homosexuals, 106
Sex, Drugs, and HIV/AIDS in Brazil (Inciardi), 241
sex-change surgery, as right, 130
Sexto Sentido (*Sixth Sense*), 278
sexual citizenship, 113
sexual identity, in Brazil, 239–40
sexuality, association with reproduction, 217
sexual orientation, definition of, 5
sexual rights: extension of to non-identity practices, 256; separating from reproductive rights, 255–56. See also LGBT rights
sex work. See prostitution
shame in homosexuals, socialization and, 107–8
shock effect, LGBT movement overdependence on, 19–20
Sierra, Sola, 382
SIGLA. See *Sociedad de Integración Gay-Lésbica Argentina*
Sikora, Schifter, 166n16
Silvestre, Lila, 151

Simons, Marlise, 359
Skocpol, Theda, 247
slavery, legacy of, and acceptance of LGBT rights, 352
Snow, D. A., 164
sociability, modes of, and counterproductive conflict within LGBT organizations, 283–89
social bonds of homosexuals: with homosexual peers, 110, 111; with those aware of homosexuality, 110; with those unaware of homosexuality, 107–10
social class: in Argentina, LGBT movement and, 393–94; in Brazil, Mascarenhas on, 189
Social Democratic Party (PDS), 178
socialization, and shame in homosexuals, 107–8
social movement field: and constitution of Costa Rican lesbian movement, 157–58; and constitution of Nicaraguan lesbian movement, 162–63; and constitution of social movements, 148–49
social movement identities. See identity of social movements
social movements, role of writing and research in, ix–xiv
social movement theory, on influence of international forces, 175
social recognition of homosexuality: adoption of informal strategies to achieve, 114–15; as beyond reach of legal system, 118–19, 119n4; factual *vs.* moral recognition, 115; forces moving Latin American culture toward, 114, 116; obstacles to, 115–16
social science research, role in Chilean feminist movement, x–xi
Sociedad de Integración Gay-Lésbica Argentina (Argentinean Society for Gay and Lesbian Integration; SIGLA), 88, 93
socioeconomic status, and homophobic attitudes, 19
sodomy, in preconquest Mexico, 61
sodomy, decriminalization of: in Argentina, 34, 37, 42n19; in Brazil, 34; in Chile, 260, 383; European Court of Human Rights and, 252; in French legal tradition, 34, 40n1; in Latin America, 34–35, 37, 42n19; in Mexico, 34
sodomy, law on: in Argentina, 37–39; in British *vs.* Spanish and Portuguese tradition, 352; in Chile, 383; French police edicts, 34–35; in Jamaica, 141; Latin American police edicts, 35–37, 40; in Nicaragua, 153, 161, 276–77; in Puerto Rico, 137
Something Else: Homosexualist Action Group (*Grupo Outra Coisa: Ação Homossexualista*), 75, 77, 83n11
Sommer, Doris, 46
Somos: Grupo de Afirmação Homossexual: associated organizations, 151; and election of 1982, 179–80, 190; founding of, 69–70, 75, 132n3, 178, 242, 401; and "gay," as term, 80; splitting of, 75, 83n1; threats against, 78
Somoza, Anastasio, 159
Spain, leftist-LGBT alliance in, 23
Spanish colonialism, legacies of, 352

Spanish conquistadors, condemnation of homosexuality, 62
Spanish penal code, decriminalization of sodomy in, 34
Spartacus: International Gay Guide, 374, 375–76
Steakley, James D., 40n1
Stein, Edward, 315, 318–19
Stonewall riots of 1969, influence of, 74, 92
Strehlke, Boris, 139
Sullivan, Andrew, 105
Sunstein, Cass, 319
Suplicy, Marta, 81
Sutherland, Jual Pablo, 259–60, 262

Tarrow, S., 146
Tatchell, Peter, 142
Taylor, V., 146
Teixeira, Paulo, 245, 246
Theory of Communicative Action (Habermas), 286–89
think tanks, role in Chilean feminist movement, xi
"The Third World and the Gay Liberation Movement" (Mascarenhas), 189
Tielman, R., 356n3
tolerance of homosexuality, discretion as condition of, 105–7, 116, 295, 337
Torch Song Trilogy (film), 276
tourism: as demonstration of LGBT economic power, 26; hospitality toward homosexuals, in Caribbean and Puerto Rico, 136–43
Toussaint L'Ouverture, François-Dominique, 136
traición travesti (transvestite treason) in Chile, 386
transgendered identity, 390–93
transgendered persons: assimilationist rights groups' reluctance to accept, 93; definition of, 5–6; desires, practices, identities and expressions of, 4t; and family discrimination, 12, 13; harassment and discrimination against, 6; and household exodus, timing of, 14; main political issues of, 5, 394; and right to sex-change surgery, 130; social class and, 16, 393–94; as term, 125; as threat to social order, 306–7
transgendered prostitutes in Brazil: construction of, as monsters, 305, 306–7, 309–10; efforts to employ in other lines of work, 309; police abuse of, 303–4, 306, 308, 310–11; public attention to, during Code of Coexistence period, 304–5; public order and, 308–9. *See also* Buenos Aires Code of Coexistence
transgender rights groups: in Argentina, 88, 89, 99n10; in Chile, 385; and debate on feminine identity, 131
Transsexuales por el Derecho a la Vida y la Identidad (Transsexuals for the Right to Life and Identity), 88, 99n10
transsexuals: definition of, 5–6, 99n2; demands prioritized by, 394; desires, practices, identities and expressions of, 4t; lack of antidiscrimination legislation on, 254; rights of, in Cuba, 271; social class of, 393–94
transvestite identity: debate on, within transvestite community, 407–8; denial of, in gay and les-

bian movement, 409–10; and social class, 393–94, 417
transvestite movement, in Argentina: agenda of, 412, 414–15; establishment of, 406–7; history of, 418–19; prostitution as issue in, 407; speech at LGBT pride march (1999), 416–18; and transvestite self-esteem, 408–9; and unmaking of gender identity, 419
transvestite movement, in Brazil, 81, 82, 124, 132n5
transvestites: in Chile, "transvestite treason" of, 385–86; definition of, 5–6, 98n2; demands prioritized by, 394; and destablization of gender norms, 425–26; and gay saunas, right of access to, 423–26; lack of antidiscrimination legislation on, 254; public decency standards and, 254; as sex workers, 6; special stigmatization of, 297
Travestis y Transgénero de Chile (Transvestites and Transgenders of Chile; *Traves Chile*), 385
Triângulo Rosa, 126, 200
truth and reconciliation commissions, and human rights progress, 19

Um Outro Olhar (An Other Look), 314–15, 321, 323, 324, 328, 329–30
United Nations Decade of the Woman, xii
United Nations Human Rights Commission, 126, 221
United Nations human rights documents, efforts to include sexual orientation in, 126
United Nations World Conference against Racism, Racial Discrimination, Xenophobia, and Related Intolerance, 126
United Nations World Conference on Women, xii
United Socialist Party of Mexico (PSUM), 178, 183
United States: expansionism, and preoccupation with masculinity, 49; as exporter of criminal gang culture, 355; hegemony of, and LGBT rights, 353–55; immigration policy on homosexuals, 359; influence on Cuban national identity, 45, 48–50
United States Virgin Islands, attitudes toward LGBT persons in, 138
universities: Chilean military junta's purging of, x–xi; globalization of, 26
urbanization, and homosexual freedom to interact, 155
Uruguay: leftists' lack of support for feminist issues, 23; progress in LGBT rights, 10; youth household exodus in, 14

validity claims: disagreements about, as source of conflict within LGBT organizations, 288–89; types of, 287–88
Vamos a Andar (periodical), 90
Varona, Enrique José, 50, 52–53
Vásquez, Tabaré, 23
Veloso, Caetano, 74
Venezuela: antidiscrimination legislation, 220–23; rejection of LGBT discrimination ban, 22–23
Venezuelan constitution: antidiscrimination provisions, defeat of, 220; general human rights provisions, 221